JAZZ

"You got to be in the sun to feel the sun.
It's that way with music, too."

—*Sidney Bechet*

JAZZ

SECOND EDITION

Scott DeVeaux

University of Virginia

Gary Giddins

The Graduate Center, City University of New York

W. W. NORTON & COMPANY

NEW YORK ■ LONDON

W. W. Norton & Company has been independent since its founding in 1923, when William Warder Norton and Mary D. Herter Norton first began publishing lectures delivered at the People's Institute, the adult education division of New York City's Cooper Union. The firm soon expanded its program beyond the Institute, publishing books by celebrated academics from America and abroad. By midcentury, the two major pillars of Norton's publishing program—trade books and college texts—were firmly established. In the 1950s, the Norton family transferred control of the company to its employees, and today—with a staff of four hundred and a comparable number of trade, college, and professional titles published each year—W. W. Norton & Company stands as the largest and oldest publishing house owned wholly by its employees.

Editor: Maribeth Payne
Developmental editor: Susan Gaustad
Media editor: Steve Hoge
Ancillaries editor: Michael Fauver
Managing editor, college: Marian Johnson
Managing editor, college digital media: Kim Yi
Production manager: Vanessa Nuttry
Marketing manager, music: Mary Dudley
Design director: Rubina Yeh
Designer: Lissi Sigillo
Media project editor: Andrew Ralston
Photo editor: Kathryn Bryan
Photo researcher: Donna Ranieri
Permissions manager: Megan Jackson
Indexer: Heather Dubnick
Music typesetter: David Botwinik
Composition: S4Carlisle
Manufacturing: LSC Commuications-Kendallville

Library of Congress Cataloging-in-Publication Data
DeVeaux, Scott Knowles.
Jazz / Scott DeVeaux, University of Virginia, Gary Giddins, The Graduate Center, City University of New York.—
Second edition.
    pages cm
Includes bibliographical references and index.
ISBN 978-0-393-93706-0 (pbk.)
1. Jazz—History and criticism. I. Giddins, Gary. II. Title.
ML3508.D47 2015
781.65—dc23

                                                                    2014038121

W. W. Norton & Company, Inc., 500 Fifth Avenue, New York, NY 10110-0017
wwnorton.com

W. W. Norton & Company Ltd., 15 Carlisle Street, London W1D 3BS
 4 5 6 7 8 9 0

To the women in my family: my grown-up daughters Amelia and Flora Thomson-DeVeaux; my still-growing twins, Lena and Celia; and most of all, my wife, Nancy Hurrelbrinck

—Scott DeVeaux

To Deborah Halper and Lea Giddins

—Gary Giddins

CONTENTS

PART III

CHAPTER 16 Fusion I: R&B, Singers, and Latin Jazz 369

CHAPTER 17 Fusion II: Jazz, Rock, and Beyond 397

CHAPTER 18 Historicism: Jazz on Jazz 427

INTRODUCTION

One of the great things about studying jazz—beyond the excitement and variety of the music itself—is its relative historical newness. It may seem like an old story that predates rock and hip-hop and your grandparents. But following its contours today, in the early years of the twenty-first century, is like what it might have meant to study Shakespeare in 1650, when you could still meet people who saw the plays as originally produced and even worked or hung out with the guy who wrote them.

The pioneers of jazz, including its preeminent soloist (Louis Armstrong) and composer (Duke Ellington), worked into the 1970s and beyond. Innovators of later jazz styles and schools are with us now. Young musicians, creating tremendous excitement at this moment, will be acclaimed as tomorrow's masters.

In other words, the dust of history has by no means settled on jazz. The canon of masterpieces is open to interpretation and adjustment. In studying the jazz past, we are also helping to define it. That goes for students as well as teachers. *Jazz* is designed to impart a basic history of jazz—a narrative arc that traces its development from nineteenth-century musical precursors to the present. It requires no prior musical knowledge or ability, only a predisposition for the enjoyment of music and the imagination to feel its expressive power.

The Plan of the Book

Each part of *Jazz* opens with an introductory overview of the period in question and its music; a timeline, situating important jazz events within a broader context of cultural and political history; and dynamic photographs that capture the mood of the era.

PART I: MUSICAL ORIENTATION This first part introduces the vocabulary necessary for discussing the basic rudiments of music and demonstrates, by recorded examples, how those rudiments function in jazz. "Musical Elements and Instruments" analyzes timbre; rhythm, polyrhythm, and swing; melody and harmony; and texture. "Jazz Form and Improvisation" delves into the area of formal structure, chiefly the twelve-bar blues and the thirty-two-bar **A A B A** popular song—forms that recur throughout jazz history. It provides a musician's-eye view of what happens on the bandstand, along with examples of essential jazz lingo like trading fours, rhythm changes, grooves, and modal improvisation.

This is the most technical section of *Jazz*. But we have attempted to clarify these points on our website ("Jazz Concepts"), with video and audio recordings by the Free Bridge Quintet, a band affiliated with the University of Virginia, that address each musical concept—from scales and blue notes to contrasting timbres of instruments to performance techniques. In addition, two pieces have been written specially for this book by the quintet's trumpeter, John D'earth—a twelve-bar blues and a thirty-two-bar song form—that put many of these concepts into action.

When a head is accompanied by the audio icon (▶), that means you can go to "Jazz Concepts" online to hear and see examples of what the section describes—brass instruments, reed instruments, trumpet mutes, homophonic texture, major scales, harmonic progressions, and so on. We suggest that you absorb this material and listen to the examples with the expectation of returning to them periodically as you progress through *Jazz*.

The four main parts of *Jazz*, described below, cover the broad sweep of the music's history and its major figures, as illustrated by seventy-seven recordings, analyzed in laymen's terms in Listening Guides. Again, you don't have to know how to read music to enjoy the guides—only how to read a clock.

PART II: EARLY JAZZ (1900–1930) After exploring the various roots of jazz (folk music, blues, minstrelsy, dance music, brass bands, ragtime), we focus on New Orleans, the birthplace of jazz, introducing its legendary (and unrecorded) founding father, Buddy Bolden, and the first artists to bring jazz to the North and, through records and tours, around the world: the Original Dixieland Jazz Band, King Oliver, Sidney Bechet, and Jelly Roll Morton. We follow them to Chicago and New York in the 1920s (the "Jazz Age"), which saw the emergence of the first great jazz soloist, singer, recording artist, and performer—Louis Armstrong—as well as a generation of improvisers inspired by him; and the phenomenon of jazz-influenced, urban dance bands, crystallized in the early triumphs of Fletcher Henderson and Duke Ellington.

PART III: THE SWING ERA Within a decade of Armstrong's first recordings as a leader, his music became the foundation for the mainstream pop music of the United States and most of the world. In this section, we discuss the social, political, and economic contexts for the extraordinary crossover of a recently localized African American vogue into the commercial market. We examine key bandleaders like Benny Goodman, Artie Shaw, and Jimmie Lunceford, and in particular the titans of big-band swing—Ellington and Count Basie. We then look at individual performers who made up the great Swing Era bands, big and small: the soloists, vocalists, and rhythm section players who transformed jazz into an increasingly sophisticated music, setting the stage for the palace coup to follow.

PART IV: MODERN JAZZ During the hard times of Depression and war, the country had danced to swing. After the war, a sober reconsideration of America's standing in the world and its problems at home brought a dark turn to the arts. In an era of *noir* movies and action painting, jazz was transformed by bebop, the exhilarating virtuoso style pioneered by Charlie Parker and Dizzy Gillespie in the 1940s—a music that favored listening over dancing and required a deeper level of concentration from the audience. Bebop led to cool jazz and hard bop, movements that dominated the 1950s, and a renaissance in jazz composition, exemplified by Thelonious Monk, Charles Mingus, Gil Evans, and George Russell. Yet the central figure in the postbop era was Miles Davis, whose bands helped to launch other pioneers, including Sonny Rollins, Bill Evans, and John Coltrane.

PART V: THE AVANT-GARDE, FUSION, HISTORICISM, AND NOW In this last section, covering the second half of jazz's first century, we abandon the usual attempt to define the music in a decade-by-decade manner. By this time, jazz began to offer alternative narratives. If bebop was a radical response to swing, the avant-garde of the late 1950s and 1960s was an even more radical response to bop, opposing all the familiar conventions of jazz: instrumentation, form, dance-beat rhythm, and tonality. Bop remained the basic language of jazz while the avant-garde developed into an ongoing parallel stream, from the tumultuous "free jazz" of Ornette Coleman and Cecil Taylor, through the musician cooperatives (the AACM) and loft jazz events of the 1970s and 1980s, to the international avant-gardism that maintains a cult-like devotion today.

In contrary fashion, another school of jazz musicians combined jazz and contemporary rock to produce fusion. Most accounts of the fusion movement begin with the electric jazz-rock of the 1970s, but fusion has a much broader history than that, and helps us to understand several major developments in postwar jazz that are usually overlooked by jazz historians. These developments originated in the big bands yet offered listener-friendly alternatives to bop: singers (Frank Sinatra, Sarah Vaughan), rhythm and blues (Louis Jordan, Nat "King" Cole), soul jazz (Jimmy Smith), and Latin jazz (Cuban and Brazilian). Jazz-rock fusion extended that tradition, from the startling syntheses of Miles Davis and Weather Report to the more fluid mixture of twenty-first-century jazz and pop heard in jam bands (Medeski, Martin and Wood), acid jazz, hip-hop jazz, and smooth jazz.

Finally, we offer a historicist view of jazz history—predicated on jazz's evolving obsession with its own history, especially after the New Orleans revivalist movement of the 1930s. The historicist sensibility played a decisive role in advancing jazz education (this book is one consequence) and the presentation of jazz at festivals throughout the world—a phenomenon that continues to flourish. Historicism led to a long-delayed recognition of jazz by establishment organizations—cultural centers, academic programs, and the committees that confer awards and grants. The avant-garde plundered the past in its irreverent way (Anthony Braxton, Arthur Blythe), leading to a dramatically conservative response by Wynton Marsalis, who made possible Jazz at Lincoln Center. Today's jazz artists have little need to choose sides. We conclude with several representative figures in contemporary jazz—including Jason Moran, Robert Glasper, Esperanza Spalding, and Vijay Iyer—who are equally at home with swinging jazz and hip-hop beats.

Within the chapters, key musical terms are highlighted in the text in boldface; these can also be found in the glossary at the back of the book, and most are demonstrated in the online "Jazz Concepts." Throughout the text, new terms are occasionally defined in the margin, or old terms redefined. When one such term is accompanied by an audio icon, that means you can hear an example of the concept being defined in "Jazz Concepts."

Each chapter ends with a list of suggestions for additional listening, including the date of the original recording. For three musicians whose careers span several parts, we provide a chronology at the end of his respective chapter—Louis Armstrong (Chapter 6), Duke Ellington (Chapter 8), and Miles Davis (Chapter 14). And each historical part (II–V) ends with a summary describing and outlining in detail the main style points of that era's music, along with lists of its major musicians.

In addition to the glossary, appendixes include a list of selected jazz musicians (with birth and death dates), categorized by primary instrument; a primer on musical notation; an essay on building a collection of jazz recordings; a filmography; and a bibliography.

The Art

We are very proud of the design of *Jazz*, and hope you will enjoy the black and white photographs—especially the work of the brilliant Herman Leonard, considered by many to be the greatest photographer ever to focus his camera on jazz. A protégé of Yousuf Karsh, Leonard is distinguished in his work by his total control of light. In the late 1940s, the peak of his jazz period, he brought his equipment to clubs, blocked out the natural light, and created his own chiaroscuro effects, emphasizing the excitement of the music and the milieu—through reflected highlights and his signature use of cigarette smoke. Leonard's New Orleans studio was destroyed by Hurricane Katrina, and he moved to California, where he died in 2010. In 2013, the William J. Clinton Presidential Library honored him with a five-month exhibition of his jazz photography. Leonard shot almost all of the full-page photographs that introduce each chapter.

The Listening Guides

Jazz provides a comprehensive overview of the music through seventy-seven selections, combining acknowledged classics (Miles Davis's "So What," Coleman Hawkins's "Body and Soul," Louis Armstrong's "West End Blues") with several unusual but illuminating tracks, ranging from Wilbur Sweatman's "Down Home Rag" (1916) to Cécile McLorin Salvant's "John Henry" (2013). Each selection is introduced by a passage in the text, designated with a listening icon (🎧), that sets the scene for the work. This is followed by a Listening Guide (carrying the same icon), in which significant musical moments are linked directly to timings along the left.

1. Below the title of the piece, you'll find basic information about the recording: the musicians, original label, date of recording, and style and form of the piece.

2. The "What to listen for" box offers some key points to help orient your listening.

3. All boldface terms are included in the glossary at the back, and most are featured in audio and/or video demonstrations online ("Jazz Concepts").

4. Occasionally a music example is provided to illustrate a distinctive melody or rhythm.

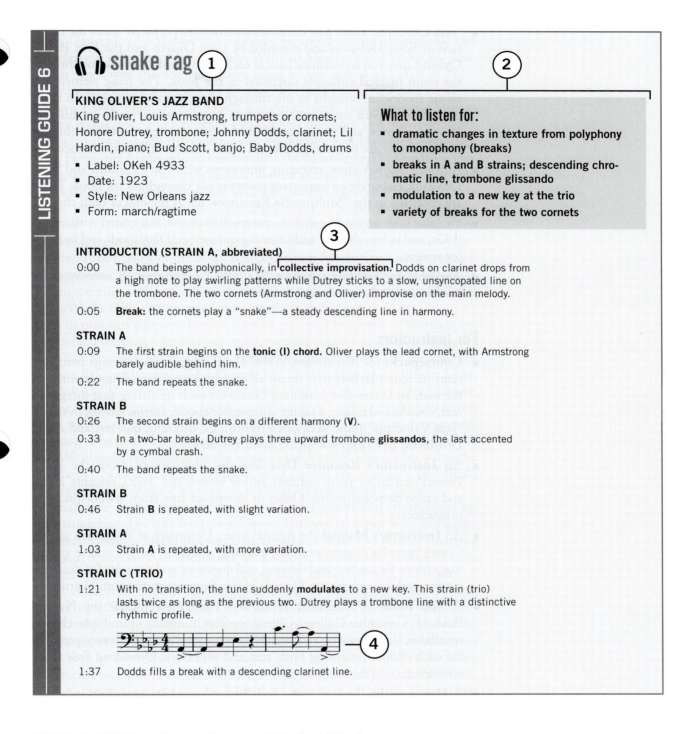

LISTENING GUIDE 6

🎧 snake rag ①

KING OLIVER'S JAZZ BAND
King Oliver, Louis Armstrong, trumpets or cornets;
Honore Dutrey, trombone; Johnny Dodds, clarinet; Lil
Hardin, piano; Bud Scott, banjo; Baby Dodds, drums
- Label: OKeh 4933
- Date: 1923
- Style: New Orleans jazz
- Form: march/ragtime

②
What to listen for:
- dramatic changes in texture from polyphony to monophony (breaks)
- breaks in A and B strains; descending chromatic line, trombone glissando
- modulation to a new key at the trio
- variety of breaks for the two cornets

INTRODUCTION (STRAIN A, abbreviated)

0:00   The band beings polyphonically, in ③ **collective improvisation.** Dodds on clarinet drops from a high note to play swirling patterns while Dutrey sticks to a slow, unsyncopated line on the trombone. The two cornets (Armstrong and Oliver) improvise on the main melody.

0:05   **Break:** the cornets play a "snake"—a steady descending line in harmony.

STRAIN A

0:09   The first strain begins on the **tonic (I) chord.** Oliver plays the lead cornet, with Armstrong barely audible behind him.

0:22   The band repeats the snake.

STRAIN B

0:26   The second strain begins on a different harmony (**V**).

0:33   In a two-bar break, Dutrey plays three upward trombone **glissandos**, the last accented by a cymbal crash.

0:40   The band repeats the snake.

STRAIN B

0:46   Strain **B** is repeated, with slight variation.

STRAIN A

1:03   Strain **A** is repeated, with more variation.

STRAIN C (TRIO)

1:21   With no transition, the tune suddenly **modulates** to a new key. This strain (trio) lasts twice as long as the previous two. Dutrey plays a trombone line with a distinctive rhythmic profile.

④

1:37   Dodds fills a break with a descending clarinet line.

TOTAL ACCESS to Recordings and Digital Media

This book offers some exciting digital features to enrich and reinforce your study of jazz. First, you have instant access to all seventy-seven recordings streamed from StudySpace or your teacher's Coursepack, as well as an Interactive Listening Guide (iLG)—combining text, visuals, and music—for each selection (wwnorton.com/total-access/jazz2).

MUSICAL ORIENTATION

Jazz has been so much a part of the world's music for the past century that almost everyone can recognize a musical work as "jazzy." We may not know exactly what jazz is, but we know it when we hear it—we respond to the familiarity of a swinging rhythm or a wailing trumpet or the spontaneity of an improvisation. But is that enough?

Obviously, a listener may derive great satisfaction from a Duke Ellington composition while knowing nothing about its chorus structure, harmonic progression, or the particularities of its instrumentation. Yet the more we know about anything, the more pleasure we take in it. Most of this book is concerned with outlining the development of jazz, showing where it came from and how it developed, offering competing theories about its history and evolution. That's the fun part: a story with fascinating characters and unpredictable twists and turns.

In this first section, however, we look at basic musical elements. Some of them will seem obvious and others complicated. Listening examples demonstrate

Late 1800s–early 1900s
- Scott Joplin, John Philip Sousa, Fisk Jubilee Singers, Buddy Bolden, Manuel Perez, W. C. Handy.
- 1914–17, World War I: James Reese Europe, Vernon and Irene Castle.
- First recordings to show shift from ragtime to jazz: Wilbur Sweatman.
- Great Migration begins, including New Orleans musicians: Freddie Keppard, King Oliver, Jelly Roll Morton.
- 1917: First jazz recordings by Original Dixieland Jazz Band.

- 1919: Will Marion Cook takes band to Europe, including Sidney Bechet.
- 1919–20, white dance bands incorporate watered-down jazz elements: Art Hickman, Paul Whiteman.

1920s: Jazz Age
- Blues divas: Ma Rainey, Bessie Smith, Mamie Smith.
- New Orleans musicians record in Chicago and New York: Jelly Roll Morton, King Oliver, Sidney Bechet, New Orleans Rhythm Kings.
- Early big bands: Fletcher Henderson, Duke Ellington, Chick Webb.
- Stride piano: Earl Hines, James P. Johnson, Fats Waller.

Gertrude "Ma" Rainey was regarded as the "Mother of the Blues." She helped to introduce several important musicians on her recordings.

Oran "Hot Lips" Page, record producer Harry Lim, pianist Dave Bowman, bassist Clyde New-combe, and Billie Holiday relax at a 1940s jam session.

In the prewar era, few musical events were more exciting than a "battle of the bands" waged before the most discerning of critics: dancers. Chick Webb led the home team at New York's Savoy Ballroom, and Fletcher Henderson was an especially notable three-time challenger—in 1927, 1928, and 1937.

specific approaches and techniques, establishing an overall context with which to consider jazz as a distinct musical art. We suggest you read these two chapters before embarking on the history, and refer back to them as you push forward. The reason is simple: jazz is most rewarding to a listener conversant with its rules. By understanding what the musician is up against—in terms of structure; or the competing claims of melody, rhythm, and harmony; or the challenge in mastering a particular instrument—you are better able to empathize with and evaluate his or her work. Happily, this basic knowledge may be acquired with virtually no musical ability or training. Most jazz, as we will see, is based on two structures and is performed on a limited number of instruments. If you can feel "time," which is how jazz musicians refer to a rhythmic pulse, and can count to four (most jazz is based on patterns of four beats), you have already mastered its most essential principles.

- Virtuoso soloists: Bix Beiderbecke, Coleman Hawkins, Benny Carter.
- Tin Pan Alley songwriters: George Gershwin, Cole Porter, Irving Berlin, Richard Rodgers, Jerome Kern, Harold Arlen, Hoagy Carmichael.
- 1925: Harlem Renaissance begins.
- 1925–28: Louis Armstrong records with the Hot Five and Hot Seven.
- 1927: Duke Ellington triumphs at the Cotton Club.
- 1929: Great Depression begins.

1930s: Swing
- Boogie-woogie comes to Café Society: Pete Johnson, Big Joe Turner.

- 1935: Swing Era is launched by Benny Goodman.
- Swing bands flourish around the country: Count Basie, Jimmy Lunceford, Artie Shaw, Glenn Miller, Cab Calloway, Duke Ellington, Andy Kirk (with Mary Lou Williams), Chick Webb.
- Jazz singing arrives: Louis Armstrong, Bing Crosby, Billie Holiday, Ella Fitzgerald, Jimmy Rushing.
- Soloists become jazz stars: Louis Armstrong, Coleman Hawkins, Fats Waller, Lester Young, Art Tatum, Django Reinhardt (first major European jazz figure), Roy Eldridge, Charlie Christian.
- Bass and drums come into their own: Jimmy Blanton, Milt Hinton, Jo Jones, Sid Catlett.
- 1939–45: World War II.

One Week Only!

Commencing

SATURDAY
JULY 14th

★

The Incomparable

FLETCHER

HENDERSON

and his FAMOUS ORCHESTRA

playing against

Chick Webb . . .

. . . and his Sensational Ban

SAVOY   World's Finest Ballroo
Lenox Ave., 140-141 S

PART I

1944–49: Bebop
- Pioneeers: Charlie Parker, Dizzy Gillespie, Kenny Clarke, Thelonious Monk, Bud Powell, Dexter Gordon, Max Roach, Sarah Vaughan.

1950s: Cool jazz and hard bop
- Cool jazz: Miles Davis, Modern Jazz Quartet, Lennie Tristano, Gil Evans, Gerry Mulligan, Stan Getz, Dave Brubeck, George Russell.
- Hard bop: Max Roach, Art Blakey, Horace Silver, Charles Mingus, John Coltrane, Sonny Rollins, Clifford Brown, Wes Montgomery.
- 1950–53: Korean War.
- 1955–68: Civil Rights Movement.

1960s–1980s:
Avant-Garde (or Free Jazz) and Loft Era
- 1960s avant-garde: Ornette Coleman, Cecil Taylor, Albert Ayler, Sonny Rollins, John Coltrane, Sun Ra, AACM, Anthony Braxton, Art Ensemble of Chicago, Andrew Hill.
- 1960s postbop: Miles Davis, Wayne Shorter, Joe Henderson.
- 1961–75: American involvement in Vietnam War.
- 1970s loft jazz: David Murray, Arthur Blythe, Leroy Jenkins, Henry Threadgill.
- 1989: Beginning of overthrow of Communist states.

Horace Silver, at piano, rehearses with his quintet: tenor saxophonist Junior Cook, trumpeter Louis Smith, bassist Gene Taylor, and drummer Louis Hayes, 1958.

Thelonious Monk (center) and Charlie Rouse (right) visit with the Prague Mime Troupe at the Village Gate in New York, 1963.

Wynton Marsalis in New Orleans, 1993.

Cab Calloway and two chorus girls at the Strand Theater in New York, 1940s.

Cecil Taylor was a controversial new-comer at the Newport Jazz Festival, 1957.

Fusion Narrative

- 1940s–1950s jazz-pop: Louis Jordan, Ray Charles, Jimmy Smith, Sarah Vaughan, Stan Getz, Frank Sinatra, Nat "King" Cole.
- 1969–70, beginning of jazz-rock: Miles Davis, Tony Williams, Herbie Hancock.
- 1970s fusion: Chick Corea, John McLaughlin, Weather Report, Pat Metheny, Jaco Pastorius, Keith Jarrett, Oregon.
- 1980–1990s smooth jazz, hip-hop, acid jazz, jam bands: Kenny G, John Scofield, Medeski, Martin and Wood.
- 2000s fusion: Robert Glasper.

Historicist Narrative

- 1930s: New Orleans revival.
- 1950s: Festivals, academia.
- 1970s: Jazz as "tradition."
- CD reissues, repertory bands, jazz in film and documentaries.
- Neoclassical (or historicist) jazz: Wynton Marsalis, SFJAZZ Collective, Betty Carter, Michael Brecker, Abdullah Ibrahim, Harry Connick Jr., Diana Krall.
- Jason Moran, Vijay Iyer, Esperanza Spalding, Cécile McLorin Salvant, and a new generation.

MUSICAL ELEMENTS AND INSTRUMENTS

EMPATHY

How does a gifted and aspiring young instrumentalist become a jazz musician? In the early 1940s, at the height of the Swing Era, Allen Eager (1927–2003) was a kid living in the Bronx, trying to master the tenor saxophone. He was a natural, with a formidable technique, and he knew just what he wanted to sound like: his idol Ben Webster, whose gruff, robust way of playing was so distinctive you could tell who it was after hearing a few notes. Webster, a saxophonist's saxophonist for years, became a major jazz star in 1940, after he joined the Duke Ellington Orchestra and recorded an unforgettable improvisation on Ellington's tune "Cotton Tail." Even now, musicians continue to study and memorize that solo.

So one evening, when Eager was fifteen and the Ellington band was playing in New York City, he took the subway into Manhattan to hear it. During a break between sets, he walked over to Webster, told him he was his favorite saxophonist, and begged him for a lesson. Webster didn't teach, but something about Eager's enthusiasm charmed him, and he agreed to have him visit the Harlem apartment building where the band boarded. When the day arrived, Webster asked him to play something. Eager assembled his tenor and played Webster's raging "Cotton Tail" solo, note for note.

Charlie Parker—blindingly fast virtuoso, bluesman, romantic ballad player—with his fellow 1949 Metronome All-Stars Lennie Tristano (piano), Eddie Safranski (bass), and Billy Bauer (guitar).

While classical music is housed in permanent concert halls like Carnegie Hall, most jazz clubs have shorter life spans. Bop City opened in 1948 at Broadway and 49th Street in Manhattan, accommodating top-line acts, but was gone within a few years.

© HERMAN LEONARD PHOTOGRAPHY LLC

Webster could hardly believe it. He woke up other Ellington musicians who were staying in neighboring rooms, exclaiming, "Listen to this white kid!" After that session, Webster invited Eager back for subsequent lessons. He never charged his student a dime. He was delighted to have such a devoted and obviously talented young disciple. Then came what Eager—when he told the story many years later—referred to as the "tragic reverse."

Eager traveled to Los Angeles, and while he was there visited a friend who put on a stack of records by the tenor saxophonist Lester Young—Webster's old friend and contemporary (they were born five months apart in 1909). In fact, Webster had gotten his start playing alongside Lester in the Young Family Band, which toured the South in the 1920s under the leadership of Lester's father. In the intervening years, Young, the star saxophonist with the Count Basie Orchestra, had developed a new way of playing the tenor, virtually the opposite of Ben's: a very smooth, evenly articulated style as compared with Webster's opulent, ornate approach. Ben was hot; Lester was cool. Eager had never paid much attention to Young, but now he fell completely in love with his serene sound. He filed his mouthpiece as Lester did in striving to mimic it.

A couple of years later, Eager returned to New York, now as a professional jazz musician with a gig at a prominent nightclub. Soon after he opened, Ben Webster proudly came by to hear and cheer his former student, only to discover another Lesterphile. "It was terrible," Eager later recalled, "a great disappointment to Ben. And it made me feel weird."

Before long, Eager emerged as a distinctive tenor saxophonist in his own right. Unusually for the time, he worked mostly with black bands, including those of Charlie Parker and Coleman Hawkins. By 1948, he had developed a sound more ethereal than Lester's, almost unearthly in its soft strength. You can hear him at his best on recordings he made with the pianist and composer Tadd Dameron. In later years, he left jazz for a long stretches of time and became known as a race car driver and exponent of LSD. But his work with Dameron remains classic jazz—shrewdly lyrical, and unmistakably beholden to the broad influence of Lester Young. Would he have arrived at his meticulous style if he had not also undergone a decisive Ben Webster period? It seems unlikely. Somehow, his double discipleship combined with other influences (he also studied clarinet with a member of the New York Philharmonic) brought Eager from a prodigious apprenticeship to a mastery of personal expression, which is the essence of jazz. This process might be described as extreme empathy.

All music—all art, all entertainment—requires empathy, but jazz requires empathy of a particular sort. Jazz musicians are inventing a musical statement (**improvising**) in that space and in that moment. In order to share in their creativity, you have to follow the twists and turns of their musical ideas while simultaneously registering their interaction with other musicians; only then can you evaluate whether a trumpet or saxophone solo, say, is a success—the soloist may be a spellbinder or a bore—and the band coherent. Sidney Bechet, the great soprano saxophonist of jazz's early years, once remarked, "You got to be in the sun to feel the sun. It's that way with music too."

One way to gain a deeper understanding is to learn some of the fundamental rules and techniques of music. Obviously, at a basic level you can simply listen to a performance and be amused, amazed, shaken, moved—you don't need anyone to tell you that you like it, or why. Most fans can recall their first exposure to jazz, whether it was a performance in a nightclub or concert hall, or on a classic recording by Louis Armstrong, Billie Holiday, John Coltrane, or Jason Moran. Often, just one encounter is enough to encourage a desire to hear more of that artist and other jazz artists.

Yet only by pressing deeper into the music, to the point where you listen like a musician, can you penetrate jazz's most rewarding mysteries. As a child, you may enjoy your first baseball game knowing only that one player pitches to another while teammates in the field strive to foil any hits. But soon you want more than that: a team to root for, understanding of rules, appreciation for tactics, statistics of varying relevance—all to intensify your involvement in the game. Jazz is similarly most rewarding to a listener conversant with its rules.

TIMBRE

Timbre refers to quality of sound, or tone color. All instruments, including the human voice, have distinct qualities—timbres—that set them apart, even when they play the same pitch. The gross differences are easy to hear: a violin sounds noticeably different from a trumpet. A tenor saxophone sounds less noticeably different from an alto saxophone. Further, timbre is something we control. We can deliberately manipulate our voices to whisper or shout, to command or console, or to express fear, love, anger, exhaustion. Jazz musicians try to lend their instruments the same qualities of human speech, though this is not as easy with a piece of metal as it is with the larynx. Some horn players use **mutes**—physical devices inserted into the bell of the instrument to distort the sounds coming out. The use of unusual sounds for expressive purposes, known as **timbre variation**, came to jazz through African American folk culture, but it lies deep within the idea of all folk traditions.

Understanding timbre is vital to an appreciation of jazz, because it is the first key to a musician's individual style. The tenor saxophonist Buddy Tate, known for his many years with the Count Basie Orchestra, once said that the first crucial step for young musicians is to find their own sound. That is a pretty radical notion. Tate didn't mean that an unfledged musician had to find a sound unlike anyone else's, just for the sake of novelty. Rather, the young musician needs to know *who* he is in order to find a sound he knows to be his own. The task is only partly a conscious one. Louis Armstrong had an ebullient personality that's reflected in his trumpet sound. Miles Davis had a more introverted personality that's reflected in his. This kind of individuality can't be taught.

THE ENSEMBLE

A jazz orchestra usually consists of trumpets, trombones, saxophones, piano, bass, and drums; a piano trio usually includes a piano, bass, and drums; a quintet usually consists of

Louis Armstrong warms up on his trumpet while trombonist Tommy Dorsey and saxophonist Bud Freeman watch.

PHOTO BY CHARLES PETERSON, COURTESY OF DON PETERSON

saxophone, trumpet, piano, bass, and drums. Yet jazz masterpieces have also been created for unaccompanied piano or saxophone; trumpet and piano; piano, bass, and guitar; organ, guitar, and drums; combined big band and symphony orchestra; multiple percussionists; and so forth, to the limit of instrumental resources and artistic imagination. At present, there is no jazz masterwork for turntable, but tomorrow there may be.

Wind Instruments (Horns)

In jazz, the largest category of instruments consists of those that produce sound by moving air—all referred to in jazz (unlike classical music) as wind instruments, or horns. The physics of wind instruments is fairly simple. Blowing on or into a tube sets a column of air in vibration, producing a particular sound. (Most wind players generate a slight wobble in pitch, known as **vibrato**.) Musicians can modify that sound by adjusting the length of the tube, or by blowing with increased intensity. The latter involves changing the embouchure, the positioning of the lips and other facial muscles—this forces the vibration to suddenly jump to a new level, raising the pitch.

▶ BRASS: The **trumpet** has an unmistakable timbre: a brittle, crisp attack with brilliant overtones. A player can vary his timbre by **half-valving**: depressing one or more of the valves only halfway. Another technique is the **shake**, a quick trill between two notes that mimics a wide vibrato. And many trumpet players carry with them a small arsenal of mutes, each with its own distinctive possibilities.

The **straight mute**, inserted directly into the bell of the instrument, quiets the sound without too much distortion. The **cup mute** adds an extension that more or less covers the bell, further attenuating the sound while rounding it out. The **Harmon mute** is a hollow mute with a hole in the center; originally the hole was filled with an adjustable sliding tube, suitable for comic effects, but most jazz musicians simply discarded the tube, creating a highly concentrated sound. Finally, the **plunger mute** is as simple as the name suggests: it's the rubber end of a sink plunger. By moving the plunger in various positions away from the bell, the player can adjust the sound so expertly that it resembles human speech. Often these mutes are used in combination. Bubber Miley, a soloist with the early Duke Ellington band, developed an unearthly sound by modifying his trumpet, already muted with a tiny, straight pixie mute, with a plunger—all the while growling in his throat.

The **trombone's** occasionally comical slide enables the player to glide seamlessly from one note to another, an effect known as a **glissando**, or **smear**. Given how difficult it is to play pitches accurately by pumping a single slide, the achievement of virtuoso jazz trombonists is remarkable.

▶ REEDS: The **clarinet**, a slim, cylindrical, wooden tube that produces a thin, occasionally shrill sound, was a standard component of the New Orleans jazz style. It achieved greater renown during the Swing Era of the 1930s, when two of

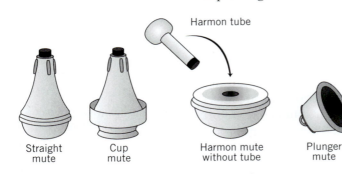

Harmon tube

Straight mute

Cup mute

Harmon mute without tube

Plunger mute

TRUMPET OR CORNET?

The similarity between the trumpet and the cornet causes much confusion in discussions of early jazz. The two instruments look and sound alike: the cornet has an extra layer of tubing and a deeper mouthpiece, producing a slightly mellower timbre. They are so similar that it is often impossible to distinguish which of the two is heard on recordings made in the 1920s. Adding to the confusion is the inclination of some commentators and musicians to refer to the trumpet as a cornet, and vice versa. Although the cornet dominated jazz at first, by 1926 it began to lose favor to the trumpet, with its brighter, more piercing sound.

FRANK DRIGGS COLLECTION

During the Swing Era, Artie Shaw rivaled Benny Goodman for popularity on the clarinet. Here, Shaw leads one of the few integrated small groups in 1945: Dodo Marmarosa (piano), Roy Eldridge (trumpet), Shaw, Barney Kessel (guitar), Morris Raymond (bass).

the most popular bandleaders, Benny Goodman and Artie Shaw, offered an inadvertent rivalry that excited fans. Beginning in the early 1960s, thanks chiefly to Eric Dolphy, the **bass clarinet** (pitched lower than the regular clarinet) found acceptance by musicians and is still often heard.

Far more common in jazz is the **saxophone**, the one wind instrument jazz can claim as its own. The kinds used most often are the **alto, tenor, soprano,** and **baritone saxophone**. In the early twentieth century, dance bands and vaudeville performers embraced the instrument as much for its parody potential as musical versatility. By 1930, thanks to such premier players as Sidney Bechet (soprano), Coleman Hawkins (tenor), Johnny Hodges and Benny Carter (alto), and Harry Carney (baritone), the saxophone had become the soul of American music: an all-purpose instrument able to play sweet or hot while suggesting tenderness or aggression.

With both saxophone and clarinet, musicians can vary the quality of pitches by flicking their tongue against the mouthpiece, **growling** into the instrument, or blowing intensely enough to produce more than one pitch, known as **multiphonics**.

New Orleans virtuoso Sidney Bechet (center) was trained on the clarinet (several are lined up on the stage floor), but he soon switched to the soprano saxophone, a straight instrument that contrasts visually with the alto saxophone (held by Otto Hardwick, right) and the tenor (Frank "Big Boy" Goudie). In the Noble Sissle band, 1928.

Rhythm Section

▶ **PIANO:** The members of the accompanying rhythm section have changed over time, as jazz has changed, but they usually number three or four, and their functions have remained stable: to provide harmony, bass, and percussion. Some instruments are naturally designed to play chords (harmony), including the **vibraphone, organ, synthesizer, electric piano, guitar**, and, in the earliest years, **banjo**. The most important, though, is the acoustic **piano**. Pianists may use the wide range of the keyboard (over seven octaves) to imitate the sound of a full orchestra or pound on the keys like a drum.

FRANK DRIGGS COLLECTION

FRANK DRIGGS COLLECTION

The "All-American" rhythm section of the Count Basie band was light yet powerful. From left to right: Walter Page, bass; Jo Jones, drums; Freddie Green, guitar; and Basie, piano. The rest of the band, crowded into the tiny bandstand at New York's Famous Door in 1938, from front row to back: Herschel Evans, Earl Warren, Jack Washington, and Lester Young, saxophones; Buck Clayton (standing), Ed Lewis, Harry Edison, trumpets; Benny Morton, Dan Minor (hidden behind Clayton), Dicky Wells, trombones.

▶ **BASS:** The **bass** is the rock on which the jazz ensemble is built. In a performance, we are naturally inclined to pay attention to the trumpet or saxophone soloist, while also registering the drums and pianist. The bass can get lost in the undercurrent unless we focus on it. Musicians are always focused on it. It has, roughly speaking, two crucial functions: playing notes that support the harmony, and providing a basic underlying rhythmic foundation. The most common instrument to fill this role is the **string bass** (also known as double bass), the same instrument used in symphony orchestras. Classical musicians usually draw a horsehair bow across the strings, a technique known as **arco**. Jazz musicians also use the bow, but they prefer the technique known as **pizzicato**: plucking the strings with their fingers. The plucked string has a percussive power that is much better suited to jazz's rhythmic nature. In the past half century, the string bass has often been supplanted by the guitar-like **electric bass**, which, though lacking the powerful natural resonance of the string bass, has the advantages of loudness and portability.

▶ **DRUMS:** The **drum kit,** or **traps** (short for "contraption"), is a one-man percussion section within the rhythm section within the band. While every jazz drummer configures the drum set in his own manner, the basic arrangement is fairly stable. The drummer sits on a stool in the center of a semicircular assembly of drums and cymbals, with the powerful **bass drum** front and center. The **snare drum**, with its penetrating, rattling sound, stands on an adjustable stand at knee level. Spreading out from it are two or more middle-size drums without snares, called **tom-toms**, which are tuned according to taste and come in various sizes.

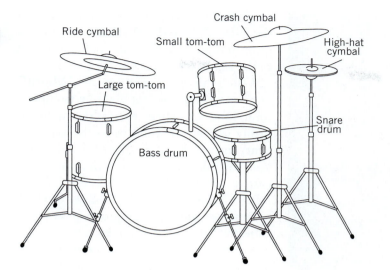

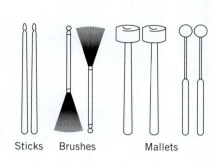

Sticks   Brushes   Mallets

A forest of cymbals provides a steely contrast to the drums below them. Two are suspended. The medium-size **ride cymbal** has a clear, focused timbre and is played more or less continuously—the band "rides" on its lithe rhythmic pulse. The slightly smaller **crash cymbal** has a splashy, indeterminate pitch, not unlike a small gong, and is used for dramatic punctuations. The third essential cymbal, the **high-hat**, consists of two shoulder-level cymbals on an upright pole with a foot pedal at its base. The pedal brings the top cymbal crashing into the lower one with a distinct *chunk*.

A jazz drummer will typically use his right foot on the bass drum pedal, his left on the high-hat pedal, his right hand wielding a stick on the ride cymbal, and his left holding a stick to play the snare drum or tom-tom. Along with wooden sticks, the drummer may use **wire brushes** to strike or literally brush the drumheads, or **mallets** for conveying a soft, quiet rumble. What distinguishes jazz drumming is the sheer virtuosity—the flexibility and subtlety—that keeps other musicians and the listener involved, a task very different from merely keeping the beat. The drummer is free to respond to whatever the soloist plays and is expected to be attentive and quick-witted enough to fill in the empty spaces or to know when not to.

Some drummers don't play the traps at all. These are the masters of Latin percussion. **Congas** are tall drums of equal height but different diameters, with the smaller one assigned the lead role. The much smaller **bongos** have two drumheads, one larger than the other, compact enough to sit between the player's knees. The **timbales** consist of two drums mounted on a stand along with a cowbell and are played with sticks by a standing musician. Among other percussion instruments are shakers (the **maraca** is a gourd filled with beans) and scrapers (the **guiro** is a gourd with ridges). In recent decades, jazz bands often include—in addition to the regular drummer—a percussionist who works with dozens of instruments: shakers, scrapers, bells, blocks, and noisemakers of every description. Percussion, like music, is a world without end.

Latin percussion

FROM POLYRHYTHM TO SWING

► Meter

Rhythm in music is directly related to biology. The beating of our hearts and the intervals of our breathing are the foundations from which humans developed dance and music. Heartbeats are relatively stable and articulate

Every drummer begins with the basic drum set, but finds a way to alter the sound to suit his particular personality. Jack DeJohnette's set-up is heavy on cymbals, ranging from the high-hat in the front to the ride in the back, with crash cymbals in between.

© CHUCK STEWART

time with a steady *thump-thump-thump* of the pulse. This "**pulse rhythm**," moving at a given **tempo** (speed), is the basic approach to rhythm used in jazz.

Listen to the opening of "Midriff" (a piece written for this book by trumpeter John D'earth), where the pulse rhythm is firmly in control. Tune in to the pulse, or **beat**, and try counting along to the music. You will likely come up with a recurring pattern: either 1-2, 1-2 or 1-2-3-4, 1-2-3-4. No one counts 1-2-3-4-5-6-7-8-9-10. That's because we *automatically* group pulses into patterns that constitute a **meter**. In jazz and most other kinds of music, the most common is **duple meter**, which means that the beats are patterned in twos or fours: every **measure**, or **bar**—indicated in notation by vertical lines—has either two or four beats, as is the case with "Midriff." Counting with these groups in mind, you will be able to hear and feel the music through the meter.

"Breath rhythm" is more elusive. Although we breathe continuously, we can speed it up or slow it down, or even (for a time) stop it altogether. In music, this can be called **rubato**, or **free rhythm**, and it is often heard in an introduction, as in the opening of Louis Armstrong's "West End Blues." Although this solo trumpet passage is played with tremendous drive, we don't feel like tapping our feet—until about fifteen seconds in, when Armstrong returns to a steady, calm pulsation.

▶ Polyrhythm

Jazz must be understood as a music that derives, in a fundamental sense, from Africa. Within the repetitive cyclic structures of jazz (discussed in Chapter 2), the music is organized by **rhythmic layers**: highly individualized parts that contrast with one another, even as they serve to create a unified whole. This simultaneous use of contrasting rhythms is known as **polyrhythm**, or **rhythmic contrast**. In a piece of African (and African American) music, *there are always at least two different rhythmic layers going on at the same time.* The most basic rhythms are the **foundation layers**—continuous, unchanging patterns whose very repetition provides a framework for the whole. In "Midriff," the bass plays a steady stream of evenly spaced notes. High above it, the drummer reinforces this pattern on the ride cymbal. These two layers are the foundation for jazz, and musicians responsible for them are said to be **keeping time**, an essential part of music making.

Foundation layers

Variable layers

Jazz soloists supply the **variable layers** of rhythm, but the rhythm section does as well. The pianist's chords may fall on the beat or in between beats. As the drummer keeps time on the ride cymbal with his right hand, his other limbs play accents on the rest of the drum kit that comment on or contradict that pulse. These layers dance above the foundation, sometimes sticking close to the beat, at other times diverging sharply from it. Every time a strong accent contradicts the basic meter, **syncopation** occurs. In most classical music, syncopation is an occasional rhythmic disruption, a temporary

Syncopation

"special effect" injected for variety. In jazz, syncopation is not an effect—it is the very air jazz breathes.

Consider, for example, what happens when you snap your fingers to "Midriff." More likely than not, your snap does not align with the **downbeat** (the first beat of every measure). If you count along, the beats you emphasize are not 1-2-3-4, but 1-**2**-3-**4**. This crucial layer in the music, the **backbeat**, offers a simple way for listeners to contribute. Whether we actually snap on the backbeat or silently respond to it in the course of listening, we add our own contrasting layer and become part of the music.

During his short career, John Coltrane became the most influential tenor saxophonist of his generation, while inspiring others to take up his secondary instrument, the soprano saxophone.

▶ Swing

If you combine the steady, four-beat rhythm in the bass and cymbal with a backbeat, you end up with a **groove**, the overall framework within which rhythmic things happen. There are many kinds of grooves. The one described here is known generically as **swing**, and it's basic to jazz. Others, like Latin and funk, draw jazz into a conversation with other musical worlds. "Swing" is a term that is impossible to define precisely (some technical aspects of swing rhythm are discussed in the Primer at the back of the book). But when all the rhythms interlock smoothly, something magical takes place and everyone in the vicinity (musicians, dancers, listeners) feels it. The band is swinging or "in the groove" or "jumping" or "feeling it together." All those clichés mean basically the same thing. Swinging spreads sunlight on everyone it touches, beginning with the members of the band.

The score of a Beethoven symphony includes all the information a conductor needs to perform it with an orchestra. A score prepared for a jazz orchestra may include the same kind of notation, but musicians unfamiliar with jazz practices, no matter how proficient, might play every note correctly and still turn out a plodding, unrecognizable performance. Similarly, if an operatic soprano who had never sung jazz sang "A Sailboat in the Moonlight," she might sing every note correctly yet capture none of Billie Holiday's lithe grace. An inability to swing (and the impossibility of notating swing) has been the ruin of many gifted instrumentalists who have tried to play jazz and failed.

MELODY AND HARMONY

▶ Melody

The basic unit of melody is the **scale**—the pitches that fall within the octave. Musical tones are named with the first seven letters of the alphabet—A, B, C, D, E, F, G—repeated over and over, and the **octave**, as shown below, is the distance from one C to the next (higher or lower), one F to the next, and so on. All you need for an understanding of the world of pitch is to grasp the patterns within the octave. The twelve notes in an octave (counting white and black keys) make up a scale by themselves, known as a **chromatic scale**, with the interval separating each note a **half step**. But it's hardly the most common scale.

◀ Chromatic scale

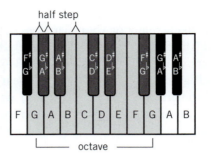

Chromatic scale (can begin on any note, here G):
G, G♯, A, A♯, B, C, C♯, D, D♯, E, F, F♯, G

Major mode

Try singing the pitches from C to C, the white keys on the piano keyboard, on the syllables *do, re, mi, fa, sol, la, ti, do* (the vast majority of people in Western culture can do this easily). This scale, the most basic in Western music, is called the **major mode**. (For our purposes, "scale" and "mode" are synonymous.) Each note is a **degree** of the scale: *do* is the first degree, *re* the second degree, and so on.

A crucial aspect of this scale is that the first degree—C (*do*) in the C major scale—is more important than the others. Melodies may not necessarily begin on *do*, but they are very likely to end on it. If you sing the first phrase of "Happy Birthday" ("Hap-py birth-day to you"), you end up floating in mid-air. That's because the last note, "you," falls on a note just short of *do*. The next phrase releases the tension, bringing the melody to its inexorable goal of *do* (on the second "you"). We call *do* the **tonic**, and music that insists on returning to the tonic (most of the music we listen to) is known as **tonal music**. The tension and release is like the use of gravity in dance. It's possible to escape the pull of gravity, but not for long.

It doesn't matter what note you choose as the tonic, because scales represent *patterns* of pitches that can be moved (or **transposed**) up or down as you like. The pattern is made up of half and whole steps: C to D is a **whole step** because there's a black key in between (C♯ or D♭). D to E is another whole step, and E to F is a half step. The complete pattern for a major scale, shown below starting on C, is W (whole step), W, H (half step), W, W, W, H.

C major scale: C, D, E, F, G, A, B, C (all white keys)

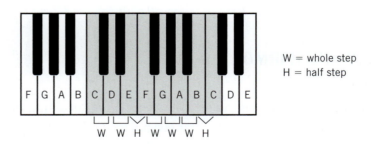

W = whole step
H = half step

The scale is named after its tonic: a C major scale begins on C, and the E♭ major scale begins on E♭. (The E♭ major scale, following the same pattern, is E♭, F, G, A♭, B♭, C, D, E♭.) Only C major stays on the white keys. For any other tonic, the pattern will inevitably involve the black keys, usually notated by **sharps** (♯) or **flats** (♭) at the beginning of a piece.

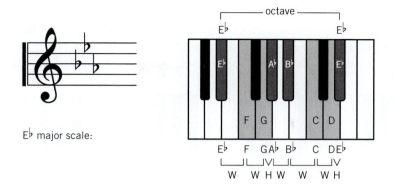

Eᵇ major scale:

The converse of the major mode is the **minor mode**, with a different half step/whole step pattern. The most important difference is in the third degree of the scale. In minor, the interval between *do* and *mi* (known as a **third**) is a half step lower; instead of moving from C to E (on the white keys), you move from C to Eᵇ. This difference may not seem like much, but it carries great emotional power. In general, minor sounds sad, moody, angry, or even tragic, while major sounds happy, peaceful, or triumphant. You need only listen to Ludwig van Beethoven's Fifth and Ninth Symphonies to hear the emotional upheaval that comes when the minor mode is thunderously replaced by the major at the end.

Minor mode

Jazz musicians also make much use of other scales, described in the Primer at the back of the book, each with its own unique pattern, sound, and expressive potential. The scale most central to the development of jazz, however, is the **blues scale**—a collection of pitches that is also an avenue into an African American cultural world. All American music—jazz, blues, gospel, pop, rhythm and blues, country and western, rock and roll, hip-hop—is influenced by its sound.

Blues scale

The blues scale, somewhere between major and minor, is actually not so much a scale as a system for creating melody. It's impossible to pin down because it takes a more relaxed approach to intonation, which in Western usage means "playing in tune." Certain notes are played with a great deal of flexibility, sliding through infinitesimal fractions (microtones) of a half step for expressive purposes—a system we might call **variable intonation**. Jazz musicians refer to these microtones as **blue notes**, or **bent notes**, and they cannot be signified in Western notation. On the piano keyboard, they are notes that would fall between the cracks.

Some of the greatest blues musicians play instruments—guitar, bass, trumpet, trombone, clarinet, saxophone—that are capable of producing subtle gradations between proper notes. The piano has no way to vary pitch like this, but it *can* approximate the sound of the blue note by playing two neighboring keys at the same time. Normally, playing both Eᵇ and E on the piano is a mistake. In jazz, this clash can spice up an improvisation; Thelonious Monk frequently used simulated blue notes to enliven his piano solos with expressive passion. In a sense, the blues is a mildly off-kilter way of looking at musical possibilities.

▶ Harmony

If you play two or more notes at the same time, you get a **chord**, the basis of harmony. The chord most fundamental to Western music is the three-note **triad**, which you can form endlessly by playing every other white key on a piano (C-E-G, D-F-A, E-G-B, and so on). Each triad takes its name from the bottom note, or **root**: a C major triad consists of C, E, and G; a D major

Chords

triad consists of D, F♯, and A. Jazz musicians can do whatever they want with harmony: they can rearrange a C major chord (with the E or G on the bottom, for example), or keep adding notes to the chord (C, E, G, B; C, E, G, B, D; and so on), producing more elaborate harmonies known as **extended chords**.

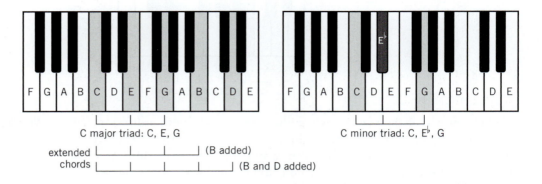

C major triad: C, E, G

C minor triad: C, E♭, G

extended ⌐—⌐—⌐ (B added)

chords ⌐—⌐—⌐—⌐ (B and D added)

Consonance/dissonance

Jazz musicians improvise over a **harmonic progression**, also known as the **changes**—a series of chords played in a strict rhythmic sequence. As the term "progression" suggests, the movement from chord to chord conveys a feeling of moving forward: **dissonant** (unstable or jarring) chords are pulled as if by gravity to **consonant** (stable) chords. The next-to-last note of "Happy Birthday," for example (on "to"), would be harmonized with the unstable V (**dominant**) chord, leading immediately to the consonant I (**tonic**) chord on the final "you."

Cadence

The end of a **phrase**, where a chord progression comes to rest (temporarily or finally), is called a **cadence**, and you can easily hear the two main kinds of cadences in the opening of "A Sailboat in the Moonlight." There are two long phrases, each beginning with the same melody but veering off to different conclusions. The first ending is a **half cadence** ("just for two") and sounds incomplete (the phrase ends on the V chord); the music couldn't stop here. The second phrase ("A soft breeze") begins like the first, but moves inexorably toward a **full cadence** ("come true"), with the melody and the harmony converging on the stable home chord (the I, or tonic). The first phrase poses a question that is answered by the second.

Of course, not all music operates according to rules of tonality. Atonal music recognizes no key center—but most jazz doesn't embrace a rigorous atonality. There is plenty of jazz that loosens the grip of tonality, creating free-floating chord progressions but not entirely banishing their pull toward tonal centers. Jazz musicians have a word for it (jazz musicians have a word for everything). When they play tonal harmonic progressions, they speak of playing "inside"; when they step outside of tonality, they play "outside." This language suggests, accurately enough, that a musician can easily move from one extreme to the other, even in the course of a solo.

TEXTURE

The balance between harmony and melody produces **texture**, of which there are three basic types: **homophony**, in which a melody is supported by harmonic accompaniment; **monophony**, where a melody exists on its own, without harmonic accompaniment; and **polyphony**, in which two or more melodies of equal interest are played at the same time.

FRANK DRIGGS COLLECTION

The year before he released his landmark album *Kind of Blue* (1959), on which "So What" is featured, Miles Davis took his new band on the road. This picture shows five of its six members at the Newport Jazz Festival in July 1958: Bill Evans, Jimmy Cobb, Paul Chambers, Davis, and John Coltrane.

▶ Homophony

Most music in and out of jazz is homophonic. We're used to hearing a strong main melody supported by a harmonic accompaniment. With homophony, the melody and the harmony are usually in separate musical layers: a guitar accompanying a singer, for example, or the pianist and bassist playing harmonies beneath Charlie Parker's saxophone in "Now's the Time." But in one important sub-category of homophonic music, the melody and harmony exist in a single layer: two or more instruments play the same phrase in the same rhythm, but with different pitches filling out the harmony, as in barbershop quartets. In jazz, this is called **block-chord texture**. Big bands depend on block chords. The first vocal trio in Paul Whiteman's "Changes" sings in block-chord harmony; the two-note harmonized figure played by three wind instruments in the theme of "So What" is also an example of block-chord texture.

Block-chord texture

Another sub-category is **countermelody**, or **obbligato**, where the subordinate instruments have melodic interest of their own, but not enough to compete with the main melody. In "A Sailboat in the Moonlight," Billie Holiday sings the main melody and tenor saxophonist Lester Young accompanies her, creating melodic ideas so rich they race shoulder to shoulder with her. Still, Young knows his place, emerging at full volume only in the **rests** (silences) between Holiday's vocal phrases.

Countermelody

▶ Monophony

When you sing in the shower, play a flute in the woods, or pick out a tune on the piano with one hand, you're creating monophony: a melody with no harmonic accompaniment. If 50,000 people sing "The Star-Spangled Banner" (melody only) in a baseball stadium without a band, it's still monophonic texture. In jazz, monophony usually occurs in solo **breaks**, when the rest of the band briefly stops playing to let a musician solo. A break, usually just two or four bars long, is a commonplace in early New Orleans jazz. It is at once a surprise that stimulates the audience and a challenge to the musician who has to fill the sudden space with a worthy moment. No matter how far jazz evolved, the break never lost its ability to impart a thrilling level of tension.

Breaks

Stop-time

Another instance of monophonic texture involves **stop-time** rhythm, created when the ensemble plays a short chord at brief intervals—say, once every bar or once every other bar—and the soloist improvises with just these interruptions from the band prodding him on. Unlike the break, which rarely lasts more than two or four bars, stop-time is open-ended, lasting as long as the musicians want.

And monophonic texture is often used to begin or end a piece. Armstrong begins "West End Blues" with what many regard as the single most significant monophonic outburst in jazz history—a radiant trumpet fanfare, or **cadenza**, that keeps us on the edge of our seat until the rest of the band finally enters. In "Body and Soul," the monophonic texture comes toward the end, as Coleman Hawkins lets the band drop out, leaving him with an unaccompanied passage that allows a heated performance to cool down.

◘ Polyphony

In polyphonic texture, two or more melody lines compete for our attention simultaneously. Polyphony is a special province of classical music, where J. S. Bach epitomizes the art of counterpoint (the intertwining of several equal voices). In jazz, polyphony is treated more casually. New Orleans jazz often features polyphonic passages in which three instruments—trumpet, trombone, and clarinet—improvise at the same time, with no one melody standing out. Polyphony faded from jazz once New Orleans style was replaced by big-band swing, with its homophonic textures. Then in the 1950s, many musicians tried to revive this technique, often by imitating models from classical music. And in avant-garde jazz, players go to great lengths to institute equality between all the members in a band.

LICKS AND RIFFS

All great jazz soloists have their own way of communicating a personal style through phrasing. Miles Davis favors short, terse phrases—a few notes surrounded by silence (or by the rhythm section's response). Charlie Parker prefers long, sinuous, virtuoso phrases that boldly fly from one point to the next. Some melodic phrases, called **licks**, are simple and basic, part of the common lore of jazz. Budding jazz musicians learn licks by listening closely to experienced soloists. The fast lick in Parker's "Now's the Time" solo, for example, pops up in many of his other solos. Although it may be disconcerting to discover that even a player as brilliant as Parker repeats the same licks, this is how improvisation works. You might compare it to speech, where a relatively limited vocabulary creates an infinity of sounds and meaning.

A **riff** is a repeated fragment of melody. In the theme of "So What," the bass plays a phrase that's answered by a two-note piano riff—barely long enough to count as a musical thought. The horns then take up the riff, continuing the repetition. Another riff is found at the beginning of "Now's the Time." In classical music, any melody that repeats insistently is known as an **ostinato** (Italian for "stubborn"), and these examples are sometimes called **ostinato riffs**. Tune like Count Basie's "One O'Clock Jump" are made of riffs—sometimes in the background, sometimes as the main melody. At their best, riffs are jazz gems: so simple anyone can play them, yet so fully capable of generating emotional and physical exultation.

The terms explained here will be used throughout the book to describe the music. Now we look at how these musical elements all come together in performance, in a miraculous combination of stable form and spontaneous improvisation.

ONLINE MULTIMEDIA RESOURCES AND REVIEW MATERIALS

Author Insight Videos

Gary Giddins encourages students to find their own way into jazz, through the personalities that strike them. Scott DeVeaux discusses the Virginia roots of players in the Dave Matthews band and the permeability of the boundary between jazz and rock.

Interactive Listening Guide

Free Bridge Quintet, "Midriff"

Jazz Concepts (audio and/or video demonstrations of terms covered here)

backbeat	drum kit	polyphony
bass	duple meter	polyrhythm
blue (bent) notes	foundation layers	saxophone
block chords	glissando (smear)	shake
break	half step	stop-time
cadence (half and full)	half-valving	swing
chord	homophony	syncopation
chromatic scale	major scale (or mode)	tonic (I) chord
clarinet	minor scale (or mode)	triad
consonant	multiphonics	trombone
countermelody	octave	trumpet
cymbals	percussion	variable layers
dissonant	phrase	whole step
dominant (V) chord	piano	
downbeat	pizzicato	

- For quick reference, review the **Chapter Overview** and **Chapter Outline**.
- Take the online **Chapter** and **Listening Quizzes**.
- Use the online **Glossary** and **Flashcards** to review important terms.

JAZZ FORM
AND IMPROVISATION

In jazz, unlike classical music, musical form is relatively straightforward. You don't have to be a musician to understand it. You only have to be able to hear patterns of eight or twelve, and distinguish between basic melodies that are designated **A** and **B**. Although it isn't necessary to know the difference between one song form and another to enjoy the flow of improvised ideas, once you understand the basics of form, something magical happens. You find yourself listening with greater insight, riding alongside the musicians and observing the choices they make.

Jazz concepts of form are derived from African music, where improvisation happens within a repeated rhythmic **cycle**. In jazz, the cycle is known as the **chorus**. Each chorus tune is a fixed rhythmic length (twelve or thirty-two measures, for example), and has its own harmonic (chord) progression.

A harmonic progression can be any size. If you've ever played "Heart and Soul" as a cyclic piano duet, over and over, you are familiar with a (very short) harmonic progression: the pianist on the left plays four chords in a certain order, then repeats them, while the pianist on the right plays melodies that fit over the progression. The tune lasts until the melody player runs out of ideas or comes up with a satisfying conclusion. Here is

Lester Young, nicknamed Pres (as in president of all saxophonists) by Billie Holiday, epitomized cool in his music, his lingo, and even the angle at which he held the tenor saxophone. A New York club, 1948.

Of all the "classic" blues singers of the 1920s, Bessie Smith was the most powerful and subtle. Wrapped in her stage regalia, as in this 1923 shot, she billed herself as the "Empress of the Blues" in theaters and tent shows across the country.

FRANK DRIGGS COLLECTION

the principle of **rhythmic contrast** in action: there are two distinct layers, one fixed (the left side's chords) and one variable.

In a jazz ensemble, the rhythm section plays the fixed chord progression in an unchanging and potentially endless circle of repeated choruses. The first and last choruses may consist of the straight tune with no improvisation, known as the **head**. In other choruses, the variable part is represented by a soloist (instrumental or vocal) embellishing and improvising over the progression.

Although a jazz chorus can, in theory, take any form, in practice musicians tend to focus on two structures for their improvisations: the **blues** and the **thirty-two-bar popular song**.

BLUES FORM

Blues form has its origin in African American folk poetry, featuring a distinctive, asymmetric three-line stanza, as in Bessie Smith's "Reckless Blues":

> *When I wasn't nothing but a child,* (4 bars)
> *When I wasn't nothing but a child,* (4 bars)
> *All you men tried to drive me wild.* (4 bars)

Each line takes up four measures, so that all three together make a **twelve-bar blues**. Each twelve bars, in purely instrumental blues as well as vocal, make up a single chorus.

Besides its twelve measures, blues form is marked by the particular harmonic scheme shown below, derived from folk practice. In its most basic form, the harmony uses only three chords: the I, or **tonic,** chord, the piece's home base (in C, this is C-E-G, or C7: C-E-G-B♭); IV, the **subdominant** chord (F-A-C, or F7: F-A-C-E♭); and V, the **dominant** chord (G-B-D, or G7: G-B-D-F). Basically, the harmony changes at the beginning of each four-measure group:

I	I	I	I	(4 bars)
IV	IV	I	I	(4 bars)
V	V	I	I	(4 bars)

At the end of each chorus (in measures 11-12), musicians often play a **turnaround**, chords that lead back to the beginning of the next chorus.

Listen to several choruses of Louis Armstrong's "West End Blues," using the guide below to help keep your place. After Armstrong's trumpet fanfare, once the band begins to play, try counting the twelve bars in each chorus, and listen for the regular changes in harmony.

▶ "West End Blues"

CHORUS I

0:16   The full ensemble begins with a I chord.

0:27   The harmony moves to IV.

0:33   The harmony resolves back to I.

0:39   The band plays a V chord.

0:44   The harmony arrives on I, followed by a turnaround.

CHORUS 2 (TROMBONE ACCOMPANIED BY WOODBLOCKS)

0:50   I chord

1:02   IV chord

1:07   I chord

1:13   V chord

1:19   I chord and turnaround

CHORUS 3 (DUET: JIMMY STRONG, CLARINET, AND LOUIS ARMSTRONG, WORDLESS VOCAL)

1:24   I chord

1:36   IV chord

1:41   I chord

1:47   V chord

1:53   I chord and turnaround

CHORUS 4 (EARL HINES, PIANO)

1:59   I chord

2:10   IV chord

2:16   I chord

2:21   V chord

2:27   I chord and turnaround

CHORUS 5 (LOUIS ARMSTRONG, TRUMPET)

2:32   I chord

2:44   IV chord

2:50   I chord

CODA (TAG ENDING)

2:56   V chord (piano, rubato)

3:12   I chord (full cadence)

To hear the blues in a more modern style, listen to Charlie Parker's "Now's the Time," recorded in 1953, twenty-five years after "West End Blues." You can hear instantly the changes that have taken place: that sizzling cymbal in the first measure tells a very different story from the clip-clopping hand cymbals of 1928. Yet for all its volatility, radically transformed rhythm, and harmonic complexity, this is still a twelve-bar blues, relying on the same underlying rhythm that guided Armstrong. Each musician takes a solo that fits precisely within the twelve-bar structure: Parker, the group's leader, has the longest solo at five choruses, followed by the pianist (two choruses) and the bass and drums (one chorus each). It should be easy to hear the blues's rhythmic structure. See if you can *feel* where the next chorus is about to begin.

▶ "Now's the Time"

CHORUS 1

0:05   Charlie Parker (alto saxophone) plays the head.

CHORUS 2

0:20   Parker repeats the head with slight variations.

CHORUS 3

0:35   Parker takes a five-chorus solo.

CHORUS 4	CHORUS 5	CHORUS 6	CHORUS 7
0:49	1:03	1:18	1:32

CHORUS 8

1:46   Al Haig (piano) takes a two-chorus solo.

CHORUS 9

2:00

CHORUS 10

2:14   Percy Heath (bass) takes a one-chorus solo.

CHORUS 11

2:28   Max Roach (drums) takes a one-chorus solo.

CHORUS 12

2:42   Parker returns to the head.

Now try following the more complete Listening Guide below for "Midriff," some of which you listened to in Chapter 1. Concepts that you will encounter throughout the book can be heard in this piece; they are highlighted in boldface type.

▶ "Midriff"

CHORUS 1

0:00   Pete Spaar begins playing a **walking bass**: a steady four beats to the bar, providing the foundations to the chords while still generating melodic interest. Behind him, Robert Jospé (drums) offers a quiet accompaniment with a **backbeat** (accents on beats 2 and 4 of each measure), played with his left foot on the high-hat cymbal pedal.

CHORUS 2

0:13   With his right hand, Jospé begins a repeated rhythmic pattern (known as the **ride pattern**) on the ride cymbal. His left hand is free to add subtle accents on the snare drum.

CHORUS 3

0:27   Bob Hallahan (piano) plays chords in a rhythmically unpredictable manner, known as **comping** (jazz slang for "accompanying").

CHORUS 4

0:41 Jeff Decker (tenor saxophone) and John D'earth (trumpet) play the **head** (the composed portion of the tune) in bare **octaves**. Its first phrase is a long string of notes that ends, suddenly, in a short rhythmic **motive** (a small musical idea). This motive is immediately echoed by the piano.

0:46 The second phrase is now treated like a **riff** (a repeated fragment of melody), repeating it with a few slight alterations to accommodate the change in harmony.

0:50 The last phrase enters a measure early, winding through the harmonies until it, too, reaches the rhythmic motive—this time, falling in a different part of the measure.

CHORUS 5

0:55 The horns repeat the head.

1:07 The third phrase is cut short on the downbeat. The band drops out, leaving space for a single soloist, D'earth, to be heard. This two-bar **monophonic** interruption of the normal **homophonic** texture is known as a **break**.

CHORUS 6

1:09 D'earth begins his two-chorus trumpet solo.

CHORUS 7

1:23 The band suddenly interrupts with a new composed section performed by the horns and the bass (even the drums second its rhythms). This is known as a **send-off riff**: a four-bar phrase that launches the soloist (sends him off) into the middle of the chorus.

1:29 D'earth continues his solo by mimicking the last phrase of the send-off riff.

CHORUS 8

1:38 The solo shifts to Decker on tenor saxophone.

CHORUS 9

1:52 Spaar suddenly restricts the bass line to a single repeated note, known as a **pedal point**. Above this steady foundation, Hallahan plays chords that shift **chromatically** up and down. Decker's improvisation becomes more dissonant—a phenomenon known in jazz as "**playing outside**."

2:01 As the musicians prepare for the next chorus, the harmonies drift back toward the normal chord progression.

CHORUS 10

2:06 The horns play a new composed section, known as the **shout chorus**. (In big bands, the shout chorus typically comes at the end of the performance; here it interrupts the flow of solos.)

2:15   The band repeats a short motive over and over, creating an over-whelming **polyrhythm.**

CHORUS 11

2:20   Dissonant notes from the end of the shout chorus introduce the next soloist, Spaar (bass). Both the drums and the piano play lightly, ensuring that the bass solo can be easily heard.

CHORUS 12

2:34   Jospé is the final soloist, fitting his drum improvisation within the twelve-bar cycle. He focuses on the drums (snare, tom-toms, bass) while keeping the backbeat on the high-hat cymbal.

CHORUS 13

2:48   The band returns to play the head.

CHORUS 14

3:03   The band repeats the head, with the piano and saxophone adding sharply dissonant asides.

CODA

3:15   The piece ends with three unsettling chords.

The blues withstood countless musical fashions to become the bedrock for rhythm and blues (in the 1940s) and rock and roll (in the 1950s), and the same basic form remains vital today. There is no such thing as a jazz musician who can't make something of a twelve-bar blues.

THIRTY-TWO-BAR POPULAR SONG FORM: A A B A

The other key form for jazz improvisation is the **thirty-two-bar A A B A** popular song. During the golden age of American songwriting, roughly from 1925 to 1960, tunes were written mostly by professional songwriters such as George Gershwin, Jerome Kern, Irving Berlin, Cole Porter, Richard Rodgers, Harold Arlen, and many others, including such jazz compatriots as Duke Ellington, Fats Waller, James P. Johnson, and Edgar Sampson.

These songs were conceived in two sections: an introductory **verse**, which helped provide a transition between spoken dialogue and song in a musical; and the thirty-two-bar section known as the **refrain**, or **chorus**—the melody that made the song successful if, as the songwriters hoped, members of the audience left the theater humming it. Verses can still be found in the sheet music, but with rare exceptions, jazz musicians have preferred to concentrate on the refrain, turning it into a continuous, repeating cycle.

The idea behind the form is simple. Compose an eight-bar phrase. Repeat it. Contrast it with a new eight-bar phrase (known as the **bridge**, or **release**). Finally, repeat the original phrase one last time. All thirty-two bars make a single chorus.

Singer Billie Holiday and tenor saxophonist Lester Young (to her right) were close colleagues from the 1930s, when they recorded tunes like "A Sailboat in the Moonlight." They hadn't seen each other in years when they appeared on a live television show in December 1957, along with tenor saxophonist Coleman Hawkins (in hat) and baritone saxophonist Gerry Mulligan. It was to be their last encounter.

A		statement (8 bars)
A		repetition (8 bars)
B (bridge)		contrast (8 bars)
A		return (8 bars)

This structure does not refer to the words, which can be written in any number of poetic forms. It refers only to the melody and harmonic progression. And unlike the blues, here composers can choose any harmonies they like.

Listen to "A Sailboat in the Moonlight," an **A A B A** song sung in a classic performance by Billie Holiday. You may notice that she doesn't sing the different **A** sections *exactly* the same, but adds subtle rhythmic variations as she goes along. Real melodic and harmonic contrast comes at the bridge, which she swings in a way the songwriters never imagined. Note also that the third chorus is abbreviated, with Holiday entering on the bridge (in order to fit the 78-rpm recording time).

▶ "A Sailboat in the Moonlight"

CHORUS 1 (BILLIE HOLIDAY, VOCAL)

A	0:08	*"A sailboat in the moonlight . . ."*
A	0:24	*"A soft breeze on a June night . . ."*
B	0:40	*"A chance to sail away . . ."*
A	0:57	*"The things, dear . . ."*

CBS/LANDOV

CHORUS 2

A	1:12	James Sherman, piano
A	1:28	
B	1:44	Buck Clayton, trumpet
A	2:00	Lester Young, tenor saxophone

CHORUS 3 (ABBREVIATED)

B	2:16	*"A chance to sail away . . ."*
A	2:32	*"The things, dear . . ."*

Musicians have found numberless ways to use the **A A B A** form as a fount for original compositions. Miles Davis's "So What" is among the best known. After an introduction, the head is made up of a bass line answered, in **call-and-response** fashion, by a two-note **riff** (repeated fragment of melody). In each eight-bar section, this mini-dialogue is played four times. At the bridge, there is a subtle but significant difference: the riff moves up a half step to a new key. It's easy to hear this **modulation** (change of key), as well as the return to the original key in the final **A** section. Once you hear this half-step change, the shape of the **A A B A** chorus is easy to follow.

▶ **call and response**
a statement by one musician or group of musicians immediately answered by another musician or group

▶ **"So What"**

CHORUS 1 (HEAD)

A	0:34	A	0:49	B	1:03	A	1:17

CHORUS 2 (MILES DAVIS, TRUMPET)

A	1:31	A	1:45	B	1:59	A	2:14

CHORUS 3

A	2:28	A	2:42	B	2:56	A	3:10

CHORUS 4 (JOHN COLTRANE, TENOR SAXOPHONE)

A	3:24	A	3:38	B	3:52	A	4:06

CHORUS 5

A	4:20	A	4:33	B	4:47	A	5:01

Many jazz composers take advantage of a loophole in copyright law. While the melody and words to a tune are legally protected, the chord progression is not. Any popular song can become the parent to thousands of new compositions, each with a new melody fitting within the **A A B A** harmonies of the original. The most famous of these is George Gershwin's "I Got Rhythm" (1930), which has engendered so many spin-offs that musicians refer to its harmonies as "rhythm changes." Listen to "The Pot Boiler," written by trumpeter John D'earth, which revisits this familiar progression with a fresh new tune.

▶ "The Pot Boiler"

CHORUS 1

| A | 0:00 | The tenor saxophone and trumpet immediately begin playing the **head**, which is considerably more intricate and rhythmically involved than "I Got Rhythm." Underneath the melody, the piano **comps** while the bass plays two beats to the bar. |

A — 0:00 — The tenor saxophone and trumpet immediately begin playing the **head**, which is considerably more intricate and rhythmically involved than "I Got Rhythm." Underneath the melody, the piano **comps** while the bass plays two beats to the bar.

A — 0:13 — While repeating the melody, the band surprises us (at 0:15) by adding an unexpected accent on the fourth beat of the measure.

0:18 — The bass line drifts into a steady, four-beat **walking bass**.

B — 0:25 — The two horns (trumpet and tenor saxophone) play short melodic phrases featuring a growling **timbre**.

A — 0:38 — The band repeats the melody once again, including a return of the accented note (at 0:40).

CHORUS 2

A — 0:50 — Jeff Decker (tenor saxophone) and John D'earth (trumpet) begin alternating short solos. This procedure, generically known as **trading fours** (trading four-bar sections), can actually take place over any set length. Here they begin by trading eight-bar solos, one for each section of the **A A B A** form. Decker opens his first solo with a pair of short **motives** (a short melodic or rhythmic idea) before unfolding a long, intricate line.

A — 1:03 — D'earth opens his response with a **fanfare** (ceremonial) rhythm.

B — 1:15 — Decker plays a string of eighth notes, decorated by tiny ornaments.

A — 1:28 — D'earth plays another fanfare. His last phrase (beginning at 1:36) lingers on **blue notes**.

CHORUS 3

A — 1:40 — The two soloists now trade fours. Decker's line continues the bluesy flavor of Dearth's last solo. Robert Jospé supports him with a relaxed tom-tom figure (*dum-dum*) on the fourth beat of the measure.

1:46 — D'earth responds to Decker's melodic gestures. He ends his line with a bluesy wail (*ba-waaa, ba-waaa*).

A — 1:52 — Decker imitates D'earth, emphasizing the same blue melodic interval.

1:59 — D'earth accelerates the rhythmic intensity, ending with a **double-time** string of 16th notes.

B — 2:05 — The soloists now begin trading two-bar solos. Decker simplifies his improvisation, using the growling timbre again.

2:08 — D'earth's response overlaps with Decker's next line.

2:11 — Decker's solo is still deliberate. D'earth responds with a short gesture.

A — 2:17 — Decker plays a short blues motive (*ba-waaa, ba-waaa*). Again, this gesture is directly imitated by D'earth.

2:24   Decker uses a wide, blustery vibrato. D'earth's line descends from a high note, signaling the end of this improvisation.

CHORUS 4

A   2:30   Bob Hallahan begins his piano solo with short, restrained gestures. D'earth should have shifted to a brief riff figure in the background (we will hear it shortly). On this recording **take**, his memory fails him: he plays a different melody before discreetly fading out. Such a mistake is not uncommon on jazz recordings, which usually preserve a complete performance, errors and all. As it turns out, D'earth preferred this take to the others.

A   2:42   As Hallahan continues, D'earth and Decker play a **riff** figure, derived from the head.

B   2:54   Hallahan fastens onto a short two-note motive, which he plays **polyrhythmically** over the chords of the bridge.

A   3:07   The riff returns underneath Hallahan's solo.

          3:16   Hallahan changes the chord progression slightly to signal the end of his improvisation.

CHORUS 5

A   3:19   The horns begin another type of trading fours—alternating four-bar solos with the drummer. Decker's improvisation is answered by a crisp syncopated response by Jospé.

A   3:30   D'earth's line is fast and unpredictable, prompting Jospé to answer with an equally complex polyrhythm.

B   3:42   Hallahan's four-bar solo ends unexpectedly with a **triplet** rhythm (where beats are divided into three parts), which Jospé quickly absorbs into his improvisation.

A   3:54   Spaar takes a four-bar bass solo. Jospé's solo ends with a long snare roll, preparing the band to return to the head.

CHORUS 6

A   4:06   The band plays the head.

A   4:18   **B**   4:31   **A**   4:43

CODA   4:53   The tempo gradually slows to a halt, allowing the tune to sink to a long held note.

More examples in this book of **A A B A** form (each with its own tune) are "Dinah," Benny Goodman (Chapter 7); "Walkin' and Swingin'," Andy Kirk with Mary Lou Williams (Chapter 8); "Ko Ko," Charlie Parker (Chapter 11); and "Tempus Fugue-It," Bud Powell (Chapter 11).

Other tunes in this book may be diagrammed a different way: **A B A C**, or **A A'**, an elegant variation on **A A B A** form. While **A A B A** adds contrast (the bridge) precisely halfway through the song, **A B A C** uses that same location to return to the opening melody.

$$\left\{\begin{array}{lll} \textbf{A} \text{ (8 bars)} & \text{statement} \\ \textbf{B} \text{ (8 bars)} & \text{contrast} \\ \textbf{A} \text{ (8 bars)} & \text{return of statement} \\ \textbf{C} \text{ (8 bars)} & \text{conclusion} \end{array}\right. \quad \text{or} \quad \left\{\begin{array}{lll} \textbf{A} \text{ (16 bars)} & \text{statement} \\ \\ \textbf{A}' \text{ (16 bars)} & \text{statement with new} \\ & \text{conclusion} \end{array}\right.$$

Tunes that fall into this form include "Hotter Than That," Louis Armstrong (Chapter 6); "Singin' the Blues," Bix Biederbecke (Chapter 6); "Star Dust," Artie Shaw (Chapter 7); and "E.S.P.," Miles Davis (Chapter 14).

IMPROVISATION

How can ensemble music made up on the spot make sense? How do musicians manage to keep together? In short, what is improvisation and how does it work? As usual with jazz riddles, the place to begin is in the rhythm section, where each instrument fills multiple roles while working to create a supple and unified underpinning.

Rhythm Section: Bass

Traditionally, the bass has the most restricted role. It provides a rhythmic foundation layer, keeping steady time in a swing groove with a continuous and even string of notes. Because this sound is the neutral backdrop for every other rhythmic gesture, the bassist has little choice but to stick to the basic pattern. But at the same time, the bass plays a crucial harmonic role. Whenever a new chord appears on the **chart** (the musical score that serves as the basis for jazz performance), the bassist is responsible for playing that chord's root. This creates a daunting challenge: he or she must produce a steady and consistent beat while fitting into a harmonic puzzle. Today's bassists do this with ease.

During Miles Davis's solo on "So What," Paul Chambers's bass line lies underneath, never calling attention to itself and never failing to fulfill its basic rhythmic and harmonic duties. Yet the line has a graceful melodic shape, a product of Chambers's creative imagination. A good bass line is a subtle form of improvisation, constantly supporting and sometimes inspiring the soloist.

Paul Chambers, seen here in 1956, was the foundation of the Miles Davis rhythm section in the 1950s, and a bassist in demand for hundreds of recording sessions.

MOSAIC IMAGES/FRANCIS WOLFF

Piano

The primary harmony instrument in the rhythm section—usually a piano, but sometimes guitar, organ, vibraphone, or electric keyboards—has a different role. Every chart specifies the chords that must be played, with musical shorthand: Cmaj7, for example, means a C major triad (C-E-G) with a major seventh (B) added. But exactly how the chords are to be played is left open. At any given moment, the pianist can play the chord in any **voicing** (arrangement of notes) or add extra notes. He or she can also use **harmonic substitutions**—harmonies that replace the existing chord progression. Compare the first and fourth choruses of Armstrong's "West End Blues." In the first, pianist Earl Hines sticks to the script, playing basic chords on the beat. By the fourth, where he is the featured soloist, he replaces these chords with a dense harmonic thicket, carving his own path through the blues form with his broad knowledge of harmony.

The pianist also provides a variable rhythmic layer, constantly adding to the rhythms to enliven the groove. He or she listens closely to the rhythmic gestures of the drummer while "feeding" chords to the soloist, or comping.

Drums

In a typical swing groove, the drummer will play a more or less constant "ride" pattern with his right hand, while accenting the backbeat on the high-hat cymbal with his left foot. The right foot, controlling the bass drum pedal, plays thunderous accents (during and just after World War II, this was referred to as **dropping bombs**), while the left hand swoops over the rest of the drum kit, adding sharp responses on the snare drum, tom-tom, or crash cymbal. This is the default rhythm. When the drummer wants to add an improvised passage, or **fill**, he can use both feet and hands to create more complicated patterns. A good drummer can play many kinds of rhythm, shifting from swing to funk to Latin to a soft ballad to free jazz.

Listening to the rhythm section ought to be a delight in itself. Still, the limelight in a jazz performance shines most on the soloist. How exactly does the saxophonist or trumpet player decide which notes to play? We can offer a few general paradigms.

FRANK DRIGGS COLLECTION

Art Tatum established the gold standard for jazz virtuosity as a piano recitalist, influencing generations of musicians with his startling harmonic substitutions. He's shown here at a celebrated jam session with clarinetist Barney Bigard, trombonist Jack Teagarden, and guitarist Al Casey at the Metropolitan Opera House, 1944.

Soloists: Melodic Paraphrase

The simplest method of improvisation takes a preexisting melody—a song known by millions or an original composition by a member of the band—and varies it. This method, **melodic paraphrase**, typically adds notes and distorts the rhythm into something that swings, but does not disguise the source material. Jazz musicians often use melodic paraphrase at the beginning and end of a performance. Many jazz classics consist entirely of paraphrase. Throughout Art Tatum's 1939 radio broadcast version of "Over the Rainbow" (Chapter 10), Tatum makes sure you can hear the melody. He is one of those rare jazz musicians who use the original melody to make their improvisation coherent at all times.

In the 1930s and 1940s, people knew the melodies (and words) to countless pop songs by heart, just as we do our favorite hits of today. Few of us are conversant with many songs from what we now call the Classic American Songbook, so in discovering jazz we find ourselves discovering those songs as well as the interpretations by great jazz stylists. It's worth noting, in this context, that Tatum's "Over the Rainbow" reversed that situation. The song, a standard that most of us do know, was generally unfamiliar to the audience that tuned in to his 1939 broadcast. *The Wizard of Oz* had opened only days before.

Harmonic and Modal Improvisation

Most jazz improvisers, however, quickly discard the original melody, which is probably the key reason some people find jazz incomprehensible. Musicians prefer to rely on the changes—a technique known as **harmonic improvisation**—and create *new* melodies that fit over the basic chord progression. Every decision must be made quickly as one chord changes to another, because melody notes that sound consonant (stable) with one chord can become painfully dissonant (unstable or jarring) in the next. When chords move fast, as they do in John Coltrane's notorious harmonic labyrinth "Giant Steps," playing them correctly becomes a superhuman task.

Another technique, **modal improvisation**, replaces a welter of chords with a stable scale or mode. Musicians who want to sound bluesy interpolate the blues scale, superimposing it over a passage as if it had no chords. In Charlie Parker's third chorus in "Now's the Time," we hear a highly skilled harmonic improviser ignore the chords and play bluesy **licks** (short melodies) that contradict the underlying harmony—even though the tune itself is a blues. In "So What," improvisers are expected to create their melodies from a scale known as the D Dorian (the piano white keys from D to D), shifting up a half step on the bridge. Modal improvisation shows that for jazz musicians, simplicity is just as important as complexity.

IN PERFORMANCE

Jazz can be played by bands of any size or by solo musicians, but—as in classical music, with its symphonic orchestras and chamber groups—there are two dominant ensembles: **big bands** and **small combos**.

Big Bands

In the 1930s, dance orchestras usually employed about sixteen musicians. These orchestras began to fade after World War II, but big bands have never completely disappeared; they switched their focus, however, from ballroom dancing to concert music. A few "ghost bands" carry on the memory of long-deceased bandleaders from the Swing Era. But most of the contemporary big bands, such as New York's Vanguard Jazz Orchestra (which plays on Monday nights at the Village Vanguard, in Greenwich Village), perform a new and modern repertory. The vast majority of big bands, however, are found at universities, where they serve as part of the jazz curriculum. As these bands are educational enterprises and not restricted by payroll, they often climb in size to twenty-five musicians.

The musicians in big bands are grouped by instrument, as they are in symphony orchestras. The sections are often designated as brass (trumpets and trombones), reeds (usually alto, tenor, and baritone saxophones, with an occasional clarinet), and rhythm (piano, bass, drums, and sometimes guitar, electric or acoustic). Because of the size of the ensemble, big bands use **arrangements**, or charts—composed scores. These arrangements often employ **block-chord texture** and play one section against another in **call-and-response** fashion. Improvisation happens only at designated moments, when limited blocks of time (from four measures to several choruses) are set aside for soloists. In this way, the big band balances composition and improvisation.

Small Combos

Jazz is usually played by small groups: a few horns plus rhythm section. The reasons are obvious: small groups are less expensive to maintain, they are a lot more mobile, they fit easily on the cramped bandstands that are fixtures in jazz clubs, and they are more accommodating to the modern jazz template of extended, free-wheeling improvisations.

Small combos reflect the informal tradition of the **jam session**, an after-hours phenomenon at which musicians gathered to play for their own enjoyment. The earliest jam sessions typically took place in out-of-the-way venues, far from the public eye. The music was meant as a form of recreation, but it also served an important function within the jazz community. Through open-ended improvisation, musicians could be heard, tested, and judged. By the 1940s, the jam session went public, becoming another way to hear jazz. Its atmosphere was different from that of a big band—no uniforms, casual bandstand behavior, a milieu of open rehearsal.

The musical format is purposefully kept simple. The head is the only composed part of the performance. The rest of the tune is improvised—as many choruses as the soloists want. A typical order of solos begins with the horn players, then proceeds through the rhythm section: piano (and/or guitar), bass, and drums. Under the bass solos, the accompaniment lightens: the drummer plays quietly and the piano plinks out a few chords. Drum solos are a different matter. They can be completely open-ended, in which case the band waits for a verbal or musical cue to come in; or they can fit precisely within the form.

A jazz club is essentially a concert hall that permits drinking and (sometimes) eating. Serious fans act as they would at a concert, but others assume that any music played in a room that serves alcohol is there as aural wallpaper. The high cost of admittance, and the inevitable shushing, tends to keep them at bay, but that same cost also keeps out many others—including budding young jazz enthusiasts. Those who do come may be puzzled by the nearly universal ritual of applauding every solo. Applause is like tipping. You do so as a matter of politesse after a number, but you ought to cheer a particular solo only when it knocks your socks off. When that happens, you are firmly situated in the sunshine of jazz, and ready to peruse its long and tangled history.

Jam sessions were informal assemblies, blending disparate musical personalities into harmony. In this session, held in a New York penthouse in 1939, Duke Ellington swaps his piano for gospel singer Sister Rosetta Tharpe's guitar. Behind them are Ellington soloists Rex Stewart (center, on cornet) and Johnny Hodges (far right, on alto saxophone), Kansas City–bred trumpeter Hot Lips Page (far left), and swing trombonist J. C. Higginbotham (to his right).

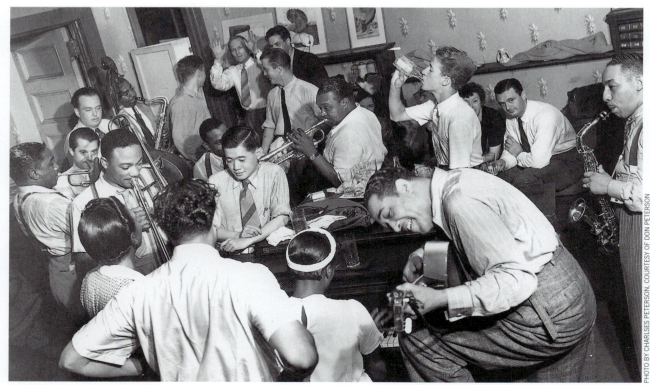

PHOTO BY CHARLISES PETERSON, COURTESY OF DON PETERSON

ONLINE MULTIMEDIA RESOURCES AND REVIEW MATERIALS

Author Insight Videos

Scott DeVeaux likens improvisation to speaking, with jazz musicians drawing on their knowledge of musical grammar to create something spontaneous; and demonstrates twelve-bar blues and thirty-two-bar popular song forms at the piano.

Interactive Listening Guides

Bessie Smith, "Reckless Blues"
Louis Armstrong, "West End Blues"
Charlie Parker, "Now's the Time"
Billie Holiday, "A Sailboat in the Moonlight"
Miles Davis, "So What"
Free Bridge Quintet, "Midriff" and "The Pot Boiler"

Jazz Concepts (audio and/or video demonstrations of terms covered here)

backbeat	melodic paraphrase	subdominant
blue note	modulation	tonic
break	motive	triplet
call and response	octave	twelve-bar blues
chart	pedal point	walking bass
dominant	polyrhythm	
harmonic improvisation	riff	

- For quick reference, review the **Chapter Overview** and **Chapter Outline**.

- Take the online **Chapter** and **Listening Quizzes**.

- Use the online **Glossary** and **Flashcards** to review important terms.

PART II

EARLY JAZZ (1900–1930)

Jazz developed as a convergence of multiple cultures. The most important factor was the importation of African slaves to a world dominated by warring European colonists—particularly the French, Spanish, and English. In striving to keep African musical traditions alive, the slaves eventually found ways to blend them with the abiding traditions of Europe, producing hybrid styles in North and South America unlike anything in the Old World. Miraculously, jazz and other forms of African American music, including spirituals, blues, and ragtime, overcame subjugation to assume dominant roles in American music.

The miracle crystallized in New Orleans, a port city that assimilated many musical influences; by the early twentieth century, it was home to a new blues-based, highly rhythmic, and improvisational way of playing music. New Orleans produced jazz's first great composers, bandleaders, instrumentalists, and teachers, as well as Louis Armstrong, the genius whose unique skills and temperament spurred the

1843
- Virginia Minstrels perform in New York: beginning of minstrelsy.

1861–65
- Civil War

1871
- Fisk Jubilee Singers begin performing.

1877
- Reconstruction ends.
- Thomas Edison invents the phonograph.

1878
- James Bland writes "Carry Me Back to Old Virginny."

1880
- John Philip Sousa takes over U.S. Marine Band, popularizing brass bands throughout the country.

1884
- Mark Twain's *The Adventures of Huckleberry Finn* published in England, in the U.S. a year later.

1886
- Statue of Liberty dedicated in New York harbor.

1893
- Chicago World's Fair; Scott Joplin performs on the Midway.

1894
- Jim Crow laws adopted in Southern states.

1896
- Ernest Hogan's "All Coons Look Alike to Me" published.
- Supreme Court, in *Plessy v. Ferguson,* allows "separate but equal" segregation of facilities.

1897
- First ragtime pieces published.

This late nineteenth-century poster of Primrose and West's Big Minstrels shows that the company offered two productions: black performers on the left, white performers on the right. All would have appeared onstage in blackface.

Mamie Smith and Her Jazz Hounds, 1922. Note teenager Coleman Hawkins, on the right, playing an alto saxophone instead of his usual tenor.

Paul Whiteman, baton raised at the upper right, leads his elephantine orchestra on one of the elaborate sets built for the movie revue *The King of Jazz*, 1930:

acceptance of jazz around the world. Armstrong had been nurtured by a strong tradition, from the first important jazz musician, Buddy Bolden, to his own mentor, King Oliver, who summoned Armstrong to Chicago to join the Creole Jazz Band.

Armstrong transformed jazz from a provincial African American folk music into an art focused less on community tradition than on the achievements of exceptional individuals. Before Armstrong, jazz had won the hearts of classical composers who reckoned it as a resource for "serious" music. After him, a generation of instrumentalists and composers proved that jazz was more than a resource: it was an emotionally and intellectually complete art in its own right. This generation included the most prolific and characteristic of American composers, Duke Ellington, and such powerful performers as vocalist Bessie Smith, saxophonist Coleman Hawkins, and cornetist Bix Beiderbecke. By the early 1930s, jazz had traveled the world, making converts everywhere.

1898
- The Broadway musical *Clorindy, or the Origin of the Cakewalk* popularizes the cakewalk.
- Spanish-American War

1899
- Joplin's "Maple Leaf Rag" published.

1900
- Sigmund Freud's *The Interpretation of Dreams* published.

1903
- Wright brothers make their first flight at Kitty Hawk, North Carolina.
- W. E. B. DuBois's *The Souls of Black Folk* published.

1904
- Ma Rainey hears the blues for the first time in St. Louis.
- Saxophones first manufactured in U.S.

1905
- Buddy Bolden at his peak in New Orleans.
- Robert Abbott founds the *Chicago Defender*.
- Einstein proposes his theory of relativity.

1906
- San Francisco earthquake kills 700.

1907
- Pablo Picasso paints *Les demoiselles d'Avignon*.

1909
- Henry Ford establishes the assembly line to produce Model Ts.
- National Association for the Advancement of Colored People (NAACP) founded.

1910
- Bert Williams becomes the first black to star in Ziegfeld's Follies.

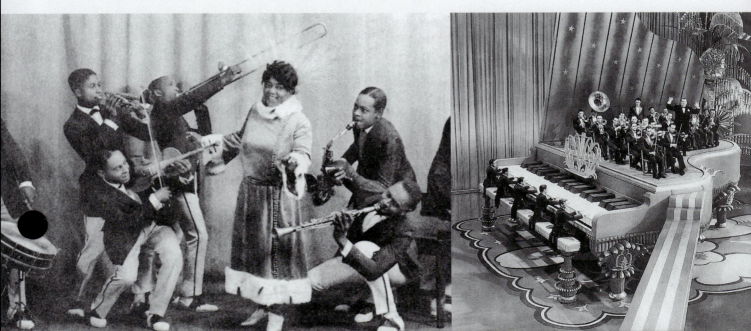

PART II

1910s
- Vernon and Irene Castle and James Reese Europe popularize dances like the turkey trot and cakewalk.

1912
- James Reese Europe performs in Carnegie Hall.
- W. C. Handy's "Memphis Blues" published.
- Sinking of the *Titanic*.

1913
- Igor Stravinsky's ballet *The Rite of Spring* premieres in Paris, causing a riot.

1914
- World War I begins in Europe.
- Charlie Chaplin makes his first short films.

1915
- D. W. Griffith's *Birth of a Nation* released, to cheers and protests.
- Franz Kafka's *The Metamorphosis* published.

1916
- Wilbur Sweatman records "Down Home Rag."

1917
- Original Dixieland Jazz Band makes the first jazz recording; beginning of the Jazz Age.
- U.S. enters World War I.
- Great Migration begins in earnest.
- Bolsheviks take power in the Russian Revolution.

1918
- World War I ends.

1919
- Prohibition (18th Amendment) becomes law.
- Chicago White Sox throw the World Series.

1920s
- Pianists (James P. Johnson, Fats Waller, Duke Ellington, Art Tatum) hit their stride in New York.

Two legends of New Orleans: trumpet player Freddy Keppard and soprano saxophonist Sidney Bechet, in Chicago, 1918.

With her bobbed hair and flowing gown, Irene Castle (shown here with her husband Vernon in 1914, the year they introduced the fox-trot in Irving Berlin's *Watch Your Step*) symbolized the new freedoms available to women at the dawn of the twentieth century.

Members of New York's music world gathered in Atlantic City, N.J., for the opening of the Vincent Youmans show *Great Day*: left to right, unknown, songwriter Harold Arlen, Fletcher Henderson (behind the wheel), trumpet player Bobby Stark, singer Lois Deppe, composer Will Marion Cook (standing), trumpet player Rex Stewart. Outside the Globe Theater, 1929.

The midtown Cotton Club, 1938. Imagine a show featuring bandleader Cab Calloway and dancer Bill "Bojangles" Robinson, plus dinner, for $1.50.

Attempts to legislate morality invariably fail, but the 18th Amendment to the Constitution proved to be catastrophic. Americans responded by drinking more than ever, generating a crime wave and unparalleled municipal corruption.

1920
- Mamie Smith's "Crazy Blues" becomes the first "race" recording hit.
- Paul Whiteman establishes his name with "Whispering."

1921
- First commercial radio broadcast.
- Eubie Blake and Noble Sissle's *Shuffle Along* premieres on Broadway.
- Arnold Schoenberg writes his first twelve-tone piece of music.

1923
- First wave of black jazz recordings: King Oliver, Jelly Roll Morton, Bessie Smith.

1924
- Premiere of George Gershwin's *Rhapsody in Blue* at Paul Whiteman's "Experiment in Modern Music" concert.

- Fletcher Henderson Orchestra opens at the Roseland Ballroom, hiring Louis Armstrong.

1925
- Armstrong begins recording with his Hot Five.
- Development of electrical recording.
- *The New Negro* published, launching the Harlem Renaissance.

1926
- Jelly Roll Morton and His Red Hot Peppers make electrical recordings.

1927
- Duke Ellington opens at the Cotton Club.
- Bix Beiderbecke records "Singin' the Blues."
- Bing Crosby introduced on Paul Whiteman recordings.
- *The Jazz Singer*, first talking picture, released.

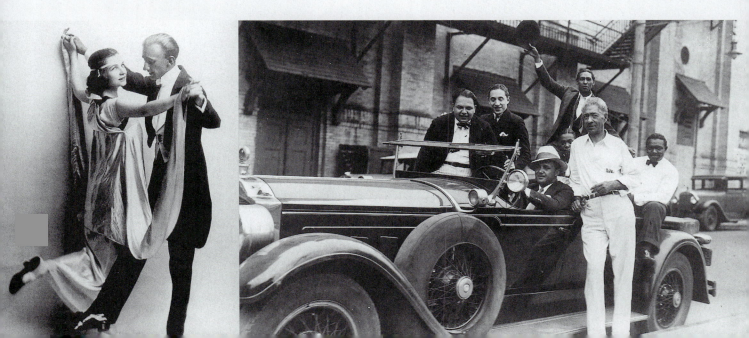

GEORGIA SEA ISLAND SINGERS
the buzzard lope

BESSIE SMITH
reckless blues

WILBUR SWEATMAN
down home rag

3

THE ROOTS OF JAZZ

JAZZ AND ETHNICITY

One evening in Mississippi, early in the twentieth century, an elegantly dressed bandleader named W. C. Handy was handed a request on the platform: would he mind letting a local band take his place for a few numbers? As he agreed, an unpromising-looking group of strangers straggled to the bandstand:

> They were led by a long-legged chocolate boy and their band consisted of just three pieces, a battered guitar, a mandolin and a worn-out bass. The music they made was pretty well in keeping with their looks. They struck up one of those over-and-over strains that seem to have no very clear beginning and certainly no ending at all. The strumming attained a disturbing monotony, but on and on it went, a kind of stuff that has long been associated with cane rows and levee camps. Thump-thump-thump went their feet on the floor. Their eyes rolled. Their shoulders swayed. And through it all that little agonizing strain persisted.

Puzzled by their sound, Handy wondered whether the crowd would chase the newcomers away. To his surprise, "A rain of silver dollars began to fall around the outlandish, stomping feet. The dancers went wild. Dollars, quarter, halves—the shower grew

African-Caribbean rhythms, imported into New Orleans as a result of the slave trade, played a powerful role in the birth of jazz. One of its later masters, the Cuban-born conguero **Chano Pozo** (seen here in 1949), gained prominence during the bebop era.

heavier. . . . There before the boys lay more money than my nine musicians were being paid for the entire engagement." From this experience, Handy had a revelation that changed his world: "Then I saw the beauty of primitive music. They had the stuff the people wanted. It touched the spot. Their music wanted polishing, but it contained the essence. Folks would pay money for it. . . . That night, a composer was born, an *American* composer."

Although Handy's description of what the band played suggests a type of folk music known as the blues, emerging from the "cane rows and levee camps" of the rural South, his immediate reaction was commercial: with a bit of professional "polishing," the music could earn untold amounts of money. From this point, Handy became inspired to notate the music, compose his own lyrics, rehearse it with his band, and eventually publish it as sheet music, all of which resulted in a popular sensation that brought him fame. "Art, in the high-brow sense, was not in my mind," he said. Yet his impulse to "improve" what he heard helped create jazz, a music now routinely heard in concert halls.

There are three categories that situate jazz within our society, and Handy's experience serves in a way to illustrate them all. Jazz is an **art form**, sometimes called "America's classical music," which can be found in or near the heart of the cultural establishment, whether in concert halls, television documentaries, or university curricula. At the same time, jazz is a **popular music**, its artists constantly negotiating with public tastes, however far removed from those tastes their instincts take them. Finally, jazz is also **folk music**. Not in the usual sense of music performed in rural isolation: jazz is distinctly urban, at home on the street corner and comfortable with modern technology. Yet on a basic level, the qualities that mark jazz as different from other musical genres stem directly from its folk origins, which, more often than not, are African American. We can therefore make the straightforward yet provocative assertion: Jazz is an African American music.

This is the kind of statement that seems designed to make some people crazy. Doesn't jazz belong to everybody? In fact, jazz musicians—including the very best of them—may be black, white, or any shade in between, just as they may be of any age, either gender, and from any part of the world. As Miles Davis once observed, if a jazz musician can play, he didn't "give a damn if he was green and had red breath." John Steinbeck found Davis's attitude to be one of jazz's signal virtues. "Let a filthy kid, unknown, unheard of and unbacked, sit in—and if he can do it—he is recognized and accepted instantly," he said. "Do you know of any other field where this is true?"

We usually construe "African American" as an indication of race—the physical characteristics of skin color we inherit through our genes; but the term also tells us about ethnicity, which helps to explain how culture makes us who we are. The difference is crucial. Race can't be changed. But because it is learned behavior, ethnicity can. We acquire it in our youth so unconsciously that our cultural habits become second nature. In the past hundred years, since the advent of recording technology, the primary way diverse peoples have shared their culture is through music. Through jazz, the whole country, the whole world, becomes more African American.

Though much of the musical grammar of jazz can be traced ultimately to Africa, the particular combination of sounds that characterize jazz—including the idea of **polyrhythm** created within a short rhythmic cycle, **blue notes**, **timbre variation**, and the spontaneous interaction of **call and response**—is uniquely African American. Its folk elements are not a fixed list of items but flexible principles that can absorb and transform whatever music its performers encounter.

FOLK TRADITIONS

Beginning in the 1600s, African American folk culture established a musical identity that survived centuries of slavery, the tumultuous decades after the Civil War, and the transition from rural to urban centers in the early twentieth century. This musical tradition was developed in several genres. One was the retelling of local history through lengthy **ballads**. The blasting of a railroad tunnel on the Virginia–West Virginia border, for example, inspired "John Henry," in which the hard-muscled, steel-driving hero fights a losing battle against modern machinery. (We'll hear a contemporary interpretation of this ballad in Chapter 19.) Other ballads, like "Staggerlee" and "Railroad Bill," celebrated the exploits of bad men—heroes of resistance who shrugged off society's constraints through their disrespectful and violent behavior. The taste for braggadocio and exaggeration, with its emphasis on sexual exploits and one-upmanship, remains prominent today in hip-hop. Another kind of secular music was the **work song**, which thrived on railroads, levees, and anywhere else music was needed to pace manual labor. And in the lonely corner of the field where the former slave continued to work, one could hear an unaccompanied **field holler**, a rhythmically loose vocal line that expressed his or her lonesome individuality.

A different folk tradition emerged in the **spiritual**, which transformed call-and-response songs into religious poetry. Beginning in 1871, the Fisk Jubilee Singers, a vocal group from a new and impoverished black college, performed a polished, carefully arranged version of spirituals before the general public. But this music was also passed on orally from parents to children and transmuted through performance in "sanctified" Pentecostal churches that were often nothing more than converted storefronts. By the 1920s, it had turned into gospel music, a rich and vibrant tradition that has never ceased to influence American music. When early jazz musicians say they learned music in the church, we may assume they acquired many of the basic skills of musical interaction from the oral tradition of the spiritual.

WILLIAM GROPPER/THE GRANGER COLLECTION, NEW YORK

The legendary steel driver John Henry has endured as the most frequently reimagined mythic figure in American history, a symbol not only of the brawny ethic of African Americans but of mankind's struggle with technology. He has been the subject of books and plays as well as music and art, including this 1945 lithograph by the politically engaged painter and cartoonist William Gropper.

🎧 "The Buzzard Lope" ("Throw Me Anywhere, Lord")

A fount of African-influenced folk culture exists on the sea islands of Georgia. Here, slaves brought directly from rice-growing West Africa worked the rice and cotton plantations; during the summer, when white residents fled inland to avoid malaria, there were only a few white overseers in charge. After Emancipation, the slaves, known as Gullahs, were left to eke out a living on their own. The result was a culture rich in African traditions, isolated from the mainland by swamps and salt marshes.

In the 1920s, bridges were built to the mainland, flooding Gullah culture with white capitalism. Lydia Parrish, a Philadelphia-bred Quaker who lived on St. Simons Island, studied the island's music closely and took it upon herself to save it from extinction. She published her findings in 1942, in *Slave Songs of the Georgia Sea Islands*. Earlier, she had used her resources to start a group eventually established as the Georgia Sea Island Singers. Zora Neale Hurston brought the folklorist Alan Lomax to hear the singers in 1935.

Twenty-five years later, he returned to the island with recording equipment, determined to preserve their music.

"The Buzzard Lope" is a spiritual dance with African origins. At death, slaves were often thrown into a field, where their bodies were devoured by buzzards. In the dance, singers gathered in a circle, leaving a piece of cloth in the center to represent the body. As they danced, individual singers would enter the ring, imitating a circling buzzard and snatching the carrion. The text is defiant: the superior power of "King Jesus" will protect the slaves, even under the most horrific conditions. The song is done in call-and-response style, with the venerable folk singer Bessie Jones taking the lead, answered by a chorus of seven men. Each separate call and response makes one cycle, with the refrain (the same words) recurring in several of them. The singers clap two rhythms: a backbeat and a polyrhythmic background (counted 3 + 3 + 2), underneath the chorus:

▶ **backbeat** in 4/4, the beats that fall on 2 and 4 (rather than on 1 and 3)

3 + 3 + 2

But when Jones enters with her call slightly ahead of the beat, the clappers extend the polyrhythm (3 + 3 + 3 + 3 + 3). Through intense repetition and syncopation, the music moves irresistibly forward until the singers abruptly cut it off.

LISTENING GUIDE 1

🎧 the buzzard lope (throw me anywhere, lord)

GEORGIA SEA ISLAND SINGERS
Bessie Jones, song leader; Joe Armstrong, Jerome Davis, John Davis, Peter Davis, Henry Morrison, Willis Proctor, Ben Ramsay, chorus

- Label: *Georgia Sea Island Songs* (New World Records, NW278)
- Date: 1960
- Style: African American folk
- Form: cyclic

What to listen for:
- cyclic structure
- body percussion (hand claps, foot stomps)
- polyrhythm
- improvisation within the call and response

CYCLE 1 (REFRAIN)

0:00   Jones begins her first phrase with a rising melody, accompanied by a quiet foot stomp:
"Throw me anywhere, Lord."

0:03   A chorus sings the **response**: a simple three-note melody, loosely harmonized:
"In that old field." The hand clapping begins in earnest.

0:05   Jones repeats her call, this time with a falling phrase.

0:08   The response descends to a **full cadence**.

CYCLE 2

0:10   Jones sings the same melody to new text:
"Don't care where you throw me/Since my Jesus own me."

0:12   The chorus sings the response, *"In that old field"* (which remains constant throughout the song).

CYCLE 3 (REFRAIN)

0:19   Jones returns to the refrain, this time varying the melody with a plaintive **blue note**.
The hand claps follow the syncopated rhythm of her melody.

CYCLE 4

0:29   Jones sings a new couplet: *"You may beat and burn me/Since my Jesus save me."*

CYCLE 5 (REFRAIN)

0:38   Behind her, you can hear a bass humming a **dissonant** note.

CYCLE 6

0:47   As Jones adds new text, the rhythm becomes more driving: *"Don't care how you treat me/Since King Jesus meet me."*

CYCLE 7

0:56   New claps (recorded more distantly) are added to the overall texture: *"Don't care how you do me/Since King Jesus choose me."*

CYCLE 8 (REFRAIN)

1:05

CYCLE 9 (REFRAIN)

1:13   Jones changes the melody, moving it triumphantly upward. The performance begins to accelerate slightly.

CYCLE 10 (REFRAIN)

1:22   She repeats the refrain, keeping the new melodic variation.

CYCLE 11

1:31   The clapping becomes more intense. Jones drives the melody upward in response: *"Don't care where you throw me/Since King Jesus own me."*

CYCLE 12

1:40   *"Don't care how you treat me/Since King Jesus meet me."*

CYCLE 13

1:49   *"Don't care how you do me/Since King Jesus choose me."*

1:54   One member of the choir enters a beat early—perhaps by mistake, or perhaps as a signal to conclude.

1:57   Jones silences the hand clapping by sustaining her last note.

BLUES

Country Blues

At the dawn of the twentieth century, the **blues** began to emerge: a new poetic genre marked by its unusual three-line stanza. Earlier forms of folk poetry usually fell into stanzas of two or four lines, but the blues took the two-line couplet and repeated the first line. It became a musical form through its distinctive chord progression in the accompaniment to ballads such as "Frankie and Johnnie," a story of romantic betrayal from St. Louis that falls roughly into a twelve-bar pattern.

Unlike the ballad, though, which is a chronological account of an event usually told in the third person, the blues is personal—a window into the singer's mind. This change in perspective matched the new mood of the time. As historian Lawrence Levin has observed, African American society had recently shifted from the communal confines of slave culture to the cold, terrifying realities of individualism. The blues was an apt and sobering metaphor for black people contemplating the true meanings of freedom.

The earliest blues melodies borrowed their rhythmic flexibility from the field holler, prompting some musicians to observe that the blues was "as old as the hills." They were accompanied by the guitar, which became widely available for the first time in the rural South in the late nineteenth century. Musicians used guitars as a blank slate for their creativity: they tuned them in unexpected ways and pressed knives, bottlenecks, and other implements against the strings to create haunting blue notes and shivery slides. This early style, later called **country blues**, was performed chiefly by solitary male musicians throughout the rural South, from the Carolinas to the Mississippi Delta into Texas. The form was loose and improvisatory, suiting the needs of the moment.

Vaudeville (Classic) Blues

The blues began to cross the boundary line into popular music as soon as the country blues caught the ear of professional entertainers. Gertrude Pritchett, a black stage singer who later became better known as "Ma" Rainey (1886–1939), heard it from a young woman in St. Louis around 1904. Asked about her peculiar style of music, she told Rainey, "It's the blues." Rainey promptly adopted the new style, and went on to fame as one of the most popular singers of what became identified as **vaudeville blues**, or **classic blues**, in which female singers were accompanied by a small band on the stages of black theater circuits in the 1910s and 1920s.

Known as the "Mother of the Blues," Rainey was a short woman with a commanding voice that could be heard in the back rows of crowded theaters or in the unfriendly acoustics of outdoor tent shows. A country bluesman, playing alone, could change the length of a blues chorus if he wanted—to eleven bars, say, or thirteen and a half. In the hands of artists like Rainey and her ensembles, the blues became more codified, falling into strict twelve-bar stanzas with written harmonic progressions. Many soon-to-be jazz musicians entered show business as backup for singers like Rainey, learning through trial and error how best to match the sound of their instruments to the singer's bluesy strains.

Ma Rainey, the "Mother of the Blues," in 1924, with blues musician "Georgia Tom," also known as Thomas Dorsey. By 1932, Dorsey had composed "Precious Lord" and turned his back on secular music, becoming the father of gospel music.

Around the same time Ma Rainey first heard the blues, cornet player W. C. Handy (1873–1958) was giving up stage time to the ragged three-piece band that wowed the crowed at the beginning of this chapter. He encountered more of "the weirdest music I had ever heard" in a Mississippi railroad station: a guitarist repeating the same line of poetry endlessly ("goin' where the Southern cross' the dog") while scraping notes on the strings with a knife. Struck by how enthusiastically Southern audiences responded to these sounds, Handy—later known as the "Father of the Blues"—began publishing blues-related popular songs, including "Memphis Blues" (1912), "Beale Street Blues" (1917), and the smash hit "St. Louis Blues" (1914).

Throughout the 1910s and early 1920s, the blues became a hot commercial property. Pop song publishers achieved major blues hits, and recording companies followed suit. By this time, blacks were crowding into Northern cities and were hungry for music from back home. The blues became their music. To satisfy their tastes (and to augment profits), record companies offered a new product: "race records," black music created for black people. The phrase sounds offensive today, as it did in the 1940s, when the trade magazine *Billboard* changed the name of its sales sheet of black recordings from "Race" to "Rhythm and Blues." But in the 1920s, the phrase was intended as respectful and accepted as such: African American newspapers frequently described their readers as "the race." The treatment of black performers, on the other hand, was far from respectful. They were paid a modest performing fee but denied a copyright royalty, and were pressured by executives to record only blues, locking them into a musical ghetto. Yet the discs sold, leaving us with a treasure of incomparable recordings.

■ BESSIE SMITH (1894–1937)

The most popular blues diva of the era, the "Empress of the Blues," Bessie Smith, possessed an extraordinarily powerful voice that she had learned to project in crowded halls long before microphones were introduced onstage. If her brassy attack was matched by a storming temperament, she also displayed a rare sensitivity in adapting her style to the demands of the recording studio. In a career that lasted only fourteen years, Smith made nearly two hundred records, beginning at OKeh Records in 1923 and establishing the standard by which other blues singers were measured. Some of her accompanists, most notably Louis Armstrong, were already familiar with the blues. For others, recording with Bessie amounted to a crash course in the music, with accompanists scurrying to match her nuances in phrasing and tone.

Smith's career peaked in 1929, the same year she made her only film appearance, as a downhearted lover in the seventeen-minute short *St. Louis Blues*. Thereafter, the Depression curtailed her audience and her earnings. In the mid-1930s, she agreed to update her sound by recording pop tunes with younger up-and-coming jazzmen. But her attempt at a comeback was cut short, in 1937, as she rode to a gig on the back roads of the Mississippi Delta. Her car plowed into the back of a truck; her arm was torn loose and she went into shock. By the time she reached a hospital, she had lost too much blood. Record producer John Hammond, who had launched his own career by producing her final recording session, angrily wrote an erroneous account claiming that Smith was taken first to a white hospital, where she died shortly after being refused admission. Actually, no one in Mississippi would have thought of taking a black woman to a white facility. Hammond may have invented the story, but the message—that her death was attributable to the casual violence that was the fabric of life for black musicians in the Deep South—rang true.

🎧 "Reckless Blues"

Louis Armstrong was not Smith's favorite accompanist: she preferred the cornetist Joe Smith (no relation), who allowed that the great singer deserved a more subservient and discreet accompanist. But on "Reckless Blues," Armstrong shows how thoroughly the language of blues had expanded by 1925 under the influence of singers like Smith.

"Reckless Blues" is a duet by two great artists, competing for our attention. Backed by Fred Longshaw's stolid chords on reed organ—as unswinging a setting as one could imagine—Smith is in command from the

Bessie Smith beams in her only film appearance, *St. Louis Blues* (1929). When her dance partner (played by Jimmy Mordecai) abandons her for another, she pours out her heart in a performance of the title tune, composed in 1914 by W. C. Handy.

start, singing each line of the stanza with simplicity and control. As the "responder" to her "call," Armstrong is alert to every gesture, filling in even the smallest spaces she provides him. His timbre is modified by two mutes: a straight mute to reduce the sound and a plunger to produce *wa-wa* effects. With each stanza, their intensity grows. Smith's lines stick to the melodic outline, but grow more opulent in timbre and more unpredictable in rhythm.

🎧 reckless blues

BESSIE SMITH
Bessie Smith, vocal; Louis Armstrong, trumpet; Fred Longshaw, reed organ
- Label: Columbia 14056-D
- Date: 1925
- Style: vaudeville blues
- Form: 12-bar blues

What to listen for:
- vaudeville (or classic) blues
- clear twelve-bar blues form
- call and response between Smith and Armstrong
- trumpet adopting blues singing style

INTRODUCTION

0:00   Over Longshaw's organ, Armstrong plays an extended blues line, his timbre distorted by a plunger mute. Throughout the piece, Longshaw remains in the background, a stable series of chords.

CHORUS 1

0:14   *"When I wasn't nothing but a child,"*
        Smith begins her first blues chorus with a descending melody.

0:28   *"When I wasn't nothing but a child,"*

0:42   *"All you men tried to drive me wild."*

CHORUS 2

0:56   *"Now I am growing old,"*
        Smith's melody follows the same basic pattern as chorus 1. On the word "now," her line is **melismatic**—several notes for a single syllable.

1:04   Armstrong's response begins with a striking **blue note.**

1:10   *"Now I am growing old,"*

1:23   *"And I've got what it takes to get all of you men told."*

CHORUS 3

1:37   *"My mama says I'm reckless, my daddy says I'm wild,"*
        As if responding to the emotional quality of the lyrics, Smith bursts in a few beats early.

1:50   *"My mama says I'm reckless, my daddy says I'm wild,"*
        Her line is intensely **syncopated**, dragging against the beat.

1:58   Armstrong lets a blue note fall agonizingly for three seconds.

2:04   *"I ain't good looking but I'm somebody's angel child."*

CHORUS 4

2:18   *"Daddy, mama wants some loving, Daddy, mama wants some hugging,"*
        Smith interrupts the usual three-line stanza with a repeated call to "Daddy." Armstrong's response mimics the word with a two-note pattern.

2:33   *"Darn it pretty papa, mama wants some loving I vow,"*
        Smith's emotions are signaled by changes in timbre.

2:40   Armstrong's response is also more emotionally involved.

2:46   *"Darn it pretty papa, mama wants some loving right now."*

CODA

2:54   In the last two measures, Armstrong and Longshaw signal the end by slowing down slightly. Longshaw's last **tonic chord** adds a blue seventh note.

POPULAR MUSIC

Minstrelsy

While the black community reveled in its own music, a good many black musicians moved toward the larger and more affluent audience of white Americans. "Mighty seldom I played for colored," recalled one violinist. "They didn't have nothing to hire you with." The deep imbalance of power between the races made it difficult for black performers to succeed. Yet black music was gradually transforming what had previously been white culture. Attentive white performers studied their black counterparts, adopting their comedic and dance styles and accompanying themselves on banjo (an instrument with African lineage) and "the bones" (a primitive form of homemade percussion). In the process, they created the most popular and influential form of entertainment in nineteenth-century America, minstrelsy.

In 1843, a quartet of white musicians called the Virginia Minstrels presented New York audiences with an evening's amusement that claimed to depict the culture of plantation slaves. They performed in blackface—a mask of burnt cork, with grotesquely exaggerated eyes and mouths. Their success was astonishing, prompting numerous imitators. Within a decade, the "minstrel show" had become the most beloved theatrical production in the country, touring everywhere on both sides of the Mason-Dixon line.

Minstrels invented new and sadly lasting stereotypes of blackness, influencing the perception of blacks particularly in areas were there were none. As "Ethiopian delineators," their wigs were mops of unruly curls, wild and woolly, and their stage clothes tattered and outrageously loud in style and color. To be sure, one of the main minstrel stereotypes, Zip Coon, was an overdressed dandy whose foppish behavior savagely parodied upper-class whites. But the most memorable characterizations were based on a poisonous racial contempt. Happy-go-lucky plantation "darkies" combined savvy musical talent with foolish, childlike behavior that no adult could

Virginia Minstrels

THE GRANGER COLLECTION, NEW YORK

Long after minstrel stage shows had passed into memory, minstrelsy's grotesque smile still remained in films like the 1939 *Swanee River*, a fictional biography of Stephen Foster, featuring Al Jolson in blackface.

Jim Crow

Black minstrel troupes

take seriously. A crippled stable hand known as Jim Crow morphed into a character so thoroughly identified with racial exploitation that the phrase "Jim Crow" became shorthand for the entire Southern legal system of post-Reconstruction segregation.

After the Civil War, something happened that caught white minstrel troupes unprepared. Major white producers organized black minstrel troupes, and white audiences soon began favoring the black troupes, which were judged more authentic—even though the black performers were obliged to play the same characters that the white imitators had created. By this point, minstrelsy was as rigorously structured as the circus, and audiences demanded the usual characters, including Tambo and Mr. Bones, the so-called endmen (men at each end of a line of performers) who made leering yet oddly impotent jokes. Blacks were pleased to get work and to travel the country, but they had to wear the burnt cork masks, wigs, and clothing, disguising their individual talents (and complexions) behind characters as fixed as the clowns in *commedia dell'arte*.

Even under these conditions, black minstrelsy created genuine stars—like Billy Kersands, a comedian whose facial muscles were so malleable he could hold a cup and saucer in his mouth. James Bland, a Howard-educated performer and songwriter, wrote several standard minstrel songs (an area dominated by the great white melodist Stephen Foster), including "O Dem Golden Slippers" and the ballad "Carry Me Back to Old Virginny," which served as Virginia's state song until 1997, when the song's racial dialect ("There's where the old darkey's heart am long'd to go") finally prompted its removal.

As jazz made its first inroads into popular culture, the minstrel show was on its last legs. Stars like the immensely versatile comedian, mime, and song-writer Bert Williams and the majestic tap dancer Bill "Bojangles" Robinson moved their acts to the vaudeville stage. Yet the minstrel show's key stereotypes lingered on and on. Radio comics used "blackvoice" dialect to keep a new generation laughing at minstrel stereotypes—the most popular radio show of the 1930s was *Amos 'n' Andy*. Through the early 1950s, film actors such as Mickey Rooney, Judy Garland, Bing Crosby, and Joan Crawford were occasionally asked to put on cork. Minstrelsy had become a show-biz staple; entertainers felt they could indulge it without acknowledging its racial slurs.

Perhaps the most unnerving aspect of minstrelsy was that it trained white audiences to expect all black entertainers, including those who came to fame long after minstrelsy's heyday, to enact characteristics of the performing fool. Louis Armstrong mugged his way through a notorious 1930s one-reeler, performing the minstrel song "Shine" in heaven, wearing a leopard skin and standing ankle-deep in soap bubbles. When Duke Ellington made his motion picture debut in a cameo appearance with Amos and Andy, however, minstrelsy was banished for three minutes; he is the same sophisticated Ellington who was seen at the Cotton Club and for the next forty years. Ironically, few whites saw these films. They were distributed almost exclusively to black theaters, where audiences were delighted to see geniuses like Ellington and Armstrong on the screen. Those audiences had no trouble getting beyond the masks, and laughed at Armstrong's inventive humor, knowing that the sound of his trumpet and the authority of his

In the late 1890s, black performers danced the cakewalk dressed in high fashion, encouraging white audiences to follow their step. This sheet music cover undercuts their elegance, however, through minstrel-style exaggeration and derisory language.

vocal delivery dispelled racist clichés, even turning them into an act of defiance. If stereotypes could not be dispelled, they could certainly be undermined.

Dance Music

After the Civil War, when blacks were pushed toward manual labor, music was one of the few skilled professions open to them. Like a butler, cook, or maid, a black musician hired to play tunes for dancing became a domestic servant, wearing livery (or the conventional black tuxedo) as a symbol of his role. His position in society was elegant and profitable, if clearly subservient. This situation held until a revolution shook the world of dance.

In late nineteenth-century America, respectable people danced at balls restricted by invitation to a small, exclusive social circle. Their favorite dances, including the quadrille and the lancer, were formal and discouraged intimacy. All that began to change early in the new century. When restaurants and cabarets threw open their dance floors to middle-class couples, a slew of new dances entered the mainstream. Sometimes known as "animal dances" (the turkey trot, bunny hug, and grizzly bear were especially

James Reese Europe (far left) was a stellar musician, conductor, arranger, and administrator. In World War I, he also proved to be a brave soldier, fighting in the trenches of France. Here he conducts his 369th Infantry Band, known as the Hellfighters, in Paris, 1919.
FRANK DRIGGS COLLECTION

popular), they were, to some, shockingly uninhibited and physical, requiring vigorous movement from the hips and lower body. Women shed their corsets, finding dance a means of physical exercise and personal expression. The advent of the phonograph enabled people to learn these snappy new dances in the privacy of their living rooms.

The most fashionable of the new steps were African American in origin; the Charleston, for example, derived its name and syncopations from the highly Africanized islands of South Carolina. Yet these dances were introduced to middle-class audiences by white experts—most famously Vernon and Irene Castle, who offered graceful interpretations that carefully removed lower-class (and lower-body) excesses. While the Castles transformed those "primitive" dances into cool, middle-class elegance, the subversively syncopated music was inescapably black, and derived from the contemporary piano (and eventually orchestral) style known as **ragtime**. "When a good orchestra plays a 'rag,'" Vernon Castle said, "one has simply *got* to move."

The Castles' ragtime was performed by a remarkable black bandleader, James Reese Europe (1881–1919). Born in Alabama, Europe moved to New York at twenty-two to perform in and conduct black musical theater. He quickly shifted his focus to dance music. When the United States entered World War I, Europe enlisted, prepared to show that black men were willing to die for their country. He fought bravely in the trenches and formed the 369th Infantry Band, known as the "Hellfighters." Today, his long-neglected recordings seem startlingly prescient, if only because his military band instrumentation favored the brasses and reeds and allowed for short breaks. Europe also pointed to the future in devising bands of different sizes: a small combo ideally suited for jazz, and an orchestra—exemplified by Europe's Hellfighters and such rival bands as Will Marion Cook's Southern Syncopated Orchestra—ideally suited for ballrooms.

James Reese Europe

John Philip Sousa brought military music to the concert stage.

John Philip Sousa

ART MUSIC

Brass Bands

Having learned during slavery that literacy meant power—why else would it be systematically denied to them?—musically inclined African Americans were drawn to the mysteries of notation and theory. In the all-black schools and universities that sprouted throughout the South after Emancipation, music became a central part of formal education. Children learned to play string instruments like the violin, and some—like Joseph Douglass, grandson of the abolitionist Frederick Douglass—became skilled performers. Musicians brought up in the concert tradition carried with them a social ambition, a dream of becoming something more in the world.

If the symphony orchestra proved a remote goal for most of these classically trained youngsters, the brass band provided a more practical alternative. An import from Britain, the brass band was originally a military institution that in peacetime became a local "people's" orchestra, with new brass instruments like the sousaphone designed for ease in marching.

The sousaphone was inspired by John Philip Sousa (1854–1932), a conductor and composer whose name was synonymous with brass band excellence. In 1892, Sousa formed his first ensemble, and for the next forty years the Sousa Band toured the world, bringing to brass band music the highest level of virtuosity and precision. He also inspired thousands of lesser ensembles, ranging in size from large professional bands (often led by former Sousa soloists) to small, local amateur groups. Indeed, it was said that "a town without its brass band is as much in need of sympathy as a church without a choir." Staffed by townspeople who mastered as much notation as necessary, local bands played for dances, concerts, and parades. Towns with a significant African American population had their own brass bands, with black players just as keen to display their skills as their white counterparts.

As the dance craze gathered steam in the early decades of the twentieth century, brass bands thinned their ranks to small dance ensembles, often led by a violinist but featuring wind instruments central to jazz: cornet, clarinet, and trombone. Cymbals, bass drum, and snare drum were combined into the modern drum set. Duple-meter marches—sometimes in a straight 2/4, at other times in a jauntier meter (6/8) with the beat divided into threes—were easily adapted for dancing.

The brass band's primary contribution to jazz turned out to be the structure of its music. The defining unit of a march is a sixteen-bar **strain**, which marries a distinctive melody to an equally identifiable chord progression.

March form

Marches are made up of a succession of strains, each usually repeated before passing on to the next. A typical march with four strains could be diagrammed as **A A B B C C D D** or **A A B B A C C D D** (with the returning **A** offering a hint of closure and transition). No attempt is made to round things off at the end by reprising the first strain.

The third, or **trio**, strain (**C**) is particularly significant. For one thing, it modulates to a new key (the subdominant, or IV), sometimes with the aid of a short introductory passage, and is often twice as long, lasting thirty-two bars instead of sixteen. Composers used the trio to change the piece's dynamics, texture, or orchestration. Many marches concentrate on the trio at the end, repeating it several times after dramatic interludes—among them Sousa's indelible classic "The Stars and Stripes Forever." Thanks to America's entry into world affairs in the Spanish-American War in 1898, this march achieved immense and lasting success as a radiant display of patriotism.

RAGTIME

While Sousa enjoyed international renown, another kind of music was coming to the fore, one that embodied—as jazz itself would—the collision of African American music with the white mainstream, absorbing and combining the disparate aspects of folk music, popular music, and art music. **Ragtime** probably got its name from the phrase "ragged time," a colorful description of African American polyrhythm.

At the time of the Civil War, "ragged time" would have been heard chiefly on the banjo, the black instrument par excellence. But over the next half century, black performers were able to take up piano—the very symbol of middle-class gentility, and yet sturdy enough to find a home in the lower-class saloons on the fringe of every urban community, white or black. Musicians who stumbled onto this instrument found that the same polyrhythms that enlivened banjo playing fit naturally under a pianist's fingers. The left hand kept a steady, two-beat rhythmic foundation: low bass notes alternating with higher chords. Against this background, the right hand was free to add contrasting rhythms that contradicted the duple meter. To "rag" a piece meant to subject it to this process of rhythmic complication.

Ragtime could mean a type of song, a dance, or a piano style. These varied associations remind us how this genre saturated American music at the turn of the century.

■ SCOTT JOPLIN (1868–1917)

The first "rags," appearing in 1897, were translations of improvised piano techniques into written form. These pieces adopted the march form, fitting their rhythmic contrast into a succession of distinct melodic strains. (March form, as it applies to jazz, is perhaps better understood as **march/ragtime form**.) Over the next two decades, thousands of rags were published—many of them by piano virtuosos who tailored their extraordinary technique to the level of the ordinary pianist. Those that have proved most durable were painstakingly notated by pianist-composers from the hinterland, none of whom was more celebrated or gifted than Scott Joplin.

Joplin was born in the backwaters of East Texas, a child of Reconstruction who believed in the power of literacy to lift black people out of poverty. He left home as a teenager to become a professional pianist, touring up and down the Mississippi River. In 1894, Joplin settled in Sedalia, Missouri, a small but bustling railroad town. There he took a leading role in the musical affairs

The few photographs that survive of ragtime composer Scott Joplin show him as impeccably dressed and intently serious.

of the black community, organizing a brass band (he also played cornet) while studying music theory at the local black college.

In 1899, he published the "Maple Leaf Rag" (named after a Sedalia saloon), a piece that wedded an irresistible polyrhythm to the harmonies and structure of a concert march. Joplin was shrewd enough to insist on royalty payments rather than the usual flat fee; the income from that one piece, which eventually sold hundreds of thousands of copies, supported him for the rest of his short-lived career. Spurred by his success, Joplin moved to St. Louis and then to New York City. He wrote more than fifty rags, some in collaboration with other pianist-composers, as well as a ballet and two operas.

Joplin did not live to witness the Jazz Age. By the time he died (from syphilis), in 1917, recordings had displaced sheet music as the most effective way to market ragtime, and Joplin was largely forgotten. True recognition came much later. In 1970, he was inducted into the Songwriters Hall of Fame; in 1976, he was awarded a Pulitzer Prize. Most surprisingly, he reached No. 3 on the Billboard pop chart in 1974, after his melodious 1903 rag "The Entertainer" was featured in the movie *The Sting*.

■ The Path to Jazz: WILBUR SWEATMAN (1882–1961)

Joplin was one of hundreds of ragtime pianists, most of them known to us only through oral history: Joe Jordan, Tom Turpin, Blind Boone, Louis Chauvin. The best of them could improvise confidently within the confines of ragtime harmony, and competed against each other in legendary contests of keyboard skill. A wealth of music that might have illuminated the transition from composed music to improvised jazz was lost, as few could or cared to notate those informal performances. But we can witness one facet of that transition by considering a friend of Joplin's, the clarinetist and saxophonist Wilbur Sweatman, whom Joplin named as executor of his will.

Multi-instrumentalist Wilbur Sweatman was a star when he performed at the Lafayette Theater in Harlem in 1923. Accompanying him is the young Duke Ellington, who had recently moved to New York from his hometown, Washington, D.C.

FRANK DRIGGS COLLECTION

Sweatman's career parallels the tumultuous changes in the ragtime era as musicians began to favor recordings over sheet music. He began performing professionally in minstrel shows and circus bands, where his signature gimmick involved playing three clarinets simultaneously. Musicians admired his know-how and showmanship. Sweatman composed several rags, of which the most successful was "Down Home Rag" (1911), a multistrain piece in march/ragtime form built around a type of polyrhythm known as **secondary ragtime**: while the meter is duple, the main melody insistently repeats a pattern of three notes, implying a **cross-rhythm**—a rhythmic layer that conflicts with the underlying meter. (This device, also called "novelty ragtime," was carried on by pianists such as George Gershwin.) When Sweatman recorded his own version, in 1916, his performance included ad-lib embellishments that hinted at a new era of bluesy improvisation. Though rarely heard, his recording survives as a crucial link between ragtime and jazz.

🎧 "Down Home Rag"

"Down Home Rag" has four strains. The first two (**A** and **B**) are nearly identical: they share a chord progression and end with the same fragment of melody. As we might expect, the trio (strain **C**) offers contrast by modulating to a nearby key; this trio, however, is the same length as the other strains. In between repetitions of **C**, the fourth strain (**D**) moves to the minor mode.

Throughout this short, exuberant recording, Sweatman is the focus of attention, performing his composed melodies with unmistakable enthusiasm. But when repeating a strain, he is just as likely to take off in unpredictable directions. It may be too much to call what he does "improvising": as with many early jazz artists, his variations have a limited range. Still, the swooping blue notes and the piercing timbre of his clarinet suggest what many ragtime musicians may have been doing in live performance at that time.

LISTENING GUIDE 3

🎧 down home rag

WILBUR SWEATMAN

Wilbur Sweatman, clarinet, with the Emerson Trio (piano, clarinet, and trombone)

- Label: Emerson 2377-1, 7161
- Date: 1916
- Style: ragtime/early jazz
- Form: march/ragtime

What to listen for:

- march/ragtime form (A A B B′ A C C′ D D′ C C′)
- contrasting trio (C) in a new key
- "secondary ragtime" (implied meter of three over meter of two)
- Sweatman's ragtime/jazz improvisation on clarinet, with blue notes

INTRODUCTION

0:00   The entire band plays an introductory figure, ending with a **half cadence**.

STRAIN A

0:04   On clarinet, Sweatman plays the main melody, with a second clarinet distantly in the background. It features a kind of polyrhythm known as **secondary ragtime**: against the duple meter, Sweatman's line implies a meter of three.

Behind Sweatman, the trombone plays a composed **countermelody**.

STRAIN A

0:12   Strain **A** is repeated.

STRAIN B

0:20   Sweatman plays a new melody over the same chord progression.

0:26   The last two bars of strain **B** are identical to those of strain **A**.

STRAIN B′

0:28   Sweatman plays a variation on the melody of **B**, which at times features **blue notes** (0:31, 0:35).

STRAIN A

0:36   After a brief pause, the band repeats strain **A**.

TRANSITION

0:44   In a four-bar chordal passage, the band **modulates** to a new key.

STRAIN C (TRIO)

0:48   Sweatman plays a new melody, constantly returning to the same high note. Once again, the trombone plays a countermelody.

STRAIN C′

0:56   While the background clarinet continues with the melody, Sweatman plays a variation, again featuring blue notes.

STRAIN D

1:05   The new strain changes mode from major to **minor**.

STRAIN D′

1:12   Sweatman's variation again features secondary ragtime.

STRAIN C′

1:20   Returning to major mode, Sweatman plays his blue note variation (heard at 1:00).

STRAIN C′

1:28   The band repeats the strain.

CODA

1:36   A single additional note ends the piece.

By the time the United States was ready to enter World War I, the basic elements for jazz were in place. For several decades, popular entertainment had been deeply affected by the rhythms and sounds of African American music. Now, despite an abiding racism so onerous it spawned the reawakening of the Ku Klux Klan, the country was ready for a genuinely new phenomenon. It came by way of the remote, dilapidated, and exotic city of New Orleans.

⊢ ADDITIONAL LISTENING ⊣	
Mississippi Fred McDowell	"Soon One Morning (Death Come a-Creepin' in My Room" (1959)
Bessie Smith	"In the House Blues" (1931)
James Reese Europe	"Too Much Mustard" (1913)
John Philip Sousa	"The Stars and Stripes Forever" (composed 1896)
Gunther Schuller	"The Entertainer" (1973)
Eubie Blake	"Stars and Stripes Forever" (1969)
Scott Joplin	"Maple Leaf Rag" (1916)
Sugar Underwood	"Dew Drop Alley" (1927)

ONLINE MULTIMEDIA RESOURCES AND REVIEW MATERIALS

Author Insight Videos

Scott DeVeaux describes how jazz grew out of the folk, popular, and art music traditions, and demonstrates ragtime examples at the piano.

Interactive Listening Guides

Georgia Sea Island Singers, "The Buzzard Lope"
Bessie Smith, "Reckless Blues"
Wilbur Sweatman, "Down Home Rag"

Jazz Concepts (audio and/or video demonstrations of terms covered here)

twelve-bar blues	call and response	minor mode
backbeat	classic (vaudeville) blues	modulation
ballad	countermelody	syncopation
blue notes	dissonance	tonic
cadence	major mode	

- For quick reference, review the **Chapter Overview** and **Chapter Outline**.
- Take the online **Chapter** and **Listening Quizzes**.
- Use the online **Glossary** and **Flashcards** to review important terms.

ORIGINAL DIXIELAND JAZZ BAND
dixie jass band one-step

JELLY ROLL MORTON
dead man blues

KING OLIVER
snake rag

RED ONION JAZZ BABIES (SIDNEY BECHET)
cake walking babies (from home)

NEW ORLEANS

THE CITY ON THE GULF

The world thinks of jazz as American, and Americans think of it as a national phenomenon—like the Mississippi, snaking through one state after another, fed by numerous tributaries such as blues, ragtime, marches, and dance bands, not to mention the overall traditions of Africa, Europe, and the Caribbean. But in the beginning, jazz was local, even provincial—a performing tradition unique to the port city of New Orleans. The style known as **New Orleans jazz** (or **Dixieland**)—featuring a highly unusual polyphonic technique called **collective improvisation**—proved irresistible enough to attract the attention of the whole country. The reasons for this tradition's birth lie in the city's geographical, racial, political, cultural, and musical peculiarities.

Southeastern Louisiana slips into the Gulf of Mexico like a well-curved shoe. New Orleans has always been the principal city on the shoe's tongue, cradled in a crescent-shaped bend of the Mississippi River, which flows down through the sole and empties into the Gulf. To the north, New Orleans faces Lake Pontchartrain, the largest inlet in the South. This watery setting not only allowed the city to grow as a major port before the railroad replaced shipping as the primary vehicle for trade, but gave New Orleans a distinct cultural character that blended elements of American commerce with those of a Caribbean island.

Jelly Roll Morton, the seminal New Orleans pianist, composer, and bandleader, at a 1926 recording session.

William Faulkner once described New Orleans as "that worldly and even foreign city," and nothing distinguishes it from the rest of the country more than its French Catholic tradition of a Mardi Gras parade, an annual event since the 1850s. Private societies, called krewes, don masks and design elaborate floats—like this boat, as commanded by the monarch Rex, in 1933.

© BETTMAN/CORBIS

Founded by France in 1718 and then relinquished as unprofitable to Spain in 1763, New Orleans was reclaimed for the French in 1803 by Napoleon, who almost immediately sold it to the United States as part of the Louisiana Purchase. Many people continued to speak French and Spanish, infusing the city with traditions of European Catholicism and culture. During a time when the South was almost entirely agricultural, it was a lively, advanced urban center with a distinct architectural look, discrete neighborhoods, and a level of sophistication associated with European capitals. New Orleans relished dances and parades, and mounted balls and celebrations to suit everyone—the rich and poor, the cultured and debauched.

Elsewhere in the United States, slaves were forced to discard their connection to Africa and accept most aspects of Western society—they were required to learn English and become Christian (and therefore Protestant). The goal was a more efficient interaction between slaves and masters, who often worked together on small landholdings. New Orleans, however, was oriented toward the Caribbean and South America. In places like Cuba and Brazil, where the slave trade remained constant until well into the nineteenth century, Africans were allowed to retain their own languages, beliefs, and customs. And those retentions carried over to New Orleans, where nearly half the population was black, whether slave or free.

Creoles of Color and Uptown Negroes

North of the Gulf of Mexico, race was divided into two distinct legal spheres—black and white. Anyone within the wide spectrum of browns, tans, and beiges (anyone believed to possess a "single drop" of black blood) was technically considered "black" and forced to live on that side of the racial division. The Caribbean world took a more pragmatic view. While continuing to enforce a barbarous society in which whites owned blacks, it acknowledged a mulatto culture and allowed that culture an intermediary social status, to the benefit of free blacks with lighter skins.

New Orleans adhered to that mulatto conception of race, producing a caste of mixed-race Negroes known as Creoles of Color. (The full description was *les gens de couleur libres*, or free people of color.) These Creoles—usually the result of black and French or Spanish alliances—evolved into a significant social group that was accorded many legal and social liberties. By 1860, most Creoles had French surnames, spoke French as well as English, attended Catholic churches, enjoyed a decent education, and worked at skilled trades—cigar making, cobbling, carpentry—that Creoles, as a group, virtually monopolized.

Their superior standing began to dissipate after the Civil War, when Reconstruction generated an increasingly intolerant racism. In 1894, Louisiana joined other Southern states in adopting the "Jim Crow" laws, which imposed and enforced a rigid color line. Two years later, the U.S. Supreme Court issued its infamous verdict in *Plessy v. Ferguson*, deciding against a light-skinned native of New Orleans (one-eighth black and seven-eighths white) who had insisted on his right to ride a streetcar in the area reserved for whites. When he lost that case, which essentially legalized segregation, the Creoles lost the last threads of their shabby aristocracy.

> **Jim Crow laws**

As their social standing fell, the Creoles, who had not lost their pride, attempted to reserve a geographical separateness from the "corn and field Negroes" pouring into New Orleans from the countryside. For a time, the dividing line was Canal Street, a large thoroughfare that begins at the Mississippi Riverfront and provides a western border for the French Quarter, home to most of the Creoles. On the other side of Canal, moving upward on the river, was the area known as Uptown, which included some of the grimmest neighborhoods in the United States. Each side had its own musical tradition; yet as Jim Crow forced the integration between Creoles and "black blacks," the two traditions collided.

> **Uptown music**

The Uptown Negroes, largely uneducated and unskilled, played a loud, upbeat, impassioned music combining elements of late nineteenth-century marching band, ragtime, and folk music. Many could not read music, and "faked" their performances by relying on an oral tradition that employed variable intonation (blue notes), rhythmic contrast, and improvisation. To Creoles, who were educated in the European manner, they failed to meet the minimum standards of professional musicianship.

> ▶ **rhythmic contrast** the simultaneous use of contrasting rhythms (polyrhythm)

As long as the Creoles remained on top, socially and musically, they landed the better-paying jobs, and were able to augment their incomes through teaching. However, their students included black Uptown players as well as downtown Creoles, and the bringing together of these two groups ultimately favored the Uptown musicians, who were on to something new: an artistry relying on improvisation, quick thinking, and a rhythmic sharpness that appealed to dancers and listeners.

Manuel Perez, the influential parade band leader and trumpeter, at home in New Orleans, 1939.

■ MANUEL PEREZ (1878–1946)

We can see a microcosm of the Creole role by looking at one of the more typical careers that figured in this cultural mix. Manuel Perez was born in New Orleans, attended a French-speaking grammar school, trained as a cigar maker (his father's profession), and studied classical music, focusing on the cornet. He soon established a local reputation, and throughout his teen years played with marching bands, dance bands, and ragtime bands, all requiring written music.

For thirty years, beginning at the dawn of the new century, Perez worked with and led the Onward Brass Band, an ensemble with as many as a dozen musicians and a great favorite at picnics

along Lake Pontchartrain as well as at the downtown dance halls. He also led small groups, including one that played on riverboats. Dozens of musicians came under his influence, whether they worked with him or took individual lessons (for which he is said to have refused payment)—among them, clarinetists Albert Nicholas and Barney Bigard, trumpeter Natty Dominique, and drummer Paul Barbarin. The jazz guitarist Danny Barker remembered Perez as "the idol of the downtown Creole colored people. To them, nobody could master the cornet like Mr. Perez." Jelly Roll Morton considered him the finest trumpeter in New Orleans (until the advent of a young jazz player, Freddie Keppard), but noted that he was a Creole from a good family and played "strictly rag time"—syncopated music, but with no improvisation.

Perez himself realized that improvisation, as practiced by the Uptown musicians, was essential for a successful band in the 1910s, and he hired Joe Oliver (the future King Oliver) as his band's improviser. Despite his prodigious technique, though, Perez found it increasingly difficult to find work for his kind of parade music, and in 1937 he returned full-time to cigar making until his death nine years later. He had lived to see the kind of parade music at which he excelled reduced to a tourist attraction and jazz itself transfigured into a worldwide phenomenon no one in 1910 could have imagined. Significantly, Manny Perez was born fifteen months after an Uptown cornetist and bandleader named Charles Joseph Bolden.

■ BUDDY BOLDEN (1877–1931) and the Birth of Jazz

In the realm of jazz myths, no one stands taller or blows louder than Buddy Bolden. He is generally acknowledged as the first important musician in jazz, and his rise to fame augurs the triumph of African American culture.

Bolden was born in New Orleans, and took up the cornet in his middle or late teens. He began working at parades and other functions in 1895, turning to music full time in 1901 or 1902. After struggling with alcoholism and depression, he suffered a mental breakdown in 1906, and was incarcerated in the state hospital for the insane, where he remained until his death in 1931. His career as musician and bandleader lasted no more than eleven years, in

Jazz begins here. The only known photograph of the Buddy Bolden Band, c. 1905: (standing) Jimmy Johnson, bass; Bolden, cornet; Willie Cornish, valve trombone; William Warner, clarinet; (seated) Jefferson Mumford, guitar; Frank Lewis, clarinet.

which time he earned the respect of almost every black musician in the city (few whites were aware of him), as well as a large public following.

The most frequent boasts concerning Bolden's prowess relate to the loudness of his playing and the seductiveness of his approach to slow blues. Jelly Roll Morton claimed that "on a still night," Bolden's cornet could be heard as far away as twelve miles, the distance between the Mississippi Riverfront and Lake Pontchartrain. On the stillest of nights, that would not be possible. Yet Bolden *would* sometimes step outside the hall his band was working and play a few phrases to attract customers in adjacent neighborhoods, who preferred his livelier, raunchier brand of music.

Although other musicians of his generation were remembered for their overall musicianship, only Bolden is consistently recalled in terms of a personal style. He was the first figure whose individuality was a decisive element, the first for whom the "how you do it" is more important than the "what you do." That made him the first jazz celebrity: the father figure on which the New Orleans story (and by extension, the jazz story) is grounded.

Did Bolden invent jazz? We can't know for

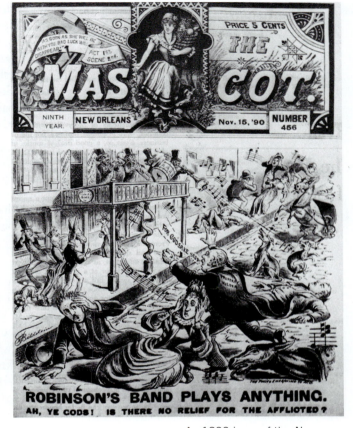

An 1890 issue of the *New Orleans Mascot* depicts white citizens pleading for mercy as a black band, hired to advertise a museum, performs some kind of new, raucous music without the aid of sheet music.

certain, but a qualified yes seems reasonable. Eyewitnesses to the musical life of New Orleans at the dawn of the twentieth century fail to cite a precursor to Bolden, or a significant rival to him during his glory days. He arrived at the right time, amid a musical cornucopia in which schooled and unschooled musicians worked together to provide a broad range of functional music—for picnics, concerts, dances, funerals, parades, and publicity events. Bolden, who could read music (he had studied with a neighbor), played in every kind of setting. The demand for music was so great that, perhaps inevitably, musicians devised ways to perform away from written scores.

In this respect, it's worth looking at a notorious illustration that appeared on the cover of the weekly newspaper the *New Orleans Mascot* in November 1890, five years before Bolden ever performed in public. It depicts four Negro musicians, three playing brass instruments and one a bass drum, all wearing top hats and producing a raucous music that has the power to send the white citizens into a panic, cupping their ears, swooning in pain, imploring the band to stop, or fainting dead away. The musicians have no music stands. Is the band playing something we might recognize as jazz? We can never know, but three things are clear: the musicians are Uptown blacks, not trained Creoles; the music is unusual enough to provoke outrage and confusion; and it is performed without sheet music.

Whatever the illustrator's musicians played added to the unique mix of New Orleans music at the turn of the century. The musicians who worked in parades (brass bands) by day and in saloons and dance halls by night had to master the technical know-how required for the former as well as the looser, bluesier ad-lib style necessary for the latter. Of the many musicians who did

New Orleans Mascot

STORYVILLE

Although Bolden played in different venues, legend invariably ties him to the saloons in or near Storyville, or "the district," as New Orleans locals called it—a zone of legalized prostitution, named for alderman Sidney Story, who wrote the bill that brought it into existence. Yet except for a few pianists, jazz musicians didn't play in bordellos. Many worked in cabarets within Storyville's precincts, but they found much of their work in parks, excursions, parades, advertising wagons, riverboats, and dances throughout the city. The dismantling of Storyville in 1917 had little effect on the exodus of jazz musicians from New Orleans. As guitarist Danny Barker remarked, "You never had to figure on getting work in the district, so it wasn't so important when it closed."

Still, it would be a mistake to dismiss Storyville as a factor in the development of New Orleans jazz. The very funkiness of its saloons undoubtedly contributed to the adoption of rhythmic blues as a central part of the repertory, along with expressive techniques that emphasized the music's seductive passion. The achingly slow "snake-hips" dancing encouraged by Bolden and the "talkative" timbre later introduced by King Oliver likely found more traction in this environment than at other social events. In rough precincts like Storyville, where white social arbiters did not breathe down their necks, musicians could explore their bonds with dancers and listeners, and let loose with the kind of artistic transgression typical of outcast communities.

both, Bolden was the one everyone talked about and imitated. George Baquet, a Creole clarinetist, recalled seeing Bolden once at the Odd Fellows and Masonic Hall—a "plenty tough" place where customers kept their hats on and interacted with the music through encouraging shouts or sexually provocative dancing. Suddenly Bolden stomped his foot, marked a few beats by banging his cornet on the floor, and began playing the rowdy ballad "Make Me a Pallet on the Floor":

> Everybody got up quick, the whole place rose and yelled out, "Oh, Mr. Bolden, play it for us, Buddy, play it!" I never heard anything like that before. I'd played "legitimate" stuff. But this! It was somethin' that pulled me! They got me up on the stand that night, and I was playing with them. After that, I didn't play "legitimate" so much.

At his peak, Bolden led several different bands, depending on the kind of music required. His best-known jazz ensemble, in place by 1905, consisted of his cornet, a valve trombonist, two clarinetists, a guitarist, a bassist, and a drummer. By the time King Oliver began to establish himself, Bolden had been hospitalized as alcoholic and schizophrenic. When he died in 1931, jazz was on the verge of international acclaim, but Bolden probably know nothing about it. Except in New Orleans, where old-timers still reminisced, he was long forgotten.

NEW ORLEANS STYLE

In the decade from Bolden's heyday until the success of recorded jazz in 1917, New Orleans musicians continued to develop their own distinctive style. We can't know precisely what their music sounded like, but by extrapolating backward from later recordings, and by drawing information from photographs and interviews, it's possible to offer a general portrait of early New Orleans jazz.

Its instrumentation derived from two sources. Brass band societies, which spawned smaller dance groups, gave the music its melody instruments: trumpet or cornet, trombone, and clarinet. Together, these instruments are called the **front line**, reflecting their position at the head of a marching band. (Fans who loyally followed a parade band came to be known as the second line.) Brass bands also, inadvertently, fostered the drum set, combining the elements of parade percussion—bass drum, snares, cymbals. The other source was string ensembles, which featured violin, banjo, mandolin, and other instruments—including guitar and bass, which became indispensable to the jazz rhythm section. The piano began to find a stable role in jazz bands with the advent of ragtime in the early decades of the twentieth century.

Originally, the earliest New Orleans bands also included a lead violinist, whose job was to play the melody straight, without improvisation or ornamentation. Against this, the cornet probably improvised a syncopated or ragged version of the melody. By 1917, the cornet had simply displaced the violinist, offering the tune in a more compact, spontaneous form, while the clarinet played a countermelody to *him*—an improvised accompaniment (mostly in eighth notes) that danced around and between the sharply articulated cornet notes. As clarinetists learned to create their own lines, they drew increasingly from the underlying chord progressions.

Similarly, the trombone originally played parts written for cello or baritone horn, but soon found its own role in filling out the ensemble. The trombone played fewer notes than the clarinet, many of them exaggerated slurs or **glissandos** (sliding from one note to the next) facilitated by the slide. (Musicians called this **tailgate trombone**, or **smear**; when bands toured the streets in a horse-drawn wagon, the trombonist sat in front on the tailgate, to minimize the risk of his slide cracking another musician's skull.)

By the time they began recording, New Orleans bands had already attained an unmistakable ensemble style. There was no obvious star or stand-out soloist. The front line improvised a dense, polyphonic texture—a **collective improvisation**, with each instrument occupying its own musical space (clarinet on top, cornet in the middle, trombone at the bottom), rhythm (clarinet is fastest, trombone slowest), and timbre. During the trio section of a piece, the band often switched to block-chord texture or, more rarely, presented a single horn plus accompaniment. Breaks and stop-time (where the band stops to let a single musician briefly solo) were common; soloing as we think of it was rare. In this sense, New Orleans jazz embodied the folk aesthetic, in which the group almost always subsumes the individual. This was especially true of the rhythm section, which provided a steady, unrelenting pulse.

Collective Improvisation

Formally, New Orleans bands usually relied on ragtime-type compositions with multiple strains (as well as the novel structure of the twelve-bar blues). At the beginning of a number, each strain was often played only once. The trio offered a point of contrast: modulating to a new key, dynamic level, or texture. The musicians' performances were tied to the composition, with little opportunity to break loose from it to play improvisations (solo or collective). Only toward the end, when the band had hit a groove with itself and with the audience that no one wanted to stop, would a strain be repeated with various embellishments, until the leader called a halt.

Forms

THE GREAT MIGRATION

Jazz began to leave New Orleans in the years of the Great Migration, the largest internal relocation of people in the history of the United States. It had started in the late nineteenth century, when former slaves began to drift away from their agricultural labors toward cities like New Orleans. With the coming of World War I, the movement became a torrent, as blacks pushed northward and ended up in the ghettos of Chicago and New York.

The migration, a long time coming, was inevitable. Very few Southern blacks owned land. Under the system of sharecropping, they were living a life of agricultural peonage, while enduring, at every turn, reminders of their second-class status. They were forced to use segregated transportation, waiting rooms, water fountains, lavatories, doorways, stairways, and theaters, as well as schools and housing. Politically powerless, they were subject to the double standards of white laws. Outside the law, the iniquity extended to murder and torture.

Robert S. Abbott founded the influential *Chicago Defender* in 1905, and helped fuel the "Great Migration" of Southern blacks to the North.

An inscribed 1913 portrait of trumpet player Freddie Keppard, one of the first musicians to take a New Orleans ensemble to Chicago and Los Angeles.

The issue was decided by economics. The United States entered World War I in 1917, on the heels of Henry Ford's introduction of the automobile assembly line. The war snatched millions of men away from the workforce and put a hold on immigration. The manpower shortage was so severe that railroads paid fares to encourage blacks to move. Newspapers like the black-owned *Chicago Defender* listed the contact numbers of people in churches and other organizations who would provide them with financial help. Agricultural interests in the South tried to stop the exodus through intimidation (they delayed travelers until their trains had left and disregarded prepaid tickets). But they could not combat the lure of decent wages and a more humane way of life.

JAZZ MOVES ON: FIRST RECORDINGS

Foremost among the black pioneers seeking to escape the South were entertainers—in minstrel troupes, tent shows, bands, and vaudeville. Perhaps the first genuinely major jazz figure to travel widely was the cornetist Freddie Keppard (1890–1933), who may have lost the chance to make the first jazz record. In 1916, the Victor Talking Machine Company invited him to make test discs to see how jazz sounded on records. Keppard refused, reportedly because he didn't want to document his music for others to steal (he was said to play with a handkerchief over his hand so other musicians couldn't see his fingering); others say he didn't like the money. Consequently, the distinction of making the first jazz records went to a white New Orleans group: the Original Dixieland Jazz Band.

■ ORIGINAL DIXIELAND JAZZ BAND

Spell it Jass, Jas, Jaz or Jazz—nothing can spoil a Jass band. Some say the Jass band originated in Chicago. Chicago says it comes from San Francisco—San Francisco being away off across the continent. Anyway a Jass band is the newest thing in the cabarets, adding greatly to the hilarity thereof.

Reading this excerpt from Victor's publicity sheet for the all-white Original Dixieland Jazz Band (ODJB), we may surmise that "jazz"—at the dawn of the "Jazz Age"—was often misspelled, that many people did not know where San Francisco was, and that no one had heard about New Orleans, though all five members of the ODJB were natives of that city. The reason for Victor's interest was that the band had come to New York to play at Reisenweber's Restaurant in January 1917, causing a sensation. It was the talk of the town, and the record industry wanted some of the action.

To most listeners, the ODJB had no precedent. Many ragtime records had preceded those of the ODJB (from as far back as 1897), and elements of jazz can be detected in records made between 1914 and 1916 by such African American performers as Bert Williams, James Reese Europe, and Wilbur Sweatman, as well as the white "Mammy singer" Al Jolson. But those elements—robust rhythms or embellishments beyond written ragtime—merely hint at the real thing. The ODJB *was* the real thing, a musical eruption genuinely new to the market.

In New Orleans at the turn of the century, there were important white ragtime players, composers, and teachers who undoubtedly influenced black jazz musicians in terms of repertory, harmony, and instrumental technique, but they don't figure in written or oral accounts of the evolution of jazz. The widely imitated five-piece instrumentation of the Original Dixieland Jazz Band, for example, originated with Freddie Keppard. Yet the white New Orleans jazz tradition is significant in its own right. The commonly accepted father of white jazz was a parade drummer named George "Papa Jack" Laine, who trained many young men who took jazz north, including most members of the ODJB. By the time the ODJB began to play in New York, its members included cornetist Nick LaRocca, trombonist Eddie Edwards, clarinetist Larry Shields, pianist Henry Ragas, and drummer Tony Sbarbaro.

The Original Dixieland Jazz Band popularized jazz (word and music) in Chicago and New York, and made the first jazz recording in 1917: Henry Ragas, Larry Shields, Eddie Edwards, Nick LaRocca, and Tony Sbarbaro.

So great was the band's initial popularity that it established the word "jazz" as part of the international vocabulary. Within five years, dozens of bands had appropriated the word. (Originally, it was "jass," but the spelling was changed after vandals repeatedly crossed out the J on the ODJB's billboards and posters.) Hotels throughout Europe began to hire what they called jazz bands (basically any kind of dance ensemble that had drums and at least one reed instrument). The 1920s would always be remembered as the **Jazz Age**.

Compared with later records by King Oliver, the New Orleans Rhythm Kings, and Jelly Roll Morton, the ODJB often sounds hokey and insincere. Still, the band played a spirited, unpretentious music, and served jazz well in several ways: its tunes became Dixieland standards; its name signaled a break with a musical past called ragtime; and a visit the band made to Europe in 1919 helped make jazz international. After its European tour, however, the band lost its verve, and finally called it quits in 1922, just in time for Morton and Oliver to redefine New Orleans jazz for all time.

🎧 "Dixie Jass Band One-Step"

This enduringly popular Dixieland theme retains ragtime's multistrain form; at the same time, the musicians burst through with their embellishments—especially the clarinetist and the drummer, and especially in the third strain (or trio). From the opening, which juxtaposes sharp **staccato** (detached) chords with collective improvisation, to its triumphant conclusion, this music is very well organized, even as it suggests the feeling of carefree spontaneity.

The trio is the most famous part of the piece, borrowed from one of the leading rags of the day ("That Teasin' Rag," written by pianist Joe Jordan in 1909) and sometimes played alone. It's a thirty-two-bar chorus, played three times. But because the chorus is made up of two similar sixteen-bar sections, we get a sense that the ensemble is playing the same melody six times, and growing increasingly rowdy with each repeat. In 1917, this outpouring of energy, underscored by repetition, had no precedent in recorded music—and it struck listeners as either exciting and optimistic or unruly and subversive. The Victor engineers did a remarkable job in capturing the sounds of the instruments, including the drummer's cymbal and woodblocks. The instrumentation allows us to hear polyphonic details as clarinet and trombone swirl around the cornet lead.

🎧 dixie jass band one-step

ORIGINAL DIXIELAND JAZZ BAND
Nick LaRocca, cornet; Eddie Edwards, trombone;
Larry Shields, clarinet; Henry Ragas, piano; Tony
Sbarbaro, drums

- Label: Victor 18255
- Date: 1917
- Style: New Orleans jazz
- Form: march/ragtime

What to listen for:

- rehearsed collective improvisation
- march/ragtime form, with modulations between the different strains
- raucous clarinet playing and trombone glissandos
- 32-bar C strain (trio), which grows rowdier and more percussive with each repeat

STRAIN A

0:00	a	The band opens with forceful **tonic** chords, surrounded by a brief silence.
0:03		A dramatic outburst (a loud trombone **glissando**, a clarinet shriek) is followed by a cymbal crash.
0:04		The band breaks into a short polyphonic passage of **collective improvisation**.
0:08	a	The material from 0:00 to 0:08 is repeated.

STRAIN B

0:16	b	A clarinet **break** introduces the next strain, which **modulates** to a new key.
0:18		The band follows with a longer passage of collective improvisation.
0:23	b′	The clarinet break returns, followed again by collective improvisation.
0:28		The strain comes to a **full cadence** on the tonic.

STRAIN A

| 0:31 | | Strain **A** is repeated. |

STRAIN B

| 0:46 | | Strain **B** is repeated. |

STRAIN C (TRIO)

1:01	c	The trio modulates to yet another key. While the trumpet plays the main melody, the clarinet plays a faster **countermelody** and the trombone adds glissandos.
1:09		The drummer adds strong **counterrhythms** on a woodblock (one of the few parts on the drum set easily captured by acoustic recording equipment).
1:16		The clarinet marks the first sixteen bars with a high note.
1:17	c′	
1:25		As we approach the final cadence, the harmonies begin to change.
1:31		A loud, raucous note on the cornet signals a repetition of the trio.

STRAIN C

1:33	c	As the band repeats the trio, the drummer increases the intensity of the polyrhythm.
1:48	c′	
1:53		The drummer plays two powerful strokes on the bass drum.
1:56		The clarinet's line often sounds like a shriek.
2:02		Another repetition is signaled by the cornet's note, played alongside a clarinet squeal.

STRAIN C

2:03	**c**	The band plays the trio one last time.
2:18	**c'**	The drummer signals the second half by hitting the bass drum, followed by a cymbal crash.
2:26		The drummer finally uses the full drum set, adding military-style rolls on the snare drum and driving the band toward the conclusion.

CODA

2:34	The band adds a four-note **coda**, a common Jazz Age ending.

■ JELLY ROLL MORTON (1890–1941)

The development of jazz may be viewed as an ongoing alliance between improvisers and composers: soloists who spontaneously create music and writers who organize frameworks for them. They influence each other, much as Creoles and Uptown blacks did. So it's fitting that the first great jazz composer was a Creole who endured expulsion from his family in order to learn from and eventually work with the kind of musicians epitomized by Buddy Bolden. Jelly Roll Morton's genius is extensively documented on records: his legacy is not a matter of speculation, unlike Bolden's—though it, too, is encrusted in myths, chiefly of Morton's own devising.

One of the most colorful characters in American music, Morton worked as a bordello pianist, pimp, pool hall hustler, and comedian before establishing himself as a fastidious musician and recording artist—a pianist, singer, composer, arranger, and music theorist. He was also a diamond-tooth dandy, insufferable braggart, occultist, and memoirist. He claimed that he had invented jazz in 1902, giving his own date of birth as 1885. In fact, New Orleans baptismal records indicate that he was born Ferdinand Joseph Lamothe in 1890. But if Morton didn't exactly invent jazz, he certainly helped to define it, propelling the New Orleans style forward at a time when no one knew precisely what jazz was.

Morton was thirty-two when he settled in Chicago, in 1922. In July of the following year, he spent two afternoons at the ramshackle Gennett Records studio in Richmond, Indiana, recording with the talented white hometown band called the New Orleans Rhythm Kings—this was the first significant integrated recording session in jazz history. At these sessions, Morton debuted a few of his tunes, the best of which show how he took the multiple-strains structure and syncopated rhythms of ragtime to a new level, emphasizing a foot-tapping beat (he called it a stomp) and tricky syncopations. One of them was "King Porter Stomp," which has four strains, the last of which became a major anthem of the Swing Era.

In Chicago, 1926, Jelly Roll Morton created his most enduring work and a pinnacle in the New Orleans style with a recording unit he called the Red Hot Peppers.

FRANK DRIGGS COLLECTION

Red Hot Peppers

Morton began recording with ensembles of seven and eight players in the fall of 1926, at the very moment that the Victor Talking Machine Company switched from acoustic to electrical technology, giving his recordings a vivid fidelity. Morton called his group the Red Hot Peppers, and Victor advertised it as "the Number One Hot Band," although it existed solely to record. To many, the Peppers sessions represent the pinnacle of the New Orleans tradition, an ideal balance between composition and improvisation. What Morton's music embodies above all is the raw, restless social energy of the early years of the century, when jazz was a new hustle and the rules had to be made before they could be broken.

🎧 "Dead Man Blues"

"Dead Man Blues" is Morton's interpretation of the New Orleans burial ritual, which he traced back to Scripture: rejoice at the death and cry at the birth. It begins with a scene-setting dialogue in the style of black minstrelsy, a comedic way of announcing Morton's intention to invoke a New Orleans funeral. This leads to the first chorus—each chorus is a twelve-bar blues—in which the musicians collectively improvise in familiar New Orleans style: you can almost see the Grand Marshal leading the mourners, gracefully prancing with his parasol. This particular performance (an alternate take) was rejected by Morton for commercial release, probably owing to the obvious gaffes made by the cornetist during his solo. On this take, however, we can hear a nimble elegance in the collective improvisation that the band failed to capture the second time around.

Morton organized his music scrupulously, going so far as to notate the parts for bass (bass lines are usually improvised), and making the most of his musicians. We are always conscious of each instrument: the tailgate smears of the trombone, the snap of the trumpet, the pretty harmonizing of the clarinets, the clanging rhythm of the banjo. For those who think of New Orleans jazz as genial chaos, with simultaneously improvised melody lines tumbling untidily on top of one another, Morton's music may come as a revelation.

While "Dead Man Blues" is a twelve-bar blues, it's also organized like a tune in march/ragtime form: choruses 1 and 2 correspond to the first strain (**A**); choruses 3 and 4, played by cornet and rhythm, to the second (**B**). The fifth and sixth choruses serve as the trio, a section of the piece for which Morton often reserved his most melodic ideas. For this recording and for these choruses, he hired two extra clarinetists to blend with Omer Simeon in playing block-chord harmonies—it's the only time they appear in the performance. In the sixth chorus, Morton introduces another of his trademark devices to increase tension: against the clarinetists' lissome melody, the trombonist Kid Ory plays a countermelody, his spare phrases adding an understated touch of drama.

By the 1930s, Morton's music was dismissed as hopelessly outdated. When he died in 1941, a revival of interest in New Orleans jazz was just getting underway, too late to help Morton, who was broke and largely ignored or belittled. Only later was he acclaimed as one of the guiding figures of early jazz—a genuinely original, thoughtful, sensitive, and permanent artist.

🎧 dead man blues

JELLY ROLL MORTON AND HIS RED HOT PEPPERS (ALTERNATE TAKE)

Jelly Roll Morton, piano; George Mitchell, cornet; Kid Ory, trombone; Omer Simeon, Barney Bigard, Darnell Howard, clarinets; Johnny St. Cyr, banjo; John Lindsay, bass; Andrew Hilaire, drums

- Label: Victor 20252
- Date: 1926
- Style: New Orleans jazz
- Form: 12-bar blues

What to listen for:

- vaudeville humor, references to New Orleans funerals at beginning
- collective improvisation alternating with clarinet and cornet solos
- clarinet trio at chorus 5, with countermelody in trombone at chorus 6

SPOKEN DIALOGUE

0:00   Morton and St. Cyr act out a vaudeville scene, with exaggerated minstrel accents, to prepare us for a New Orleans funeral.

> Morton: *"What's that I hear at twelve o'clock in the daytime? Church bells ringing?"*
> St. Cyr: *"Oh, man, you don't hear no church bells ringing twelve o'clock in the day."*
> Morton: *"Don't tell me—somebody must be dead!"*
> St. Cyr: *"Ain't nobody dead. Somebody must be dead drunk."*
> Morton: *"Don't tell me, I think there's a fyoo-neral!"*
> St. Cyr: *"Well, looky here! I believe I do hear a funeral! I believe I hear that tram-bone blowin'!"*

INTRODUCTION

0:18   A trombone **glissando** introduces a somber march, played by the band in **block-chord** texture. The tune comes from the beginning of the traditional hymn "Flee as a Bird to the Mountain," usually performed during the procession to the cemetery.

CHORUS 1

0:33   Suddenly, as if the funeral ceremony were over, the band swings into a faster tempo. The texture is **polyphonic**, with each instrument contributing its individual melodic line to the **collective improvisation**. The bass plays a variety of patterns: the relaxed two-beat pattern at the opening adjusts at times to four beats to the bar (0:41) or even eight beats to the bar (0:48).

CHORUS 2

0:55   Simeon plays a clarinet solo marked by **variable intonation** (or **blue notes**). Underneath, Morton plays a delicate **counterpoint** (creating a polyphonic texture) on the piano.

CHORUS 3

1:18   Mitchell's cornet solo begins roughly, marred by several obvious errors (1:19, 1:27).

CHORUS 4

1:40   As Mitchell continues his solo, he plays with more accuracy and confidence.

CHORUS 5 (TRIO)

2:03   Two other clarinets (Bigard and Howard) join Simeon, playing a simple melody in block-chord texture. The rhythm section responds to each line with a loud accent.

CHORUS 6

2:26   As the clarinets repeat their block-chord line, Ory adds a subtle bluesy **countermelody.**

CHORUS 7

2:48   The band improvises polyphonically in a climactic chorus of collective improvisation.

CODA

3:11   In a witty coda, Morton brings back the clarinet trio, only to cut it short with a final accent by the rhythm section.

■ KING OLIVER (1885–1938)

If New Orleans jazz started out, in the Bolden era, as local gumbo flavored by the great variety of music available in that city, by 1922 the gumbo was traveled and seasoned. Instrumental mastery had increased, hundreds of new pieces had been written, and the New Orleans style had assimilated flavors of the cities in which it prospered. Jazz had become a fad in the late teens, tricked up with comical routines and instrumental gimmicks. In refusing to cheapen or remodel his music, Joseph "King" Oliver brought New Orleans jazz to an enduring plateau.

Born in rural Louisiana, Oliver moved to New Orleans in early childhood and turned to music (relatively late in life) around 1905, the peak of Buddy Bolden's reign. He served a long apprenticeship as a cornetist in various brass bands and saloon groups, finally achieving local renown in an orchestra led by trombonist Kid Ory, who billed him as King Oliver in 1917, cementing his place as Bolden's heir.

Oliver presented quite a sight. Self-conscious about his blind and pro-truding left eye, the result of a childhood accident (some people called him Popeye), he played seated or leaning against a wall, sporting a derby rakishly angled to cover the affliction, and used an arsenal of mutes to vary his timbre: a rubber plunger, pop bottle, bucket, glass, doorknob, or hat. Oliver's love of muting devices had an immense influence on jazz, and eventually led to the manufacture of professional mutes. Richard M. Jones, a pianist who later became an important record producer, recalled Oliver's resourcefulness one night when his band was playing at a Storyville dance hall called Abadie's and his rival, Freddie Keppard, had drawn a larger crowd across the street at Pete Lala's:

> I was sitting at the piano and Joe Oliver came over to me and commanded in a nervous harsh voice "Get in B-flat." He didn't even mention a tune, just "Get in B-flat." I did, and Joe walked out on the sidewalk, lifted his horn to his lips, and blew the most beautiful stuff I ever heard. People started pouring out of the other spots to see who was blowing all that horn. Before long our place was full and Joe came in, smiling, and said "Now that SOB won't bother me no more." From then on, our place was full every night.

King Oliver's Jazz Band

In 1918, Oliver moved to Chicago (he played in the band that cheered the White Sox at the fixed 1919 World Series), and after several years on the road returned there in 1922 to play at Lincoln Gardens, a swanky, black-owned nightclub on the Southside (Chicago's black district). It was there he formed his most famous group, King Oliver's Jazz Band (sometimes called his Creole Jazz Band).

With one exception, Oliver recruited musicians who had come north from New Orleans: trombonist Honore Dutrey, clarinetist Johnny Dodds, drummer Warren "Baby" Dodds (Johnny's brother), and bassist and banjoist Bill Johnson (who had founded the Original Creole Band and hired Oliver when he first arrived in Chicago). The ringer was pianist Lil Hardin, from Memphis by way of Fisk University in Nashville. The band was an imme-diate success, but Oliver, suffering from pyorrhea, a disease of the gums, wanted a second cornetist to punch up the front line and spell him when his

SPECIAL RELEASE
"DIPPER MOUTH BLUES"
"WHERE DID YOU STAY LAST NIGHT"?
on OKeh Record No 4918
played by KING OLIVER'S JAZZ BAND
ON SALE AT YOUR DEALERS

FRANK DRIGGS COLLECTION

King Oliver's Jazz Band promotes its latest OKeh Record in Chicago, 1923. Oliver stands tall at the center. Louis Armstrong, with one leg over the sign, sits beside pianist Lil Hardin, soon to be his wife.

embouchure (positioning of the lips and other facial muscles) failed. Weeks into the job, he cabled New Orleans for twenty-year-old Louis Armstrong to join him. Oliver had mentored Louis, who later remembered him as a man who "would stop and show the kids in New Orleans anything they want to know about their music."

Armstrong arrives

With Armstrong on board, respectfully playing second cornet, the great ensemble was now complete. King Oliver's Jazz Band attracted black and white musicians alike, who stopped by when their own engagements were finished. They had never heard anything like it. Nor had they seen a dance hall like Lincoln Gardens, one of the largest ballrooms (it could accommodate a thousand dancers) in the Midwest. A mirrored ball refracted the light over dozens of tables ringing the dance floor, where fans and musicians sat riveted by the band's collective power.

Unlike Morton's Red Hot Peppers band, which existed only in the recording studio, Oliver's Jazz Band played for audiences, including many people who, like him, had moved to Chicago from the South. Oliver had to be responsive to the moods and desires of dancers and listeners alike. Despite the occasional use of "Creole" in its name, his band embodied the ascendancy of the Uptown improvised approach over the Creole written tradition. They performed a rigorously collective music, its most salient characteristic a polyphonic attack—similar to the style established, albeit more superficially, by the Original Dixieland Jazz Band.

In April 1923, King Oliver's Jazz Band loaded their instruments into a couple of Model T Fords and traveled the short trip to Richmond, Indiana, to make their first recordings for Gennett Records. Gennett had been recording jazz since 1919, but only white bands and not very good ones.

A typical set-up for an early acoustic recording: Rosario Bourdon, a major figure in the development of the Victor Talking Machine Company, conducts its ensemble at the RCA-Victor Studios in Camden, N.J., 1928. The musicians play into a horn attached to a recording apparatus in the adjoining room. Note the cellist's custom-built high chair.

With Oliver and Morton, it recognized the commercial potential of music aimed at black audiences. Other labels formed subsidiaries to promote race records, but not Gennett, which saw no reason to segregate its product.

On these selections, Oliver used two-bar breaks, stop-time choruses, and other devices to vary the texture, but the most memorable moments occur when the entire ensemble builds its head of steam. Because of the limitations of acoustic recording, it may be hard at first to distinguish between the front-line instruments, but eventually you begin to isolate the separate voices—the piping clarinet, the trombone skirting the edges, the two cornets buoying each other. Yet the important thing is not the discrete components, but the marvel of a music in which each instrument contributes to the whole as judiciously as if a master composer had plotted every move.

A useful introduction to the Gennetts is Oliver's trademark number, "Dippermouth Blues," in part because so much of it is given to solos. During the Swing Era, bandleader Fletcher Henderson orchestrated Oliver's solo as "Sugar Foot Stomp." "Snake Rag" is a more typical performance in that the ensemble is the star performer.

GENNETT RECORDS

The Gennett studio was a squat, rectangular building built a few feet from railroad tracks, which meant frequent disruptions as trains bustled through Richmond. The recording space was a room lined with wood planks. From one wall, a megaphone-shaped horn, about eighteen inches in diameter, jutted out through a black curtain. The musicians had to figure out a way to position themselves around the horn so that the music—traveling through the horn into a stylus (an engraving phonograph needle in the adjoining room), which transmitted the sound onto a lateral disc— would be well balanced. In other words, the only audio mixing they could do was in deciding where to stand. This was the acoustic method of recording. No other method was available in 1923, which is the main reason Oliver's Creole Jazz Band records have always been more difficult to listen to than Morton's electrically recorded 1926 sessions.

🎧 "Snake Rag"

As its title suggests, "Snake Rag" is a rag, following the march/ragtime structure of several disparate strains. (Oliver recorded this piece twice: for Gennett in April 1923 and for OKeh Records two months later. The more accomplished OKeh performance is featured here.) This sly piece, disrupted by a series of pungent two-part breaks, takes its name from Oliver's slang for complicated chromatic lines: he called them "snakes," and the snake here is the descending chromatic scale played, unaccompanied, by the cornets at the end of the **A** and **B** strains. The last strain, or trio, is twice as long: thirty-two bars instead of sixteen. The fact that it is played three times in succession contributes to the buildup in excitement and ferment. Yet notice how steady the underlying pulse remains.

▶ **chromatic** moving by half step

During the trio, Oliver and Armstrong play quite different two-bar breaks (at the same time), accompanied by the trombone. These breaks preserve an aspect of the band's presentation at Lincoln Gardens that had become a signature routine, and a mystery to visiting musicians. They couldn't figure out how the two cornetists managed to harmonize perfectly on apparently ad-libbed passages. Armstrong later explained that seconds before each break, Oliver would mime the fingering of the upcoming part on his cornet, which cued him as to which break they would play. The two examples on this recording are exceptionally expressive, and we can imagine the audience cheering them on.

As influential as his music proved to be—Louis Armstrong, Bix Beiderbecke, and Duke Ellington all borrowed from him—Oliver enjoyed only a brief time in the sun. As his gums continued to worsen, he tried to modernize the New Orleans sound with larger ensembles, but the arrangements failed to find an audience. By 1935, he couldn't play at all; plagued by illness and bad business decisions, he settled in Savannah, Georgia, where he worked as a pool-room janitor and ran a fruit stand. He was broke but not broken when Armstrong ran in to him, in 1938:

> He was standing there in his shirtsleeves. No tears. Just glad to see us. Just another day. He had that spirit. I gave him about $150 I had in my pocket, and Luis Russell and Red Allen, Pops Foster, Albert Nicholas, Paul Barbarin—they all used to be his boys—they gave him what they had. And that night we played a dance, and we look over and there's Joe standing in the wings. He was sharp like the old Joe Oliver of 1915. . . . And pretty soon he died—most people said it was a heart attack. I think it was a broken heart.

🎧 snake rag

KING OLIVER'S JAZZ BAND

King Oliver, Louis Armstrong, trumpets or cornets; Honore Dutrey, trombone; Johnny Dodds, clarinet; Lil Hardin, piano; Bud Scott, banjo; Baby Dodds, drums

- Label: OKeh 4933
- Date: 1923
- Style: New Orleans jazz
- Form: march/ragtime

What to listen for:

- dramatic changes in texture from polyphony to monophony (breaks)
- breaks in A and B strains; descending chromatic line, trombone glissando
- modulation to a new key at the trio
- variety of breaks for the two cornets

INTRODUCTION (STRAIN A, abbreviated)

0:00   The band beings polyphonically, in **collective improvisation.** Dodds on clarinet drops from a high note to play swirling patterns while Dutrey sticks to a slow, unsyncopated line on the trombone. The two cornets (Armstrong and Oliver) improvise on the main melody.

0:05   **Break:** the cornets play a "snake"—a steady descending line in harmony.

STRAIN A

0:09   The first strain begins on the **tonic (I) chord.** Oliver plays the lead cornet, with Armstrong barely audible behind him.

0:22   The band repeats the snake.

STRAIN B

0:26   The second strain begins on a different harmony (**V**).

0:33   In a two-bar break, Dutrey plays three upward trombone **glissandos**, the last accented by a cymbal crash.

0:40   The band repeats the snake.

STRAIN B

0:46   Strain **B** is repeated, with slight variation.

STRAIN A

1:03   Strain **A** is repeated, with more variation.

STRAIN C (TRIO)

1:21   With no transition, the tune suddenly **modulates** to a new key. This strain (trio) lasts twice as long as the previous two. Dutrey plays a trombone line with a distinctive rhythmic profile.

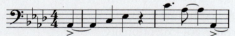

1:37   Dodds fills a break with a descending clarinet line.

STRAIN C

1:58   Strain **C** is repeated, with considerable variation.

2:13   During a break, Oliver and Armstrong play a bluesy and complex **riff.**

2:32   Break: Scott sings out in full voice, "Oh, sweet mama!"

STRAIN C

2:34   On this third appearance of strain **C**, the collective improvisation becomes freer and more intense.

2:50   For the final break, the cornets play a new passage, ending with a lengthy **blue note**.

CODA

3:10   The band tacks on an additional two measures before the cymbal finally cuts them off.

■ SIDNEY BECHET (1897–1959)

Sidney Bechet, who played clarinet and soprano saxophone, is considered by some to be the first great improviser in jazz history. During the early years of jazz, when the saxophone was on the margins of this music, Bechet turned the instrument into one of its leading voices. He was a moody, impassioned man whose tendency toward violence occasionally landed him in jail; but his emotions were imparted through the very timbre of his playing. He was one of the music's first global stars: he spent a good deal of the Jazz Age overseas, and was among the first Americans to perform in the Soviet Union in the 1920s.

Bechet was born in New Orleans to a musical Creole family. Primarily self-taught on the clarinet, he played in every important marching band in the city, occasionally doubling on cornet. In 1916, he left to travel with touring bands; one took him up to Chicago, where, three years later, he attracted the attention of Will Marion Cook (1869–1944). A classically trained violinist and conductor, Cook made his name as a songwriter and composer. In later years, he organized the first concerts in New York devoted exclusively to black composers, including jazz musicians. When he and Bechet met, Cook was about to take his Southern Syncopated Orchestra to London, and he recruited Bechet—a momentous decision.

Will Marion Cook and London

In London, Bechet purchased a straight (no bell curve) soprano saxophone, the instrument with which he ultimately made his mark. He also played clarinet in several prestigious halls with Cook's orchestra (they appeared before King George V), inspiring the first serious essay written about jazz. This lengthy review, by the conductor Ernest Ansermet, singled out "an extraordinary clarinet virtuoso who is, so it seems, the first of his race to have composed perfectly formed blues on the clarinet." He concluded:

> I wish to set down the name of this artist; as for myself, I shall never forget it—it is Sidney Bechet. When one has tried so often to rediscover in the past one of those figures to whom we owe the advent of our art,—those men of the 17th and 18th centuries, for example, who made expressive works of dance airs, clearing the way for Haydn and Mozart who mark, not the starting point, but the first milestone—what a moving thing it is to meet this very black, fat boy with white teeth and that narrow forehead, who is very glad one likes what he does, but who can say nothing of his art, save that he follows his "own way," and when one thinks that his "own way" is perhaps the highway the whole world will travel tomorrow.

By the time Cook left England, Europe had taken American Negro music to its heart, an affection that would continue throughout the twentieth century. Bechet liked the way he was treated there and, with a contingent of musicians from the Southern Syncopated, played in both Paris and London, clearing the way for an invasion of black entertainers. But his involvement in a violent argument in London ended with his deportation in 1921.

The volatile Bechet did not like playing second fiddle to anyone; in jazz, that meant playing clarinet in support of the cornet. On the soprano saxophone, with its commanding, piercing sound, he could dominate any ensemble. What's more, he had begun to think of himself not as a member of a fixed group but as a virtuoso soloist—a new category of which he was perhaps the prime example.

Clarence Williams's Blue Five

In New York, Bechet reunited with an old buddy from New Orleans—the pianist, song publisher, and record producer Clarence Williams (1893–1965), who asked him to participate in a series of recordings billed as Clarence Williams's Blue Five. These records document, for the first time, Bechet's extraordinary stylistic maturity. On their dynamic 1924 recording "Cake Walking Babies (from Home)," Bechet proved himself to be the only musician of that era who could stand head to head with Louis Armstrong—occasionally, as in this instance, standing a bit taller.

🎧 "Cake Walking Babies (from Home)"

Recorded in New York, where jazz and Tin Pan Alley pop songs first became inextricably entwined, "Cake Walking Babies (from Home)" combines New Orleans jazz polyphony with the popular music of the day. The title refers to the **cakewalk**, a comic dance supposedly dating from the time of slavery and one of the first dances to cross over from black to white society. As a song publisher who put his name on songs he may or may not have worked on, Clarence Williams saw records as a way to boost sheet music sales, and usually included vocal choruses on his recordings to promote words and music. The vocal chorus of "Cake Walking Babies" underscores the high-stepping cheerfulness of this forty-bar song (singer Alberta Hunter went on to enjoy a long career as an entertainer, mixing blues and standards).

The rest of the performance offers a different kind of excitement, as cornet and soprano saxophone transform the usual New Orleans front line into a battle of wits. The first chorus begins with the usual collective improvisation. Bechet seems to anticipate Armstrong's every rest, filling those spaces with melodic figures. This chorus is followed by a statement of the sixteen-bar verse—a seldom-heard contrasting melody used as a way of introducing the chorus. The vocal (second) chorus is accompanied only by banjo and piano, and is lively if dated. It's hard to imagine a singer today performing in this style, whereas the bravura interpretations by Armstrong and Bechet, especially in choruses 3 and 4 (the last two), would be impressive in any day.

LISTENING GUIDE 7

🎧 cake walking babies (from home)

THE RED ONION JAZZ BABIES
Louis Armstrong, cornet; Charlie Irvis, trombone; Sidney Bechet, soprano saxophone; Lil Armstrong, piano; Buddy Christian, banjo; Clarence Todd and Alberta Hunter, vocals
- Label: Gennett 5627
- Date: 1924
- Style: New Orleans jazz
- Form: verse/chorus; chorus is 40-bar popular song (**A B A′ C A″**)

What to listen for:
- New Orleans–style collective improvisation
- a "duel" between two great jazz soloists, Armstrong and Bechet, especially in choruses 3 and 4
- triplets in the Bechet breaks

CHORUS 1

0:00	**A**	The three horns (Armstrong on cornet, Bechet on soprano saxophone, Irvis on trombone) play in **collective improvisation**. While Armstrong plays the melodic lead, Bechet competes for attention with his aggressive, fluid improvisation.
0:08	**B**	
0:17	**A'**	
0:25	**C**	Armstrong closely paraphrases the original melody (which we will hear in its entirety at 1:00).
0:34	**A"**	

VERSE

0:42		Armstrong and Bechet loosely paraphrase the original melody; the trombone adds a lively response.
0:47		While Armstrong sticks close to the tune, Bechet improvises with more freedom.

CHORUS 2 (SONG)

0:59	**A**	Hunter sings the song, harmonized by Todd (his extra lyrics are in parentheses); the two are accompanied by banjo and piano. *"Here they come (oh, here we come!), those strutting syncopators!* *Going some (oh, going some!), look at those demonstrators!"*
1:08	**B**	*"Talk of [the] town, Green and Brown, picking 'em up and laying 'em down!"*
1:16	**A'**	*"Prancing fools (oh, prancing fools!), that's what we like to call 'em,* *They're in a class all alone!"*
1:24	**C**	*"The only way for them to lose is to cheat 'em,* *You may tie 'em, but you'll never beat 'em!"*
1:33	**A"**	*"Strut that stuff, they don't do nothing different,* *Cake walking babies from home!"*
1:39		Underneath the vocalists' last notes, the horns begin playing.

CHORUS 3

1:41	**A**	The instruments resume their collective improvisation. Armstrong plays more freely and with greater intensity. Bechet's timbre is hard and penetrating.
1:49	**B**	
1:56		Bechet plays a two-bar **break** in **triplets**, a rhythm that srongly divides the beat into threes.

1:58	**A'**	
2:06	**C**	**Stop-time**: Armstrong improvises a complex syncopated line in his upper register.
2:14		At the end of the passage, Armstrong plays his last note with a growl.
2:15	**A"**	
2:22		The horns sustain a long note, a signal that another chorus is coming.

CHORUS 4

2:24	**A**	The two soloists differ dramatically in style: Armstrong plays sparsely, with intense syncopation, while Bechet smoothes out into lengthy strings of eighth notes.
2:32	**B**	
2:38		Irvis plays a gruff trombone solo during the break.
2:40	**A'**	
2:49	**C**	Stop-time: Bechet begins with a rough series of slurs and improvises a rhythm that shifts unpredictably between triplets and jazzy syncopation.
2:58	**A"**	To signal the end of the piece, both Armstrong and Bechet play repeated riffs.

In 1925, Bechet returned to Europe with the musical *Revue Negre*, starring singer and dancer Josephine Baker. He played in Berlin, Amsterdam, and Moscow, where he met up with his most important partner, Louisiana-born trumpet player Tommy Ladnier. Together, in New York in the early 1930s, the two formed the New Orleans Feetwarmers and made records that confirmed Bechet's uniquely florid yet exacting style. He continued to make dozens of memorable records ("Summertime") demonstrating a broad repertory, advanced sense of harmony, and adventurous spirit. His 1941 version of "The Sheik of Araby" employed overdubbing to allow him to play all the parts: clarinet, soprano saxophone, tenor saxophone, bass, and drums—a neat trick, especially at a time when audio tape didn't exist.

Bechet's dominance of the soprano saxophone was so complete that he remained its chief exponent until his death in 1959. By then, he had become one of the most beloved musicians in Europe, especially France, where he settled in 1951. His records graced every café jukebox (one of his compositions, "Petite Fleur," became a national phenomenon), and a memorial bust was unveiled in Nice.

New Orleans Style Today

New Orleans jazz has never disappeared, though generations of modern jazz enthusiasts have done their best to ignore it. The tradition is kept alive, quite naturally, at New Orleans's Preservation Hall, a popular tourist attraction located in a small eighteenth-century building in the French Quarter, a few blocks from the Mississippi River. Bands and societies devoted to New Orleans or Dixieland jazz can be found all over the world, from New Jersey to Brazil, Denmark, and Japan. No matter where it is played, the repertory, instrumentation, polyphonic front line, and marchlike rhythm section remain essentially the same. So does the attitude, which ranges from happiness to exultation, and is usually nostalgic though rarely sentimental. Dixieland musicians often wear straw hats and sleeve garters as if to announce that they are part of a musical tradition sufficient unto itself, a thing apart from the evolution of jazz, complete in its own right.

ADDITIONAL LISTENING	
Bunk Johnson	"C. C. Rider" (1944)
Freddie Keppard	"Stock Yards Strut" (1926)
Original Dixieland Jazz Band	"Tiger Rag," "Livery Stable Blues" (both 1917)
Jelly Roll Morton	"Doctor Jazz," "King Porter Stomp" (both 1926), "Buddy Bolden's Blues" (1938), "I Thought I Heard Buddy Bolden Say" (1939)
King Oliver	"Dippermouth Blues," "High Society" (both 1923)
Sidney Bechet	"Maple Leaf Rag" (1932), "Summertime" (1939), "Make Me a Pallet on the Floor" (1940), "Weary Blues" (1945)

ONLINE MULTIMEDIA RESOURCES & REVIEW MATERIALS

Author Insight Videos

Gary Giddins discusses, among other topics, New Orleans as the birthplace of jazz, the new form of music based on improvisation that resulted from the clash of European and African cultures, and the earliest jazz recordings.

Interactive Listening Guides

Original Dixieland Jazz Band, "Dixie Jass Band One-Step"
Jelly Roll Morton, "Dead Man Blues"
King Oliver, "Snake Rag"
Red Onion Jazz Babies (Sidney Bechet), "Cake Walking Babies (from Home)"

Jazz Concepts (audio and/or video demonstrations of terms covered here)

block chords	countermelody	staccato
blue note	glissando	stop-time
break	modulation	tailgate trombone
cadence	polyphonic texture	(or smear)
chromatic scale	rhythmic contrast	tonic
collective improvisation	riff	triplets

- For quick reference, review the **Chapter Overview** and **Chapter Outline.**
- Take the online **Chapter** and **Listening Quizzes.**
- Use the online **Glossary** and **Flashcards** to review important terms.

PAUL WHITEMAN
changes

FLETCHER HENDERSON
copenhagen

JAMES P. JOHNSON
you've got to be modernistic

DUKE ELLINGTON
black and tan fantasy

NEW YORK IN THE 1920s

ARABIAN NIGHTS

New York City, particularly the borough of Manhattan, has served as the focus for jazz's evolution from the late 1920s to the present. While New Orleans, Chicago, Kansas City, and Los Angeles all enjoyed intense associations with specific eras in jazz, nearly all the great jazz musicians had to make their way to New York to cement a genuine, enduring success. Three interlocking spheres of influence contributed to New York's centrality, especially in the early years.

Commercial: The country's entertainment infrastructure—concert halls, theaters, museums, galleries, radio and television, newspapers and magazines, book publishers, and record labels, not to mention managers, agents, bookers, and publicists—took root in New York in the closing years of the nineteenth century and never left.

Sociological: The years of the Great Migration from South to North coincided with a massive East-to-West emigration from Europe to the United States. Jazz is unusual as an art form in that a majority of its performers have belonged to ethnic minorities. Most of the major figures in jazz history who were not African American derived from immigrant families that originated in Italy, Ireland, Germany, and Russia. (An underexplored area is the involvement of Native Americans, especially in jazz's formative years in the

Duke Ellington conducts his orchestra from the piano at the Olympia Theater in Paris, 1958.

85

▶ **pentatonic scale** five-note scale, as C D E G A

late nineteenth and early twentieth centuries.) Middle European Jews, whose music involved a blues-like use of the pentatonic scale and a feel for improvisation, were especially drawn to jazz. An alliance between black musicians and Jewish songwriters helped to define jazz for three decades.

Musical: The city's most significant contribution to jazz was the development of large bands and orchestrations: the influx of jazz musicians in the 1920s from New Orleans, Chicago, and elsewhere overlapped with the growing enthusiasm for ballroom dancing, generating a demand for elegant orchestras. These were jazz's first important big bands. Small wonder that when a young and untested Duke Ellington arrived in New York for the first time in 1923 and surveyed the bright lights that extended from one end of Manhattan to the other, he exclaimed, "Why, it is just like the Arabian Nights!" The possibilities were limitless and the soundtrack was jazz.

TRANSFORMATIONS

In the 1920s, recordings, radio, and movies were refined in ways that changed forever the customs and habits of American lives. The development of electrical recording (in 1925) as a replacement for the primitive technology of acoustical recording meant that records, formerly inadequate for reproducing certain instruments and vocal ranges, now boasted a stunning fidelity that especially benefited jazz, with its drums and cymbals and intricately entwined wind instruments. The recording industry, in a slump since 1920, came back to life with dramatically reduced prices in phonographs and discs.

Radio, which had been little more than a hobby for most people, blighted by static and requiring headphones, sprang to life as a broadcast medium in 1921 (KDKA in Pittsburgh), achieving a lifelike clarity with the invention of the carbon microphone and, subsequently, the much-improved condenser microphone. The first radio networks (NBC, CBS) united the nation with simultaneous broadcasts. Advances in radio and recording gave entertainment seekers a kind of permission to stay at home—a permission that quickly became a national habit, as people grew emotionally attached to broadcasts or obsessed with collecting records. The cinema responded to these technological challenges with an innovation of its own. In 1927, Warner Bros. introduced the first feature film with synchronized dialogue—an adaptation of a Broadway play significantly, if deceptively, called *The Jazz Singer*.

As technology encouraged people to stay put, nightlife received an unintended boost. In 1920, a Republican Congress passed—over President Wilson's veto—the Eighteenth Amendment to the Constitution, prohibiting the manufacture, transporting, and sale of alcohol. Under Prohibition, it was legal to drink and even purchase alcoholic beverages, but since no one could legally sell (or manufacture) it, the amendment's principal effect was to create a vast web of organized crime.

In the 1920s, Fletcher Henderson led the orchestra at the Roseland Ballroom, one of the most gloried dance halls in America, at Broadway and 51st in New York.

FRANK DRIGGS COLLECTION

By the next year, the country was pockmarked with tens of thousands of illicit saloons, memorably tagged as speakeasies. Their gangster owners competed for customers by hiring the most talented musicians, singers, comedians, and dancers around. In mob-controlled cities like Chicago, Kansas City, and New York, many of these nightspots stayed open through breakfast, and jazz was perfectly suited to an industry that required music to flow as liberally as beer. All the composers in town could not have written enough music to fill the order, but improvisers could spin an infinite number of variations on blues and pop songs. Musicians follow the lure of work, and—until it was repealed in 1932—Prohibition provided a lot of work.

DANCE BANDS AND SYMPHONIC JAZZ

A cursory look at early jazz suggests a long dry spell between the 1917 triumph by the Original Dixieland Jazz Band and the classic recordings of King Oliver and others in 1923. Yet the interim was a period of great ferment, especially in New York, where jazz came face to face with a simmering pot of musical styles: Tin Pan Alley popular songs, ragtime, New Orleans jazz, marching bands (especially popular after 1918, in the aftermath of World War I), and vaudeville, which featured anything that could keep an audience attentive during a fifteen-minute act—comical saxophones, blues divas, self-styled jazz or ragtime dancers. Jazz also found its way into elaborate ballrooms and concert halls. Oddly enough, two leading figures in this process, Art Hickman and Paul Whiteman, came east from San Francisco.

Art Hickman

Hickman (1886–1930), a pianist, drummer, and songwriter, encountered jazz in the honky-tonks of the Barbary Coast in San Francisco, where he believed jazz originated: "Negroes playing it. Eye shades, sleeves up, cigars in mouth. Gin and liquor and smoke and filth. But music!" In 1913, Hickman organized a dance band, which soon included two saxophonists. Though he did not harmonize them in the manner of a reed section (where two or more reed instruments play in harmony), he did assign them prominent roles, creating a smoother sound than the brass-heavy ensembles associated with New Orleans jazz and marching bands. The dual saxophones gave an appealing character to a band that otherwise consisted of trumpet, trombone, violin, and a rigid rhythm section with two or three banjos (a remnant from minstrelsy). Hickman's success served to establish saxophones as an abiding component in the jazz ensemble.

■ PAUL WHITEMAN (1890–1967)

In 1919, the Victor Talking Machine Company brought Hickman's band to New York with great fanfare. But Hickman disliked the city and hurried back to San Francisco, leaving room for a successor—a far more formidable figure. It may be difficult now to appreciate how incredibly popular bandleader Paul Whiteman was in the 1920s. Tall and corpulent, with a round and much caricatured face, he was the first American pop-music superstar of the twentieth century, a phenomenon at home and abroad—as celebrated as Charlie Chaplin and Mickey Mouse.

Born in Denver, Whiteman studied viola and began to attract attention when, after moving west to play in the San Francisco Symphony Orchestra, he organized a Barbary Coast ragtime outfit in his off hours. He formed his first ballroom band in 1919, achieving success in Los Angeles, Atlantic City,

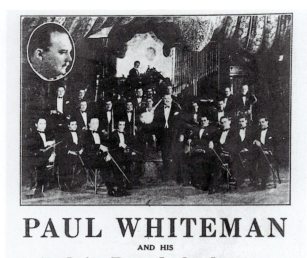

PAUL WHITEMAN
AND HIS
Palais Royal Orchestra
WILL OFFER
An Experiment in Modern Music

Zez Confrey
and
George Gershwin

New Typically American Compositions by Victor Herbert, George Gershwin and Zez Confrey will be played for the first time.

AEOLIAN CONCERT HALL
Tuesday, Feb. 12th (LINCOLN'S BIRTHDAY) at 3 P. M.
Tickets now on Sale, 55c. to $2.20

Victor Records   Chickering Pianos   Buescher Instruments

Bandleader Paul Whiteman sought to legitimize American music in a 1924 concert at Aeolian Hall that introduced George Gershwin's jazz-influenced concert piece *Rhapsody in Blue*, performed with the composer at the piano.

FRANK DRIGGS COLLECTION

and finally New York, where he became an immediate favorite at the ritzy Palais Royal.

Up to this point, Whiteman had been thoroughly outshone by Hickman. The tables turned in 1920, when Victor released Whiteman's first recordings, "Whispering" and "Japanese Sandman," which sold well over a million copies. Whiteman built a much larger band, producing a more lavish and flexible sound. He conducted with a graceful if oblivious pomp, demonstrating an appealing personality and making news by fiercely arguing the merits of American music.

Whiteman, more than anyone else, embodied the struggle over what kind of music jazz would ultimately be. Would it be a scrappy, no-holds-barred improvisational music built on the raw emotions and techniques of the New Orleans style, or a quasi-symphonic adaptation, with only vestigial elements to suggest the source of inspiration? Was jazz merely a resource, a primitive music from which art music could be developed, or was it an art in itself?

In 1924, Whiteman set out to prove his contention that jazz could be the foundation for American classical music with a concert—he called it "An Experiment in Modern Music"—at New York's Aeolian Hall, a crucial moment in twentieth-century musical history. He opened with a crude performance of the Original Dixieland Jazz Band's "Livery Stable Blues," played for laughs as an example of jazz in its "true naked form," and closed with a new work he had commissioned from the ingenious Broadway songwriter George Gershwin (1898–1937)—*Rhapsody in Blue*, performed with the composer at the piano. The response to Whiteman's singular Americana was so fervent that he was promoted as the "King of Jazz" and originator of **symphonic jazz**, a phrase he coined. Symphonic jazz represented a fusion of musical styles—in this instance, of Negro folk art and the high-culture paradigm of Europe.

Bing Crosby and Bill Challis

Meanwhile, hardly anyone—certainly no one in the media—noticed that in the very year of Whiteman's Aeolian Hall triumph, a relatively unknown Louis Armstrong had arrived in New York to take a seat in Fletcher Henderson's orchestra. Whiteman, however, did notice, and in 1926 he decided it was time for the King of Jazz to hire a few jazz musicians. Initially, he wanted to recruit black musicians, but his management convinced him that he couldn't get away with a racially integrated band: he would lose bookings, and the black musicians would be barred from white hotels and restaurants. Whiteman countered that no one could stop him from hiring black arrangers; he traded orchestrations with Henderson and added the prolific African American composer William Grant Still to his staff.

Whiteman's first important jazz hire came from vaudeville: singer Bing Crosby (1903–1977). Never before had a popular bandleader hired a full-time

Bing Crosby, advertised on a Broadway billboard, brought jazz rhythms and inflections to popular ballads, revolutionizing radio and breaking the all-time house record at the Paramount Theater in New York, 1931.

singer; in the past, instrumentalists had assumed the vocal chores. During his first week with the Whiteman band, in Chicago in 1926, Crosby heard Armstrong perform, and was astonished by his ability to combine a powerful art with bawdy comedy, ranging from risqué jokes to parodies of a Southern preacher. Crosby would become the most popular singer in the first half of the twentieth century, a decisive force on records and radio and in the movies—and a major link between jazz and the mainstream. He helped to make Armstrong's musical approach accessible to the white public by adapting rhythmic and improvisational elements of Armstrong's singing style to his own. In turn, Crosby inspired Armstrong to add romantic ballads to his repertory—they often recorded the same songs within weeks of each other. They would work together, on and off, for the next four decades.

Whiteman next signed up the most admired young white jazz instrumentalists in the country, including cornetist Bix Beiderbecke, saxophonist Frank Trumbauer, guitarist Eddie Lang, and violinist Joe Venuti (see Chapter 6). An especially influential new recruit was the stubbornly original arranger Bill Challis, who had an uncanny ability to combine every aspect of Whiteman's orchestra—jazz, pop, and classical elements alike. Thanks to Challis and the other new additions, Whiteman was able to release innovative jazz records in the years 1927–29, until financial considerations exacerbated by the Great Depression obliged him to return to a more reliably profitable pop format.

🎧 "Changes"

In 1927, the Whiteman band served as a microcosm of the three-way battle involving jazz, symphonic jazz, and pop. Bill Challis favored Crosby and the jazz players, but when the band's old (symphonic) guard complained of neglect, he found ways to bring everyone into the mix. His arrangement of Walter Donaldson's "Changes" opens with strings, incorporates pop and jazz singing, and climaxes with a roaring Bix Beiderbecke solo, the sound of his cornet tightened by a straight mute inserted into the bell of his horn.

The title itself is significant, suggesting changes in the band, changes in taste as ballroom music assimilated the vitality of jazz, and changes in improvisation techniques as harmonic progressions (noted in the lyrics) took the place of elaborations of the melody. The title also signifies broader cultural changes that were transforming the United States. In the several months before the recording was made, Charles Lindbergh had flown the Atlantic Ocean, Babe Ruth had hit sixty home runs, and talking pictures had premiered. The national mood was optimistic, as reflected in songs like "Good News," "Hallelujah," "'S Wonderful," "Smile," "There'll Be Some Changes Made," and many others.

Challis emphasizes changes between new and old with contrasting rhythms and vocal groups. Rhythmically, a **Charleston beat** (two emphatic beats followed by a rest), usually enunciated by the trumpets, alternates with the more even rhythms stated by the violins. The performance never sticks to any one sound, preferring to cut back and forth between strings, brasses, saxophones, and voices, with solo spots interspersed.

Although six vocalists are listed among the personnel, they never sing in tandem. Three of them, representing Whiteman's old guard, were full-time instrumentalists (trombonist Jack Fulton and violinists Charles Gaylord and Austin Young) who were occasionally deputized to sing pop refrains. Shortly after Crosby and his pianist and harmonizing partner Al Rinker joined Whiteman, they recruited singer-pianist Harry Barris to form a novel group called the Rhythm Boys. Of the singers, Crosby was by far the most gifted. Accordingly, Challis divided the vocal chorus into sections, employing both vocal trios and Crosby as soloist. The chorus begins with the old guard ("Beautiful changes"), then—with Barris signaling the change by imitating a cymbal ("pah")—switches to the Rhythm Boys, who blend high-pitched harmonies and a unified **scat** break (wordless vocalizing). This is followed by the old guard setting up a solo by Crosby, who mimics a trombone slide on the words "weatherman" and "Dixieland." Crosby's solo leads to the record's flash point: Beiderbecke's improvisation.

🎧 **changes**

LISTENING GUIDE 8

PAUL WHITEMAN

Paul Whiteman, director; Henry Busse, Charlie Margulis, trumpets; Bix Beiderbecke, cornet; Frank Trumbauer, C-melody saxophone; Wilbur Hall, Tommy Dorsey, trombones; Chester Hazlett, Hal McLean, clarinets/alto saxophones; Jimmy Dorsey, Nye Mayhew, Charles Strickfaden, clarinets, alto and baritone saxophones; Kurt Dieterle, Mischa Russell, Mario Perry, Matt Malneck, violins; Harry Perrella, piano; Mike Pingitore, banjo; Mike Trafficante, brass bass; Steve Brown, string bass; Harold McDonald, drums; Bing Crosby, Al Rinker, Harry Barris, Jack Fulton, Charles Gaylord, Austin Young, vocals

- Label: Victor 21103
- Date: 1927
- Style: early New York big band
- Form: 32-bar popular song (**A B C A'**), with interlude and verses

What to listen for:
- full instrumentation of a large commercial dance band, including strings
- **Charleston rhythm**
- vocalists: "sweet" trio vs. "jazz" trio (with scat-singing)
- Beiderbecke's "hot" cornet solo

INTRODUCTION

0:00   The brass section rises through unstable **chromatic** harmonies until it finally settles on a **consonant** chord.

SONG (D-flat major)

0:10 **A**   The saxophones play the melody, decorated above by short, syncopated trumpet chords and supported by the strings. Underneath, the banjo and piano play four beats to the bar, while the bas plays two beats.

0:19 **B**   The melody shifts to the violins.

0:28 **C**   The trumpets play a jaunty **Charleston rhythm,** answered first by the saxophones, then by the strings.

0:38 **A'**   The saxophones return to the opening melody, which moves toward a **full cadence.**

INTERLUDE

0:45   The rhythmic accompaniment temporarily stops. Over changing orchestral textures (including a violin solo), the piece **modulates** to a new key.

VERSE 1 (16-bar A A B A)

0:52 **A**   The trumpets and strings return to the Charleston rhythm, underscored by the trombones' offbeat accents. The phrase begins in **minor** but ends in **major.**

0:56 **A**

1:01 **B**   For the bridge, the saxophones quietly sustain chords.

1:05 **A**

SONG (E-flat major)

1:10 **A**   *"Beautiful changes in different keys, beautiful changes and harmonies."*
The "sweet" vocal trio harmonizes the melody in **block-chord** harmony, accompanied by the rhythm section (string bass, banjo, drums).

1:19 **B**   *"He starts in C, then changes to D. He's foolin' around most any old key."*
The harmonies shift away from the tonic, matching the intent of the words.

1:28   **Break:** Barris introduces the "jazz" vocal trio (Rhythm Boys) by imitating a quiet cymbal stroke ("pah").

1:29 **C**   *"Watch that—hear that minor strain! Ba-dum, ba-dum,"*
The Rhythm Boys adapt to the new style by singing a more detached and "cooler" series of chords.

1:35   *"Bada(ba)da-lada(bada-lada)-la-dum!"*
During a break, the vocalists imitate **scat-singing,** changing the dynamics to match the rhythm.

1:38 **A'**   *"There's so many babies that he can squeeze, and he's always changing those keys!"*
The first trio returns to set up Crosby's solo.

1:46   The voices retreat to background chords.

VERSE 2

1:47   *"First, he changes into B, changes into C, changes into D, changes into E,*
As easy as the weatherman! Now, he's getting kinda cold, getting kinda hot,
Listen, I forgot, since he was a tot, he's been the talk of Dixieland!"
Crosby sings the verse with ease, ending each phrase with a rich, resonant timbre.

SONG

2:05 **A**   While the voices continue their background harmony, Beiderbecke takes a cornet solo with a sharp, focused sound. Underneath him, the bass switches to a four-beat **walking bass.**

2:14 **B**

2:24 **C**   The full band returns with the Charleston rhythm.

2:33 **A'**   In full **block-chord** texture, the band plays a written-out version of the melody with syncopations.

CODA

2:40   The tempo moves to **free rhythm.** Over sustained chords, a saxophone plays a short solo.

2:49   As the chords dissipate, all that's left is the sound of a bell.

■ FLETCHER HENDERSON (1897–1952)

Like every other bandleader in New York, black and white, Fletcher Henderson initially looked to Whiteman for inspiration, seeking to emulate his opulent sound and diverse repertory as well as his public success. Yet he would ultimately take big-band music down a very different, far more influential route as he developed into an outstanding arranger.

An unassuming, soft-spoken man who initially had no particular allegiance to jazz, Henderson, like Whiteman, grew up in a middle-class home with parents who disdained jazz. Born in Cuthbert, Georgia, he studied classical music with his mother. Soon after traveling to New York in 1920 for postgraduate study in chemistry, he learned how to play piano well enough to record with Ethel Waters and Bessie Smith. He went on to organize dance bands for nightclubs and ballrooms.

In 1924, Henderson began a lengthy engagement at the luxurious Roseland Ballroom at 51st Street and Broadway, New York's preeminent dance palace. As a black musician working in midtown venues with exclusively white clienteles, Henderson offered polished and conventional dance music: fox-trots, tangos, and waltzes. At the same time, he had access to the best black musicians, including an attention-getting young saxophonist named Coleman Hawkins, and, like Whiteman, felt a need to keep up with the ever-changing dance scene.

By 1926, Henderson's band was widely regarded as the best jazz orchestra anywhere, a standing it began to lose the following year, with the rise of Duke Ellington and other bandleaders who elaborated on the approach pioneered

Fletcher Henderson, seated at the piano, organized the first great black orchestra in New York and introduced many major jazz musicians. The 1924 edition of his band included tenor saxophonist Coleman Hawkins (third from left) and trumpet player Louis Armstrong (sixth from left).

by Henderson and his chief arranger, Don Redman. Although Henderson never achieved a popular renown equal to that of Ellington, Count Basie, Benny Goodman, and other big-band stars, his influence among musicians increased during the 1930s, as he produced a stream of compositions and arrangements that helped to define big-band music in the Swing Era. Over the decade 1924–34, the orchestra grew to an average of fifteen musicians: typically three trumpets, two to three trombones, up to five reeds, and four rhythm (piano, bass or tuba, banjo or guitar, drums). This basic big-band instrumentation, notwithstanding numerous variations, remains unchanged even now.

When, in that banner year of 1924, Henderson decided to add a third trumpet player, he sought the hottest soloist he could find, Louis Armstrong. At first, Henderson's well-paid, spiffily dressed musicians didn't know what to make of a country boy like Louis. But Armstrong brought with him essential ingredients that the band lacked: the bracing authority of swing, the power of blues, and the improvisational logic of a born storyteller.

The standard had been raised, and no one understood that better than Don Redman (1900–1964), who later acknowledged that he changed his orchestration style to accommodate Armstrong's daring. In recordings like "Copenhagen" and "Sugar Foot Stomp" (an ingenious adaptation of King Oliver's "Dippermouth Blues," with Armstrong playing Oliver's solo), Redman's writing began to take on a commanding directness and sharper rhythmic gait. Nor was his fanciful use of breaks and popular melodies lost on Armstrong, who employed them in the Hot Five sessions he initiated after his year with Henderson (see Chapter 6). Redman's writing not only launched big-band jazz, but also served as a link between King Oliver's Jazz Band (1923) and Armstrong's seminal Hot Five (1925).

Don Redman

🎧 "Copenhagen"

Several historic threads come together in Fletcher Henderson's 1924 recording of "Copenhagen," a multistrain composition by a Midwestern bandleader (Charlie Davis), named not for the capital of Denmark but after a favorite brand of snuff. The Wolverines, a scrappy little band featuring Bix Beiderbecke, had recorded it in May, and its publisher issued a stock arrangement of the song. To this Don Redman added his own variations, employing aspects of New Orleans jazz (orchestrated polyphony), block-chord harmonies (standard for large dance orchestras), brief breaks, hot solos, old-fashioned two-beat dance rhythms, and sectional call and response. Conceived in the ragtime tradition, the piece combines twelve-bar blues with sixteen-bar ragtime strains.

Louis Armstrong's jolting blues chorus is an undoubted highlight in a performance also notable for the spirit of the ensemble and of individual contributions such as Charlie Green's trombone smears and Buster Bailey's whirling clarinet. Bailey joined Henderson around the same time as Armstrong, extending the New Orleans tradition of clarinet obbligato into big-band jazz a decade before, as we will see, the clarinet came to symbolize the Swing Era. Note the contrasting trios featuring three clarinets in the **B** strain and three trumpets in the **D** strain, and compare the notated polyphony in the **A** strain with the improvised polyphony (played against block-chord trumpets) in the **E** strain. The harmonically surprising finish is an arranger's trick, which in 1924 inclined listeners to shake their heads in wonder and move the needle back to the beginning.

🎧 copenhagen

FLETCHER HENDERSON

Fletcher Henderson, piano; Elmer Chambers, Howard Scott, Louis Armstrong, trumpets; Charlie Green, trombone; Buster Bailey, clarinet; Don Redman, clarinet and alto saxophone; Coleman Hawkins, clarinet and tenor saxophone; Charlie Dixon, banjo; Ralph Escudero, tuba; Kaiser Marshall, drums

- Label: Vocalion 14926
- Date: 1924
- Style: early big band
- Form: march/ragtime

What to listen for:
- 16-bar ragtime strains alternating with 12-bar blues
- sectional arranging: clarinet trios (**B** strain) and trumpet trios (**D**)
- notated polyphony (**A**) vs. improvised polyphony (**E**)
- unexpected ending

STRAIN A (16 bars)

0:00 The saxophones and trumpets move up and down through the **chromatic scale** in **block-chord** harmony.

0:04 Led by a trombone, the entire band responds with a cleverly written-out imitation of **collective improvisation.**

0:09 The opening passage is now given to clarinets playing in their lowest register. The response, once again, is scored collective improvisation.

STRAIN B (12-bar blues)

0:17 A high-pitched clarinet trio plays a bluesy melody. Underneath, the rhythm section (piano, banjo, drums, tuba) plays a lively two-beat accompaniment, with the drummer and banjo player adding a strong **backbeat.**

STRAIN B

0:29 A repetition of the previous twelve bars.

STRAIN B

0:42 Armstrong plays a well-rehearsed solo (the same solo can be heard on another take). His playing is hard-driving, with a swing rhythm and a bluesy sensibility.

STRAIN C (16 bars)

0:54 The full band plays a series of syncopated block chords, punctuated by cymbal crashes. Again, the response is scored polyphony.

1:02 The previous eight-bar section is repeated.

STRAIN D (16 bars)

1:11 A trio of trumpets plays a melody in a simple three-note rhythm.

1:17 During a two-bar **break,** the trumpets are interrupted by the clarinet trio performing a disorienting, rising **glissando.**

STRAIN A

1:28 The opening of strain **A** is played by the clarinet trio in its highest register.

1:36 The same passage is played by the saxophones.

STRAIN E (12-bar blues)

1:44 The trombone plays an introductory melody.

1:48 While the trumpets play in block-chord harmony, the clarinet and trombone improvise in New Orleans style.

STRAIN E

1:57 The repetition of strain **E** has a looser, more improvised feeling: the trombone plays with more glissando, while the clarinet sustains its high pitch for four measures.

STRAIN F (16 bars)

2:09   As the trumpet trio plays block-chord harmonies, the clarinet improvises busily underneath.

2:16   The break is divided between the banjo and the tenor saxophone.

CODA

2:26   The band returns to strain **A**.

2:34   Without pause, the band suddenly shifts to the beginning of strain **C**.

2:38   A high-pitched clarinet trio reintroduces strain **A**.

2:45   The band moves to block chords that descend precipitously outside the piece's tonality. With this surprising gesture, the piece abruptly ends.

Throughout his career, Henderson continued to provide a showcase for the finest black musicians in New York. A short list of major jazz figures who worked with him includes, in addition to the remarkable trinity of Armstrong, Hawkins, and Redman, trumpet players Rex Stewart, Henry "Red" Allen, Roy Eldridge; trombonists J. C. Higginbotham, Dicky Wells; clarinetists and saxophonists Benny Carter (also a major composer-arranger), Lester Young, Ben Webster, Chu Berry, Omer Simeon; bassists John Kirby, Israel Crosby; drummers Kaiser Marshall, Sidney Catlett; and arranger Horace Henderson (his brother). No other big-band leader can lay claim to such a roll. We will encounter Henderson again as an accidental architect of the Benny Goodman Orchestra.

THE ALLEY AND THE STAGE

In New York's midtown section, Broadway, the thoroughfare running north to south, offered plays, musicals, ballet, opera, revues, movies, vaudeville, and every other kind of show business. Midtown was also home to Tin Pan Alley, the first songwriting factory of its kind. The name has come to represent the popular music written for the stage and cinema from the 1890s through the 1950s, until rock and roll began to change the business. Originally, it was the nickname for buildings on 28th Street between Broadway and Sixth Avenue, where music publishers had their offices and passersby could hear the cacophony of a dozen or more competing pianos—songwriters demonstrating their wares. The Alley introduced the idea of the professional songwriter, who wrote specific songs to order: ballads, novelties, patriotic anthems, rhythm songs, and so forth, as commissioned by performers or to meet a public demand.

By the middle 1920s, the most sophisticated generation of songwriters ever assembled was in place. Rejecting the sentimental formulas that had dominated pop songs during the previous thirty years, they wrote music and words that were original, intelligent, and frequently beautiful, with advanced harmonic underpinnings that gave them a particularly modern and enduring appeal. The songs this generation wrote remain the core of the classic American songbook, and were vital to the development of jazz. The songwriters, influenced by jazz rhythms and blues scales, came of age with Armstrong-inspired improvisers who required new and more intricate material than the blues and ragtime strains that had served their predecessors. The two groups were ideally matched: a composer like George Gershwin actively

George Gershwin, seen here c. 1928, wrote pop songs for Broadway, concert works for symphony orchestra, and the opera *Porgy and Bess*, incarnating the influence of jazz on all forms of American music.

Bert Williams, the most successful black entertainer in history until his death in 1922, was forced to perform in blackface, but he broke down several racial barriers: he appeared on Broadway and became the first major Victor recording artist, in 1901.

The public never saw Williams looking as he does in the publicity shot; he deeply resented having to perform exclusively in blackface.

BOTH: FRANK DRIGGS COLLECTION

tried to capture the jazz spirit, and an improviser like Coleman Hawkins found inspiration in Gershwin's melodies and harmonies.

Among the most masterly and prolific of the new Tin Pan Alley songwriters, the resourceful and adaptable street-smart Irving Berlin (from New York) and the younger, Yale-educated, well traveled, and smart-set ColePorter (from Indiana) were unusual in writing both words and music. For the most part, pop songs were contrived by teams, including composers George Gershwin, Jerome Kern, Harold Arlen, Richard Rodgers, Vincent Youmans, and Hoagy Carmichael, and lyricists Ira Gershwin, Lorenz Hart, Oscar Hammerstein II, Dorothy Fields, and E. Y. Harburg.

Although whites, and especially Jews, dominated the Alley, black songwriters turned out some of the best-known classics in the American songbook. Among them were Spencer Williams ("I Ain't Got Nobody," "Basin Street Blues"), Maceo Pinkard ("Sweet Georgia Brown," "Sugar"), Henry Creamer and Turner Layton ("Way Down Yonder in New Orleans," "After You've Gone"), Shelton Brooks ("Some of These Days"), Chris Smith ("Ballin' the Jack," "Cake Walking Babies [from Home]"), James P. Johnson ("If I Could Be with You One Hour Tonight," "Charleston"), and Noble Sissle and Eubie Blake ("Memories of You," "I'm Just Wild About Harry"). And any account of pantheon songwriters in the 1920s would have to include composers Duke Ellington and Fats Waller and lyricist Andy Razaf.

THE HARLEM RENAISSANCE

In 1904, the Afro-American Realty Company organized a campaign—not unlike the *Chicago Defender*'s crusade to bring Southern blacks to Chicago—to lure African Americans to Harlem, a vast, mostly white settlement stretching from 110th Street to 155th Street. The movement accelerated over the next fifteen years, producing a massive migration involving especially large numbers of Southern and West Indian Negroes that was matched by a simultaneous exodus of whites. By 1920, central Harlem had become what poet and memoirist James Weldon Johnson described as "not merely a Negro colony or community, [but] a city within a city, the greatest Negro city in the world."

In 1925, philosopher and critic Alain Locke edited a book of essays called *The New Negro*, one of the most influential manifestos ever published in the United States. Locke's anthology argued that African American artists represented a political and cultural force in literature, art, dance, and theater—it was the foundation for what would become known as the Harlem Renaissance. Most leaders of this renaissance disliked jazz, which seemed to them coarse, commercial music wrapped up in stereotypes they preferred to leave behind.

Unhappily, the very forces that turned Harlem into a cultural carnival also turned it into a slum and a profit center for organized crime. The crammed residents, unable to spread out to racially restricted neighborhoods, fell victim to landlords who increased the rents while partitioning apartments into ever-smaller units. As an added insult, mobsters financed ornate nightclubs—including the Cotton Club, which featured top black performers and sexy floor shows—that refused entrance to black patrons. In these Harlem getaways, the New Negro was banned from witnessing the fruits of his own renaissance.

STRIDE

Fittingly, the city that established orchestral jazz also encouraged the ripening of the most orchestral brand of jazz piano, initially known as "Harlem style" but eventually recognized internationally as **stride piano**. Here was an aggressive, competitive, joyous way of playing piano that directly reflected the musical vigor of New York. Where ragtime was graceful and polished, stride was impetuous, flashy, and loud. Where ragtime produced a contained repertory, stride was open to anything. The evolution from one to the other occurred gradually.

Like ragtime, stride began as a composed music made up of multiple strains. Then, just as ragtimers had competed in contests of virtuosity, the East Coast stride players began to add their own flourishes and rhythms, eventually developing an offshoot that was livelier, faster, and more propulsive. Perhaps the most remarkable parallel between ragtime and stride is that each style gave birth to the foremost African American composers of its time. Ragtime's pedigree from Scott Joplin to Jelly Roll Morton was more than equaled by stride pianists of the 1920s, who, through their disciples, shaped jazz piano and jazz composition for decades to come—a lineage that includes James P. Johnson, Fats Waller, Duke Ellington, Art Tatum, and Thelonious Monk.

The name "stride" describes the motion of the pianist's left hand, striding back and forth from low to high in the bass clef. On the first and third beats, the pianist plays either a single low note or a low chord, usually involving a tenth—an octave plus a third (for example, a low C together with an E, ten white keys higher). Tenths require large hands, so resourceful pianists without the necessary reach perfected "broken tenths": the notes played in rapid succession instead of simultaneously. On the second and fourth beats, the pianist plays a three- or four-note chord in the upper part of

James P. Johnson, the most influential of the pioneering stride pianists and a Broadway composer whose songs include the 1920s anthem "Charleston," at a 1930s jam session.

PHOTO BY CHARLES PETERSON, COURTESY OF DON PETERSON

the bass clef. The masters of stride created intricate harmonic and rhythmic patterns that kept the left hand from becoming a mechanical rhythm device. They also developed tricks for the right hand that allowed it to embellish melodies with luscious glissandos, producing a richer texture than traditional ragtime.

Rent parties

Stride pianists found they could earn a livelihood by hiring out for Harlem "rent parties." These get-togethers, a social phenomenon of the 1920s, arose from people's need to meet ever-higher rents. Friends and neighbors would congregate for food and music, making contributions to a communal kitty. As the average living room could not accommodate a band, the pianist had to be loud and steady enough to suit dancers and be heard over the volume of conversation. Inevitably, stride pianists achieved a high social standing. They competed with each other on the piano and in personal style—with tailored suits, rakish derbies, expensive cigars, and colorful personalities.

■ JAMES P. JOHNSON (1894–1955)

James P. Johnson, the "Father of Stride Piano," perfected the East Coast style as a progressive leap from its ragtime roots. Almost every major jazz pianist who came along in the 1920s and 1930s—not just Waller, Tatum, and Ellington, but also Earl Hines, Count Basie, and Teddy Wilson—learned from him. Although he never achieved the fame of his protégés, stride revivalists regard him as the most accomplished innovator of the stride style.

Johnson was born in New Brunswick, New Jersey, where his mother sang in the Methodist Church and taught him songs at the piano. He later credited the **ring-shout dances** (the earliest known African American performing tradition, combining religious songs and West African dances) and brass bands he heard as a child as important influences. After the family moved to New York in 1908, he studied classical piano and encountered like-minded ragtimers—especially Eubie Blake and Luckey Roberts, who was regarded by his colleagues as the best pianist in New York. Beginning in 1918, Johnson punched out a series of influential piano rolls, including an early version of "Carolina Shout," which became an anthem and a test piece—a kind of "Maple Leaf Rag" for New York's piano elite. As ragtime had become popular through widely distributed sheet music, stride found a smaller but dedicated audience through piano rolls.

In 1921, Johnson finally initiated a series of sensational disc recordings, including a definitive "Carolina Shout," "Keep Off the Grass," and "Worried and Lonesome Blues," and two years later wrote perhaps the single most widely recognized melody of the 1920s, "Charleston." While continuing to write songs and play piano, Johnson also produced shows and composed classical pieces (including *De-Organizer*, in collaboration with the poet Langston Hughes, in 1940). By the time a stroke incapacitated him in 1951, Thelonious Monk and Erroll Garner were extending Johnson's keyboard style into modern jazz.

THE PLAYER PIANO

The player piano, a hugely popular entertainment apparatus in middle- and upper-class American homes, served two functions: as a regular piano and as a machine capable of playing music inscribed on piano rolls. These were rolls of paper perforated with tiny squares representing the notes; as the squares rolled over a "tracker bar," they triggered a suction device that, in turn, controlled a lever of the keyboard. Piano rolls could be purchased like records, and were often made by celebrated musicians. As there was no limit to the number of squares that could be cut into a roll, some pianists (notably Gershwin) would secretly cut the same roll twice, adding accompanying notes the second time—the first instance of overdubbing. (Stymied customers trying to imitate such a roll complained that Gershwin had four hands; turns out, he did.) The player piano operated as a teaching tool: you could play the roll at any speed, and slow it down enough to study the depressed keys. Ellington and Waller, among others, learned to emulate Johnson's vibrant attack by slowing down a roll of "Carolina Shout" and placing their fingers on the depressed keys.

🎧 "You've Got to Be Modernistic"

The transition from ragtime to stride, from formal composition to jazz variations, is illuminated in Johnson's dazzling 1930 recording of "You've Got to Be Modernistic." Consider two aspects of its modernism. First, the introduction and first two strains are ornamented by advanced harmonies, drawing on the **whole-tone scale**, that keep the listener in a state of perpetual surprise. Second, Johnson switches midway from the formalism of ragtime to the theme and variations of jazz: the structure consists of three sixteen-bar strains (with a four-bar interlude), but with the introduction of strain **C**, the piece romps through seven choruses of variations with no reprise of strains **A** or **B**.

Significantly, the **C** strain, unlike the virtuosic **A** and **B** strains, has the most traditional melody. It begins with a two-bar riff (which Johnson later set to the words "You've got to be modernistic!"), yet suggests a simple Scott Joplin–style ragtime harmony in measures 7 and 8. Johnson, for all his flashing speed and hairpin changes, always exercises a composer's control. Each strain is so distinct from the others (and in the **C** series, one chorus accents blue notes, another bass notes, another an insistent triple-chord pattern) that the listener is never lulled by repetition or familiarity. The entire performance is a well-ordered whirlwind.

▶ **whole-tone scale** six-note scale, each note a whole step from the next

LISTENING GUIDE 10

🎧 you've got to be modernistic

JAMES P. JOHNSON, PIANO
- Label: Brunswick 4762
- Date: 1930
- Style: Harlem stride
- Form: march/ragtime (**A B A C**)

What to listen for:
- stride piano accompaniment: a steady alternation of bass note and chord
- whole-tone harmonies in introduction, strain **A**, and interlude
- trio (**C**) played seven times, with jazzy riffs
- pianistic blue notes

INTRODUCTION

0:00   After an opening left-hand chord, Johnson's right hand plays a series of descending **whole-tone** chords (triads derived from the whole-tone scale).

STRAIN A

0:04   Johnson plays the main melody in **stride** style, with the left hand alternating between bass notes and chords.

0:07   The end of the first phrase is marked by a syncopation in the left hand. The melody leads to a **chromatic** passage.

0:12   The opening melody is repeated.

0:16   A rising series of whole-tone chords resolves in a **full cadence**.

STRAIN A

0:20   Following march/ragtime form, Johnson repeats the strain.

0:29   He shifts the pattern in his left hand, playing the bass note one beat early and temporarily disrupting the accompaniment with a polyrhythm.

STRAIN B

0:35   The next strain begins with left-hand bass notes alternating with right-hand chords. The pattern descends chromatically.

STRAIN B

0:50   Johnson repeats the strain an octave higher, adding a bluesy figure.

STRAIN A

1:05   The right hand is even higher, near the top of the piano keyboard.

INTERLUDE

1:20   To **modulate** to a new key, Johnson brings back the whole-tone harmonies and texture of the introduction.

STRAIN C (TRIO)

1:24   The trio is built around repetitions of a short **riff**.

STRAIN C

1:39   As before, the repetition is played an octave higher. The end of the riff pattern is reduced to an emphatic **blue note**, achieved by playing two adjacent notes at the same time.

STRAIN C

1:54   The melody is now in the bass line, with the left hand playing each note twice.

2:01   The rhythmic pattern in the left hand intensifies to three notes in a row.

STRAIN C

2:09   The right hand plays widespread chords in a **polyrhythm** against the basic meter.

2:17   Here (and again at 2:23), Johnson disrupts the accompaniment by shifting the position of the bass note.

STRAIN C

2:24   Against the same harmonic background, Johnson improvises a new riff.

STRAIN C

2:39   Johnson begins his riff pattern with a held-out chord.

2:45   For two measures, the right and left hands play together rhythmically.

2:47   The riff pattern shifts to the downbeat, changing the groove.

STRAIN C

2:54   Johnson plays his right-hand chords in a quick three-note repetition (similar to what we heard in the left hand at 2:03).

3:07   With a few short chords, he brings the piece to an end.

◼ DUKE ELLINGTON BEGINS (1899–1974)

As the most important composer that jazz—and arguably the United States—has produced, Duke Ellington played a vital role in every decade of its development, from the 1920s until his death in 1974. His music is probably more widely performed than that of any other jazz composer. Ellington achieved distinction in many roles: composer, arranger, songwriter, bandleader, pianist, producer. He wrote music of every kind, including pop songs and blues; ballets and opera; theater, film, and television scores; suites, concertos, and symphonies; music for personal homages and public dedications; and, most significantly, thousands of instrumental miniatures.

All of his music contains decisive elements of jazz, even where there is no improvisation. He made thousands of recordings, more than any other composer or bandleader, some inadvertently (he rarely discouraged fans with tape recorders) and others privately and at his own expense, to be released posthumously.

Ellington's early breakthrough, in the late 1920s and early 1930s, defined four aspects of New York's musical culture. The first three were strictly musical. (1) He clarified the nature of big-band jazz, demonstrating potential beyond Whiteman's imagination or Henderson's achievement. (2) He solidified the influence of stride piano as a jazz factor, employing it not only as a pianist himself but also as a foundation in orchestrations. (3) He proved that the most individual and adventurous of jazz writing could also be applied to popular songs.

The fourth area concerned his persona and proved no less vital to the standing of jazz and especially its relationship to the Harlem Renaissance. Ellington, a handsome, well-mannered, witty, and serious man, violated assumptions about jazz as a low and unlettered music. A largely self-taught artist, Ellington earned his regal nickname with an innate dignity that musicians, black and white, were quick to embrace. In his refusal to accept racial limitations, he became an authentic hero to black communities across the country for nearly half a century.

Edward Kennedy Ellington was born in Washington, D.C., to a middle-class family who encouraged his talent for music and art. His first composition, "Soda Fountain Rag," written at fourteen, mimicked James P. Johnson's

Duke Ellington—composer, arranger, orchestra leader, pianist—is regarded by many as the most accomplished figure in American music. Gifted musicians devoted their lives to his band, including baritone saxophonist Harry Carney (to left of guitarist in front), alto saxophonist Johnny Hodges (far right in middle row), clarinetist Barney Bigard (to his left, here playing saxophone), and trumpet player Cootie Williams (above Hodges). Ellington is pictured at the piano and on the bass drum played by Sonny Greer, 1938.

FRANK DRIGGS COLLECTION

"Carolina Shout." As a high school senior, Ellington organized a five-piece band and found enough work to keep him going until he readied himself to try New York, in 1923.

At New York's Kentucky Club, he enlarged the band, focusing on growling, vocalized brasses and finding a creative ally in Bubber Miley, an innovative trumpet player from South Carolina inspired by King Oliver's muting effects. By late 1926, Ellington began to reveal a style of his own that was influenced by Miley, whose almost macabre, blues-ridden mewling—quite unlike Armstrong's open-horn majesty—was ideally suited to Ellington's theatrical bent. In crafting pieces with and for Miley, Ellington ignored Don Redman's method of contrasting reeds and brasses, and combined his instruments to create odd voicings, thereby introducing a new sound into American music. As presented in his first major works, "East St. Louis Toodle-O," "Black and Tan Fantasy," and two vividly different approaches to the blues, "The Blues I Love to Sing" and "Creole Love Call" (in which he used wordless singing as he would an instrument), the overall effect was mysterious, audacious, and carnal.

The Cotton Club

Ellington's career took a giant leap on December 4, 1927, when he opened at Harlem's Cotton Club. Although this segregated citadel was thought to represent the height of New York sophistication, it actually exploited tired minstrel clichés. The bandstand design replicated a Southern mansion with large white columns and a painted backdrop of weeping willows and slave quarters. A mixture of Southern Negro and African motifs (featuring capering light-skinned women) encouraged frank sexuality. For Ellington, though, the whole experience was enlightening. He learned much about show business by working with other composers (including the great songwriter Harold Arlen), choreographers, directors, set designers, and dancers. As the headliner for the next three years, Ellington became a major celebrity in New York and—through the Cotton Club's radio transmissions—the country. His reputation quickly spread to Europe.

At Harlem's world-famous, mob-run Cotton Club, the audience was white and the entertainment black, or at least a lighter shade of beige. Women dancers auditioning for the chorus line, pictured here, were subjected to the brown paper bag test: if her complexion was darker than an ordinary shopping bag, she could not dance there.

© BETTMANN/CORBIS

Ellington was finding legitimate musical subjects in racial pride, quite a turn from Tin Pan Alley's coon and Mammy songs, and sexual desire, an equally sweeping break with the Alley's depictions of romantic innocence. He was not a Broadway composer who borrowed from jazz, like Gershwin, but a true jazz composer—with enormous vitality and humor, and a gift for sensuous melodies, richly textured harmonies, and rollicking rhythms that reflected his love of stride piano. As the band grew in size, it gathered a cast of **Ellingtonians**, musicians who stayed with him for years, decades, and in some instances entire careers—stylists such as alto saxophonist Johnny Hodges, baritone saxophonist Harry Carney, trumpeter (and successor to Miley) Cootie Williams, trombonist Joe "Tricky Sam" Nanton, clarinetist Barney Bigard, and bassist Wellman Braud. Upon leaving the Cotton Club in 1931, the fifteen-piece band now known as Duke Ellington and His Famous Orchestra traveled the world, and in the process defined the future of jazz with a 1932 song title: "It Don't Mean a Thing (if It Ain't Got That Swing)."

🎧 "Black and Tan Fantasy"

A great deal of Ellington's music is **programmatic**, attempting to describe specific places, people, or events. The tongue-in-cheek attitude of Ellington's arresting "Black and Tan Fantasy" can be appreciated without a back story, but it's perhaps more compelling if the satirical point is taken into account. Unlike the Cotton Club, which refused to admit blacks, other Harlem clubs catered exclusively to African Americans. And some, which were regarded as a pinnacle of liberality, invited members of both races. These were known as the "black and tan" clubs. Ellington's piece works as a response to the idea that these small, overlooked speakeasies absolved a racially divided society. "Black and Tan Fantasy" contrasts a characteristic twelve-bar blues by Miley with a flouncy sixteen-bar melody by Ellington. Miley's theme, the black part of the equation, was based on a spiritual he had learned from his mother. Ellington's, the tan part, draws on the ragtime traditions that lingered in the 1920s. As the two strains merge in a climactic evocation of Frédéric Chopin's "Funeral March," the piece buries the illusions of an era. Yet while black and tans disappeared, the "Fantasy" remained a steady, much revised number in Ellington's book—an American classic.

LISTENING GUIDE 11

🎧 black and tan fantasy

DUKE ELLINGTON AND HIS ORCHESTRA
Duke Ellington, piano; Bubber Miley, Louis Metcalf, trumpets; Joe "Tricky Sam" Nanton, trombone; Otto Hardwick, Rudy Jackson, Harry Carney, saxophones; Fred Guy, banjo; Wellman Braud, bass; Sonny Greer, drums

- Label: Victor 21137
- Date: 1927
- Style: early New York big band
- Form: 12-bar blues (with a contrasting 16-bar interlude)

What to listen for:

- the growling timbre of Ellington's horns
- clash between blues harmony and contrasting pop-song material
- the expressive use of mutes by Miley (trumpet) and Nanton (trombone) in their solos
- Ellington's stride piano

CHORUS 1 (12-bar blues)

0:00 Over a steady beat in the rhythm section, Miley (trumpet) and Nanton (trombone) play a simple, bluesy melody in the **minor mode**. The unusual sound they elicit from their tightly muted horns is an excellent example of **timbre variation**.

0:25 A cymbal crash signals the appearance of new material.

INTERLUDE (16 bars)

0:26 The harmonic progression suddenly changes with an unexpected chord that eventually turns to the **major mode**. The melody is played by Hardwick (alto saxophone) in a "sweet" style, with thick vibrato, a sultry tone, and exaggerated **glissandos**.

0:38 During a two-measure **break**, the band plays a **turnaround**—a complicated bit of chromatic harmony designed to connect one section with the next.

0:42 Repeat of the opening melody.

0:54 The horns play a series of chords, then stop. The drummer plays several strokes on the cymbal, muting the vibration with his free hand.

CHORUS 2

0:58 Over a major-mode blues progression, Miley takes a solo. For the first four bars, he restricts himself to a high, tightly muted note.

1:06 Miley plays expressive bluesy phrases, constantly changing the position of his **plunger mute** over the **pixie mute** to produce new sounds that seem eerily vocal (wa-wa).

CHORUS 3

1:23 Miley begins with a pair of phrases reaching upward to an expressive **blue note**.

1:25 The cymbal responds, as if in sympathy.

1:26 In the next phrase, Miley thickens the timbre by growling into his horn.

CHORUS 4

1:47 The band drops out while Ellington plays a cleverly arranged **stride piano** solo.

1:51 The left hand plays in **broken octaves:** the lower note of each octave anticipates the beat.

1:58 Ellington plays a striking **harmonic substitution**.

CHORUS 5

2:11 Nanton begins his solo on tightly muted trombone.

2:15 He loosens the plunger mute, increasing the volume and heightening the intensity of the unusual timbre.

2:27 Nanton precedes his last phrase with a bizarre gesture, sounding somewhere between insane laughter and a donkey's whinny.

CHORUS 6

2:36 Miley returns for an explosive bluesy statement, featuring quick repeated notes. Each phrase is answered by a sharp accent from the rhythm section.

2:50 As the harmony changes, the band enters, reinforcing Miley's moan.

CODA

2:57 With Miley in the lead, the band ends by quoting Chopin's "Funeral March"— returning the piece to the minor mode.

To appreciate the amazing progress jazz made in the 1920s, you could do worse than listen to "Black and Tan Fantasy" back-to-back with Jelly Roll Morton's "Dead Man Blues," which also involves a satiric fantasy that invokes death and was recorded the previous year. The differences between them exceed questions of musical technique—Morton's polyphony and Ellington's alternating themes. Far more significant is the difference in perspective. Morton's piece looked back, celebrating the traditions from which he sprang. Ellington's looked at the present in a provocative way that promised a vital future.

In the music of Ellington and others who achieved success in the jazz world of Prohibition New York, we hear little deference to jazz's Southern roots. Their music, channeling the city's cosmopolitanism, is smart, urban, fast moving, glittery, independent, and motivated. In liberating jazz from its roots, the Ellington generation is ready to take on everything the entertainment business and the world can throw at it. This sense of a second youth, of a new start, became a motive in the development of jazz, as each subsequent generation strove to remake the music in its own image.

ADDITIONAL LISTENING

George Gershwin / Paul Whiteman	*Rhapsody in Blue* (1927)
Bert Williams	"Nobody" (1906)
Art Hickman	"Rose Room" (1919)
Paul Whiteman	"Whispering" (1920), "From Monday On" (1928)
Fletcher Henderson	"Dirty Blues" (1923), "Shanghai Shuffle" (1924), "Sugar Foot Stomp" (1925), "King Porter Stomp" (1928)
James P. Johnson	"Carolina Shout," "Keep Off the Grass" (both 1921), "Worried and Lonesome Blues" (1923), "Charleston" (1924)
Duke Ellington	"East St. Louis Toodle-oo" (1926), "Creole Love Call" (1927), "The Mooche" (1928)

ONLINE MULTIMEDIA RESOURCES AND REVIEW MATERIALS

Author Insight Videos

Gary Giddins explains why New York provided an ideal environment for jazz in the 1920s, how Louis Armstrong raised the bar after he joined Fletcher Henderson's band in 1924, and how Duke Ellington's "Black and Tan Fantasy" gave a "new start" to jazz.

Interactive Listening Guides

Paul Whiteman, "Changes"
Fletcher Henderson, "Copenhagen"
James P. Johnson, "You've Got to Be Modernistic"
Duke Ellington, "Black and Tan Fantasy"

Jazz Concepts (audio and/or video demonstrations of terms covered here)

backbeat	collective improvisation	pentatonic scale
block chords	consonant	plunger mute
blue note	glissando	polyrhythm
break	major mode	riff
broken octaves	minor mode	walking bass
cadence	modulation	whole-tone scale
chromatic harmony and scale	octave	whole-tone chord

- For quick reference, review the **Chapter Overview** and **Chapter Outline**.
- Take the online **Chapter** and **Listening Quizzes**.
- Use the online **Glossary** and **Flashcards** to review important terms.

6

LOUIS ARMSTRONG AND THE FIRST GREAT SOLOISTS

■ LOUIS ARMSTRONG (1901–1971)

Louis Armstrong is the single most important figure in the development of jazz. His ascension in the 1920s transformed the social music of New Orleans into an art that, in the words of composer Gunther Schuller, "had the potential capacity to compete with the highest order of previously known musical expression," an art in which musicians of every geographical and racial background could find their own voice. He remains the only major figure in Western music to influence the music of his era equally as an instrumentalist and a singer. Within a decade, he codified the artistic standards of jazz, and his influence did not stop there. It penetrated every arena of Western music: symphonic trumpet players emulated his bright vibrato, and popular and country performers adapted his phrasing, spontaneity, and natural sound.

Armstrong was also one of the most beloved musicians of the twentieth century—the man who, more than anyone else, conveyed the feeling and pleasure of jazz to audiences throughout the world. The matter of his popularity is important, because it had cultural and political ramifications beyond music. Though raised in unimaginable poverty and racial segregation, he was able to present his music in a generous way that welcomed and exhilarated new listeners. At a time when jazz was denounced from political

Louis Armstrong, described by Bing Crosby as "the beginning and the end of music in America," radiated an energy that seemed to transcend his artistry. Paris, 1960.

and religious pulpits as primitive, unskilled, immoral, and even degenerate, Armstrong used his outsize personality to soothe fears and neutralize dissent. America had never experienced anything like him. He seemed to combine nineteenth-century minstrel humor and a nearly obsequious desire to please with an art so thunderously personal and powerful that audiences of every stripe were drawn to him. By the 1950s, he was widely accepted as a national "ambassador of good will" and of America's most admirable qualities. For Duke Ellington, he was "the epitome of the kind of American who goes beyond the rules, a truly good and original man."

Armstrong's influence may be measured, in large part, by his innovations in five areas.

BLUES: He emphatically established the blues scale and blues feeling as jazz's harmonic foundation at a time when significant jazz figures, especially those on the Eastern Seaboard, thought the blues might be a mere fashion, like ragtime.

IMPROVISATION: Armstrong established jazz as music that prizes individual expression. His records showed that an improvised music could have the weight and durability of written music. But to compete on Armstrong's level, a musician had to do more than master an instrument; he had to make the instrument an extension of his self.

SINGING: As a boy, Armstrong mastered **scat-singing**—using nonsense syllables instead of words, with the same improvisational brio and expressive candor as an instrumentalist. With his 1926 recording "Heebie Jeebies," he introduced a true jazz vocal style, dependent on mastery of pitch and time as well as fast reflexes and imagination. He soon proved as agile with written lyrics as with scat phrases. Almost instantly, Armstrong's influence was heard in the work of singers as diverse as Bing Crosby and Billie Holiday.

REPERTORY: In the 1930s, New Orleans "purists" argued that jazz musicians should confine themselves to original New Orleans jazz themes, and avoid popular tunes as lacking in authenticity. Armstrong created masterworks based on Tin Pan Alley songs, showing that pop music could broaden jazz's potential both musically and commercially.

RHYTHM: Perhaps Armstrong's greatest contribution was to teach the world to swing. He introduced a new rhythmic energy that would eventually become second nature to people everywhere. His approach to rhythm exemplified the contagiously joyous, bawdy, accessible, human nature of his music.

Early Years

Not the least miraculous aspect of Armstrong's achievement is that it was forged from such bleak beginnings. He was born, on August 4, 1901, to an unwed teenager (no older than sixteen) and a laborer who abandoned them, in an area of New Orleans so devastated by violence, crime, and prostitution that residents called it "the Battlefield." At age seven, Louis was already working, delivering coal to prostitutes by night and helping with a rag-and-bone cart by day, blowing a tinhorn to announce the cart's arrival. He organized a quartet to sing for pennies on street corners (the Singing Fools), and received his first cornet from the immigrant Jewish family that owned the rag-and-bone business; the first tune he learned to play, he recalled, was "Home, Sweet Home."

Armstrong, known in childhood by several nicknames, including Little Louis, Dippermouth, and Satchelmouth, sits at the very center of the brass band at the New Orleans Colored Waif's Home, where he was incarcerated in 1913.

FRANK DRIGGS COLLECTION

In the early hours of New Year's Day, 1913, Louis was apprehended for shooting blanks in the air and was sent to the New Orleans Colored Waif's Home for Boys for eighteen months. There, he received rudimentary musical instruction from the home's bandmaster, and progressed from tambourine to bugle to cornet and ultimately leader of the institution's band. After his discharge, Louis apprenticed with his idol, Joe Oliver, running errands in return for lessons.

His career began in earnest in 1918 with two jobs. When Oliver left for Chicago, he suggested that Louis replace him in the band he had co-led with trombonist Kid Ory. A short time later, Louis was recruited to play on Mississippi riverboat excursions. In order to prove himself eighteen and thus legally responsible, he applied for a draft card, backdating his birth to 1900— July 4, 1900, a patriotic date that became famously associated with him, and the only birthday he ever acknowledged.

Armstrong spent three years on riverboats operated by the Streckfus Steamboat Line, working under the leadership of Fate Marable, This was a decisive engagement on several counts: he greatly improved his ability to read a music score; he learned to adapt the earthy music of New Orleans to written arrangements; he absorbed a variety of songs beyond the New Orleans repertory; he saw another part of the world and experienced a different kind of audience (exclusively white, except for the one night a week reserved for black customers); and he grew accustomed to the rigors of traveling from one engagement to another, establishing a lifelong pattern.

Riverboat years

With Oliver and Henderson

One restriction, though, galled him: Marable refused to let him sing. Partly for that reason, Armstrong quit in September 1921, and returned to Ory's band. During this period, his reputation spread throughout the region. The

Louis first experienced the world beyond Louisiana when he worked in Fate Marable's orchestra on the excursion boat *S.S. Capitol*, 1920: Henry Kimball, bass: Boyd Atkins, violin; Marable, piano; Johnny St. Cyr, banjo; David Jones and Norman Mason, saxophones; Armstrong, cornet; George Brashear, trombone; Baby Dodds, drums. Note the sign warning patrons not to stand "in front of orchestra."

FRANK DRIGGS COLLECTION

celebrated New York singer and actress Ethel Waters toured New Orleans with her then little-known pianist, Fletcher Henderson, and attempted to lure him to New York. But Armstrong resolved not to leave his hometown unless Joe Oliver himself sent for him. That summons arrived in August 1922, in the form of a wire inviting him to become a member of Oliver's Jazz Band at Lincoln Gardens, on Chicago's Southside.

Chicago, 1922

In Oliver's band, Armstrong usually played second trumpet (or cornet), though he occasionally played lead, as on "Dippermouth Blues." If the trumpet breaks he harmonized with Oliver astonished musicians, the brilliance of his timbre was overwhelming. In Oliver's pianist, Armstrong found his second of four wives. The well-educated Memphis-born Lil Hardin encouraged Louis to leave Oliver and establish himself as a leader. He resisted at first, but in 1924, when Fletcher Henderson, now leading a much-admired orchestra in New York, offered him a seat in the band, he accepted.

New York, 1924

Armstrong spent little more than a year in New York, which turned out to be a crucial period for him and for jazz. In a time of strict segregation, Henderson's dance band hired the best black musicians of the day—much as his counterpart and friend Paul Whiteman did with white musicians. Henderson's men—street-smart, well dressed, self-assured—initially viewed Armstrong as a rube, a newcomer from the country who had made a modest name for himself in Chicago playing in an idiom that was already deemed old-fashioned. The mockery ceased when they heard his trumpet. Armstrong's authority and originality, his profound feeling for blues, and his irresistible, heart-pounding rhythmic drive converted them all.

During his fourteen months with Henderson, Armstrong recorded more than three dozen numbers with the band (including "Sugar Foot Stomp," the orchestration of Oliver's "Dippermouth Blues"). With Armstrong on board, Henderson's men played with a more prominent beat, while embracing the blues and longer solos. Each of the band's fine musicians sought in his own way to reproduce something of Armstrong's clarion attack, exciting rhythms, and diverse emotions. Every bandleader wanted to hire a soloist in his mold, from Paul Whiteman to Duke Ellington. Armstrong was also the accompanist of choice for blues divas like Bessie Smith ("Everything I did with her, I like," he recalled), Ma Rainey, Sippie Wallace, and Bertha Hill, among others.

Armstrong's association with Henderson ended, in part, because of dis-agreement (again) over one of his talents. Like Louis's boss on the Mississippi riverboat, Henderson would not let him sing—beyond a brief scat break on one record ("Everybody Loves My Baby"). Louis, confident of a vocal ability that everyone else denounced because of his gravelly timbre, angrily returned to Chicago in late 1925.

The Hot Five and Seven

Back in Chicago, Armstrong earned his living playing in a pit orchestra that accompanied silent movies. But before the year 1925 was out, OKeh Records invited him to make his first records as a leader. Armstrong agreed, with the proviso that he would choose the music and musicians; whether he also notified the company of his intention to sing and speak on the recordings we don't know. Other than his wife Lil, he surrounded himself with New Orleanians, three musicians he had already worked with: clarinetist Johnny Dodds and banjoist Johnny St. Cyr in Oliver's band, and trombonist Kid Ory in New Orleans. Louis called his band the Hot Five, and unlike Oliver's group, it existed only to record.

It would be difficult to overstate the impact of the discs made by the Hot Five and Hot Seven (the same instrumentation plus tuba and drums) between 1925 and 1928—sixty-five titles in all, not including similar sessions in which Armstrong appeared as a **sideman** (any musician employed by a bandleader), in support of vocalists or other bandleaders. Here at last we witness jazz's

The most influential small band in jazz history, Louis Armstrong and His Hot Five, existed only to make records: Armstrong, trumpet; Johnny St. Cyr, banjo; Johnny Dodds, clarinet and saxophone; Kid Ory, trombone; Lil Hardin Armstrong, piano. Chicago, 1926.

rapid evolution from a group concept dominated by polyphony to a showcase for soloists and individual expression. The modest embellishments heard in Oliver and Morton performances give way here to daring improvisations; two- and four-bar breaks are extended to solos of a full chorus or more; and the multiple strains of ragtime are winnowed down to the single-theme choruses of popular song and blues. Each of these elements can be found in other recordings of the day, but the force of Armstrong's creativity and instrumental control—the vitality and spirit—impart the sensation of a great art coming into flower.

🎧 "Hotter Than That"

This 1927 Hot Five recording is an illuminating example of the way Armstrong revolutionized the New Orleans tradition. The thirty-two-bar chorus is based on the chords of the main strain of "Tiger Rag," a New Orleans jazz tune, popularized in 1918 by the Original Dixieland Jazz Band, though no one knows who wrote it. An unusual aspect of this performance is the addition of a guest, the pioneer guitarist Lonnie Johnson. Johnson, a native of New Orleans, apprenticed on riverboats and went on to enjoy two dramatically different careers: as one of the first jazz guitar soloists in the 1920s and as a popular blues singer-guitarist of the 1940s and after. His very presence reminds us that long after New Orleans generated jazz, the city also provided sustenance for rhythm and blues and rock and roll.

The group's banjoist, Johnny St. Cyr, doesn't play on "Hotter Than That," so that the dialogue between Armstrong and Johnson is emphasized. Armstrong plays the first chorus, which is entirely improvised: there is no written theme to set up the improvisations, only a harmonic underpinning borrowed from "Tiger Rag." The third chorus features one of his most memorable scat-singing vocals. Listen to what follows the mid-chorus break, where Armstrong sings counterrhythms of enormous complexity. Try counting four beats to a measure here, and you may find yourself losing your moorings, because his phrases are in opposition to the ground beat—a technique that later became standard in jazz.

LISTENING GUIDE 12

🎧 hotter than that

LOUIS ARMSTRONG AND HIS HOT FIVE
Louis Armstrong, trumpet; Kid Ory, trombone; Johnny Dodds, clarinet; Lil Hardin Armstrong, piano; Lonnie Johnson, guitar

- Label: OKeh 8535
- Date: 1927
- Style: New Orleans Jazz
- Form: 32-bar popular song (**A B A C**)

What to listen for:
- polyphonic collective improvisation vs. homophonic solos
- Armstrong's soloing and scat-singing
- his intense improvised polyrhythms
- dialogue between voice and guitar

INTRODUCTION

0:00	The band begins with **collective improvisation**, with Armstrong's trumpet clearly in front. The remaining instruments provide support: the trombone plays simple single-note figures, while the clarinet is distantly in the background. The harmonies are those of the last eight bars of the chorus.

CHORUS 1

0:09	**A**	Armstrong begins his improvisation. Many of his notes are **ghosted**—played so lightly that they're almost inaudible.
0:18	**B**	
0:25		Trumpet **break**.
0:27	**A**	Coming out of the break, Armstrong places accents on the **backbeat**, before finishing with a quick **triplet** figure.
0:36	**C**	Armstrong emphasizes a high note with a **shake**—an extra vibrato at the end.
0:43		During a two-measure break, Dodds begins his clarinet solo.

CHORUS 2

0:45	**A**	Dodds plays his solo in the clarinet's upper register. Beneath him, Hardin plays rhythmic piano fills.
0:54	**B**	
1:02		Dodds's clarinet break ends on a **blue note**.
1:03	**A**	
1:12	**C**	
1:19		A **scat-singing** break introduces the next solo, by Armstrong.

CHORUS 3

1:21	**A**	Armstrong begins his solo by singing on-the-beat quarter notes, backed by the guitar's bluesy improvised lines. The timbre of his voice is rough but pleasant.
1:30	**B**	As his melodic ideas take flight, he stretches the beat in unpredictable ways.
1:36		Scat-singing break.
1:39	**A**	Armstrong ingeniously uses melody, rhythm, and scat syllables to create a strong sense of **polyrhythm**.
1:47	**C**	

INTERLUDE

| 1:55 | | In a loose extension of the previous chorus, Armstrong exchanges intimate, bluesy moans with Johnson's guitar. |
| 2:13 | | Hardin on piano calls the band together with four bars of **octaves**. |

CHORUS 4

2:17	**A**	Ory takes a sharply accented trombone solo, which echoes the beginning of Armstrong's scat solo.
2:26	**B**	
2:33		Trumpet break: Armstrong interrupts Ory's solo with a rocket-like string of quick notes, ending with a high B-flat.
2:35	**A**	Collective improvisation, with Armstrong hitting his high note again and again in a short, syncopated riff.
2:43	**C**	The last eight bars are in **stop-time**: Armstrong generates tension by playing unpredictable short lines.

CODA

| 2:50 | | Johnson and Armstrong exchange brief solos. |
| 2:56 | | Johnson's line ends on a dissonant **diminished-seventh chord**, which leaves the harmony suspended. |

🎧 "West End Blues"

One of the most fabled performances in all of recorded music took place at a session (June 28, 1928) that at first did not seem very promising. The band began with "Don't Jive Me," which aside from being the first tune to use the word "jive" in a title, shows little distinction, and was shelved by the record company until 1940, when it was first released. Incredibly, the band segued from that to "West End Blues," beginning with a cadenza that is often interpreted as the call to arms of a new world-shaking art, unmatched to this day in its concision, power, and relentless invention. The keening momentum of this monophonic trumpet passage cannot be precisely notated because the note values are craftily altered by Armstrong's embouchure technique and extremely supple phrasing. Each subsequent twelve-bar chorus, in what is essentially a banal blues composed by King Oliver, is different from its neighbors; those involving Armstrong bring to fruition ideas he had explored at previous sessions.

The **theme chorus** (or head), with Armstrong in the lead, is followed by a staid trombone solo backed by woodblocks. The next chorus also features two instruments—the clarinet and Armstrong's voice—in an exchange of soft, lyrical improvised phrases, Armstrong's wordless singing suggesting an inspired kind of humming. This was an idea he had used more aggressively in exchanges with the clarinetist on "Skid-Dat-De-Dat" and with the guitarist on "Hotter Than That," but never with as delicate a touch as here. An expansive salon-style piano solo by Earl Hines enriches the performance's harmonic palette and offers a distinctive emotional break that sets up Armstrong's dramatic return. Armstrong the trumpeter now holds one perfect, unwavering note for four measures, and then caroms into a series of fervent descending **arpeggios** (notes of a chord played one after the other rather than simultaneously) in a melodic-rhythmic idea he had first employed on "S.O.L. Blues," before bringing in the ensemble to complete the chorus. The concluding piano and clop-cymbal finish is a stoical anticlimax. Few composers have imparted as much emotional, formal pleasure in three minutes.

LISTENING GUIDE 13

🎧 west end blues

LOUIS ARMSTRONG AND HIS HOT FIVE
Armstrong, trumpet, vocal; Fred Robinson, trombone; Jimmy Strong, clarinet; Earl Hines, piano; Mancy Cara, banjo; Zutty Singleton, drums

- Label: OKeh 8597
- Date: 1928
- Style: New Orleans jazz
- Form: 12-bar blues

What to listen for:

- Armstrong's introductory cadenza, one of the most famous passages in jazz
- loose, bluesy phrases over a simple chord progression
- Armstrong as scat-singing vocalist (chorus 3)
- Hines's delicate piano solo (chorus 4)
- Armstrong's sustained high B-flat in chorus 5

INTRODUCTION

0:00   Armstrong launches into a **cadenza** with vigorous, forceful notes. These soon shift into **triplets** (notes divided into three parts) as his line spirals upward toward a climax on a high note.

0:05   After a brief pause, the melodic line cascades downward, gradually losing speed and volume as it comes to rest on its final note.

0:13   The band enters, playing a **dominant (V)** chord.

CHORUS 1

0:16   Armstrong plays the main melody. The clarinet (Strong) loosely harmonizes behind him, while the trombone (Robinson) plays a supporting line featuring **glissandos**. On piano, Hines marks time with simple chords on every beat.

0:44   Armstrong returns to the triplet rhythms of the cadenza, ascending toward another high note.

CHORUS 2

0:50   The melody passes to Robinson on trombone. Underneath him, the drummer (Singleton) plays patterns on woodblocks, while Hines switches to playing the chords in **tremolo** (the speedy alternation of two or more notes).

CHORUS 3

1:24   In a **call-and-response** pattern, the clarinet plays short fragments drawn from the melody, while Armstrong answers him, singing with **scat syllables**.

1:36   Armstrong's responses become longer and rhythmically more intricate.

1:53   On the **turnaround** (the last two measures of the chorus), Armstrong and Strong harmonize over the descending chords.

CHORUS 4

1:59   Hines's solo is flashy and delicate, featuring long decorative passages. His left-hand stride accompaniment (alternating bass notes with chords) fills out the simple blues progression with **harmonic substitutions**.

2:10   As the harmony shifts to IV, Hines suddenly attacks the piano with renewed energy. His aggressive playing suggests **double-time** (a temporary doubling of the tempo).

2:20   Gradually, he lets the tension subside.

CHORUS 5

2:32   Armstrong starts the melody a full octave higher. Once he reaches the top note, he sustains it, holding the high B-flat for four agonizingly slow measures. Underneath, the accompanying harmony swells in volume.

2:44   Armstrong releases the tension through a series of short bluesy phrases, each one placed just before or after the beat. These phrases gradually melt into longer, more intricate phrases.

CODA

2:56   Hines plays a series of descending chords.

3:04   Armstrong plays one last phrase, holding his final note through the band's **rubato** (rhythmically flexible) chords.

3:15   The drummer signals the end with a hollow cymbal clap.

▪ ENTER EARL HINES (1903–1983)

In 1926, Armstrong was hired as featured soloist with the Carroll Dickerson Orchestra, at the Sunset Café in Chicago. For the first time, his name was up in lights, as "the world's greatest trumpet player." White musicians, including Bing Crosby, Bix Beiderbecke, and the very young Benny Goodman, flocked to hear him. Throughout that year and the next, Armstrong studio units produced such benchmark recordings as "Hotter Than That," "Potato Head Blues," "Wild Man Blues," "Willie the Weeper," and "Struttin' with Some

FRANK DRIGGS COLLECTION

Earl Hines earned the nickname "Fatha" for the originality of his piano style, making him an ideal partner for Armstrong. Chicago, 1926.

Barbecue." But something just as special was developing at the Sunset. While on tour, Dickerson had recruited a young pianist from Pittsburgh, Earl Hines, an utterly original stylist who subverted the techniques on which other jazz pianists relied.

Hines was content neither to play on-the-beat background chords, in the manner of Lil Armstrong, nor to confine himself to the propulsive rhythms of stride or "boogie-woogie" (a Midwestern phenomenon in which the pianist's left hand plays eight beats to every bar; see Chapter 8). He preferred to combine those approaches, with the result that his idiosyncratic style seemed to play games with the rhythm. Above all, he was determined to use the piano much as Armstrong used the trumpet, as a solo instrument improvising single-line melodies. To make them audible, he developed an ability to improvise in **tremolos** (the speedy alternation of two or more notes, creating a pianistic version of the brass man's vibrato) and octaves or tenths: instead of hitting one note at a time with his right hand, he hit two with vibrantly percussive force—his reach was so large that jealous competitors spread the rumor that he had had the webbing between his fingers surgically removed.

Hines and Armstrong hit it off immediately. As Hines recalled, "I was amazed to find a trumpeter like Louis who was playing everything that I was trying to do on the piano. So, there were the two of us expressing the same spirit." For the 1928 Hot Five recordings, Armstrong changed the personnel to employ Hines and the younger musicians he worked with in Dickerson's band at the Sunset Café and at New York's Savoy Ballroom. The new recordings, representing a marked advance on their sensational predecessors, included the seminal "West End Blues," "Basin Street Blues," "Muggles," "St. James Infirmary," and the tour de force "Tight Like This," in which Armstrong develops three thematic choruses of architectural grandeur. The best example of the interplay between Armstrong and Hines came about at the end of a session, when the ensemble had finished for the day. The two men improvised a duet on an old Armstrong rag they had played in concert, "Weather Bird." Worried that fans of the Hot Five would object, the record company did not release it until 1930.

🎧 "Weather Bird"

"Weather Bird" has a dizzying stop-and-go momentum, punched up with humor, competitive daring, and an unanticipated beauty. Armstrong wrote "Weather Bird" for King Oliver and recorded it with him in 1923. Unlike his other compositions, it uses the traditional ragtime structure of three sixteen-bar strains. On Oliver's record, the piece is played as a ragtime march, with a stop-time section and brief breaks (including one by the twin trumpets); there is no sustained improvisation.

Armstrong and Hines follow the same format, but turn the piece into a friendly battle, packed with broken rhythms, shifty jabs and feints, until the grand finale: a sixteen-bar coda, during which they exchange phrases with a mocking "where-are-we-going-with-this" wariness, concluded by Armstrong's exquisitely timed ascending scale, cradled by Hines's final chords.

🎧 **weather bird**

LOUIS ARMSTRONG AND EARL HINES

Louis Armstrong, trumpet; Earl Hines, piano

- Label: OKeh 41454
- Date: 1928
- Style: early jazz
- Form: march/ragtime

What to listen for:

- improvised call and response between trumpet and piano
- great soloists pushing each other to their limits
- cadence figure at the end of each strain
- unpredictable rhythms
- exchange between soloists in the coda, figuring out how to end the piece

INTRODUCTION

0:00   Armstrong plays the opening melody on trumpet, discreetly backed by Hines's piano.

STRAIN A

0:04   Armstrong displays his command of **dynamics** (volume, or degrees of loudness and softness). Some notes are played at full volume; others (**ghosted**) are so soft that they virtually disappear. Underneath him, Hines plays surprising syncopations, undermining the steady rhythm: he has no intention of playing the well-behaved accompanist. His style is not ragtime or stride, but a more idiosyncratic mixture.

0:13   The strain comes to rest on a **half cadence**.

0:18   The harmonies begin a drive to a **full cadence**. (We will call this passage, already heard in the introduction, the *cadence figure*.)

STRAIN B

0:23   A new strain, marked by a striking melodic phrase. Armstrong primarily sticks to the original tune, leaving room for Hines to improvise.

0:28   Armstrong plays a static ragtime polyrhythm, against which Hines adds his own melodies and rhythms.

0:33   At times, they seem to read each other's minds: Armstrong plays a short phrase that Hines instantly echoes; a few seconds later, when Armstrong briefly rests, Hines pounces in with a dramatic flourish.

0:39   Armstrong ends his line with the last few notes of the *cadence figure*.

STRAIN B

0:41   Hines begins to solo in **stride** piano style.

0:49   At the place where a break would normally occur in early jazz, he suddenly shifts to a new pianistic texture. For the next several measures, his playing is highly polyrhythmic and unpredictable.

0:56   As the strain ends, he returns to a more normal texture, clearly playing the *cadence figure*.

STRAIN A

1:00   Armstrong repeats the melody for strain **A**, embellishing it, and then abandoning it for outright improvisation.

1:14   He returns to the *cadence figure*.

INTERLUDE

1:18   A transitional passage: Armstrong and Hines begin with simple syncopated figures, but rapidly increase the rhythmic intensity to unnerving levels.

STRAIN C (TRIO)

1:23   Unusually, the trio doesn't modulate: it's in the same key as the first two strains. Hines plays a piano solo.

1:32   Hines pushes his improvisation so far that it outraces even his own abilities: we can occasionally hear mistakes.

1:37   At the end of the strain, he dissolves tension by returning to a variation of the *cadence figure*.

STRAIN C

1:41   After a **break** featuring Armstrong, the two men test each other's mettle, phrasing both *on* and *off* the beat, in a kind of **call-and-response** match.

1:51   During another break, Armstrong ascends to a new high note.

1:58   He returns to the *cadence figure*.

STRAIN C

2:00   The call-and-response roles are reversed: Hines begins with a break, Armstrong responding.

2:10   During an oddly impromptu break, Hines plays a disorienting rhythm ending on an aggressively **dissonant** note, resolved—at the last second—with a **consonance**.

2:14   Armstrong plays the *cadence figure* with an interesting rhythmic twist.

CODA

2:18   Once again, Armstrong begins with a break.

2:20   Hines responds with dissonant harmonies, suggesting that he wants to end the piece.

2:22   Armstrong answers, matching the dissonance in his melodic line.

2:25   Hines moves toward a final cadence. The exchanges become shorter, as the two musicians try to figure out where to go.

2:32   Suddenly, Armstrong begins a new phrase, ascending slowly but with steady acceleration, virtually eliminating all previous sense of meter.

2:36   In response to Armstrong's high note, Hines adds the concluding harmonies.

By the end of the 1920s, the fad of naming jazz bands after New Orleans had virtually disappeared. And the arrival, in those same years, of gifted and original white musicians underscored the reality that jazz had the potential to become an idiom of universal acceptance. Armstrong seemed to be offering jazz as a gift to anyone who could feel and master it, of any region or race. "Jazz is only what you are," as he put it. By 1929, dozens of forceful musical personalities, some of them older and more experienced than Armstrong, were following suit. They forged a music in which the soloist emerged as prince of the realm, in which the best composers and arrangers were those who made the most creative use of their soloists. Among the most remarkable of those soloists were Bix Beiderbecke and Coleman Hawkins.

■ BIX BEIDERBECKE (1903–1931)

Leon Beiderbecke, known throughout his life as Bix (a corruption of his middle name, Bismark), was born in Davenport, Iowa. His mother played church organ and encouraged her son to pick out melodies on the family piano. Bix took a few lessons but relied chiefly on his exceptional musical ear.

Beiderbecke belonged to the first generation of musicians who learned about jazz from recordings. This kind of introduction had an immediate threefold influence. First, young people were exposed to jazz without having to live in a particular area or sneak into off-limits places (saloons) where it was performed. Second, owning records encouraged, through repeated plays, study and memorization. Third, records freed the imagination of young listeners to interpret jazz as they pleased, without the constricting influence of tradition. In the era before network radio, recordings could bring a New Orleans jazz ensemble, and the faraway world it represented, into non-Southern towns like the stolid German-American community of Davenport.

Bix was fourteen when the Original Dixieland Jazz Band issued its first records, and they affected him deeply—much to the vexation of his parents, whose abhorrence of jazz and Beiderbecke's association with it never lessened. He taught himself cornet by mimicking and harmonizing with recorded performances. In 1921, as a result of neglecting his homework to haunt jazz clubs, his parents sent him to Lake Forrest Academy in Illinois, a move that Bix experienced with anguish but one that put him within train-hopping distance of Chicago. Soon he was making regular visits to Lincoln Gardens and other Chicago nightclubs, soaking up the music of King Oliver, Louis Armstrong, the New Orleans Rhythm Kings, and other bands that passed through town. More truancies led to his expulsion from Lake Forrest, and in 1923 he joined the Wolverines—the first band of Northern whites formed in imitation of the New Orleans style.

Bix Beiderbecke, seen here in 1923, was the first major white jazz star and the first to acquire a mythological aura after his early death.

Chicago Style

Late in 1924, Beiderbecke recorded with the Sioux City Six, alongside C-melody saxophonist Frank Trumbauer (1901–1956)—the beginning of a lifelong association. The C-melody saxophone enjoyed popularity in the early years of the twentieth century because of its strong limber sound—suggesting a cross between an alto and a tenor—and because it's in the key of C, the same as the piano. It never made much headway in jazz; Trumbauer was its only important exponent. He presided over the most admired white small-group jazz records of the 1920s, and his sweet-with-out-being-corny timbre, lyricism, phrasing, and songlike use of smears and glides introduced a delicacy to saxophone playing that made an indelible impression on several major black saxophonists, notably Lester Young and Benny Carter.

Frank Trumbauer

Beiderbecke and Trumbauer became the figureheads for a generation of white jazz musicians (almost all born between 1904 and 1909) often referred to as the Austin High Gang, after those who had attended Chicago's Austin High School: pianist Joe Sullivan, drummer Dave Tough, tenor saxophonist Bud Freeman, cornetist Jimmy McPartland, and clarinetist Frank Teschemacher. Their associates, white musicians who had either grown up in Chicago or, like Beiderbecke, gravitated there from other points in the Midwest, included clarinetists Benny Goodman, Pee Wee Russell, and Don Murray, guitarist Eddie Condon, bass saxophonist Adrian Rollini, and drummer Gene Krupa. Collectively, they created the **Chicago style**, which began by imitating New Orleans bands and evolved into a more slapdash, aggressively rhythmic school that combined expansive solos with polyphonic theme statements. Their music represented both homage to black jazz and a rebellion against the gentility of the white middle class. Eddie Condon proudly recalled of an early performance: "One of the ladies told me it was just like having the Indians in town again."

Beiderbecke's flamelike career, cut short at twenty-eight, chiefly from alcoholism, strengthened white musicians' rebellious conviction, despite the financial security Bix had achieved in his last years as featured soloist in Paul Whiteman's orchestra (see "Changes" in Chapter 5). Largely unknown to the public during his life, his gentle genius accrued in death the lineaments of martyrdom. Bix recorded between 1924 and 1930, and the high-water mark of his legacy is the series of sessions made in 1927 with Trumbauer (they were initially released as Frankie Trumbauer and His Orchestra) and the influential and serenely capable guitarist Eddie Lang. "Singin' the Blues," one of the most imitated of all recordings, is generally considered their masterpiece.

🎧 "Singin' the Blues"

Three things to keep in mind while listening to this recording: (1) the source material is a popular song, introduced in 1920; (2) the song is never actually played as written except in the eight-bar ensemble passage following the cornet solo; (3) the tempo and feeling of the performance are those of a ballad. These aspects were considered novel in 1927, when jazz musicians rarely drew on Tin Pan Alley songs, when improvisers embellished the written melody instead of displacing it with original variations, and when contemplative tempos were usually reserved for the blues.

This performance is dominated by full-chorus solos by Trumbauer and Beiderbecke, accompanied by Lang, whose firm second- and fourth-beat accents and fluid, responsive arpeggios give it much of its propulsion and charm. Trumbauer's virtues are beautifully displayed in this, his most famous solo. Beiderbecke's solo conveys instantly the qualities that so startled his contemporaries. Jazz is a music of individuality, and therefore of sensibility. Beiderbecke introduced a new sensibility, quite different from the extroverted Armstrong. There is a shy politeness to Bix's playing, as he rings each note with the precision of a percussionist hitting chimes. He plots his variations with great care—as Lang does his accompaniment, playing with greater harmonic daring to match Bix's melodies.

The two long solos on "Singin' the Blues" quickly entered the lexicon of jazz, and have since been incessantly studied and imitated. Fletcher Henderson recorded a version in which his reed section played the Trumbauer solo and cornetist Rex Stewart played Bix's improvisation, as though they were composed pieces of music, which in this instance they were (by virtue of being played from a written score). These solos are also believed to be the first to which lyrics were written (a process that came to be known as "vocalese" when it blossomed in the 1950s).

🎧 singin' the blues

FRANKIE TRUMBAUER AND HIS ORCHESTRA

Frankie Trumbauer, C-melody saxophone; Bix Beiderbecke, cornet; Bill Rank, trombone; Jimmy Dorsey, clarinet; Doc Ryker, alto saxophone; Paul Mertz, piano; Eddie Lang, guitar; Chauncey Morehouse, drums

- Label: OKeh 40772
- Date: 1927
- Style: Chicago-style jazz
- Form: 32-bar popular song (**A B A' C**)

What to listen for:
- **chorus 1: Trumbauer's fluid solo on C-melody saxophone, answered by Lang's inventive guitar**
- **chorus 2: Beiderbecke's introverted, delicate cornet solo**
- **Chicago-style collective improvisation and solos**

INTRODUCTION

0:00		In a passage arranged by Bill Challis, the horns enter in **block-chord** texture, accompanied by fills on the cymbals.

CHORUS 1

0:07	**A**	Trumbauer begins his solo on C-melody saxophone, swooping up to his first note, accompanied by Lang on guitar (with the pianist distantly in the background).
0:16		Lang's accompaniment occasionally provides improvised **countermelodies**.
0:21	**B**	Trumbauer's high note is preceded by a lengthy scooped entrance.
0:31		A two-measure **break** features Trumbauer's subtle phrases. The break ends with guitar chords and a cymbal crash.
0:35	**A'**	
0:41		A passage by Trumbauer in rapid **triplets** is neatly extended by Lang's guitar.
0:49	**C**	
0:59		Trumbauer's concluding break is fast and unpredictable.

CHORUS 2

1:03	**A**	Beiderbecke enters on cornet. He plays with a cool, introverted feeling, pulling back in volume at the end of each phrase.
1:17	**B**	His melody features the hint of a **blue note**.
1:28		On his break, Beiderbecke improvises a fast passage that ends with delicately played repeated notes.
1:31	**A'**	He suddenly erupts into a dramatic upward rip. This heated emotion quickly subsides, as if he were letting off a bit of steam.
1:46	**C**	
1:52		To bring his solo to a close, he hints at bluesy playing.

CHORUS 3

2:00	**A**	The band states the original melody of the song, disguised by a mild version of New Orleans polyphony. The drummer adds accents on the cymbals.
2:15	**B**	Dorsey's clarinet solo loosely suggests Beiderbecke's restrained style.
2:26		Dorsey's break ends almost in a whisper.
2:29	**A'**	The band returns with collective improvisation, with Beiderbecke's cornet on top.
2:44	**C**	
2:46		A one-measure break features Lang playing a rapid upward **arpeggio** on guitar.
2:51		Beiderbecke begins his last line with another aggressive rip, followed by short riffs on a repeated note.
2:58		A cymbal stroke brings the piece to a close.

FRANK DRIGGS COLLECTION

Coleman Hawkins, shown here in 1949, was known for his powerful timbre and rhapsodic improvisational style. He established the tenor saxophone as the most iconic instrument in jazz.

■ COLEMAN HAWKINS (1904–1969)

In contrast with Beiderbecke's meteoric career, Coleman Hawkins's spanned five decades of jazz history, at the end of which he had become one of its universally admired patriarchs. His great period came in the 1930s and 1940s, but it was in the 1920s that he created an almost universally imitated template for playing tenor saxophone.

Hawkins, born in St. Joseph, Missouri, began learning piano at age five from his mother, a teacher and organist. He also studied cello, and added the C-melody saxophone at nine; as a teenager, he played both instruments professionally at Kansas City dances. In 1922, Hawkins joined with Mamie Smith and Her Jazzhounds; that summer he took up the tenor saxophone. Touring with Smith, he traveled from Kansas City to Chicago and eventually to both coasts, electing to stay in New York to freelance with top musicians. When Fletcher Henderson heard Hawkins with Wilbur Sweatman's band, he engaged him for a record session and then for a spot in his new orchestra. Hawkins stayed with Henderson for eleven years, establishing himself as the leading figure on his instrument.

From the beginning, he demonstrated tremendous authority, bringing to the saxophone qualities more often associated with the cello: wide vibrato, dynamics, and a huge sound. What he lacked in swing, blues sensibility, and emotional clarity became clear to him when Henderson hired Louis Armstrong in 1924. During the next few years, he strove to adapt Armstrong's style to the tenor saxophone. An early indication of his increasing maturity was an explosive solo on Henderson's 1926 record "Stampede," a great success among musicians and often cited by the next generation of tenor saxophonists as a decisive influence on their education.

"One Hour"

Hawkins's 1939 masterpiece "Body and Soul" has been called the greatest of all jazz solos (we take up his later career and this piece in Chapter 9), but it was a decade in the making, and the 1929 "One Hour" was a benchmark in that process. Up to this point, Hawkins's playing had conspicuously lacked a **legato**, or smooth attack. His phrasing had consisted of clearly articulated notes, even at very fast tempos. An essential component of swing was missing: relaxation. Nor was there any romance in his music. In "One Hour," improvised variations on James P. Johnson's song "If I Could Be with You One Hour Tonight," Hawkins unveiled a radically new approach to the tenor saxophone—one that brought a new romantic expressiveness to jazz, transcending the smooth melodicism of Trumbauer with nearly rapturous power. (A Listening Guide is available online.)

SATCHMO'S WORLD

Louis Armstrong's Hot Five and Seven emancipated jazz from the conventions of an inherited, ritualized tradition, and paved the way for a new music. They sold well by the standards of "race" labels, distributed to targeted urban communities, but they caused barely a ripple in the mainstream compared with popular white musicians of the day, like Paul Whiteman and singers Al Jolson and Gene Austin. Musicians, however, eagerly awaited every new Armstrong release, and his reputation in jazz circles grew accordingly.

After the last of the Hot Five sessions in 1928, Armstrong went on the road with Carroll Dickerson, performing in Detroit and at Harlem's Savoy Ballroom. His next record date, in March 1929, was a double milestone. It included the first integrated jazz ensemble that was generally acknowledged as such: the band released only one track—an impromptu blues, "Knockin' a Jug"—but its personnel (three blacks, three whites) symbolized the fact that jazz had crossed the racial divide and had produced a new crop of musicians who had the technical and creative abilities to function as soloists. Each of the three white participants would enjoy an important career: guitarist Eddie Lang (featured in "Singin' the Blues"), trombonist Jack Teagarden, and pianist Joe Sullivan.

At the same recording session, Armstrong **fronted** (a front man is the nominal star of a band, but not really its leader or music director) a completely different integrated, ten-piece orchestra, under the musical direction of Luis Russell, a Panamanian-born pianist, arranger, and bandleader who as a teenager had won a $3,000 lottery and used the prize to move to New Orleans. This band not only mingled black and white, but also encompassed a broad geographical sweep, with musicians from South America, New Orleans, Georgia, Alabama, Indiana, and Boston. For those paying attention, the lesson was clear: jazz had a global, pan-racial future. The orchestra recorded two numbers that day, one of which was "I Can't Give You Anything but Love," a New York show tune by the team of Jimmy McHugh and Dorothy Fields. This was the record that proved how effective a singer Armstrong could be with pop material and how completely he could reinvent it as jazz.

Luis Russell

There was no stopping him now. Weeks later, in July 1929, he achieved a major hit with Fats Waller's song "Ain't Misbehavin'," and during the next few years (1930–33) recorded every kind of song, from "St. Louis Blues" and "Tiger Rag" to "Star Dust" and "Song of the Islands." Younger musicians and fans, black and white, imitated everything he did. The clarinetist Mezz Mezzrow recalled people copying his trademark white handkerchiefs, his slouch, his slang, his growl, and his fondness for marijuana: "All the raggedy kids, especially those who became vipers [pot smokers], were so inspired with self-respect after digging how neat and natty Louis was, they started to dress up real good."

After long engagements in Los Angeles, New York, and Chicago and tours that took in most of the Midwest and Northeast, Armstrong sailed for Europe in 1932, triumphing in London and Paris. One British journalist mispronounced one of Louis's nicknames (Satchelmouth) as "Satchmo," and the name stuck for good. He returned to Europe to even greater acclaim in 1933 and 1934—thousands greeted him at the train station in Copenhagen. By this time, he had begun to star in short films, which invariably employed demeaning stereotypes. Yet Armstrong transcended them, seemingly winking at the audience, who venerated him as a great artist who subverted the clichés of minstrelsy.

Europe/films

By 1935 and 1936, the Swing Era had been launched, and the whole country wanted to dance to big-band jazz. Armstrong took on a powerful manager, Joe Glaser, whose control of his career began with a lucrative Decca Records contract that lasted nearly twenty years. Armstrong published his first (heavily ghostwritten) autobiography, *Swing That Music*, and received star billing for a cameo appearance in a Bing Crosby movie, *Pennies from Heaven*. He released dozens of hit records, appeared in other movies, and became the first black performer to host a nationally sponsored radio show.

After fronting a big band for more than fifteen years, Louis Armstrong returned to a small group with his aptly named All Stars: Sidney Catlett, drums; Barney Bigard, clarinet; Armstrong, trumpet; Earl Hines, piano; Jack Teagarden, trombone; and Arvell Shaw, bass, at the Blue Note in Chicago, 1948.

FRANK DRIGGS COLLECTION

In this period (the mid-1930s), Armstrong's voice developed into a surprisingly mellow tenor, and he was widely acclaimed as one of the great singers in jazz or popular music. His trumpet playing achieved an astonishing brilliance, famous for intricate high-note flourishes and melody statements that imparted unsuspected depths to familiar songs. Among his great big-band recordings are a glittering remake of "Struttin' with Some Barbecue," "Swing That Music," "Jubilee," "Love Walked In," "Ev'ntide," "I Double Dare You," and "Skeleton in the Closet."

Things began to sour during World War II. The younger audience had discovered rhythm and blues, and many forward-looking musicians were entranced by new jazz styles, later known as bebop or cool jazz, and shunned the good-natured, old-fashioned show business presentation Armstrong had come to represent. His appearance in a 1946 Hollywood travesty, *New Orleans,* had the beneficial result of encouraging him to return to a small-band format for the first time in seventeen years. Subsequent triumphs at New York's Carnegie Hall and Town Hall in 1947 led to the formation of an integrated sextet billed as Louis Armstrong and His All Stars, the unit he would lead for the rest of his life.

The All Stars ▶ In its early years, the All Stars really *were* stars, including his old friend trombonist Jack Teagarden, clarinetist Barney Bigard (formerly of Duke Ellington's Orchestra), drummer Sid Catlett (an audience favorite who had played in the big bands of Fletcher Henderson and Benny Goodman), and his early partner Earl Hines, who had himself become a major bandleader during the Swing Era. Armstrong continued to make movies and hit records throughout the 1950s, regularly appearing on television, traveling constantly, and earning his reputation as America's ambassador of good will. In the latter part of that decade, however, he found himself at the center of a political storm.

Africa and Arkansas

In 1956, CBS News arranged for Armstrong to visit Africa as part of a documentary film it was preparing about him. When he arrived in Accra, in Ghana, thousands stormed the tarmac to see him; his performance at the stadium of "(What Did I Do to Be So) Black and Blue," for an audience of 100,000, brought Prime Minister Kwame Nkrumah to tears. Inspired by Ghana's independence, Armstrong faced a quandary on his return home: how to deal with the fight for civil rights in his own country. He insisted on touring the South with an integrated band or not at all, even when the audiences were segregated (with blacks in the balcony). Early in 1957, at one such concert in Knoxville, Tennessee, a stick of dynamite was hurled at the theater. Armstrong managed to avert panic by reassuring the audience, "That's all right folks, it's just the phone."

His humor failed him that September, though, when Arkansas governor Orval Faubus ordered the National Guard to block the admission of black students to Little Rock's Central High School. "The way they are treating my people in the South, the government can go to hell," he told a reporter. Meanwhile, the U.S. government, determined to capitalize on Armstrong's African success, planned to send him to the Soviet Union as part of the 1950s cultural exchange program. Armstrong balked: "The people over there ask me what's wrong with my country, what am I supposed to say?" When President Eisenhower finally sent federal troops to Arkansas, Armstrong sent him a supportive telegram. Yet the FBI investigated him, a conservative columnist called for a boycott of his concerts and records, and a few black entertainers criticized him for speaking out.

At the same time, others characterized him as an Uncle Tom, confusing his persona as an entertainer with minstrel attitudes. His demeanor ("aggressively happy," in writer Truman Capote's words) made them uncomfortable. He was now a confusing figure: irresistible as an entertainer and artist, even to many of his detractors, but an embarrassing vestige of the era when black performers grinned and shuffled. By the mid-1960s, the controversy had passed. The totally surprising success of "Hello, Dolly!" in 1964 triggered one of the great reassessments in entertainment history: although Armstrong had never stopped touring, recording, and broadcasting, he was once again beloved by all. In his last years, he devoted much of his energy to writing an unfinished memoir, detailing the grueling hardships of his youth in New Orleans. His death, on July 6, 1971, was mourned worldwide. Incredibly, seventeen years later, Satchmo had the best-selling record in the country, with the rediscovery (thanks to a film score) of the previously ignored "What a Wonderful World."

© HERB SNITZER

The public rarely saw the private side of Armstrong, shown here at rest during a road tour in 1960. Note the Star of David, a gift from the Jewish family who befriended him as a small boy (the owners of the rag-and-bone business), and the skin graft on his upper lip, necessitated by his flair for high notes. The cigarette is just that—not his favorite natural herb, which he also smoked daily.

Jazz Personalized

The arc of Armstrong's life was, in many ways, the arc of jazz. In 1929, Armstrong achieved the beginnings of a mainstream acceptance, while such musicians as Bix Beiderbecke and Coleman Hawkins embodied the importance of individual expression and the emotional potential of a music just coming into its own. In the 1930s, a generation of musicians would similarly personalize jazz, removing most of its ties to New Orleans and the Chicago and New York of the 1920s—to the degree that many old-timers scarcely recognized it. In the process of modernization, these younger players achieved something that now seems miraculous. They transformed jazz into the world's best-known popular music. The change was so dramatic that many fans and musicians refused to call it jazz: they called it swing.

LOUIS ARMSTRONG CHRONOLOGY		
1901	Born August 4 in New Orleans.	
1913	Sent to New Orleans Colored Waif's Home; joins band.	Learns New Orleans style.
1918–21	Mississippi riverboats, Fate Marable.	
1922	Chicago: King Oliver's Creole Jazz Band.	Plays 2nd cornet, New Orleans style.
1923	Recordings with King Oliver.	
1924–25	New York: Fletcher Henderson; recordings with Clarence Williams's Blue Five (Sidney Bechet), Bessie Smith.	Soloist, big-band.
1925	Back to Chicago.	
1925–28	Hot Five/Hot Seven recordings.	Combines solo improvisation with New Orleans style.
1926	Featured soloist, Carroll Dickerson, Sunset Café.	Soloist in live performance.
1928	Recordings with Earl Hines.	
1929	New York: fronts big band (Luis Russell).	
1932–34	Tours of Europe.	
1935	Signs with Joe Glaser; major recording artist.	Swing Era band.
1947	Abandons big band; forms Armstrong's All Stars.	Return to New Orleans style.
1957	Little Rock controversy.	
1964	No.1 hit: "Hello, Dolly!"	
1971	Dies July 6 in New York City.	

┤ ADDITIONAL LISTENING ├	
Louis Armstrong	"Potato Head Blues," "Struttin' with Some Barbecue," "St. James Infirmary," "Basin Street Blues," "Tight Like This" (all 1928); "I Can't Give You Anything but Love," "(What Did I Do to Be So) Black and Blue" (both 1929)
Bix Beiderbecke	"I'm Comin' Virginia," "In a Mist" (both 1927)
Coleman Hawkins	"The Stampede" (1926), "One Hour" (1929), "Heartbreak Blues" (1933), "Hocus Pocus" (1934)

ONLINE MULTIMEDIA RESOURCES AND REVIEW MATERIALS

Author Insight Videos

Gary Giddins describes Armstrong's musical innovations, his own unforgettable encounter with Armstrong as a college student, and how jazz came to be the world's best-known popular music.

Interactive Listening Guides

Louis Armstrong, "Hotter Than That"
Louis Armstrong, "West End Blues"
Louis Armstrong / Earl Hines, "Weather Bird"
Frank Trumbauer / Bix Beiderbecke, "Singin' the Blues"

Jazz Concepts (audio and/or video demonstrations of terms covered here)

arpeggio	consonance	octave
backbeat	countermelody	polyrhythm
block chords	dissonance	riff
blue note	dominant chord	rubato
break	double-time	tremolo
cadence	ghosted notes	triplets
cadenza	glissando	
call and response	legato	

- For quick reference, review the **Chapter Overview** and **Chapter Outline**.
- Take the online **Chapter and Listening Quizzes**.
- Use the online **Glossary** and **Flashcards** to review important terms.

PRECURSORS TO JAZZ

Jazz embodied the collision of African American music with the white mainstream, combining elements of folk music, popular music, and art music.

Folk music techniques that made their way into jazz include polyrhythm, call and response, cyclic form, blue notes (variable intonation), and timbre variation. "Classic" or "vaudeville" blues solidified the 12-bar blues form.

Popular music influences include minstrelsy and dance music.

Art music was represented by brass bands, which contributed instrumentation—cornet, clarinet, trombone, percussion—and march/ragtime form: 16-bar strains (usually **A A B B A C C D D**), with the **C** strain (trio) twice as long and in a different key.

Before 1917, the music that combined all these elements was ragtime: in popular songs, dances, and a piano style organized in march-like strains, with a steady two-beat rhythm in the left hand and contrasting rhythms in the right.

Major musicians

- Blues: Ma Rainey, Bessie Smith
- Dance: Vernon and Irene Castle, James Reese Europe
- Ragtime: Scott Joplin (piano), Wilbur Sweatman (clarinet)

In New Orleans, ragtime, blues, march music, and social dance combined in their turn to produce the music we know as jazz. The transformation was already complete as musicians began to make recordings.

NEW ORLEANS STYLE

By the time they began recording in 1917, New Orleans bands had attained an unmistakable ensemble style.

Texture

- largely polyphonic
- occasional homophonic passages
- breaks: monophonic

Instrumentation

- cornet/trumpet, clarinet, trombone ("front line")
- rhythm section: string bass or tuba, acoustic guitar, piano, drums

Form

- march/ragtime
- 12-bar blues
- occasional 32-bar popular song (**A B A C**)

Special techniques

- collective improvisation (polyphonic)
- stop-time
- breaks

Major New Orleans bands

- Buddy Bolden
- Original Dixieland Jazz Band
- Creole Jazz Band (to 1916: Freddie Keppard)
- King Oliver's Jazz Band
- Jelly Roll Morton and His Red Hot Peppers

Major New Orleans musicians

Cornet/trumpet

- Buddy Bolden
- Freddie Keppard
- Nick LaRocca
- Joseph "King" Oliver
- Louis Armstrong

Clarinet

- George Bacquet
- Johnny Dodds
- Sidney Bechet (and soprano saxophone)

Piano

- Jelly Roll Morton

BIG BANDS BEFORE 1930

The 1920s saw a migration of jazz musicians from New Orleans, Chicago, and elsewhere to New York, the center of the entertainment infrastructure. Here, the growing enthusiasm for ballroom dancing led to the establishment of the first important big bands. New York also encouraged the ripening of the most orchestral brand of jazz piano, stride.

Texture
- homophonic

Instrumentation
- sections of trumpets, trombones, saxophones/clarinets
- rhythm section: tuba, banjo, piano, drums

Form
- 32-bar popular song (**A A B A, A B A C**)
- 12-bar blues
- occasional march/ragtime

Special techniques
- two-beat groove
- block-chord texture

Major early big bands
- Paul Whiteman
- Fletcher Henderson
- Duke Ellington
- McKinney's Cotton Pickers (Don Redman)

Early stride pianists
- James P. Johnson
- Eubie Blake
- Luckey Roberts

Ellingtonians (early)
Saxophone
- Johnny Hodges (alto)
- Harry Carney (baritone)

Clarinet
- Barney Bigard

Trumpet
- Bubber Miley
- Cootie Williams

Trombone
- Joe "Tricky Sam" Nanton

Bass
- Wellman Braud

Piano
- Duke Ellington

LOUIS ARMSTRONG

Guided by Armstrong's vitality and contagious spirit, jazz evolved from ensemble music characterized by polyphony to music that featured soloists and daring improvisation; the multiple strains of ragtime become single-themed choruses of popular songs and blues; two- and four-bar breaks become solos of a full chorus or more.

In addition, Armstrong
- established the blues as jazz's melodic and spiritual foundation;
- introduced scat-singing;
- created brilliant improvisations on popular songs;
- introduced a new rhythmic energy: swing.

Some Armstrong-influenced soloists
Saxophone
- Frank Trumbauer (C-melody)
- Coleman Hawkins (tenor)

Clarinet
- Pee Wee Russell
- Benny Goodman

Trumpet/cornet
- Bix Beiderbecke
- Cootie Williams

Trombone
- Jack Teagarden

PART III

THE SWING ERA

I took ten years for jazz to develop from an often disdained urban phenomenon, played mostly by young male musicians for black audiences, into a national obsession that crossed geographical, generational, gender, and racial borders. Louis Armstrong inaugurated his Hot Five recordings in November 1925; Benny Goodman inadvertently launched the Swing Era in August 1935. In the decade that followed, "jazz" was used almost exclusively to describe traditional New Orleans music. The new word was "swing," which encompassed "hot" orchestras, like those of Duke Ellington and Count Basie, and "sweet" bands, like those of Sammy Kaye and Hal Kemp, which had virtually nothing to do with jazz. Many bands played both hot and sweet in attempting to create stylish dance music that combined elements of jazz with lush instrumentation and pop songs.

The swing bands revived a music industry considered moribund in the dark days of the Depression, and lifted the country's spirits during the darker days of World War II. Even the Nazis, who spurned jazz as a symptom of American

1920s
- Territory dance bands proliferate across country.

1922
- James Joyce's *Ulysses* published.
- T. S. Eliot's *The Wasteland* published.

1925
- The Ku Klux Klan marches in Washington, D.C.
- John Scopes convicted in Tennessee for teaching evolution.
- F. Scott Fitzgerald's *The Great Gatsby* published.
- Ernest Hemingway's *In Our Time* published.

1926
- Savoy Ballroom opens in New York.
- First national radio network (NBC).

1927
- Charles Lindbergh flies solo across the Atlantic.

1928
- Mickey Mouse makes first screen appearance.

1929
- *St. Louis Blues*, featuring Bessie Smith, released.
- Stock market crashes, Great Depression begins.
- William Faulkner's *The Sound and the Fury* published.

1930s
- Guitar replaces banjo, string bass replaces tuba in jazz bands.
- Stride and boogie-woogie piano styles at their peak.

1930
- George Gershwin composes "I Got Rhythm."
- Warner Bros. launches gangster film cycle with *Little Caesar*.

1931
- Cab Calloway records "Minnie the Moocher."
- Universal launches horror film cycle with *Frankenstein* and *Dracula*.

Roy Eldridge, a terror on the trumpet, respectfully known as "Little Jazz" or just plain "Jazz," poses in front of the Savoy Ballroom in the 1930s.

Rosie the Riveter was a familiar symbol for feminine power during World War II.

The phenomenal popularity of Benny Goodman's dance band launched the Swing Era. New York, 1937–38.

Mary Lou Williams, "the lady who swings the band," was the chief arranger and pianist for Andy Kirk's Clouds of Joy. Cleveland, 1937.

degeneracy, were forced to issue imitation swing records to attract listeners to their broadcasts in occupied countries. In the United States, swing created new styles in slang, dress, and especially dance—an energetic, athletic "jitterbugging" that kept ballrooms jumping from coast to coast. Millions of fans debated the merits of bands and knew the names of key soloists: in that era, jazz and pop were largely inseparable.

Yet there was more to swing than big bands and riotous dancing. A new virtuosity had taken hold—a technical bravura that advanced the harmonic and rhythmic underpinnings of jazz, spurring innovations that would last long after the Swing Era had faded. Jazz singing came into its own, the guitar found a new voice through electronic amplification, and orchestrating became an art in its own right. If jazz of the 1920s, created in times of plenty, illuminated a defiant individualism, the Swing Era responded to years of hardship and war with a collective spirit that expressed a carefree, even blissful optimism.

1932
- Duke Ellington records "It Don't Mean a Thing (if It Ain't Got That Swing)."
- Unemployment in the U.S. reaches 14 million.
- Franklin D. Roosevelt elected president.

1932–34
- Louis Armstrong tours Europe.

1933
- Billie Holiday makes first recordings.
- Duke Ellington tours Europe.
- Recording industry at nadir: only 4 million records sold.
- Prohibition repealed.
- Adolf Hitler becomes chancellor of Germany.

1934
- Fats Waller makes first recordings.
- Jimmie Lunceford band performs at the Cotton Club.
- The Quintette du Hot Club de France (with Django Reinhardt) performs in Paris.
- Ella Fitzgerald wins talent competition at the Apollo Theater in New York.
- *Le jazz hot*, *Down Beat* magazines founded.
- Dust Bowl begins (lasting till 1939).
- Frank Capra's *It Happened One Night* released.

1935
- Benny Goodman band, at the Palomar Ballroom in California, launches Swing Era; Goodman begins recording with integrated trio.
- Billie Holiday records with top musicians, including Teddy Wilson.
- Ella Fitzgerald records with Chick Webb.
- George Gershwin's opera *Porgy and Bess* opens in New York.
- Popular Front formed.

PART III

1936
- Count Basie takes band to New York.
- Lester Young records "Oh! Lady Be Good."
- Gibson Company produces first electric guitar.
- Jazz clubs thrive on New York's 52nd Street.
- Jesse Owens wins four gold medals at Berlin Olympics.
- *Life* magazine founded.
- Charlie Chaplin's *Modern Times* released.
- Fred Astaire/Ginger Rogers film *Swing Time* released.

1936–39
- Spanish Civil War

1937
- Mary Lou Williams and Andy Kirk band in New York.
- Count Basie band performs at Savoy, records "One O'Clock Jump."
- Hindenburg explodes in New Jersey.

- Pablo Picasso paints *Guernica*.
- *Snow White and the Seven Dwarfs* released.
- Oscar Hammerstein/Jerome Kern musical *Show Boat* opens in New York.

1938
- Benny Goodman concert at Carnegie Hall (January).
- "From Spirituals to Swing" concert at Carnegie Hall (December).
- Ella Fitzgerald records "A-Tisket, a-Tasket."
- Billy Strayhorn joins Duke Ellington.
- Germany annexes Austria.
- Orson Welles's radio broadcast "The War of the Worlds" creates national panic.

1939
- Coleman Hawkins records "Body and Soul."
- Billie Holiday records "Strange Fruit."
- Glenn Miller records "In the Mood."

The Original Blue Devils defined Kansas City jazz. Lester Young stands to the left and Buster Smith to the right of leader Alvin Burroughs, 1932.

The most famous dance hall in America: the Savoy Ballroom on Lenox Avenue, Harlem, 1940.

In this shot from George Stevens's *Swing Time,* you can sense the thumping yet gravity-defying rhythmic elation Fred Astaire and Ginger Rogers brought to swing dancing. It would be hard to overstate the contagious joy of Fred's ingenious choreography and Ginger's plucky collaboration during very bad times.

Ella Fitzgerald, "the first lady of song," brought the stars out, including Swedish clarinetist Stan Hasselgård (behind Ellington), Duke Ellington, Benny Goodman, and music publisher Jack Robbins. New York, 1949.

Fats Waller and His Rhythm (including saxophonist Gene Sedric and trumpet player Herman Autrey) recording with the Deep River Boys at the RCA-Victor studios in New York, 1942.

- Lester Young records "Lester Leaps In" with Count Basie.
- Benny Goodman hires Charlie Christian.
- World War II begins in Europe.
- John Steinbeck's *The Grapes of Wrath* published.
- *Gone with the Wind*, *The Wizard of Oz*, *Young Mr. Lincoln* released.

1940
- Duke Ellington records "Concerto for Cootie," "Conga Brava," "Ko-Ko."
- Cootie Williams leaves Duke Ellington's band.
- Winston Churchill becomes prime minister of Britain.
- The Blitz: bombing of England.

1941
- Duke Ellington records "Take the 'A' Train."
- Japan bombs Pearl Harbor, U.S. enters war.
- *Citizen Kane*, *The Maltese Falcon* released.

1942
- Glenn Miller forms Air Force band.
- Bing Crosby records "White Christmas."

1943
- Duke Ellington performs *Black, Brown and Beige* at Carnegie Hall.

1944
- Glenn Miller's plane disappears over English Channel.
- Allies invade Normandy, France (D-Day).

1945
- U.S. drops atomic bombs on Hiroshima and Nagasaki; World War II ends.
- Franklin D. Roosevelt dies, Harry S. Truman becomes president.

FLETCHER HENDERSON
blue lou

BENNY GOODMAN
dinah

ARTIE SHAW
star dust

JIMMIE LUNCEFORD
annie laurie

7

SWING BANDS

FROM JAZZ TO SWING

In the 1930s, jazz became the world's popular music under the name of **swing**. We call this period the Swing Era, to distinguish it from the jazz of the 1920s. It was mostly **big-band** music, performed by large dance orchestras divided into sections of trumpets, saxophones, and trombones, as well as rhythm. Although swing was a new music to the casual consumer, it retained the basic elements of jazz we have already seen: polyrhythm, blues phrasing, timbre variation. And though it used written music more than previous forms of jazz, swing continued to balance composition against spontaneous improvisation.

The Depression

Swing was bounded by two crucial events in American culture. The first was the Great Depression, which began with a stock market crash in October 1929. The Depression ruined the banking system, cast millions into unemployment, and shifted America's political landscape. African Americans played a significant role in the new coalition—along with organized labor, Southern whites, and the dispossessed poor—that swept the Democratic candidate, President Franklin Roosevelt, to the presidency in 1932. Roosevelt swiftly launched the New Deal, a blizzard of programs that stretched the nation's political and economic resources to help the unemployed and hurting. He was

Buddy Rich, one of the flashiest virtuoso drummers of the Swing Era, caught here in the middle of a solo, 1954.

reelected an unparalleled three times, but for all his efforts, recovery was slow and laborious until the second event, World War II, transformed the country into a powerhouse of unprecedented strength.

Although swing came of age during this hardest of times, it hardly reflected the era's deep anxiety. Like movies, swing was a counterstatement to reality—an upbeat, slickly packaged commodity to distract people from their daily cares—and produced many great artists. It was a teenager's music, the first in the nation's history, loud and brash and demanding an exuberant physical response. Swing's improvisatory flair and buoyant energy encouraged America to recover from an emotional malaise; no less than the ingenuity of the New Deal, swing made average citizens feel alive, alert, and engaged.

World War II
After the bombing of Pearl Harbor in 1941 and America's entry into war, the fight against fascism required the involvement of all the country's industries, resources, and manpower—not least the world of entertainment. For four long years, while the country was on edge, shifting unsteadily from steely grimness to giddy recklessness, swing drew avid and anxious patrons to ballrooms and theaters. For many people, swing exemplified what Americans were fighting for: compared with Nazi or Japanese authoritarianism, the casual, participatory nature of swing, yoking together people from different backgrounds, was a rousing statement of democracy. At the war's end, hundreds of thousands of servicemen returned home to their families and jobs, shutting down the hyperactive dancing culture that had formed the basis for countless orchestras, national and local. It was the end of an era—and with the introduction of atomic warfare, the beginning of a new one.

Swing and Economics

The Depression nearly destroyed the record companies. At a time when people could barely afford food and rent, the price of a record (one dollar, sometimes two) was too much to bear. Besides, why spend money on records when music was available over the radio for free? Sales of records plunged—from over 100 million in 1929 to 4 million in 1933. Familiar jazz labels like Gennett, OKeh, and the once-dominant Columbia went bankrupt or were bought up by speculators. The only major label that survived the early 1930s was Victor, because it had been amalgamated with the RCA radio network.

Things began to look up a few years later, thanks to the invention of the jukebox, the garish record-selecting machine that filled restaurants or bars with music for a nickel a side. By the late 1930s, the business had begun to turn around, and people who had declared records a thing of the past wanted into it. Three labels, "the majors," as they were known—Columbia (bought by CBS), Victor, and Decca—produced about 90 percent of the recordings Americans listened to.

Similar patterns of concentration could be found in other media. Millions of families listened to the weekly or daily radio broadcasts of comedians, singers, classical concerts,

By the early 1930s, all Americans had to scrounge for meals. New York soup kitchen, 1931.

soap operas, serials, movie and literary adaptations, quiz shows, and anything else that the market would bear—all on just three national networks. In 1939, two-thirds of the public went to the movies at least once a week. Popular songs were at their peak: every week Tin Pan Alley companies published new tunes by Gershwin, Kern, Arlen, Rodgers, Berlin, or Porter, and competed to get singers and orchestras to perform them. All the entertainment branches intersected, however distrustful they had been of each other.

A swing tune might be blasted over a restaurant's jukebox or on a late-night radio broadcast; it might be sung in the soundtrack of a movie or performed live in a nightclub or theater. It was this commercial buzz that made jazz-as-popular-music possible. Musicians poured into the field from all over, and as competition for the best jobs increased, musical standards rose precipitously. A sideman was now expected to play his instrument flawlessly, sight-read efficiently, and improvise convincingly. Dance bands offered steady work at a respectable salary, making music one of the few skilled crafts open to African Americans.

Still, swing was situated on the fault line of race. Its dance steps were worked out on the floor of black ballrooms, and its orchestral arrangements mimicked the call and response of black churches. Yet most of the money went into white pockets, and many black musicians felt that their music had been "stolen"—a feeling that would later help to fuel the postwar musical revolution known as bebop.

Though much of white America was dancing to an African American beat, whites were not especially interested in the music's origins. How many knew that "Stompin' at the Savoy" referred to a Harlem dance palace, or that Duke Ellington coined the word "swing" three years before Benny Goodman made it an American byword, or that much of Goodman's music was crafted for him by Fletcher Henderson and Edgar Sampson, the composer-arranger for Chick Webb's immensely influential Harlem-based band, or that much of their after-school "jive" talk was black slang? Blacks and whites could play together in jam sessions, but racially mixed bands were no more tolerated than integrated army units. Swing would help to change that.

Swing and Dance

At the core of swing is its groove: a steady, unaccented four-beats-to-the-bar foundation, perfect for dancing. This was not in itself new. We hear the same groove in records by Louis Armstrong; we even hear it emerging in passages by Jelly Roll Morton's Red Hot Peppers. But in the early 1930s—when Ellington issued his dictum "It Don't Mean a Thing (if It Ain't Got That Swing)"—the four-beat groove became firmly established as the standard for hot dance music.

The swing dance style emerged from New York's Savoy Ballroom, which **The Savoy** opened for business in 1926. The Savoy was an enormous space, filling an entire block in Harlem. Like other new dance halls, it offered a luxurious environment for a modest fee. Entering by the marble staircase, dancers saw "fancy wall decorations all over, thick patterned carpets on the floor, soft benches for sitting, round tables for drinking, and a heavy brass railing all around the long, polished dance floor." Although the Savoy was most closely associated with the big band led by drummer Chick Webb, his orchestra often engaged in "battles" with other bands, the two alternating sets on opposite sides of

Two dancers in the midst of executing a daring "air step" at the Savoy Ballroom in Harlem, during the early 1940s.

the hall. Harlem was proud of the Savoy, and opened its doors to white visitors from downtown and around the world; but unlike the Cotton Club, its primary constituency was the black neighborhood surrounding it.

The Savoy dance style came to be known as the Lindy Hop—after Charles Lindbergh, whose 1927 flight across the Atlantic signified a thrilling triumph for youth and ambition in the Jazz Age. The steady four-four beat opened up all kinds of possibilities; in one professional's opinion, a good dancer "takes the unvarying accent, and dances *against* it." The new dance was more "African": lower to the ground, demanding flexibility in the knee and hip joints. There was also greater room for improvisation. While the fox-trot or waltz insisted that couples remain linked arm-in-arm, the Lindy Hop featured "breakaways" where the partners could separate at arm's length to execute their own steps. The best dancers began adding new acrobatic variations, including "air steps," in which the female was thrown heedlessly (but always with grace) over her partner's shoulders. White observers were amazed. Author Carl Van Vechten, who watched safely from the sidelines, described its movements as "epileptic," but added that "to observe the Lindy Hop being performed at first induces gooseflesh, and second, intense excitement, akin to religious mania."

Rhythm section

To help bands adjust to the new groove, major changes were made in the rhythm section. While the bass drum continued to play a rock-solid four-beat pulse, the tuba, commonly used in large dance bands of the 1920s, was replaced by the string bass. During the early years of recording, the tuba was able to project a clear, huffing sound. But the string bass had always been a specialty of New Orleans, and many players, including Wellman Braud in Duke Ellington's band, showed that the instrument had a special percussive flavor when the strings were given a pizzicato "slap." Change came gradually in the late 1920s, once word got around about how well the string bass worked. Tuba players realized that they'd better switch instruments if they wanted to keep working in dance bands.

The banjo, with its loud and raucous tone, was replaced with the guitar, which provided a more subtle, secure pulsation (*chunk-chunk*) in the foundation rhythm. As the saying went, the guitar was more felt than heard. Listeners experienced the combined sound of bass, guitar, and drums as a sonic force that rippled through and beyond cavernous dance halls. "If you were on the first floor, and the dance hall was upstairs," Count Basie remembered, "that was what you would hear, that steady *rump, rump, rump, rump* in that medium tempo."

Arrangements

To fit the new groove, arrangers learned to write elaborate lines for an entire section, harmonized in block chords, called *soli*. Arrangements could also arise spontaneously out of oral practice. This approach was especially popular in Kansas City, but even in New York, where bands prided themselves on their musical literacy, musicians could take improvised riffs and harmonize them on the spot. The result, known as a **head arrangement**, was an unwritten arrangement created by the entire band. One musician compared it to child's play—"a lot of kids playing in the mud, having a big time."

PHOTO BY CHARLES PETERSON, COURTESY OF DON PETERSON

Fletcher Henderson, whose arrangements featuring call-and-response riffs helped to launch the Swing Era, gathered some of his all-stars for a reunion performance at Café Society, 1941. Left to right: J. C. Higginbotham, Buster Bailey, Sandy Williams (behind Bailey), Henderson (at piano), "Big Sid" Catlett, John Kirby, Henry Red Allen, Benny Carter, Russell Procope.

Both kinds of arrangements, written and unwritten, could be heard in the hundreds of 1930s records by Fletcher Henderson, whose "King Porter Stomp"—derived from one strain of a piano piece by Jelly Roll Morton, now shorn of its original two-beat rhythm and march/ragtime form—became an exemplary anthem for the entire era. Henderson emerged as swing's most representative arranger. His genius for rhythmic swing and melodic simplicity was so effective that it inspired countless imitations. He was fond of short, memorable riffs in call and response: saxophones responding to trumpets, for example. He would write only a few choice choruses and leave the remainder of the arrangement open for solos accompanied by discreet, long-held chords or short riffs. The final climactic chorus, often known as a **shout chorus**, would dissolve the piece in an ecstatic wail.

🎧 "Blue Lou"

The early Henderson band was dramatically effective in person: "We used to rock the walls," remembered Coleman Hawkins. But it was notoriously imperfect in the studio. Some of the best-known records from the early 1930s sounded, according to Hawkins, "like cats and dogs fighting." By 1936, the band had perfected its public presentation, and is in particularly splendid form on "Blue Lou."

The piece was composed by Edgar Sampson, a saxophonist with the Henderson band who became an arranger for Henderson and later for Benny Goodman (among his tunes are "Stompin' at the Savoy" and "Don't Be That Way"). It was arranged in the Henderson style by Fletcher's brother Horace, who oriented it toward the band's chief soloists: the brilliant trumpeter Roy Eldridge and one of Coleman Hawkins's most brilliant followers on tenor saxophone, Chu Berry (see Chapter 9).

Like many swing tunes, "Blue Lou" is built around a simple idea. The tune is in major, but the opening riff (a descending two-note figure) introduces a flatted scale degree from the minor mode. That peculiarity gives the piece its tension, and gives musically astute soloists an idea to use in their harmonic improvisation—as Chu Berry does at the beginning of his solo, where he mimics the opening riff, and as Roy Eldridge does in the last eight bars of his solo, where the dissonant flatted note is blasted at the top of his range.

Although "Blue Lou" begins with a relaxed two-beat feeling, the four-four dance groove gradually takes over. The first chorus introduces the original tune (note how the tune is expanded in the second **A** section into an elaborate *soli*), while the fourth (and last) chorus deforms it through ecstatic starts and stops. But the piece doesn't end there: with half a minute to go, there is a sudden modulation to the unusual key of A major (notoriously difficult for brass instruments). The new sixteen-bar section doesn't last long, but its presence suggests that this arrangement may have been flexible. Perhaps the drum stroke that precedes the modulation was a cue to follow in case the band wanted to keep dancers on the floor. Eldridge's solo at the end sounds as though it could have gone on forever.

🎧 blue lou

FLETCHER HENDERSON AND HIS ORCHESTRA
Dick Vance, Joe Thomas, Roy Eldridge, trumpets; Fernando Arbello, Ed Cuffee, trombones; Buster Bailey, Scoops Carey, alto saxophones; Elmer Williams, Chu Berry, tenor saxophones; Horace Henderson, piano; Bob Lessey, guitar; John Kirby, bass; Sidney Catlett, drums

- Label: Vocalion/OKeh 3211
- Date: 1936
- Style: big-band swing
- Form: 32-bar popular song (**A A B A**)

What to listen for:
- two-note riff at beginning, echoed in trumpet (chorus 2) and tenor saxophone (chorus 3) solos
- *soli* by saxophones in chorus 1 and by trumpets in chorus 4
- modulation to new key and new 16-bar tune at chorus 5

CHORUS 1

0:00	**A**	The tune begins immediately with the saxophones playing a simple yet dissonant two-note **riff**, colored with a note borrowed from the **minor mode**.
0:01		The saxophone section is immediately answered by the brass, with short chords.
0:05		The saxophones continue with a *soli*—a simple syncopated melody.
0:09	**A**	The chord progression is repeated, but the saxophones now play a complicated *soli* in the style of an improvisation.
0:19	**B**	On the bridge, the tune **modulates** to a new key. The saxophone section plays another simple riff, answered by brief chords from the brass.
0:29	**A**	Return of the opening two-note riff.

CHORUS 2

0:38	**A**	Eldridge takes a dominating trumpet solo, jumping quickly from his lower to his highest register. Behind him, the saxophone section plays jumpy background riffs or sustained chords.

0:48	**A**	
0:57	**B**	On muted trombone, Cuffee plays a **melodic paraphrase** of chorus 1's bridge.
1:06	**A**	Searching for a dramatic reentry, Eldridge begins in his highest register, playing the first few dissonant notes slightly out of tune.

CHORUS 3

1:16	**A**	Berry, on tenor saxophone, begins his solo with the opening two-note riff. Underneath him, the brass section swells in volume on background harmonies.
1:25	**A**	
1:35	**B**	As Berry increases in intensity, the bass finally begins playing a **walking-bass** line.
1:44	**A**	

CHORUS 4

1:53	**A**	The brass section plays a simpler *soli*, with short **staccato** notes, opening up a lot of space.
2:03	**A**	
2:12	**B**	Berry returns to take an eight-bar solo, accompanied only by the rhythm section.
2:22	**A**	As if interrupting, the trumpets reenter on a new variation (of the original two-note riff).

CHORUS 5 (NEW TUNE: 16-bar A A)

2:31	**A**	Signaled by a drum shot, the tune suddenly modulates to a new key, A major, offering a new melody over a new harmonic progression. The bass returns to a (mostly) two-beat feel.
2:41	**A**	

CODA

2:50		The band repeats a short, four-measure harmonic figure.
2:54		As the figure is taken up by the saxophones, Eldridge takes a muted solo.
3:03		Eldridge's solo is cut short by a brief cadence figure, ending the piece.

▪ BENNY GOODMAN (1909–1986)

In the early 1930s, the music industry resembled the nation by being as firmly divided by race as ever. "Hot" music was known to be a black specialty. White musicians drawn to jazz had to confront the fact that much of their best music would be played not on the bandstand but only for fun, at after-hours jam sessions. Future swing bandleaders like Artie Shaw, Glenn Miller, and Tommy and Jimmy Dorsey gravitated toward jazz, mastered it, and added their own innovations—but most of their jobs found them playing long nights of demanding, uninspiring arrangements in genteel dance bands and radio orchestras while dreaming of getting away to play some real jazz. That changed with the astonishing breakthrough of the Benny Goodman orchestra.

Goodman grew up in the slums of Chicago, where his father, a recent immigrant from Warsaw, worked in the stockyards. The boy showed a prodigious talent on the clarinet, which gave him a way out of menial labor. By the 1920s, he was an elegant soloist with a decided penchant for the blues, distinguishing himself in bands and on records with musicians inclined toward jazz, from bandleader and drummer Ben Pollack to vaudeville showman and sentimental clarinetist Ted Lewis.

Goodman moved to New York, where his tastes led him to create a band that would bridge the gap between the jazz he loved and the commercial realities he had to heed. Taking his cue from vocalist Mildred Bailey, who advised him to "get a Harlem book" of arrangements, he hired some of the best underemployed black arrangers in the business: Benny Carter, Edgar Sampson, and Fletcher Henderson, who was struggling to hold his own band together and glad of the extra cash.

Let's Dance!

In 1935, Goodman's band was featured as the "hot" orchestra on a national radio program broadcast from New York, *Let's Dance!*—one of three bands that played consecutive sets before a live audience. Benny's band went on last, when most New Yorkers were asleep. When the band went on a national tour that May, its reception seemed to get worse with each city, reaching a nadir in Salt Lake City and Denver; at that point, his management suggested that they cancel the rest of the tour. But Benny persevered and, in August, arrived at the Palomar Ballroom in Los Angeles. He opened with one of the mild pieces that the dance hall owners had been insisting on; the audience of young people looked puzzled. Goodman then decided that if he was going to die, he would die playing the music he cared about—he called for one of the Henderson arrangements, and before the band had played four bars, the place went crazy.

No one had taken into account the fact that those late-night broadcasts, when he was allowed to play jazz because few people were listening, were airing in prime time on the West Coast. He had inadvertently created a fan base, and when they heard him go into "King Porter Stomp," the kids cheered in recognition. Goodman's swing repertory suddenly found its audience. Through their vigorous, almost violent enthusiasm for this new Harlem-based sound, white teenagers awakened the music industry and launched the Swing Era. By the time he returned to New York, he was the hottest commodity in show business.

The quartet led by Benny Goodman brought racial integration to the public and invaluable opportunities to its members. Within a few years, each musician—pianist Teddy Wilson, vibraphonist Lionel Hampton, and drummer Gene Krupa—had become a bandleader. New York's Paramount Theater, 1937.

FRANK DRIGGS COLLECTION

Goodman's band blended his swing rhythms with up-to-date arrangements of current pop songs. The first chorus would be recognizable enough to satisfy Tin Pan Alley, even as the rest transported its listeners into jazz. As historian James Maher remembered: "He arrived with 'Blue Skies.' . . . I mean, everybody knew Irving Berlin! So we were home free." Goodman managed to both satisfy the jitterbugs and make swing acceptable to the cultured middle classes. One of his most memorable achievements was to bring jazz and its audience to New York's Carnegie Hall, a citadel of musical respectability, in January 1938. The musicians may have felt out of place (like a "whore in church," as trumpeter Harry James described it), but the band's rousing success cemented jazz's place in contemporary American culture.

Teddy Wilson, the cool and elegant pianist with the Benny Goodman Quartet, briefly led his own big band in the late 1930s.

The Goodman Trio and Quartet

Goodman also pioneered the return of small groups, including a trio with the same instrumentation (clarinet, piano, drums) that Jelly Roll Morton had once used, recasting them as a kind of swing chamber music—relaxed and spontaneous, yet highly polished and refined. The most remarkable thing about Goodman's trio, beyond the music, was that it was integrated—not a big deal on records, but a landmark in concert. Goodman had bonded musically with a dazzling young pianist, Teddy Wilson, and after the Palomar, he had the clout to include black musicians as a regular part of his shows. Yet for Goodman, this was not about making a social statement. He was simply, by all accounts, determined to play with musicians who stimulated him.

Teddy Wilson

Teddy Wilson's role model was Earl Hines, whom he admired for his superb stride technique. But where Hines was breathtakingly daring in his improvisation, Wilson's style was smooth and polished, cool and controlled even at high speed. Goodman compromised with segregation by presenting Wilson not as a full member of the band but as a "special guest," playing only with what was called the Benny Goodman Trio (the third member was drummer Gene Krupa). Within a few years, Goodman's "band-within-the-band" had been widely imitated in the industry by Cab Calloway (the Cab Jivers), Artie Shaw (the Gramercy Five), Tommy Dorsey (the Clambake Seven), and Woody Herman (the Woodchoppers), among others.

Lionel Hampton

The trio expanded to a quartet when Goodman added Lionel Hampton in 1936. Hampton was originally a drummer who had played with Louis Armstrong's big band in the early 1930s. At a recording session, Armstrong rolled a vibraphone out of the shadows and asked Hampton to play it. A new instrument at the time, the vibraphone uses rotating discs and amplification to enhance the sound of a metal xylophone. Within a few years, Hampton shifted to the vibes as his main instrument. His extroverted energy, combined with the histrionic glamour of Gene Krupa, was a crucial part of the quartet's popular appeal. After leaving Goodman in the early 1940s to form his own band, Hampton carried his reckless energy into rhythm and blues, ultimately linking jazz with rock and roll.

🎧 "Dinah"

"Dinah," a thirty-two-bar **A A B A** pop song composed in 1925, first became popular in Goodman's teenage years, and might have had a short shelf life like most tunes, lasting no more than six months. But jazz musicians were attracted to its harmonic structure, which was similar to that of "I Got Rhythm": an opening **A** section firmly in the tonic, followed by a bridge with more elaborate harmonic movement. "Dinah" became an evergreen, or **standard**—a permanent addition to the jazz repertory.

In the Goodman Quartet's 1936 recording, the mood is exuberant and playful, even bewildering: during Hampton's introduction, it's virtually impossible to hear where the downbeat is. The four musicians play in an informal jam-session spirit, exercising their freedom to listen and interact spontaneously. In the first **A** section, Goodman plays the melody with delicacy and circumspection; but in the bridge, he obliterates it in a lengthy string of fast notes. When Hampton plays in the second chorus, he shifts between simple riff figures and complicated harmonic substitutions of his own devising.

The performance heats up steadily, as it might in an impromptu jam session. Krupa begins with a steady two-beat foundation, but soon barges in with his snare drum and tom-tom accents. Goodman's later improvisations have little to do with the original melody. In his brief solo spot, Wilson shows the kind of delicate filigree he could weave around the harmonies of the bridge. At the end, the three soloists coincide in a kind of ecstatic polyphony. It's not chaotic, however, and the ending is tightly controlled.

LISTENING GUIDE 17

🎧 dinah

BENNY GOODMAN QUARTET
Benny Goodman, clarinet; Lionel Hampton, vibraphone; Teddy Wilson, piano; Gene Krupa, drums

- Label: Victor 25398
- Date: 1936
- Style: small combo swing
- Form: 32-bar popular song (**A A B A**)

What to listen for:
- Goodman's melodic paraphrase of this jam-session standard
- exuberant solo improvisation (choruses 2–4)
- polyphonic improvisation (chorus 5)
- tightly controlled ending

INTRODUCTION

| 0:00 | | Hampton begins at a brisk tempo, playing a short introductory passage on the vibes. He's joined seconds later by Krupa on drums. |

CHORUS 1

0:04	**A**	The rest of the band enters. Goodman takes the lead on the clarinet, delicately paraphrasing the original melody. Behind him, Krupa thumps a two-beat pattern on the bass drum.
0:12	**A**	Wilson quietly plays a contrasting accompaniment.
0:20	**B**	As Goodman begins to improvise, Wilson plays a simpler **stride** accompaniment.
0:28	**A**	Goodman returns to the original melody.

CHORUS 2

0:36	**A**	Hampton takes a solo, prompting Krupa to play **polyrhythms** on the tom-tom drums.
0:43	**A**	As Hampton warms up, his line becomes a long, continuous string of even eighth notes, occasionally punctuated by Krupa's quick drum strokes.
0:51	**B**	
0:59	**A**	

CHORUS 3

1:07	A	Hampton divides a **cross-rhythm** between his two hands.
1:13		Krupa plays a disorienting snare-drum accent just before his bass drum stroke.
1:15	A	
1:22	B	
1:30	A	To conclude his solo, Hampton plays a few simple notes polyrhythmically.

CHORUS 4

1:37	A	Goodman begins his solo with a bluesy phrase.
1:45	A	
1:53	B	Wilson plays a discreet solo over the bridge.
1:58		At the end of the bridge, Wilson embellishes the chord progression with a **harmonic substitution**.
2:00	A	With a strikingly high entrance, Goodman concludes his solo.

CHORUS 5

2:08	A	The three soloists play together: Wilson's riffs are responded to by Goodman, who paraphrases parts of "Dinah" before abandoning the melody in improvisation.
2:16	A	
2:23	B	**Break:** Hampton plays an unaccompanied solo, interrupted every two beats by a brief chord from Wilson.
2:29		Krupa reenters, followed by Goodman.
2:31	A	The entire band plays an untrammeled polyphonic conclusion.
2:38		The piece ends discreetly with a bass drum thump.

JOHN HAMMOND AND OTHER FANS

The interracial Goodman Quartet was encouraged by the most influential jazz entrepreneur and activist of the period, John Hammond (1910–1987). A list of artists whose careers Hammond helped would include Bessie Smith, Fletcher Henderson, Goodman, Billie Holiday, Count Basie, and Charlie Christian—and in a later generation, Bob Dylan, Aretha Franklin, George Benson, and Bruce Springsteen. He was no musician (although he was an amateur violinist for a while), but his intense commitment and political convictions make him a significant figure in jazz history.

Born into a wealthy New York family, Hammond developed two passions. The first was a love of black jazz and folk music, which to him seemed infinitely superior to any other kind. "There was no white pianist to compare with Fats Waller," he said, "no white band as good as Fletcher Henderson's, no blues singer like Bessie Smith." The second was a hatred of racial injustice. Although raised on prejudice typical of his time (his mother once explained to him that black people were "different" because "their skulls harden when they are twelve"), he became outraged by inequality.

Benny Goodman (wearing a sweater vest) converses with his bespectacled guitarist, Charlie Christian, during a 1940 recording session for Columbia Records. John Hammond is seated in the left corner.

Hammond used a long-running association with Columbia Records to champion the music he admired. He became a ubiquitous figure in nightclubs, standing out with his conservative crewcut and uninhibited enthusiasm. He made possible hundreds of recording dates for his latest discoveries. Some black musicians did not relish his overbearing personality—he was criticized for his patriarchal attitude. But few nonmusicians came close to Hammond in shaping the course of jazz.

Hammond was the most conspicuous and connected member of a new generation of ardent fans. The Swing Era saw the emergence of jazz record collectors—young men of privileged backgrounds who combed through discarded vinyl at flea markets and junk shops looking for forgotten old recordings. To distinguish one recording from another, they duly noted all the pertinent information: personnel, dates, matrix numbers (the codes inscribed on the disc that identify a particular master disc), release numbers. This data formed the beginnings of record classification, and was eventually collated and published **Discographies** ▶ as **discographies**—an indispensable source for researchers. "Hot Clubs" were formed in towns throughout the country, bringing together fans and sponsoring public jam sessions. To suit their reading tastes, new mass-market magazines like *Down Beat* and *Metronome* and smaller fan-based journals like *Jazz Information* emerged. From their pages came the first American jazz critics, among them Leonard Feather, George T. Simon, and Hammond himself.

A FEW MAJOR SWING BANDS (AMONG MANY)

As the dance business boomed, the number of new bands exploded. By 1940, there were hundreds of bands—some leaning toward conventional dance music, others specializing in hard-driving swing, and still others who worked both sides of the divide (Tommy Dorsey, a limited improviser but innovative trombonist and hard-line bandleader with an infallible ear for talent, was especially good at this). Benny Goodman's own band was a seedbed for bandleaders: they emerged from his trumpet section (Bunny Berigan and Harry James), saxophone section (Vido Musso and Toots Mondello), and quartet (Wilson, Krupa, and Hampton). A few major figures like Fats Waller and Art Tatum continued to pilot small groups, but as most of the established figures, including Louis Armstrong and Earl Hines, switched to big bands, a wave of orchestral might rolled over the music industry—for a few years, it was easier for a booking agency to tour a big band than a small one.

■ ARTIE SHAW (1910–2004)

One of the most gifted and eccentric figures in jazz history was Goodman's bête noir, Artie Shaw, a rival as leader and clarinetist. Like Goodman, Shaw was a child of the ghetto. Born to Jewish immigrants on the Lower East Side of Manhattan, he quickly discovered that his prodigious skill on saxophone and clarinet was a ticket into the world of studio bands and dance orchestras. By 1930, he was studying with pianist Willie "the Lion" Smith in Harlem and listening to Armstrong, Hines, and the influential Chicago-based clarinetist Jimmie Noone, who had made a much-admired series of small-group recordings with Hines.

During the early 1930s, Shaw lived a double life, working studio gigs like the CBS radio orchestra (playing for what he disdained as "soap and cereal

Artie Shaw, who dropped his civilian life to join the service during World War II, crowds his Navy Band onto the deck of the *U.S.S. Saratoga*, 1944.

FRANK DRIGGS COLLECTION

programs") and jamming in Harlem with the Lion and others. "I was actually living the life of a Negro musician," he recalled, "adopting Negro values and attitudes, and accepting the Negro out-group point of view not only about music but life in general." A self-taught man who read extensively and stored everything in his steel-trap memory, he hoped to earn a few thousand dollars in music so that he could quit and write a book. To his surprise, he became astronomically successful after the band he formed in 1938 sold millions of copies of "Begin the Beguine." He claimed to hate the fame, but celebrity had its privileges: he was married eight times, including to movie queens Lana Turner, Ava Gardner, and Evelyn Keyes. His personal life, musical success, and dark good looks kept him on the pages of Hollywood magazines.

Yet he disdained the jitterbugging fans who screamed with wild enthusiasm and demanded to hear his hits again and again, played exactly like the record. Shaw also protested against the mute acceptance of segregation, and fought it by hiring black arrangers, singers (including Billie Holiday and Lena Horne), and musicians—notably Roy Eldridge, who had already made social history by becoming the first black musician to sit in a white trumpet section (not as a "special guest") in Gene Krupa's band.

Periodically, Shaw walked away from his band and show business—always a front-page story—to brood in silence, only to return to even greater acclaim. Finally, in 1954, after completing a superb series of small-group recordings, he retired from playing altogether. He published a memoir, novellas, and short stories, and spent much time trying to explain to bewildered fans how a man could abandon such an extraordinary talent.

VOICES

Roy Eldridge, one of the top trumpet players of the Swing Era (see Chapter 9), was a black soloist in otherwise white bands led by Gene Krupa and Artie Shaw. Years later, he explained why he would never cross racial barriers again:

> We arrived in one town and the rest of the band checks in. I can't get into their hotel, so I keep my bags and start riding around looking for another place, where someone's supposed to have made a reservation for us . . . then the clerk, when he sees that I'm the Mr. Eldridge the reservation was made for, suddenly discovers that one of their regular tenants just arrived and took the last available room. . . .

One night the tension got so bad I flipped. I could feel it right up to my neck while I was playing "Rockin' Chair"; I started trembling, ran off the stand, and threw up. They carried me to the doctor's. I had a hundred-and-five fever; my nerves were shot. . . . Later on, when I was with Artie Shaw, I went to a place where we were supposed to play a dance, and they wouldn't even let me in the place. "This is a white dance," they said, and there was my name right outside, Roy "Little Jazz" Eldridge. . . . Man, when you're on the stage, you're great, but as soon as you come off, you're nothing. It's not worth the glory, not worth the money, not worth anything. Never again!

🎧 "Star Dust"

Shaw's various bands reflected his restless temperament. At times he wanted to satisfy his fans' desire for "the loudest band in the whole goddamn world." At others, he attempted to bridge the gap between jazz and classical music. His first claim to fame came in 1936 when he wrote, for the musicians' community, a piece for clarinet, string quartet (two violins, viola, cello), and rhythm. In 1940, now a celebrity, he enriched his swing band with a nine-piece string section, intelligently used by arranger Lennie Hayton.

"Star Dust," which dates from this period, is a restrained and lyrical performance, focusing on the haunting melody written by Hoagy Carmichael in 1927. The soloists treat the tune with love and ingenuity. In the opening chorus, trumpeter Billy Butterfield uses a rich vibrato and lyrical sense of embellishment to paraphrase the famous melody. Subsequent soloists explore the tune's mood of romantic sentiment in their own creations. Jack Jenney's brief but melting trombone solo is a highlight, notable for his expressive leap up an octave into the

---

LISTENING GUIDE 18

🎧 star dust

ARTIE SHAW AND HIS ORCHESTRA

Artie Shaw, clarinet; George Wendt, J. Cathcart, Billy Butterfield, trumpets; Jack Jenney, Vernon Brown, trombones; Bud Bassey, Neely Plumb, alto saxophones; Les Robinson, Jerry Jerome, tenor saxophones; Johnny Guarnieri, piano; Al Hendrickson, guitar; Jud DeNaut, bass; Nick Fatool, drums; T. Boardman, T. Klages, B. Bower, Bob Morrow, Al Beller, E. Lamas, violins; A. Harshman, K. Collins, violas; F. Goerner, cello

- Label: Victor 27230
- Date: 1940
- Style: big-band swing
- Form: 32-bar popular song (**A B A C**)

What to listen for:
- big-band instrumentation (with strings)
- Shaw's virtuosic paraphrase of the tune
- Jenney's trombone solo

INTRODUCTION

0:00   Tentatively holding out each note, an unaccompanied trumpet soloist (Butterfield) plays the first few notes of the tune.

CHORUS 1

0:05   **A**   With a gentle slide, he signals the band to enter. Underneath, the saxophone section plays long-held chords in a slow, measured tempo.

0:14   Immediately after a dramatic chord change, the string section emerges from the background.

0:27   **B**

0:49   **A**   The string section plays an elaborate variation on the main melody.

1:10   **C**   The trumpet returns on a high note, while the accompaniment returns a few seconds later (1:14).

1:21   For the final statement of the tune, the entire band enters.

INTERLUDE

1:29   The band **modulates** for the next chorus.

CHORUS 2

1:40   **A**   Shaw enters for his clarinet solo, with a highly decorated version of the melody that moves into **double-time**.

2:02   **B**   As Shaw begins exploring the chords through **harmonic improvisation**, his line becomes a string of eighth notes.

2:13   Shaw's line climaxes on a dramatic high note.

2:25   **A**   Jenney enters on trombone, playing a beautiful solo with subtle ornaments.

2:47   **C**   With the strings hovering in the background, the band takes over the melody. The drummer underscores the excitement with cymbals.

2:57   The last phrase is signaled by a sharp, syncopated accent.

3:01   **Break:** the band drops out, leaving Shaw to conclude the melody unaccompanied.

CODA

3:04   Shaw continues his line, improvising harmonically.

3:07   On a rising series of chords, the band reenters.

3:13   The string section emerges with its own **dissonant** harmonic progression, which finally resolves (by 3:18) to the **tonic** chord.

3:23   The strings have the last word, adding a decorative skein of dissonance over the final chord.

trombone's upper register. So is Shaw's. He was a brilliant technician on clarinet, and a fluid and supple improviser. This solo is finely sculpted, suggesting the reach of a great violinist when it climaxes in the stratosphere on a high A.

◾ JIMMIE LUNCEFORD (1902–1947)

Jimmie Lunceford fit few swing stereotypes—like Paul Whiteman, with whose father Lunceford had studied as a high school student in Denver, he appeared onstage as a baton-waving conductor, not as a star instrumentalist. As a youth, he studied saxophone as well as guitar and trombone, but in his maturity he never played his favorite instrument, the alto saxophone, with his band. He was instead a stern taskmaster and disciplinarian who brought an air of the school classroom with him onto the bandstand.

A fastidious, athletic man, Lunceford felt at ease in positions of authority. Nicknamed "the Professor," he drilled his band like a martinet, insisting on impeccable appearance ("he checked their socks," one bandleader remembered)

The genial Jimmie Lunceford wields his baton at the Fiesta Danceteria in New York, 1940. At the microphone is James "Trummy" Young, a trombonist who also sang on tunes like "'Tain't What You Do (It's the Way That You Do It)."

FRANK DRIGGS COLLECTION

and exacting musicianship through endless rehearsals. He refused to accept sloppy behavior, demanding that his musicians adhere to the three P's: punctuality, precision, and presentation. The result was a band that embodied the best in black middle-class dignity, with Lunceford at its center. "Until I met Jimmie, I'd never met anybody of whom I felt any intellectual fear," recalled his arranger Sy Oliver. "The musicians don't all realize it, but that man raised them. He changed their lives."

🎧 "Annie Laurie"

Lunceford demanded professionalism on every level. He had the slickest-looking band of the day, with smartly tailored musicians waving derby mutes and twirling their instruments while playing with an exactitude that set standards for ensemble virtuosity. He also had an unusual sense of whimsy that

VOICES

With the gradual decline of vaudeville, dance bands were often thrust onto the stage to pick up the slack, and the Lunceford band was always eager to put on a show. Trombonist Eddie Durham described one at the Apollo Theater:

> They would come out and play a dance routine. The Shim Sham Shimmy was popular then and six of the guys would come down and dance to it—like a tap dance, crossing their feet and sliding. Then Willie Smith would put his bonnet on and sing a sort of nursery rhythm. [Trumpeter] Eddie Tompkins hit the high notes and did a Louis Armstrong deal. Then they had a Guy Lombardo bit and a Paul Whiteman bit—see, they imitated bands. The lights would go down next and they'd all lay down their horns and come out to sing as a glee club. . . . The next number, they'd be throwing their horns and hats up to the ceiling. That was all novelty, and I liked it.

took its repertory to places few jazz bands traveled. "Annie Laurie" is a brilliant example of the band's individuality, and particularly of Sy Oliver's highly original style of arranging. Oliver (1910–1988), who also played trumpet and sang, was at a crossroads when he met with Lunceford in 1933. He considered giving up music and returning to school, but was so impressed by the band's accurate handling of his music that he signed up. Over the next six years, he wrote dozens of witty, imaginative charts, turning such unlikely tunes as "Organ Grinder's Swing" or "Put On Your Old Grey Bonnet" into swing masterworks.

Oliver insisted on the two-beat rhythmic feeling that became the band's signature: the music was written in four but executed in a manner to emphasize the backbeat. Dancers loved it. His writing combined unified trumpet **shakes** (quick trills) and trombone smears, baritone saxophone voice-leading, a vital bass line, and dynamic drumming. He applied all his techniques to the old ballad "Annie Laurie" (published in 1838)—a musical setting by Scottish composer Alicia Ann Spottiswood to a seventeenth-century love poem. Its dramatic octave leap in the first measure evokes the Scottish folk tradition, and it became a great favorite in America after P. T. Barnum presented the "Swedish Nightingale" Jenny Lind singing it. Oliver, adapting the melody into thirty-two-bar song form, treats it with respect, yet creates a swinging euphoria that recalls the polyphonic revelry of New Orleans jazz. The excitement is unrelenting, from the starting-in-the-middle beginning to the first **B** section, where a swooning high-note chord from the saxophones and Jimmy Crawford's forceful drums combine with the brasses to create an emotional flash fire; to the rip-snorting entrance by trombonist and singer James "Trummy" Young, the band's best-known soloist; to the thrilling climax.

In 1939, the popular bandleader and trombonist Tommy Dorsey hired Oliver as chief arranger for his band, which also recruited the young Frank Sinatra and the dazzling drummer Buddy Rich. After the war, Oliver became house arranger and producer at Decca Records—one of the first black executives at a major label. The Lunceford band continued to soar with young hotshot arrangers, notably Gerald Wilson and Billy Moore. After the leader's death, saxophonist Joe Thomas and pianist Eddie Wilcox tried to keep it going, but by 1948 the big-band era was over. Trummy Young went on to achieve international recognition as a member of Louis Armstrong's All-Stars.

🎧 Annie Laurie

JIMMIE LUNCEFORD AND HIS ORCHESTRA
Jimmie Lunceford, director; Eddie Tompkins, Paul Webster, trumpets; Sy Oliver, trumpet and arranger; Elmer Crumbley, Russell Bowles, James "Trummy" Young, trombones; Willie Smith, Earl Carruthers, Ted Buckner, Dan Grissom, Joe Thomas, saxophones; Edwin Wilcox, piano; Al Norris, guitar; Moses Allen, bass; Jimmy Crawford, drums

- Label: Decca 1569
- Date: 1937
- Style: big-band swing
- Form: 32-bar popular song (**A A B C**)

What to listen for:

- wit and precision of the Lunceford Orchestra
- Oliver's clever arrangement of a Scottish melody
- contrasting solos by Thomas and Young

INTRODUCTION

0:00   The performance begins at the tune's climax—the end of the bridge, where the melody is at its peak and the harmony at its most remote—and moves toward its final **cadence**.

CHORUS 1

0:14 **A** Playing in **block-chord** harmonies, the brass section transforms the traditional melody with jazzy **syncopation** and occasional blue notes.

0:23   At the end of the phrase, the saxophone section responds with a **riff**.

0:26 **A** The band repeats the opening phrase, but steers the conclusion toward a full cadence.

0:35   To signal the end, the entire band (including the drums) blasts out a series of chords.

0:37 **B** The trumpet section interacts with the saxophones and trombones.

0:43   Crawford signals intensity with cymbal crashes.

0:49 **C** The saxophones, followed by the brass, allow the melody to taper off.

0:57   Entering two bars early, Thomas begins his solo on tenor saxophone.

CHORUS 2

1:01 **A** Thomas plays the melody, accompanied by gentle riffs in the brass. A few seconds later, he shifts to harmonic improvisation.

1:12 **A** Broadening his tone with a wide vibrato, he plays blues phrases.

1:24 **B** The trombones play a simplified version of the melody, decorated by the brass section's intricate variations.

1:36 **C** Thomas reenters on a hoarse, guttural **blue note**.

1:44   With a dramatic flourish, Young announces his solo on trombone with fast, slurred fanfares.

CHORUS 3 (HALF CHORUS)

1:47 **A** Young's solo is another melodic paraphrase, with subtle rhythmic variations that fall between the beats. Underneath him, the saxophones play detached, rhythmic chords.

1:59 **A**

CHORUS 4

2:10 **A** The saxophones enter with a simple paraphrase of the melody.

2:17   They're answered by Webster, with a phrase reminiscent of Louis Armstrong.

2:22 **A** The band returns with a more syncopated version of the melody.

2:29   Webster answers with dramatic bursts into the trumpet's highest range.

2:34 **B** At the arrangement's climax, the trumpet, saxophone, and trombone sections interact with fury.

2:46 **C** The saxophones take the lead, followed closely by the brass.

CODA

2:55   Sparked by Crawford's drumming, the band returns to the opening of the Introduction.

2:57   As Crawford plays heavily on the **backbeat**, the saxophones play syncopated chords, alternating with a rising scale from the trombones.

3:07   The trombone line rises to the tonic, prompting a concluding series of chords.

The Lunceford band's downfall can be traced to the leader's stingy salaries, which cost him the loyalty of Oliver and several of his most noted sidemen, and his grueling work schedule. The sheer volume of touring was unbelievable: to give one example, the band played in Providence, Rhode Island, on one night; in Martinsburg, West Virginia, the next; and the following night in Clemson, South Carolina. Lunceford died at forty-five, of a heart attack while signing autographs.

■ GLENN MILLER (1904–1944)

As America entered the war, its most popular bandleader was Glenn Miller, an owl-eyed trombonist who brought swing firmly into mainstream entertainment. It was decidedly not Miller's intention to join the jazz canon. Instead, the unmistakable sound of his arrangements, with their lush blend of clarinet and saxophones, aimed straight at the white mainstream audience, who heard his music as the embodiment of the Swing Era and of modern pop music.

Miller grew up in a Midwestern household where he absorbed his parents' habits of discipline and self-control. As a teenager, he developed a taste for jazzy dance music, prompting him to drop out of college to become a musician. When he started his own dance band in 1938, Miller refused the path laid out by Goodman. He knew what his audiences wanted: unfiltered melodies, a smooth, danceable rhythm, and above all, a distinctive sound. To achieve the latter, he topped his saxophone section with a wide, pulsating clarinet (played by Willie Schwartz), creating a warm, mellifluous timbre that became his calling card. The sound can be heard on Miller's theme song, the lushly romantic "Moonlight Serenade," as well as on numerous other hit records ("A String of Pearls," "In the Mood") that dominated the charts in the early 1940s. Indeed, Miller's tunes were so popular that early in 1942, when shellac was limited, RCA-Victor scaled back production of all other records so that it could press millions of copies of "Chattanooga Choo Choo."

That same year, Miller became the best-known bandleader to offer his services to the armed forces. The enormous Glenn Miller Army Air Force Band featured forty-two musicians and combined strings and brass. Like

Seen here in 1943, at a British Air Force base, Glenn Miller leads his uniformed Army Air Force Band before a large audience with tents in the rear. A year later, his plane disappeared over the English Channel.

Paul Whiteman before him, Miller included jazz as part of an eclectic mixture that offered something for everybody. His disappearance in December 1944, when his plane flew over the English Channel and never landed, was mourned as a national tragedy. Decades later, it was discovered that he may have been killed by a U.S. bomber, dropping its unexploded munitions on Miller's unseen plane.

■ CAB CALLOWAY (1907–1994)

Cab Calloway was a curiously ambivalent icon of black culture during the Swing Era. To whites, he offered an entrée into the black ghetto: through his singing, with its suggestive use of slang, they could catch a glimpse of an alluring world of illicit drugs and sex. To blacks, he represented hope: he showed how a man with talent and ambition could rise to the top of the music business. He wowed the cats in New York's Harlem with his stylish, zoot-suited flair and straight hair, which invariably ended up falling over his forehead. Sammy Davis Jr. included himself among the thousands of black kids who, he said, jumped up and down before a mirror trying to get their hair to do that. The African American establishment was more impressed with his flaunted material success.

Calloway grew up in Baltimore in the black middle class. He studied classical singing, but in the evenings, unsuspected by his teacher (or his mother, who expected her son to become a lawyer like his father), he discovered the joys of singing jazz. In the late 1920s, Calloway formed his own band, the Alabamians, which he took to New York's Savoy Ballroom. His big break came in 1930, when the Cotton Club asked him to replace Duke Ellington.

The Cotton Club's staff songwriter Harold Arlen and lyricist Ted Koehler crafted new songs to match Calloway's exuberant personality with fantastic scenes meant to evoke Harlem's exotic underground. In "Kickin' the Gong Around" (a reference to opium and cocaine), Smokey Joe searches for his drug-addict girlfriend, Minnie. Calloway took that scenario a step further in "Minnie the Moocher," enriching the moody, minor-mode song with rhyming slang to turn Minnie into a powerful central character (the "toughest frail" with "a heart as big as a whale"). His performances of "Minnie" famously climaxed with a scat-singing call and response—as Cab's expressive wails of "hi-de-ho" were echoed by the band and audience.

Calloway was a fine singer, his voice ranging from a deep baritone to a high tenor. He was also a shrewd businessman who continually improved his band with the best musicians money could buy. He was unafraid to take his black band down South, where their New York hipness often attracted the hostile attention of racists ("We were not docile Negroes," he said). His band traveled in style, in its own Pullman car, with Calloway's lime-green Lincoln stashed in its cargo. "Cab was like a breath of fresh air," his bassist Milt Hinton remembered. "He said, 'I feel obligated to try to show these people that there's a better way of life—that entertainment is higher than this.'"

By the late 1930s, Calloway was deeply immersed in jazz. He hired the best upcoming soloists, including tenor saxophonist Chu Berry, drummer Cozy Cole, and the young trumpet wizard Dizzy Gillespie, who tormented Calloway with his modernist playing and zany antics. After Calloway's band folded in the late 1940s, he developed a solo act in nightclubs, and worked as an actor in movies and on Broadway. As late as 1980, at seventy-three in the movie *The Blues Brothers*, his every step radiated class and style.

As a commercial product, swing necessarily tended toward certain formulas, of which the Fletcher Henderson arranging style (riffs in call and response) was the most obvious. Anyone could imitate this style, it was said, and many did. Yet at the same time, swing allowed for individual creativity of a high order. In the next chapter, we consider the music of two bandleaders who were especially bold and influential in bending the rules of swing to their own advantage: the Kansas City swing style of Count Basie and the mature compositions of Duke Ellington.

ADDITIONAL LISTENING	
Fletcher Henderson	"Sugar Foot Stomp" (1925), "New King Porter Stomp" (1932)
Benny Goodman	"Blue Skies," "Stomping at the Savoy" (both 1938)
Artie Shaw	"Nightmare" (1937), "Begin the Beguine" (1938)
Jimmie Lunceford	"The Organ Grinder's Swing" (1936), "For Dancers Only" (1937), "'Tain't What You Do (It's the Way That You Do It)" (1939)
Glenn Miller	"Moonlight Serenade" (1938), "In the Mood" (1939)
Cab Calloway	"Minnie the Moocher" (1931)

ONLINE MULTIMEDIA RESOURCES AND REVIEW MATERIALS

Author Insight Videos

Scott DeVeaux discusses the business revolution brought about by Benny Goodman's breakthrough, swing as the soundtrack to the New Deal, why Goodman sought out Harlem arrangements for his swing band, women in swing bands, and territory bands.

Interactive Listening Guides

Fletcher Henderson, "Blue Lou"
Benny Goodman, "Dinah"
Artie Shaw, "Stardust"
Jimmie Lunceford, "Annie Laurie"

Jazz Concepts (audio and/or video demonstrations of terms covered here)

backbeat	harmonic improvisation	staccato
block chords	minor mode	swing
blue note	modulation	syncopation
break	polyrhythm	tonic
cadence	riff	walking bass
dissonance	shake	

- For quick reference, review the **Chapter Overview** and **Chapter Outline**.
- Take the online **Chapter** and **Listening Quizzes**.
- Use the online **Glossary** and **Flashcards** to review important terms.

8

COUNT BASIE
AND DUKE ELLINGTON

THE SOUTHWEST AND BOOGIE-WOOGIE

As their aristocratic nicknames suggest, two swing bandleaders—William "Count" Basie and Duke Ellington—tower over their contemporaries. People who know little about jazz have heard of them. They transcend the Swing Era, in part because they remained on the road so much longer than the others, but also because their music is intrinsic to the development of jazz. Yet without the Swing Era, Basie might never have come into his own, and Ellington almost certainly would not have enjoyed the commercial and artistic clout that generated his astonishing outpouring of masterpieces.

Although swing was a national music, one region was strong enough to pull that national sound in a new direction. In jazz parlance, the Southwest was not, as we would have it today, the desert regions north of Mexico, but rather the area south and west of the Mississippi, including Missouri, Oklahoma, and Texas, with its urban headquarters in Kansas City. African Americans had known about the Southwest since the end of the Civil War, when, seeking economic opportunity and social freedom, they began heading toward what they called "the territory."

The impact of the Southwest on the nation's musical taste is apparent in the rise of the blues piano style known as **boogie-woogie**. The provenance of boogie-woogie is

Count Basie accomplished the most with the least effort. Here we see his good humor in action, at the Newport Jazz Festival, 1955.

© HERMAN LEONARD PHOTOGRAPHY LLC

uncertain, but one early nickname—"fast Western"—suggests the Southwest, while other bits of oral evidence point to east Texas and Louisiana. The style spread rapidly during the 1920s, following the urbanizing trend of the Great Migration, and secured a home in the Midwest, especially in Kansas City and Chicago. As with ragtime, boogie-woogie was built on a firm rhythmic foundation in the left hand. But unlike ragtime, or stride, which turned the four-beat measure into a two-beat feeling by alternating bass notes and chords, boogie-woogie doubled the pace with fierce, rhythmic **ostinatos**. Known as "chains" for their repetitive quality, these patterns divide each beat in two, so that the four-beat measure now has an eight-beat pulse, a nonstop torrent of sound in the pianist's left hand. Against it, the right hand is free to play bluesy patterns in percussive cross-rhythms—rhythms that conflict with the underlying meter.

Rhythmic foundation

Boogie-woogie was a social music—tumultuous and inexpensive, perfect for dancing and blues singing. In speakeasies, hard-working pianists played through the night for a few dollars. Much as stride served as an ideal accompaniment at New York rent parties, boogie-woogie provided the preferred rhythmic punch in the Midwest. Like its later progeny, rock and roll, its thunderous sound cut through the tumult, spurring dancers onto the floor. The music found its way onto recordings in the 1920s (Meade Lux Lewis's "Honky Tonk Train Blues" in 1927, Clarence "Pine Top" Smith's "Pine Top's Boogie Woogie" in 1928), but in the early 1930s struggled to survive. It was too rhythmically complicated to transfer to the printed page, and record companies were cutting back sharply on black dance music.

Yet just a few years later, boogie-woogie made a sudden turnaround and became a craze with the white mainstream audience. This startling comeback can be credited to a revival of vernacular music, which began as a self-conscious attempt to publicize black folk traditions; its central figure, once again, was John Hammond. Having seen black dance music marketed successfully as swing, Hammond decided to go further: why not show the world how swing was based on neglected traditions, such as blues, gospel, and boogie-woogie? He scoured the countryside looking for performers and brought them together for a concert, "From Spirituals to Swing," held at Carnegie Hall in 1938, the same year as Benny Goodman's coup. For the first time, an audience heard the now-familiar sounds of swing juxtaposed with the Southern harmonica playing of blind Sonny Terry, the Chicago-style country blues of Big Bill Broonzy, and gospel by the Golden Gate Quartet and Sister Rosetta Tharpe. To represent boogie-woogie, Hammond hired Meade Lux Lewis and Albert Ammons from Chicago, and pianist Pete Johnson and singer Big Joe Turner from the Sunset Café in Kansas City. The concert program encouraged the audience to "forget you are in Carnegie Hall" and relax into the spirit of Kansas City.

In the wake of John Hammond's "From Spirituals to Swing" concert, Café Society offered its New York patrons the finest in boogie-woogie: Meade Lux Lewis, Big Joe Turner (with his face turned), Albert Ammons, Pete Johnson, 1939.

Soon boogie-woogie became mainstsream, as pianists everywhere were expected to learn its thumping rhythms. The Andrews Sisters sang a tune about "the boogie-woogie bugle boy of Company B" during World War II. The underground music of black Kansas City and Chicago had become part of the all-American soundtrack.

🎧 "It's All Right, Baby"

Pete Johnson had worked as a manual laborer (shining shoes among other jobs) before discovering that the piano could offer better money for less work. At a speakeasy where he earned $3 (plus tips) playing literally all night, he became famous for a hard-driving, percussive blues that seemed never to end. Big Joe Turner, a young man with an intensely powerful voice, worked across the room as the bartender, serving beer for $.15 in tin cans. Turner would sing from behind the bar, and occasionally step outside to the sidewalk to sing down the street—a method of luring in customers that he referred to as "calling the children home," much as Buddy Bolden and King Oliver had done in New Orleans. From about 1933, they performed regularly at the Sunset Café.

Johnson and Turner were not new to New York: Hammond had brought them east in 1936, hoping to drum up excitement for their music. But at the "From Spirituals to Swing" concert, they had to compress their loose, casual backroom flavor into a tight three minutes—as at a record session. Fortunately, they had done precisely that two years earlier with a recording of "Roll 'Em Pete," a number roughly recast as "It's All Right, Baby" at Carnegie. Turner seems right at home from the outset. After a long, languorous introductory phrase ("Well, it's all . . . right . . . then!"), he barks encouragement to Johnson and keeps lively time with his feet while singing the three-line blues stanzas. After several choruses of Johnson's percussive playing, Turner's words melt down to throaty shouts, serving as calls to Johnson's inventive responses. Not for nothing were Turner and singers like him often called blues shouters. This exhilarating performance captures, like few others, the ambience of Sunset Café craziness—until the business-like, abrupt ending makes it clear that the professionals were fully in charge all along.

LISTENING GUIDE 20

🎧 it's all right, baby

PETE JOHNSON AND BIG JOE TURNER

Pete Johnson, piano; Big Joe Turner, vocal

- Label: *From Spirituals to Swing: 1938 & 1939 Carnegie Hall Concerts* (Vanguard 169-171-2)
- Date: 1938
- Style: boogie-woogie
- Form: 12-bar blues

What to listen for:

- solid, rocking rhythm
- Kansas City–style boogie-woogie piano: 12-bar blues, left-hand ostinato
- powerful and varied blues singing
- call and response between voice and piano

CHORUS 1

0:00   Johnson opens with a dramatic series of repeated chords on the piano.

0:05   (sung) *"Well, it's all . . . right . . . then!"*
       As the harmony shifts to IV, Johnson begins a boogie-woogie **ostinato.** Turner enters with a broad, sweeping phrase.

0:09   (spoken) *"Yeah, papa."*
        While commenting on Johnson's solid groove, Turner adds an additional rhythmic layer
        by tapping his feet.

CHORUS 2

0:14   *"That's all right, baby, that's all right for you.*
        [unintelligible] *for you, babe, that's the way you do."*
        Turner sings his first full chorus, full of subtle variations in rhythm. His first line begins
        on the **offbeat**, then shifts to the **downbeat**. Johnson's left hand continues the ostinato,
        while the right hand retreats to simple lower-register chords.

0:27   Johnson responds to Turner's melodies with a low melodic **riff**.

CHORUS 3

0:29   *"Well, you're so beautiful, but you've got to die someday.*
        All I want [is] a little lovin' just before you pass away."
        At the end of his first line, Turner escapes into an expressive **blue note**.

CHORUS 4

0:44   *"Baby, what's the matter now? Tryin' to quit me, babe, where you don't know how."*
        Behind Turner's vocal, Johnson begins playing short riffs.

CHORUS 5

0:59   *"Roll 'em, boy . . . let 'em jump for joy. Yeah, man, happy as a baby boy.*
        Well, just got another brand-new choo-choo toy."
        Turner jumps in ahead of the bar line. In response, Johnson plays a familiar
        boogie-woogie riff.

1:12   (spoken) *"Ah, pick it, papa!"*

CHORUS 6

1:14   Spurred by Turner's foot stomp and hand clap on the **backbeat**, Johnson begins
        his two-chorus solo.

1:16   (spoken) *"Yeah, yeah!"*

1:24   (spoken) *"Way down, way down!"*

CHORUS 7

1:28   Johnson suddenly plays a high-pitched series of repeated notes at the top
        of the keyboard.

1:35   As Johnson returns to the middle register, Turner chuckles appreciatively.

1:39   (spoken) *"Solid, pops, solid!"*

CHORUS 8

1:43   *"Yes, yes! Yes, I know!"*
        Turner's simple phrase becomes a call, prompting a response from Johnson's piano.

1:45   Each time Turner repeats his phrase, he varies it in pitch and rhythm.

CHORUS 9

1:57   *"Well, all right, then!"*
        Without taking a breath, Turner launches into a new phrase, again answered
        by Johnson.

CHORUS 10

2:12   *"Bye . . . bye!"*
        Turner transforms his two-syllable phrase into a lengthy, expressive arc that spans
        several measures.

CODA

2:24   *"Bye-bye, baby, bye-bye!"*
        Johnson suddenly cuts off the boogie-woogie ostinato. With a few simple gestures,
        Johnson and Turner dismantle the rhythmic momentum and bring the performance
        to a close. Thunderous applause follows.

■ Territory Bands: ANDY KIRK (1898–1992) and MARY LOU WILLIAMS (1910–1981)

During the 1920s and early 1930s, thousands of dance bands crisscrossed the United States. Known as **territory bands**, they worked a geographic area no more than a day's drive from their headquarters. Some "territories" were close to the center of the music business in New York, while others ranged from the Southeast to the upper Midwest (where the polkas of Lawrence Welk held sway) to Northern California. Some were white, others were black. Some specialized in "hot" swing, while others purveyed a more genteel music. A surprising number, including the Melodears, the Prairie View Co-Eds, and the International Sweethearts of Rhythm, were all-female. A few were even religious, like the mysteriously bearded and gentile House of David band, sponsored by a commune in Michigan. Bands often sported names that had little contact with reality: Art Bronson's Bostonians, for example, were based in Salinas, Kansas. Only a few territory bands ever set foot in a recording studio.

One that did and became a national favorite began as the Twelve Clouds of Joy, led by tuba player Andy Kirk. The group lived a typical life for a territory band during the Depression—constant touring under the constant threat of financial failure (sometimes they were paid in fried chicken; other times they stole corn and roasted the kernels). Kirk proved his swing bona fides with an exciting recording of "Christopher Columbus," a big hit that put the band on its feet. Soon thereafter, "Until the Real Thing Comes Along" (with the band now called Clouds of Joy, sung by Pha Terrell) roared to No. 1 on the pop charts, became Kirk's theme song, and popularized a black crooning style (a high-pitched male voice) that was new to the public and spawned many imitators, most successfully a vocal group called the Ink Spots.

It wasn't crooning, however, that made Kirk's band important. The musical genius of the group was the pianist and arranger Mary Lou Williams, whose approach to big-band writing caught the ear of everyone from Duke Ellington and Benny Goodman (they both commissioned work from her) to an unknown teenager named Thelonious Monk. She had grown up in Pittsburgh, where she learned to play piano by listening to the local master Earl Hines and records by Jelly Roll Morton and James P. Johnson. Her talent was evident by age fourteen, when she left home to join a vaudeville show; a few years later, she married John Williams, who joined the Kirk band as a saxophonist. She remained backstage, occasionally earning money by driving the bus and styling hair, until 1929, when one day the band's pianist didn't show up for a recording session. Williams volunteered to sit in, having already learned the band's repertory by ear (she had perfect pitch and an uncanny memory). She was hired on the spot, and even began to record as a sideman, usually as Mary Leo Burley.

At first, unable to read music, Williams relied on her exceptional ear to negotiate difficult musical situations. But she soon mastered music theory. "She'd be sitting up at the foot of the bed, legs crossed like an Indian,"

After leaving the Andy Kirk band, Mary Lou Williams, seen here in 1949, led her own band for several years at New York's Café Society.

DUNCAN SCHIEDT COLLECTION

Kirk recounts, "just writing and writing." As an accompanist and band soloist, Williams was a powerful force. "I listened to how a pianist pushed, like Count Basie," she said, "and *I* pushed."

According to Williams, though she had recorded with the band in 1929, in Kansas City, Kirk dithered about bringing her to Chicago the following year until his record producer, Jack Kapp, insisted that the band "didn't sound the same" without her. She traveled alone, arriving at the studio in April after a hellish journey, having been raped on the train. While the band warmed up, Kapp asked her to play a couple of numbers. "I have always done my best composing while playing," Williams told the Smithsonian Institute's Jazz Oral History Project regarding that session: "I was almost scared to death, but got going, remembering the night life of K.C."

The two solo piano pieces, "Night Life" and "Drag 'Em," the first sides released under her own name, are dazzling improvisations that interweave tricky cross-rhythms, hesitations, tremolos, and a stomp. She never falters, while showing how much piano she had soaked up from Eubie Blake, James P. Johnson, Fats Waller, and Earl Hines in the development of an obstinately self-sufficient pianistic personality. Those solos were little noted at the time, but she returned with the Kirk band in the new era of 1936. Her forcefulness established her as the most prominent female instrumentalist in jazz or swing. As one of her arrangements put it, she was "the lady who swings the band." She once proudly claimed that she played "heavy, like a man"—an assessment that says more about her social upbringing than her playing. She strenuously avoided cheesecake shots, an obligation most women musicians and singers fulfilled to generate publicity. Insiders accepted her as someone in the know, someone to learn from.

🎧 "Walkin' and Swingin'"

"Walkin' and Swingin'" was written by Mary Lou Williams in 1936, shortly after the agent Joe Glaser had taken control of the Twelve Clouds of Joy's bookings and vetted their contract with Decca Records. Although Williams's arrangement earned her only a few dollars—a small bonus to her salary as pianist—she was satisfied that the piece furthered her reputation as a performer and arranger, and helped pave the way for her to eventually lead her own smaller bands. Though not a big hit, "Walkin' and Swingin'" is the piece most often used by today's jazz repertory ensembles to capture the quality of the band and of Williams's early writing style.

The piece begins with a harmonic novelty—a dissonance from the minor mode that resolves to the major. Yet its most striking innovation was a response to the band's small size: while most arrangers depended on four or five saxophones to fill out their harmonies, Kirk's band had only three. Williams's solution was ingenious: she asked one of the trumpet players to "talk into a hat"—to use a metal derby mute—to help it blend with the saxophones. The mood is sly and conversational, as if the collective voice of the band had continually new things to say. One of Williams's most memorable melodic ideas appears near the end of the second chorus (1:12)—her friend Thelonious Monk combined it with a lick from Ellington's "Ducky Wucky" to create his own tune, "Rhythm-a-ning," first recorded in 1957. Others, less friendly, also took from her. Her composition "What's Your Story, Morning Glory?" was lifted whole and turned into the standard pop tune "Black Coffee."

🎧 walkin' and swingin'

ANDY KIRK AND HIS TWELVE CLOUDS OF JOY
Harry "Big Jim" Lawson, Paul King, Earl Thompson, trumpets; Ted Donnelly, Henry Wells, trombones; John Williams, John Harrington, alto saxophones; Dick Wilson, tenor saxophone; Mary Lou Williams, piano; Ted Robinson, guitar; Booker Collins, bass; Ben Thigpen, drums

- Label: Decca 809
- Date: 1936
- Style: big-band swing
- Form: 32-bar popular song (**A A B A**)

What to listen for:
- swing groove (two-beat bass line, switching to four-beat)
- ingenious *soli* by saxophone/trumpet section in chorus 2
- Williams's intricate solo, featuring blue notes

CHORUS 1

0:00	**A**	The saxophones begin a long, swooping melody, supported by a **riff** in the brass that seesaws between two notes. The bass plays a two-beat pattern (although we still feel the overall four-beat framework).
0:08		After the saxophone melody finishes, the brass section emerges with a brief figure on the **offbeats**.
0:10	**A**	
0:20	**B**	The piece **modulates** to a new key. The brass take the lead, with the saxophones quietly in the background.
0:30	**A**	The tune modulates back to the original key.

INTERLUDE

0:38		The saxophones, topped by a solo trumpet, extend the seesawing riff to a **full cadence**.

CHORUS 2

0:43	**A**	The piece modulates again, this time to yet a different key. The saxophone/trumpet combination plays a chorus-long passage in **block-chord** texture (*soli*). By subtly changing dynamics and rhythm, the band suggests an improvising soloist.
0:52	**A**	As it passes over the same chord progression, the band plays shorter, more propulsive figures.
1:02	**B**	Again the tune modulates, with the written-out *soli* line rising and falling over the chords.
1:12	**A**	The *soli* settles into a simple, on-the-beat riff.

CHORUS 3

1:21	**A**	Williams begins her piano solo, interspersing punchy percussive phrases with delicate, intricate runs.
1:31	**A**	She simulates a **blue note** by crushing two notes together.
1:41	**B**	Wilson plays a tenor saxophone solo, accompanied by background riffs.
1:50	**A**	Williams returns to continue her solo.
1:56		She plays a riff that sounds like an improvisation. But when the band immediately repeats it (in a two-bar **break**), we realize that the entire passage is part of Williams's arrangement.

CHORUS 4 (abbreviated)

2:00	**A**	In a **shout chorus**, the saxophones return to their seesawing riff while the bass switches to a four-beat pattern. Above them, the brass punctuate strongly on the offbeat.

2:08	A	In the next section (which arrives two bars early), a simple brass riff is answered by the saxophones.
2:17	B	As the arrangement reaches its climax, saxophones scurry beneath a brass high note.
2:28	A	The brass play a new two-note riff, answered by the saxophones.
2:35		The two-note riff falls to a final cadence.

In 1942, tiring of continuous band travel, Williams left Kirk's band and took a spot at Barney Josephson's Café Society in New York, the country's first completely integrated nightclub. She also became more active as a composer, recording elaborate pieces such as *Zodiac Suite* (1945). Her interest in complex chromatic harmonies (she called them "zombie chords") pulled her into the bebop revolution of the 1940s, where she assumed a position of leadership. Her apartment on Hamilton Terrace in Harlem became a gathering place for such musicians as Dizzy Gillespie, Kenny Clarke, Bud Powell, and especially Thelonious Monk, whom she took on as a protégé. Gillespie credited her with helping them to rethink the formation of chords. In the 1960s and 70s, Williams became a devoted teacher of jazz history, organized bands of different sizes, composed religious oratorios, recorded, and played concerts featuring lengthy pieces designed to show the evolution of jazz, from ragtime to modal. She remained a fearless champion of jazz in all its forms.

■ COUNT BASIE (1904–1984)

Most of the major figures in Kansas City jazz were not raised there, but they did hail from the South and Southwest. Not William "Count" Basie, by far the most famous Kansas City bandleader of them all: he grew up in Red Bank, on the New Jersey shore, not far from New York City. He learned his trade in New York in the mid-1920s, studying the work of the stride masters (Fats Waller gave him lessons on pipe organ) while trying to avoid direct competition with pianists like James P. Johnson, who were far above him in ability. When the chance came to leave town as the accompanist for a touring vaudeville show, he grabbed it.

Count Basie could look suave and elegant, as in this 1939 portrait. Yet to his musicians he was "ol' Base," an unpretentious bandleader who made sure the music never traveled far from its core elements—the blues and the dance groove.

DUNCAN SCHIEDT COLLECTION

In 1927, Basie found himself stranded in Kansas City, recovering from spinal meningitis. Within a year, he was freelancing with bands and singers, accompanying silent movies, and going out on short tours. One morning, from his window at the Red Wing Hotel in Tulsa, he heard a new type of jazz played by a territory band from Oklahoma City, the Blue Devils, who were using the back of a truck as a bandstand. "I had never heard anything like that band in my life," he remembered. "Everybody seemed to be having so much fun just being up there playing together. . . . you just couldn't help wishing that you were a part of it."

Basie became an irregular member of the Blue Devils, which was nominally led by the bassist Walter Page. Like many other groups of the time, it was a "commonwealth" band, distributing its funds evenly among its members and relying on group consensus for decisions. This informality ultimately spelled disaster. As one band member remembered, "Whenever we wanted to do something, accept a job, we have to sit down and have a discussion. . . . Seven would vote for it and six would vote against it."

By the time the band dissolved in 1933, Basie and Page had already been scooped up by the most prosperous band in the Kansas City region, led by Benny Moten (1894–1935). Moten was a skilled ragtime pianist but an even more successful businessman. In Kansas City, he dealt shrewdly with the powerful city organization led by Tom Pendergast, whose *laissez-faire* attitude toward illegal activities guaranteed a boisterous night life. Pendergast's grip on Kansas City was as clenched as Al Capone's on Chicago. In Tom's Town, as it was known throughout the Southwest, violators of Prohibition were rarely convicted and saloons stayed open all night. Black musicians didn't escape racism in Kansas City (it "might as well have been Gulfport, Mississippi," one performer remembered), but they could always find work.

Benny Moten

In 1935, Benny Moten's life came to an unexpected end after a botched tonsillectomy. His demise, while devastating for many musicians, inadvertently helped to launch Basie. He retreated to the Reno Club in Kansas City, where he gathered together several of Moten's musicians in the course of creating his own band. This tiny, L-shaped saloon was so small that Walter Page often had to sit on a stool outside and lean in the window. Basie's band was also small, with only nine pieces—three trumpets, three saxophones, and three in the rhythm section—and managed to create music without written arrangements. "I don't think we had over four or five sheets of music up there," Basie recalled. "We had our own thing, and we could always play some more blues and call it something."

Head Arrangements and Jam Sessions

The unwritten music created by Basie's band was based on **head arrangements**, so called because the music, created collectively (as noted in Chapter 7), was stored in the heads of the musicians who played it. Head arrangements typified the casual but competitive and creative atmosphere of the jam session in Kansas City. A club like the Sunset Café would typically hire only a pianist and drummer, expecting the rest of the music to be created by musicians who dropped by in the course of an evening. "It wasn't unusual for one number to go on about an hour or an hour and a half," the drummer Jo Jones recalled. "Nobody got tired. They didn't tell me at that time they used to change drummers, so I just sat there and played the whole time for pure joy."

Although only one soloist played at a time, the mood of the jam session was collective, with horn players waiting their turn to join in. If one musician played a riff, others nearby would harmonize it, searching for notes to fit the riff into a block-chord texture. According to bassist Gene Ramey, this skill derived from black folk traditions. It reminded him of "revival meetings, where the preacher and the people are singing, and there's happenings all around." The more musicians, the more notes were needed: a saxophonist might add extra extended notes to standard chords to avoid "stepping on" someone else's "line" (i.e., to avoid playing the same basic chord tone). At the same time, since this spontaneous music was created by professionals, it had a slick, orchestral polish. All that was needed to transfer it to the dance band was a group of musicians capable of remembering what they had played.

For dance bands, head arrangements offered special flexibility. Some became fixed arrangements, written down to preserve the order of riffs. But in the heat of performance, musicians could stretch the tune to extraordinary lengths. New riffs could be created to match the dancers' ingenuity. Basie was particularly skilled at creating head arrangements from the piano, by cuing the saxophones with one keyboard riff and the brasses with another. "When you play a battle of music, it's the head arrangements that you could play for about ten minutes and get the dancers going," remembered Teddy Wilson, whose music-reading dance band could not keep up with Kansas City–style spontaneity. Once the Basie band began playing "One O'Clock Jump," the contest was over: "That was the end of the dance!"

The Basie Band

One night in 1936, John Hammond happened to hear Basie's band on the shortwave radio built into his car, and soon traveled to Kansas City to hear the band for himself. Entranced with its loose, easy swing, Hammond—who hit it off with Basie from the start—was determined to bring the band into the commercial mainstream. Although Basie was under contract with Decca, Hammond grabbed Basie, his vocalist Jimmy Rushing, and four of his key musicians to secretly make their first records for Columbia under the pseudonym Jones-Smith Incorporated (see p. 192).

For Basie's musicians, moving from the Reno Club was not easy. Some of their instruments were held together with rubber bands and string. Some members left, while others were added to raise their number from nine to thirteen, and later to the industry standard of fifteen. On the road to New York, when asked to play conventional dance music ("I don't think I even knew what a goddamn tango was," Basie remembered), the band floundered. "By the time you read this," a Chicago newspaper opined, "they will be on their way back to Kansas City." But over the long road trip, Basie worked out the musical kinks. In 1937, having made it to New York, the band began practicing in earnest in the basement of Harlem's Woodside Hotel, developing their own repertory. As Basie later remembered:

> It was like the Blue Devils. We always had somebody in those sections who was a leader, who could start something and get those ensembles going. I mean while somebody would be soloing in the reed section, the brasses would have something going in the background, and the reed section would have something to go with that. And while the brass section had something going, somebody in the reed section might be playing a solo....
>
> Those guys knew just where to come in.... And the thing about it that was so fantastic was this: *Once those guys played something, they could damn near play it exactly the same the next night....* And a lot of times the heads that we made down there in that basement were a lot better than things that were written out.

Basie was no composer, but he worked closely with trombonist Eddie Durham to cast these collectively created charts into permanent form. He also edited many an elaborate chart down to a clean, uncluttered piece, in accordance with the maxim "less is more." The result was not technically dazzling—few Kansas City arrangements are swing landmarks—but Basie made history by insisting on simplicity and establishing and sustaining the most irresistible rhythmic pulse of the day. His name became synonymous with "time." If Benny Goodman was "King of the Swing Era," everyone knew that Basie was the "King of Swing"; you could not listen to him without dancing or at least tapping a foot. His own piano technique, though still

grounded in the techniques of stride, melted away as he remade himself as the most laconic pianist ever. Yet every note he played helped the band swing. "The Count don't do much," one band member explained, "but he does it better than anyone else."

The most crucial characteristic of Kansas City jazz was its distinctive groove of four beats to the bar, and at its core was bassist Walter Page, a large man nicknamed "Big 'Un" who made dancers happy by evening out the beat. The drummer, Jo Jones—like Page, a veteran of the Blue Devils— played with extraordinary lightness and a keen sense of ensemble. Guitarist Freddie Green was added in 1937, recommended by John Hammond, who had spotted him at a club in New York's Greenwich Village. The propulsive lightness of what became known as the "All-American Rhythm Section" was perhaps the band's most far-reaching innovation. "When you listen to that Basie section," bassist Gene Ramey remembered, "the drums didn't sound any louder than the guitar, the piano—it was all balanced. . . . It showed the rhythm section was 'teaming.'"

Basie's soloists initially included, on trumpet, the bright and buoyant Buck Clayton and Harry Edison, nicknamed "Sweets" in ironic tribute to his caustic tone and witty, low-register solos, often distorted with the derby mute. The trombone section included Eddie Durham, who was also one of the earliest electric guitarists, and Dickie Wells, whose solos are often identifiable by his ironically expressive tone. Vocalist Jimmy Rushing had an uncannily

The Apollo Theater demanded the most of any band performing there, including the Count Basie band. Beneath drummer Jo Jones (on platform), Lester Young matches the exuberance of his playing by raising his tenor saxophone to its limit.

 Rhythm section

 Soloists

serene way of singing blues lyrics and of making standards sound, if not quite like blues, then certainly like vehicles expressly conceived for him.

One reason the Basie band became famous was its dueling tenor saxophonists: the ingenious Lester Young, the band's most celebrated and influential soloist, played with a swift, blissful grace; and Herschel Evans, a powerful saxophonist from Denton, Texas, embodied a full-bodied approach to the tenor known as "Texas style." They sat on opposite sides of the saxophone section and played as though they were in open competition, with crowds cheering each soloist. This two-tenor rivalry (with Buddy Tate taking Evans's place in 1939) was widely imitated by other swing bandleaders.

🎧 "One O'Clock Jump"

"One O'Clock Jump" was a fluid, twelve-bar blues arrangement that had evolved gradually for more than a decade before finding its final form; only after it was recorded was it notated so that the copyright could be reserved. Many of its riffs were collected over the years by Basie long-timers like saxophonist Buster Smith, trumpeter Hot Lips Page, and trombonist Eddie Durham. The main theme (not played until the ninth chorus on the recording) can be heard in the 1920s Don Redman arrangement "Six or Seven Times." Originality was hardly the issue: like the blues itself, these riffs were assumed to be public property. It wasn't what you did, but how you did it.

There is little else holding the piece together. The band knew it as "Blue Balls," an admittedly indecent title they never expected to make public. When the tune was finally performed on the radio, community standards ("You can't call it *that!*") forced a change. "One O'Clock Jump" presumably commemorates the hour of the morning it was first broadcast. Stark and even elemental, it was tremendously effective and became Basie's first hit.

Basie begins with a piano solo that locks the rhythm section into its groove. He often insisted on starting off on his own, playing several choruses until the tempo felt right—"just like you were mixing mash and yeast to make whiskey," his trumpet player Harry "Sweets" Edison once said, "and you keep tasting it." A sudden modulation switches from Basie's favorite key (F major) to the distant key the horn players preferred (D-flat major). The arrangement is primarily a string of solos, featuring the best of the Basie band with riff accompaniment. Then comes what might be called a rhythm section solo (chorus 7): Basie is the main voice, but his minimal jabs divert our attention to the light, clear sound of what was widely thought of as the best rhythm section of the Swing Era.

The last three choruses consist of interlocking riffs. The famous version is the commercial recording, a 78-rpm disc limited by technology to three minutes. Some radio broadcasts extended the piece for several minutes; musicians have said it could go on for half an hour. The maximum length, one supposes, depended on the fortitude of the musicians. Like African music, it could be extended to suit any occasion.

🎧 one o'clock jump

COUNT BASIE AND HIS ORCHESTRA
Count Basie, piano; Buck Clayton, Ed Lewis, Bobby Moore, trumpets; George Hunt, Dan Minor, trombones; Earl Warren, alto saxophone; Jack Washington, baritone saxophone; Herschel Evans, Lester Young, tenor saxophones; Freddie Green, guitar; Walter Page, bass; Jo Jones, drums

- Label: Decca 1363
- Date: 1937
- Style: Kansas City swing
- Form: 12-bar blues

What to listen for:
- Kansas-City-style head arrangement
- string of solos, accompanied by riffs
- steady rhythm section, highlighted in chorus 7
- Young's solo in chorus 5 (including false fingerings)

INTRODUCTION

0:00   Basie begins with a **vamp**—a short, repeated figure in the left hand. Other members of the rhythm section enter gingerly, as if feeling Basie's tempo and groove.

CHORUS 1

0:11   With the rhythm section now in full gear, Basie begins his solo with a clear melodic statement. His left hand, playing a spare and tentative **stride** accompaniment, blends in with the consistent on-beat attacks of the guitar, bass, and drums.

CHORUS 2

0:28   Basie suddenly attacks the piano in octaves, ending his phrases with a **tremolo** (a rapid shaking of the notes in a chord).

0:43   Closing off the introduction, Basie quickly **modulates** to a new key.

CHORUS 3

0:45   On the tenor saxophone, Evans plays a stately chorus with full **vibrato**. Behind him, the muted trumpets play a simple, two-note harmonized riff.

CHORUS 4

1:02   Hunt (trombone) takes over smoothly for the next chorus, accompanied by a background riff by the saxophones. The drummer moves the pulse to the high-hat cymbal.

1:15   The trombonist uses his slide to create **blue notes**.

CHORUS 5

1:19   Young (tenor saxophone) begins his chorus with **false fingerings**—playing the same note with different fingerings to create new timbres. To match the accompanying riff, the drummer adjusts his pattern to a bass-drum accent every other measure.

CHORUS 6

1:36   On trumpet, Clayton starts his solo with a simple riff (resembling the beginning of "When the Saints Go Marching In"). Behind him, the saxophones play a long descending riff. The drummer returns to playing the high-hat cymbal with occasional snare-drum **backbeats**.

CHORUS 7

1:53   Basie plays sparely, accompanied only by the rhythm section. Each of his chords has a distinctive sound: high-pitched, spanning slightly over an octave. The bass, drums, and guitar play unflaggingly.

2:02   For a few measures, the bass plays slightly sharp (above pitch).

CHORUS 8

2:10   The band reenters with overlapping riffs: a simple melody, played by the saxophones, is interwoven with three trumpet chords. Both are answered by a trombone chord.

CHORUS 9

2:27 The riffs remain the same except for the saxophonists', who play the melody usually recognized as the theme to "One O'Clock Jump."

CHORUS 10

2:43 The saxophones change to a simple, unharmonized riff. The drummer reinforces the trombone chord with a sharp accent on the snare drum.

2:57 With a short series of chords, the saxophones signal the end.

Later Basie Basie's incalculably influential Swing Era period lasted from his recording debut in 1936 to the late 1940s. Like other bandleaders, Basie struggled after World War II and finally broke up the band, reducing his group to an octet in 1948. Several years later, when he decided to revive his big band, only Freddie Green was left from the original crew. The rest of the musicians were drawn from the large number of excellent studio musicians and from soloists who had come of age with bebop. This group, known as the "New Testament" Basie band in theological deference to its predecessor, was a decidedly different outfit. The head arrangements were gone, replaced by sturdy written scores. The new musicians were equally at home with "mainstream" swing and modern jazz, and were accustomed to a written repertory. Basie often joked about his musical turnabout. "You know, don't you," he once said, "that if the lights go out on this band, the music will stop!"

Basie came to exemplify the swing sound in the 1950s and after; he was the ideal choice for singers such as Frank Sinatra, Sarah Vaughan, Tony Bennett, and Billy Eckstine, who wanted to spark their mainstream pop with the drive of an orchestra that had lost none of its strength or wit. For thirty years, Basie toured the world as a roving ambassador of swing. At the end, he sat in a wheelchair, supervising his band and continuing to play spare piano—the twilight of a splendid career.

■ THE INCOMPARABLE ELLINGTON

From his arrival at Harlem's swank Cotton Club in the late 1920s until the middle 1930s, Duke Ellington displaced Fletcher Henderson as the most prominent black bandleader in the world. With the advent of the Swing Era, however, it felt almost ludicrous to talk about Ellington primarily in terms of race, despite his astute focus on race as thematic material. He was America's great composer, America's great bandleader—acknowledged as such by nearly everyone, including the public. His renown was international, his influence pandemic. He was of swing and beyond swing.

Ellington would not have been comfortable with the designation "jazz composer." For one thing, he disliked the word "jazz," which he sensed tended to marginalize the creativity of black musicians. Sometimes he claimed that he wrote "Negro folk music." He described Ella Fitzgerald and other artists for whom he had the greatest esteem as "beyond category," a term that applies—as he knew very well—equally to himself. In what category do you place a pianist, bandleader, composer, and arranger who created an ensemble unlike any other and wrote practically every kind of Western music other than grand opera—from ragtime to rock and roll, from blues to ballet, from stage and film scores to tone poems, oratorios, and sacred concerts, not to mention works for instrumental combinations from piano-bass duets to symphony orchestra. A proudly black artist, whose subject matter never departed for long from African American history and life, he also wrote about the full breadth of America and much of the world.

Classical music has taught us to think of composers working in isolation, scribbling music on manuscript paper for others to perform. Ellington *did* work this way. Whenever he traveled, he carried a pad of paper and a pencil. At odd moments throughout the day, and in the unlikeliest places (often on the train, in hotel rooms loud with partying, or alone at night), he jotted down ideas as they came to him. The Smithsonian Institution's Ellington Archive contains mountains of sheet music, often transcribed into individual parts by his copyists.

As composer

But turning his musical ideas into actual pieces required collaboration with his musicians, a process that could devolve into chaos. Writer Richard Boyer, who traveled with the band in 1944, described such moments as a "creative free-for-all" that sounded "like a political convention" or "a zoo at feeding time": "Perhaps a musician will get up and say, 'No, Duke! It just can't be that way!' and demonstrate on his instrument his conception of the phrase or bar under consideration. Often, too, this idea may outrage a colleague, who replies on *his* instrument with *his* conception, and the two players argue back and forth not with words but with blasts from trumpet or trombone." And in truth, Ellington's orchestral parts were often a nightmare. Dizzy Gillespie, who joined the band briefly in the 1940s, recalled the complicated jumble of his trumpet parts. "I'm supposed to remember that you jump from 'A' to the first three bars of 'Z,' and then jump back to 'Q,' play eight bars of that, then jump over to the next part, and then play the solo." Other scores, though, especially his later pieces, show the tight control of a musical architect.

It's not surprising that Ellington's stature as composer has been frequently misunderstood. The most notorious case came in 1965 when the music committee for the Pulitzer Prize unanimously recommended him for an award to honor the entire body of his achievement, but was overruled by the Pulitzer board, which chose to give no award that year. The sixty-six-year-old composer responded: "Fate is being kind to me. Fate doesn't want me to be too famous too young." In 1999, a quarter century after his death, the board

DUNCAN SCHIEDT COLLECTION

In 1929, few knew that the young bandleader Duke Ellington took his composing seriously. Yet we can feel here the focused intent he brought to the challenges of organizing his band's sound.

finally did bestow a lifetime achievement award; by then, even the Pulitzer could no longer pretend that Ellington was a minor or passing figure.

Unlike those of other composers, Ellington scores are starting points. Instead, his legacy has been comprehensively preserved on recordings, thousands of them. Unlike swing bands that sounded much better live than on record, Ellington was "at the height of his creative powers" in a recording studio. For the first half of his career, he squeezed hundreds of recordings into the three-minute limit dictated by the 78-rpm format. His first attempts at longer pieces were spread out awkwardly over several discs, but eventually technology caught up with him. By the 1950s, the LP made it easy for him to conceive his music in broader terms. He was among the first composers to write specifically for microgroove.

Ellingtonians

Ellington's music proved inimitable because the sonorities he relied on derived from musicians he worked with year in and year out. "You can't write music right," he once said, "unless you know how the man that'll play it plays poker." Among Ellington's most remarkable achievements was his ability to command the loyalties of outstanding musicians for decades—in some instances for the entire duration of their professional lives.

By 1935, Ellington had already gathered an ensemble easily recognized by the musical (and personal) quirks that stimulated his imagination: brass players who specialized in muted effects and vocalized timbres, saxophonists with a noble or blustery or heartbreakingly romantic attack, and radically different trombonists (understated and overstated) who nonetheless blended together like pigments of color. For each of these voices, Ellington created pieces that set them off as a fine jeweler sets off his prized stones.

Harry Carney

Some of his most valued associates joined him in the early years. The baritone saxophonist Harry Carney was barely seventeen when he signed up with Ellington in 1927, earning the nickname Youth, which clung to him through the forty-seven years he remained with the band. His deep, rich sonority was an integral part of Ellington's sound, floating to wherever it was needed but generally anchoring the band. Most saxophone sections assigned the lead voice to the alto saxophone. Ellington's music was made instantly recognizable by his voice-leading baritone. Miles Davis once said of Carney, "If he wasn't in the band, the band wouldn't be Duke."

VOICES

In 1944, when journalist Richard Boyer spent weeks traveling with the Ellington band for a three-part *New Yorker* profile, Ellington revealed how he perceived his process of artistic creation:

You've got to write with certain men in mind. You write just for their abilities and natural tendencies and give them places where they do their best—certain entrances and exits and background stuff. You got to know each man to know what he'll react well to. One guy likes very simple ornamentation; another guy likes ornamentation better than the theme because it gives him a feeling of being a second mind. Every musician has his favorite licks and you gotta write to them. . . . I might think of a wonderful thing for an oboe, but I ain't got no oboe and it doesn't interest me. My band is my instrument.

Other musicians lasted far less long, but exerted a powerful influence. Bubber Miley in some ways epitomized Ellington's musical values—his motto was "If it ain't got swing, it ain't worth playin'"—but his behavior was impossible. After drinking too much, he would crawl under the piano to sleep it off. Ellington let him go in 1929, hiring Cootie Williams in his place. True to form, Ellington did not tell Williams what to do. He simply let the new musician listen carefully and realize, after playing in the trumpet section for a while, that something was missing—and that it was up to him to provide it. Williams laughed when he first heard Tricky Sam Nanton's yowling trombone, but soon took on the esoteric art of mutes to create his own idiosyncratic sounds.

Cootie Williams

Playing with Sidney Bechet in the mid-1920s gave Ellington a taste for the elegant simplicity and earthy quality of the New Orleans clarinet. His love of that "all wood" sound led him to lure Barney Bigard, a sometime tenor saxophonist, back to his original instrument. Bigard had learned to play the clarinet in New Orleans through an old-fashioned system of fingering that was harder to play but was thought to offer a richer, more open timbre. After fifteen years with Ellington, he became a member of the Louis Armstrong All-Stars.

Barney Bigard

No Ellington voice was more important than that of the alto saxophonist Johnny Hodges (1906–1970), who joined the group in 1928 and remained, excepting one five-year sabbatical, for nearly five decades. Ellington had been searching for a saxophonist with the visceral punch and stylish elegance of Sidney Bechet, and in Hodges he found someone who had already taken Bechet as his model. He immediately became one of Ellington's main soloists, his notes slicing the air with unassailable authority, sometimes projecting a spirited blues-wise toughness, at other times a gentle lyricism that could turn on a dime to dark, passionate romanticism.

Johnny Hodges

Ellington's trombonists, in addition to Tricky Sam Nanton, were an interesting pair. Lawrence Brown was a dignified man who brought a lithe middle-register grace to the trombone, occasionally enriched by the more orchestral characteristics associated with a cello. Alongside him was the Puerto Rican valve trombonist Juan Tizol, who joined the band in 1929 (an extremely early instance of integration, though not one that was widely noted beyond musical circles), carving out a niche for himself as the band's "legitimate" (or classical) trombone player, incapable of improvising but perfect for realizing a written part with a beautiful, polished tone. He was also one of the few people Ellington trusted to copy out parts for the rest of the band.

Cootie Williams, brought on board in the early 1930s to replace Bubber Miley, was one of Ellington's favorite musicians, using a plunger mute over a pixie mute to create otherworldly sounds. He's seen here with the Benny Goodman Orchestra, 1940.

🎧 "Mood Indigo"

According to Ellington, his 1930 tune "Mood Indigo" was inspired by a plaintive scene. While having his back rubbed between shows, he described it to a newspaper reporter:

"It's just a little story about a little girl and a little boy. They're about eight and the little girl loves the little boy. They never speak of it, of course, but she just likes the way he wears his hat. Every day he comes by her house at a certain time and she sits in her window and waits." Duke's voice dropped solemnly. The masseur, sensing the climax, eased up, and Duke said evenly, "Then one day he doesn't come." There was silence until Duke added: "'Mood Indigo' just tells how she feels."

DUNCAN SCHIEDT COLLECTION

That was the explanation given to casual observers, and an instance of Ellington's quick-witted verbal dexterity. He invented things like that all the time. In fact, the melody for "Mood Indigo" came to Ellington from Barney Bigard (who had probably acquired it from his New Orleans teacher, Lorenzo Tio). But Ellington made it his own by adding a memorable bridge and casting the whole thing in a daringly original arrangement. The instrumentation at the beginning suggests, superficially, New Orleans jazz—clarinet, trumpet, and trombone—but the sound is as different as night from day. The brass players (Nanton and trumpeter Arthur Whetsol) are distant and deliberately muted, holding their sound in check and playing in the high range, while the clarinet, instead of being the highest instrument, is plunged into its deep and rich lower register.

According to Ellington, this unusual combination represented, at least in part, an adjustment to technology. In the recording studio, a faulty microphone reacted strangely to the sound of his horns, producing an illusory pitch that ruined several takes. Eventually, Ellington decided to work with what he had, and adjusted the horns so that the microphone's errant tone became "centralized" in the overall sound. However it was achieved, the opening bars of "Mood Indigo" are unearthly and mystifying—the source of conductor-pianist André Previn's famous comment: "Duke merely lifts a finger, three horns make a sound, and I don't know what it is!"

🎧 mood indigo

DUKE ELLINGTON AND HIS ORCHESTRA

Duke Ellington, piano; Arthur Whetsol, Freddy Jenkins, Cootie Williams, trumpets; Joe "Tricky Sam" Nanton, Juan Tizol, trombones; Johnny Hodges, alto saxophone and clarinet; Harry Carney, baritone saxophone and clarinet; Barney Bigard, clarinet; Fred Guy, banjo; Wellman Braud, bass; Sonny Greer, drums

- Label: Victor 22587-A
- Date: 1930
- Style: early big band
- Form: 16-bar popular song

What to listen for:

- unusual instrumentation: muted brass and low-register clarinet (chorus 1), clarinet trio (chorus 2)
- a quiet mood of melancholy: low dynamics and blue notes
- Bigard's expressive clarinet solo in chorus 3

CHORUS 1 (16 bars)

0:00   Williams, Nanton, and Bigard play their three horns (trumpet, trombone, and clarinet) in **block-chord** texture, but the trumpet and trombone are on top, heavily muted, while the clarinet is in its lowest register. Guy plays a steady, thrumming beat on the banjo.

0:15   To connect from one harmony to another, Ellington plays a **chromatic scale** on the piano.

0:22   Nanton's trombone, producing unearthly sounds from a combination of straight pixie mute, plunger mute, and throat growls, can be briefly heard on its own.

INTERLUDE

0:43   On piano, Ellington provides breathing space between the first two choruses.

CHORUS 2

0:54   Williams (trumpet) continues reharmonizing the theme, this time supported by a clarinet trio (with Hodges and Carney joining Bigard on clarinet).

1:15   Williams ascends to a long-sustained top note, leaving room for the clarinets to take the lead.

1:36   A brief flourish by the brass signals the next chorus.

CHORUS 3

1:37   Bigard plays a new melody on clarinet, over a background of sustained brass chords. While the banjo continues its steady thrumming, the bass often doubles its pace to eight beats to the bar.

2:04   For several bars, Bigard chooses pitches that clash with Ellington's elusive harmony.

CHORUS 4

2:20   The final chorus reprises the unusual instrumentation of the opening chorus.

3:01   The banjo finally comes to a rest on a **tremolo** chord, punctuated by a single piano note.

In the Swing Era

In 1933, Ellington took his band to England and France, where knowledgeable critics and adulatory fans who compared his music to Shakespeare made him realize how much larger his ambitions could be. Back home, he divided his time between theaters and dance halls. From dancing came the maxim that he turned into a song in 1932: "It don't mean a thing if it ain't got that swing." He continued to develop the persona he had introduced at the Cotton Club in 1927, becoming familiar to millions the world over for his flashy, natty suits, the wide, welcoming grin, the extravagant style of speaking that made him an aristocrat of the swing world. In the film *Symphony in Black* (1935), Ellington plays himself: an urban sophisticate writing and conducting a score about black manual labor and rural worship.

A trio of Ellington's musicians on a city street in the early 1930s. Alto saxophonist Johnny Hodges (left), guitarist Fred Guy, and clarinetist Barney Bigard, a New Orleans Creole so pale that he once petitioned the Los Angeles musicians' union (unsuccessfully) to admit him as white.

For all his personal charisma and charm (he was a ladies' man of legendary accomplishment), Ellington sensed the responsibilities that came with being a black celebrity. He became a "race man," a spokesperson for black America, and whenever possible reminded his audiences about race consciousness. In 1941, he insisted that the black man was the country's "creative voice": "It was a happy day in America when the first unhappy slave was landed on its shores. There, in our tortured induction into this 'land of liberty,' we built its most graceful civilization. Its wealth, its flowering fields and handsome homes; its pretty traditions; its guarded leisure and its music, were all our creations." Black audiences everywhere understood this message. When his band toured the country, passing through cities and small towns with their splendid uniforms and evocative sounds, they were "news from the great wide world." Author Ralph Ellison, who heard him in Oklahoma, asked: "Where in the white community, in any white community, could there have been found images, examples such as these? Who were so worldly, who so elegant, and who so mockingly creative?"

In 1943, the jazz, pop, and classical worlds met in a moment of rare solidarity to acknowledge his debut at Carnegie Hall and the premiere of his most ambitious work to date, *Black, Brown and Beige*. This forty-eight-minute piece conveyed in tones the history of the American Negro. Unfortunately

Black, Brown and Beige

for Ellington, jazz fans initially found his symphonic rhetoric pretentious, while classical critics declined to hear it as a serious work. "I guess *serious* is a confusing word," Ellington mused. "We take our American music seriously." One movement, however, became an enduring standard, the hymn "Come Sunday" (lyrics were added shortly after the premiere), and over the years the entire work, which Ellington revised from time to time, attracted increased respect. *Black, Brown and Beige* turned out to be the capstone to Ellington's most remarkable period, 1939 to 1943, when the addition of arranger Billy Strayhorn, bassist Jimmy Blanton, trumpeter-violinist-singer Ray Nance, and Ben Webster, the gruff, hard-blowing tenor saxophonist he had been trying to recruit for years, combined to stimulate him to a creative peak.

🎧 "Conga Brava"

By 1940, the Cotton Club was safely stored in Ellington's past. But the habits of mind that had been formed there—"exotic" evocations of distant lands, unusual timbres—continued to shape new compositions, as exemplified by "Conga Brava." It was probably a successor to an earlier piece, "Caravan," co-written with Juan Tizol. The opening melody—Tizol's contribution—is admirably suited to his trombone, played here with unfailing classical excellence evocative of Romantic opera. ("I don't feel the pop tunes," Tizol once said, "but I feel 'La Gioconda' and 'La Bohème.' I like pure romantic flavor.") This opening mood, however, is complicated seconds later by Barney Bigard's elaborate improvised curlicues and snarling commentary by Cootie Williams, Rex Stewart, and Joe Nanton. Ellington covers a staggering amount of territory in his customary three minutes, from a Kansas City–style blowing session for Ben Webster to a stunning virtuosic *soli* for the brass. Playing by ear, Webster adds new notes to the chords, extending them into more dissonant territory and enriching Ellington's harmonic palette. Ultimately, though, all these moments are folded back into the mood of the opening. It's as though Ellington has taken us on a short but eventful trip, eventually escorting us gently home.

LISTENING GUIDE 24

🎧 conga brava

DUKE ELLINGTON AND HIS FAMOUS ORCHESTRA
Duke Ellington, piano; Wallace Jones, Rex Stewart, Cootie Williams, trumpets; Joe "Tricky Sam" Nanton, Lawrence Brown, Juan Tizol, trombones; Johnny Hodges, Otto Hardwick, alto saxophones; Ben Webster, tenor saxophone; Harry Carney, baritone saxophone; Barney Bigard, clarinet; Fred Guy, banjo; Jimmy Blanton, bass; Sonny Greer, drums

- Label: Victor 26577
- Date: 1940
- Style: big-band jazz
- Form: extended popular song (**A A B A**)

What to listen for:
- contributions by Ellington soloists: Tizol, Webster, Bigard, Stewart, Williams, Nanton
- unusual timbres (muted brass)
- smooth shifts between Latin and swing grooves
- dramatic changes in texture from solos to virtuosic block-chord passages

INTRODUCTION

0:00		The rhythm section establishes a Latin groove, contrasting a syncopated bass line with an **ostinato** pattern by Ellington on piano. Greer (drums) plays a disorienting accent on the fourth beat of the measure.

CHORUS 1

0:04	**A** (20 bars)	Tizol enters with a long, lingering melody on the valve trombone. Ellington continues his **ostinato**, adjusting it up and down to suit the harmonies.
0:21		Tizol holds out the last note of his melody. Underneath, Bigard enters with a clarinet **countermelody**.
0:24	**A** (20 bars)	Tizol repeats his long melody. In place of Ellington's ostinato, a trio of muted brass (Williams, Nanton, Stewart) accompanies him with snarling, syncopated chords.
0:41		Bigard reenters underneath Tizol's last note; the brass chords continue.
0:44	**B** (8 bars)	The groove shifts from Latin to straightforward swing. Over a new harmonic progression, Bigard's low-register solo competes for our attention with the brass chords.
0:52	**A** (6 bars)	The band as a whole enters in a brief passage in **block-chord** texture, ending on the dominant chord.

CHORUS 2

0:59	**A** (20 bars)	Firmly within the swing groove, Webster enters on tenor saxophone for a "blowing chorus" accompanied by the rhythm section. The harmonic progression is the same as in chorus 1.
1:13		In bars 15 and 16, Ellington marks the closing of the first section with two simple chords.
1:17		The bass drops down to the lower octave.
1:19	**A** (20 bars)	Webster continues his solo.
1:33		Ellington again plays his two simple chords.
1:36		In his last phrase, Webster increases the volume and intensity of his playing.
1:39	**B** (8 bars)	The muted brass trio returns in block-chord texture.
1:47	**A** (20 bars)	The saxophones enter in rich harmonies, reestablishing the opening melody. The drums stay within the swing groove, but recall the Latin opening by again accenting the fourth beat of the measure.
1:51		Against the melody, Stewart (trumpet) improvises a countermelody.
2:05		Ellington briefly reprises his ostinato figure.

INTERLUDE (based on A)

2:07		The brass enter with a rhythmically brilliant *soli*. Greer (drums) answers each of the first two phrases with an accent on the fourth beat.
2:17		A repeat of the *soli*.
2:22		Halfway through, the harmony heads toward a cadence, ending with a **dominant** chord.

INTRODUCTION

2:28		A sudden drop in volume signals the return of the Latin groove.

CHORUS 3 (abbreviated)

2:32	**A**	Tizol (trombone) plays the opening melody, once again accompanied only by the rhythm section.

CODA

2:52		Over the opening vamp, the band fades out.

The Later Years

After a long period on top, Ellington was due for a fall. It came with the decline of the Swing Era in the middle 1940s and continued for nearly a decade. The strain of continuous touring over twenty years had exhausted his musicians; one trumpet player claimed that he slept for nearly a year after leaving the band. More tellingly, Ellington suffered his first on-the-job death when Tricky Sam Nanton was felled by a stroke in 1946. Other musicians left to cash in on their growing reputations: Cootie Williams, Ben Webster, Juan Tizol, Rex Stewart, Johnny Hodges, and Lawrence Brown.

With the rise of modern jazz, Ellington's music no longer seemed central. He stubbornly kept his band together by pouring in his own royalties—fittingly enough, considering the band's contributions to several of his most lucrative songs. Yet he seemed to be having doubts about the value of his own achievement, judging from the radical and often misguided renovations he made on several of his classic works. He played for ice skaters and county fairs, wrote mambos and rhythm and blues, and waited.

Newport, 1956

The turnaround came, spectacularly, in 1956. Johnny Hodges and Lawrence Brown had returned to the band, and Ellington had recruited several gifted musicians, including tenor saxophonist Paul Gonsalves, who reflected the influences of Ben Webster and the harmonic advances of the bop generation—Gonsalves had worked with Dizzy Gillespie and Count Basie before joining Ellington in 1950. The band was in prime form when it was invited to the third Newport Jazz Festival, one of the first of the new summer extravaganzas that helped to transform the way jazz was heard and promoted.

Ellington came on late at night, after waiting for what seemed an eternity ("What are we—the animal act, acrobats?" he complained). Members of the audience had begun to head for the parking lot, but when the band broke into a two-part piece from 1937, "Diminuendo and Crescendo in Blue," the exodus came to a halt. In between the band's two parts, there was an open-ended blues solo, assigned to Gonsalves, who instantly created a contagious and growing musical energy. As the tension mounted, Ellington kept the solo going. A blonde woman in the crowd began dancing, and the audience went wild. Jo Jones helped to beat out time with a rolled newspaper on the stage apron. Gonsalves played a full twenty-seven blues choruses, earning him Ellington's nightly introduction for the next eighteen years as "the hero of the Newport Jazz Festival." The whole proceeding, preserved on tape but improved with some studio dubbing, was issued as *Ellington at Newport*, the best-selling album of Ellington's career. The Newport triumph put Ellington on the cover of *Time* magazine. A new era had begun.

In his last twenty years, Ellington took advantage of the space afforded by new LP recordings to write lengthy pieces. Most were suites—collections of characteristic Ellington miniatures loosely organized around a theme. He also worked as a film composer (*Anatomy of a Murder, Paris Blues*), and joined forces with traditionalists, including Louis Armstrong, Count Basie, and Ella Fitzgerald, and modernists, including Dizzy Gillespie, John Coltrane, Charles Mingus, Max Roach, and Ray Brown.

■ BILLY STRAYHORN (1915–1967)

Ellington's devoted partner in all this late activity was the ingeniously versatile yet personally reserved Billy Strayhorn, a composer in his own right as well as Ellington's co-composer, rehearsal pianist, deputy conductor, and occasional lyricist. He was Ellington's closest associate for twenty-eight years, the one man to whom any musical task could be reliably delegated. His first classic tune, "Lush Life" (a major hit for Nat "King" Cole, who slightly simplified the challenging harmonies), written as a teenager, reflected his love of densely chromatic music and his sense of isolation as a black man who refused to compromise his homosexuality. Ellington said the song brought him to tears.

Strayhorn joined Ellington in 1938. His first tune with the band was based on the directions Ellington gave him to his apartment: when you get to Manhattan, take the A train (rather than the D train, which headed off to the Bronx) to reach Harlem. "Take the 'A' Train" relied heavily on swing conventions, but its harmonic ingenuity and the sureness of its orchestral textures provided the band with a new classic.

Nicknamed "Swee' Pea" (after the baby in "Popeye"), Strayhorn steadily rose in stature through the 1950s and 1960s. The two composers worked so closely, sharing insights and completing one another's phrases, that it is often impossible to separate their work—on, for example, *Such Sweet Thunder* and *Far East Suite*. Most of the major works, including the larger suites

Duke Ellington used his wiles to convince his musicians to do exactly what he wanted, but he treated Billy Strayhorn (right), a brilliant composer who was an essential figure in the post-1930s Ellington band, with unwavering friendship and respect. This picture dates from 1960, when they were in Paris to score the film *Paris Blues*.

from the 1950s, carry both their names as composers. A significant number of pieces were the work of Strayhorn alone: "Satin Doll" (Ellington's last pop hit), "Chelsea Bridge," "A Flower Is a Lovesome Thing," "Day Dream," "Rain Check," "Something to Live For," and "Lotus Blossom," among many others.

"Blood Count"

As Strayhorn turned fifty, his health began to fail, and within two years he was in around-the-clock treatment in a New York hospital, where he continued to compose. One of the tunes was originally entitled "Blue Cloud"; but as he became mesmerized by his declining vital signs, it was reconceived as "Blood Count," his last composition. "That was the last thing he had to say," a close friend remembered. "And it wasn't 'Good-bye' or 'Thank you' or anything phony like that. It was 'This is how I feel . . . like it or leave it.'" Before Strayhorn died, Ellington performed an effective but preliminary arrangement of it in concert, allowing the composer to hear it on tape. Shortly afterward, Strayhorn slipped into oblivion. The band recorded the piece three months later, as part of an emotional tribute to Strayhorn—one of Ellington's magisterial albums—entitled "*. . . and his mother called him Bill.*"

The tune begins with more harmonic ambiguity than was usual for Strayhorn. We don't know where we are or where we're heading. In this bleak territory, Johnny Hodges, Strayhorn's favorite soloist (he wrote several pieces for him, including "Day Dream" and "Chelsea Bridge"), plays the lead melody with his characteristic knife-edged timbre, controlled vibrato, and unnerving glissandos. The piece proceeds with quiet resignation, first through D minor, then D major, until the second bridge (in chorus 2), when it erupts in a violent *crescendo*. It's as if the normally serene Hodges, overwhelmed by the resentment and impatience Strayhorn had encoded in the chromatic harmonies, explodes into an outpouring of grief, pressing against the physical limitations of his alto saxophone.

The moment subsides, and as the piece draws to a close, we can hear one of Strayhorn's dramatic farewell gestures. Over a coursing **pedal point**, the harmonies drop chromatically, one by one, toward the tonic. It's a bittersweet climax to a bittersweet tribute. The original LP recording ends with an almost unbearably private moment: while the band files out of the recording studio, Ellington sits at the piano playing "Lotus Blossom" over and over, hushing the departing musicians through his devotion. In the album's notes, Ellington offered this eulogy:

> His greatest virtue, I think, was his honesty—not only to others but to himself. . . . He demanded freedom of expression and lived in what we consider the most important of moral freedoms: freedom from hate, unconditionally; freedom from all self-pity (even throughout all the pain and bad news); freedom from fear of possibly doing something that might help another more than it might help himself; and freedom from the kind of pride that could make a man feel he was better than his brother or neighbor.

🎧 blood count

LISTENING GUIDE 25

DUKE ELLINGTON AND HIS ORCHESTRA
Duke Ellington, piano; Cat Anderson, Mercer
Ellington, Herbie Jones, Cootie Williams, trumpets;
Lawrence Brown, Buster Cooper, trombones; Chuck
Connors, bass trombone; Johnny Hodges, Russell
Procope, Jimmy Hamilton, alto saxophones; Paul
Gonsalves, tenor saxophone; Harry Carney, baritone
saxophone; Aaron Bell, bass; Steve Little, drums

- Label: RCA LSP-3906
- Date: 1967
- Style: big band
- Form: 32-bar popular song (**A A′ B A′**)

What to listen for:
- **harmonic ambiguity, resigned mood**
- **unusual brass timbres**
- **a dramatic explosion by Hodges in chorus 2**
- **rising and falling chromatic harmonies**

CHORUS 1 (32 bars)

0:00	**A**	Hodges (alto saxophone) begins playing melodic fragments over ambiguous harmonies. The band accompanies with slow, sustained harmonies and occasional **chromatic** lines. The bass plays two beats to the bar. The drums add color with the cymbals, with occasional accents on the tom-toms.
0:17		The harmony settles into a new key area in the **minor mode**, with the bass holding a **pedal point**. The saxophones increase tension with a gradually rising chromatic line. Hodges repeats a short, quick motive.
0:34	**A′**	A return to the opening melody.
0:50		The harmony is now in the **major mode**.
1:08	**B**	The new melodic phrase starts on a high pitch, descending sharply to a **blue note**.
1:16		By manipulating his embouchure, Hodges slides up to the high note.
1:33		The harmony rises **chromatically**.
1:41	**A′**	Hodges returns to the opening melody, expressing his emotions through swelling dynamics.
1:58		As the harmony settles into the major mode, the mood is hushed and expectant.
2:12		Driven by a drum roll, the band rises suddenly in a dramatic **crescendo**.

CHORUS 2 (abbreviated)

2:15	**B**	The band has the melody. Hodges improvises furiously in response.
2:31		As the intensity of his line increases, Hodges's tone thickens. Some of his individual notes are almost forced out, like barks.
2:39		Over a chromatic rise in harmony, he plays a violent two-note rising motive.
2:45		At the end of the phrase, the dynamics begin to abate.
2:48	**A′**	In a return to the opening, Hodges now sounds resigned, reflective.

CODA

3:20	The music continues quietly in the same vein.
3:37	The harmony has reached the **dominant**, preparing for the final cadence. Over a pedal point, the harmony falls chromatically. Hodges plays simple, mournful figures with a quiet, bluesy feeling.
3:45	The bass finally reaches the **tonic**, but the baritone saxophone continues to hold its note until the end.
3:47	The brass section, tightly muted, continues the chromatic falling chords.
3:52	Hodges uses **variable intonation** to color his melodies.
4:01	In his last phrase, Hodges plays a phrase from the opening of the tune, leaving us feeling unsettled.

As if to prove he could survive without Strayhorn, Ellington immersed himself in work during his last six years, accepting commissions that ranged from ballets to public occasions (a tone poem for the 150th anniversary of Jacksonville, Florida). He reserved his finest efforts for suites reflecting his travels, among them the *Latin American Suite* and *The Afro-Eurasian Eclipse*. His death was mourned as the end of an era and of a career that could never be duplicated—no other composer would ever manage to have his own orchestra at his beck and call for half a century.

DUKE ELLINGTON CHRONOLOGY		
1899	Born April 29 in Washington, D.C.	
1923	Arrives in New York.	
1927	Opens at the Cotton Club.	"Black and Tan Fantasy"
1929	Bubber Miley leaves, replaced by Cootie Williams.	
1930		"Mood Indigo"
1932		"It Don't Mean a Thing (if It Ain't Got That Swing)," "Sophisticated Lady"
1933	Tours Europe.	
1938	Billy Strayhorn joins the band.	
1939	Jimmy Blanton and Ben Webster join the band.	
1940		"Conga Brava"
1941		*Jump for Joy* (musical)
1943	Performs at Carnegie Hall.	*Black, Brown and Beige*
1951	Johnny Hodges leaves to form his own band.	
1955	Hodges returns.	
1956	Triumph at the Newport Jazz Festival.	*Such Sweet Thunder*
1965	Offer of Pulitzer Prize overruled.	
1966		*Far East Suite*
1967	Strayhorn dies.	"Blood Count"
1974	Ellington dies, May 24, in New York City.	

ADDITIONAL LISTENING	
Clarence "Pine Top" Smith	"Pine Top's Boogie Woogie" (1928)
The Blue Devils	"Squabblin'" (1929)
Andy Kirk (with Mary Lou Williams)	"The Lady Who Swings the Band" (1936)
Mary Lou Williams	"Little Joe from Chicago" (1939)
Bennie Moten	"Toby" (1932)
Count Basie	"Every Tub," "Blue and Sentimental," "Doggin' Around," "Jumpin' at the Woodside" (all 1938), "Lil' Darling" (1957)
Duke Ellington	"It Don't Mean a Thing (if It Ain't Got That Swing)" (1932), "Ko-Ko" (1940), "Concerto for Cootie" (1940), "Chelsea Bridge" (1941), *Black, Brown and Beige* (1943), "Diminuendo and Crescendo in Blue" (1956), "The Star-Crossed Lovers" (1957)

ONLINE MULTIMEDIA RESOURCES AND REVIEW MATERIALS

Author Insight Videos

Scott DeVeaux discusses Ellington's importance as a composer, how he made the most of individual musicians' timbre, and his partnership with Billy Strayhorn; Basie's use of head arrangements; and Kansas City boogie-woogie.

Interactive Listening Guides

Pete Johnson / Big Joe Turner, "It's All Right, Baby"
Andy Kirk / Mary Lou Williams, "Walkin' and Swingin' "
Count Basie, "One O'Clock Jump"
Duke Ellington, "Mood Indigo"
Duke Ellington, "Conga Brava"
Duke Ellington, "Blood Count"

Jazz Concepts (audio and/or video demonstrations of terms covered here)

backbeat	countermelody	modulation
block chords	dominant	ostinato
blue notes	downbeat	pedal point
break	false fingerings	riff
cadence	major mode	tonic
chromatic scale	minor mode	tremolo

- For quick reference, review the **Chapter Overview** and **Chapter Outline**.
- Take the online **Chapter** and **Listening Quizzes**.
- Use the online **Glossary** and **Flashcards** to review important terms.

A WORLD OF SOLOISTS

JAMMIN' THE BLUES

During the Swing Era, the leading bands were almost as well known for their star performers as for their overall styles. These soloists, like actors in a play, were assigned specific parts, which rarely allotted them as much as a full chorus and often no more than eight measures. As a result, they developed styles so distinct that fans tuning in to radio broadcasts could quickly identify them by their timbres, melodies, and rhythmic phrases.

Still, soloists were merely components in a larger unit, shining only as bright as the leader permitted. One way they worked off their frustrations at the restrictions imposed on them was in improvised jam sessions, usually played after hours. In the 1940s, when the wartime draft depleted the ranks of virtually all major orchestras, staged jam sessions became popular with the public. Soloists also found relief in small-group bands, which many successful orchestra leaders—Goodman, Ellington, and Woody Herman—formed as supplementary units.

The increasing popularity of soloists portended a new respect for jazz musicians. As free agents, they enjoyed diverse professional opportunities—working on records, in pit bands, and even in movie and radio studios, though most of those well-paid positions were reserved for white musicians. Beginning in the 1930s, fans voted for their

Billie Holiday, the quintessential jazz vocalist, has an angel over her shoulder, partly obscured by smoke at this 1949 recording session.

favorite bands, soloists, and singers in magazine polls. The friendly and not-so-friendly rivalries helped to spur a rapid development in musical technique. Compare, say, Armstrong's 1928 "West End Blues" and Coleman Hawkins's 1939 "Body and Soul," and you cannot fail to hear daunting developments in harmony, rhythm, and technical agility.

In 1944, as the Swing Era ground to a standstill, Norman Granz, a producer of staged jam sessions, hired photographer Gjon Mili to direct the classic ten-minute film *Jammin' the Blues*, which featured soloists who had become famous for their work with Count Basie, Lionel Hampton, and other bandleaders. Fastidiously directed, photographed, and edited, this film captured an informal letting-go by musicians in an environment free of written scores and other constraints. It foreshadowed the turnaround in jazz that took place in the postwar years, as small groups and extended improvisations replaced the checks and balances of big bands.

■ COLEMAN HAWKINS

No one exemplifies the rise of the independent soloist better than Coleman Hawkins. We have already seen how he adapted Armstrong's ideas during his years with Fletcher Henderson, eventually producing a legato style that refined the jazz ballad. But Hawkins's overall impact went way beyond that performance and era.

In his later years, Hawkins modestly claimed, "People always say I invented the jazz tenor—it isn't true. . . . Why, gangs of tenors would be coming into New York all the time from bands on the road." The saxophone had been around for sixty years before Hawkins's birth, occasionally used in symphonic music but best known as a starchy novelty instrument. The first important saxophonists in jazz focused on soprano (Sidney Bechet) and C-melody (Frank Trumbauer), but those instruments disappeared or declined in popularity as Hawkins established the tenor as the embodiment of jazz—much as the guitar came to signify rock and roll. Imbuing the instrument with individuality, passion, dignity, and romance, Hawkins erased its association with comic antics. He made the goose-necked horn look cool, virile, and even dangerous.

Coleman Hawkins, nicknamed "Bean," performed with characteristic passion at the second annual Newport Jazz Festival, 1955.

Musicians called him "Hawk" or "Bean" (as in "He's got a lot on the bean"). During his eleven years with the Henderson band (1923–34), Hawkins had few rivals and no peers. His style was now considered the "correct" one, characterized by heavy vibrato, powerful timbre, emotional zeal, and a harmonic ingenuity that fascinated musicians. His great musical innovation, beyond remaking the tenor saxophone in his own image, was to change the emphasis in improvisation from embellishing the melody to creating variations based on the song's harmonies.

Hawkins mastered chords and the way they relate to each other by developing a style based on arpeggios. In an **arpeggio**, a chord's notes are played successively, one at a time. They can be played in any order: a C7 chord may be arpeggiated as C, E, G, B-flat or in reverse or in another sequence entirely. Hawkins found myriad ways to maneuver through chords by breaking them down into these component notes, which he shaped into powerful rhythmic melodies. In the course of breaking them down, he frequently added harmonic substitutions—chords richer and more intricate than those the composer had provided.

In 1934, Hawkins signed with British bandleader Jack Hylton to tour England. He set sail expecting to stay for six months, but, bowled over by the size and enthusiasm of crowds that greeted him at every stop, ended up living in Europe for the next five years. During this time, he performed and recorded in London, Paris, the Hague, Zurich, and elsewhere, establishing an international paradigm for the tenor saxophone and jazz. While he was gone, a serious rival appeared in Lester Young, who offered an almost diametrically opposed approach that attracted many adherents. Hawkins kept up with the American scene and the newer crop of tenor saxophonists through recordings; he expressed particular admiration for Ben Webster.

In July 1939, weeks before Germany invaded Poland, Hawkins had no choice but to return to the United States, where observers wondered if he could retain his standing as the No. 1 tenor saxophonist. In September, he appeared on a Lionel Hampton session alongside two tenors who had been influenced by him, Webster and Chu Berry (who had recently enjoyed success with a recording he and Roy Eldridge made of "Body and Soul"), as well as an unknown trumpet player, Dizzy Gillespie. This session was a warm-up for Hawkins.

Across the Atlantic

🎧 "Body and Soul"

A month later, Hawkins conducted his own session, which unexpectedly turned out to be one of jazz's seismic events. The idea was to showcase the nine-piece band he commanded at a New York nightclub, Kelly's Stables. The band spent most of the session nailing down the three complicated arrangements Hawkins had prepared; but the record label needed a fourth side in order to release two discs. The producer cajoled him into playing an ad-lib rendition of a song he had performed at the nightclub, "Body and Soul." Hawkins wasn't happy about it, but he agreed to play it once, without rehearsal.

Hawkins's "Body and Soul" is a pinnacle in jazz improvisation. Recorded entirely off the cuff, it has the weight and logic of formal composition and the tension and energy of spontaneous invention. John Green had composed the thirty-two-bar **A A B A** melody for a Broadway revue in 1930, and it quickly became a favorite among "torch singers"—women who specialized in heart-on-sleeve laments. Louis Armstrong adapted the tune as a jazz piece, and memorable renditions followed by Benny Goodman, guitarist Django Reinhardt, and Berry-Eldridge. Hawkins's version confirmed it as a jazz and pop standard, and made it an everlasting challenge to other tenor saxophonists.

After the piano introduction by Gene Rodgers, the performance is all Hawkins for two choruses and a coda. He begins briskly, his tone smooth as worn felt. Then, after two measures, something unusual happens: "Body and Soul" disappears. Hawkins heads into new territory, extending his initial phrase into an original melodic arc. His spiraling phrases, representing a zenith of the arpeggio style, advance with assurance and deliberation, building tension. Hawkins later described the climactic passages as a kind of sexual release. This record proved to be a critical milestone and a tremendous commercial success.

🎧 body and soul

COLEMAN HAWKINS

Tommy Lindsay, Joe Guy, trumpets; Earl Hardy, trombone; Jackie Fields, Eustis Moore, alto saxophones; Coleman Hawkins, tenor saxophone; Gene Rodgers, piano; William Oscar Smith, bass; Arthur Herbert, drums

- Label: Bluebird B-10253
- Date: 1939
- Style: small group swing
- Form: 32-bar popular song (**A A B A**)

What to listen for:
- Hawkins's melodic paraphrase (at beginning) *and* harmonic improvisation
- a gradual build from the romantic opening to the exciting leaps at the climax
- double-time passages (played at twice the speed of the ground rhythm)
- chromatic harmony

INTRODUCTION

0:00		Rodgers (piano) plays a four-bar introduction in D-flat major.

CHORUS 1

0:10	**A**	Hawkins plays a decorated version of the original melody of "Body and Soul"—the opening phrases (in the lower register) with a breathy tone and somewhat behind the beat. Behind him, the piano keeps time by playing on every beat, with the bass tending to play every other beat. The cymbals slightly emphasize the backbeat.
0:31	**A**	Hawkins's phrases curve upward as they begin to escape the gravity of the original melody.
0:51	**B**	A **modulation** leads to the bridge, in the distant key of D major.
1:08		Through a **chromatic** chord sequence, the tune modulates back to D-flat major.
1:11	**A**	Hawkins's improvisation is now securely in **double-time**, moving in 16th notes, twice as fast as the accompaniment.

CHORUS 2

1:32	**A**	The horns enter, playing a solid chordal background behind Hawkins's solo. He begins adding even faster figures (32nd notes).
1:47		The improvised line uses **sequences**: short melodic patterns repeated on different pitches.
1:52	**A**	
2:00		An intense, piercing entry in the upper register (over a **diminished-seventh chord**).
2:13	**B**	During the second bridge, the horns drop out, leaving Hawkins accompanied only by the rhythm section.
2:33	**A**	The horns reenter; with a series of ascending leaps, Hawkins's solo suddenly reaches its climax.

CODA

2:48		During the last two bars of the second chorus, Hawkins allows both the horn and rhythm sections to dissipate. He continues to play with no accompaniment, his line dropping in register and volume.
2:56		He holds his final note, signaling the end to the rest of the band, which enters (somewhat untidily) on the **tonic** chord.

Hawkins's recording of "Body and Soul" scored on the pop charts for six weeks in the beginning of 1940—audiences demanded he play it at virtually every appearance. Significantly, they clamored not for the original song, but for his recorded improvisation. In later years, he performed the 1939 solo as if it were the written theme, following it with additional variations. Just about every important tenor saxophonist in jazz eventually took a shot at "Body and Soul," from Lester Young and Ben Webster to Sonny Rollins and John Coltrane to David Murray and Joshua Redman. Charlie Parker memorized the solo, quoting from it on his first radio broadcasts.

The idea of improvising on the harmonic foundation of songs advanced the development of modern jazz, as it emerged after the war. Adventurous musicians like Parker, Dizzy Gillespie, and Bud Powell were encouraged to forge their own paths. Hawkins himself, however, continued to work in the swing style with which he felt most comfortable, though he often played with young modernists—and, in fact, hired Thelonious Monk when others kept their distance.

The Hawkins School

Hawkins's impact on jazz was not unlike that of Louis Armstrong. His solos on Fletcher Henderson's records so mesmerized musicians around the country that many who had taken up the C-melody saxophone after hearing Trumbauer switched to the tenor. Hawkins's combustible riff-laden solo on Henderson's "The Stampede" (1926) was especially influential: for the first time, the tenor leaped from the band, punching and feinting with the dynamism of a trumpet. During the next decade, Hawkins's primacy was nearly absolute—except in Kansas City and the Southwest, where an indigenous tenor saxophone style took root, exemplified by Lester Young.

It's a measure of Hawkins's power that Ben Webster (1909–1973), born in Kansas City, chose him as his muse—knowing his music only from 78-rpm records—over Lester Young, with whom he traveled. Webster arrived in New York in 1932 as a member of Benny Moten's orchestra, and worked with several key bandleaders—including Andy Kirk, Fletcher Henderson, Cab Calloway, and Teddy Wilson—before Duke Ellington recruited him; with Ellington, he made his name.

Musicians nicknamed Webster "the Brute" for his rambunctious playing and capricious temper. Trumpeter and memoirist Rex Stewart, who worked

Ben Webster

© JACK TOWERS, COURTESY OF DUNCAN SCHIEDT COLLECTION

The Duke Ellington Orchestra had the most illustrious reed and brass sections in jazz history, especially after Ellington recruited tenor saxophonist Ben Webster. Top row: Rex Stewart, trumpet; Ray Nance, violin and trumpet; Wallace Jones, trumpet; Sonny Greer (top, partly obscured), drums; Joe Nanton, Juan Tizol, Lawrence Brown, trombones. Bottom row: Barney Bigard, clarinet; Johnny Hodges, Otto Hardwick, alto saxophones; Ben Webster, tenor; Harry Carney, baritone. Onstage at Sioux Falls, South Dakota, 1939.

alongside him in both the Henderson and Ellington bands, wrote that in his early period, "he blew with unrestrained savagery, buzzing and growling through chord changes like a prehistoric monster challenging a foe. With the passage of time, this fire has given way to tender, introspective declamations of maturing and reflective beauty." Webster's gruff yet empathic style established him as one of the three great pillars of prewar tenor saxophone, along with Hawkins and Young. Of the three, Webster ripened the most in later years; his mellow playing in the 1950s and 1960s is arguably more distinctive and satisfying than the innovative triumphs of his youth.

Chu Berry

Leon "Chu" Berry (1908–1941), born in West Virginia, began on alto saxophone and switched to tenor in 1929. A year later, he traveled with a band to New York and soon became a musical mainstay, working and recording with such important musicians as Benny Carter and Charlie Johnson (who led a popular group at Small's Paradise in Harlem). As Hawkins toured Europe, Berry took his spot as Henderson's tenor soloist from 1935 to 1937, where he displayed his characteristic rhythmic drive, weighty timbre, and ability to remain melodically relaxed at a speedy tempo—an aspect of his playing that impressed the young Charlie Parker. Berry achieved his greatest success in 1937 when he joined the Cab Calloway band, a tenure tragically cut short by his death in an automobile accident, at thirty-three.

Roy Eldridge

Roy Eldridge (1911–1989), born in Pittsburgh, was an outstanding high-speed, high-note, harmonically daring, bravura trumpet player. He inherited Armstrong's mantle as the most original and influential brass man of the Swing Era, and set the stage for the ascension of Dizzy Gillespie (who called him "the messiah of our generation"). Eldridge moved to New York in 1930, and within two years his competitive spirit and short size had earned him the nickname "Little Jazz"; among musicians, he was known simply as "Jazz." He closely studied Armstrong, but his primary stimulation came from saxophonists. One admirer was Hawkins. "He told me he liked my playing from some records he heard in Europe," Eldridge said. "He was saying, 'Man, this cat ain't playing harsh like the rest of them cats. He's kind of playing more or less like a saxophone, lot of legato things, playing changes.' But he didn't realize that I was playing some of his stuff, and Pres's [Lester Young's] and Chu's."

Eldridge joined Henderson in 1935, and left a year later to form his own eight-piece group. That band's few recordings, like "Heckler's Hop" and "Wabash Stomp," raised the bar on jazz trumpet and on jazz's emotional resources. His penchant for stratospheric climaxes thrilled jazz fans. His timbre was unmistakably personal, bright yet coated with grit, as effective on ballads as on showstoppers—making him a natural for backing singers, including Ella Fitzgerald and Billie Holiday.

In the 1940s, Eldridge became a focal point in the battle for integration in the entertainment world, as the first black musician to sit in a white orchestra, Gene Krupa's band (1941–43; see p. 148), but his stay was of primary importance for his breakthroughs as an artist. His classic trumpet solos, including

Roy Eldridge (trumpet) and Chu Berry (tenor saxophone) were among the most exciting soloists of the Swing Era, and close friends who appeared together on recording sessions and with the Fletcher Henderson band. In this picture, they were just getting started as members of Teddy Hill's Orchestra, in 1935.

DUNCAN SCHEDT COLLECTION

what many consider his masterpiece, "Rockin' Chair," remain benchmark performances, as are his solos with Artie Shaw's band in 1944 and his participation in after-hours Harlem sessions that contributed to the birth of bebop.

■ LESTER YOUNG (1909–1959)
and the Lestorian Mode

Lester Young's tenor saxophone style was initially considered so radical that he was hooted out of the Henderson band. Born in Mississippi, Young grew up in New Orleans, where his father, W. H. Young, trained him and his siblings to play a variety of instruments (Lester played violin, drums, trumpet, and several kinds of saxophone) so that they could form the Young Family Band. An ardent admirer of Frank Trumbauer, whose records he carried everywhere, Lester sought to reproduce Trumbauer's lighter, vibratoless sound on tenor. According to Ben Webster, Lester developed a distinctive tenor saxophone timbre as early as 1929.

In 1933, after performing in the Midwest with King Oliver, Benny Moten, the Blue Devils, and others, he settled in Kansas City, where he joined the Basie band. When Fletcher Henderson's band came to town in December of that year, Young and Hawkins squared off at a legendary jam session involving several tenor saxophonists including Webster, lasting all night and into the morning. By most accounts, Young emerged the victor.

After Hawkins departed for Europe in 1934, Henderson convinced Young to come to New York. He didn't last long there, however: the other musicians in Henderson's band ridiculed his light sound and introverted personal style. Henderson reluctantly let him go, after lecturing his musicians that Lester played better than any of them, and Young worked his way back to Kansas City, where he returned to Count Basie. Basie's sizzling, rangy swing was an ideal platform for Young; unlike Henderson's detailed arrangements, Basie's were streamlined and blues-driven. His soloists were encouraged to improvise at length, accompanied by the rhythm section and the ad-libbed head riffs. In that atmosphere, Young created a free-floating style, wheeling and diving like a gull, banking with low, funky riffs that pleased dancers and listeners alike. Stan Getz, one of countless young musicians who began by imitating Young, called his style of playing the Lestorian Mode—a fount of ideas expressing a new freedom in jazz.

Young's way of improvising on a song differed from Hawkins's in almost every particular. Where Hawkins arpeggiated each chord in a harmonic progression, Young created melodic phrases that touched down on some chords and ignored others. Given, for example, an eight-measure passage with a dozen or so chords, Young would improvise a melody that fit the overall harmonic framework without detailing every harmony. He also had a more liberal attitude toward dissonance and rhythm. One of his favorite gambits was to repeat a note while slightly altering its pitch (often by using false fingering), making it a bit flat. And while Hawkins's phrases were tied to the beat, Young's sometimes disregarded the beat, creating an uninhibited counterrhythm.

At a 1948 recording session, Lester Young was beckoned from his instrument and music. He put his cigarette on a Coke bottle and hung his famous porkpie hat on his saxophone case. Photographer Herman Leonard took one look and recognized an iconic still life— and created a classic of jazz photography.

With Basie

© HERMAN LEONARD PHOTOGRAPHY LLC.

When Basie brought his band to Chicago and New York, in 1936, the world was ready for Lester, though he would always remain something of an outsider. More than any other musician, Young introduced the idea of "cool," in musical style and personal affect. Shy and diffident, he stood aloof from most conventions. "I'm looking for something soft," he said. "I can't stand that loud noise. It's got to be sweetness, you dig? Sweetness can be funky, filthy or anything." He famously wore a broad-brimmed porkpie hat—a kind of Western fedora with a flat top—and narrow knit ties. When he played, he held the saxophone aloft and at a horizontal angle, almost like a flute. He spoke a colorful, obscure slang of his own invention, some of which became a part of jazz diction, including his nicknames for musicians. He called Billie Holiday "Lady Day"; she returned the favor by nicknaming him "Pres" (as in president of all saxophonists). Both honorifics stuck.

Many of the musicians who went on to pioneer modern jazz worshiped Young, learning his solos and imitating his look. White saxophonists (like Stan Getz, Zoot Sims, Al Cohn, and Allen Eager) tended to focus on his lyricism and feathery timbre in the upper register. Black saxophonists (like Dexter Gordon, Wardell Gray, Hank Mobley, and Illinois Jacquet) preferred his blues riffs and darker timbre in the middle and lower registers. Dexter Gordon observed, "Zoot and I worked in a club in Hollywood. He was playing Lester and I was playing Lester, but there was always a difference." Young's style was so stirring and varied that it spurred the Swing Era, bebop, *and* rhythm and blues.

🎧 "Oh! Lady Be Good"

In "Oh! Lady Be Good," you can hear the youthful zest of Lester Young's style at its peak—indeed, this two-chorus solo is often cited as his finest work on records. All the attributes he brought to jazz are apparent, from the initial entrance, followed by a rest and a long rolling phrase, to the slurred (connected) notes, polyrhythms, staccato single notes, pitch variation, and unfailing swing that make this improvisation a riveting experience. The song, by George and Ira Gershwin, originated in their score for the 1924 Broadway musical *Lady, Be Good*. Count Basie plays the melody; Young leaves it behind, inventing melodies that float over the song's chords.

"Jones-Smith Incorporated" was the pseudonym created by John Hammond when he determined to be the first to record Basie, despite Basie's contract with Decca. The session was held early one morning in Chicago, after the band had played through the night. To release the records, Hammond took the names of trumpeter Carl "Tatti" Smith and drummer Jo Jones, pretending it was a new group—fooling no one who had ever heard Basie or Young.

Young's life changed irrevocably when he was drafted, in October 1944—he was starring in *Jammin' the Blues* when he received the summons. After admitting to officers that he smoked marijuana, and additionally nettling them with his perplexing lingo, Young was subjected to a ninety-five-minute trial and sentenced to a year of hard labor at a debilitation barracks (D.B.) in Georgia. Although he announced his return to civilian life nine months later with a triumphant 1945 recording, "D.B. Blues," he never completely recovered from the incarceration and soon surrendered to alcoholism. Charles Mingus's tribute "Goodbye Pork Pie Hat" expresses the feeling of loss that accompanied Young's death, at forty-nine.

🎧 oh! lady be good

JONES-SMITH INCORPORATED

Carl Smith, trumpet; Lester Young, tenor saxophone;
Count Basie, piano; Walter Page, bass; Jo Jones,
drums

- Label: Vocalion 3459
- Date: 1936
- Style: Kansas City swing
- Form: 32-bar popular song (**A A B A**)

What to listen for:

- **Young's two-chorus solo (choruses 2 and 3): unpredictable rhythms, relaxed and bluesy**
- **Jones's cool, quiet drumming (with the beat on the high-hat cymbal)**

CHORUS 1

0:00	**A**	Basie begins by stating the melody to the song with his right hand. Behind him, Jones on drums plays quietly on the high-hat cymbal.
0:10	**A**	At times, Basie begins to show traces of a **stride** foundation in his left hand.
0:20	**B**	
0:29		The drums begin to build intensity by playing a **backbeat**.
0:30	**A**	

CHORUS 2

0:40	**A**	Young enters with a three-note statement, accompanied by a drum accent. His phrases are inflected with notes from the blues. Behind him, Basie plays chords on the beat.
0:51	**A**	
0:59		In one of the phrases, Young bends one of his pitches.
1:01	**B**	He begins to build intensity by starting phrases with accented, scooped notes.
1:11	**A**	He creates **polyrhythms** out of a single note.
1:16		Another striking use of variable intonation.

CHORUS 3

1:21	**A**	Young's second chorus begins higher in pitch and adds faster rhythmic values, prompting Page to relax from four beats to two beats to the measure.
1:32	**A**	Beginning with a scooped note, Young creates polyrhythms from a short phrase. Page returns to four beats to the measure.
1:42	**B**	At the bridge, Young plays a descending phrase that becomes polyrhythmic through off-center repetition; the drummer responds with a drum roll.
1:48		Young reaches the high point of his solo.
1:52	**A**	He starts the last section with a dramatic **syncopation**, followed by another off-center repetition.
2:00		Young's last phrase bids us a bluesy farewell.

CHORUS 4

2:03	**A**	Smith begins his trumpet solo. Behind him, Young starts playing a background **riff** figure.
2:13	**A**	
2:23	**B**	Smith's solo and Young's syncopated riff tangle in a complex polyrhythmic interaction.
2:34	**A**	

CHORUS 5 (abbreviated)

2:44	**B**	While the drums drop out, the bass line quietly rises to a higher register. Basie plays a simple piano solo.
2:54	**A**	With a sudden increase in volume, the two horns and the drums reenter for a climactic final chorus.

OVER THERE

Having spread out from New Orleans and the South to Chicago, New York, Kansas City, California, and other parts of the United States, jazz leaped the oceans as quickly as recordings could carry it. Adherents listened to and learned to play jazz in Europe, Asia, South America, Australia, and Africa, as it returned to the nations whose emigrants had first transported its musical ingredients.

Two contrary factors stimulated jazz's growth abroad. First, it was recognized as a serious, exhilarating new art. When Armstrong, Ellington, Fats Waller, and Hawkins appeared in France, England, Holland, and Denmark, they received the kind of respect due major artists, and many black musicians, singers, and dancers followed their lead. Racism continued to rear its head, but it was not supported by laws that defined its victims as second-class citizens. In France, Negro entertainers were considered chic.

The second factor tried to quash the first. In the Soviet Union and Germany, jazz was illegal, and thus came to represent rebellion and liberty. Music that prized personal expression as its highest aesthetic goal could not help but exemplify the lure of freedom and democracy. In these societies, jazz flourished underground. When Benny Goodman toured Moscow in the 1950s, he was amazed to discover that he had thousands of Russian fans who referred to his records by catalog numbers—a practice once intended to fool spies.

The Nazis banned jazz as decadent, the product of barbaric blacks and Jews. Then as the world moved toward war, German leaders were obliged to face the fact that in the countries they occupied, citizens were far more likely to listen to the local radio stations, which played jazz constantly, than to German broadcasts. Instead of combating the jazz craze, they tried to join it, as German musicians recorded (unintentionally hilarious) imitations of American swing hits. After the war, liberated cities like Paris, Copenhagen, and Amsterdam treated jazz musicians as heroes.

Wherever jazz landed, it developed a bond with local musical practices. Argentina's tango, Brazil's samba, and Cuba's clave influenced jazz and were influenced by it in turn. Jazz similarly mixed with the music of Africa, Japan, Finland, and Hawaii, generating new compounds. American jazz musicians remained stars in all these places, but local musicians also achieved fame. In 1971, Duke Ellington introduced *The Afro-Eurasian Eclipse* by pointing out that as various cultures lose their provincial identities, "it's most improbable that anyone will ever know exactly who is enjoying the shadow of whom."

■ DJANGO REINHARDT (1910–1953)

Only one European jazz artist was universally conceded a seat at the table of prime movers—those figures who decisively changed the way jazz is played. Django Reinhardt was born in a Gypsy caravan passing through Belgium. He and his two younger siblings grew up in a settlement near Paris. Their father, an itinerant entertainer, abandoned the family when Django was five, and their mother supported them by weaving baskets and making bracelets from artillery shells found on World War I battlefields.

Django learned violin and banjo from relatives before taking up guitar, which he began playing professionally at twelve. Then in 1928, shortly before he turned nineteen, he was struck by a tragedy that would have ended the ambitions of most musicians: his caravan caught fire and he was trapped inside. His left hand, which held tight the blanket that saved him, suffered severe burns and mutilation—the fourth and fifth fingers folded inward like a claw. Determined to continue with the guitar despite this setback, he developed a way of playing single notes and chords with only two fingers and his thumb; at the same time, he had to learn to arch his hand so that the damaged fingers did not get in the way.

Within a few years, Reinhardt created new fingerings to play chords while perfecting rapid-fire single-line improvisations that ranged over the entire length of the fret board. His right hand picked the strings with such percussive strength that, long before the introduction of the electric guitar, his sound had a vital, piercing tone. With the help of a microphone, he had no trouble being heard. Reinhardt's love of music was transformed by the first jazz records to reach Paris. When he heard duets by guitarist Eddie Lang and violinist Joe Venuti, he recognized an immediate kinship with jazz improvisation and rhythm. At a time when most American guitarists played little more than rhythm and chords, Reinhardt emerged as a soloist of stunning originality and a deeply personal romanticism.

The turning point for European jazz came in 1934 (the same year Coleman Hawkins embarked on his five-year visit). A couple of years earlier, a few French fans, including critics Hugues Panassié and Charles Delaunay, had formed the Hot Club de France, an influential organization for enthusiasts and musicians. Then in 1934, Panassié published *Le jazz hot*, the first serious critical book on jazz in any language—and the first to suggest the preeminent role of African Americans. He and Delaunay prepared to launch a magazine, *Jazz Hot* (still in existence today), and a band to represent the club's musical point of view: Quintette du Hot Club de France.

The Quintette, which arose out of informal jam sessions, included two powerful and like-minded soloists—Reinhardt and violinist Stephane Grappelli—with an unusual rhythm section of two guitars and bass. Recordings by the Quintette drew high praise in Europe and were avidly sought in the United States. If Bix Beiderbecke had shown that whites could master jazz with individuality, the Quintette du Hot Club demonstrated that Europeans could do the same. It confirmed the idea that jazz, though American in origin, was a musical art of universal potential.

Given Reinhardt's immediate acceptance by Americans (after the war, Ellington would sponsor his only visit to the United States), Delaunay began recording him with visiting Americans: Hawkins, Benny Carter, violinist Eddie South, trumpeter Bill Coleman, clarinetist Barney Bigard, and others. Hawkins was the most prominent of the guest soloists, but Carter was perhaps the most significant: in addition to playing superb alto saxophone and trumpet, he wrote arrangements that epitomized international jazz.

Django Reinhardt acquired his first Gibson electric guitar, shown here, during his only visit to New York, in 1946, as a guest of Duke Ellington. During that same trip, he also got to meet a playful Paul Whiteman, whose 1920s orchestra helped to introduce the brilliant, tragic guitarist Eddie Lang, a decisive influence on the young Django.

© EF/AP/CORBIS

Quintette du Hot Club de France

PHOTO BY CHARLES PETERSON, COURTESY OF DON PETERSON

Benny Carter—multi-instrumentalist, composer, arranger, and orchestra leader—was known among musicians as the King because he did everything with originality and panache. New York, 1941.

■ BENNY CARTER (1907–2003)

Press agents and pundits could call who they liked king, but musicians privately reserved the royal epithet for a hero of the Swing Era who received little popular acclaim: the modest, soft-spoken jack-of-all-musical-trades Benny Carter. Born in New York City, Carter learned piano from his mother, but was largely self-taught as an instrumentalist (clarinet, tenor and soprano saxophone, trombone, and piano), composer, and arranger. He formed his own orchestra in 1932.

Carter's importance to jazz has four components: instrumentalist, composer-arranger, bandleader, and social activist. Along with Johnny Hodges, Carter established the alto saxophone as a major jazz instrument, paralleling Hawkins's impact on tenor. He played with an unruffled, melodic flair, underscored by compositional logic. He also developed a personal approach on trumpet, which he played less frequently but with memorable aplomb.

As a composer, Carter emerged in the 1930s as one of the most accomplished tunesmiths in jazz ("When Lights Are Low" and "Blues in My Heart" became popular standards). He was the first important jazz arranger to cut away the complex ornamentation of most dance bands, setting a standard for swing that would soon be echoed in the arrangements of Fletcher Henderson and Count Basie. The most imitated trademark in Carter's orchestrations was his writing for the reed section, which could swing with the impulsiveness of an improvised solo: the highlight of many of his works is a chorus by unified saxophones (*soli*).

As a bandleader, Carter enjoyed little commercial success; at a time when most bands courted dancers, he concentrated on musical refinement. Yet he was so much admired by fellow musicians that he had his pick of players. Musicians who worked in his bands in the swing years include Ben Webster, Chu Berry, Teddy Wilson, Dizzy Gillespie, trombonists Vic Dickenson and J. J. Johnson, drummer Max Roach, and Miles Davis.

As an activist, Carter steadfastly fought racism by opening doors closed to African Americans. In 1937, two years after arriving in Europe, he organized, at a Dutch resort, the first integrated and international orchestra in jazz history. Determined to create similar opportunities at home, he worked his way into the Hollywood studio system, one of the last bastions of segregation in the entertainment world. There, his temperament (mild-mannered but very tough), business savvy, and uncommon versatility allowed him to crack the "color bar." As a result, he enjoyed a rare level of financial security in jazz, living in Beverly Hills and driving a Rolls Royce. He worked on dramatic and musical films and more than two dozen television programs, beginning with the l950s police series *M Squad*. In 1978, Carter was inducted into the Black Filmmakers Hall of Fame. It was at that point that he revived his career as a soloist, achieving his greatest success as a touring jazz musician in his seventies and eighties.

🎧 "I'm Coming, Virginia"

Many of Carter's stylistic strengths are apparent in his 1938 treatment of the 1926 standard "I'm Coming, Virginia," by black songwriters Will Marion Cook (the man who brought Sidney Bechet to Europe in 1919) and Donald

Heywood. Carter leads an integrated and pan-national ensemble (it was recorded in Paris) in an arrangement that offers his own exceptional alto saxophone solo, a chorus by Django Reinhardt, and a signature climax featuring a four-part voicing of the saxophones. By the middle and late twentieth century, the world outside the United States produced countless accomplished jazz musicians, some of them achieving international renown and exercising an influence that would be absorbed by American players abroad and at home. For Europe, the spark that ignited that jazz fever was fanned in the short period before the war when travelers like Carter and Hawkins made common cause, inviting the world's musicians to join in. They wanted to spread jazz, not keep it to themselves.

🎧 i'm coming, virginia

LISTENING GUIDE 28

BENNY CARTER AND HIS ORCHESTRA
Benny Carter, Fletcher Allen, alto saxophones; Bertie King, Alix Combelle, tenor saxophones; Yorke de Souza, piano; Django Reinhardt, guitar; Len Harrison, bass; Robert Montmarché, drums

- Label: Swing (F)20
- Date: 1938
- Style: big-band swing
- Form: 24-bar popular song (**A A' B**)

What to listen for:
- Reinhardt's acoustic guitar solo (chorus 3)
- Carter's supple arrangements for saxophone *soli* (choruses 1 and 5)

INTRODUCTION

0:00   The piano plays a four-bar introduction, lightly accompanied by the drums.

CHORUS 1

0:05   **A**   The four saxophones enter with a *soli* in **block-chord** harmony. This arrangement by Carter is based on the original tune, but varies it through new rhythmic patterns reminiscent of speech.

0:16   **A'**

0:28   **B**

INTERLUDE

0:39   The saxophones continue their block-chord texture, accompanied only by a faint pulse on the bass drum.

CHORUS 2

0:44   **A**   The Belgian tenor saxophonist Combelle takes a solo. Behind him, Reinhardt on guitar plays a heavy eight-beats-to-the bar pattern.

0:55   **A'**

0:58   Reinhardt relaxes into a more normal texture, playing chords on the **backbeat.**

1:06   **B**

CHORUS 3

1:18   **A**   Reinhardt enters with a dissonant harmonic **arpeggio** on guitar. Underneath him, the piano plays a stiff accompaniment.

1:22   Reinhardt plays a **blue note**, which tails off at the end of a phrase.

1:29   **A'**

1:40   **B**

CHORUS 4

1:51	**A**	Carter takes a solo. The other saxophones support him with simple chords in the background.
2:02	**A'**	
2:14	**B**	

INTERLUDE

| 2:22 | | The tenor saxophones interrupt with a **syncopated** phrase. The full band then plays a series of chords that modulate to a new key. |

CHORUS 5

2:28	**A**	The saxophone section reenters, this time with a much freer and rhythmically varied *soli*. It begins with a new riff in bare **octaves**, followed by a tumultuous plunge in block-chord harmonies.
2:37		Reinhardt interjects a brief phrase in octaves.
2:39	**A'**	
2:41		For dramatic relief, Carter reduces the sound of the ensemble to an octave.
2:50	**B**	
2:56		A familiar chord progression leads to the final cadence.

■ Women in Jazz: VALAIDA SNOW (1904–1956)

During the war, women were on the rise. While men were in uniform, Rosie the Riveter—arms flexed in determination—symbolized the readiness of women to work for their nation's defense, whether on factory floors or on the bandstand. The entertainment business, however, stubbornly maintained its prejudices. The piano was considered "feminine," providing fewer barriers for the likes of Julia Lee and Mary Lou Williams, but wind and percussion instruments were regarded as the exclusive province of men. "Have you ever heard a woman saxophonist who didn't get a quavering tone with absolutely uncontrolled vibrato?" complained one critic in a 1938 issue of *Down Beat* magazine. "The mind may be willing, but the flesh is weak!" It was one thing to travel in an all-women ensemble (the International Sweethearts of Rhythm and the Harlem Playgirls were among the hardest-swinging territory bands of the day), but the majority of women associated with male outfits functioned as dancers and singers, showing off their bodies in luxurious or skimpy clothing.

Even the best of them had to tough it out. While touring with the Count Basie band, Billie Holiday ruined her stockings by playing craps on the floor of the bus, and finally quit in disgust. Anita O'Day, touring with Gene Krupa's band, grew tired of the expense of maintaining evening gowns and insisted on wearing the same band jacket that the men wore. This prompted accusations of lesbianism, leading O'Day to wonder, "What does a jacket or shirt have to do with anyone's sex life?" Only a few women made names for themselves as instrumentalists in male bands: trumpeters

Valaida Snow could dance and play most string and reed instruments, but she won fame as a trumpet player, singer, and bandleader—a remarkable achievement for a woman in the 1930s. She's pictured here, sleek and masterly, leading the orchestra for the British production of the Broadway success *Blackbirds of 1934,* at London's Coliseum that year.

Billie Rodgers and Norma Carson, vibraphonist Marjorie Hymans, trombonist Melba Liston. Ultimately, the pressures of the road proved too much for most women, whose careers were cut short by family duties, marriage, or social convention.

One of the more remarkable careers of the Swing Era was that of Valaida Snow, born in Chattanooga, Tennessee. Fortunately for her, there was no prejudice against performing in her family: her father was an entertainer, while her mother studied music at Howard University. Snow, who was born with perfect pitch, mastered a variety of instruments (cello, bass, violin, guitar, harp, and saxophone) before settling on the trumpet. Unlike most of the soloists we've followed so far, her career was centered on vaudeville, taking advantage of her skills in singing and dancing. She moved to New York in 1922 to star in Barron Wilkins's Harlem cabaret; two years later, she appeared in Eubie Blake's revue *The Chocolate Dandies* alongside the vivacious dancer Josephine Baker. Baker moved on to Paris to headline *La Revue Nègre,* where her erotic dancing made her a sensational international success. Snow went overseas as well, beginning with a trip to London in 1926 with *Lew Leslie's Blackbirds.* From that point on, she was in continual motion, traveling as far afield as Shanghai and Moscow, and returning periodically to perform in Chicago and New York.

Snow's appeal was multifaceted. She was an excellent trumpet player and singer, her style modeled on Louis Armstrong's, which she often combined with dancing: in one stage act, she brandished her trumpet while hoofing on top of a huge bass drum. Armstrong remembered her specialty number at the Sunset Café in Chicago: she lined up seven pairs of shoes at the front of the stage, ranging from tap shoes to Dutch clogs, Turkish slippers, and Russian boots, and did a specialty dance in each pair. Backstage, she was an efficient manager, often serving as music director for the bands or orchestras that accompanied her act. Earl Hines recalled her riding in a Mercedes, driven by her chauffeur: "She used to dress luxuriously and look very glamorous. She was just a beautiful and exceptionally talented woman."

🎧 "You're Driving Me Crazy"

This brisk, upbeat selection was paradoxically rife with a daring political subtext. Snow, having made all her pre-war records in Europe, never having enjoyed comparable opportunities in the United States, was in no hurry to return home when war broke out. Unlike other American jazz musicians who were greeted rapturously in Denmark (including Louis Armstrong, Coleman Hawkins, and Fats Waller), she thought she could stick it out. "You're Driving Me Crazy" is from a session she recorded in Copenhagen in tandem with Winstrup Olesen's Swingband three months *after* the Nazis invaded Denmark. Two years later, she was allowed to return to the United States, but a remarkable bond had formed between the Danes and jazz, which they embraced as the dissident music of liberation. Those who continued to play it, like Leo Mathisen (heard here) and violinist Svend Asmussen, were regarded as heroes. To combat the popularity of jazz on radio, the Nazi station vainly tried to compete with hastily assembled and farcical German jazz bands.

VOICES

Another trumpet player, Clora Bryant (b. 1927), described what it took for a woman to advance her career in jazz:

I missed a lot of opportunities. See, the agents—well, sometimes there would be a couch-like thing, see? I said, "Well, if you can't hire me for my trumpet playing, forget it." And the club owners. They'd want you to sit there and drink, like a B-girl.... You drink Coca-Cola and the customer gets charged for a drink, see? But I wasn't raised that way, so I probably missed a lot of chances. A lot of the women in music playing horns and instruments, they were in it for the glamour and the hoopla—that made it easier to get connections. But from the jump, mine was strictly for music, and it still is.

"You're Driving Me Crazy" is a fine example of the way Valaida (she was billed with her first name only) and Danish musicians found a common language in swing—specifically the improvisational style of Armstrong and the ensemble brio of Fats Waller (see Chapter 10). From the first notes of her vocal, she fashions small embellishments to the melody, taking greater liberties as she continues, until she is freely improvising in the last section of the first chorus, even tossing a couple of Armstrongian growls into the mix. Mathisen (a musical humorist and singer in his own right) anchors the rhythm with his strong left hand and emerges for a brief, showy solo, but this is Valaida's show all the way. As relaxed as she is commanding, she demonstrates in her climactic trumpet solo a bright, powerful sound and a stirring authority that ought to have earned her more respect than she received when she resumed her career in Chicago.

🎧 you're driving me crazy

VALAIDA SNOW

Valaida Snow, trumpet and vocal; Winstrup Olesen, tenor saxophone; Kai Moeller, clarinet; Leo Mathisen, piano; Helge Jacobsen, guitar; Christian Jensen, bass; Kai Fischer, drums

- Label: Tono 21165
- Date: 1940
- Style: swing
- Form: 32-bar popular song (**A A B A**)

What to listen for:

- Snow's adaptation of Armstrong's vocal style
- Danish musicians performing in American swing style
- Snow's brilliant trumpet technique

INTRODUCTION

0:00		A sprightly four-bar passage by Mathisen on piano introduces the singer.

CHORUS 1

0:05	**A**	Over a relaxed, two-beat bass line, Snow sings the first line: *"Baby, you're driving me crazy!"* Behind her, Moeller and Olesen add **countermelodies.**
0:16	**A**	Snow draws out certain notes for expressive potential.
0:27	**B**	*"Who were the friends who were near me to cheer me, believe me, they knew, You were the one who would hurt me, and desert me when I needed you!"*
0:39	**A**	She sings the line *"Oh, can't you see you're driving me crazy!"* with a degree of rhythmic freedom, only to hurry for the last line: *"What did I do? What did I do to you?"*

CHORUS 2

0:50	**A**	Snow repeats the lyrics with a fierce **staccato.**
0:55		On the syllable "oh!," she growls the notes.
0:59		She urges the band: *"Swing it, boys, swing it!"*
1:01	**A**	
1:09		She ends with a **scat-singing** phrase.
1:12	**B**	Moeller takes a clarinet solo, interrupted by Snow's comments: *"Oh, yeah! Ai-ee, ai-ee."*
1:23	**A**	Introduced by Snow (*"C'mon, Leo, talk to me!"*), Mathisen plays a florid piano solo.

	CHORUS 3		
1:34	**A**	As the band **modulates** upward to a new key, Snow begins her trumpet solo. Behind her, Moeller and Olesen play **riff** figures.	
1:45	**A**	Her second phrase reaches upward before descending stepwise.	
1:56	**B**	Olesen takes a brief solo, occasionally roughening his tone.	
2:07	**A**	Snow completes her solo, with Olesen and Moeller playing **counterpoint** behind her.	
2:17		On her last note, Snow exits on a high F.	

SINGERS: LADY DAY AND THE FIRST LADY OF SONG

Singers have a peculiar relationship to jazz. Instrumentalists model themselves on the flexibility and expressiveness of the voice, while singers aim for the rhythmic freedom of instrumentalists. But there is a crucial difference: singers for the most part concentrate on melody, leaving the abstractions of ad-lib variations to instrumentalists. They occupy a middle ground between jazz and commercial entertainment, with a far greater chance of acceptance by the mainstream. Louis Armstrong reached more people singing than playing trumpet.

In the early days of the dance bands, instrumentalists who could carry a tune "doubled" as vocalists. If audience members could hear lyrics, they were more likely to enjoy and remember the melody. That's how hits were made: people left theaters and ballrooms humming melodies and seeking them out in sheet music and on records. Inevitably, dedicated singers were added to the payroll. When Paul Whiteman recruited the first full-time singers in a dance band—Bing Crosby in 1926 and Mildred Bailey in 1929—he introduced a new and frequently rivalrous relationship between instrumentalists and singers. Crosby in particular created a template for the jazz-influenced pop singer who gains ever-greater popularity by singing every kind of song, and then translates that success into movie and broadcast stardom.

Many women singers, however talented, doubled as sexual adornments and were obliged to pose flirtatiously for *Down Beat* and *Metronome*, the leading swing journals. They were routinely referred to with bird synonyms: a female band singer was a thrush, a canary, a sparrow, a chick or chickadee. Such images were far removed from those associated with 1920s blues divas like Bessie Smith and Ma Rainey, who were depicted as tough and independent. Where blues singers used double entendres to celebrate sex, these younger performers tended to either pine for their men or offer cheerful courtship fantasies. Great vocal artists emerged even so, including two particularly ingenious singers who incarnated contrary views of life. Billie Holiday and Ella Fitzgerald, each in her way, exemplify a degree of cultural resilience beyond the scope of all but a few instrumentalists.

Bing Crosby and Mildred Bailey were childhood neighbors in Washington State, though they first met in Los Angeles, where Mildred worked in a speakeasy and helped Crosby get auditions in vaudeville. Paul Whiteman hired them as the first full-time male and female vocalists to tour with a big band. Here they rehearse for a radio show, c. 1949.

FRANK DRIGGS COLLECTION

Billie Holiday recorded Lewis Allen's "Strange Fruit," a vivid description of a lynching and the first widely noted song about racism in American popular music, for the small Commodore label after Columbia Records refused. The band included Jimmy McGlin, guitar; John Williams, bass; and Eddie Dougherty, drums. New York, April 1939.

PHOTO BY CHARLES PETERSON, COURTESY OF DON PETERSON

■ BILLIE HOLIDAY (1915–1959)

The life of Billie Holiday is shrouded in myths. Born in Philadelphia and raised in Baltimore, she was the illegitimate daughter of a teenage guitarist, Clarence Holiday, who declined to acknowledge his paternity until she became a professional. Her young mother moved to New York soon after Billie's birth, leaving her in the care of abusive relatives. At ten, Holiday was remanded to a school for delinquent girls. In 1929, she joined her mother in New York, where she worked at menial labor and was arrested for prostitution. She began singing a year later, and by 1933 was ensconced at a Harlem club, where John Hammond heard her and invited her to record with Benny Goodman's still-unknown band. Soon thereafter, she wowed the notoriously demanding audience at the Apollo Theater.

In 1935, Hammond built a series of recording sessions around her, directed by Teddy Wilson and involving top musicians of the day, including Artie Shaw, Goodman, Roy Eldridge, Johnny Hodges, and several members of the Basie band, most significantly Lester Young, with whom she shared one of the most musically fertile partnerships in jazz. Holiday briefly worked with big bands—first Basie and then Shaw—but mostly sang in nightclubs, including, in 1939, New York's new and defiantly integrated Café Society. Her records, which were made with the growing jukebox market in mind, sold well, and her recording of "Strange Fruit" (1939), the vivid depiction of a Southern lynching, enhanced her standing with the New York intelligentsia. Her growing fame included a fling in Hollywood: she was cast as a singing maid in the film *New Orleans*, but walked off the set before it was finished.

Holiday suffered a long, public downfall that was caused by her dependency on narcotics and a thug who married her, encouraged her addiction, and betrayed her to the police to save himself. After a sensationalized drawn-out trial in 1947, she was jailed for eight months and deprived of her cabaret card—the permit (abolished in 1960) necessary for working in New York nightclubs. In the 1950s, Holiday continued to command a loyal following, recording with large ensembles and all-star small bands, though her voice weakened. She began to focus on ballads, developing a more mannered, expressive style. As her voice declined, she experienced a few musical reprieves, including a triumphant 1957 appearance on a television broadcast, *The Sound of Jazz*, in which she was supported by an astonishing band that included Young, Hawkins, Webster, Eldridge, and the bebop baritone saxophonist Gerry Mulligan. At the time she died, at forty-four, her voice was little more than a whisper, yet through good times and bad, she was always Lady Day, the enchantress with the white carnation in her hair, a hot-tempered yet sweetly generous truthteller who didn't know how to fake a performance.

Often cited as jazz's greatest vocalist, Holiday initially drew inspiration from Ethel Waters, Bessie Smith, and Louis Armstrong. The Armstrong influence proved decisive: from him, she learned to swing, paraphrase and embellish a melody, and impart a blues feeling to everything she sang. She does not fit the cliché of the jazz singer: scat-singing held no interest for her, and she rarely sang blues. Her range was limited to about an octave and a half, and her voice had a thin, edgy timbre. None of this mattered, because she had a gift for altering a melody in such a way as to make it extremely personal. She managed to imbue even the most insufferably trite numbers with such profound import that some of them—"What a Little Moonlight Can Do," "Miss Brown to You," "A Sunbonnet Blue"—became her signature songs. After her death, Frank Sinatra, born in the same year as Holiday, called her "unquestionably the most important influence on American popular singing in the last twenty years."

Jazz musicians adored her phrasing, which is at once guileless and clever and always rhythmically assured. They considered her one of them—a jazz artist of the first rank. Her musical romance with Young is unequaled, suggesting an intimate solidarity in performances like "A Sailboat in the Moonlight," which begins as singer-and-accompaniment and becomes a true collaboration between two comparable personalities riding out the night.

VOICES

The musical relationship between Billie Holiday and Lester Young was one of the warmest in jazz history. Holiday presented her side in her autobiography, *Lady Sings the Blues*:

> For my money Lester was the world's greatest. I loved his music, and some of my favorite recordings are the ones with Lester's pretty solos. I remember how the late Herschel Evans used to hate me. Whenever Basie had an arranger work out something for me, I'd tell him I wanted Lester to solo behind me. That always made Herschel salty. It wasn't that I didn't love his playing. It was just that I liked Lester's more. Lester sings with his horn; you listen to him and can almost hear the words. People think he's cocky and secure, but you can hurt his feelings in two seconds. I know, because I found out once that I had. We've been hungry together, and I'll always love him and his horn.

🎧 "A Sailboat in the Moonlight"

"A Sailboat in the Moonlight" is Holiday alchemy. The Carmen Lombardo melody was a No. 1 hit for his brother, Guy Lombardo and His Royal Canadians (a band that specialized in sugary music with no jazz content). Its sentimental cadences emphasize a thoroughly banal lyric. Yet Holiday, abetted by Young and Count Basie's rhythm section as led by a good Teddy Wilson imitator (Jimmy Sherman), is rhythmically inspired and genuinely touching. How does she do it? The transformation begins immediately as she replaces the song's corny ascending melody with a repeated pitch, each of three notes ("A sail-boat") articulated for rhythmic effect—not unlike the way Young begins many of his solos. From then on, she alters this note and that, stretches one at the expense of another, never obscuring the appealing qualities of the song (which has the saving grace of pretty harmonies). She makes the fantasy of sailing away with her lover to a remote rendezvous a dream worth cherishing.

🎧 a sailboat in the moonlight

BILLIE HOLIDAY

Billie Holiday, vocal; Buck Clayton, trumpet; Edmond Hall, clarinet; Lester Young, tenor saxophone; James Sherman, piano; Freddy Green, guitar; Walter Page, bass; Jo Jones, drums

- Label: Vocalion/OKeh 3605
- Date: 1937
- Style: swing
- Form: 32-bar popular song (**A A B A**)

What to listen for:

- **Holiday's melodic paraphrasing and rhythmic variations**
- **Young's expressive countermelodies and responses to Holiday**

INTRODUCTION

| 0:00 | | Clayton on trumpet plays a matched set of phrases, each ending on a **half cadence** (on the dominant). Jones accompanies on the high-hat cymbal. |

CHORUS 1

0:08	**A**	"A sailboat in the moonlight and you. Wouldn't that be heaven, a heaven just for two?" As Holiday sings the song, she paraphrases the melody and swings hard against the beat. Young on tenor saxophone plays both underneath the solo (**countermelody**) and in answer to it (**call and response**). In the background, the clarinet plays sustained notes. The bass (Page) plays a simple accompaniment of two beats to the bar.
0:21		Over the **turnaround**, Young responds to Holiday by raising his volume and playing a phrase that lags noticeably behind the beat.
0:24	**A**	"A soft breeze on a June night and you. What a perfect setting for letting dreams come true!" Holiday continues to add rhythmic variations, while Young improvises a new line.
0:40	**B**	"A chance to sail away to Sweetheart Bay beneath the stars that shine, A chance to drift, for you to lift your tender lips to mine!" The bridge provides contrast by moving to unexpected new harmonies.
0:57	**A**	"The things, dear, that I long for are few: Just give me a sailboat in the moonlight and you!" Holiday falls farther behind the beat.
1:03		She emphasizes the tune's title by singing the last phrase with a sharper timbre.

CHORUS 2

1:12	**A**	Sherman plays a light, spare piano solo. Behind him, Jones switches to a dry, **staccato** accompaniment on the cymbals. Page on bass occasionally fills in the texture by adding extra notes.
1:28	**A**	
1:44	**B**	Clayton (trumpet) enters. Jones returns to a splashier high-hat sound, responding to the trumpet's phrases with sharp snare-drum accents.
1:53		In the background, someone shouts "Yeah!"
2:00	**A**	Young plays an eight-bar solo in a smooth, relaxed style.
2:09		The last phrase of the solo wraps things up by descending through a bluesy phrase to the **tonic**.

CHORUS 3 (abbreviated)

2:16 **B** *"A chance to sail away to Sweetheart Bay beneath the stars that shine. A chance to drift, for you to lift your tender lips to mine!"*
Holiday returns, her notes falling unpredictably within the measure. Young retreats to accompaniment, joining Hall (clarinet), who plays sustained notes deep in the background.

2:24 Holiday suddenly sings firmly on the beat, with the rhythm section instead of against it, helping to intensify the sense of groove.

2:32 **A** *"The things, dear, that I long for are few: Just give me a sailboat in the moonlight and you!"*
As if responding to Holiday, Page switches to a steady **walking bass** (four beats to the bar).

2:38 Holiday marks her last phrase by repeatedly hitting her highest pitch.

CODA

2:44 At the end of the vocal, the accompanying instruments (piano, tenor saxophone, and clarinet) combine in a brief polyphonic clamor.

■ ELLA FITZGERALD (1917-1996)

If Billie Holiday is a singer associated with emotional pain—a wounded sparrow, in songbird parlance—Ella Fitzgerald is the irrepressible spirit of musical joy. Like Holiday, she rarely sang the blues, but where Billie had an unmistakable feeling for them, Ella saw blues as just another song form, useful for up-tempo scat improvisations. Her vocal equipment was also the opposite of Holiday's: she had four octaves at her disposal, and was not averse to adding high falsetto cries and low growls. In her peak years, her timbre had a luscious, ripe quality. She was an accomplished, peerless scat-singer, one of very few who could improvise on chords as imaginatively as the best instrumentalists. Shy and demure in her personal style and extremely private, she came vivaciously to life in scat vocals, reaching emotional peaks that verged on euphoria, delighting audiences and mesmerizing musicians.

Fitzgerald was born in Virginia and raised in Yonkers, New York, where she sang in church and taught herself to dance. By 1934, she had dropped out of school and was living off her wits on the streets. That November, she entered the Apollo Theater's amateur night as a dancer, but at the last minute chose to sing. Fitzgerald, who lacked Holiday's great physical beauty, was hooted when she walked onstage—a big, clunky girl, awkward in manner and badly dressed—until she broke into song. Her enchantingly girlish voice and dynamic rhythm triumphed, and she won the competition.

Because of her looks, however, bandleaders refused to hire her until Chick Webb heard her and was instantly hooked. He became her legal guardian, bought her clothes, and restructured his band to feature a voice he predicted would be heard for decades. From the summer of 1935, she was present on most of his record

Ella Fitzgerald, the voice of exuberant joy and vivacious swing, made an effortless transition from swing to bop to mainstream pop, maintaining top echelon stardom until her death. She is pictured here at the peak of the Swing Era with drummer Bill Beason at the Savoy Ballroom, 1940.

sessions. Webb's best-selling 1938 recording of "A-Tisket, a-Tasket," based on an old nursery rhyme she set to a catchy melody (arranged by future film composer Van Alexander), made her famous. Within months she was billed as the "First Lady of Swing"—in later years the "First Lady of Song."

After Webb's death, Fitzgerald recorded dozens of ballads, swingers (up-tempo songs that swing), and novelties, effortlessly making the transition to bebop (her "Air Mail Special" is a bop version of a swing classic). Norman Granz recruited her for his Jazz at the Philharmonic concert tours (he also signed Holiday; see Chapter 11), and became her personal manager, building a new record label, Verve, around her. Fitzgerald's innovative songbook albums, each devoted to one songwriter, garnered tremendous acclaim in the 1950s and 1960s. She was regarded universally as the gold standard for both jazz and pop singing.

🎧 "Blue Skies"

"Blue Skies," a pop standard frequently adapted by jazz musicians, was recorded for the album *Ella Fitzgerald Sings the Irving Berlin Songbook*. But her rendition is so adventurous (it's more Ella than Berlin), it was initially dropped from that album and included on another, *Get Happy!*—an emblematic Fitzgerald title (a typical Holiday title, by contrast, is *Songs for Distingué Lovers*). She begins with a scat intro, employing cantorial phrases that suggest Jewish liturgical music. She sings the lyric at a medium clip, accompanied by Harry "Sweets" Edison's trumpet obbligato, mildly embellishing the melody, yet making every phrase swing. Then she takes off on a three-chorus scat improvisation, singing variations with the imagination of an instrumentalist. With typical high-flying nonchalance, she quotes from Richard Wagner's "Wedding March" in chorus 2, and a few bars of Gershwin's *Rhapsody in Blue* in the last chorus before reprising the lyric for the final bridge. She never runs out of steam or breath, carrying the rhythm like an ocean current.

LISTENING GUIDE 31

🎧 blue skies

ELLA FITZGERALD

Ella Fitzgerald, vocal, with Paul Weston Orchestra: John Best, Pete Candoli, Harry Edison, Don Fagerquist, Manny Klein, trumpets; Ed Kusby, Dick Noel, William Schaefer, trombones; Juan Tizol, valve trombone; Gene Cipriano, Chuck Gentry, Leonard Hartman, Matty Matlock, Ted Nash, Babe Russin, Fred Stulce, woodwinds; Paul Smith, piano; Barney Kessel, guitar; Joe Mondragon, bass; Alvin Stoller, drums

- Label: *Ella Fitzgerald Sings the Irving Berlin Songbook* (Verve 830-2)
- Date: 1958
- Style: big-band swing
- Form: 32-bar popular song (**A A B A**)

What to listen for:
- Fitzgerald's imaginative scat-singing, with instrumental-like motives and riffs
- her varied rhythm and unusual vocal timbres
- unexpected quotations

INTRODUCTION

0:00   Over sustained orchestra chords, Fitzgerald begins to **scat-sing**, using open, resonant nonsense syllables ("da," "la") instead of words. The vocal line lazily moves through **arpeggios**: notes drawn from the underlying chords.

0:17   As the accompanying instruments come to rest on a dominant chord, the vocal line falls to its lowest note.

CHORUS 1

0:22   **A**   *"Blue skies smiling at me, nothing but blue skies do I see."*
Fitzgerald sings the melody to "Blue Skies" with its original text. In each **A** section, the melody gradually falls from the **minor** into the **major mode** (at "nothing but *blue* skies"). Behind her, the rhythm section plays a steady, even pulse, with **countermelodies** from muted trumpet (Edison) and piano.

0:34   **A**   *"Bluebirds singing a song, nothing but bluebirds all day long."*
Fitzgerald adds slight decorative touches to individual notes, and alters the melody at phrase's end (0:43).

0:46   **B**   *"Never saw the sun shining so bright, never saw things going so right.*
Noticing the days hurrying by, when you're in love, my, how they fly."
As the melody moves into the major mode and a higher register, the saxophones counter with a restrained lower accompanying line.

0:58   **A**   *"Blue days, all of them gone, nothing but blue skies from now on."*

1:08   The saxophones begin playing a riff.

CHORUS 2

1:11   **A**   Picking up on the rhythm and melody of the saxophone riff, Fitzgerald begins scatting.

1:17   For a few measures, she sings slightly behind the beat, adding rhythmic tension.

1:23   **A**   Using variable intonation (**blue note**), she gradually pulls the first note upward.

1:29   Using her head voice (higher register), she sings a series of relaxed **triplets,** followed by a quotation from Wagner's "Wedding March."

1:35   **B**   As the saxophones play gruff chords, Fitzgerald hints at singing in **double-time.**

1:42   She sings a phrase, then repeats it at a higher pitch level as the song returns to its original minor key.

1:47   **A**   Starting on a dramatic high note, she launches into a loose, bluesy phrase.

1:53   She sings a three-note motive; repeating it, she turns it into a **polyrhythmic** motive.

CHORUS 3

1:59   **A**   As the accompaniment intensifies, Fitzgerald digs into the beat, turning her line into a riff figure and using more percussive syllables ("bop," "dee-yowwww").

2:05   Searching for more consonants, she begins a new phrase with a misplaced (but arresting) "sssssssss" sound.

2:11   **A**   Fitzgerald marks the arrival at the next **A** section with a startling **dissonance**. She repeats it several more times to make it clear to the casual listener that it's not a mistake.

2:23   **B**   Picking up on a phrase she's just sung, she bounces back and forth between two notes in the major scale.

2:29   A lengthy phrase finally ends on the downbeat of the next **A** section.

2:35   **A**   More complicated rhythmic figures suddenly precede an extended passage in her upper register.

CHORUS 4

2:47   **A**   As the background orchestra reaches the peak of its intensity, Fitzgerald retreats to a simple riff figure.

2:54   She quotes a famous theme from Gershwin's *Rhapsody in Blue.*

3:00   **A**   She begins each phrase by leaning on the tonic, sometimes decorating it unexpectedly with **triplets.**

| 3:12 | B | *"I never saw the sun shining so bright, never saw things going so right.*
Noticing the days hurrying by, when you're in love, my how they fly."
The band retreats to a simpler texture. Fitzgerald returns to the song's lyrics
and, at times, its original melody. |
| 3:24 | A | *"Blue days, all of them gone, nothing but blue skies from now on."*
The last lines are distorted into soaring arpeggios. |

CODA

| 3:34 | As Fitzgerald hits her high note, the band plays two sharp dominant chords,
then drops out to let her add a bit more scat-singing. |
| 3:37 | The tune ends with a caterwauling of chords, piano phrases, and drumming. |

As swing soloists developed their virtuoso techniques, the rhythm section had to make even more radical changes in order to keep up. As we will see in the next chapter, by the end of the Swing Era, every instrument of the ensemble could be featured, at least potentially, as a soloist. With rhythm players showing greater and greater flair in their individual roles as accompanists, the very nature and function of the rhythm section began to change.

ADDITIONAL LISTENING

Fletcher Henderson	"Queer Notions" (1933)
Coleman Hawkins	"Picasso" (1948)
Bud Freeman	"The Eel" (1939)
Chu Berry and Roy Eldridge	"Body and Soul" (1938)
Lester Young	"D. B. Blues" (1945)
Benny Carter	"When Lights Are Low" (1936)
Django Reinhardt	"Nuages" (1942)
Benny Goodman	"Solo Flight" (1941)
Teddy Wilson	"Blues in C Sharp Minor" (1936)
Duke Ellington	"Jack the Bear" (1940)
Count Basie	"Clap Hands, Here Comes Charlie" (1939)
Billie Holiday	"Strange Fruit" (1939)
Ella Fitzgerald	"Air Mail Special" (1952)

ONLINE MULTIMEDIA RESOURCES AND REVIEW MATERIALS

Author Insight Videos

Gary Giddins discusses the significance of jam sessions in the 1940s, the different tenor saxophone styles of Coleman Hawkins and Lester Young, jazz overseas, and how racial barriers began to be broken down.

Interactive Listening Guides

Coleman Hawkins, "Body and Soul"
Count Basie / Lester Young, "Oh! Lady Be Good"
Benny Carter / Django Reinhardt, "I'm Coming, Virginia"
Valaida Snow, "You're Driving Me Crazy"
Billie Holiday, "A Sailboat in the Moonlight"
Ella Fitzgerald, "Blue Skies"

Jazz Concepts (audio and/or video demonstrations of terms covered here)

arpeggio	dissonance	shake
backbeat	double-time	staccato
block chords	major mode	syncopation
blue note	minor mode	riff
cadence	modulation	tonic
call and response	octave	triplets
chromatic	polyrhythm	walking bass
countermelody	sequence	

- For quick reference, review the **Chapter Overview** and **Chapter Outline**.
- Take the online **Chapter** and **Listening Quizzes**.
- Use the online **Glossary** and **Flashcards** to review important terms.

FATS WALLER
christopher columbus

ART TATUM
over the rainbow

CHARLIE CHRISTIAN
swing to bop (topsy)

10

RHYTHM
IN TRANSITION

RHYTHM IS OUR BUSINESS

In May 1935, the No. 1 record in the country was Jimmie Lunceford's "Rhythm Is Our Business." If rhythm defined the swing bands, its foundation lay in the rhythm section, which was undergoing a thorough overhaul. In bands big and small, the pianists, guitarists, bassists, and drummers fused into a unified rhythmic front, supplying the beat and marking the harmonies. Each of the leading bands presented a distinct, well-designed rhythmic attack that complemented its particular style. The rhythm sections of Ellington, Basie, and Lunceford, for example, sounded nothing alike. And just as the soloists were champing at the bit of big-band constraints, rhythm players of the 1930s and early 1940s were developing techniques and ideas that demanded more attention than they usually received. In the process, they helped set the stage for postwar modern jazz.

PIANO

Although swing bands, especially those led by pianists (Ellington, Basie, Earl Hines, Teddy Wilson), allowed piano solos, pianist-bandleaders limited themselves to introductions, solo choruses, and an occasional mini-concerto. Long before jazz, however, the

Jo Jones, the Count Basie drummer who was said to play like the wind, changed the feeling of swing with his brisk attack on the high-hat cymbal. New York, 1950.

Fats Waller, a master of comic poses and satirical interpretations of Tin Pan Alley songs, popularized stride piano and composed such classic jazz themes as "Ain't Misbehavin'" and the all-time jam-session favorite "Honeysuckle Rose." He's pictured here on a 1939 magazine cover.

DUNCAN SCHIEDT COLLECTION

piano had enjoyed a history of self-sufficiency. We saw how pianists achieved prominence with stride and boogie-woogie—these keyboard styles prospered and peaked in the 1930s.

■ FATS WALLER (1904–1943)

Thomas "Fats" Waller achieved, during a brief but incredibly prolific career, a matchless standing in jazz and pop, straddling the dividing line with his humor and instrumental technique. A radiant pianist, canny vocalist, musical satirist, and important songwriter, he made more than 500 records (most within a span of eight years), and succeeded as a composer on Broadway and as an entertainer in movies.

Waller was born in New York City, the son of a Baptist lay preacher. His mother taught him piano and organ, instilling in him a lasting love for the music of J. S. Bach. When Fats was in his mid-teens, he came under the spell of James P. Johnson. Like other stride pianists, Waller found work at rent parties, and also participated in "cutting contests"—largely amiable, usually respectful, but deadly serious keyboard competitions—winning admirers with his flawless keyboard touch and outgoing, ebullient personality. If he lacked Johnson's imaginative bass lines and breakneck speed, he was a more expressive interpreter of blues and ballads, exhibiting greater subtlety and a fluent rhythmic feeling that perfectly meshed with swing. By the late 1920s, Waller had become a prominent figure in jazz and theater, thanks chiefly to the widely performed songs he wrote for theatrical revues. Louis Armstrong established several of his songs as standards—including "Ain't Misbehavin'," "(What Did I Do to Be So) Black and Blue," and "Honeysuckle Rose." (After Ellington, Waller remains jazz's most enduring pop songwriter.)

In 1934, RCA-Victor signed up Fats Waller and His Rhythm, a six-piece band. During the next five years, Waller was rarely absent from the pop charts. Adapting the guise of a Harlem dandy—in a derby, vest, and tailored pinstripes—he created satirical gems with painfully sentimental material like "The Curse of an Aching Heart." At the same time, he could be touchingly sincere with good songs, like "I'm Gonna Sit Right Down and Write Myself a Letter." He possessed a mildly strident voice of surprising suppleness, using his middle octave for straightforward singing, low notes for rude asides, high ones for feminine mockery. And he created several impeccable solo piano works that suggested an artistic potential far beyond his studio repertory. Fats's immense success put him in a bind: RCA wanted nothing but hits, and jazz lovers failed to appreciate the artistry of his clowning. Significantly, at the time of his death (from pneumonia, at thirty-nine), Waller the recording artist had yet to record some of the finest songs by Waller the composer.

🎧 "Christopher Columbus"

"Christopher Columbus" represents Waller in a typically uproarious mood, very funny and very musical. The melody, by Chu Berry, who adapted the chords to "I Got Rhythm" for the bridge, generated several hits in 1936, though Waller's version (subtitled "A Rhythm Cocktail") was not among them. Fletcher Henderson, Benny Goodman, Andy Kirk, and Teddy Wilson all scored with it, but the tune didn't become a jazz hallmark until 1938, when Goodman incorporated it as the secondary theme in his version of "Sing, Sing, Sing." Andy Razaf, Waller's friend and favorite lyricist, wrote the hare-brained words, which Waller mocks, drawing on each of his vocal registers.

This performance shows Waller integrating stride piano into small-group swing, emphasizing rhythmic power—especially the cross-rhythms in his dashing solo chorus. His band remained fairly stable during the RCA years, with two prominent supporting roles taken by saxophonist and clarinet-ist Gene Sedric and trumpet player Herman Autrey. Accomplished musicians, Sedric and Autrey were nonetheless second-string players who reflect the dominating influences of the period: Sedric shows the inspiration of Hawkins and Chu Berry, while Autrey blends the sound and temperament of Armstrong and Roy Eldridge. The rhythm section has its hands full keeping up with Waller.

🎧 christopher columbus (a rhythm cocktail)

LISTENING GUIDE 32

FATS WALLER AND HIS RHYTHM
Herman Autrey, trumpet; Gene Sedric, tenor saxophone; Fats Waller, piano and vocal; Albert Casey, guitar; Charles Turner, bass; Arnold Boling, drums

- Label: Victor 25295
- Date: 1936
- Style: small-group swing
- Form: 32-bar popular song (**A A B A**)

What to listen for:
- **Waller's stride piano, and cross-rhythms in chorus 4**
- his humorous changes in vocal timbre
- background riffs played behind solos

INTRODUCTION

0:00   Waller plays the simple opening riff in **octaves**.

0:04   When the riff is repeated, it quickly subsides into a **stride** accompaniment.

CHORUS 1 (extended)

0:07   **A**   As the rest of the rhythm section enters in the first two sections of a 32-bar form, Waller begins to sing.
"Mister Christopher Columbus sailed the sea without a compass.
When his men began a rumpus,
(spoken gruffly) *Up spoke Christopher Columbus, yes!"*
He changes the timbre of his voice for comic effect.

0:22   **A**   *"There's land somewhere, until we get there,*
We will not go wrong if we sing, swing a song.
Since the world is round-o, we'll be safe and sound-o.
Till our goal is found-o, we'll just keep rhythm bound-o."
The band continues with another 16-bar **A A** section. Columbus is parodied in a high-pitched sing-song that gradually falls to Waller's normal speaking voice.

0:36   **B**   (sung) *"Since the crew was makin' merry—*
(spoken) *Mary got up and went home!*
There came a yell for Isabel, and they brought the rum and Isabel."
This section, which serves as the bridge to the broader 32-bar **A A B A** form, borrows its chord progression from "I Got Rhythm."

0:43   **A**   *"No more mutiny, no! What a time at sea!*
With diplomacy, Christory made history! Yes!"
A return to the **A** section.

CHORUS 2 (abbreviated)

0:50 **A** (sung) *"Mister Christopher Columbus! Uh-huh!*
He used rhythm as a compass! Yes, yes! Music ended all the rumpus! Yes!
Wise old Christopher Columbus! [spoken] *Latch on, Christy! Yeah!"*
Waller reduces the melody line to a simple riff. Each line of text is answered
by a short exclamation, as if Waller were in **call and response** with himself.

CHORUS 3

1:04 **A** Sedric takes a tenor saxophone solo, spurred on by Waller's enthusiastic replies
("yes, yes!").

1:11 **A**

1:18 **B** Waller signals the bridge by playing a two-note background line.

1:25 **A**

CHORUS 4

1:33 **A** Waller plays the opening melody in exuberant stride style, emphasizing the offbeats.

1:40 **A**

1:47 **B** Over the bridge, he plays a complicated **cross-rhythmic** pattern.

1:52 He signals the end of the bridge with a descending octave pattern.

1:54 **A**

2:00 At the end of the chorus, Waller interjects an excited "Yes!"

CHORUS 5

2:01 **A** Autrey (trumpet) enters with an excited single-note pattern. Behind him, Sedric
(tenor saxophone) plays a bluesy riff.

2:08 **A**

2:15 **B** During the bridge, the riff temporarily disappears (it will reappear during the
last **A** section).

2:22 **A**

CODA

2:30 (spoken) *"Well, look-a there! Christy's grabbed the Santa Maria,*
And he's going back! Yeah! Ahhhh, look-a there!"
The band moves suddenly to a quieter volume, with Waller playing the opening
riff. In response, Autrey plays his own trumpet riff while Waller improvises some
concluding remarks.

2:43 *"Uh-huh. . . . In the year 1492, Columbus sailed the ocean bluuuuue!*
(quickly) *What'd I say?"*
The band drops out entirely, leaving Waller the last word.

■ ART TATUM (1909–1956)

The peculiar nature of Art Tatum's genius is epitomized by the fact that twenty-first century listeners respond to his records much as 1930s listeners did—with gawking amazement. Whatever we may think of his music, there is no getting around his spectacular dexterity. The fact that he was legally blind magnifies his legend. The son of amateur musicians, Tatum was born in Toledo, Ohio, with cataracts on both eyes. Minor gains made through operations were undone when he was mugged as a teenager and lost all sight in his left eye, retaining a sliver of light in the right.

Tatum began picking out melodies at three, led his own bands at seventeen, and signed a two-year radio contract before he was twenty. His reputation spread quickly. While passing through Ohio, Duke Ellington sought him out and encouraged him to head for New York, where the competition would raise his sights and sharpen his wits. The New York stride pianists instantly acknowledged his superiority, a capitulation made easier by his friendly, unassuming demeanor.

Most accomplished artists in any field have achieved a measure of virtuosity; still, when it comes to Tatum, there is a temptation to call him a virtuoso and then retire the word. No other jazz player is so closely associated with dazzling, superhuman nimbleness. That's because his style is fundamentally inseparable from his technique. Tatum was championed by some of the great classical pianists of his time, including George Gershwin, Sergei Rachmaninoff, and Vladimir Horowitz. Jazz pianists universally regarded him as peerless. Waller, whom Tatum often named as his inspiration (you can hear the influence in Tatum's use of stride), once interrupted a number when Tatum entered a club where he was performing, and announced, "Ladies and gentlemen, I play piano, but God is in the house tonight!" Pianist Hank Jones has said that when he first heard Tatum's records, he felt certain they were "tricks" achieved through overdubbing.

Tatum was indefatigable. He worked in top nightclubs and then dropped by dives and after-hours joints, where he would play till dawn. He'd first play a two-handed run to test the keyboard; if a particular piano was out of tune or worse, he would avoid the bad or missing keys for the rest of the night. But though he was a frequent guest on radio broadcasts, he was never embraced by the mainstream. He appeared in few concert halls and recorded mostly for independent labels.

Unexpectedly, he found his greatest popular success leading a trio with guitar (Tiny Grimes) and bass (Slam Stewart). Audiences enjoyed watching the three instrumentalists challenge each other with oddball quotations from songs other than the ones they were playing. Tatum, however, was primarily a solo pianist and as such, a fount of surprises. He developed set routines on many of his favorite songs, but no matter how often he played them, he was able to astound the listener with harmonic substitutions of unbelievable complexity. Charlie Parker and Charles Mingus named him as a primary influence.

Banjoist Elmer Snowden, the original leader of what became the Duke Ellington band, stands beside two incomparable pianists in a Greenwich Village nightclub, 1942: Art Tatum (right), who claimed Fats Waller as his primary influence, and Waller (center), who introduced Tatum to a nightclub audience by saying, "I play piano, but God is in the house tonight!"

DUNCAN SCHIEDT COLLECTION

🎧 "Over the Rainbow"

Tatum's 1939 "Over the Rainbow"—the first of his five surviving versions, recorded over a sixteen-year span—was made when the song was new to the public. It was written by Harold Arlen and E. Y. Harburg for *The Wizard of Oz*, a movie that debuted only days before Tatum made this recording to be broadcast on radio. The fact that he brings so much feeling and control to a song new to his repertory is impressive; that he understands the mechanics of the song well enough to rewire its harmonies and deconstruct its melody is extraordinary.

This was one of many performances made by Tatum and other musicians for a company called Standard Transcriptions, which produced recordings exclusively for radio stations. Transcriptions, as the discs were called, could not be sold in stores. Broadcasters preferred creating their own music libraries to paying licensing fees to air commercial recordings. Eventually, the networks cut a deal with the labels, and transcription discs disappeared. In some ways, however, transcriptions were superior to records: fidelity was enhanced because the discs were larger (sixteen inches instead of the usual ten), and the artists had more latitude in terms of length. This performance is a minute longer than a record would have allowed. Even so, Tatum has to hurry to squeeze in his ending.

LISTENING GUIDE 33

🎧 over the rainbow

ART TATUM, PIANO
- Label: Music & Arts #2
- Date: 1939
- Style: stride piano
- Form: 32-bar popular song (**A A B A**)

What to listen for:
- melodic paraphrase: clear statements or reminders of the melody throughout, with complicated harmonic substitutions
- dazzling virtuosic runs

INTRODUCTION

0:00		Tatum begins with an intensely dissonant **dominant chord**, rolled up from the bottom. It's answered by a pair of **octaves** in the right hand.

CHORUS 1

0:07	**A**	Tatum plays the melody harmonized by chords, without the stride accompaniment. He plays **rubato**, adjusting the tempo for expressive purposes (sometimes accelerating slightly, at other times slowing down dramatically).
0:12		The first of many descending runs into the bass register.
0:19		He decorates the end of the first **A** section with new chords and a dramatic upward-sweeping run.
0:23	**A**	For the second **A** section, he repeats the melody. Throughout, he plays the melody with faithful accuracy, but alters the chord progression with **harmonic substitutions**.
0:36	**B**	Tatum plays the bridge simply, accompanied only by sparse chords in the left hand.
0:40		Where the original tune is harmonically static, he adds a new series of chords.
0:52		He marks the end of the bridge with several runs.
0:57	**A**	Return of the original melody, now beginning in the bass register. At times, the harmony is intensely **dissonant**.
1:08		He begins to move into a steady tempo.

CHORUS 2

1:17	**A**	In a moderate, relaxed tempo, Tatum uses a **stride** accompaniment in his left hand.
1:31		At the cadence, he throws in melodic lines that suggest a bluesy feeling.
1:36	**A**	
1:38		He replaces the original melody with a complicated, dissonant 16th-note line, featuring harmonic substitutions. The intensity of this passage is "erased" a few seconds later by a descending fast run.
1:55	**B**	Once again, Tatum plays the melody to the bridge accompanied by simple left-hand chords.
2:01		As the phrase ends, the harmonies suddenly move into unexpected chromatic territory.

2:13		As Tatum nears the end of the bridge, his melodic line becomes increasingly fast and dissonant; it resolves directly on the downbeat of the new **A** section.
2:15	**A**	
2:20		As he settles into his groove, the harmonies take on more of a bluesy tinge.

CHORUS 3

2:36	**A**	
2:51		Over the last two measures of the **A** section, Tatum's improvisation drifts out of the main key and accelerates as it heads for a resolution on the downbeat of the next section.
2:56	**A**	
3:02		Over a few simple chords, he plays a blindingly fast passage.
3:11		Another bluesy cadence figure.
3:16	**B**	The bridge, which had been a point of relaxation, suddenly becomes more intense: over steady eighth-note chords in the left hand, the harmonization departs radically from the original.
3:26		Finally, Tatum resolves to the tonic harmony.
3:31		Suddenly, as if under extreme time pressure, he speeds up the performance and races through the rest of the tune in record time.
3:33	**A**	

PLUGGING IN

In the 1930s, as we have seen, the guitar replaced the banjo in jazz bands (except those that played in the traditional New Orleans vein). Its role emphasized rhythm and harmony. The guitar had earned prominence as a solo instrument in the 1920s, when Eddie Lang and Lonnie Johnson appeared on records with Bix Beiderbecke, Joe Venuti, Armstrong, and Ellington; but now the great rhythm guitarists did little more than strum a steady four-to-the-bar *chunk-chunk-chunk-chunk*, reinforcing the pulse of the drummer and bassist.

The problem was volume. Whether the band was large or small, the guitar lacked the dynamic presence of other instruments. Various attempts were made to amplify it, using resonators, external microphones, and pick-ups (magnets coiled with wire that transmit an electrical impulse from the strings to an amplifier). Meanwhile, recordings by Django Reinhardt showed that the guitar was a jazz instrument of barely explored potential.

In the early 1930s, the Gibson Company began building prototypes for an electric guitar, achieving a breakthrough in 1936. In the late 1940s, Gibson introduced the solid body electric guitar, and within a decade it was the representative instrument of rock and roll, urban blues, and country music. Those early technological advances meant little, however, until one remarkable musician showed that the electric guitar was more than a loud acoustic guitar: it was a separate instrument with a timbre and personality of its own.

▨ CHARLIE CHRISTIAN (1916–1942)

In a career of tragic brevity (only twenty-three months in the public spotlight), Christian transformed the guitar and provided yet another channel of momentum to the younger musicians who would soon introduce bebop. In his hands, the guitar acquired the same rhythmic suppleness and dynamic confidence associated with the saxophone and trumpet. His warm, radiant sound had a suitably electrifying effect.

Charlie Christian, seen here in 1940, was the first prominent electric guitarist. He was initially met with skepticism, until he used amplification to liberate the guitar from the rhythm section and establish it as a powerful solo instrument.

FRANK DRIGGS COLLECTION

Charlie Christian was born in Texas and grew up in a poor section of Oklahoma City, where, according to his neighbor, novelist Ralph Ellison, he was a wonder in grade school, playing guitars made from cigar boxes and taking up trumpet, piano, and bass. In 1938, Christian hooked up an electric pick-up to his acoustic guitar, and word of his prodigious gifts spread. Mary Lou Williams raved about him to John Hammond, who in 1939 arranged for him to audition for Benny Goodman. At first reluctant to hire a guitarist, Goodman changed his mind when he heard Christian's limber phrases soaring over the rhythm section.

Goodman signed Christian to his sextet, which made weekly radio broadcasts, and featured him on records with the big band. Extremely laconic, Christian usually let his music speak for him, yet three months after he signed with Goodman, he lent his name to a Chicago newspaper article (presumably ghostwritten) whose headline read "Guitarmen, Wake Up and Pluck! Wire for Sound; Let 'em Hear You Play." The article argued that a guitarist is "more than just a robot plunking on a gadget to keep the rhythm going," and that "electrical amplification has given guitarists a new lease on life."

Christian made his case on record after record. Seemingly overnight, a flood of guitarists plugged in, determined to capture the spare clarity of Christian's solos—every phrase enunciated, logical, and decisive. Recording with some of the finest musicians of the era, Christian always stood out with his ricocheting riffs, inspired melodies, and deep blues feeling. One of his most successful acolytes, Barney Kessel, later compared his importance to that of Thomas Edison. That may seem like an exaggeration, yet by the time Christian succumbed to tuberculosis at twenty-five, few would have argued the point. He had given the electric guitar a permanent lease on life.

🎧 "Swing to Bop" ("Topsy")

This performance, one of Christian's best, exists by accident. In 1941, an engineer named Jerry Newman took his wire recorder (a predecessor to the tape recorder) to Harlem after-hours clubs to document jam sessions. The sessions at Minton's Playhouse proved especially illuminating, because the rhythm section included two men who later figured as key bebop innovators, drummer Kenny Clarke and pianist Thelonious Monk. Among the soloists who dropped by to jam were adventurous swing stars like Christian, Roy Eldridge, saxophonist Don Byas, and fledgling modernist Dizzy Gillespie.

When, years later, Newman's wire recordings were released commercially, they were greeted as a revelation, capturing the first steps in what proved to be the transformation from swing to bebop. Newman in fact released this track as "Swing to Bop," a title that couldn't have existed in 1941 because the word "bop" had not yet been coined. The tune is actually "Topsy," a swing hit by Eddie Durham and Edgar Battle, though the melody isn't played: Newman began recording this number during the middle of Christian's first chorus. (This excerpt consists only of his six-chorus solo.) Christian is inspired by the song's harmonies, consistently varying his riffs and rhythmic accents, building on motives and playing with a relaxed lucidity—notice, too, how the harmonies of the bridge, especially, *always* liberate his melodic imagination.

🎧 swing to bop (topsy)

CHARLIE CHRISTIAN

Charlie Christian, electric guitar; Kenny Clarke, drums; unknown piano, bass

- Label: *Live Sessions at Minton's* (Everest FS-219)
- Date: 1941
- Style: small-group swing
- Form: 32-bar popular song (**A A' B A**)

What to listen for:
- wide-open jam session
- **Christian's innovative polyrhythmic phrases**
- bluesy riffs in the A sections, long harmonic lines in the bridge
- **Clarke interacting with Christian**

CHORUS 1

0:00	**A**	The recording fades in at the beginning of Christian's first chorus on electric guitar. He's just completing the first **A** section of the tune.
0:03	**A'**	For the **A'** section, the harmony changes to IV for four bars. In the background, the pianist loudly plays a **stride** accompaniment.
0:12	**B**	As the piano retreats to **comping**, the **walking bass** gradually takes over as the rhythmic foundation.
0:21	**A**	Christian's tone hardens. He begins playing a simple three-note figure, shifting it in different rhythmic positions in the measure.

CHORUS 2

0:29	**A**	The three-note motive now becomes the beginning of a longer, more involved phrase, including **triplets**.
0:38	**A'**	
0:47	**B**	As he enters the more complex chord changes of the bridge, Christian draws on harmonic improvisation in long, flowing lines. Clarke occasionally interrupts with bass drum accents.
0:56	**A**	The harmony returns to the tonic, and Christian turns the three-note motive into short repeated riffs.

CHORUS 3

1:05	**A**	The next chorus begins with a new riff, loosely based on the three-note motive.
1:13	**A'**	
1:19		A final bluesy phrase rounds out the **A'** section. It's followed by silence.
1:22	**B**	Christian begins the bridge on a high note. The drums strongly accent the **backbeat**.
1:31	**A**	Christian's line becomes detached, falling firmly on the **offbeat**.

CHORUS 4

1:40	**A**	Christian repeats a simple riff. When he precedes it with a syncopation, Clarke coincides with accents on the snare drum.
1:48	**A'**	The line suddenly rises to match the harmony.
1:57	**B**	A sudden return to straight eighth-note patterns, **arpeggiating** the underlying chords.
2:06	**A**	
2:11		The line ends with a single note, decorated with **tremolos** and repeated in a cross-rhythmic pattern.

CHORUS 5

2:15	**A**	The fifth chorus begins with a riff that uses the tremolo pattern to create a new **polyrhythm** (three beats against four).
2:23	**A'**	The line concentrates on a single note, played rhythmically on the beat and building intensity through repetition.
2:32	**B**	Christian begins two beats early with a driving, descending **chromatic** pattern. Within a few seconds, the pattern gets "turned around"—shifting on an eighth note earlier, creating cross-rhythmic intensity.
2:41	**A**	The line again falls strongly on the offbeat.
2:49		Christian and Clarke coincide on strong offbeat accents.

CHORUS 6

2:50	**A**	Christian plays a new riff, starting with the **flat fifth**.
2:58	**A'**	He plays a pattern with strong rhythmic contrast, prompting Clarke to match it with drum accents.
3:04		Christian plays a phrase that accents the weakest notes in the measure (one-and-two-*and*, three-and-four-*and*).
3:07	**B**	Once again, he launches himself into the tune's chord pattern.
3:16	**A**	After the climactic final phrase, Christian retreats, allowing another instrument (trumpet) to continue the jam session.

BASS

Of all the instruments in the jazz ensemble, the bass was the slowest in reaching maturity. One reason is that since the bass traditionally served to bind the rhythm section, firming the tempo and outlining the harmonic progression, bassists had little incentive to expand their technical abilities. Until the late 1930s, the average bass solo was a predictable four-to-the-bar walk. Technique was so lacking that poor intonation was commonplace even in some of the top bands.

Walter Page

There were a few exceptions. Walter Page (1900–1957), who codified the walking bass, developed his style in the middle 1920s, while leading the Blue Devils in Oklahoma. After he joined with Count Basie in Kansas City, Basie built his rhythm section on the metronomic reliability of Page's walking bass: pizzicato notes in stable, stepwise patterns, usually four evenly stated pitches per measure.

Milt Hinton

Milt Hinton (1910–2000), a much-loved musician, expanded the bass walk by using more advanced harmonies and syncopating his rhythmic support with inventive melodic figures. Initially known for his long stay with Cab Calloway and a shorter one with Louis Armstrong, he became the most in-demand and frequently recorded bassist of his generation, shifting effortlessly from Bing Crosby and Billie Holiday to Aretha Franklin and Bobby Darin. At jam sessions with Dizzy Gillespie and other young modernists,

Count Basie's All American Rhythm Section brought a sizzling excitement to the Swing Era. Guitarist Freddie Green, drummer Jo Jones, bassist Walter Page, and Basie recording for Decca in New York, 1938.

he showed he could master the latest chord changes. Hinton also won respect as an important jazz photographer, whose candid shots document the life of musicians touring the South as no one else's ever did.

Another remarkable bassist was the prodigy Israel Crosby (1919–1962), who became famous in the 1950s and 60s for his virtuoso turns with the Ahmad Jamal Trio. He began recording at sixteen, with pianists Jess Stacey, Albert Ammons, and Teddy Wilson (Crosby created a powerful **ostinato**—a repeated melodic phrase, with the same pitches—for Wilson's "Blues in C Sharp Minor") and drummer Gene Krupa. He also spent three years with Fletcher Henderson's orchestra (1936–39). In each situation, he was encouraged to play solos that demonstrated a melodic and rhythmic confidence rare in those days.

Israel Crosby

By contrast, the best-known bassist of the Swing Era, John Kirby (1908–1952), was famous not because of his playing, which was conventional and flawed, but because he led one of the most popular small jazz bands of its day (1937–42), an unusually minimalist sextet that prefigured the cool style of the 1950s. Slam Stewart also won fame in this period, as part of the duo Slim and Slam (with singer-guitarist-humorist Slim Gaillard) and later as a member of the Art Tatum Trio. Stewart was known for his ability to simultaneously scat-sing and improvise bass lines played with a bow.

John Kirby / Slam Stewart

Oddly enough, the man who did the most to advance the cause of the bass didn't play it. Duke Ellington, partial to the lower end of the musical spectrum, wrote arrangements in the 1920s that required the elaborate participation of his Louisiana-born bassist, Wellman Braud. With Ellington, Braud helped to develop the walking bass and popularized the bowing technique, heard in tandem with the wind instruments.

Wellman Braud

■ JIMMY BLANTON (1918–1942)

Ellington's greatest contribution to jazz bass, however, came with his discovery of Jimmy Blanton, the man who became such a central figure in the key edition of the Ellington band, which also introduced Ben Webster, that the band was later referred to by fans as "the Blanton-Webster band." Blanton's brief life and career parallels that of Charlie Christian (they succumbed to the same illness, Blanton at twenty-three), and his transformation of jazz bass was every bit as complete as Christian's remaking of the guitar. In little more than two years— the same period in which Christian emerged (1939–41)—Blanton changed the way the bass was played and, by extension, the nature of the rhythm section.

His attributes included a Tatumesque grounding in harmony that allowed him to add substitute chords; a distinctly attractive and supple timbre; and an authoritative rhythmic pulse. Blanton recorded the first bass solos that departed from the walking-bass style in favor of a freely melodic conception. In his hands, the bass, no longer a cumbersome instrument, could maneuver with speed and flexibility. Blanton's work buoyed Ellington's music with a metrical panache in such works as "Jack the Bear," "Ko-Ko," and "Concerto for Cootie."

DRUMMERS STEP OUT

Unlike the bass, the drums quickly reached a high plateau of accomplishment in the Swing Era. Because drums played a loud, dominant, visibly important role in the jazz band, they focused the attention of the audience. As a result, they became a selling point and drummers became showmen: they tossed their sticks in the air and surrounded themselves with exotic instruments, design-ing and even illuminating their bass drum heads. At the same time, a genuine

Jimmy Blanton (c. 1940), a discovery of Duke Ellington, who wrote the first bass concertos for him, revolutionized the instru-ment and its role in the rhythm section, replacing the walking 4/4 approach with melodic, harmonic, rhythmic, and tonal nuances.

FRANK DRIGGS COLLECTION

Chick Webb (c. 1939), a dwarfed hunchback whose drums were scaled to order, advanced big-band jazz and drumming as the indefatigable King of the Savoy Ballroom, finding commercial success as he launched the career of Ella Fitzgerald.

DUNCAN SCHIEDT COLLECTION

Gene Krupa

Jo Jones

musical virtuosity emerged, as drummers competed to create distinct and imaginative ways to keep time, shape arrangements, and inspire soloists.

William Henry Webb (1909–1939), nicknamed Chick for his small size, was the first great swing drummer and the first to lead his own orchestra, a fiercely competitive outfit that ruled New York's Savoy Ballroom in the early 1930s. He didn't look the part of a powerful drummer and commanding bandleader: mangled by spinal tuberculosis, Webb was a dwarfed hunchback who lived most of his short life in pain. Drums of reduced size were built to accommodate him. Even so, his drumming had a titanic power, and even by contemporary standards his short solos and rattling breaks impart a jolt: each stroke has the articulation of a gunshot. Gene Krupa said of Webb, "When he really let go, you had a feeling that the entire atmosphere in the place was being charged. When he felt like it, he could down any of us." A generous nurturer of talent—Ellington turned to him to find young musicians—he hit the big time when he discovered Ella Fitzgerald.

Webb's rim shots and explosive breaks gave his music a unique kick. In 1937, he enjoyed the satisfaction of engaging in a "battle of the bands" at the Savoy with Goodman and trouncing him. The victory was particularly sweet because Goodman's drummer was the nationally publicized Krupa, who at the end faced Webb and bowed down in respect. But Webb didn't have long to savor his success; he died at thirty, of tuberculosis and pleurisy.

Gene Krupa (1909–1973), one of the white Chicagoans who congregated around Bix Beiderbecke and the Austin High guys, was the first drummer to achieve the status of a matinee idol. During four years with Goodman's band (1934–38), he created a sensation with his dramatic solos, characterized by facial contortions, broad arm movements, and hair falling over his brow. His trademark was an ominous, repetitive figure played on the tom-toms ("Sing, Sing, Sing"). In 1938, given his growing fan base, Krupa was encouraged to leave Goodman to start his own band, which proved adventurous and tasteful, and made social and musical history by hiring Roy Eldridge.

No less mesmerizing and more musically accomplished was Jo Jones (1911–1985), who created the fleet four-four drive that made Count Basie's rhythm section a swing touchstone. It was said that "he played like the wind." His great innovation was to transfer the foundation rhythm from the snare and bass drums to the high-hat cymbal: this created a tremendous fluidity, replacing *thump-thump-thump* with a sibilant *ching-a-ching-ching*. Jones created some of the most exciting moments of the era, announcing pieces on the high-hat, as in "Clap Hands, Here Comes Charlie," or spurring the soloists with razor-sharp stick work (note his accompaniment to Lester Young and Buck Clayton on "One O'Clock Jump"). In later years, he was reverently known as Papa Jo; on some nights, he would walk through the clubs he worked and drum on every surface.

The Swing Era defined and unified American culture as no other style of music ever had or would—even the 1960s era of the Beatles, which evoked the optimism and broad reach of swing, exposed a "generation gap." Swing was innovated by men and women in their thirties, and if their initial audiences were young, their music almost immediately suspended all gaps. Swing was bigger than jazz. Country music performers like Bob Wills organized Western swing bands; comic personalities like Kay Kyser fronted novelty swing bands. Some liked it hot, others sweet; some liked it highbrow, others lowdown.

The irony of swing is that it flourished during the Depression, when luxury was in short supply except in popular culture; this was also the era of cinematic spectaculars like *Gone with the Wind* and *The Wizard of Oz*, of Fred

Astaire / Ginger Rogers musicals and Cary Grant / Irene Dunne comedies, when actors played characters who wore tuxedos and gowns and hobnobbed with the very rich in laughably glamorous settings. That fantasy crashed in the aftermath of the war. The music that dominated the next decade of American life emanated directly from swing bands—not from its stars, but rather from its mavericks, musicians considered tangential to or insignificant in the world of swing. They would lay the groundwork for rhythm and blues, salsa, star vocalists, and a way of playing jazz that was more intellectual and demanding than its predecessors. True to form, the mainstream press tagged it with a silly onomatopoetic name that it could never discard: bebop.

ADDITIONAL LISTENING	
Fats Waller	"I'm Gonna Sit Right Down and Write Myself a Letter" (1935), "Honeysuckle Rose" (1951)
Art Tatum and Ben Webster	*The Tatum Group Masterpieces,* vol. 8 (1956)
Louis Armstrong and Sid Catlett	"Steak Face" (1947)
Teddy Wilson	"Blues in C Sharp Minor" (1936)
Chick Webb	"Don't Be That Way" (1934), "A-Tisket, a-Tasket" (1938)
Gene Krupa	"Let Me Off Uptown" (1941)
Roy Eldridge	"Rockin' Chair" (1946)

ONLINE MULTIMEDIA RESOURCES AND REVIEW MATERIALS

Author Insight Videos

Gary Giddins describes changes in the way the rhythm section interacted with the rest of the band in the 1930s, how Charlie Christian opened doors for jazz guitarists, how jazz unified the whole country during the Swing Era, and how this unity later broke down into discrete audiences who defined themselves by the music they listened to.

Interactive Listening Guides

Fats Waller, "Christopher Columbus"
Art Tatum, "Over the Rainbow"
Charlie Christian, "Swing to Bop" ("Topsy")

Jazz Concepts (audio and/or video demonstrations of terms covered here)

arco	dissonance	rubato
arpeggio	dominant	tonic
backbeat	octave	tremolo
call and response	polyrhythm	triplets
chromatic	riff	walking bass

- For quick reference, review the **Chapter Overview** and **Chapter Outline**.

- Take the online **Chapter** and **Listening Quizzes**.

- Use the online **Glossary** and **Flashcards** to review important terms.

SWING BANDS AFTER 1930

Swing, a buoyant, exuberant (mostly big-band) music that inspired teenage dancers to acrobatic feats, unified American culture as no other style ever had. The same tune might be played on the radio or a jukebox, on a movie soundtrack, or by a big band (hot or sweet) or small band. With its well-defined melodies, big-band swing was simple and accessible, and continued to balance composition against spontaneous improvisation.

Texture
- homophonic

Rhythm
- clearly articulated four beats to the bar

Instrumentation
- sections of trumpets, trombones, saxophones
- rhythm section: string bass, acoustic guitar, piano, drums

Form and repertory
- 32-bar popular song (**A A B A, A B A C**), 12-bar blues
- current pop songs

Special techniques
- call-and-response riffs
- improvised solos over simple backgrounds

Big bands
- Benny Goodman
- Fletcher Henderson
- Artie Shaw
- Jimmie Lunceford
- Cab Calloway
- Glenn Miller
- Gene Krupa

COUNT BASIE AND DUKE ELLINGTON

In the 1920s, thousands of local dance bands known as territory bands covered the country. In the same period, a new piano style called boogie-woogie developed in the Southwest and spread rapidly, securing a home in Kansas City and Chicago: a 12-bar blues, with a strong left-hand rhythmic ostinato that divided each measure into eight.

The most famous Kansas City pianist and bandleader was Count Basie, whose music making conveyed above all simplicity. Kansas City swing followed the same style as the big bands above, except that it placed more emphasis on head arrangements and soloists and featured a lighter rhythm section.

In the years before 1935, Duke Ellington was the dominant black name in dance bands. In a career spanning half a century, Ellington established a legacy through recordings that proves him to be, arguably, America's greatest composer.

Boogie-woogie pianists
- Pete Johnson
- Meade Lux Lewis

Territory bandleaders and musicians
- Benny Moten
- Walter Page
- Andy Kirk
- Mary Lou Williams

Count Basie Orchestra, 1930s–1940s
- Lester Young, tenor saxophone
- Herschel Evans, tenor saxophone
- Buck Clayton, trumpet
- Harry "Sweets" Edison, trumpet
- Eddie Durham, trombone
- Jo Jones, drums
- Freddie Green, guitar
- Walter Page, bass
- Jimmy Rushing, vocal

Duke Ellington Orchestra, 1940–
- Ben Webster, tenor saxophone
- Juan Tizol, trombone
- Lawrence Brown, trombone
- Rex Stewart, trumpet
- Billy Strayhorn, arranger/composer

- Sonny Greer, drums
- Jimmy Blanton, bass
- Johnny Hodges, alto saxophone
- Harry Carney, baritone saxophone
- Barney Bigard, clarinet
- Ivie Anderson, vocal

SWING-ERA SOLOISTS

Soloists in big bands and smaller groups developed distinct personal syles that listeners could readily identify. Their popularity increased throughout the 1930s, portending a new respect for jazz musicians. At the same time, rhythm-section musicians developed technical skills and harmonic and rhythmic ideas that demanded attention.

Alto saxophone
- Benny Carter

Tenor saxophone
- Coleman Hawkins
- Ben Webster
- Lester Young
- Chu Berry

Trumpet
- Roy Eldridge
- Valaida Snow

Guitar
- Django Reinhardt
- Charlie Christian (electric)

Piano
- Fats Waller
- Art Tatum

Bass
- Milt Hinton
- Jimmy Blanton
- Walter Page
- Israel Crosby
- John Kirby
- Slam Stewart

Drums
- Chick Webb
- Sid Catlett
- Gene Krupa
- Jo Jones
- Buddy Rich

Vocalists
- Billie Holiday
- Ella Fitzgerald
- Mildred Bailey
- Ethel Waters

PART IV

MODERN JAZZ

The war transformed the economy, speeded the pace of life, and spurred the demand for civil rights. Segregated black troops who had fought to liberate foreign lands from tyranny were more determined to liberate themselves from a second-class citizenship. Many young musicians, black and white, found a bond and a social message in the jazz represented by the incendiary brilliance of Charlie Parker and Dizzy Gillespie. Their music, which became known as bebop, emerged from the swing bands and found its own setting in small bands. In an era of rockets and atom bombs, bebop favored art over entertainment, unleashing supersonic tempos and volatile rhythms that frightened many listeners accustomed to the steady, stamping beat of swing.

Bebop became the standard language of jazz improvisation, yet it accommodated various musical styles, or schools. The West Coast fostered a cool way of playing, while the East Coast came up with a more visceral brew called hard

1940
- Charlie Parker joins Jay McShann's orchestra in Kansas City.

1941
- Parker begins playing in Minton's Playhouse jam sessions.

1944
- Dizzy Gillespie's band plays on New York's 52nd Street, known as Swing Street.
- Norman Granz establishes Jazz at the Philharmonic and produces *Jammin' the Blues*, featuring Lester Young.
- *Going My Way,* starring Jazz Age crooner Bing Crosby, is top-grossing movie of the year.

1945
- Charlie Parker records "Ko Ko."
- Parker and Gillespie take their band to Los Angeles.
- United Nations founded.

1946
- Jackie Robinson becomes the first African American in major league baseball.

- "Hollywood 10" blacklisted by the House Un-American Activities Committee.

1947
- Louis Armstrong forms his All Stars band.
- Woody Herman forms his Second Herd, known as the Four Brothers band.
- Tennessee Williams's *A Streetcar Named Desire* (with Marlon Brando) opens on Broadway.

1948
- The last important clubs on New York's 52nd Street close.
- Dizzy Gillespie performs at Nice Jazz Festival in France.
- Billie Holiday breaks records at Carnegie Hall concerts.
- Microgrooves—LP $33\frac{1}{3}$ rpm and 45 rpm—are introduced.
- Apartheid imposed in South Africa.
- State of Israel founded.
- *The Texaco Star Theater*, starring Milton Berle, debuts on television.

Coleman Hawkins (left) led a prophetic session in 1944 at the Spotlight Club in New York, with one of his disciples, tenor saxophonist Don Byas (third from left), and an unknown pianist he championed named Thelonious Monk.

It happened here: In 1968, civil rights activists were blocked by National Guardsmen brandishing bayonets on Beale Street in Memphis. The demonstrators were also flanked by tanks.

Alto saxophonist Cannonball Adderley, a former schoolteacher from Tampa, Florida, became an overnight sensation after sitting in at New York's Club Bohemia.

bop. The revival of church, classical, and Latin influences led to soul jazz, Third Stream, and salsa. Miles Davis, one of the most influential and restless bop musicians, contributed innovations to all of these schools. His use of modes and free styles of improvisation also helped to ignite the avant-garde, which created a jazz rift more disputatious than the swing/bop schism.

Like jazz before and after, bop reflected the times. The relief and triumph that attended the Allied victory led almost instantly to disillusionment and paranoia, as the fear of nuclear devastation and Communist infiltration and demands for racial equality generated social discord. Television responded with a homogenized view of American life, emphasizing middle-class satisfactions. Jazz no longer served as an optimistic booster. If it now alienated much of the audience that had rallied around swing, it attracted a younger audience that admired its irreverence and subtlety. It was championed by beatniks, hedonists, students, and intellectuals.

1949

- "Rhythm and blues" displaces the label "race records."
- The club Birdland, named after Charlie Parker, opens in New York.
- Paris Jazz Festival brings Parker, Miles Davis, and other young musicians to Europe.
- West German Federal Republic and East German Democratic Republic established.
- Mao Tse-Tung establishes the People's Republic of China.
- First flight of a passenger jet aircraft.
- George Orwell's *1984* published.
- Carol Reed directs Graham Greene's film script for *The Third Man.*
- Arthur Miller's *Death of a Salesman* opens on Broadway.

1949–50

- Miles Davis leads "Birth of the Cool" sessions.

1950–53

- Korean War

1951

- Dave Brubeck organizes quartet with Paul Desmond.
- J. D. Salinger's *Catcher in the Rye* published.

1952

- John Lewis forms Modern Jazz Quartet (in New York).
- Gerry Mulligan organizes a "piano-less" quartet (in California).
- First pocket-sized transitor radios sold.
- Edward R. Murrow's *See It Now* comes to TV, helping to bring down Senator Joseph McCarthy.
- Ralph Ellison's *The Invisible Man* published.

1953

- Art Blakey and Horace Silver form the Jazz Messengers.
- George Russell publishes *Lydian Chromatic Concept.*

1954

- Miles Davis records "Walkin'."
- Clifford Brown and Max Roach form quintet.
- Supreme Court, in *Brown v. Board of Education of Topeka*, finds segregation in public schools unconstitutional.

CHARLIE PARKER
ko ko

CHARLIE PARKER
embraceable you

CHARLIE PARKER
now's the time

BUD POWELL
tempus fugue-it

DEXTER GORDON
long tall dexter

BEBOP

BEBOP AND JAM SESSIONS

In the mid-1940s, the swing jazz that had risen from its New Orleans origins to become an extroverted popular music turned a sharp corner with the sounds known as **bebop**, or **bop**. Jazz was suddenly an isolated music, appearing in tiny cramped night-clubs rather than brightly lit dance halls. Its music—small-combo tunes with peculiar names such as "Salt Peanuts" and "Ornithology"—was complex, dense, and difficult to grasp. It traded in a mass audience for a jazz cult (fans were often characterized as beatniks or intellectuals) that revered musicians known by terse, elliptical names, real or bestowed: Bird (Charlie Parker), Diz (Dizzy Gillespie), Klook (Kenny Clarke), Monk (Thelonious Monk), Bud (Bud Powell), Dex (Dexter Gordon). Like swing, bebop was still a music that prized virtuosity; if anything, its standards were higher. But most people saw it as an outsider's music, steeped in drug abuse and tainted with an atmosphere of racial hostility.

Jazz historians, taking a cue from musicians and fans, initially described bebop as a revolution, emphatically breaking with the past. In 1949, the incalculably influential alto saxophonist Charlie Parker insisted that bebop was a new music, something "entirely separate and apart" from the jazz that had preceded it. Historians today, however, tend to

Few saxophonists seemed more elegant than **Dexter Gordon**, who made looking cool a top priority for the bebop generation. New York, Royal Roost, 1948, with drummer Kenny Clarke.

treat bebop as an evolution from swing, placing it firmly in the center of the jazz tradition while acknowledging that its status was altered to that of self-conscious art music. The evolutionary view links bop to a particular backstage phenomenon of the Swing Era: the jam session.

Dropping Bombs at Minton's

The swing musician's day began in the evening, as people drifted toward theaters and ballrooms for their after-work entertainment. By the time those audiences went home to bed, musicians in large cities, especially Manhattan, were gearing up for more work. "The average musician hated to go home in those days," remembered Sonny Greer, Duke Ellington's drummer. "He was always seeking some place where someone was playing something he ought to hear." Free of the constraints of the bandstand, musicians could come and go in these places as they pleased.

To keep players from wandering in who didn't belong, jam sessions offered a series of musical obstacles. The simplest way to make an inexperienced interloper feel unwelcome was to count off a tune at a ridiculously fast tempo or play it in an unfamiliar key. Sometimes tunes would modulate up a half step with every chorus, challenging everyone's ability to transpose. Favorite tunes like "I Got Rhythm" would be recast with blisteringly difficult harmonic substitutions. Those who could take the heat were welcome; those who couldn't went home to practice. In this way, the musicians who would become the bebop generation had their musical skills continually tested. When Ben Webster first heard Parker play, he asked, "Man, is that cat crazy?" and reportedly grabbed the horn away, exclaiming, "That horn ain't supposed to sound that fast."

Charlie Parker and other young Turks could be heard regularly at Minton's Playhouse, on 118th Street in Harlem, which hosted some of the most celebrated jam sessions in Manhattan. Many of the innovations that took place there reflected its professional clientele's hunger for musical challenge. Consider, for example, how bebop changed drumming. As Kenny Clarke once explained it, his technical breakthrough came when he was playing for a swing band led by Teddy Hill in the late 1930s. During an exceptionally fast arrangement of "Ol' Man River," he found it nearly impossible to keep time in the usual fashion by striking his bass drum for each beat. Suddenly it occurred to him to shift the pulse to the ride cymbal. This innovation gave him two new tactics: a shimmering cymbal that became the lighter, more flexible foundation for all of modern jazz, and the powerful bass drum now filling in the holes in the band's arrangements with its thunderous booms.

When Hill moved to Minton's Playhouse in 1940, he brought Clarke into the rhythm section, where he soon earned the nickname "Klook" because his combined snare drum and bass drum hits evoked a "klook-mop"

Minton's Playhouse opened for business in 1940. By 1947, it was famous enough as the birthplace of bebop that this photograph was staged for posterity. From the left: pianist/composer Thelonious Monk, trumpet players Howard McGhee and Roy Eldridge, and bandleader/manager Teddy Hill.

© WILLIAM P. GOTTLIEB

sound. Given the startup of the war, especially the recently endured Battle of Britain, Clarke's style of unexpected bass drum explosions was referred to as **dropping bombs**. Young, hip musicians fell in love with Clarke's simmering polyrhythms. Drummers like Max Roach and Art Blakey found in his playing the methods they needed for a more modern style.

Over this new accompaniment, the rhythms played by soloists (inspired by Lester Young's and Charlie Christian's fluid, discontinuous approach) were disorienting and unpredictable. Listeners were startled by the spurts of fast notes, ending abruptly with a two-note gesture that inspired the scat syllables "be-bop" or "re-bop." Older musicians were not amused. While jamming at Minton's, Fats Waller supposedly yelled out, "Stop that crazy boppin' and a-stoppin' and play that jive like the rest of us guys!"

Pianists who came of age with the stripped-down playing of Count Basie dropped stride patterns in favor of **comping**—the rhythmically unpredictable skein of accompanying chords that complemented the drummer's strokes and added yet another layer to the rhythmic mix. The acoustic guitar's insistent chording (*chunk chunk chunk*) that once thickened the sound of a swing rhythm section was superfluous in the context of bebop's ride cymbal and walking-bass line. Guitarists either steered clear of bebop or, following Charlie Christian's lead, switched to electric amplification, which allowed them to take a more active, syncopated role in the rhythm section or step into the limelight as soloist.

The bassists' role didn't change—they remained timekeepers at the bottom of the texture—yet thanks to the jam session, as well as the instantly influential Jimmy Blanton, who had begun to undergird the Ellington band in the years directly preceding Minton's, a new generation of bass players raised the level of virtuosity. One of the most impressive musicians to expand on Blanton's innovations was Oscar Pettiford, a young musician of Choctaw and Cherokee ancestry. On a 1943 Coleman Hawkins recording of "The Man I Love," Pettiford plays a wonderfully melodic solo made intensely rhythmic by his gasps of breath between each phrase.

While Kenny Clarke devised his new techniques as a swing drummer in the 1930s, he came alive in after-hours jam sessions. As a member of the house band at Minton's Playhouse, he was central to the birth of modern jazz.

Oscar Pettiford

"Nobody Plays Those Changes"

Bebop was famous—and sometimes reviled—for its complex, dissonant harmonies. To be sure, these sounds had been part of the jazz vocabulary for years. Art Tatum turned popular songs into harmonic minefields through the complexity of his chord substitutions, leaving other musicians—including a nineteen-year-old Charlie Parker, who worked as a dishwasher in a restaurant that featured Tatum—to shake their heads in wonder. Arrangers listened closely to Duke Ellington's instrumentation, trying to decipher how he voiced his astringent chords. Improvisers took their cue from Coleman Hawkins, who showed in "Body and Soul" how to use dense chromatic harmonies in popular song.

The challenge for the bebop generation came in translating these dissonant harmonies into a vocabulary all musicians could share. Soloists and members

Bebop was the music of small clubs like Bop City in San Francisco. Crowded into this room one night in 1951 were Dizzy Gillespie (right, at the piano) and fellow trumpet players Kenny Dorham (standing to his left) and Miles Davis (head bowed, to his right); singer Betty Bennett; saxophonist Jimmy Heath (facing camera directly below her) and his brother, bassist Percy Heath (kneeling, to his right); vibraharpist Milt Jackson (kneeling, bottom left, facing left); and drummer Roy Porter (far left in back row, smoking cigarette).

FRANK DRIGGS COLLECTION

of the rhythm section had to learn to coordinate. This could be done deliberately, as when Dizzy Gillespie and bassist Milt Hinton got together on the roof of the Cotton Club and planned substitute harmonies for that evening's jam sessions. At other times, there was the shock of discovery. When Charlie Parker first heard pianist Tadd Dameron's unusual chord voicings, he was so pleased he kissed him on the cheek. "That's what I've been hearing all my life," he said, "but nobody plays those changes."

 **tritone / flatted fifth** the interval of three whole steps

The new harmonies fastened onto dissonances like the **tritone**—the chromatic interval known to the Middle Ages as the "devil in music" and to the beboppers as the **flatted fifth.** Other extended notes (sixths, flat ninths) were added to the palette, making the job of harmonic improvisation that much more difficult. "With bop, you had to *know*," trumpet player Howard McGhee stated firmly. "Not feel; you had to *know* what you were doing."

At the same time, nonmusical forces—racial and economic—were driving musicians out of swing into the unknown future, and these forces formed the basis for the notion that bop was revolutionary. During the Swing Era, black bands were barred from two kinds of jobs: a sponsored prime-time radio show (such as *The Camel Cavalcade,* subsidized by Camel cigarettes) and a lengthy engagement at a major hotel ballroom or dance hall in New York City. These latter jobs offered free late-night broadcasts, invaluable for publicity, as well as a chance to rest from the rigors of travel. For several months of the year, the musicians in top white bands could unpack their bags, rehearse new tunes, and live with their families.

On the road

The top black bands were obliged to stay on the road. A few, like Ellington's and Cab Calloway's, could afford the comforts of a private railroad car, but the rest toured the country in rattletrap buses. Continuous travel was enough to exhaust even the hardiest musicians, especially when it took them into the heart of the Jim Crow South. As highly visible African American celebrities headquartered in New York, these jazz musicians aroused the ire of white Southerners, from the man on the street to uniformed police. Musicians had to eat at "colored" restaurants, sit in the Jim Crow car of a railroad, and avoid eye contact with white women—or risk violence. Milt Hinton, touring with Calloway, shot photographs of musicians pissing on whites-only signs or shaking their heads in disbelief.

Under these circumstances, musicians became bitter—especially younger ones, impatient with the hypocrisy that protected racism while allowing the country to boast of its crusade against totalitarian injustice. The most talented quit the swing bands, sometimes out of exhaustion, sometimes disgust. Increasingly, they turned toward the jam sessions, hoping to find some way to carry on their music outside the system. Bebop absorbed their energy: it was subversive, "uppity," daring, and hell-bent on social change. "There was a message to our music," proclaimed Kenny Clarke. "Whatever you go into, go into it *intelligently*.... The idea was to wake up, look around you, there's something to do." By the early 1940s, a new approach to jazz, based on progressive chromatic harmonies and supported by an interactive rhythm section, was in place. The final piece in the puzzle was a new kind of virtuoso soloist, taking standards of improvisational excellence to unforeseen levels.

■ CHARLIE PARKER (1920–1955)

One of the most gifted instrumentalists in music history, Charlie Parker earned his nickname early in his apprenticeship, while touring with a Kansas City–based territory band led by the boogie-woogie pianist Jay McShann. On a short trip, for which the band traveled in a small caravan of cars, Parker's ride ran over a chicken. He yelled at the driver to stop and, to everyone's amusement, rushed to the dying bird and carried it back to the car. When the band arrived that night at a boarding house, he proudly presented the freshly killed chicken as the main ingredient for his meal. His bandmates teasingly called him Yardbird, but as the name got shortened over time to Bird, the joking aspect disappeared, to be replaced by an unmistakable reverence. Within five years, the name Bird signified melodious beauty, elusivenesss, and quickness of flight.

Parker, who was born in Kansas and grew up in Missouri's Kansas City, didn't seem at first to have any special gift for music. He played baritone horn in his high school marching band, pecking out notes in the accompaniment. Eventually, he picked up the alto saxophone, teaching himself to play by ear standard jazz fare like Fats Waller's "Honeysuckle Rose." When he tried to sit in on jam sessions, though, he met only humiliation. According to a well-traveled legend, after he sat in on "Body and Soul" and flailed around in the wrong key, the drummer Jo Jones gonged him out by tossing his ride cymbal on the floor. That kind of experience spurred him into a furious regimen of practicing. During one summer in the Ozarks, he learned how to play fluently in *every* key—an uncommon achievement even for established players.

He listened to famous alto saxophonists of the day, but paid most attention to the tenors; he played his favorite records by Chu Berry, Coleman Hawkins, and Lester Young repeatedly, and memorized Young's 1936 solo on "Oh! Lady Be Good." (Parker's own improvisation

Throughout his brief career, alto saxophonist Charlie Parker appeared with a long list of trumpet players. In the late 1940s, his bandstand partner was young Miles Davis (right), barely out of his teens.

FRANK DRIGGS COLLECTION

on that song became one of *his* most imitated solos, and remains a textbook example of how to transform a pop tune with deep blues feeling.) By the time he returned to Kansas City in late 1937, his rhythm had become supercharged: one musician conveyed the impression of Parker's speed by playing a Young record twice as fast. Now an expert soloist, Parker quickly earned a position in the McShann orchestra, a top band in Kansas City. But he also began using alcohol and pills; still in his teens, he soon found his way to heroin, a substance that eventually controlled much of his life.

Parker's playing struck people at first as both bluesy and modern. For his solo on McShann's "Hootie Blues" (1941), he upgraded the twelve-bar blues with new chromatic chord progressions and enlivened it with rapid flurries of notes. He also proved that he could be a model citizen in a swing band, blending beautifully in the saxophone section and devising endlessly varied riffs behind soloists during head arrangements. Members of the jazz elite began talking about him—both his phenomenal playing and his dependency on drugs. Some had seen him rise from a stupor, practically nodding out on the bandstand, to play a magnificent solo. But McShann and other bandleaders found it too taxing to keep him. Instead, Parker settled into a precarious New York existence where narcotics were available and jam sessions offered a place to musically stretch out. He became a magnet for a network of musicians similarly attuned to what he once called the "real advanced New York style."

■ DIZZY GILLESPIE (1917–1993)

The musician most attuned to Parker's achievement, and the intellectual force behind the music that would be called bebop, was an extravagantly talented trumpet player John Birks "Dizzy" Gillespie. His astounding solos, crackling in the upper register and accelerating to speeds not thought possible, matched Parker's note for note, but seemed to many listeners even more dramatic—expecially when ripping into the trumpet's upper register. The excitement he generated combined with a razor-sharp wit, organizational savvy, and steady hand brought him a larger audience than Parker, in a career that lasted more than fifty years. If Parker was bebop's inspiration, the Pied Piper of modern jazz, Gillespie pulled the style into shape like a master craftsman.

Like Parker, Gillespie came to New York from the provinces. He grew up in Cheraw, South Carolina, and taught himself trumpet so unconventionally that he damaged his neck muscles, causing his cheeks to protrude, frog-like, when he played. He earned a scholarship to the Laurinburg Institute, across the border in North Carolina, where he studied trumpet and piano. After hearing broadcasts of great jazz players, especially Roy Eldridge, he headed north—first to Philadelphia, joining local bands, and later to New York.

This combo, which debuted at the Onyx Club on 52nd Street in late 1943, was probably the first bebop band. From left to right: Max Roach, drums; Budd Johnson, tenor saxophone; Oscar Pettiford, bass; George Wallington, piano; and Dizzy Gillespie, trumpet.

FRANK DRIGGS COLLECTION

By 1939, Gillespie had reached the top of the heap. For the next several years, he was employed by the Cab Calloway Orchestra, perhaps the most lucrative black band in existence. He thrived in this atmosphere, flying high in the trumpet section and creating such tunes as "Pickin' the Cabbage," a 1940 Calloway recording that combines a hip harmonic bite with a Latin groove. Still, he couldn't help feeling dissatisfaction with the status quo: "I worked hard while I played with Cab, and practiced constantly. I could seldom get much encouragement from the guys in Cab's band. Mostly they talked about real estate or something, never talked about music. That atmosphere kept me acting wiggy and getting into a lot of mischief."

With Calloway

Gillespie had earned his nickname back in Philadelphia for his fiery temperament and wicked sense of humor. He brought this unpredictable behavior onto the Calloway bandstand, devising practical jokes and irritating the bandleader with his wildly experimental solos. One night in 1941, a spitball flew directly into Calloway's spotlight. Gillespie was innocent of the crime (a fellow musician had thrown it), but it was the kind of thing Dizzy did and Calloway assumed he was the culprit. Gillespie was fired—a stroke of fortune in that it spurred him into action. He now worked as a freelance musician and composer, earning a living through whatever means possible, including the jam-session performances that led to the establishment of bebop.

In Miles Davis's words, Gillespie was bebop's "head and hands," the "one who kept it all together." Gillespie was quick to grasp the music's novelties and was generous enough to spread them as far as possible. In jam sessions, he showed pianists how to play the appropriate chords, and sat on the drum stool to demonstrate to drummers the more flexible, interactive style. He absorbed the creativity of others as well, noting chords created by Mary Lou Williams or Thelonious Monk and working them into new tunes and arrangements. Thanks to his piano skills, Gillespie was fully aware of the harmonic possibilities of bebop. He loved the edge that dissonant chords gave his melodies, among them "Salt Peanuts," a bracingly fast reworking of "I Got Rhythm": its title was sung to a riff based on a bebop drum lick (the quick alternation of snare and bass drum). "A Night in Tunisia" offered a more exotic groove. Completed in 1942 as the Allied troops invaded North Africa, "Tunisia" adapted modern chord changes to a Latin bass line, deepening Gillespie's fascination with Caribbean music.

On 52nd Street

Gillespie and Parker first crossed paths in the early 1940s. Parker reveled in Gillespie's brilliant sound and his deep knowledge of harmony. Gillespie focused on the fluidity of Parker's phrases: "Charlie Parker brought the rhythm," he said. "The *way* he played those notes." The two worked side by side in 1942, when Earl Hines hired them for his big band (with Parker switching to tenor saxophone). Two years later, they again joined forces when Hines's vocalist, Billy Eckstine, started his own band. With Gillespie serving as music director, Eckstine's was the first big band to fully embrace bop.

Tunes like "Salt Peanuts" and "A Night in Tunisia," with their tricky interludes, elaborate breaks, and sudden shifts in texture, now seem naturally adaptable to the big-band environment. Yet the nascent style of modern jazz never found its way to a mass audience, and by the end of 1944 Dizzy and Bird had quit the Eckstine band, turning instead to small groups as the

Charlie Parker and Dizzy Gillespie posed together in 1951 at Birdland, the Broadway club named in Parker's honor. To their left is bassist Tommy Potter, while looking on from the right is the young saxophonist John Coltrane.

Bebop arrives

best way to present their music. The kind of group Parker and Gillespie had in mind was nothing like the winnowed ensembles that the big bands had offered for contrast. It would have to embody the daring and impetuousness of a jam session, but rehearsed and charged—it would have to pin your ears back.

By the time Gillespie brought a quintet to 52nd Street, the emergent style was known as **bebop**, or less frequently rebop, the scat syllables reflecting the new rhythmic style. In tightening up the go-for-broke music heard at Minton's, it added a new and challenging wrinkle: at the beginning of a tune, where one might expect to hear a familiar harmonized melody, the horns played a bare, sinuous theme in disjointed rhythms, confusing those not already familiar with the Harlem jam sessions and offering no clue of what was to come. In this way, the jam-session style, already shielded from the public, became a way of transmuting blues and standards into a new repertory. The white swing drummer Dave Tough, who heard the 1944 band, remembered its uncanny impact: "As we walked in, see, these cats snatched up their horns and blew crazy stuff. One would stop all of a sudden and another would start for no reason at all. We never could tell when a solo was supposed to begin or end. Then they all quit at once and walked off the stand. It scared us."

BIRD ON RECORD

The first true bebop records date from early 1945, a chaotic period just before the end of the war that saw the emergence of small, independent record labels—Savoy, Apollo, Dial—with a view toward a low-cost way of entering the business: no arrangements, occasional vocals, plenty of blues, but mostly just let the musicians do their thing. Startling as these were, the real shock came with Parker's first session under his own name, recorded late in 1945 and released early the following year.

🎧 "Ko Ko"

"Cherokee," written by British bandleader Ray Noble in 1938 and turned into a popular hit the following year by Charlie Barnet, was an alleged tribute to Native Americans, with lyrics to match ("Sweet Indian maiden / Since I first met you / I can't forget you / Cherokee sweetheart"). Musicians were intrigued by its sixty-four-bar form, twice the length of the standard **A A B A**. Soloists shied away from the bridge, though, which jumped precipitously to a distant key and wound its way back home through continuous modulation. When Count Basie recorded this tune in 1939 (on two sides of a 78-rpm disc), the bridge appeared only during the head. The rest of the time, the soloists stayed with the simpler harmonies of the **A** section.

Parker practiced this tune assiduously as a kid in Kansas City and later in New York, reveling in its difficult harmonic progression. He once recalled that it was while working through its changes with a New York guitarist named Biddy Fleet that he had the epiphany that changed his music—the realization that any note, no matter how dissonant, could be made to resolve in a chord. The song soon became his favorite showpiece. To accommodate him, McShann's band concocted a loose head arrangement. When they finally made it to the Savoy Ballroom, Parker celebrated his New York debut by letting loose a "Cherokee" solo that seemed never to end, with the band spontaneously supplying riffs behind him. Like many others who heard that performance via radio, the trumpet player Howard McGhee was struck dumb with amazement: "I had never heard anything like that in my *life*," he remembered. "Here's a guy who's playing everything that he wants to play . . . and *playing* it, you know. I never heard nobody play a horn like that—that *complete*."

"Cherokee" was transformed into "Ko Ko" in 1945, when Parker brought a new quintet to the studio of Savoy Records. Originally a radio-parts store in Newark, New Jersey, Savoy expanded into a recording operation despite the relentless miserliness of its owner, Herman Lubinsky. Like other small record company owners, Lubinsky tried to avoid copyrighted tunes. So it's no surprise that on the first take, after Parker and Gillespie follow an abstract introduction with the melody to "Cherokee," someone shouts, "Hold it!" This was probably Parker, who, royalties aside, must have realized that a full chorus of the melody would limit his solo time. In any case, a subsequent take left the "Cherokee" melody out altogether. The name "Ko Ko" may have been borrowed unconsciously from the 1940 Ellington recording of the same name. "Naming-day at Savoy," one critic has said, "must have been an exhilarating, if random, experience."

The recording session was comically misassembled. Bud Powell was supposed to be the pianist, but in his absence Argonne Thornton (later known

Savoy Records

as Sadik Hakim) was hastily recruited. Gillespie, who showed up primarily for moral support, substituted on piano on some tunes. Miles Davis, a new member (at nineteen) of Parker's band, played trumpet on most of the session, but was not up to the blazing eight-bar exchanges at the beginning and end of "Ko Ko," so Gillespie took up the trumpet for those elaborate passages. Gillespie sounds like the pianist on the released (master) take; but Thornton must be the pianist on the false start, when Gillespie is clearly on trumpet. Somehow, out of this chaos came a bellwether jazz masterpiece—bop's equivalent of Louis Armstrong's "West End Blues." Parker's two white-hot choruses (only on repeated listening does it become evident that, for all his speed and seeming volatility, Parker plays melodies and riffs), preceded by the boldly disorienting introduction and followed by a lightning-fast Max Roach drum solo, constituted a music so startlingly different that it demanded a new name: *bebop*, at once an insider's term and a trivialization of the music, stuck to it like crazy glue.

🎧 ko ko

CHARLIE PARKER'S RE-BOPPERS
Charlie Parker, alto saxophone; Dizzy Gillespie, trumpet; Curley Russell, bass; Argonne "Dense" Thornton, piano; Max Roach, drums
- Label: Take 1 (fragment)—Savoy MG-12079; master take—Savoy 597
- Date: 1945
- Style: bebop
- Form: 64-bar popular song (**A A B A**; each section lasts 16 bars)

What to listen for:
- extremely fast tempo
- Parker and Gillespie playing precomposed melody in octaves in the disorienting introduction and coda
- Parker's constantly shifting accents, disruptive two-note "be-bop" rhythm
- Roach's dropping bombs

TAKE 1 (fragment)

INTRODUCTION

0:00 In an elusive introduction, Gillespie and Parker play a single composed line in bare **octaves**. There's no harmonic accompaniment; the only rhythmic backdrop is the snare drum, played lightly by Roach with brushes.

0:06 Gillespie plays a trumpet solo that implies a harmonic background through skillful improvisation. Many of the notes are **ghosted**—played so quietly that they are suggested rather than stated.

0:12 Parker enters with his own fluid line, overlapping slightly with the trumpet. The drums add **cross-rhythms**.

0:18 A loud "thump" on the bass drum pulls the two instruments back together. Gillespie plays a high note, followed immediately by a note an octave lower from Parker. As the two instruments continue without accompaniment, Roach exchanges his brushes for drum sticks.

CHORUS 1

0:24 **A** The two horns begin playing the melody to "Cherokee," with Parker adding a harmonized line. At the phrase's end, Parker switches to a rapid bebop-style **countermelody**.

0:33 Someone—probably Parker, who has stopped playing—shouts, "Hey, hey! Hold it!" and whistles and claps his hands loudly. The tape suddenly ends.

MASTER TAKE

INTRODUCTION

0:00   The opening is identical to the previous take.

0:06   Gillespie's solo is nearly identical to the previous take, suggesting that he had carefully prepared his line.

0:12   Parker's solo is strikingly different, underscoring the unpredictability of his improvisations.

CHORUS 1 (abbreviated)

0:25 **A** Parker begins improvising in a steady stream to the chord progression to "Cherokee." Roach marks time through a shadowy halo on the ride cymbal. The bass is **walking**, and the piano **comps**.

0:35   The rhythms in Parker's improvisation are disorienting, not simply because the tempo is extraordinarily fast, but because the accents are constantly shifting: sometimes on the beat, sometimes off.

0:37 **A** Parker's line continues through this **A** section, in a phrase that recalls the opening of the solo. The drummer's improvisation is more intense and interactive.

0:50 **B** The bridge to "Cherokee" begins with a sudden shift away from the home key to more distant harmonies. Parker marks it by a relatively simple melodic phrase that ends with piercing, bluesy notes.

1:03 **A**

1:05   Two sharp drum accents signal the start of another Parker phrase.

1:13   Parker prepares for his next chorus by resting on a single note, echoed by the piano and accents from the bass drum.

CHORUS 2

1:16 **A** Parker suddenly demonstrates his encyclopedic knowledge of jazz's history by quoting the famous piccolo **obbligato** from the New Orleans march "High Society."

1:29 **A**

1:41 **B** The piano marks the harmonic progression through simple chords. Parker disorients the listener with rhythms that alternately accent the strong and weak beats of the measure.

1:54 **A** A line that started toward the end of the bridge continues through the beginning of this **A** section, ending on the disruptive two-note "be-bop" rhythm.

2:01   Parker's improvised line is interrupted by a squeak from his notoriously unreliable reed.

CHORUS 3 (abbreviated)

2:07 **A** Roach begins his chorus-long solo with a simple alternating of the bass and snare drums, followed by a lengthy passage on the snare drum.

2:12   The snare drum pattern continues, occasionally punctuated by accents from the bass drum.

2:18 **A**

2:21   Roach plays a pattern of accents on the downbeat of each measure, before turning them into a cross-rhythm.

2:28   With a sudden two-note figure (*ch-bop!*), Roach ends his solo.

CODA

2:30   In a repetition of the introduction, Gillespie and Parker play the opening passage.

2:36   Gillespie improvises harmonically, while Roach quietly plays the backbeat behind him.

2:42   Parker fluently improvises on a harmonic progression that circles wildly through many key centers.

2:52   The back-and-forth octave exchange, which had previously served to introduce the first chorus, now returns as the piece's sudden and inconclusive end.

🎧 "Embraceable You"

Parker had an extraordinary musical memory. Through brief snippets quoted in his solos (such as the piccolo line from "High Society" in "Ko Ko" or a snippet of Armstrong's "West End Blues" cadenza played during a concert version of the same piece), we can get a sense of how much music he processed and stored. He also loved classical composers, especially Stravinsky, whose early modernist pieces (*Petrushka, The Firebird*) deeply impressed him, as well as hundreds of popular songs. His companion of several years, Chan Parker, recalled him walking around the house bellowing Mario Lanza's hit "Be My Love," and referring to "All the Things You Are" as "YATAG," an acronym of his favorite line from the lyric, "you are the angel glow."

"Embraceable You," recorded in 1947, is the best known of his several interpretations of the chord changes to George Gershwin's celebrated ballad; on none of them, however, does he play the actual tune—in fact, he usually gave his recorded interpretations new titles, like "Meandering" and "Quasimodo." Yet here he uses Gershwin's title, sacrificing his potential royalties, perhaps because he knew he had achieved something especially fine and wanted people to know how inventive it was. Instead of beginning with the melody, Parker introduces a two-bar phrase from a relatively obscure song, "A Table in the Corner," composed by Dana Suesse (who in her earlier years had been promoted as "the girl Gershwin") and recorded by Artie Shaw, in 1939. We can't know how he happened to think of it while playing this take—he doesn't use it on the other take recorded at the same session—but he makes this fragment fit into the harmonic progression of "Embraceable You" hand in glove, developing and modulating the phrase as though he had been working on it for years.

The remainder is a dazzling rhythmic swirl. Parker plays with a softness and earnestness that beautifully captures the song's romantic essence. Yet he barely touches down on Gershwin's melody, floating instead on rapid and constantly shifting phrases, playing a stream of thirty-second notes at a paradoxically very slow tempo. As is typical for a bebop recording, Parker's solo comes first, leaving Miles Davis the unenviable job of following him. Davis may have felt like Howard McGhee, who also followed Parker on recordings in the 1940s. "I used to hate to go to work," McGhee remembered, "knowing he would put a heavy whipping on me. And yet I couldn't wait to get there, because I knew what I was going to hear when I got there. And damn, he didn't never let me down."

LISTENING GUIDE 36

🎧 embraceable you

CHARLIE PARKER
Charlie Parker, alto saxophone; Miles Davis, trumpet; Duke Jordan, piano; Tommy Potter, bass; Max Roach, drums

- Label: Dial 1024
- Date: 1947
- Style: bebop
- Form: 32-bar popular song (**A B A C**)

What to listen for:
- extremely slow tempo
- Parker's improvisation within a romantic ballad
- his use of sequences, merely hinting at the song's melody
- early Davis solo

INTRODUCTION

0:00   The piano builds an introduction around a questioning four-note motive.

CHORUS 1

0:13   **A**   Parker quotes the melody to "A Table in a Corner." The accompaniment is simple: a slow **walking-bass** line, quiet piano chords, and the drums played almost inaudibly with brushes.

0:27   Having taken his quotation as far as it will go over the chord progression to "Embraceable You," Parker moves to bebop-style improvisation.

0:31   Over the next two measures, he plays a phrase that lags slightly behind the beat.

0:41   **B**   The high accented notes in his line derive from the melody to "Embraceable You" ("*Just* one look at *you* brings out the *gyp*-sy in me").

0:51   As Parker focuses his line onto one note, his tone becomes rougher and more intimate.

0:54   His rhythmic feeling begins to fall into **double-time**.

1:00   Shifting suddenly to a more **staccato** articulation, Parker plays a line that's rhythmically unpredictable.

1:07   The next double-time lick is one of his favorites.

1:10   **A**

1:17   Parker plays a lick, then transposes it by **sequence**, starting on a different pitch.

1:26   An impassioned entry results in a blown note.

1:29   The next phrase begins on a high note.

1:33   Parker plays another motive in sequence, moving it higher and higher.

1:38   Over a dominant chord, he raises the tension level by playing bebop dissonances.

1:40   **C**   After a silence, Parker continues in double-time.

1:50   He begins his last phrase with a different rhythmic groove and more staccato articulation. His line emphasizes high notes on the downbeat, falling from there.

CHORUS 2 (abbreviated)

2:09   **B**   Davis begins quietly playing a lyrical line on muted trumpet. His line is restrained and simple, lacking Parker's dramatic rhythmic changes.

2:38   To signal the return to the **A** section, Roach adds a discreet roll with his brushes.

2:40   **A**   As Davis continues his solo, Parker plays hushed **countermelodies** behind him.

3:03   Roach suggests a double-time groove, but Davis declines to follow.

3:10   **C**

3:19   Davis's improvisation, which is primarily **stepwise** (moving to adjacent notes), is interrupted by an octave lick; he repeats the lick a few seconds later.

3:26   The two horns together play the conclusion of "Embraceable You."

CODA

3:34   Underneath the horns' held-out note, the bass continues to walk while Roach plays a final roll.

🎧 "Now's the Time"

Parker once described bebop as the collision of New York's progressive intensity with the Midwestern blues. While some working-class blacks were alienated by bebop's intellectual complexity, he knew they would respond to what he called "red beans and rice music." There were many kinds of blues in the 1940s. As African Americans adjusted to the demands of the industrial North, the blues reflected time and place. In addition to the swing bands, there were the harsh reinventions of Southern blues in Muddy Waters's electrified, Chicago-based take on the Mississippi Delta and in the guitar virtuosity of the Texan T-Bone Walker. Parker added to the mix by melding blues vocal nuances to chromatic harmonies while perfecting a sweepingly fluid sense of rhythm. He showed how the blues could be made modern, and many of the more traditional blues musicians showed they understood this by adopting his harmonies and rhythms.

"Now's the Time" is one of Parker's most direct statements, built on a single riff, repeated and varied throughout the twelve bars. One of his early compositions, it was first recorded on the same 1945 session as "Ko Ko." Four years later, Savoy's proprietors conveniently ignored Parker's authorship and retooled it as "The Huckle-Buck" for a rhythm and blues saxophonist, Paul Williams. "The one was jazz, the other was rock and roll, and we were hungry," explained go-between producer Teddy Reig. "And Lubinsky owned everything anyway." Linked in the public mind with a slow, erotic dance, "The Huckle-Buck" became a huge hit. It was soon covered by musicians ranging from Lucky Millinder to Frank Sinatra to Louis Armstrong. Even rock and roll singer Chubby Checker had a top-ten hit with it in 1961. Parker earned nothing from this—much as Duke Ellington and Mary Lou Williams earned nothing when his "Happy-Go-Lucky Local" was turned into the pop hit "Night Train," and her "What's Your Story, Morning Glory?" was appropriated as "Black Coffee."

This quartet version of "Now's the Time" was made toward the end of Parker's short life, at an inspired 1953 session (one of Parker's finest compositions, "Confirmation," was recorded at the same date). Backing Parker was the elegant pianist Al Haig, who combined the light touch of swing players like Teddy Wilson with the fleet and harmonically dauntless vision of the preeminent bop pianist, Bud Powell. By this point, Parker was recording for one of Norman Granz's class labels (Clef, which later became Verve), and the fidelity is excellent. Rhythm section nuances, dimly audible in 1940s recordings, now take sonic precedence. As a result, we can fully appreciate Max Roach's drumming, particularly his masterly interaction with Parker—a superb example of heightened musical reflexes.

LISTENING GUIDE 37

🎧 now's the time

CHARLIE PARKER QUARTET
Charlie Parker, alto saxophone; Al Haig, piano; Percy Heath, bass; Max Roach, drums

- Label: Clef EPC208
- Date: 1953
- Style: bebop
- Form: 12-bar blues

What to listen for:
- explosive five-chorus Parker solo, at times imitating speech
- interaction between Parker and Roach
- solos by Roach and Heath

INTRODUCTION

0:00   Haig (piano) plays a four-bar introduction, accompanied by Roach's high-hat cymbal.

CHORUS 1 (HEAD)

0:05   Parker plays the opening **riff**. Roach answers in **call and response**.

0:10   As the harmony moves to IV, Parker ends his riff with a syncopated accent, doubled by the drums.

CHORUS 2 (HEAD)

0:20 In repeating the previous twelve bars, Parker leaves slight room for improvisation (notice the ad-lib interpolation at 0:22).

CHORUS 3

0:35 Parker begins his five-chorus solo.

0:40 Over the "bluesiest" part of the progression (where the harmony moves to IV), Parker plays slightly behind the beat.

CHORUS 4

0:49 Beginning of chorus.

0:53 Parker adds to his bluesy sound with a brief stuttering figure.

CHORUS 5

1:03 As he warms up, his rhythm imitates the looser, conversational quality of speech.

CHORUS 6

1:18 He takes a simple phrase and turns it into a complex **polyrhythm**.

CHORUS 7

1:32 Beginning of chorus.

1:44 Parker's last line signals the end of his solo, but still leaves us hanging.

CHORUS 8

1:46 After a brief pause, Haig begins his piano solo.

CHORUS 9

2:00 Haig's chorus begins with simple phrases, moves to fast, complicated phrases, and then returns to the style of the opening.

CHORUS 10

2:14 Heath (bass) takes a solo, accompanied by a tightly muffled cymbal and brief piano chords.

CHORUS 11

2:28 Roach takes a solo, alternating between the snare drum and bass drum.

CHORUS 12 (HEAD)

2:42 A repetition of the opening, but with more intense response from the rhythm section.

CODA

2:54 With a slight *ritard* (slowing down), Parker brings the piece to its end.

Bird's Last Flight

The collaboration between Charlie Parker and Dizzy Gillespie lasted only a few years. It foundered in early 1946, weeks after they took their band to Los Angeles in hopes of publicizing their radical new music on the West Coast. California proved indifferent, even hostile. Disappointed, Gillespie took the band back to New York. But Parker, still in thrall to drugs, cashed in his airplane ticket to pay his connection. He remained in Southern California for a year, sinking deeper into heroin addiction in a place where suppliers were few and ruthless. He not only titled a tune after a drug dealer ("Moose the Mooche"), but signed away his royalties for that record in the hope of keeping his supplies intact. When the heroin ran out, he began mixing alcohol and barbiturates.

In July 1947, Parker strolled through his hotel lobby one night wearing only his socks, and was arrested after accidentally setting fire to his bed.

Convinced he was schizophrenic, the police committed him to the state hospital at Camarillo, where he remained for another six months. Though he returned to New York free (briefly) of his drug addiction, for the remainder of his life his genius was steadily undercut by physical and professional decline. Miles Davis, who played with him on and off for several years, finally left in disgust in 1949, fed up with his "childish, stupid" behavior.

In his more ambitious mode, Parker found a trace of commercial success through Norman Granz, who supported and recorded him, introducing new contexts in the process—including a Latin rhythm section, vocal choirs, and all-star jams (Parker's solo on "Funky Blues" is a highlight, with Johnny Hodges and Benny Carter sharing the performance). When Parker expressed his longing to record with strings, Granz commissioned an album's worth of arrangements in which his alto saxophone was cushioned in much the same way vocal stars were featured in the bosom of violins, cellos, and even a harp. Today, *Bird with Strings* is regarded by musicians as one of his crowning achievements. In the early 1950s, Parker enjoyed two triumphant tours of Europe, where he was greeted as a major artist and charmed everyone. He also continued to perform straight-ahead bebop and made some of his finest recordings in 1953, including a stirring version of the song that symbolized his calamity in Los Angeles, "Lover Man."

With strings

But Parker's addiction to alcohol proved even more ruinous than drugs. As he became increasingly unreliable, he was barred from the nightclub named in his honor, Birdland, and occasionally turned up playing with amateurs in storefronts. Bloated and sluggish, his intonation slackened. Jazz itself was beginning to move beyond him. Even so, he might have bounced back as he had done before, but when his two-year-old daughter Pree died of pneumonia, he crumpled and never fully recovered—there was a 1954 suicide attempt followed by a voluntary commitment in the psychiatric facility at Bellevue Hospital. He was thirty-four at the time of his death in 1955, but the coroner estimated the age of his enervated body as fifty-three. His passing received little notice in the press, most of it sensationalistic since he had died in the hotel apartment of a famous jazz patron, Baroness Pannonica de Königswarter, a Rothschild heiress. For musicians, his passing was a dark turning point. As soon as the news got out, someone began scrawling "Bird Lives!" on Greenwich Village walls, a phrase that morphed into an ongoing obituary.

The Elder Statesman

Dizzy Gillespie offered a different model. His career demonstrated how bebop could be the musical and professional foundation for working jazz musicians. On returning from California in 1946, he formed a big band, adapting his bebop arrangements to the full resources of a swing dance orchestra, but added touches that would ultimately have as large an influence on modern jazz as bop itself. In commissioning compositions from a young ex-drummer named George Russell, Gillespie introduced modality into big-band jazz, anticipating aspects of the 1950s and 1960s avant-garde before the public had made peace with bop. At the same time, he almost single-handedly spurred the Afro-Cuban jazz movement: he hired the great Cuban percussionist and composer Chano Pozo and teamed up with several major Latin jazz figures, including Mario Bauzá, Machito, and Chico O'Farrill, setting the stage for salsa and other rhythmic cross-cultural fusions (see Chapter 16).

Gillespie soon created a matchless stage persona appropriate for his time: like Louis Armstrong, he balanced his artistry against his wit and penchant for genial silliness. He brought his bebop-flavored big-band entertainment to cheering crowds well into the 1950s, and occasionally fronted large bands for the rest of his life. A signature ploy was to say that he would now introduce the musicians and then turn and introduce them to each other. This may not sound like much, but it always got a big laugh, erasing the intimidation factor at a time when jazz was remaking itself as a listener's rather than a dancer's music. Through it all, Dizzy's exhilarating bebop lines soared, the trumpet section performing dazzling block-chord-textured phrases that sounded as close to his as possible.

As bebop declined in popularity through the 1950s, Gillespie remained clean-living, gregarious, and generous to a fault. Never without a band, big or small, he nurtured the careers of such musicians as John Lewis, Ray Brown, Milt Jackson, John Coltrane, Yusef Lateef, Jimmy Heath, Paul Gonsalves, Percy Heath, Quincy Jones, Lee Morgan, Melba Liston, Wynton Kelly, and on and on. In the 1950s, when the State Department began to realize that jazz could be used as an overseas weapon of propaganda, Gillespie took his band on official tours, carefully balancing his patriotism against his insistence on speaking openly about the state of American race relations.

His goatee, his beret, his specially raised trumpet (designed to compensate for a lifetime habit of playing with the bell pointed down), and especially his distended cheeks made him instantly recognizable. In the 1960s, Gillespie took a leadership role in introducing bossa nova and organized one of the great quintets of his career, with his former big-band sideman and now-established saxophone and flute star James Moody and the prodigious young pianist Kenny Barron. Nor did he cease to maintain his standing as a resolute master of the jam session, recording impromptu encounters with players of every generation, from Mary Lou Williams, Bobby Hackett, Benny Carter, Count Basie, and the idol of his youth, Roy Eldridge, to Sonny Rollins, Stan Getz, Freddie Hubbard, and the avant-garde saxophonist Sam Rivers, who became a member of his last small band. As jazz continued to build on its increasing sense of history and tradition, Gillespie remained a central figure until his death in 1993, which, unlike that of Charlie Parker, was front page news everywhere.

One night in 1953, an accident on stage pushed the bell of Dizzy Gillespie's trumpet upward. Realizing that this new design compensated for a lifetime habit of looking down while playing, Gillespie asked a trumpet manufacturer to make all of his horns that way.

THE BEBOP GENERATION

Parker and Gillespie were only the most visible part of the bebop generation. In the 1940s, hundreds of young musicians, mostly but not exclusively black, were swept up into the new jazz, pulled by a modernist sensitivity to previously unseen social and musical realities. The path was not easy. Some musicians, watching Charlie Parker, concluded that his musical achievements

VOICES

Poet, dramatist, and jazz critic Amiri Baraka captured the renewed sense of purpose felt by bebop fans in the 1940s:

I listened to bebop after school, over and over. At first it was strange and the strangeness itself was strangely alluring. Bebop! I listened and listened. And began learning the names of musicians and times and places and events. Bird, Diz, Max, Klook, Monk, Miles, Getz, and eventually secondary jive like Down Beat, Metronome . . . And I wasn't even sure what the music was. Bebop! A new language a new tongue and vision for a generally more advanced group in our generation. Bebop was a staging area for a new sensibility growing to maturity. And the beboppers themselves were blowing the sound to attract the growing, the developing, the about-to-see. . . .

My father had asked me one day, "Why do you want to be a bopper?" Who knows what I said. I couldn't have explained it then. Bebop suggested another mode of being. Another way of living. Another way of perceiving reality— connected to the one I'd had—blue/black and brown but also pushing past that to something else. Strangeness. Weirdness. The unknown!

were somehow associated with drugs and became hooked on heroin. Theodore "Fats" Navarro, one of Gillespie's most brilliant followers on trumpet, made just a few dozen recordings before succumbing to addiction.

The technical achievements of this generation were remarkable. Who would have imagined, on first hearing Parker play in the early 1940s, that anyone could equal him in speed and fury? Yet hard on his heels came the alto saxophonist Sonny Stitt, whose style so closely resembled Parker's that for a time he switched to tenor, hoping to avoid the unflattering comparison. As for the tenor saxophone, Parker's influence was filtered through Coleman Hawkins's harmonic mastery and Lester Young's cool idiom, resulting in the syntheses pioneered by Lucky Thompson, Don Byas, and Illinois Jacquet, until it was unleashed in the thoroughly renovated yet varied styles of players like Dexter Gordon, Stan Getz, Zoot Sims, Gene Ammons, and Wardell Gray. The trombonist J. J. Johnson kept pace with his peers by jettisoning his instrument's limited rips and smears for a cool, angular, and unbelievably swift sound. Bebop spread to the baritone saxophone (Serge Chaloff, Gerry Mulligan, Leo Parker), the vibraphone (Milt Jackson), the harmonica (Toots Thielemans), and every other instrument playing jazz.

■ BUD POWELL (1924–1966)

Bud Powell, the finest pianist of the bebop generation, and arguably the most influential keyboard player of the past seventy years, came by his talent naturally. His father was a New York stride pianist, his older brother played trumpet, and his younger brother Richie also became a bop pianist. Powell was drilled in classical music technique, studying Bach and Chopin, while becoming fascinated by jazz. As a teenager, he frequented Minton's Playhouse, where Thelonious Monk spotted his talents: "I was the only one who dug him," Monk once said. "Nobody understood what he was playing." In return, Powell showed a stubborn loyalty to Monk's music throughout his life.

Powell dropped out of high school to join the swing band of Cootie Williams, then on leave from Duke Ellington, where he fit in beautifully, as broadcast recordings show. But while he was touring with the band in Philadelphia, he was unjustly apprehended by the police and brutally beaten, leaving him with crippling headaches—the beginning of a long nightmare that may have been complicated by a form of epilepsy. For a full third of his adult life, Powell was subjected to "psychiatric supervision" that was often hostile and punitive, including dousing with ammoniated water, hardly unique for blacks in that period. He was incarcerated and medicated, and underwent electroshock treatments so severe that they affected his memory. Combine this confusion with a weakness for alcohol so profound that a single drink might leave him slumped against a wall, and it's hard to believe that he was able to function at all, let alone forge a career as a radiant stylist, virtually reinventing jazz piano and codifying the modern piano trio.

It would be hard to overstate Powell's impact. His ingenious technique and originality as an improviser and composer established the foundation for all pianists to follow. Long after bop had faded, Powell remained a source of inspiration for pianists as varied as the harmonically engrossed Bill Evans and the rhythmically unfettered Cecil Taylor. In other words, there is jazz piano Before Powell and After Powell. While his left hand played a neutral backdrop of chords, his right hand would explode into a blindingly intricate improvisatory cascade, rivaling (and even surpassing) Parker and Gillespie in rhythmic imagination. Watching Powell play was almost frighteningly intense. The jazz critic Ira Gitler, who observed him at close quarters, described him as "one with the music itself": "Right leg digging into the floor at an odd angle, pants leg up to almost the top of the shin, shoulders hunched, upper lip tight against the teeth, mouth emitting an accompanying guttural song to what the steel fingers were playing, vein in temple throbbing violently as perspiration popped out all over his scalp and ran down his face and neck." Yet for all his virtuosity—and this is perhaps the central achievement of his art—Powell was always emotionally candid and decisive. He never played a flourish just to play a flourish.

The unstable but brilliant Bud Powell transferred bebop's electric pace to the piano keyboard. He's seen performing at Birdland in 1949.

© HERMAN LEONARD PHOTOGRAPHY LLC

Sometimes Powell used block chords: combining his two hands to play a melody supported by fat chords, like a big-band *soli*. On other occasions, he played stride piano, borrowing from the overshadowing presence of Art Tatum. He did far more than any other pianist to pioneer the now-standard piano trio format (with bass and drums), replacing the rhythm guitar favored by Tatum with the rhythmic power of drummers like Roy Haynes, Art Blakey, and Max Roach.

By the end of the 1950s, Powell had moved to France, where adoring crowds watched him gradually disintegrate. There were times when he returned to his youthful self, performing at the peak of his ability. On other occasions he would play haltingly or stop, staring blankly at the wall with what Miles Davis once described as a "secret, faraway smile." In the mid-1960s, he returned to New York, where he died of tuberculosis. His funeral cortege steadily swelled as it moved through Harlem. Like Charlie Parker, Powell was a visionary whose legacy lay as much in what he might have done as in what he actually did.

🎧 "Tempus Fugue-It"

Early 1949 was a good time for Bud Powell. He had just emerged from Creedmore Sanitorium, where he had been incarcerated for several months, and was raring to make a record for Clef. It was a brief window, as he soon returned to Creedmore for more treatment. Difficult as it may be to imagine musical creativity taking place under these conditions, Powell seemed untouchably inspired, ready to display not only his pianistic fancy but also his talent as a composer. He was a remarkable tunesmith whose work ranged from the pure delight of "Bouncing with Bud" to the forbiddingly haunted "Glass Enclosure" to the bop march "Dance of the Infidels," which begins with a harmonized bugle call. Drawing on his knowledge of Baroque counterpoint and his command of modern jazz harmony, he couched his tunes and many of his arrangements of pop songs in intricate structures. In light of his mental instability, it's telling that some of his best-known tunes have painfully self-reflective titles, like "Hallucinations" and "Un Poco Loco." The latter is an insistently aggressive, utterly original Latin tune, pitting Powell's frenetic energy against Max Roach's clanging cowbell and polyrhythmic accompaniment.

On the 1949 sessions, accompanied by Ray Brown and Roach, he turned out a number of masterpieces. A dazzlingly fast and boldly reharmonized "Cherokee" visited and challenged territory previously claimed by Charlie Parker, while the easygoing "Celia" (dedicated to his infant daughter) explored the gentle side of bop, combining relaxed triplets and his canny use of syncopated rests. The darkly colored "Tempus Fugue-It" is a tempestuous performance that nonetheless suggests Powell's witting familiarity with Baroque polyphony (namely, the fugue) and the Latin proverb *Tempus fugit*. The form is standard thirty-two-bar **A A B A,** with the **A** section barely moving from the tonic. Harmonic variety is pushed to the bridge, which moves rapidly from chord to chord. "Tempus Fugue-It" shows Powell pushing his technique to the limit. There are undoubtedly a few miscalculations that later record producers, armed with tape and digital technology, would have edited out—but they would have robbed this performance of its blunt intensity.

🎧 tempus fugue-it

BUD POWELL
Bud Powell, piano; Ray Brown, bass; Max Roach, drums

- Label: Clef 11045
- Date: 1949
- Style: bebop
- Form: 32-bar popular song (**A A B A**)

What to listen for:
- Powell's translation of bebop soloing to piano
- his complex chords, changes, and polyrhythmic ostinatos
- his simple octaves at the end of chorus 2
- harmonic variety in the bridge section

INTRODUCTION

0:00		Powell jumps in unaccompanied, playing a line in **octaves**. Its last few notes are accented by the drums.
0:04		He juxtaposes a dissonant note in the right hand with syncopated chords in the left.

CHORUS 1 (HEAD)

0:07	**A**	The opening melody is a sinuous bebop line with stops and starts. Each empty beat is filled in by a subtle brush hit on the drums.
0:14	**A**	
0:20	**B**	The melody is nearly overshadowed by a powerful bass line played in octaves by the left hand.
0:25		Dissonant chords are decorated with fast **grace notes** (ornamental, quickly played notes).
0:27	**A**	

INTERLUDE

0:34		Disjointed chords enter in unexpected rhythms, doubled by the bass and drums.
0:37		During a two-measure **break**, Powell begins his solo.

CHORUS 2

0:39	**A**	Powell plays a fast, elaborate melody in the right hand. When the melody pauses, we can hear his left hand alternating neutral, open harmonies with a sharp dissonance (the **flatted fifth**) deep in the bass.
0:45	**A**	He fills the next eight bars with a continuous phrase.
0:51	**B**	As the harmonies change, he improvises a line that matches the notes of each chord.
0:58	**A**	The drums interact with the line, adding sharp accents with the brushes.
1:01		Powell ends the chorus with simple octaves. The left hand maintains tension by lingering on the dissonant interval.

CHORUS 3

1:04	**A**	Powell plays a short fragment over and over that clashes **polyrhythmically** with the meter.
1:10	**A**	The same polyrhythmic effect is created by a new melodic fragment.
1:17	**B**	Over the rapidly moving harmony, Powell begins a line that disappears a few measures later, as if his concentration were temporarily thrown off.
1:20		After a few beats, he begins a new line that continues well into the next **A** section.
1:23	**A**	

CHORUS 4

1:29	**A**	Powell repeats the fragment from the previous chorus, with less precision.
1:35	**A**	In an apparent miscalculation, he begins playing the chords to the bridge. After a bar or two, he realizes his mistake and seamlessly corrects himself.
1:41	**B**	Now he plays the correct chords with exactitude.
1:45		For a few beats, he's suddenly disrupted from the groove, playing a few notes out of rhythm.
1:47	**A**	Within a few seconds, he returns to his brilliantly quick improvised line.

CHORUS 5 (HEAD)

1:53	**A**	Powell plays the head an octave higher, matching pitch to the heat of performance.
1:59	**A**	
2:06	**B**	
2:12	**A**	

CODA

2:18		As a signal for the ending, Powell repeats the last phrase.
2:19		He holds out the last chord, a dissonantly voiced tonic, with a **tremolo**.

JAZZ IN LOS ANGELES: CENTRAL AVENUE

Bebop was born in Harlem and nurtured on New York's 52nd Street, but despite a confused initial reception, it also resonated three thousand miles away on the West Coast. Though geographically remote, Southern California had rivaled New York as the center of the national entertainment industry since the birth of film. And jazz had been a part of California life ever since vaudeville brought the music west early in the century. Restless New Orleans musicians used California as a convenient second home, easily reachable by railroad lines running direct from the Crescent City. It was in Los Angeles, in 1922, that the first recording by a black jazz band (led by trombonist Kid Ory) was made—a year before King Oliver's band.

The Los Angeles jazz scene spread along Central Avenue, the core of a narrow, all-black neighborhood, thirty blocks long and only a few blocks wide. ("Housing covenants" in other neighborhoods prevented white residents from selling their property to people of other races.) This crowded and lively avenue was a mecca for entertainment, offering its share of blues, comedy, dance, and early rhythm and blues. In 1945, that scene began to include modern jazz, with Coleman Hawkins's quintet, bop groups led by trumpet player Howard McGhee, and the star-crossed visitation by Dizzy Gillespie and Charlie Parker's quintet. Musicians adopted the new language as quickly as possible. Soon there was a bevy of California bebop practitioners, led by the charismatic tenor saxophonist Dexter Gordon.

■ DEXTER GORDON (1923–1990)

Gordon was a product of the black middle class. His father, a jazz-loving doctor, counted Lionel Hampton and Duke Ellington among his celebrity patients and took his young son to hear the big swing bands that came regularly to the Coast. At the integrated Jefferson High School in Los Angeles, Dexter studied clarinet with Sam Browne, the school's first black teacher, but soon switched from clarinet to saxophone, with Browne keeping him after school to practice his scales.

Like many aspiring tenor players, Gordon initially saw Coleman Hawkins as the model for harmonic improvisation. But his creative inspiration was Lester Young, whom he first heard when the Basie band came to Los Angeles in 1939. Young's "bittersweet approach" to melody and rhythm mesmerized him. "When Pres appeared, we all started listening to him alone. Pres had an entirely new sound, one we seemed to be waiting for." Gordon was introduced to bebop in New York, where he studied music theory with Dizzy Gillespie.

His first encounter with Charlie Parker's penetrating authority left him speechless. Under Parker's influence, he headed into the bop orbit, adding a new level of rhythmic intensity to his music while picking up a debilitating addiction to heroin.

Of the new bebop saxophonists, Gordon was the most flamboyant. On the street, he cut a fine figure, dressing in the latest style with wide-shouldered suits accentuating his lanky frame and topped by a wide-brimmed hat that made him seem "about seven feet tall." But it was his musical style that turned people's heads. Gordon combined the looseness of Young, playing slightly behind the beat, with Parker's rhythmic intricacies. He was also quirky and humorous, with a charming habit of interpolating into his solos fragments of popular songs, suggesting that just beneath the language of bebop lay a world made up of beautiful Tin Pan Alley melodies. Gordon's improvisational style was forged in after-hours jam sessions, where he could be ruthlessly efficient, using his quick-witted command of phrases and his broad, implacable timbre to leave his competitors

About his elegant look, Dexter Gordon once told the young Miles Davis, "It ain't got nothing to do with money, it's got something to do with hipness." New York, 1948.

© HERMAN LEONARD PHOTOGRAPHY LLC

helpless. One of his partners was Wardell Gray, a fellow saxophonist from Oklahoma City. A memento of their sessions was "The Chase" (1947), a frenzied tenor saxophone battle spread out over two sides of a 78-rpm recording for Dial. Featuring Gordon and Gray trading eight-, four-, and finally two-bar segments, it was one of the longest jazz improvisations on record.

Wardell Gray

🎧 "Long Tall Dexter"

In January 1946, Gordon recorded a youthful, emergized group for Savoy Records. The rhythm section included Bud Powell (twenty-one), Max Roach (twenty-two), and veteran bassist Curley Russell (at twenty-eight the oldest musician present). The trumpet player was Leonard Hawkins, a high-school friend of Roach's from Brooklyn who was making his recording debut. But the focus was on Gordon, as the titles from that day's work made clear: "Dexter Rides Again," "Dexter Digs In," and a blues that took a nickname inspired by Gordon's six-foot-five-inch frame, "Long Tall Dexter." The tune is built on a riff as elemental and effective as the one in Parker's "Now's the Time," and like Parker's strategically introduces an unexpected bit of dissonance (0:13).

Gordon's five-chorus solo on "Long Tall Dexter" is, from its dramatic beginning, a perfectly paced tour de force, a condensation of what he might use to triumph in a jam session. After he and Hawkins play a **send-off riff** (a composed segment that takes up the first four bars of a chorus), Gordon enters on an unexpected note, held for a long time before dissolving into a dissonance. The remainder of this chorus is spare and restrained, setting up what's to come. In chorus 4, he expands the range of his solo, sending his line into a number of sharp dissonances (e.g., at 0:51). But it's with chorus 5 that he begins ratcheting up the intensity. Restricting himself to a single note, he punches out riffs with rhythms so unpredictable that Powell and Roach are virtually pulled into the conversation. From here the riffs keep piling on, until at the beginning of chorus 7 he mounts a climax of virtuosic display. Early on, Gordon drops to a honking low note—the sort of gesture that would soon be a staple of nearly all rhythm and blues saxophonists. And in the solo's last few measures, he cools down the temperature with false fingerings, a delicate and inventive way of emphasizing a closing nod to the blues.

LISTENING GUIDE 39

🎧 long tall dexter

DEXTER GORDON QUINTET
Dexter Gordon, tenor saxophone; Leonard Hawkins, trumpet; Bud Powell, piano; Curley Russell, bass; Max Roach, drums

- Label: Dial 603
- Date: 1946
- Style: bebop
- Form: 12-bar blues

What to listen for:
- simple 12-bar blues riff, spiced with dissonance
- send-off riff in chorus 3
- Gordon's masterful five-chorus solo (choruses 3–7)

INTRODUCTION

0:00   Over a shimmer of cymbals, Roach creates a complex **polyrhythm** on the drums, alternating strokes on the snare and bass drum.

CHORUS 1 (HEAD)

0:04   Gordon (tenor saxophone) and Hawkins (trumpet) play the simple riff-based melody in **octaves**. Underneath, Powell comps with dense, **dissonant** chords on piano.

0:07   Hawkins adds a slight but noticeable rhythmic decoration to the head.

0:08   Roach punctuates the end of the phrase with a sharp snare-drum accent.

0:09   As the harmony changes from I to IV, the riff figure adjusts by flatting one of the notes.

0:13   The horns play a simple ascending scale. When the harmony changes to V, they move it up a half step, creating an intense dissonance.

CHORUS 2 (HEAD)

0:18   As is typical for bebop blues, the head is repeated.

0:31   Gordon lets his last note tail off.

CHORUS 3

0:32   The two horns play a **send-off riff**—a composed four-bar melody designed to lead directly to the next soloist. This riff is built on a **harmonic substitution**, beginning with a remote harmony that modulates quickly back home to the **tonic**.

0:34   At its conclusion, the send-off riff becomes stridently dissonant, featuring **flatted fifths** against the prevailing harmony.

0:37   As the harmony shifts to IV, Gordon enters with a long-held note that finally descends to yet another dissonance, the chord's flatted fifth.

0:45   Roach punctuates the chorus's end with a few loud **fills**.

CHORUS 4

0:46   Gordon plays even strings of notes that climb into his highest register.

0:51   He plays a prominently dissonant note over the IV chord.

CHORUS 5

1:00   Gordon plays punchy, short riffs in continually changing rhythms. The drummer and pianist respond by filling in the spaces.

1:09   After reaching its melodic peak, the phrase winds down.

CHORUS 6

1:15   Gordon starts a new riff, maintaining a simple rhythm (long, short-short) while shifting the pitch in sequence.

1:20   Over the IV chord, he drops down to a sonorous low note. When he repeats the figure, the note moves up a half step to a sharp dissonance.

1:25   As the chorus ends, he plays a rhythmically intricate riff.

CHORUS 7

1:29   Gordon compresses the riff into a long, complex phrase that finally ends in a repeated note.

1:39   Using **false fingering**, he creates a note with a hollow timbre. Because it's slightly less than a half step higher and falls on the third degree of the scale, it has a distinctly bluesy tone.

CHORUS 8

1:43   Slightly off-microphone, Hawkins enters with the send-off riff. Gordon enters after a moment's hesitation.

1:48   Hawkins's solo begins with a simple two-note phrase. Immediately afterward, the drums stop playing for a several beats, creating an unexpected sense of space.

1:52   Hawkins plays the rest of his solo with a broad, open tone, **ghosted** notes, and occasional rapid bebop-style decorations.

1:57   Roach responds with rapid fills.

CHORUS 9

1:58   As Hawkins digs in to a short riff, his timbre becomes coarser.

2:03   For a brief moment, he makes an apparent mistake: he hits a note that contradicts the IV harmony underneath.

CHORUS 10

2:12   Powell enters in octaves, emphasizing the first note with a "crushed" grace note. In the background, you can hear his rough singing.

2:16   He accompanies his intricate right-hand melodies with simple lines and two-note "shells" of chords in the left.

CHORUS 11

2:27   Powell suggests a faster, double-time feeling.

CHORUS 12

2:41   Instead of reprising the head, the two horns play a different (if equally simple) riff-based tune.

2:46   As the harmony shifts, the riff's top-most note is flatted.

CODA

2:54   A final new melodic phrase closes out the piece.

2:56   At the piece's end, Roach continues playing.

2:58   Powell has the last word with a dissonant lick that ends a **tritone** away from the tonic.

For Gordon, the 1950s were a mess. His career was twice interrupted by jail sentences for heroin use, culminating with a stint in California's Folsom Prison. But in the next decade, he firmly reestablished his reputation as one of the finest saxophonists of his generation, recording masterful albums for Blue Note, including *Go!* and *Our Man in Paris*. Gordon spent fourteen years in Europe, where black musicians could take refuge from racial prejudice. When he returned home to New York and opened at the Village Vanguard in 1976, he received a rousing welcome (see Chapter 18). In his last years, Gordon occupied a role he was never to relinquish—the gracious elder statesman of acoustic jazz. Shrewd promotion by Columbia helped his new albums succeed, and films gave him fame way beyond bebop. He surprised everyone by winning a well-deserved Oscar nomination for his lead role (inspired by the lives of Lester Young and Bud Powell) in Bertrand Tavernier's 1986 film *'Round Midnight*.

AFTERMATH: BEBOP AND POP

For a brief time in the late 1940s, bebop was aggressively marketed as popular music. Its public face was Dizzy Gillespie, whose goatee, glasses, and beret gave cartoonists a convenient shorthand for jazz modernism. But jazz slang was parodied (endless repetitions of "cool," "daddy-o") and ultimately became 1950s beatnik clichés. Bing Crosby and Patti Andrews (of the Andrews Sisters) recorded a parody lyric called "Bebop Spoken Here," which left their usually reliable fans nonplussed. Gillespie contributed to the confusion when he appeared in *Life* magazine in 1948, exchanging a "bebop handshake" with Benny Carter, their high fives supposedly representing the flatted fifth. "There was no such thing in real life," Gillespie later protested. "It was just a bunch of horseplay that we went through so they could pretend we were something weird. . . . We were helping to make bebop seem like just another fad, which it wasn't."

At the same time that bebop failed as popular music, it steadily gained strength among musicians. As professionals, they saw it less as a fashion than a musical system to be mastered. To be a jazz musician meant learning to play like Charlie Parker and Dizzy Gillespie. That part remains true today—more

MILES DAVIS
venus de milo

MODERN JAZZ QUARTET
vendome

HORACE SILVER
song for my father

CLIFFORD BROWN
a night in tunisia

SONNY ROLLINS
i'm an old cowhand

12

THE 1950s:
COOL JAZZ AND HARD BOP

NEW SCHOOLS

Bebop created a kind of Rubicon that many fans, critics, and musicians of the 1940s could not cross. They had come to jazz in the years of swing, when it functioned as dance music and entertainment, and they dismissed the new way of playing as a fad; when it failed to fade, they lost interest in jazz. Far from fading, bop became so much the language of jazz that its influence proved retroactive: even young musicians who still played in swing or traditional styles adapted elements of the new harmonies, rhythms, and melodies. Still, the very intricacy of bebop made it a more introverted listening experience. The music had evolved, and no single musician—not Louis Armstrong or Duke Ellington or Charlie Parker—could be depicted as a defining figure for its entire canvas. Jazz now had a convoluted history: from New Orleans style to swing to bop. In the 1950s, additional styles grew out of bebop—cool jazz, hard bop, funk, avant-garde, and others—leading jazz historians to speak in terms of schools, as if it had splintered off into discrete realms.

It's important to remember that bebop did not cause the first schism in jazz. Hidebound critics in the 1920s attacked Armstrong and Ellington for sacrificing "authenticity"— Armstrong because he interpreted popular songs, Ellington because he orchestrated

Dave Brubeck pioneered unusual time signatures and became emblematic of jazz as a hip, sophisticated, modern music for the age of affluence. Los Angeles, 1953.

Gerry Mulligan, the only baritone saxophonist to become a major jazz star, was also an influential composer and arranger. In this photo taken in the 1950s, he's backed by his longtime bassist Bill Crow.

Chet Baker

Chico Hamilton

a few Mulligan compositions that combined polyphony and simultaneous meters in ways that built on the achievements of the nonet. These arrangements influenced a generation of jazz composers.

In 1952, Mulligan returned to Los Angeles and accepted a Mondays-only job at a small restaurant called the Haig, distinguished by its white picket fence and location: across the street from the Hollywood nightclub called the Cocoanut Grove. There he formed a quartet consisting of baritone saxophone, trumpet, bass, and drums. According to legend, the Haig's bandstand was too small to accommodate a grand piano. An article in *Time* magazine drew attention to the "piano-less" group and its balmy music, which was thought to personify the laid-back temperament of Southern California. As crowds descended on the Haig, the quartet recorded a version of the Rodgers and Hart ballad "My Funny Valentine" that sold unusually well. The breezily swinging lyricism of cool jazz had found its star.

Without a piano to fill out the harmony, Mulligan and his young Oklahoma-born trumpet player, Chet Baker, expanded the contours of their music with contrapuntal interplay. Sometimes they achieved genuine two-part polyphony; at other times, one simply supported the other by playing whole notes to signify the song's chord sequence. Baker, an intuitive improviser, played almost exclusively in the middle register in a style that superficially resembled that of Miles Davis, but with lighter timbre and less dramatic force; he also won admirers as a soft-voiced ballad singer. The quartet's drummer, Chico Hamilton, known for the quiet rolling rhythms he created with mallets, later became an important bandleader in his own right. As an African American, Hamilton automatically symbolized postwar integration in jazz and the society at large.

The Gerry Mulligan Quartet lasted little more than a year before each man went his own way, yet its popularity was so lasting that Mulligan and Hamilton appeared in movies, while actors playing jazz musicians mimicked Baker's baby-face looks and surly attitude. In later years, Mulligan divided his time between small groups and big bands, writing several jazz standards ("Rocker," "Line for Lyons," "Festive Minor") and winning polls as best baritone saxophonist for twenty years.

■ JOHN LEWIS (1920–2001) and the MODERN JAZZ QUARTET

The Modern Jazz Quartet (MJQ) emerged, in some ways, as a reverse image of the Gerry Mulligan Quartet. It was an African American East Coast band that lasted more than four decades with only one change in personnel. As such, it was called the longest-running chamber group in or out of jazz. Created by pianist John Lewis, who had written two of the Davis nonet pieces, it was a genuine cooperative, with each member assigned specific extra-musical duties such as travel arrangements, finances, and public relations. Lewis was in charge of the music; his arrangements reflected a lifelong fascination with polyphony and counter-point, and the conviction that J. S. Bach and blues were compatible.

Lewis was raised in Albuquerque and studied at the Manhattan School of Music while working with Dizzy Gillespie and participating in recording sessions with Charlie Parker and other modernists. He immediately demonstrated a unique piano style: spare, light, melodic yet rhythmically firm and persistently inflected with the blues. Gillespie encouraged him to compose for his band and to work up separate pieces that featured only the rhythm section, which consisted of Lewis, drummer Kenny Clarke, vibraphonist Milt Jackson, and bassist Ray Brown—the nucleus of the MJQ.

Pianist and composer John Lewis created the Modern Jazz Quartet, the most durable small band in jazz history (1952–97), with vibes virtuoso Milt Jackson (behind him).

By 1952, Lewis believed he had found the right musicians and the right concept. Milt Jackson, a native of Detroit, was the first major vibraphone player in a decade, since Lionel Hampton and Red Norvo in the 1930s. The vibes perfectly complemented the chimes-like sound Lewis coaxed from the piano, as well as offering a dramatic contrast: Jackson played with teeming energy, less subtle than Lewis and drenched in gospel-like figures he had learned in the church. Clarke, the most established member of the group, played with rambunctious enthusiasm yet also created an unmistakably tasteful brand of timekeeping with brushes or sticks. After two years, he moved to Europe and was replaced by Connie Kay. The least experienced member was bassist Percy Heath, a replacement for Ray Brown.

Lewis was determined to undo popular misconceptions about jazz, not only in the manner of his music but in its presentation. He had ideas about the way the quartet should dress (in identical tuxedos or suits, in the tradition of the swing bands), enter and exit the stage, and introduce pieces. Every performance was to be regarded as a concert.

Only after the MJQ was lauded in Europe did the American critics get on board. By the late 1950s, it ranked as one of the world's most successful jazz ensembles. In appearance and manner, the group seemed genteel and cerebral. But its music was, in fact, profoundly rhythmic and emotionally intense—in other words, cool on the surface, hot at the core.

Lewis, like Ellington, benefited from the loyalties of his musicians. The MJQ survived forty-two years, forty of them with the same musicians. During those forty years, Lewis merged his ensemble with symphony orchestras, chamber groups, big bands, singers, and individual guest soloists. He wrote many benchmark works, including "Django," "England's Carol," "Afternoon in Paris," "Two Degrees East, Three Degrees West," "Little David's Fugue," the film scores *Odds Against Tomorrow* and *No Sun in Venice*, the ballet *The Comedy*, and the suite *A Day in Dubrovnik*. Lewis also functioned as an

VOICES

John Lewis's idea that the MJQ's performances were concerts, no matter the venue, puzzled many. As Percy Heath recalled:

We had a hard time getting people to quiet down and listen. At that time in nightclubs, people were talking about hanging out. In order to break that down, instead of trying to play over the conversation, we'd use reverse psychology and play softer. Suddenly, they knew we were up there and realized the conversation was louder than the music. Of course, if it got too loud, we'd come off—just stop playing and walk off. It didn't take long for them to realize they were wasting their time, because we weren't going to entertain them in that sense. We didn't have funny acts, we didn't have any costumes. We were conservatively dressed, we played conservative music, and if you didn't listen you didn't get it. We were four instruments going along horizontally, contrapuntally. There was no back-up and soloist, the concept was changing.

educator and jazz activist, directing the Lenox (Massachusetts) School of Jazz between 1957 and 1960 and the Monterey (California) Jazz Festival between 1958 and 1982. And as an early proponent of performing jazz classics with the respect given classical repertory, he co-founded and conducted Orchestra U.S.A. (1962) and the American Jazz Orchestra (1986–92).

Third Stream

The most controversial of Lewis's alliances, with composer, conductor, and musicologist Gunther Schuller, gave birth to a short-lived idiom that Schuller called the Third Stream—a synthesis of elements in "Western art music" with "ethnic or vernacular" music. For several years, composers from both worlds self-consciously contributed to this movement. Their music was not cool per se, but it had been stimulated in an environment nurtured by cool's architects. Although classical techniques would continue to figure in jazz as sources of creative inspiration, the movement soon faded and the term "Third Stream" fell into disuse.

🎧 "Vendome'

"Vendome" was the third of four selections recorded by the Modern Jazz Quartet at its very first session, in 1952, and it captures the group in a state of becoming. This selection is often scorned by critics, and was similarly disdained by members of the MJQ. Lewis, who composed and painstakingly rehearsed it, put the case against it tersely in a 1959 interview, during the height of the MJQ's worldwide acclaim: "Some of the music we've played, 'Vendome' for instance, was very unnatural when we started playing. On the record it is not natural at all. Now it has become natural, but it has taken a long time." When he was once asked about the bass part, Percy Heath laughed: "Did you think 'Vendome' was improvised?" This number was the first of the group's **fugues**—a Baroque polyphonic form in which a short melody or phrase (the fugue **subject**) is introduced by one part and successively taken up by others—and Lewis, determined to get the counterpoint right, wrote Heath's part. He would continue to write bass and drum parts until all the musicians felt so comfortable with the form that they could improvise and swing his fugues with enchanting panache—as though it were the most natural thing in the world.

Yet though Lewis's later fugues (including subsequent renditions of "Vendome") are more confidently performed and configured than this one, there is something to be said for the excitement of a performance that breaks new ground. With nothing to prove, "Vendome" has actually aged well. And its uncommon split personality is itself a source of pleasure, as it switches between the original canonical theme and the improvisations, which are wedded to the chord changes of Jerome Kern's "All the Things You Are," a favorite song of the bop players for its intricate harmonies. Significantly, the first of the pieces recorded that day was a straight-ahead version of Kern's tune. While bop musicians frequently improvised on a song's changes without alluding to the melody (as Charlie Parker did on "Embraceable You"), plunking a familiar harmonic sequence into a new work was unusual; a few years later, George Russell did something similar in "Concerto for Billy the Kid." Lewis explained that in 1952, he had yet to find a way to make counterpoint swing, but the back-and-forth between his catchy fugue and the jazz sections allows "Vendome" to cast its own spell, helped along by Kenny Clarke's drums, beating a steady path throughout the piece; and Milt Jackson's uncanny ability to make everything he plays sound offhanded and easy. The interplay between Jackson and Lewis grew increasingly sure over time, but is already impressive here—a consequence of the years they had spent together in Dizzy Gillespie's rhythm section.

🎧 vendome

MODERN JAZZ QUARTET

John Lewis, piano; Milt Jackson, vibraphone; Percy Heath, bass; Kenny Clarke, drums

- Label: Prestige LP7059
- Date: 1952
- Style: cool jazz
- Form: fugue, including the pop song "All the Things You Are"

What to listen for:

- **Lewis's fugal composition**
- **Third Stream mixture of classical and jazz**
- **Jackson's soulful improvising on vibes**

FUGUE

0:00	Jackson states the fugue **subject** (theme) in C minor on the vibes. He's accompanied by Heath on bass and (very discreetly) by Clarke with brushes.
0:05	Lewis plays the "answer"—the second appearance of the fugue subject, in the **dominant** (**V**)—on piano.
0:10	Jackson returns the fugue subject to its original key. Lewis adds **counterpoint** in his right hand.
0:15	With his left hand, Lewis plays the fourth entrance of the fugue subject, creating three independent voices: Jackson's line on the vibes, and two lines played on the piano.

"ALL THE THINGS YOU ARE"

0:20	A	The band suddenly switches to the chord progression of Jerome Kern's song. Over Heath's walking-bass line, Jackson improvises a melody.
0:33	A	The tune **modulates** upward to a new key.

FUGUE

0:45	Lewis returns us to the fugue, stating the subject on the piano. Jackson follows a few bars later.
0:54	A **trill** in the piano and a new accompaniment rhythm in the bass, ♩ 𝅗𝅥 ♩, signal an "episode"—a free section with no entries of the subject. Lewis's piano line begins in C minor but soon modulates to other keys.
1:14	Jackson plays the fugue subject in the major mode.
1:23	Over a **pedal point**, Jackson and Lewis trade imitative counterpoint.
1:37	In a dense **polyphonic** texture, the fugue subject is played by Heath on the bass, with Jackson answering on the vibes.

"ALL THE THINGS YOU ARE"

1:49	Intro	The shift to the jazz section is made clear by Clarke's subtle **backbeat** and Jackson's fluid, bluesy lines.
2:02	A	Jackson improvises freely over the first eight bars of the tune (in the distant key of B minor).

FUGUE

2:11	As Jackson continues his solo, Heath's descending bass line forces the harmonies through a series of modulations.

2:38	Finally the bass lands on the dominant of C minor. Underneath Jackson's bluesy **licks**, Lewis prepares us for the return to the home key.
2:48	Jackson returns to the fugue subject. It's interrupted by a *stretto*—a polyphonic overlap with another entry of the fugue subject (by Lewis). In quick order, the bass, vibes, and piano rapidly state the theme.
3:00	As the bass stays fixed on the dominant, Lewis and Jackson play descending **diminished-seventh chords.**
3:04	A final series of chords lands us triumphantly on C major.

HEATING THE COOL AND CHANGING THE TIME

Lightness was a significant aspect of cool jazz. Lester Young's influence on a generation of tenor saxophonists produced two approaches that tended to break down along racial lines. Black tenors (like Dexter Gordon, Wardell Gray, Illinois Jacquet, and Gene Ammons) modified Young's legato (smooth) phrasing into a more forthright attack, emphasizing the expressive robustness of his style. White tenors (like Stan Getz, Zoot Sims, Al Cohn, and Allen Eager) focused instead on Young's airy lyricism. The most accomplished "white Lesters" worked together in the Woody Herman Orchestra. After Herman recorded Jimmy Giuffre's "Four Brothers," a fast bop piece that featured the reed section, the title phrase was used to define that reed section and any tenor who approximated that style ("the Lestorian mode," in Getz's phrase). These saxophonists perfected timbres that avoided vibrato while aiming for a high, transparent sound. Gerry Mulligan made the baritone saxophone sound almost like a tenor; Giuffre made the tenor sound almost like an alto; and Paul Desmond made the alto sound almost like a flute.

The "Four Brothers" sound—three tenor saxophones and a baritone saxophone—was named after a piece created for Woody Herman's 1947 orchestra. At a 1957 reunion recording session, the brothers were (left to right) Herbie Steward, Al Cohn, Zoot Sims, and Serge Chaloff.

■ DAVE BRUBECK (1920–2012)

Paul Desmond made his name with the Dave Brubeck Quartet, the most popular jazz group of the 1950s. Brubeck grew up in Concord, California, in a musical family; his first instructor was his mother, a classical pianist. He later studied with composer Darius Milhaud, whose 1923 ballet *La Création du monde* was one of the first orchestral works to employ blues harmonies. In 1951, Brubeck hooked up with Desmond and organized his first quartet (piano, alto saxophone, bass, drums). Success was almost immediate. He was pictured on the cover of *Time* in 1954, a rare acknowledgment for a jazz musician, and won acclaim from younger listeners by playing and recording on college campuses.

The Brubeck Quartet blew both hot and cool, in the contrast between Desmond's ethereal saxophone and Brubeck's heavy-handed piano. Both musicians excelled at unusual chord substitutions, but where Desmond improvised appealing melodies, Brubeck built his solos in a pattern that began with single-note phrases and climaxed with repetitive blocks of chords,

JAZZ GRAPHICS
Art and Commerce

The most significant visual documentation of jazz is achieved through photography, as exemplified in the images used throughout this book, and film. Photographs and movies allow us to see the great figures of jazz history in their prime and in settings particular to their eras. Yet jazz is also documented in the related but significantly different field of graphic design. All art is subject to marketing ploys. Just as book designers want you to judge a book by its cover, those who devise album jackets, concert posters, movie ads, and magazines hope to catch your attention with pictorial design.

Good graphic design provides us not only with the pleasure of aesthetically striking and informative images, but also historical insight into the way corporations sought to entice customers. In this section, we focus on the marketing of written and recorded jazz during the past century, beginning with sheet music, which was the most important outlet for new songs well into the 1920s. Unlike the plain covers on classical music scores, the sheet music for popular songs often had flamboyant and even witty covers that illustrated the themes or lyrics of the songs. We then look at the four types of recordings that dominated the market until the advent of the MP3 and other digital systems: 78-rpm records, LPs, 45s, and CDs.

"It's Nobody's Business but My Own," a satire of womanizing black preachers, was written by a white team (Skidmore and Walker) for the legendary comedian Bert Williams, a black man who had to perform in blackface makeup. He introduced it in the Ziegfeld Follies and recorded it in 1919. The stereotype drawings underscore the fact that it's a Negro dialect song.

"Big Indian Chief," a "two-step" ragtime number by the black songwriting team of Bob Cole and J. Rosamund Johnson, advertises its origin in a college production and implies (note the staff running across the top of the page) that it has a lyric; in fact, the sheet music is a piano instrumental of a song that was interpolated into an all-white 1904 musical, *An English Daisy*, after it was imported from London to Broadway.

All materials are from the Gary Giddins Collection.

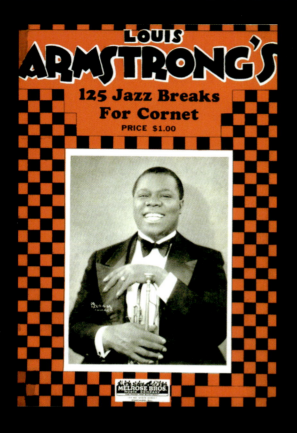

"Louis Armstrong's 125 Jazz Breaks for Cornet" is one of two portfolios that Armstrong created exclusively for the Chicago-based Melrose Publishing Company. He recorded the breaks and solos, which Melrose transcribed as sheet music—before destroying the discs! This volume came out in 1927, when relatively few people beyond jazz musicians and a small coterie of fans had heard of Louis Armstrong.

Eddie Green, a white song and dance man, wrote "A Good Man Is Hard to Find" in 1918, for the pioneering black music publishing company operated by W. C. Handy and Harry Pace. Its title became a catchphrase in American culture, and the song a jazz standard in the "red hot mama" mode, as popularized by Sophie Tucker and Bessie Smith. The sheet music, however, emphasizes the debonair vaudevillian Jack Norworth and depicts a high-born lady sharing the "Matrimonial News" with a parrot, as ships arrive on the horizon.

Alberta Hunter and Lovie Austin were well-known performers and songwriters in 1923, when they wrote "Chirpin' the Blues" (not a chirpy number: "It takes a worried woman to chirp this weary song"). Hunter recorded it that year, and Bessie Smith never recorded it at all; yet, as the more promising and charismatic star, she is glowingly featured on the sheet music cover.

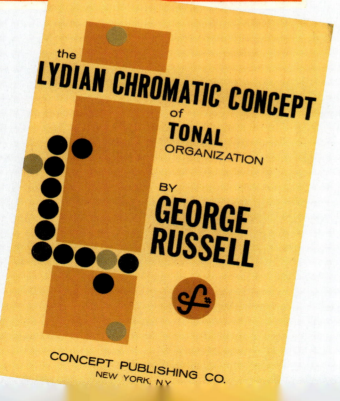

During the Swing Era, nothing sold sheet music better than endorsements from the most popular bandleaders, so when Mills Music reissued a piano arrangement of Fats Waller's 1929 classic "Ain't Misbehavin'" in 1945, it used a photo of Harry James, promoting his recent recording (lower left-hand corner), even though his version was only a minor commercial hit.

George Russell's *Lydian Chromatic Concept of Tonal Organization* is his argument on behalf of modes or scales as a way of systematizing harmony. Although his theory led directly to Miles Davis's *Kind of Blue*, his text of some 100 pages, as published in 1959, complete with graphs and paper slide rule, was too arcane for all but dedicated musicologists. The design, reminiscent of the Dutch painter Piet Mondrian, indicates modernism.

The plain white sheet music cover for Thelonious Monk's " 'Round Midnight" indicates a musical seriousness and economical decision, as the song initially had marginal status as a pop hit. Note that the composer is listed third, after the lyricist and the bandleader who introduced the 1944 song, which Monk himself did not record until 1947.

Three projects involving Louis Armstrong show how graphic design figures in the promotion of jazz publications and concerts. *Swing That Music* (1939), the first (heavily ghostwritten) book issued under his name, forgoes a photograph in favor of reverberant musical notes and the names of many musicians, who are represented in the book merely by transcriptions of the way they might play the title song. The introduction by nasal pop singer Rudy Vallee, by no means a jazz performer, perceptively argues that Armstrong is the preeminent influence on contemporary vocalists. A 1947 issue of *Jazz Record*, aimed at collectors, uses a 1920s photo of Armstrong to underscore its concern with jazz's early years. The 1953 "Jazz Concert Programme" was sold during the historic tour undertaken by Armstrong and Benny Goodman, until illness forced Goodman to quit. Such programs invariably included publicity photographs of the participating musicians, with short biographies. Fans could purchase them and, between sets, ask musicians to sign their respective pages. Even at the height of its popularity, jazz stars were generally accessible to the fans.

Most early 78-rpm recordings were ten inches in diameter and were sold in plain wrapping-paper sleeves with holes to reveal the labels. The short-lived Emerson Phonograph Company offered an arty sleeve design with jester and dancer (reflecting a late nineteenth-century graphic style) and a label logo involving the Statue of Liberty. "7 Inch Double Disc" refers to the diameter (the same as postwar 45s) and the fact that there is a different tune on each side—many 78s were recorded on one side only. "Honey Boy" is a 1916 raggy dance version of a minstrel song, played by a marching band.

Paramount Records was a leader in "Race Records," which targeted the African American market. The company is remembered for its extraordinary catalog advertisements, which were generally free of minstrel stereotypes and focused on the story content of the lyrics. The handout for "Keep a Knocking and You Can't Get In," a 1928 disc by the obscure vocalist and kazoo player James "Boodle It" Wiggins, boasts of the label's "electric method" of recording.

Ma Rainey had only been recording for three months when, in early 1924, Paramount put her picture on the 78 label and gave her the uncommon possessive credit: " 'Ma' Rainey's Dream Blues." This was testament to her great popularity as a performer, which the company hoped would extend to her records.

Paramount's ad for a 1922 recording by Alberta Hunter bills her as "The Idol of Dreamland" (a Chicago club) and "the most popular colored artist that ever appeared on the theatrical stage." Hunter, despite her work as a composer and performer of blues, had a versatile, mostly pop-oriented repertory, but in the 1920s every black woman singer was pigeonholed as a blues singer. After working as a nurse for two decades, Hunter enjoyed her greatest success in an astonishing New York comeback, in 1977, at the age of eighty-two. She continued to perform until her death in 1984.

Few record companies survived the Depression—even the formerly prosperous Columbia Records went into receivership. That began to change in the late 1930s, as the popularity of performers like Bing Crosby, Louis Armstrong, and the swing bands generated record sales. By 1940, there were three major American labels: Victor had been sustained by the RCA radio network; Decca began operating in 1934, with British financing; and Columbia was bought and relaunched by the CBS network. Audiences now clamored for older records that had long ago disappeared from shops. The labels responded with a new concept: *albums*— usually four discs in plain sleeves bound with a pictorial cover.

HOT JAZZ CLASSICS • SET C-38

$7.00

THE DUKE

Album #5 in a series of re-issues of the original records that made jazz history

COLUMBIA RECORDS

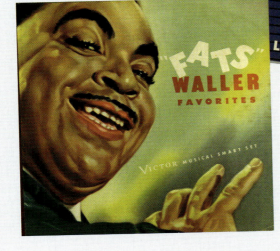

"FATS" WALLER FAVORITES

VICTOR MUSICAL SMART SET

The Duke was the fifth in a series of albums collecting Ellington's Columbia recordings from the 1920s and 1930s. Note that the photograph emphasizes Ellington's supreme elegance and his association with the piano, as indicated by a thin black line—and that the name *Ellington* appears nowhere. Victor tested the market for Fats Waller by offering a compilation of "Favorites," commissioning a buoyant and colorful painting to attract customers. Boyd Raeburn, a bandleader, saxophonist, and arranger, played music that combined the headiest elements of bebop and classical music (especially Stravinsky)— something a record buyer might guess from the fantastic drawing on his 1946 *Innovations*, released by the small Jewel label: faces and instruments melt together along with an angel, a goatee, and dark glasses. Like crazy, man.

INNOVATIONS BY

JEWEL RECORDS

The entertainment industry was completely revolutionized in the postwar years with the introduction of magnetic tape and television. In the recording business, the big innovation was microgroove, which Columbia and RCA-Victor innovated simultaneously, but along different lines. In the end, the industry accepted RCA's seven-inch, donut-hole 45-rpm disc as a vehicle for single tracks, replacing the 78, and for Extended Play (EP) 45s (two songs per side). Columbia's twelve-inch Long Playing (LP) disc would serve as an extension of the album format, which was particularly suitable for classical music and jazz.

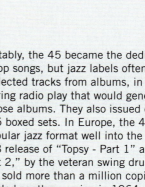

Inevitably, the 45 became the dedicated format for pop songs, but jazz labels often issued 45s of selected tracks from albums, in the hope of securing radio play that would generate interest in those albums. They also issued entire albums as 45 boxed sets. In Europe, the 45 remained a popular jazz format well into the 1960s. The 1958 release of "Topsy - Part 1" and "Topsy - Part 2," by the veteran swing drummer Cozy Cole, sold more than a million copies; Cole recorded another version in 1964, for Coral, that didn't do nearly as well, but served the purpose of keeping his name alive. "The Genius of Art Tatum" is an EP, No. 23 in a series of 27, containing the 69 piano solos Tatum recorded in December 1953; they were later released as ten LPs or four CDs—today, Tatum's complete works would fit on an iPod along with a few thousand other tracks. Note the painting by David Stone Martin, one of the most prolific and ubiquitous jazz artists of the 1950s. "John Coltrane" is another EP, containing two longish tracks, made specifically for the European market.

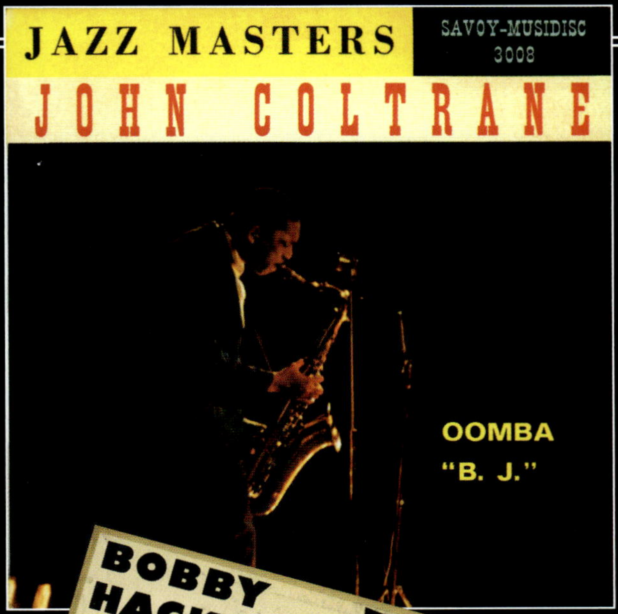

JAZZ MASTERS

JOHN COLTRANE

OOMBA
"B. J."

BOBBY HACKETT
Trumpet Solos

The Brunswick
LONG PLAY 33 RECORD
BL 58014

Program

IRVING BERLIN
SOFT LIGHTS AND SWEET MUSIC
HOWARD DIETZ · ARTHUR SCHWARTZ
IF THERE IS SOMEONE LOVELIER THAN YOU
VERNON DUKE
WHAT IS THERE TO SAY?
GEORGE GERSHWIN
SOON · BUT NOT FOR ME
COLE PORTER
EASY TO LOVE
RICHARD RODGERS · LORENZ HART
WITH A SONG IN MY HEART
JOHNNY MERCER · GORDON JENKINS
BERNARD HANIGHEN
WHEN A WOMAN LOVES A MAN

With Orchestra Directed by
BILL CHALLIS
and
BOBBY HACKETT

BRUNSWICK LONG PLAY MICROGROOVE
UNBREAKABLE RECORD BL 58014

CL 637

COLUMBIA
LP

Lady Day

A collection
of classic jazz
interpretations by
Billie
Holiday
with all-star
accompaniments

Miss Brown to You   I Wished on the Moon
What a Little Moonlight Can Do
If You Were Mine   Summertime
Billie's Blues   I Must Have That Man!
Foolin' Myself   Easy Living
Me, Myself and I   A Sailboat in the Moonlight
I Cried for You

LPs also came in two formats. The ten-inch disc was briefly popular in the 1950s. It was less expensive than the twelve-inch and contained less music—typically, four tracks per side instead of six. "Bobby Hackett Trumpet Solos," released in 1950, gives equal emphasis to the musician, the songs and their composers, and the fact (posted on the upper right and lower left of the cover) that Long Play Microgroove Records were "unbreakable," an advantage over the brittle 78. From the first, the LP was used to package classic recordings. Billie Holiday's *Lady Day*, a compilation of her 1930s sides, introduced her early work to a new generation, and reminded older fans of how she had once sounded. The design is highly dramatic, with its oddly shadowed photograph blocked by large white letters and only the dancing red and blue letters for contrast.

The twelve-inch LP dominated the adult-listening market for nearly thirty-five years, ultimately giving way to CDs in the middle 1980s. Record collectors cherished them in a way that surpassed their feelings for 78s and was never equaled by the CD. One reason, some have speculated, is that cardboard is more "human" than plastic. Another reason is that tremendous care was expended on the cover graphics and liner notes, making the LP a more complete experience. The twelve-inch cover was more challenging and rewarding to visual artists than the five-inch CD booklet. Most important, the 35-to-50-minute playing time held the listener's attention, while the 75 minutes of music often crammed onto a CD exhausted the listener's patience, especially as the individual tracks also grew in length.

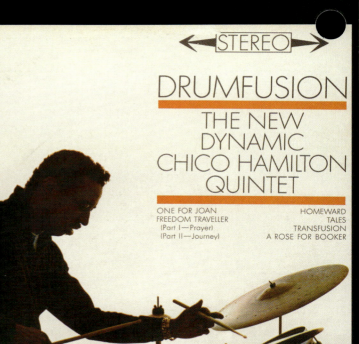

All the major labels offered extensive reissue programs to exploit their catalogs and provide an inexpensive means of producing product to keep national distributors interested in the labels' output. *Don Redman: Master of the Big Band* comes from one of the best of the 1960s reissue series, RCA-Vintage, which creatively assembled tracks of classic and relatively obscure jazz, pop, blues, and folk. Customers who came to trust the consistent good taste of a series like Vintage might purchase LPs by people they had never heard of, inevitably expanding their own knowledge of prewar American music.

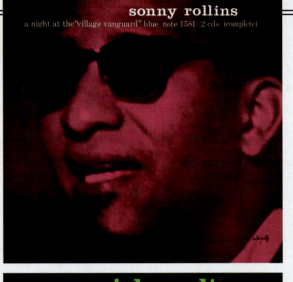

sonny rollins
a night at the "village vanguard" blue note 1581 2 cds (complete)

john coltrane
BLUE TRAIN blue note 53428

Chico Hamilton's *Drumfusion*, a 1962 Columbia album, takes an aggressive approach by labeling the music "Dynamic" and serving up a dynamic cover, with its largely silhouetted Hamilton, uppercase lettering, and black trim. Also boldly noted is the stereo option, at a time when you could pay slightly less for a monaural version. The cover includes the names of the selections rather than the musicians, though this album helped to launch the career of tenor saxophonist Charles Lloyd. Blue Note usually took the opposite approach, promoting the names of the sidemen, but for two singularly important 1957 releases, John Coltrane's *Blue Train* and Sonny Rollins's *A Night at the Village Vanguard*, it focused on the leaders in close-up studies. No catalog of album covers is more celebrated than that of Blue Note, designed by Reid Miles and featuring the black and white photography (here color tinted) of the label's co-owner, Francis Wolff. These two covers are CD reissues—Blue Note music without Blue Note graphics is unthinkable.

One of the most unusual and arresting of album covers, for *Undercurrent,* by Bill Evans and Jim Hall (United Artists, 1962), has no design and no information—just a dreamlike black and white photograph by Toni Frissell of a woman who seems to be floating underwater. If you turn it upside down, you can see that it really shows a woman in a nightgown diving into a lake.

By the 1960s, jazz covers had become an art in their own right. Classical music albums usually settled for reproductions of famous paintings or posed portraits of the artists, and pop albums tended toward straightforward or romantic depictions of the performers. One especially influential cover was Dave Brubeck's *Time Out*. In 1959, a Columbia Records producer thought Brubeck's album so unmarketable that he refused to release it until the pianist mounted a protest. Why? All the selections were originals based on odd time signatures, and Neil Fujita's painting (which Brubeck insisted on) was thought too perplexing for the average consumer. *Time Out* remains one of the best-selling jazz albums of all time.

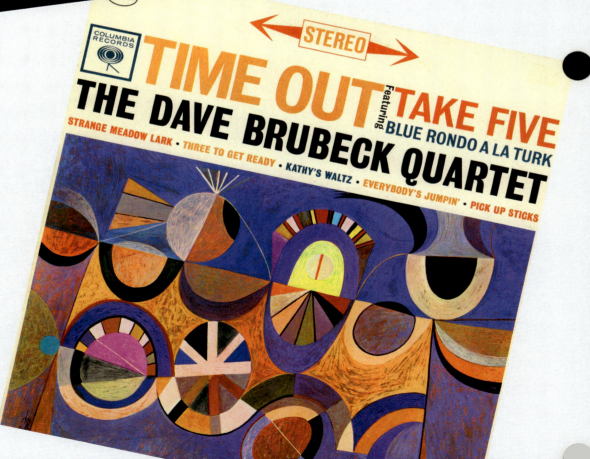

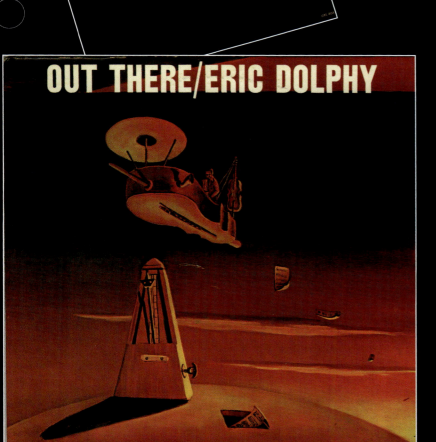

LOVE FOR SALE CECIL TAYLOR Trio and Quintet
UA HI-FIDELITY

MILES *Sketches of Spain* arranged and conducted by Gil Evans
Columbia

OUT THERE/ERIC DOLPHY
PRESTIGE/NEW JAZZ 8252
Prophet

The release of Miles Davis's third LP arranged by Gil Evans, *Sketches of Spain*, was an event in 1960, a fusion of jazz and flamenco, its searing emotionalism conveyed by the classic simplicity of the uncredited cover—three layers of color in a manner reminiscent of the paintings of Mark Rothko, with a small full-figure silhouette of the trumpet player confronting a bull charging his first name; no last name necessary. The cover of Verve's 1963 landmark album *Getz / Gilberto* was widely imitated for its use of an abstract painting by the Puerto Rican–born artist Olga Albizu, confirming the idea that bossa nova was indeed a new style. The surreal illustration for Eric Dolphy's 1960 Prestige album *Out There* (signed by Prophet) telegraphs the idea that this music is not merely modern, but far out. On the other hand, United Artists came up with one of the most laughably deceptive covers in presenting the avant-garde Cecil Taylor's 1959 *Love for Sale* as a conventional interpretation of Cole Porter.

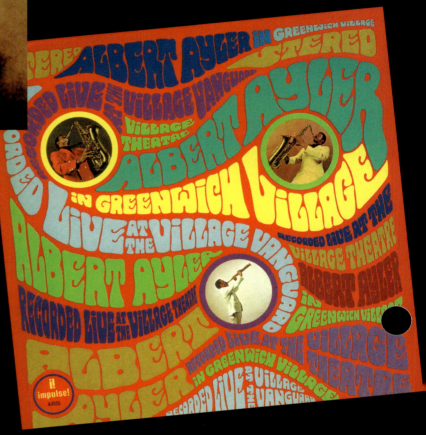

"The New Wave of Jazz is on Impulse!"—so proclaimed a major new label of 1960s jazz, known for its gatefold covers with orange spines (they stood out on record shelves) and a name with a built-in exclamation point. For a 1963 Charles Mingus album, it combined a close-up profile from a Joe Alper photograph with a kinetic typeface, repeating his name five times: *Mingus Mingus Mingus Mingus Mingus*. What more did you need to know? By the middle of the decade, rock covers brought a new style to graphic design, venturing into psychedelic whirls and colors. One of the first jazz covers to go that route was *Albert Ayler in Greenwich Village*, a 1966 Impulse! title, which, in its way, was as deceptive as Cecil Taylor's *Love for Sale*.

Miles Davis rejected Summer of Love graphics in favor of a startling new style for his breakout fusion album, *Bitches Brew*. The stunning cover art by Mati Klarwein and the startlingly crude title (by the standards of Columbia Records and of 1969) told listeners they were entering a brave new world before they put the platter on the turntable. No previous jazz album looked remotely like this. A couple of years later, a more naturalistic approach was back in favor. For Archie Shepp's 1972 *Attica Blues*, Impulse! countered the album's political theme (the riots at Attica prison) with a pensive study of the artist at work.

A decade after that, LPs were fighting a losing battle to CDs, even though the first digital discs had inferior sound; people bought records they already owned in the shiny new format, just as collectors of 78s had repurchased their favorites on microgroove. Usually the labels miniaturized the original LP cover art. But on occasion, they would contract a new one. When Chiaroscuro released Mary Lou Williams's 1971 *Nitelife* as a 1998 CD, the producer Hank O'Neal added a second disc of performances and commissioned a colorful painting by Richard Merkin, which made the music seem more urgent and contemporary.

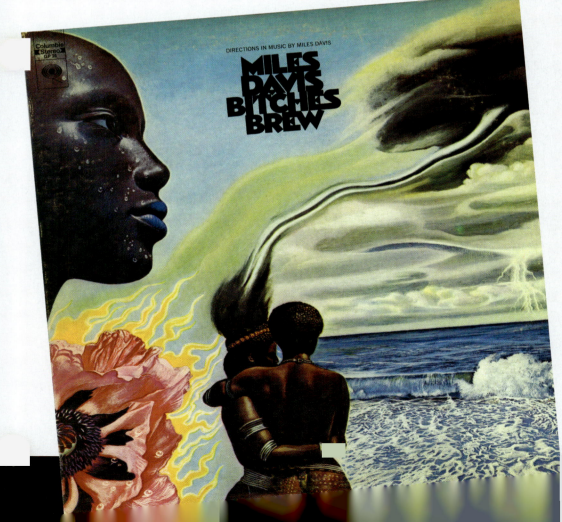

The diminutive size of CDs changed the nature of graphic design. More creative effort was expended on fancy boxed sets and oddly designed packages than on the typical single-disc album. Cover art was dominated by photographs rather than paintings or ornamental typeface. Of course, there are many exceptions, and graphic artists continue to find effective ways of communicating something about the artist or the music. For Danilo Perez's 2000 *Motherland*, Verve posed the pianist against an expansion bridge to evoke the connection he establishes between jazz and the music of his native Panama and other South American countries. You wouldn't know it from the cover, but Diana Krall's 2001 *The Look of Love* presents the singer-pianist, usually heard leading a trio, with a large orchestra; instead, Verve focuses entirely on her, especially her legs. The consumer can have no doubt that Jason Moran's 2002 *Modernistic* will live up to its title: Blue Note's design by P. R. Brown returns to basic black and white, but in a fashionably modern way, combining an alert eyeball and computer-like font to excite the buyer's curiosity.

generating either excitement or tedium, depending on the listener's taste. Brubeck's primary trademark was an innovative use of irregular meters such as 5/4 and 9/4. After decades of jazz played almost exclusively in 4/4 (even waltzes were rare), his approach to time was exotic, charming, and frequently catchy. Brubeck's 1959 album *Time Out* became a national phenomenon, especially his "Blue Rondo à la Turk" (in 9/4) and Desmond's "Take Five" (in 5/4), which was released as a hit single. A composition in 5/4 might be counted as 2 plus 3 or the reverse: "Blue Rondo à la Turk" breaks down to 1-2, 1-2, 1-2, 1-2-3. By the end of the twentieth century, unusual time signatures, some borrowed from Eastern music, were commonplace.

HARD BOP

The most profound counterstatement to cool jazz was essentially a revival of bop but with a harder edge. By the middle 1950s, the umbrella term **hard bop** was adopted by critics to describe a populous East Coast school of jazz that placed itself in direct opposition to the more arid precincts of cool. Ironically, Miles Davis helped pilot the turn. Put off by underfed, overintellectualized music that claimed to be derived from his nonet, he switched directions in 1954, with recordings ("Walkin'," "Blue and Boogie") that restored jazz's earthy directness.

Born largely of musicians who came to New York from the nation's inner cities, especially Detroit and Philadelphia, hard bop was said to reflect the intensity and hustling tempo of city life. To these musicians, the cool school represented a more tranquil, stress-free environment. This idea paints a superficial gloss on the relationship between art and geography; obviously, West Coast musicians were as stressed as anyone else. Still, it seems fair to suggest that the West Coast school's expression of life's irritations was relatively introverted, while the East Coast's was relatively extroverted.

One instantly apparent difference concerned timbre. If cool jazz aimed for a light timbre, hard bop preferred a sound that was heavy, dark, impassioned. The tenor replaced the alto as the saxophone of choice, and drummers worked in an assertive style that drove the soloists. Some hard bop bands winnowed bop's harmonic complexity in favor of elemental chords reminiscent of the sanctified church or rhythm and blues, creating a subset of hard bop called **soul jazz** (see Chapter 16). In effect, the soul musicians were attempting to reconnect modern jazz to popular music. Ultimately, the contrast between cool and hard bop, though unmistakable, was not radical enough to suggest a schism like the one that divided swing and bop. Some musicians, like pianists Sonny Clark and Hampton Hawes, played in both schools. Cool and hard bop represented the natural development of bop in a changing world. Part of the change was technological.

Microgroove and Long Solos

In 1948, Columbia Records patented a recording process called microgroove, or long-playing records (LPs): twelve-inch platters that turned at 33 1/3 revolutions per minute and accommodated about twenty minutes of music per side with excellent fidelity. They were manufactured from a flexible plastic (or vinyl) that was promoted as unbreakable. By contrast, the three-minute 78-rpm platter that had dominated the industry for half a century was extremely brittle and easily shattered. As Columbia announced its breakthrough, its competitor RCA-Victor introduced a similar system, also using microgrooves and improved vinyl, but smaller and with less playing time, a speed of 45 rpm, and a large donut-hole in its center. The industry quickly accepted both technologies, reserving the LP for serious or extended works and the 45 for pop songs no longer than those heard on 78s. The LP had an immediate impact on jazz, particularly on the new generation of hard bop musicians.

When the LP arrived (almost simultaneously with the introduction of audio tape), it not only opened the door to extensive live recording, but also influenced the way music was played in the studio. Duke Ellington was one of the first to take advantage of the liberty it afforded him, composing extended works specifically for the new medium.

Partly because of the LP, hard bop bands were inclined toward longer solos. Shunning counterpoint and complicated ensemble arrangements, they relied on extended improvisations. The average performance consisted of a head, solos by some or all the band members, and a reprise of the head. As the lengthy improvisations threatened to alienate audiences accustomed to shorter solos, major labels like Columbia and RCA were disinclined to pursue hard bop. But new, independent labels were delighted to take up the slack, among them Blue Note, Prestige, Contemporary, and Riverside. They realized that a large segment of the audience was ready for a style of jazz that was at once expansive and closer to its roots.

One way the bands maintained the interest of a mainstream audience with their long solos was to fortify the beat with a pronounced backbeat. In the 1950s, jazz fans congregated in nightclubs where physical reactions like foot-tapping and finger-snapping amounted to a kind of dancing while seated. The independent record companies liked the longer tracks for another reason: the fewer tunes on an album, the less they had to pay in songwriter royalties.

■ ART BLAKEY (1919–1990)

Art Blakey was the primary figurehead of hard bop. Raised amid the Pittsburgh steel mills, he began on piano, switched to drums, and made his way to New York in 1942 to work with Mary Lou Williams. Two years later, Dizzy Gillespie recruited him for the Billy Eckstine band, positioning him to become one of the most influential percussionists of the bop era. Blakey had an earthier approach than Kenny Clarke and Max Roach, and was their equal in finding precisely the right rhythmic figures or timbres to complement and inspire a soloist. He became famous for his **press-roll**: an intense rumbling on the snare drum, usually at a turn-around, which had the effect of boosting a soloist into the air for a few seconds and then setting him down in the next chorus. Blakey's attentiveness made him an ideal drummer for Thelonious Monk, with whom he had a long association—even though Monk's own music was quirky and convoluted while Blakey's was brash and straightforward.

Drummer Art Blakey pushed his Jazz Messengers to the pinnacle of hard bop for more than three decades, graduating dozens of major musicians, from Clifford Brown to Wynton Marsalis.

© CHUCK STEWART

In 1953, Blakey and pianist-composer Horace Silver formed a quintet (trumpet, tenor saxophone, piano, bass, and drums) called the Jazz Messengers. They made a few live recordings (including *A Night in Birdland*, with trumpet player Clifford Brown), and within two years had codified hard bop as quintet music that combined bebop complexity with blunt simplicity (in bluesy or gospel-inspired themes and backbeat rhythms). In 1956, after Silver left to organize his own quintet, Blakey formally assumed leadership, and the band became Art Blakey and His Jazz Messengers.

Jazz Messengers

The number of important musicians who either began or matured in Blakey's groups is remarkable: trumpet players Kenny Dorham, Lee Morgan, Freddie Hubbard, Woody Shaw, and Wynton Marsalis; saxophonists Hank Mobley, Jackie McLean, Benny Golson, Wayne Shorter, and Branford Marsalis; and pianists Cedar Walton, John Hicks, Keith Jarrett, Joanne Brackeen, and Mulgrew Miller, among many others. Blakey telegraphed the consistent attitude of his music in classic album titles: *Moanin', Drum Suite, The Freedom Rider, The Big Beat, Indestructible, Hard Bop, Straight Ahead.*

■ HORACE SILVER (1928–2014)

In the three years he worked with Blakey, Horace Silver composed several of the tunes that incarnated the hard bop aesthetic. Born and raised in Connecticut, Silver was discovered at twenty-one by Stan Getz, who took him on tour and into recording studios. During the next few years, he worked with major musicians, including Coleman Hawkins, Lester Young, and Charlie Parker; he appeared with Miles Davis on the 1954 sessions that helped turn the tide from cool to hard. Beyond his ability to filter bop through gospel, rhythm and blues, and folk-song structures, Silver brought to his music an uncanny ability to create catchy melodies that sounded familiar and new at the same time. One of his earliest pieces, "Opus de Funk" (1953), a play on Stan Getz's "Opus de Bop" (1946), popularized a word for Silver's brand of soulful jazz: funky. Partly derived from nineteenth-century slang for spoiled tobacco, "funky" also has a long history in African American usage to describe any kind of foul odor. (Jelly Roll Morton used it in his version of "I Thought I Heard Buddy Bolden Say.") Thanks to Silver, the term was reborn to signify basic back-to-roots musical values. Many of his tunes became jazz standards; several attracted lyricists and vocalists. Significantly, a few were covered by pop or soul artists, including "Doodlin'," "Señor Blues," "Peace," and "Song for My Father."

🎧 "Song for My Father"

By 1965, when Blue Note released the album *Song for My Father*, Silver was one of the most acclaimed artists on the label, highly regarded as a composer, pianist, and leader of a hard-hitting quintet. This album, especially the title selection, proved to be a watershed. Even the cover art signaled a departure: instead of the usual moody, black-and-white head shot of the session leader, it offered a full-color portrait of a jaunty older man, wearing a panama hat and smoking a

Horace Silver, seen here in the 1950s, established funk as the quintessence of soulful, rhythmically propulsive jazz, and wrote tunes like "The Preacher" and "Song for My Father," which were played by bands that ranged from Dixieland to rock.

© CHUCK STEWART

cigar—Silver's father, the inspiration for his first extended foray into rhythms and melodies he associated with his father's years on the island of Maio in Cape Verde. Previously, Silver was known for compositions grounded in the church ("The Preacher"), blues ("Home Cookin'"), and bop ("Cookin' at the Continental"). "Song for My Father" suggests a new accent straightaway, with its four-note vamp—an unforgettable pace-setting phrase. Throughout the album, he uses similar vamps, which became a distinctive signature of his music. The album was a tremendous hit, and "Song for My Father" was adopted as a standard in jazz and beyond: James Brown recorded his own instrumental version, and the vamp turned up in recordings by Earth, Wind and Fire and Steely Dan, among others.

This is a spacious performance in which every detail stands out. With only two wind instruments, Silver makes us conscious of his carefully calculated harmonies. The frequent breaks key up the tension, and the rhythm section plays with an unhurried cohesiveness that, by its very restraint, highlights the rhythmic conceits of the solos by Silver and the exceptional Joe Henderson, himself an important Blue Note artist in the 1960s. Like Count Basie, Silver holds his technique in a less-is-more reserve, making every note count. By contrast, Henderson, in a career-lifting improvisation, begins with a simple melodic phrase and then builds exciting, ardent rhythmic arcs, demonstrating the trademark edginess of timbre (for example, at 4:40 and 5:11) that distinguished him from other major tenor saxophonists of the period. The finale is notable: for a while, the piece seems to be heading for a fade-out, a cliché Silver spurns in favor of a triumphant full stop.

LISTENING GUIDE 42

🎧 song for my father

HORACE SILVER

Horace Silver, piano; Joe Henderson, tenor saxophone; Carmell Jones, trumpet; Teddy Smith, bass; Roger Humphries, drums

- Label: *Song for My Father*, Blue Note BLP4185
- Date: 1964
- Style: hard bop
- Form: 24-bar popular song (**A A B**)

What to listen for:

- Silver's catchy composition
- his simple bluesy piano playing
- Henderson's complex virtuoso solo

0:01		Against a Latin beat, Silver's left hand (doubled by Smith on bass) plays a simple Latin bass line:

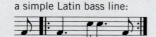

CHORUS 1 (HEAD)

0:09	**A**	Jones (trumpet) and Henderson (tenor saxophone) play the opening phrase of the melody (doubled by Silver), ending on a long-held harmonic **second** (interval of a **whole step**).
0:16		The continuation is also harmonized by a pungent whole step. After a brief pause, it concludes with more harmonious **thirds**.
0:24	**A**	The melody is repeated.
0:39	**B**	The melody continues in short phrases, harmonized in parallel thirds.
0:50		The ending, while consonant, sounds tentative because it features unusual notes of the scale.

CHORUS 2 (HEAD)

0:54	**A**	The second chorus repeats the melody. Instead of doubling the horns, Silver accompanies with rich chords.
1:06		At the conclusion, he adds a **syncopated** dance beat.
1:10	**A**	The melody is repeated.
1:25	**B**	

CHORUS 3 (SILVER SOLO)

1:40	**A**	Silver's solo emerges from his chordal accompaniment.
1:50		After the short **break**, he plays a simple bluesy phrase.
1:55	**A**	His playing, decorated with **grace notes**, is simple and rhythmically direct.
2:05		The conclusion is the same as for the first **A** section.
2:10	**B**	

CHORUS 4

2:26	**A**	By harmonizing his melody in parallel **fourths**, Silver creates a vaguely "Oriental" effect.
2:35		His bluesy response is more biting and syncopated.
2:41	**A**	
2:51		The bluesy response is the same as above.
2:56	**B**	Silver's playing gradually becomes denser and more varied.

CHORUS 5

3:11	**A**	He plays two notes at a time, harmonized initially with the whole step, in short phrases.
3:21		Over the break, he hits the tonic repeatedly on the **backbeat**.
3:26	**A**	A harsh interval alternates with a simple bluesy figure.
3:41	**B**	Using both hands, Silver plays forceful chords.
3:51		He concludes his solo with the bluesy figure first heard at 1:50.

CHORUS 6 (HENDERSON SOLO)

3:56	**A**	Henderson builds from Silver's solo, relying on similar blues phrases.
4:11	**A**	He plays with one blues motive at a much faster rhythmic level; when the harmony changes, he **transposes** it.
4:21		For the break, he switches to a new rhythm, a lengthy passage in **triplets**.
4:26	**B**	After taking a breath, Henderson launches into fast bebop-style passages.
4:36		The chorus reaches its climax on a strained high note.
4:39		The next chorus's opening motive is launched a measure early.

CHORUS 7

4:41	**A**	
4:47		A lengthy pause precedes a new motive, transposed to fit the harmonies.
4:56	**A**	Henderson's third chorus latches on to a repeated note, which he maintains even as the harmony moves.
5:06		Over the break, he transforms the repeated note into a blues **lick**.
5:11	**B**	At the peak of his solo, his decorations become even faster, linking his motives together into chains.

INTERLUDE

5:26		Henderson's solo spills over into an interlude. While his line gradually recedes in intensity, Silver continues the simple bass line.

CHORUS 8

5:45	**A**	The band repeats the head.
6:00	**A**	
6:15	**B**	

CODA	
6:30	Silver plays his syncopated rhythm four times, gradually decreasing in volume.
6:44	He plays a harshly dissonant lick repeatedly, changing its rhythm.
6:55	Quieter licks, occasionally interrupted by outbursts, fade into the bass line.
7:13	Silver ends the tune efficiently with emphatic lower **octaves**.

THREE SOLOISTS

By the 1960s, few observers could doubt that the unofficial rivalry between cool and hot had been decided in favor of hot. The stars of cool jazz retained their popularity, but most—including Stan Getz, Zoot Sims, and Al Cohn—had begun to play in an unmistakably harder style, reflecting the East Coast movement's impact. Moreover, the whole direction of jazz had developed an increasingly aggressive attitude, which would culminate in the raucous howls of the avant-garde. The tenor saxophone had long since supplanted the trumpet as the most vital instrument in jazz, and many of the tenors who defined 1960s jazz by exploring the middle ground between bebop and radical avant-gardism had learned their trade playing hard bop—among them John Coltrane in Miles Davis's band, Wayne Shorter in Art Blakey's band, and Joe Henderson in Horace Silver's band. Three major soloists who found their own paths amid the competing jazz schools were Clifford Brown, Sonny Rollins, and Wes Montgomery.

Clifford Brown (trumpet) and Sonny Rollins (tenor saxophone) brought a new inventiveness and spirit to jazz and their instruments, teaming briefly in the classic band co-led by Brown and drummer Max Roach in 1956.

© CHUCK STEWART

■ CLIFFORD BROWN (1930–1956)

The career of Clifford Brown lasted barely four years, but in that time he became one of the most admired and beloved musicians of his day. His death in an automobile accident at age twenty-five was mourned as a catastrophe for jazz. Born in Wilmington, Delaware, he took up trumpet at thirteen and attracted attention for his remarkable facility while studying at Maryland State College. After playing in Philadelphia and touring with a rhythm and blues band, word quickly spread that "he had it all"—gorgeous tone, virtuoso technique, infallible time, and a bottomless well of creative ideas. Nor was his importance exclusively musical. At a time when the jazz ranks were devastated by heroin addiction, Brown embodied an entirely different attitude. Here was an immensely likable young man whose musical ability rivaled that of Charlie Parker, but who had none of Parker's bad habits. He didn't smoke or drink, let alone take drugs, and his example inspired other musicians to change the way they lived.

Brown received encouragement from Dizzy Gillespie, Red Rodney, and especially Fats Navarro, with whom he shared a particular stylistic bond: each man was noted for his unusually rich timbre. It was an Art Blakey engagement at Birdland in early 1954 that made Brown the talk of the jazz elite: the two albums recorded at Birdland helped to clinch his growing reputation.

In the summer of 1954, Max Roach brought Brown to Los Angeles to make a concert recording. That event resulted in the formation of the Clifford Brown / Max Roach Quintet, with which Brown was associated for the remainder of his short life. Often cited as the last great bebop ensemble, the quintet influenced the emerging hard bop bands with its exciting vitality and canny arrangements, including a few unlikely pieces ("Delilah," from the score of the film *Samson and Delilah*) and originals by Brown: "Joy Spring," "Daahoud," and "The Blues Walk" became jazz standards. Brown conquered Los Angeles as easily as he had New York, recording with the new quintet as well as with Zoot Sims and singer Dinah Washington. The latter association generated other requests from singers; on returning to New York, he made landmark albums with Sarah Vaughan and Helen Merrill, as well as the most successful jazz album with strings since Charlie Parker's.

Brown/Roach Quintet

Brown's work as a trumpet player penetrated every aspect of jazz on both coasts but especially in the East, where a succession of hard bop trumpeters modeled themselves after him, determined to replicate his radiant sound and infectious enthusiasm. He offered an alternate approach to the meditative calculations of Miles Davis, and remained for decades a paradigm for upcoming trumpet players, including all those who succeeded him in Art Blakey's Jazz Messengers.

🎧 "A Night in Tunisia"

Clifford Brown's "A Night in Tunisia" is a posthumous recording, one of many that have turned up since the introduction of portable recording devices. A few weeks before he died, in 1956, Brown sat in with the local band at a small jazz club in Philadelphia. Three numbers were taped, though the tape didn't surface until the early 1970s, when it was released to tremendous acclaim by Columbia Records. His five-chorus solo on this Gillespie classic is an inspired romp that, because of its length and the relaxed ambience, allows us a glimpse into the way Brown thinks in the heat of action, using various gambits, pivotal notes, and motives; and altering speed, range, and meter as he produces a stream of stimulating musical ideas. This performance is also interesting for showing a great musician accompanied by a journeyman group—the jazz equivalent of a garage band—working hard to keep up (the drummer, who owned the jazz club, is especially alert) and not always succeeding, while an avid audience adds percussion-like fills with its shouts and hollers. Brown's solo achieved theatrical renown in 1999, when it was heard in Warren Leight's play *Side Man*: one character plays the recently discovered tape for a couple of friends, who marvel and gasp in response.

🎧 a night in tunisia (excerpt)

CLIFFORD BROWN

Clifford Brown, trumpet; Mel "Ziggy" Vines, Billy Root, tenor saxophones; Sam Dockery, piano; Ace Tesone, bass; Ellis Tollin, drums

- Label: Columbia KC32284
- Date: 1956
- Style: hard bop
- Form: 32-bar popular song (**A A B A**), with an interlude

What to listen for:

- Brown's exploration of range and rhythm
- his use of motives to control portions of his extended improvised solo
- support by drums
- live audience interaction

INTRODUCTION

| 0:00 | | The rhythm section plays a **vamp:** an open-ended, two-measure figure in a Latin groove, with an asymmetric, syncopated bass line. Conversation can be heard in the background. |
| 0:12 | | A saxophone enters, playing a background riff. |

CHORUS 1 (HEAD)

0:17	**A**	Brown enters, playing the tune on the trumpet over the two-chord progression of the vamp. Every time he reaches for the high note, it falls slightly behind the beat.
0:28	**A**	Brown repeats the **A** section, adding a melodic variation at 0:32.
0:39	**B**	For the bridge, the accompanying horns drop out, leaving Brown alone on the melody. The rhythm section leaves the Latin groove behind for a straight bebop-style four-four, with walking bass.
0:49	**A**	The band returns to the Latin groove of the opening.

INTERLUDE (16 bars)

| 0:59 | | The band plays a complicated interlude, designed to connect the head with the solos. The horns play a short riff with a constant rhythm; the melody changes slightly with each chord. Not everyone in the band knows this passage: the bass drops out entirely, while the pianist does his best to approximate the chords. |
| 1:15 | | The interlude ends with a four-measure **break**. Brown plays a string of clean, even eighth notes that reach a peak at 1:17. |

CHORUS 2

1:20	**A**	Brown's descending line connects smoothly with his solo, drawing applause from the crowd. The piano enters on the downbeat, the drums following a beat later.
1:31	**A**	Brown's playing remains relaxed and relatively simple.
1:42	**B**	At the bridge, Brown plays a descending line that interrupts the smooth rhythmic flow with unexpected **polyrhythmic** accents.
1:52	**A**	

CHORUS 3

2:03	**A**	The new chorus begins with a four-note motive, played in a simple descending pattern; it's answered by another four-note pattern, this one ascending.
2:12		The phrase ends with enough space for an excited fan to yell, "Hey, Brownie!"
2:13	**A**	Brown plays a fanfare-like statement on a high-pitched note—A, the fifth scale degree of the home key of D minor.
2:24	**B**	Playing in the upper register of his trumpet, he starts a line that will continue throughout the bridge.
2:32		The lengthy phrase is finally rounded off with a quick two-note figure, prompting cries of "Oh, yeah!" from the excited crowd.
2:34	**A**	Brown now plays with the two-note figure, placing it in different parts of the measure; the drummer responds by playing unexpected bass drum accents (**dropping bombs**).

CHORUS 4

2:45   **A**   Brown returns to a high A, playing a series of **triplets** that encourage the drummer to follow his rhythm.

2:51   Aiming for a climax, he hits and holds a sharply **dissonant** note.

2:55   **A**   Again returning to a high A, Brown plays a sharp, detached **cross-rhythm** that's instantly reinforced by syncopated bass-drum accents.

3:06   **B**

3:14   Brown suddenly breaks into a quick, upward run.

3:17   **A**   Seizing on the run as a compositional idea, he folds it into a series of repeated phrases, each ascending higher than the last. He follows this with a rapid descending sequence based on a four-note motive.

CHORUS 5

3:27   **A**   Once again, Brown begins by blasting out a high A, but quickly shifts to a series of triplets. The accent for the triplet falls on the normally unaccented last note of each group.

3:38   **A**   Brown plays a pair of phrases, each beginning with insistent triplets.

3:48   **B**   The bridge begins with a fast barrage of notes.

3:57   The drummer marks the end of the bridge with an intense **fill**.

3:58   **A**   Brown's fast solo passage begins to disintegrate into shorter fragments.

CHORUS 6

4:09   **A**   Brown begins again on a high A, playing a line strikingly similar to the line heard at 2:13.

4:15   Playing at the very top of his register, he squeaks out a line that's slightly out of tune until it descends into normal range.

4:19   **A**   For the last time, he begins on a high A before quickly descending.

4:30   **B**

4:40   **A**   During his last melodic pattern, Brown plays dissonant intervals within a rhythm drawn from the "Night in Tunisia" theme.

4:51   His solo ends. As the excerpt fades out, a tenor saxophone solo begins.

■ SONNY ROLLINS (b. 1930)

One of the most influential tenor saxophonists in jazz history, Sonny Rollins initially played a role in jazz similar to that of Clifford Brown. In the 1950s, countless young saxophonists and some older ones tried to assimilate his creative energy, brawny timbre, and rhythmic authority. He projected a measure of individuality and power—in the tradition of Louis Armstrong and Rollins's idol, Coleman Hawkins—that could not be contained in a conventional band. Unlike Brown, however, Rollins enjoyed a long, vigorous career, performing for sixty years, snatching a few rest periods along the way to refuel but always challenging himself to change, even to the point of taking on different musical identities. At times, when he seemed to have reached an artistic peak, he would turn a sharp corner, altering his sound, repertory, and instrumentation. Rollins represents continuity with the jazz past (through his use of pop tunes and swinging rhythms), while pointing the way to a promising future.

Born and raised in Harlem, Rollins studied piano and alto saxophone before taking up the tenor at sixteen. Two years later, Thelonious Monk invited him to participate in a program of rehearsals that went on for months, boosting his confidence and ambition. At nineteen, Rollins recorded as a sideman with Bud Powell and J. J. Johnson, among others, combining the

Sonny Rollins, one of the most admired saxophonists and tune writers of the 1950s, focused on the lower register and never ceased pushing himself to greater heights. He's shown here in 1965.

© CHUCK STEWART

gruff heaviness of Hawkins's sound with the quicksilver facility of Charlie Parker. Recording with Miles Davis a few years later, he revealed an unusual capacity for writing jazz pieces that other musicians jumped at the chance to perform ("Airegin," "Oleo"); with the Clifford Brown / Max Roach Quintet, he introduced the first widely noted bebop waltz, "Valse Hot."

In 1955, Rollins achieved an impressive stylistic breakthrough with the quartet album *Worktime*, following it a year later with *Saxophone Colossus*, one of the most lauded albums of the era. In 1959, depleted by a decade of work and puzzled by the new stylistic currents, Rollins put his career on hold for more than two years, which he devoted to intense practicing. It was the first of three sabbaticals, each a restorative that led him toward further experimentation and ultimately into the heart of the avant-garde. Although Rollins has remained faithful to bop, he has taken its harmonic complexity, vigorous swing, and melodic invention into diverse areas. These include calypso ("St. Thomas" was the first of many highly rhythmic jazz calypsos), avant-garde (he pioneered the piano-less saxophone-bass-drums trio), and rock (he has recorded with the Rolling Stones).

Rollins's solos are characterized by humor and his idiosyncratic approaches to timbre, motives, cadenzas, and—a nonmusical word—ebullience.

TIMBRE: Rollins's timbre is something of a paradox in that it has changed several times, yet is always recognizably his. In the early 1950s, his tone was harsh and splintered, almost grating. A few years later, in what is generally considered his first great period (1955–59), he produced an enormously attractive timbre: commanding, virile, and smooth as oak. He continued to experiment with his tone, eventually producing, in the late 1970s, a capacious, bigger-than-life timbre remarkable in its expressiveness.

MOTIVES: Rollins broke with bebop's tendency to favor harmonic improvisation. Instead of discarding the melody after the head, he paraphrases key phrases (motives) during his improvisation as touchstones, reminding the listener that he is elaborating on a particular song and not just its harmonic underpinnings.

CADENZAS: The cadenza is an integral part of jazz, not unrelated to the breaks that characterized early New Orleans jazz; Louis Armstrong's "West End Blues" cadenza signaled jazz's independence and maturity as a serious art form. But no one has done as much with cadenzas as Rollins, who makes them an integral part of live and recorded performances. His sometimes go on longer than the ensemble sections, and almost always generate audience excitement.

EBULLIENCE: Rollins's ebullience works best in concert, particularly in the outdoor and stadium settings he has favored since the 1980s, where audiences are primed to follow him in search of ecstatic release. It doesn't work in studio recordings, where repetition quickly palls. As a result, Rollins has split his music into two modes: the concert mode, which aims for a spiritual intensity, and the studio mode, which is systematic and frequently pithy. The two modes come together in his best live recordings.

"I'm an Old Cowhand"

Rollins had never been to California when he signed with the Los Angeles–based label Contemporary Records to record the 1957 album *Way Out West*.

But he had been recording like mad—in 1956 alone, he participated as leader or sideman in fifteen sessions that produced a dozen albums. The shocking death that year of Clifford Brown had taken the wind out of him, and he looked forward to the change in scenery. Yet typically, the venture put him in mind of a pun, on which he centered the project. A lifelong fan of Westerns, he suggested posing on the cover in Western regalia. The resulting photograph by William Claxton—portraying Rollins in a desert of cactus and bleached bones, wearing a ten-gallon hat and (empty) holster, the bell of his tenor saxophone emerging from his side like the barrel of a small cannon—was one of the era's most celebrated jackets. In addition to two originals (including the title tune) and two standard ballads, he underscored the theme with two ersatz cowboy songs, "Wagon Wheels," from the 1934 *Ziegfeld Follies*, and "I'm an Old Cowhand," from the 1936 Bing Crosby movie *Rhythm on the Range*.

Few jazz musicians knew Tin Pan Alley as well as Rollins, who often chose unlikely songs as vehicles for improvisation. Johnny Mercer's "I'm an Old Cowhand" suited him as much for its satirical attitude as its spare chords and loping melody. In the 1950s, almost anyone familiar with American popular music would have known the song and the fun it pokes at phony cowboys. (Sample lyric: "I know all the songs that the cowboys know / 'Bout the big corral where the doggies go / 'Cause I learned them all on the radio / Yippie-i-o-ki-ay"). This posture is wittily conveyed by Shelly Manne's introductory stick work. But Rollins was after more than fun and games. He also wanted to record an album with just bass and drums, no piano, guitar, or secondary wind instrument—as in Gerry Mulligan's piano-less quartet—to state the harmonies. This was a rather avant-garde gesture, which the Western theme helped make accessible, as did Rollins's lucid command of thematic variation: no matter how far out he goes, the listener is always aware that he's elaborating on "I'm an Old Cowhand." Manne, a major force in West Coast jazz who later operated the jazz club Shelly's Manne-Hole, and Ray Brown, the influential bass virtuoso associated with the Oscar Peterson Trio, were ideal companions for Rollins's loose-limbed improvisation, a style known as strolling. Wherever he goes, they are on his heels. Note his changeable timbre—for example, the roundhouse low notes at 00:39–00:49, and the stateliness of his sound at 1:16–1:24, which matches the swagger of his melodic phrases. Note the sheer authority of his swing.

🎧 i'm an old cowhand (from the rio grande)

SONNY ROLLINS
Sonny Rollins, tenor saxophone; Shelly Manne, drums; Ray Brown, bass

- Label: *Way Out West*, Contemporary
- Date: 1957
- Style: hard bop
- Form: 18-bar popular song, **A** (8) **B** (6) **C** (4)

What to listen for:
- piano-less trio format
- Rollins's sly improvisation, switching from bebop to melodic paraphrase
- his humorous use of popular song

0:00	Manne kicks off a sly, funky version of a cowboy groove, capped by a distinctive **syncopation** on the bass drum.

CHORUS 1

0:11   **A**   Beginning with a **break**, Rollins plays the opening melody ("I'm an old cowhand, from the Rio Grande"). Each phrase is answered by an improvisation on bass from Brown.

0:22   **B**   A quick **press-roll** signals the switch by the drums and bass to a straightforward swing feeling.

0:31   **C**   For the cowboy nonsense syllables ("Yippie-i-o-ki-ay"), the groove returns to the opening.

CHORUS 2

0:37   **A**   Rollins repeats the melody, augmented by syncopation and unexpected lower notes. Brown provides looser, more comical answers.

0:49   **B**

0:58   **C**

CHORUS 3

1:03   **A**   With a few squeaks to show for his effort, Rollins improvises the opening section of the song in bebop style.

1:15   **B**   He offers a pair of matched phrases to substitute for the repeating melody of the original song.

1:24   **C**

CHORUS 4

1:30   **A**   Rollins's second chorus begins with a forceful statement.

1:41   **B**   He plays another pair of matched phrases; the second has a slight but significant difference.

1:50   **C**   He ends the chorus with a *cadence phrase*, followed by a paraphrase of the melody.

CHORUS 5

1:56   **A**

2:01   Rollins's melodic phrase, which briefly clashes with the swing groove, is followed by a smooth bebop passage.

2:08   **B**   He offers another pair of phrases, each culminating in a semi-comic climax. (The first high note is squeaked, the other muffed.)

2:16   **C**   He repeats the *cadence phrase* from chorus 4.

CHORUS 6

2:22   **A**   Rollins's next chorus begins at a higher pitch level before descending to low notes.

2:34   **B**   His paraphrase of the melody falls in the cracks between the beats.

2:42   **C**   A bluesy shrug is followed by a return of the *cadence phrase*.

CHORUS 7

2:49   **A**   After Rollins ends his solo inconclusively, Brown begins his solo on bass. Underneath him, Manne plays the ride-cymbal pattern, augmented with a steady **backbeat** and occasional snare-drum accents.

3:00   **B**

3:08   **C**   Brown rounds off his chorus with a distinctly bluesy phrase.

CHORUS 8

3:13   **A**   Rollins plays a single note, as if he were about to start playing. Brown begins with a walking bass, but after the saxophone remains silent, he returns to his solo.

3:24   **B**   Brown plays a high note, slightly out of tune, but forces it to fit his solo by turning it into a **chromatic** figure.

3:33   **C**   Again, Brown's solo ends with a firm conclusion.

CHORUS 9

3:40   **A**   Manne's solo begins with a series of short, disconnected rhythmic gestures.

3:50   **B**   He adds **triplet** rhythms.

3:59   **C**   The closing section is rhythmically intricate, mixing snare-drum strokes with the ride cymbal.

CHORUS 10

4:04	A	Over a steady snare-drum passage, Manne intermingles hard drum strokes with the pitched sound of two tom-toms.
4:13		Gradually, he returns to the more disjointed style of the solo's opening.
4:15	B	
4:23	C	He emphatically ends his solo with a moment's silence.

CHORUS 11

4:29	A	As Manne returns to the opening cowboy groove, Rollins and Brown humorously exchange phrases.
4:40	B	Rollins returns to the original melody, enthusiastically dramatizing the tune's repeated notes.
4:48	C	
4:53		After a pause, he returns to his bebop-style improvisation.

CODA

4:54		Rollins and Brown continue their musical conversation.
4:59		Suddenly Rollins takes his melody up a **half step**; Brown hears it and immediately adjusts. This harmonic substitution, which resolves downward two measures later, becomes the basis for the coda.
5:10		Rollins switches to **double-time**.
5:15		After a pause, he returns to his original manner, the 16th notes now absorbed into decorative phrases.
5:29		Rollins begins dissolving the piece by stuttering on a single note. Brown drops out, leaving Manne and Rollins to end the tune.

■ WES MONTGOMERY (1923–1968)

The arrival of Charlie Christian in the late 1930s opened the floodgates to electric guitarists who played in a linear style, adapting the single-line phrasing of horn players. Several combined linear solos with chords, voicing them in ways unique to the six-string configuration of the guitar. Those who achieved prominence in the 1950s include Barney Kessel, Tal Farlow, Jim Hall, and Kenny Burrell—each took Christian's example and developed a distinctive style of his own. None, however, had the impact of Wes Montgomery, who radically altered the instrument's sound with his innovative approach to chordal harmonies.

Born in Indianapolis, Montgomery was twenty and married when he bought an electric guitar and amplifier, and began spending hours at night after work teaching himself to play. When his wife complained that the amplifier was too loud, he dispensed with the pick and used his thumb, achieving unparalleled mastery with this technique as well as a remarkably mellow tone. Montgomery elaborated on that dulcet sound by playing in octaves. From octaves, he moved on to full and intricate chords, manipulating them with the same speed and dexterity of his single-line improvisations, continuing to pluck and strum with his thumb. Soon he developed a signature approach to soloing: after a theme statement, he would play choruses of single-line phrases, followed by choruses of more rhythmically intense octaves, climaxing with hard-riffing chords. In 1948, he went on tour with Lionel Hampton's big band.

Montgomery was thirty-four when alto saxophonist Cannonball Adderley heard him and alerted his record label to this major undiscovered talent. From the moment Montgomery arrived in New York, the critical reception

▶ **octave** two notes with the same letter name, an eighth apart

Wes Montgomery set a new standard for jazz guitar and innovated a new style of soloing, combining single-note phrases, octaves, and rhythmic chords, and became a 1960s pop star in the bargain.

was highly favorable; guitarists gawked at his impossibly fast thumb, and he came to be regarded as a musician's musician. Then in the early 1960s, the guitar moved to the center of America's musical consciousness, and Montgomery's alluring octaves were seen as having great commercial potential. As he switched affiliations from a jazz label to a pop label, in 1967, he emerged as a mainstream recording star, performing with large studio ensembles in easy-listening arrangements of pop songs that featured his octaves and minimized improvisation. Those records failed to reflect the stimulating jazz he continued to play in live performance, but firmly established him as one of the best-selling musicians of his time.

Sadly, Montgomery did not have long to enjoy his skyrocketing success. The 1965 album *Goin' out of My Head* received a Grammy Award, and his more commercial debut on the pop label A&M, *A Day in the Life*, was cited as the best-selling jazz album of 1967. From that point on, his record producers demanded he hew to the proven formula: familiar tunes played with octaves, backed by a large, easy-listening ensemble, with few improvised solos to confuse the target audience. In 1968, he died suddenly of a heart attack, at forty-three.

Montgomery's career was interpreted by many as a jazz parable, with the moral being: for every album an artist does for the company, he ought to insist on doing one for himself. In concert, Montgomery continued to perform brilliantly, rarely playing the pop tunes that made him famous and never touring with large ensembles. Yet none of that work was formally documented after 1965. Indeed, the impact of his popular success was so pervasive that after his death, Verve released tracks by his quartet with an overdubbed string ensemble to simulate the pop recordings. Decades later, those magnificent tracks were released as Montgomery (and a first-class rhythm section including pianist Wynton Kelly) performed them, to much acclaim. By then, virtually every jazz guitarist had studied and many had mastered his octaves and harmonies.

ADDITIONAL LISTENING	
Claude Thornhill	"Donna Lee" (1947)
Miles Davis	"Boplicity" (1949)
Stan Kenton	"City of Glass" (1951)
Gerry Mulligan	"My Funny Valentine" (1953), "Festive Minor" (1959)
Modern Jazz Quartet	"All the Things You Are" (1952), "Django" (1954)
John Lewis and the Modern Jazz Quartet	"England's Carol (God Rest Ye Merry Gentlemen)" (1960)
Dave Brubeck	"Blue Rondo à la Turk," "Take Five" (both 1959)
Art Blakey	"Moanin'" (1958)
Horace Silver	"The Preacher" (1955), "Señor Blues" (1956)

⊣ ADDITIONAL LISTENING ⊢	
Max Roach / Clifford Brown Quintet	"Joy Spring," "Delilah" (both 1954)
Sonny Rollins	"St. Thomas," "Blue Seven" (both 1956)
Wes Montgomery	"Four on Six," "Airegin" (both 1960), "Twisted Blues" (1965)
Lennie Tristano	"Subconscious-Lee," "Wow" (both 1949), "Requiem" (1955)
Tadd Dameron	"Lady Bird" (1948)

ONLINE MULTIMEDIA RESOURCES AND REVIEW MATERIALS

Author Insight Videos

Gary Giddins explains how "jazz" came to be an umbrella term that signified different styles in the 1950s; describes how jazz musicians, who have always drawn on classical music, began to do this more consciously in the 1950s; and discusses Sonny Rollins's innovations as a soloist.

Interactive Listening Guides

Miles Davis, "Venus de Milo"
Modern Jazz Quartet, "Vendome"
Horace Silver, "Song for My Father"
Clifford Brown, "A Night in Tunisia"
Sonny Rollins, "I'm an Old Cowhand"

Jazz Concepts (audio and/or video demonstrations of terms covered here)

backbeat	dominant	polyrhythm
block chords	half, whole steps	riff
break	legato	syncopation
cadenza	modulation	transposition
chromatic scale	octave	tremolo
countermelody	pedal point	triad
dissonance	polyphonic	triplets

- For quick reference, review the **Chapter Overview** and **Chapter Outline**.

- Take the online **Chapter** and **Listening Quizzes**.

- Use the online **Glossary** and **Flashcards** to review important terms.

13

THELONIOUS MONK
thelonious

THELONIOUS MONK
rhythm-a-ning

CHARLES MINGUS
boogie stop shuffle

GIL EVANS
king porter stomp

GEORGE RUSSELL
concerto for billy the kid

JAZZ COMPOSITION IN THE 1950s

Composition is not easily defined in music driven by improvisation. Before the advent of records, formal composition was something committed to a written score. From the twentieth century on, records often supplanted or eliminated the need for scores, making the idea of improvisation-as-lasting-music possible. Coleman Hawkins's "Body and Soul" has been published as a score, but the truest representation of the work must be his recording, which alone documents such essential components as his timbre and rhythmic pulse. Simply by calling it Coleman Hawkins's "Body and Soul," we contest the traditional attribution of composition, since the performance is based on a published melody by John Green. Indeed, international copyright laws fail to acknowledge the improviser's contribution at all: the "mechanical" (or composer) royalties that accrue from sales of the record are divided between the song's composer, lyricist, and publisher. Hawkins does not participate in the profits, even though virtually every melodic phrase he plays after the first two bars is his own invention.

Hawkins was trained to do something classical composers don't do: compose durable music spontaneously. His solo on "Body and Soul" became so renowned that it was subsequently transcribed and arranged for ensembles to perform. But that's one of several exceptions that prove the rule, which may be stated as follows: A composition is a musical work that may be played by any number of musicians and bands while

Thelonious Monk, a powerful force at the jam sessions that fed the birth of modern jazz, works on a score at Minton's Playhouse in Harlem, 1948.

remaining basically unchanged; an improvisation, though it may prove as durable and adaptable as a composition, exists first and foremost as a particular performance.

In the wake of bebop, the nature of jazz composition changed. In addition to borrowing from classical music, popular music, and their contemporaries in jazz, composers began reinvestigating the jazz past, which by now had its own tradition of compositional systems and procedures. They combined modern jazz with such techniques as polyphony, stride piano, short breaks, and cadenzas, as well as standard jazz and pop themes. In this period, jazz began to produce full-time composers who did not necessarily work as instrumentalists.

The four composers examined here represent four approaches to expanding the jazz canvas. Thelonious Monk worked almost exclusively with blues and song forms, rarely composing themes longer than thirty-two bars. Charles Mingus also worked with conventional forms, adding effects from gospel, ragtime, bop, classical music, and other sources, and expanding those forms into longer works. Gil Evans focused on the music of other composers, radically altering it into imaginative new pieces. George Russell introduced modalism into jazz, which spurred fresh ways of looking at harmony and the connection between improvisation and composition.

■ THELONIOUS MONK (1917–1982)

After Duke Ellington, Thelonious Monk is the most widely performed of all jazz composers. This is remarkable when you consider the differences in their output: Ellington wrote between 1,500 and 2,000 pieces, while Monk wrote around 70. Though he composed no hits and only one song ("'Round Midnight") that achieved a marginal mainstream acceptance, every jazz player knows at least a few Monk pieces: they have been adapted for swing band, Dixieland, cool jazz, hard bop, avant-garde, and classical music settings. With the addition of lyrics, they have found increasing favor with singers. Although in his early years Monk was regarded as an eccentric, difficult, and (incredibly) not very talented pianist, his music is widely loved today, even among people who have no interest in or feeling for jazz.

Born in North Carolina, Monk was four when his family moved to New York. In grade school, he began absorbing his older sister's piano lessons; when she quit, he became her teacher's favorite student. Around 1940, he was recruited by Kenny Clarke to play in the house band at Minton's Playhouse. The after-hours jam sessions and cutting contests at Minton's, where he accompanied Charlie Christian, Dizzy Gillespie, and other advanced musicians, placed him at the center of bebop's development. The dazzling Bud Powell, whom Monk mentored, admired his quirky rhythmic attack and progressive harmonies. Yet that very quirkiness as a composer and pianist—his percussive keyboard style was mocked by many critics and fans—necessitated that he work as a leader of his own band and only rarely as a sideman. His family felt that he was afflicted with bipolar disorder, an extreme form of depression, which may have been

Ridiculed as a charlatan for his unorthodox style, Thelonious Monk proved his bona fides to skeptics by recording an album of Duke Ellington tunes, backed by his partner from Minton's, drummer Kenny Clarke, in 1955.

PHOTO BY CAROLE RIEFF © CAROLE RIEFF ARCHIVE

MONK'S 71

A worklist of the seventy-one compositions attributed to Monk (some were written in collaboration with other musicians or had lyrics subsequently added) suggests the gearing up, development, pinnacle years, and slowing down of his genius. The dates denote the earliest recorded versions by Monk, not necessarily the year of composition; where a decade is given, Monk never recorded the tune.

1940s: "52nd Street Theme" (aka "The Theme"), "Harlem Is Awful Messy"

1946: "Introspection"

1947: "Humph," "In Walked Bud," "Off Minor," "'Round Midnight," "Ruby, My Dear," "Thelonious," "Well, You Needn't," "Who Knows?"

1948: "Epistrophy," "Evidence," "I Mean You," "Misterioso"

1950s: "Two Timer" (aka "Five Will Get You Ten")

1951: "Ask Me Now," "Criss Cross," "Eronel," "Four in One," "Straight, No Chaser"

1952: "Bemsha Swing," "Bye-Ya," "Hornin' In," "Let's Cool One," "Little Rootie Tootie," "Monk's Dream," "Monk's Mood," "Reflections," "Sixteen," "Skippy," "Trinkle Tinkle"

1953: "Friday the 13th," "Let's Call This," "Think of One"

1954: "Blue Monk," "Hackensack," "Locomotive," "Nutty," "We See," "Work"

1955: "Brake's Sake," "Gallop's Gallop," "Shuffle Boil"

1956: "Ba-lue Bolivar Ba-lues-are," "Brilliant Corners," "Pannonica"

1957: "Crepuscule with Nellie," "Functional," "Light Blue," "Rhythm-a-ning"

1958: "Blues Five Spot," "Coming on the Hudson"

1959: "Bluehawk," "Jackie-ing," "Played Twice," "Round Lights"

1960: "San Francisco Holiday"

1961: "Bright Mississippi"

1963: "Oska T"

1964: "Monk's Point," "North of the Sunset," "Stuffy Turkey," "Teo"

1966: "Green Chimneys"

1967: "Boo Boo's Birthday," "Ugly Beauty"

1968: "Raise Four"

1971: "Blue Sphere," "Something in Blue"

1972: "A Merrier Christmas"

---

exacerbated by his fondness for drink and amphetamines. Monk was known for his mood swings (long silences in speech and in music, staring into space) and episodes of idiosyncratic behavior: onstage dancing (he would twitchingly whirl in a circle as the other musicians soloed), frequent all-nighters, and an obsessive concentration on a few compositions.

The most important of Monk's early compositions was the ballad "'Round Midnight," which trumpet player Cootie Williams recorded in a big-band version in 1944, with Powell on piano. Williams made it his theme song, and after lyrics were added (by Bernie Hanighen), singers began to perform it. As word of Monk's unusual music spread, he found an important admirer in Alfred Lion, whose record company, Blue Note, signed him in 1947 and documented much of his most important work over the next five years. In 1955, Monk signed with a new independent label, Riverside; his third Riverside album, *Brilliant Corners*, which featured Sonny Rollins and Max Roach, was hailed as a major jazz event in 1956. The following year, he took up a historic six-month residency at the Five Spot, leading a quartet that included tenor saxophonist John Coltrane. Monk was taken up as a hero of the beats and of a generation of self-defined outlaw artists. A magnificent example of the collaboration with Coltrane was recorded at a Carnegie Hall concert for overseas broadcast by the Voice of

● **"'Round Midnight"**

● **With Coltrane**

America; it remained unknown here until 2005, when the tape was discovered in the Library of Congress and released on Blue Note.

Monk's fame steadily grew. In 1962, he was signed by Columbia Records, the country's premier record label, and two years later *Time* ran a cover story about him that cinched his standing as one of jazz's most admired musicians. Monk's quartet, with his longtime saxophonist Charlie Rouse, toured the world, finally reaping the rewards of his refusal to compromise. As he once witheringly remarked, "I say play your own way. Don't play what the public wants—you play what you want and let the public pick up on what you are doing—even if it does take them fifteen, twenty years."

Monk made his last records in 1971, and appeared in concert only a few times after that. By the middle 1970s, he had slipped into seclusion; soon he stopped speaking to anyone but his wife and a few friends. He spent his last years in the home of his longtime friend and supporter Baroness Pannonica de Königswarter, and died of a stroke in 1982. In 2006, he received a belated Pulitzer Prize in music.

Style

Monk's compositions are abstractions of the song forms that had always predominated in jazz and popular music: **A A B A** tunes and blues. In some instances, he altered standard harmonic progressions with whole-tone and bizarre substitutions, so that "Just You, Just Me" became "Evidence," "Blue Skies" became "In Walked Bud," and "Sweet Georgia Brown" became "Bright Mississippi." The particular dissonances he favored—including minor ninths, flatted fifths (tritones), and minor seconds (half steps)—had been widely regarded as mistakes until he established them as essential components in jazz harmony. Monk played minor seconds, for example (two adjacent notes on the piano), as though his finger had accidentally hit the crack between the keys, making them both ring and forcing the listener to accept that jarring sound as a routine part of his musical language. Nellie Monk, his wife, described an incident in their home life that suggests a parallel with the way Monk altered the way we hear jazz: "I used to have a phobia about pictures or anything on a wall hanging just

Monk occasionally stood and danced in jerky, circular movements while another member of his band soloed. Here he responds to his longtime tenor saxophonist Charlie Rouse, 1960s.

FRANK DRIGGS COLLECTION

a little bit crooked. Thelonious cured me. He nailed a clock to the wall at a very slight angle, just enough to make me furious. We argued about it for two hours, but he wouldn't let me change it. Finally, I got used to it. Now anything can hang at any angle, and it doesn't bother me at all."

In "Thelonious," which is chock-a-block with dissonances, there is a revealing moment about two minutes in, where he concludes an arpeggio by landing on the wrong note. He then plays the right one, and combines them so as to resolve the error, making it a viable part of the performance. (Musicians call this a "save.") A fastidious composer-improviser, Monk believed that a meaningful improvisation should flow from and develop the composed theme. Unsurprisingly, his compositions sound like his improvisations, and his improvisations often sound like his compositions—even when he didn't write the theme. For example, classical pianists have transcribed his solo interpretations of pop songs like "I Should Care" or "April in Paris," performing them as if they were Monk originals. His music has altered our perception of harmony, space, swing, and melody, all while remaining tied to the traditions from which it sprang.

🎧 "Thelonious"

A product of Monk's first session as a leader, "Thelonious" is considered his first masterpiece, a work that shuns the usual theme-and-variations format of bop and shows off his compositional ingenuity and fierce independence. In 1947, a *Billboard* reviewer called it a "controversial jazz disking worked out on a one note riff." But that repeated note, a B-flat (sometimes doubled as a B-flat octave), is a deceptively simple front for the descending chromatic chords that shadow this thirty-six-bar variant on the **A A B A** song. The **A** sections are eight bars, the bridge is ten, and the last **A** section includes a two-bar coda. This pattern demands heightened attention from musicians, who, as a matter of habit, tend to think in terms of four eight-bar sections. As John Coltrane observed, "I always had to be alert with Monk, because if you didn't keep aware all the time of what was going on, you'd suddenly feel as if you'd stepped into an empty elevator shaft." In "Thelonious," the three wind instruments are used to voice (build) the chords, and the only soloists are piano and, briefly, drums. The result is a kind of short-form piano concerto, incorporating various elements of jazz history from stride to bop.

LISTENING GUIDE 45

🎧 thelonious

THELONIOUS MONK
Idrees Sulieman, trumpet; Danny Quebec West, alto saxophone; Billy Smith, tenor saxophone; Thelonious Monk, piano; Gene Ramey, bass; Art Blakey, drums

- Label: BLP 1510
- Date: 1947
- Style: bebop, Monk-style
- Form: 36-bar popular song (**A A B A**; the bridge and the last **A** section are 10 rather than 8 bars long)

What to listen for:
- insistent repeated note, over chromatic chords
- unusual number of measures in B and last A
- Monk's unusual improvising, including stride piano in chorus 3

INTRODUCTION

0:00   Unaccompanied, Monk plays the main theme of the piece: a syncopated figure on the first note of the scale (the tonic). Pianistically, it's simple, built comfortably around an **octave**.

0:02   As Monk continues, he's joined by Blakey on cymbals. The theme ends on a **blue third**, which Monk holds out.

0:04   Blakey plays a brief solo, alternating snare drum with bass drum. In the background, we can hear Monk's voice counting off time.

CHORUS 1 (HEAD)

0:08   **A**   The entire band plays the theme: Monk's insistent, repetitive octave, supported by descending **chromatic** chords in the horns. The bass line for the **A** section remains consistent throughout the performance.

0:18   **A**

0:27   **B**   The bridge begins with a *cadence figure*, deriving its rhythm from the **A** section and promising a conclusion to its chromatic harmonies. But the harmony is *not* resolved: instead, the melody blends into a slower line that floats above ambiguous harmonies.

0:31   When the melody reaches the tonic, it's supported not by conventional harmony but by the **whole-tone scale**, which distorts our sense of tonality.

0:32   The melody slowly descends by half step.

0:37   As the melody reaches a half cadence, Monk connects the bridge to the concluding **A** section with a whole-tone scale.

0:38   **A**

0:47   The chorus ends with the *cadence figure* heard at the opening of the bridge, this time resolving to the tonic in the second bar.

CHORUS 2

0:49   **A**   Monk begins his solo with simple melodic fragments, all derived from his opening octave.

0:58   **A**   Suddenly, responding to the harmonies implied by the chromatic bass line, he shifts to a bebop-style improvised line.

1:07   **B**   Monk begins the bridge by paraphrasing its melody.

1:12   With a few dissonant notes and unexpected silences, he complicates his connection to the underlying harmony.

1:17   He finally returns to the tonic octave—a full bar early.

1:19   **A**   Monk plays a syncopated pattern with the tonic octave in the highest register of the piano, accompanied by only the bass and drums.

1:28   At the end of the chorus, he returns to the middle of the piano to play the *cadence figure*.

CHORUS 3

1:30   **A**   Sounding uncannily like a ragtime piano player, Monk begins playing in **stride** style, firmly doubling the bass line.

1:39   **A**   With his left hand shifting restlessly between chromatic chords, his right hand remains firmly rooted in the tonic.

1:48   **B**   Monk starts the bridge by once again paraphrasing its melody.

1:52   He "misses" a note by a half step, corrects it, and returns to a literal statement of the melody.

2:00   **A**

2:02   A new three-note motive borrows its rhythm from the bebop standard "Salt Peanuts."

2:09   Monk plays the *cadence figure*, connecting it seamlessly to the beginning of the next chorus.

CHORUS 4

2:11   **A**   Once again, the chorus begins with an unaccompanied statement of the main theme.

2:16   Fastening onto a short chromatic **triplet**, Monk pulls it down the length of the piano.

2:20   **A**   He plays a long, involved melodic line based on the chromatic harmony.

2:29	**B**	The bridge begins in the upper octave; Monk plays it delicately.
2:41	**A**	The band returns with a full statement of the theme.
CODA		
2:50		The band plays the *cadence figure*, stopping on the next-to-last chord. While the horns hold out the unresolved harmony, Monk plays a lengthy descending whole-tone scale.
2:56		He ends his improvisation with a striking high note.
2:58		A three-note stroke from the drummer closes the performance.

🎧 "Rhythm-a-ning"

One of Monk's best-known pieces, "Rhythm-a-ning" has a long history, which testifies to his gift for collating bits of music and renewing them in his own way. The **A A B A** tune is based on the chord changes of "I Got Rhythm," but the primary eight-bar melody draws on two big-band recordings of the 1930s: Duke Ellington's "Ducky Wucky" (1932) for two measures, and Mary Lou Williams's "Walkin' and Swingin'" for four. Williams's lick was later picked up by Charlie Christian and other musicians, but only Monk turned it into a postbop classic, in part by connecting it seamlessly to the Ellington figure and adding a bridge of modern harmonies.

Although he wrote the piece much earlier, Monk did not record "Rhythm-a-ning" until 1957, at which point it became a regular part of his repertory. An especially fine version dates from five years later, the period when he first signed with Columbia Records. Tenor saxophonist Charlie Rouse was Monk's most consistent partner; he joined the quartet in 1959 and stayed for eleven years. His soft, sandy sound suggests an extraordinary affinity with Monk's piano, and his quick-witted responses provide countless moments of give and take with Monk's comping. This performance is taken at a medium up-tempo, flowing smoothly through the introduction, theme, two choruses by Rouse, two choruses by Monk, theme, and coda. But close listening discloses how much each musician relies on Monk's cues and the demands of the piece. The drummer states the rhythm but also responds to rhythmic ideas introduced on piano. Rouse improvises variations on the theme, but also echoes melodic suggestions played by Monk. The bassist enables the others with his rock-solid harmonic and rhythmic foundation.

Charlie Rouse

LISTENING GUIDE 46

🎧 rhythm-a-ning

THELONIOUS MONK
Charlie Rouse, tenor saxophone; Thelonious Monk, piano; John Ore, bass; Frankie Dunlop, drums

- Label: Columbia CL2038
- Date: 1962
- Style: bebop, Monk-style
- Form: 32-bar popular song (**A A B A**)

What to listen for:
- Monk's comping and Rouse's responses
- Monk's dissonant minor seconds (half steps) and right-hand ostinato
- drum's offbeat accents

INTRODUCTION

0:00   Monk plays the opening **riff** on solo piano. At various points, he plays several adjacent keys (**minor seconds**, or **half steps**) simultaneously—sometimes deliberately (as in the underlying harmony) but other times apparently from "sloppy" technique.

0:05   The second part of the tune is a repeated three-note riff, its last note falling in unexpected places and given extra weight by Monk, who doubles it in his left hand.

CHORUS 1 (HEAD)

0:09   **A**   With a cymbal crash, the entire band enters. Rouse (tenor saxophone) and Ore (bass) join the piano on the melody, with the drums reinforcing its syncopations.

0:19   **A**

0:28   **B**   Over the chord progression to "I Got Rhythm," Monk continues the rhythm of the three-note riff, accenting the last note of each phrase.

0:36   A rising scale ends with a startling, splatted **dissonance**.

0:37   **A**

CHORUS 2

0:47   **A**   The first solo, by Rouse, is introduced by Monk's **comping**. Monk plays a dissonant chord that lands squarely on the opening beat of the chorus, then falls silent. Rouse paraphrases the theme's melody, accompanied by a crisp **backbeat** in the drums. This pattern (a chord on the **downbeat**, followed by four measures of silence) continues throughout the **A** sections of this chorus.

0:56   **A**   Rouse moves away from the melody toward bebop-style lines. The drums similarly drift from the backbeat into more interactive rhythms.

1:05   **B**

1:10   Monk's chords become more frequent, falling every other beat.

1:15   **A**   Monk returns to his spare comping.

CHORUS 3

1:24   **A**   Monk signals a new chorus, still Rouse's, by placidly repeating a single chord until stopping altogether.

1:33   **A**   Rouse plays a phrase derived from the theme, then clashes with the bass line by repeating it a half step higher.

1:43   **B**   Monk begins a new pattern of accompaniment, and Rouse improvises in response.

1:52   **A**   Monk returns to his favorite chord.

CHORUS 4

2:01   **A**   Monk begins his solo by borrowing a common harmonic pattern from bebop. He shifts to a distant chord and returns by a series of substitute chords to the tonic four bars later. (Since the bass immediately responds to Monk's chords, we can assume that this substitution was planned.)

2:10   **A**   Monk repeats his harmonic substitution, improvising a more dissonant line on top.

2:19   **B**   On the bridge, he plays dissonant **whole-tone** fragments in his right hand against loud single notes in his left hand. The drums disorient us by playing consistently on the offbeat.

2:29   **A**   Monk returns to the theme, occasionally altered by dissonant half-step splats and left-hand notes.

2:34   The last phrase reaches for a dissonant high note—the tritone, or **flatted fifth**.

CHORUS 5

2:38   **A**   Playing entirely in the upper register of the piano, Monk builds a line that consistently accents the dissonant flatted fifth.

2:47   **A**   He turns the flatted-fifth pattern into an **ostinato** in the right hand. The only accompaniment is the drum's accents and an occasional open fifth in the left hand.

2:56   **B**   Infusing his harmonies with the whole-tone scale, Monk transforms the "I Got Rhythm" progression into a series of unsettling sounds.

3:05   **A**   He turns the opening theme into a descending scale that interacts with the improvised drum part.

CHORUS 6 (HEAD)

3:14	**A**	The band returns to repeat the head.
3:21		Monk responds to the theme with a dissonant **chord cluster** (with closely spaced notes), emphasizing the flatted fifth.
3:23	**A**	
3:31	**B**	The bridge begins an octave lower than in the beginning.
3:40	**A**	

CODA

3:48		Over the last sustained piano chord, Monk repeats a jarringly dissonant minor ninth.

■ CHARLES MINGUS (1922–1979)

Charles Mingus was a bigger-than-life figure who made an indelible mark in many areas of jazz. As a bassist, he was among the most accomplished virtuosos of his time. As a composer, he expanded the variety and scope of American music, assimilating influences as far ranging as the sanctified church, New Orleans polyphony, swing, bop, Romantic classical music, and modern classical music. As a spokesman, he made jazz relevant to the civil rights era. As a memoirist, he brought new insights into the tribulations of African American artists trying to surmount the constrictions of prejudice.

Charles Mingus wrote grand tone poems, suites, jazz standards, parodies, and threnodies while leading his cutting-edge Jazz Workshop and maintaining his stature as one of the greatest bass players of all time. From the 1960s.

Born in Nogales, Arizona, Mingus was only three months old when his family moved to Watts, an area of Los Angeles with a large population of blacks and Mexican Americans. The family belonged to the African Methodist Episcopal Church, where Charles heard the gospel music that had a lasting influence on him. He played piano, trombone, and cello before taking up the bass in high school, studying with the excellent jazz bassist Red Callender and with Callender's teacher, Herman Rheinschagen, formerly of the New York Philharmonic. In later years, Mingus recalled being advised to switch from cello to bass because as a black man he could not succeed in classical music and would find work only if he learned to "slap that bass, Charlie!"

Mingus worked in diverse ensembles, including big bands led by Louis Armstrong and Lionel Hampton; but not until 1950, when he came to New York with the Red Norvo Trio, did he receive national attention. His virtuosity made him a mainstay of the city's best musicians, resulting in important engagements with Charlie Parker, Bud Powell, Stan Getz, Miles Davis, and the Duke Ellington Orchestra, among others.

In 1956, Mingus signed with Atlantic Records and created his breakthrough album, *Pithecanthropus Erectus*, which demonstrated how explosive yet lyrical his music could be. The following year, he completed his more significant second Atlantic album, *The Clown*, which placed him in the forefront of advanced jazz thinkers. This album, played by a quintet he called the Charles Mingus Jazz Workshop, combined rousing passions with an almost nostalgic serenity, and demonstrated to anyone in doubt that Mingus might be the finest bass player alive, in or out of jazz. It also proved that he could produce a compelling work with little more than a fragment of composed music. The lead-off selection, "Haitian Fight Song," opens with a thunderous bass cadenza—"bass slapping" taken to a new and stirring level. The written material consists of two riffs amounting to about eight bars, plus a twelve-bar blues format for the solos.

The Clown

Jazz Workshop

VOICES

For Mingus, Duke Ellington was "the Hero," the uncontested model for the jazz bandleader as composer. In his youth, Mingus spent a brief time in the band—until he had a falling out with trombonist Juan Tizol, who allegedly brandished a knife in Mingus's direciton as the band started to play "Take the 'A' Train." In his autobiography, Mingus finishes the story in Ellington's own words:

> "Now, Charles," he says, looking amused, putting Cartier links into the cuffs of his beautiful handmade shirt, "you could have forewarned me—you left me out of the act entirely! At least you could have let me cue in a few chords as you ran through that Nijinsky routine. . . . I must say I never saw a large man so agile—I never saw *anybody* make such tremendous leaps! The gambado over the piano carrying your bass was colossal. When you exited after that I thought, 'That man's really afraid of Juan's knife and at the speed he's going he's probably home in bed by now.' But no, back you came through the same door with your bass still intact. For a moment I was hopeful you'd decided to sit down and play but instead you slashed Juan's chair in two with a fire axe! Really, Charles, that's destructive. Everybody knows Juan has a knife, but nobody ever took it seriously—he likes to pull it out and show it to people, you understand. So I'm afraid, Charles—I never fire anybody—you'll have to quit my band. I don't need any new problems. Juan's an old problem, I can cope with that, but you seem to have a whole bag of new tricks. I must ask you to be kind enough to give me your notice, Mingus." The charming way he says it, it's like he's paying you a compliment. Feeling honored, you shake hands and resign.

Mingus became increasingly notorious for outspoken comments on and off the bandstand. One piece, "Gunslinging Bird" (also known as "If Charlie Parker Was a Gunslinger, There'd Be a Whole Lot of Dead Copycats"), expressed his loathing for musicians who played clichés or failed to find original, personal ways of measuring up to his music. During public performances, he would occasionally stop a piece to berate a musician and then begin again. Mingus's comments turned political after 1957, when President Eisenhower reluctantly sent federal troops to force Arkansas governor Orville Faubus to integrate Little Rock's Central High School. In 1959, Mingus recorded "Fables of Faubus," a piece that satirizes Faubus with its whimsically satiric theme. Columbia Records, however, refused to let him sing his lyric, which he recorded for a smaller label (Candid) the following year, proclaiming Faubus "ridiculous" and "a fool." As the civil rights era heated up, other jazz musicians followed Mingus's example of speaking out through their music.

"Fables of Faubus"

Mingus frequently rewrote pieces, revising scores within minutes of performing and recording them. From the 1970s.

For all his insistence on originality, Mingus remained respectful of jazz traditions. He never tired of citing as his core inspirations Ellington, Tatum, Parker, and the church, though his music took in far more than that. Mingus was the first composer of his generation to pay indelible tributes to great figures of the past, including Lester Young, the subject of his famous threnody (perhaps the best known of his tunes) "Goodbye Pork Pie Hat," and Jelly Roll Morton, in the affectionate parody "Jelly Roll."

As the Jazz Workshop developed, Mingus retreated from writing out his ideas in favor of a more flexible form of collaboration with his musicians. This policy worked for shorter pieces, but caused problems as he continued to compose exceedingly long orchestral works that required an organizational discipline he often lacked. In a famous 1962 debacle, he held a concert at New York's Town Hall for which he was so unprepared that the musicians were seen correcting their scores as the curtains parted. Mingus began hiring arrangers and copyists to help organize his pieces; however many hands were involved, though, the end product always sounded like unadulterated Mingus.

Mingus's large body of work (some 300 compositions) spans cool jazz and hard bop while combining daunting experimentalism with visceral pleasure. Some of his music, with its heady, polyphonic textures, gloomy dissonances, and intimations of outright terror, is as difficult for musicians to master as it is for listeners to understand. Mingus died in 1979 at fifty-six, from the effects of amyotrophic lateral sclerosis (Lou Gehrig's disease). He composed and conducted his final works from a wheelchair.

🎧 "Boogie Stop Shuffle"

Mingus generates express-train momentum with "Boogie Stop Shuffle," a twelve-bar blues that builds vibrantly on the eight-to-the-bar rhythms of boogie-woogie. Although he has only seven instruments at his disposal, he achieves a staggering variety of textures. The soloists express themselves freely, yet the main impression is of a tightly organized work in which the improvisations serve to elaborate on the composer's vision. The head alone requires the first five choruses, with its ostinato (repeated melody), staccato chords, unison moaning, three-note riff, and bop variation punctuated first by cymbals (fourth chorus) and then by piano (fifth chorus). The expeditious tempo means that each of the eighteen choruses is played in about eleven seconds.

All the musicians heard here were important figures in the Jazz Workshop, especially Dannie Richmond, formerly a rhythm and blues tenor saxophonist who switched to drums under Mingus's tutelage and became his second in command. Pianist Horace Parlan developed a powerful left-hand style to compensate for the fact that his right hand was partly paralyzed by polio. The key soloist here, Booker Ervin, was one of the most recognizable tenor saxophonists of his generation, known for his huge sound and relentless energy. This is the original recording of "Boogie Stop Shuffle" as edited by Mingus for the Columbia album *Mingus Ah Um.* After his death, Columbia reissued the album with the cuts restored. In some cases, such restorations are welcome. In this instance, Mingus knew what he was doing: increasing the excitement of the performance by cutting inessential passages and enabling the tenor saxophone to make an especially dramatic entrance. Incidentally, fans of the Spider-Man movies may experience déjà vu: the theme song is suspiciously similar to "Boogie Stop Shuffle."

🎧 boogie stop shuffle (edited version)

LISTENING GUIDE 47

CHARLES MINGUS

Willie Dennis, trombone; John Handy, alto saxophone; Shafi Hadi, Booker Ervin, tenor saxophones; Horace Parlan, piano; Charles Mingus, bass; Dannie Richmond, drums

- Label: Columbia CL1370
- Date: 1959
- Style: experimental hard bop
- Form: 12-bar blues

What to listen for:
- ostinato in 12-bar blues
- shifts between boogie-woogie and bebop grooves
- solos by Ervin, Parlan, and Richmond

CHORUS 1

0:00   The piece opens with an **ostinato riff** played by the tenor saxophones, piano, and bass, in a rhythm reminiscent of a **boogie-woogie** left hand. As the blues harmony changes, the riff moves in **sequence**.

CHORUS 2

0:11   Parlan (piano) and Mingus (bass) continue the ostinato. Above it, the horns (three saxophones and trombone) mark the end of the ostinato's phrases with sharp, **dissonant** chords. These chords are extended, containing major triads that clash with the prevailing minor tonality.

0:19   By controlling their volume and bending pitches, the saxophones manage to match their sound to that of the trombone with a plunger mute.

CHORUS 3

0:22   The phrase played by the horns spills over into the next chorus. Each line now begins with a crisp, three-note riff on the same chords.

CHORUS 4

0:34   Suddenly the horns switch to a bebop-style line, played in unison. The bass ostinato continues underneath.

CHORUS 5

0:45   As the horns repeat the same line, the groove changes to a more standard bebop feeling: Mingus switches to a more conventional **walking-bass** line, while Parlan begins to **comp**.

CHORUS 6

0:55   A barely audible shift marks the spot where Mingus edited out the first two choruses of Ervin's tenor saxophone solo. What was originally his third chorus begins dramatically with a series of upward rips, supported by **block-chord** riffs by the saxophones and trombone.

CHORUS 7

1:07   Ervin uses **false fingering** while the background horns continue their riffs.

CHORUS 8

1:18   The horns and the bass return to the riff. Above them, Parlan oscillates between three piano chords.

CHORUS 9

1:29   In the upper register, Parlan plays a short, bluesy phrase, its endless repetitions forming a **cross-rhythm** against the background riff.

CHORUS 10

1:40   The groove switches once again, with the bass moving to a walking pattern. Parlan begins to improvise.

1:48   Toward the end of the chorus, Parlan lands on a harsh, bluesy dissonance.

CHORUS 11

1:52   Parlan continues on the same chord, effectively blurring the boundary between the two choruses.

CHORUS 12

2:03   Another bit of editing eliminates five choruses from the original. The ostinato returns in the bass, accompanied by a slow, mournful **countermelody** by the alto saxophone. Richmond on drums, preparing for a solo, plays more aggressively.

CHORUS 13

2:14   Richmond takes a solo. The first phrase fits neatly over the first four bars of blues form.

CHORUS 14

2:25   Beginning of chorus.

2:28   Richmond plays a phrase that alternates between the snare drum and the tom-toms.

CHORUS 15

2:35   The ostinato bass line returns, supported by the horn chords from chorus 2.

CHORUS 16

2:47   A repeat of chorus 3.

CHORUS 17

2:58   A repeat of chorus 4.

CHORUS 18

3:09   A repeat of chorus 5.

CODA

3:18   As the horns sustain their last chord, the rhythm comes to a halt.
The sound of the chord pulsates as individual horns change their volume.

3:21   The alto saxophone adds an anguished squeal. The other horns join in, creating polyphonic chaos.

3:28   Inspired by the moment, Richmond begins an impromptu free-rhythm drum solo.

3:36   With a final cymbal crash, the tune comes to an end.

■ GIL EVANS (1912–1988)

Gil Evans occupies a unique place in jazz: he composed several memorable pieces ("La Nevada" and "Flute Song" among them), but he was primarily an arranger who, in Gunther Schuller's words, "elevated arranging virtually to the art of composition." He achieved national recognition in 1957 when he reunited with Miles Davis for the groundbreaking album *Miles Ahead*, where he crafted a series of trumpet concertos that emphasized the power and expressiveness of Davis's playing. He also wrote transitional interludes between selections, replacing the usual silences between tracks—a technique that remained unexplored until the Beatles did the same thing a decade later in *Sgt. Pepper's Lonely Hearts Club Band*.

Miles Ahead established Evans as a recording artist in his own right, piloting his albums with hand-picked ensembles. His choice of material ranged widely—from operetta to folk-blues to mainstream pop—but the majority of tunes were drawn directly from jazz. Evans's reinventions of classic jazz pieces stimulated a revival of interest in jazz history. His music was characterized by a generous use of counterpoint, sonorous slow-moving chords, and a sound palette that combined very low instruments with very high ones. For Evans, a melody was a skeleton to be dressed from the ground up in his own harmonies, countermelodies, timbres, and rhythms. The same might be said of most good arrangers, but few performed this task with his imagination or matched his ability to phrase passages so that they simulated the spontaneity of a good improvisation. As for his transformations of contemporary music, John Lewis spoke for many when he said that

VOICES

Despite their obvious differences in age, race, and experience, Miles Davis and Gil Evans formed a deep and long-lasting partnership. In his autobiography, Davis recalled his first stunned impressions of this lanky outsider:

When I first met him, he used to come to listen to Bird when I was in the band. He'd come in with a whole bag of "horseradishes"—that's what we used to call radishes—that he'd be eating with salt. Here was this tall, thin, white guy from Canada who was hipper than hip. I mean, I didn't know *any* white people like him.

Evans's version of "Django" taught him things about his own composition he had not previously realized.

Evans is best known for his use of the concerto form. In addition to Davis, he built works around soprano saxophonist Steve Lacy, mellophonist Don Elliott, trumpeter Johnny Coles, and guitarist Kenny Burrell, among others. In 1958, he adapted classic jazz themes for an album, *New Bottle, Old Wine*, featuring Julian "Cannonball" Adderley (1928–1975), an alto saxophonist who had been acclaimed as "the new Bird" shortly after moving to New York in 1955. The instrumentation is pure Evans, favoring nine brasses (trumpets, trombones, bass trombone, French horn, and tuba). Other than Adderley, he uses only two woodwind players, and assigns them atypical jazz instruments: flute, piccolo, and bass clarinet.

Cannonball Adderley

By 1970, Evans had begun to jettison the music that had made him famous, and, like Miles Davis, with whom he maintained a close friendship, added percussion instruments to his rhythm section and embraced a free-spirited fusion of jazz and rock. His 1969 album *Gil Evans*, though little noted at the time, was a major statement in that direction, preceding Davis's heralded *Bitches Brew*. A planned collaboration with Jimi Hendrix was halted by Hendrix's death; instead, Evans recorded orchestral versions of the rock guitarist's music—"Up from the Skies" is a superior example. By the 1970s and 1980s, having created an orchestra as steadfast as Ellington's, he routinely extended and revised pieces on the bandstand with physical gestures, piano chords, and vocal commands. Until his death in 1988, Evans continued to lead his band while also writing film scores, mentoring young composers, and working with rock stars like Sting.

Arranger Gil Evans (foreground) and trumpet player Miles Davis enjoyed one of the most fruitful partnerships in jazz. Here they record a radical rethinking of Gershwin's opera *Porgy and Bess*, New York, 1958.

© VERNON L. SMITH SR.

🎧 "King Porter Stomp"

Other than W. C. Handy's "St. Louis Blues," Jelly Roll Morton's 1923 piano piece "King Porter Stomp" was the oldest work on *New Bottle, Old Wine*. (In fact, it may have been older than Handy's tune, if we can believe Morton's claim that he composed it as a teenager.) In 1958, the title would still have been familiar to jazz fans because of the Fletcher Henderson arrangement that Benny Goodman turned into a 1935 hit. But while Henderson's arrangement employed only one strain of Morton's piece, Evans returned to the 1923 original and adapted all four strains, including Morton's tricky upbeat syncopations in the **A** strain, which did not readily fit in with the Swing Era. Evans makes it swing harder than ever even as he transforms Morton's piece with dissonant harmonies and slashing bop-influenced phrases. The interaction between Adderley's improvisations and the written ensemble passages recalls the give-and-take perfected by Ellington in pieces like "In a Mellotone." Whether the ensemble initiates or responds in its exchanges with Adderley, it engenders the illusion of unstoppable energy.

🎧 king porter stomp

GIL EVANS

John Coles, Louis Mucci, Ernie Royal, trumpets; Joe Bennett, Frank Rehak, Tom Mitchell, trombones; Julius Watkins, French horn; Harvey Philips, tuba; Cannonball Adderley, alto saxophone; Jerry Sanfino, reeds; Gil Evans, piano; Chuck Wayne, guitar; Paul Chambers, bass; Art Blakey, drums

- Label: World Pacific WP1246
- Date: 1958
- Style: modernist big band
- Form: march/ragtime

What to listen for:

- Adderley's improvisation and the ensemble's response
- Evans's bold rhythms and inventive horn *soli*
- arpeggiated theme in strain B, Jelly Roll Morton's theme in strain D

INTRODUCTION

0:00   Blakey (drums) plays a vigorous roll on the tom-toms, keeping the **backbeat** on the high-hat cymbal.

0:06   By pressing on the heads, he produces a subtle descent in pitch.

0:07   The horns enter unaccompanied on sustained chords. Over this background, Adderley (on alto saxophone) improvises.

STRAIN A

0:15   Adderley begins to solo over the rhythm section, while the low brass (trombones, tuba, horn) play short chords on the fourth beat of each measure.

0:26   All the horns join in on an extended *soli*, each horn occupying its own melody part, ending in a **tritone**-colored cadence.

STRAIN A

0:30   Adderley's solo continues, accompanied by lower brass chords.

0:35   The solo is interrupted by a line played by the trumpet and trombones.

0:39   Adderley reenters, accompanied only by the bass and drums.

STRAIN B

0:45   The new strain, starting in the minor mode, is marked by an **arpeggiated** theme scored delicately for guitar, piano, and clarinet.

0:49   The theme is answered by a sassy melody for the trumpets.

0:53   The arpeggiated theme is played again, this time in a higher register.

0:56   Once again, it's answered by the band.

STRAIN B

1:01   The arpeggiated theme is heard again, this time scored for trombone, alto saxophone, and clarinet. Underneath it, the lower brass reinforce the bass line.

1:05   The theme is followed by quiet **trills** from the reeds over a descending bass line.

1:09   The theme makes one more appearance.

1:12   The band responds with loud brass *soli*.

1:15   During a **break**, Adderley begins a solo.

TRANSITION

1:17   The composed line, **modulating** from the key of the first two strains to the key of the trio, is bolstered by rich *soli* scoring.

STRAIN C

1:21   In a new key, Adderley plays over just the drums and the bass.

1:29   He accidentally makes a distorted honking sound on a low note. Emboldened, he returns to this sound again and again—essentially turning a mistake into a motive.

STRAIN C

1:37   Under Adderley's solo, a low-pitched line for the trombones and the tuba descends, then ascends, through the **chromatic scale**. The guitar begins playing the chords to the tune very softly.

STRAIN D

1:53   The band now plays the piece's main theme, recognizably the same as it was originally written by Jelly Roll Morton.

1:57   As it continues, the theme is paraphrased—its harmonies and melodies changed.

2:01   Halfway through, when the melody is repeated, the rhythms are distorted.

2:08   During a one-bar break, the brass instruments (with Adderley on top) play a *soli*.

STRAIN D

2:09   Borrowing again from Jelly Roll Morton, the brass instruments play a riff made up of restrained and delicate chords, most of them falling securely on the beat.

STRAIN D

2:25   The brass chords turn into a background for an Adderley solo.

STRAIN D

2:42   The band plays a *soli* with familiar Swing Era rhythms, but its harmonies are unusually dissonant.

2:50   Adderley improvises a response.

STRAIN D

2:58   The *soli* becomes rhythmically sparse and its harmonies increasingly dissonant.

3:03   The band suddenly switches to a riff taken straight from the 1930s arrangement by Fletcher Henderson.

CODA

3:10   The coda—once again borrowed from Henderson—begins with a short riff fragment played over and over, creating a **cross-rhythm** against the underlying meter.

3:13   The drums stop: the horns ascend with a richly voiced *soli* to the final tonic chord.

■ GEORGE RUSSELL (1923–2009)

Among the major jazz figures in the bop and postbop eras, George Russell is singular on two counts. First, he worked exclusively as a composer-bandleader, not as an instrumentalist; second, he devoted much of his life to formulating an intricate musical theory, published in 1953 and revised in 2001 as *George Russell's Lydian Chromatic Concept of Tonal Organization, Volume One: The Art and Science of Tonal Gravity*. As a result of his thesis and challenging music, Russell is generally perceived as an archetypal jazz intellectual—too difficult for the general public.

This is hardly fair. While some of his music was considered ahead of its time and presents challenges even today, a great deal is entertaining in a peculiarly pop-oriented way: his 1957 masterpiece "All About Rosie," for example, is based on a universal playground tune and never fails to charm audiences on those rare occasions when it is performed. His 1959 suite *New York, N.Y.*, which combines three original pieces with three adaptations of popular songs that celebrate Manhattan, was recorded with a rhyming rhythmic narration by singer Jon Hendricks that prefigures rap. Almost all of Russell's music since the 1970s incorporates funk and even disco rhythms. Russell is the de facto father of modal jazz, the harmonic approach that produced such classics as Miles Davis's *Kind of Blue*, John Coltrane's *Giant Steps*, and Herbie Hancock's *Maiden Voyage*.

Born out of wedlock to a racially mixed couple, Russell was adopted and raised by a black family in Cincinnati. In high school, he took up drums, but later described the experience of hearing the extraordinary Max Roach as marking the end of his ambition to play and the beginning of his determination to compose. His theory was inspired in part by a conversation with Miles Davis, who wanted Russell to help him understand how chords relate to each other. Russell began to analyze chords in terms of related scales, which ultimately led him to the conclusion that using fewer chords, and translating chords into their underlying scales or modes, would incline the improviser to think more melodically. Ultimately, it would even lead to the undoing of song and blues form. This was the basis for **modalism** as an improvisational method. As Davis realized: "It's not like when you base stuff on chords, and you know at the end of thirty-two bars that the chords have run out and there's nothing to do but repeat what you've done with variations. I was moving away from that and into more melodic ways of doing things. And in the modal way I saw all kind of possibilities." The "modal way" would come to dominate jazz in the 1960s, particularly in the realm of jazz-rock fusion.

Russell rejected the idea of major and minor keys and the harmonic rules contingent on them; instead, he advocated superimposing different scales, so as to eliminate a tonal center. Charlie Parker showed that any note could be made to fit harmonically within a chord. Russell believed that any chord could be made to fit within a scale. Instead of improvising against a scrim of two or more chords in each measure, a musician could replace all the chords in, say, an eight-bar passage with one scale. The harmonic progression would no longer guide the direction of the piece. Instead, as Davis realized, "The challenge here, when you work in the modal way, is to see how inventive you can be melodically."

Some of the best examples of what Russell intended may be found in his own work, beginning with "Cubana Be / Cubana Bop," a two-part arrangement he wrote for Dizzy Gillespie in 1947 that fused jazz and Afro-Cuban music and introduced modal orchestral writing. Not until 1956 did he record under his own name: the result, *Jazz Workshop*, by the George Russell Smalltet, is among his finest achievements.

© CHUCK STEWART

George Russell (seen here in the 1950s), the only major figure in jazz who did not play an instrument or sing, argued for the use of modes or scales as a substitute for chord changes with his Lydian Chromatic Concept and, more significantly, his challenging compositions.

Bill Evans revitalized the piano trio as a boldly interactive ensemble, emphasizing a harmonic and melodic discourse between piano and bass. This photo, taken in Copenhagen in 1964, captures better than most his singular keyboard posture—eyes shut tight and back hunched over so that his face is only a few inches removed from his hands.

© JAZZ SIGN/LEBRECHT/THE IMAGE WORKS

🎧 "Concerto for Billy the Kid"

Russell was held in great esteem by the most advanced jazz musicians of the 1950s, and he surrounded himself with many of them, including John Coltrane and Max Roach. But he also had a good ear for raw talent. His most influential discovery was the pianist Bill Evans, whom he eventually introduced to Davis. Evans had appeared on a few record sessions yet was virtually unknown when Russell recruited him for *Jazz Workshop*. To showcase his immense talent, Russell conceived "Concerto for Billy the Kid." Evans's rigorous solo, coming to a head in his whirling stop-time cadenza, is far removed from the more meditative approach that later became his signature, but it remains one of his most compelling performances.

Working with only six musicians in this piece, Russell creates tremendous harmonic density. His clashing scales give the performance a distinctly modernistic edge, though he also uses a standard chord progression (from the 1942 Raye-DePaul standard "I'll Remember April," an enduring favorite among jazz musicians) for the Evans sequence. In creating a harmonic landscape that obliterates tonal centers, Russell makes his sextet sound like a much larger ensemble. For all the dissonances, rhythmic changes, and fragmented melodies, the piece swings with a pure-jazz élan. The inventiveness of the composer and his soloists never wavers. After more than half a century, "Concerto for Billy the Kid" sounds not only fresh but avant-garde, in the truest sense of the term. It would sound modern if it were written and recorded today.

LISTENING GUIDE 49

🎧 concerto for billy the kid

GEORGE RUSSELL

Art Farmer, trumpet; Hal McKusick, alto saxophone; Bill Evans, piano; Barry Galbraith, electric guitar; Milt Hinton, bass; Paul Motian, drums

- Label: Victor LPM1372
- Date: 1956
- Style: modernist small-group composition
- Form: original, including 32-bar **A A'** and 48-bar **A B A**

What to listen for:

- Latin rhythms at beginning and elsewhere
- Evans's stop-time cadenza in right hand and rhythmically tricky improvisation
- Evans's and Motian's sharp accents on dissonant chords

INTRODUCTION

0:00	The drums begin by playing a Latin groove: a syncopated rhythm on the cymbals alternates with the bass drum on the main beats and the snare drum on the backbeat.
0:05	Above the groove, two horns (muted trumpet and alto saxophone) play two independent lines in dissonant **counterpoint**. The rhythms are disjointed and unpredictable.
0:09	The horns become stuck on a dissonant interval—the **major second**, or **whole step**. They move this interval up and down. They are joined by Hinton on bass (doubled by piano), repeating two notes a **half step** apart. (This bass line will remain in place for most of the introduction.)

0:24		The horns switch to a new key and begin a new **ostinato** that clashes, polyrhythmically, with the meter. Evans (piano) and Galbraith (guitar) improvise **countermelodies**.
0:34		The horns begin a new ostinato in **call and response** with the guitar.
0:44		The ostinato changes slightly, fitting more securely into the measure. Evans adds complicated responses.
0:58		Farmer (trumpet) removes his mute. The ostinato becomes a more engaging Latin riff, forming a four-bar pattern. Underneath it, Hinton plays a syncopated bass line.
1:11		In a dramatic cadence, the harmony finally reaches the tonic. The drums improvise during a short two-bar **break**.

CHORUS 1 (32 bars, A A')

| 1:15 | **A** | The rhythm section sets up a new Latin groove, with an unexpected syncopation on one beat. Evans plays a peculiar twisting line in **octaves** on piano, moving dissonantly through the chord structure. |
| 1:28 | **A'** | As the chord progression begins over again, Evans's melody continues to dance above the harmonies. |

CHORUS 2

| 1:42 | **A** | The horns repeat Evans's line note for note. Underneath, Evans plays a syncopated chordal pattern typically found in Latin accompaniments, locking into the asymmetrical bass line. |
| 1:56 | **A'** | |

TRANSITION

| 2:11 | | The walking-bass line rises and falls **chromatically**, while melodic themes are tossed between the instruments. |
| 2:21 | | The band returns to the Latin groove and the melodic ideas previously heard in the introduction. |

CHORUS 3 (48-bar A B A, each section 16 bars)

2:28	**A**	This new chord progression—based on "I'll Remember April"—begins with an extended passage of **stop-time**. Evans improvises for four bars in a single melodic line.
2:31		The band plays the next chord with a single sharp gesture. Evans continues to improvise.
2:42	**B**	The band's chords are irregular, often syncopated.
2:56	**A**	Evans's improvisations are so rhythmically slippery that the band misplays its next stop-time entrance.
3:08		A **walking bass** reestablishes a more conventional groove.

CHORUS 4

3:09	**A**	Evans plays a full chorus solo, featuring his right hand only.
3:23	**B**	He distorts the meter by relentlessly repeating a polyrhythmic **triplet** figure.
3:37	**A**	He switches to a series of bluesy gestures.

INTERRUPTION

| 3:50 | | The chorus is interrupted when the bass (doubled by piano) suddenly establishes a new triple meter. Against this, the horns play a dissonant line, harmonized in fourths (**quartal chords**). |

CHORUS 5

3:55	**A**	We return to the piano solo, a full five bars into this chorus.
3:58		Evans joins with the drummer in playing sharp accents (or "kicks") on harshly dissonant chords.
4:05	**B**	Farmer takes a trumpet solo.
4:12		Underneath, McKusick (alto saxophone) adds a background line, harmonizing with the guitar's chords.

| 4:19 | **A** | McKusick plays a melody previously heard in the introduction (at 0:34). |
| 4:26 | | The trumpet suddenly joins the saxophone in quartal harmonies, fitting obliquely over the harmonic progression. |

CODA

| 4:31 | | As the bass drops out, the instruments revisit ideas from the beginning of the introduction. |
| 4:39 | | Evans plays the final gesture on piano. |

The *Jazz Workshop* album received glowing reviews. As a result, and despite poor sales, it provoked enough interest to enable Russell to sign with other labels and to tour with a small group. He initiated an especially productive collaboration with the saxophonist Eric Dolphy, who played an important role in the burgeoning avant-garde of the 1960s. But even after more critical success with "All About Rosie" and *New York, N.Y.*, Russell found it increasingly difficult to find work in the United States. In 1963, he moved to Scandinavia, accepting a teaching post at the University of Sweden, touring with his sextet (which included some of the most admired young improvisers in Europe), and writing longer and more challenging pieces.

Russell returned to the United States in 1969 to teach at the New England Conservatory. Among his later works, *The London Concert* (1989) documents the bravura spirit, rhythmic ebullience, and remarkable beauty Russell could produce onstage; the album includes his arrangement of Davis's "So What," built not on the theme but rather on Davis's 1959 improvisation. Russell remained a controversial figure: the Jazz at Lincoln Center program in New York notoriously refused to present him on the grounds that his orchestra used electric bass.

┤ ADDITIONAL LISTENING ├

Thelonious Monk	"'Round Midnight" (1947), "I Should Care" (1948), "Brilliant Corners" (1956)
Charles Mingus	"Haitian Fight Song" (1955), *Pithecanthropus Erectus* (1956), "Goodbye Pork Pie Hat," "Fables of Faubus" (both 1959)
Miles Davis and Gil Evans	*Miles Ahead* (1957), *Porgy and Bess* (1958)
Gil Evans	"La Nevada" (1960), "Up from the Skies" (1974)
Dizzy Gillespie (George Russell)	"Cubana Be / Cubana Bop" (1947)
George Russell	"All About Rosie" (1957), *New York, N.Y.* (1958), "Ezz-thetic" (1961)

ONLINE MULTIMEDIA RESOURCES AND REVIEW MATERIALS

Author Insight Vides

Gary Giddins explains how improvisation has always been present in jazz even as composers were assuming more control in the 1950s, taking works of Gil Evans and Charles Mingus as examples.

Interactive Listening Guides

Thelonious Monk, "Thelonious"
Thelonious Monk, "Rhythm-a-ning"
Charles Mingus, "Boogie Stop Shuffle"
Gil Evans, "King Porter Stomp"
George Russell, "Concerto for Billy the Kid"

Jazz Concepts (audio and/or video demonstrations of terms covered here)

arpeggio	countermelody	quartal chords
backbeat	dissonance	riff
block chords	false fingering	sequence
blue note	flatted fifth (tritone)	stop-time
break	half, whole steps	tonic
cadence	modulation	triplets
call and response	octave	walking bass
chromatic scale	ostinato riff	whole-tone scale

- For quick reference, review the **Chapter Overview** and **Chapter Outline**.
- Take the online **Chapter** and **Listening Quizzes**.
- Use the online **Glossary** and **Flashcards** to review important terms.

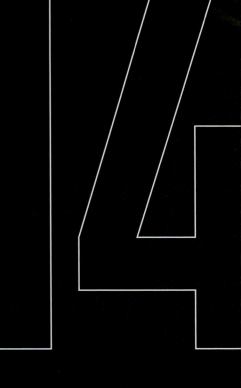

MODALITY: MILES DAVIS AND JOHN COLTRANE

■ **The Sorcerer: MILES DAVIS (1926–1991)**

No one looms larger than Miles Davis in postwar jazz, because no one had a greater capacity for change. His innovations, signaling what he called "new directions," altered the musical landscape at least six times in the two decades of his greatest impact.

- In 1949–50, his nonet helped launch cool jazz.
- In 1954, his "Walkin'" session provided an impetus for hard bop.
- From 1957 to 1960, Davis's three major collaborations with Gil Evans enlarged the scope of jazz composition, big-band music, and recording projects, projecting a meditative mood new in jazz.
- In 1959, *Kind of Blue*, the culmination of Davis's experiments with modal improvisation, transformed jazz performance and replaced bebop's harmonic complexity with a scalar approach that favored melody and nuance.
- In 1963–67, his second quintet, in such recordings as *E.S.P.* and *Nefertiti*, incorporated elements of the avant-garde.
- In 1969, *Bitches Brew* initiated an era of jazz-rock fusion, shifting the emphasis from melody to rhythm.

At twenty-three, **Miles Davis** had served a rigorous apprenticeship with Charlie Parker and was now (1949) about to launch the cool jazz movement with his nonet.

Davis's work involved a continuous rethinking of the four primary elements that define jazz and most other kinds of music: harmony, melody, rhythm, and instrumentation. Yet despite all the contextual changes that his music underwent, his approach to the trumpet remained ardently personal and consistent. In the 1950s especially, his power as a performer had the effect of resolving musical opposites while leading jazz to a multifaceted future that broadened its audience. By the 1970s, he had achieved the rare distinction of remaining on the edge of jazz innovation while borrowing techniques from avant-garde classical music and signaling a rapprochement with the latest currents in both black and white pop music.

Handsome and charismatic, Davis emerged as the archetypal modern jazz musician (distant, unflappable, romantic) and the civil-rights-era black man (self-reliant, outspoken, confident). Imitated for his personal and musical attributes, including his dress and candor, Davis generated a series of epithets: he was the man who walked on eggshells, the Prince of Darkness, the Sorcerer. Amiri Baraka described him as "my ultimate culture hero: artist, cool man, bad dude, hipster, clear as daylight and funky as revelation."

Early Years

Miles Dewey Davis III was born in Alton, Illinois, to a wealthy black family (his father was a prominent dental surgeon) who moved to East St. Louis when he was a year old. Davis's comfortable background instilled in him unshakable self-possession. He studied trumpet in school, and when Billy Eckstine's orchestra visited St. Louis in 1944, he sat in alongside Dizzy Gillespie (who advised him to learn piano and harmony) and Charlie Parker. Davis soon persuaded his father to send him to New York to study at the Juilliard School, where he attended classes for a year and took piano lessons before dropping out to pursue his real goal: learning from and working with Parker.

In 1945, Parker hired the nineteen-year-old Miles for his quintet and first recording date. Davis soloed with affecting resolve on "Now's the Time" and "Billie's Bounce," but (as we have seen) lacked sufficient technique to play on the pièce de résistance, "Ko Ko." He was attempting to forge a trumpet style in the shadow of Gillespie's (and Parker's) blazing virtuosity—an ambition that virtually doomed him to failure. In Parker's quintet, Davis had to solo after the leader in almost every piece, and the contrast did not favor him.

Davis's approach was different: he preferred the middle register to the more exciting high register, and focused on timbre and melody, playing fewer and longer notes. For a short time, he attempted to compensate for his perceived limitations by writing excessively intricate tunes—such as "Sippin' at Bells," a blues with so many chord changes that the blues feeling is nullified. Parker, switching to tenor saxophone, played as a sideman on Davis's first session as a leader and commented, sarcastically, that some of those changes were too complicated for a "country boy" like him.

In early 1949, having just broken with Parker, Davis began to experiment with the musicians and composers who would form the historic nonet. That same year, he visited Paris to play the first Festival International de Jazz, an important presentation of old and young musicians, which gave him a more positive perspective, given the respect that jazz and his own music enjoyed in Europe. He was now increasingly recognized for the emotional and rhythmic restraint of his solos. But if his acceptance in Europe buoyed Davis's spirits, it also added to his bitterness and disillusionment about the realities of race in America. He had resisted the lure of narcotics during his years with Parker, but now descended into heroin addiction, which took him through circles of hell utterly foreign to his privileged upbringing. Heroin hooked him for four years, during which time he completed *Birth of the Cool*.

A turning point came in 1954, when, after suffering withdrawal from heroin and recuperating at his father's farm, he returned to jazz with renewed energy and ambition. He now faced the double challenge of reestablishing himself as a serious force in jazz and as a reliable professional. Under contract to Prestige Records, he presided over five remarkable sessions with many of the best musicians of the day, and an exemplary rhythm section—the first of several in his career—consisting of Horace Silver, Percy Heath, and Kenny Clarke, that helped introduce hard bop. These performances revealed Davis to be a toughened, street-wise musician, thoroughly in charge of his timbre and playing with steely conviction. His evenly phrased solos, combined with his dark good looks and quietly pugnacious stance, introduced a new kind of black masculinity in American entertainment, at once tender and invincible. His coiled power came fully to the fore in "Walkin'" (1954), an extended, endlessly inventive performance that turned the jazz tide back to forthright, blues-driven improvisations.

Two months after "Walkin'," at a session with Sonny Rollins, Davis debuted three Rollins compositions that became instant jazz standards ("Airegin," "Oleo," "Doxy") and demonstrated a little-known device that would become emblematic of his style. The **Harmon mute**, unlike other metal mutes, is held in place by a cork ring, forcing the musician's entire air column into the appliance to produce a thin, vulnerable humming sound. The mute only augmented the brooding intensity of Davis's music.

With Percy Heath on bass and "Birth of the Cool" colleague Gerry Mulligan on baritone saxophone, Davis (center) gave a triumphant, drugs-free performance at the Newport Jazz Festival, Rhode Island, in 1955.

● **"Walkin'"**

Star Time

In the summer of 1955, Davis made a brief but much-acclaimed appearance at the Newport (Rhode Island) Jazz Festival, creating a stir with his version of Monk's "'Round Midnight." It was the first time most critics and fans had ever seen a Harmon mute. On the basis of this performance, Davis signed a contract with Columbia Records—a major career leap beyond independent jazz labels like Prestige. Davis, however, still owed Prestige three years under his existing contract, which he fulfilled by recording five albums of music at two marathon sessions. The proliferation of Davis albums in the late 1950s from both labels (the Prestiges were memorably titled with descriptive gerunds: *Relaxin'*, *Steamin'*, *Cookin'*, *Workin'*) boosted his celebrity.

For the cover of his debut Columbia album, *'Round About Midnight* (1955), Davis was photographed through a red lens, wearing dark glasses, embracing his trumpet, unsmiling—an iconic image. That album also introduced his

First quintet

first great quintet, one of the most admired small bands in history, with tenor saxophonist John Coltrane, pianist Red Garland, bassist Paul Chambers, and drummer Philly Joe Jones. Miles's old friend Gil Evans crafted the arrangement of "'Round Midnight," adding a tempo change and making the quintet sound fuller than on the other selections.

Three aspects of this quintet were particularly noticeable. The contrast between Davis's sparing, poignant solos and Coltrane's more demonstrative virtuosity reversed the earlier disparity between Parker and Davis, this time favoring Davis; the rhythm section boasted an assertive independence, thanks to Jones's insistent attack and Chambers's authoritative pulse; and the diverse repertory combined original pieces with pop songs dating back to the 1920s or borrowed from recent Broadway shows. In this regard, Davis was also influenced by Frank Sinatra, who was revitalizing his own career at the same time, often with old songs that were considered too dated or corny for modern jazz. By adapting such unlikely songs as "Bye Bye Blackbird" (from a 1926 revue), "The Surrey with the Fringe on Top" (from the 1943 show *Oklahoma!*), and "If I Were a Bell" (from the 1950 show *Guys and Dolls*), Davis opened up jazz repertory and affirmed that old saw: "'Taint what you do, it's the way that you do it."

Gil Evans and a Night at the Movies

After the success of *'Round About Midnight* and mindful that Prestige would soon be issuing annual albums by the quintet, Davis's gifted producer, George Avakian, suggested an orchestral album; without hesitation, Davis chose Gil Evans as the arranger. After several discussions, Miles and Gil settled on a nineteen-piece ensemble, extending the sonorities of the nonet's French horns and tuba to include flutes, piccolos, and harp. Davis would be the only soloist. The result, *Miles Ahead*, was a hit with the critics and public and a benchmark in recording history. Evans composed links between the selections, something never done before, to create the illusion of a tone poem without breaks.

Miles Ahead

Meanwhile, Davis had disbanded his quintet, partly in disgust because a few of his musicians had been derailed by drugs. At a loss for what to do next, he agreed to a tour of Europe. Upon arriving, he learned that several engagements had been canceled, but he was offered something more intriguing: the chance to compose a film score for a French police thriller starring Jeanne Moreau and directed by Louis Malle. Gambling on Davis's ingenuity, Malle asked him to improvise the score at one late-night session, creating music cues as he watched the picture, *Ascenseur pour l'échafaud* (*Elevator to the Gallows*). Davis improvised on scales instead of chords, simplifying the music harmonically and maximizing emotional content with slow, drawn-out phrases—often based on nothing more than a D minor scale. The international success of *Ascenseur* inspired a vogue for movies with scores by or featuring jazz stars, but for Davis it was a personal "eureka moment," and he returned home eager to elaborate on this new way of improvising.

Ascenseur pour l'échafaud

His first problem was to reorganize his band. One musician he wanted to work with was alto saxophonist Cannonball Adderley, whom he recruited in 1958. Davis had fired Coltrane because of his dependency on stimulants, but Coltrane had by now experienced what he later described as a rebirth, inspirational and (after working a year with Thelonious Monk) musical, and

Arranger Gil Evans and Davis take a break during the momentous Columbia Records sessions that produced *Porgy and Bess*, 1958.

was rehired. Davis's new band—a sextet made up of trumpet, two saxophones, and his old rhythm section (Garland, Chambers, and Jones)—recorded *Milestones* (1958), his most mature work to date, exploring devices he had used in the film.

Three weeks later, Davis returned to the studio for an ambitious project with Gil Evans, a reconceived version of George Gershwin's 1935 opera *Porgy and Bess*. Unlike the aggressively free-spirited music he made with his sextet, Davis's work with Evans on *Porgy* and the 1960 *Sketches of Spain* (a fusion of jazz with Spanish classical and folk music) possessed a sensuous luster that appealed to people who lacked the patience for long jazz improvisations.

> **Porgy and Bess / Sketches of Spain**

Kind of Blue

In 1959, the year between *Porgy and Bess* and *Sketches of Spain*, Davis regrouped his sextet to record a few unrehearsed musical ideas that he had been toying with and soon released as *Kind of Blue*. This album represented the fruition of the modal approach he had been working on since the film scoring in Paris, and would alter the playing habits of countless musicians. Here, in contrast to the strenuous orchestral projects with Evans, Davis kept the compositional demands simple. Determined to stimulate each of his musicians, he did not show them the pieces until they arrived at the recording sessions. His goal was nothing less than to banish the clichés of modern jazz.

By now, jazz had been fixated for fifteen years on chromatic harmony and the technical challenge of improvising smoothly and efficiently within it. Followers of Charlie Parker, liberated by his innovations, often made chord

Kind of Blue, the 1959 best-selling jazz recording of the LP era, popularized modality and changed the nature of improvisation: (left to right) John Coltrane, tenor saxophone; Cannonball Adderley, alto saxophone; Miles Davis; Bill Evans, piano.

progressions more concentrated and difficult; harmonic improvisation became a task rather like running hurdles, clearing a new obstacle every few yards. In his early years, Davis had tried to prove himself precisely in that manner. But **modal jazz** sent him in the opposite direction: fewer chords and less concentrated harmonies—or rather, scales that override harmonies, clearing away the hurdles. Modal improvisation was not new to jazz. It is, in essence, an abiding idea found in early jazz in the use of the blues scale. In the 1950s, though, it emerged as a specific technique in reaction to the busyness of bop harmony. It offered a solution to the problem of revitalizing the relationship between improvised melodies and the foundations on which those improvisations are based.

As we have seen, Davis was not alone in trying to move jazz beyond chord changes. Charles Mingus, who publicly excoriated musicians for "copying Bird," wrote pieces with minimal harmonies to provoke fresh approaches, Dave Brubeck sought to inspire musicians with novel meters, and George Russell created his Lydian concept as a theoretical justification for modal jazz. For that matter, an as-yet-unknown avant-garde was just over the horizon, more than willing to run roughshod over all of jazz's ground rules. Yet the dark, flowing introspection of *Kind of Blue*, probably the best-selling jazz album ever, caught the spirit of the times like no other recording. The modal arrangements and moderate tempos underscored Davis's strengths and not his weaknesses, encouraging his predilection for the middle range, his measured lyricism, his reserved disposition. It also provided an ideal middle ground between his laid-back ("walking on eggshells") style and the exuberance of the saxophonists, especially Coltrane, who even in the absence of chord changes filled every scale and space with an almost garrulous intensity.

In order to realize this project, Davis made a couple of changes in the rhythm section. He hired drummer Jimmy Cobb, a musician steeped in hard bop, as a replacement for Philly Joe Jones. On one track only, "Freddie Freeloader," Davis used his group's recently hired pianist, Jamaican-born Wynton Kelly, a veteran of hard bop who would remain with the band through 1962. For the remaining four selections, Davis recruited Bill Evans, who had been his pianist in 1958. Evans's return to the fold for the two days it took to record *Kind of Blue* proved to be a crucial component in the album's success and that of his own career.

■ BILL EVANS (1929–1980)

One of the most influential musicians of his generation, Bill Evans was on the verge of achieving recognition when George Russell introduced him to Davis. Like Davis, he too possessed an instantly identifiable sound on his instrument.

Born in Plainfield, New Jersey, Evans began classical piano and violin studies at six, and worked in dance bands as a teenager. After wowing critics with his work for Russell, he was invited to record with his own trio in 1956. His debut album, earnestly titled (by his producer) *New Jazz Conceptions*, introduced "Waltz for Debby," a classic jazz ballad that marked him as a composer of promise. For the next two years, he recorded as a sideman with Davis, Mingus, Adderley, Gunther Schuller, Chet Baker, and others, finally returning to the studio under his own steam in 1958 with an album called *Everybody Digs Bill Evans*, festooned with admiring quotations from other musicians. A highlight of this session was his spontaneous "Peace Piece," improvised freely over a simple alternation of tonic and dominant chords.

Bill Evans (center) created an ideal trio with bassist Scott LaFaro (left) and drummer Paul Motian, pictured here in 1961 at the Village Vanguard, where they made their most memorable recordings.

In 1959, Evans made a significant leap, first with his work on *Kind of Blue*, and later that year with his third album, *Portrait in Jazz*. Drawing on his classical background and modal jazz, he developed an original approach to voicing harmonies that made his chords sound fresh and open-ended. *Portrait in Jazz* also premiered a new approach to the piano trio, in which each member was a fully active participant. In the usual bebop piano trio as perfected by Bud Powell, the pianist was almost always the central figure. Powell liked interacting with a vigorous drummer, but his bassists typically marked the harmonies and followed his lead. Evans favored the bassist, who was free to respond with strong melodic ideas of his own. He found ideal allies in the soft and responsive punctuations of drummer Paul Motian and the superb intonation, smooth timbre, and melodic fancies of bassist Scott LaFaro. The early death of LaFaro shortly after the group reached its peak (*The Complete Village Vanguard Recordings, 1961*) disrupted Evans's progress for a few years, but he rebounded with a series of interdependent trios, and continued to compose challenging, introspective tunes, among them "Peri's Scope," "Turn Out the Stars," and "Very Early."

VOICING CHORDS

"Voicing" refers to the way notes or instruments are combined. We have already encountered instrumental voicings with big bands. Chord voicings similarly refer to the choices a musician makes in constructing harmony. Bill Evans was especially good at voicing chords in ways that made them sound fresh and open-ended: for example, instead of letting a definite C chord (C-E-G, with the root C at the bottom) advance to a definite F chord (F-A-C), his C chord might have the E or G on the bottom, and the F chord the A or C at the bottom, so that we hear the progression in a new way. If you drop the root notes altogether and add the interval of a ninth to each chord—D for the C chord and G for the F chord—you've come a long way from the original harmonies while staying within the original chord changes, and the possibilities for voicing seem limitless. Evans had a genius for realizing those possibilities.

Evans's best-known composition (and one of Davis's most moving recordings) is "Blue in Green," first performed on *Kind of Blue*. It's a ten-measure circular sequence of chords that, as Evans configured them, has no obvious beginning or ending. Its hypnotic quality continues to challenge instrumentalists and singers today. Elsewhere, his **quartal harmonies** (built on fourths rather than thirds) help to define the modal achievement of *Kind of Blue*. The piece that popularized modal jazz is the album's opening selection, "So What."

🎧 "So What"

"So What" presents modal jazz in the context of a thirty-two-bar **A A B A** tune, which makes the piece's only harmonic change stand out like a red tuxedo. The **A** sections are based on the D Dorian mode (on a piano keyboard, the white keys from D to D) and the bridge, a half step higher, shifts to the E-flat Dorian mode (same scale, same intervals, starting on E-flat). In practice, this means that musicians improvise mostly on a D minor triad. A great deal of Davis's lyrical solo, particularly in the opening measures, employs just the triad's three notes (D-F-A). Yet he found the experience melodically liberating, and his variations—lucid, moving, and memorable—don't sound the least bit constricted or forced. This beautifully executed solo has been much studied and imitated: the singer Eddie Jefferson put lyrics to it, and George Russell orchestrated it for his band.

The fascinating opening episode by the rhythm section is thought to be sketched by Gil Evans. Paul Chambers's bass prompts a three-note piano phrase, leading to a bass-like figure played in tandem by bass and piano, followed by the pianist's enigmatic, Spanish-style chords and the bassist's introduction of a swing beat and the theme. Davis continued to play the piece for years, at ever-faster tempos. By the middle 1960s, modal jazz was everywhere, as young musicians rose to the test of improvising without the supportive guideposts of chord changes.

🎧 so what

LISTENING GUIDE 50

MILES DAVIS

Miles Davis, trumpet; John Coltrane, tenor saxophone; Cannonball Adderley, alto saxophone; Bill Evans, piano; Paul Chambers, bass; Jimmy Cobb, drums

- Label: *Kind of Blue,* Columbia CL1355
- Date: 1959
- Style: modal jazz
- Form: 32-bar popular song (**A A B A**)

What to listen for:
- two-note riff ("So what!") in response to bass; first in piano, then horns
- bridge a half step higher than A sections
- modal improvisation
- contrast in styles between soloists

INTRODUCTION

0:00	Chambers quietly plays a rising bass line, evoking a two-note response from Evans on the piano: this prefigures, in slow tempo, the main head. The chords drift ambivalently, fitting no particular key area.
0:13	In a slightly faster tempo, Chambers and Evans combine on a precomposed melody.
0:20	The bass drops a step. Evans drifts elusively between chords.
0:30	After a pause, Chambers rumbles incoherently in the bass's lowest register.

CHORUS 1 (HEAD)

0:34	**A**	Suddenly striking up a steady tempo, Chambers plays a repetitive riff, answered by Evans with the famous two-note "So What" chord in **quartal** harmony (voiced in fourths). Cobb quietly supports on drums.
0:49	**A**	The response is now voiced by the three wind instruments. Cobb ratchets up the intensity by adding a **backbeat** on the high-hat cymbal.
1:03	**B**	In a subtle change, Chambers moves a half step higher. The horns play the riff in the new key.
1:17	**A**	All the instruments drop back to the original key.

CHORUS 2

1:31	**A**	Davis begins his two-chorus solo. He plays a few short phrases, answered by Evans with the riff.
1:37		Davis continues with a longer phrase. As it reaches its melodic peak, he pulls slightly behind the beat.
1:45	**A**	He plays short, concise phrases, leaving ample space for the rhythm section.
1:59	**B**	Evans moves a densely voiced **chord cluster** (with closely spaced notes) up a half step to signal the bridge. Davis plays over the harmonic cluster.
2:07		Evans returns to the "So What" motive.
2:14	**A**	The shift downward is signaled by a sharp drum accent.

CHORUS 3

2:28	**A**	Davis plays a hauntingly lyrical, sustained passage over a rhythmically active but harmonically static bass **ostinato**.
2:42	**A**	Chambers returns to a **walking bass**.
2:56	**B**	With a surprising dissonance, Davis signals modulation one beat early.
3:10	**A**	A drum crash leads the return back to the original key. Davis reprises his lyrical passage.
3:19		Davis's last phrase has a bluesy tinge.

CHORUS 4

3:24	**A**	While Cobb plays strong accents at the end of Davis's solo, Coltrane begins his two-chorus tenor saxophone solo with the same restrained mood.
3:38	**A**	Suddenly he switches to a more intense style of improvising, with flurries of fast notes. Evans responds with a peculiar **comping** pattern: holding a few notes, releasing others.
3:52	**B**	Cobb plays interactively on the snare drum, prodding Coltrane to greater intensity.
4:02		As Coltrane reaches the upper limits of his phrase, his timbre coarsens.
4:06	**A**	He plays a phrase in his lower register, repeating and extending it.
4:18		Cobb adds a Latin polyrhythm.

CHORUS 5

4:20	**A**	As in chorus 3, Chambers moves to a bass ostinato. Coltrane's line aims toward a melodic peak.
4:33	**A**	The bass returns to a walking-bass pattern.
4:47	**B**	His improvisation lingers around a single note.
5:01	**A**	His last phrase begins in his highest register.

CHORUS 6

5:15	**A**	The rhythm section quiets down to allow Adderley (alto saxophone) to enter, mimicking Coltrane's extensive **double-time** lines.
5:29	**A**	For a moment Adderley digs into the groove, but soon returns to his double-time improvisation.
5:41		He suddenly moves up a half step, clashing against the background. Evans responds with the appropriate chord several seconds later.
5:42	**B**	
5:56	**A**	Adderley returns to the tonic by repeating, on varied tones, a two-note motive.

CHORUS 7

6:10	**A**	Adderley plays a pair of phrases in the same rhythm.
6:24	**A**	He begins a simple rhythmic phrase with blues inflections, but once again moves back to faster passages.
6:38	**B**	A high-pitched phrase elicits a delayed chord from Evans.
6:51	**A**	Adderley's return comes a beat early.
7:00		His last phrase is distinctly bluesy.

CHORUS 8

7:05	**A**	The horns enter with the "So What" riff, shifting their role from the response to the call. Evans plays dense, dissonant chords.
7:19	**A**	Evans plays slow, single-note lines, recalling Davis's lyrical phrases.
7:33	**B**	On the bridge, he returns to short, dissonant chord clusters.
7:47	**A**	Back in the home key, he plays thinner chords: two notes a mere step apart.

CHORUS 9

8:02	**A**	Evans shifts the "So What" riff back to its original position. The bass continues to walk.
8:16	**A**	Chambers plays the call, with the horns joining Evans in responding with the "So What" chords.
8:30	**B**	
8:44	**A**	

CODA

| 8:58 | | Evans continues to respond to the bass, while the other instruments drop out. The music fades to silence. |

🎧 "Witchcraft"

Much as film fans like to single out 1939 as Hollywood's *annus mirabilis*, jazz lovers tend to champion 1959, which produced, besides *Kind of Blue*, such eminent albums as Dave Brubeck's *Time Out*, Ornette Coleman's *The Shape of Jazz to Come*, Charles Mingus's *Mingus Ah Um*, John Coltrane's *Giant Steps*, *Thelonious Monk Orchestra at Town Hall*, Duke Ellington's *Jazz Party*, and several more. One of the most significant of them, Bill Evans's *Portrait in Jazz*, slipped in at the end, recorded in a single day (December 28). Yet the album changed forever the texture, technique, and aspiration of the piano trio. Evans sought to develop a trio based on spontaneous interaction between the musicians. As he put it: if the bass player "hears an idea that he wants to answer, why should he just keep playing a 4/4 background?" Still, he couldn't pull it off until he found the right players.

The year was a crucial one for Evans. He had worked on *Kind of Blue* in March and April, and Davis encouraged him to embark as a leader in his own right. He tried a succession of bassists and drummers while supporting himself with sideman work. In October, he signed to a record session by clarinetist Tony Scott. The bassist was twenty-three-year-old Scott LaFaro—a native, curiously enough, of Irvington, New Jersey, not twenty-five minutes from Evans's hometown of Plainfield. They had met a couple of years earlier at an audition, and Evans's response then was mixed. Scott was undoubtedly a virtuoso, but, as Evans recalled, "ideas were rolling out on top of each other; he could barely handle it. It was like a bucking horse." Time had tamed him. With a no-less-compatible Philadelphia-born drummer, Paul Motian, they landed a long club engagement and prepared to record.

"Witchcraft" was their breakthrough performance, the second number recorded at the session. Within the first five seconds, LaFaro abandons the walking approach for an ascending line that seems to announce, "I'm ready for anything." At no time do we feel we are listening to a pianist backed by rhythm. Piano and bass are locked in conversation, and while the performance is, in some respects, a conventional swinging romp on a pop tune (popularized by Frank Sinatra), the great pleasure it affords is in the intense mutuality of the dialogue. Motian wisely keeps to the background with his elegantly pattering brushes; but he, too, developed an assertively interactive style, and you can hear the beginnings of it in the final twenty seconds of the fifth chorus, as he underscores the pianist's accents and dynamics.

Tragically, LaFaro was killed eighteen months later in a car accident. The "first" Evans trio, as it was known, recorded only four albums, two of them at its last gig at the Village Vanguard, ten days before LaFaro's death. Evans was shattered, yet with the discovery of another gifted bassist, Chuck Israels, the second trio and those that followed enabled him to continue and elaborate his explorations until his own premature death in 1980.

🎧 witchcraft

BILL EVANS TRIO

Bill Evans, piano; Scott LaFaro, bass; Paul Motian, drums

- Label: *Portrait in Jazz*, Riverside RLP12-315
- Date: 1959
- Style: contemporary piano trio
- Form: 40-bar popular song (**A A' B C A"**)

What to listen for:
- Evans's use of different piano techniques (block chords, single-note lines)
- LaFaro's loose interaction with Evans
- transformation of a complex popular song into a vehicle for improvisation

CHORUS 1 (HEAD)

0:00	A	Evans plays the melody in **block chords**. LaFaro begins by fulfilling his expected role—playing roots and keeping time—but soon breaks free with an ascending solo line in **triplets**.
0:05		Having reached the highest note, LaFaro breaks off to rejoin Evans on the next downbeat.
0:10	A'	
0:19		LaFaro plays a triplet figure that will serve as an **ostinato** pattern.
0:21	B	Switching to a more conventional piano texture (melody in the right hand, chords in the left), Evans plays the melody's distinctive ascending octave (corresponding to the phrase "It's witchcraft!").
0:31	C	LaFaro locks into a swinging **walking-bass** line. Evans continues the melody, contrasting it with a syncopated **chromatic** line in his left hand.
0:41	A"	Evans returns to the opening block chords. LaFaro plays in **call and response** with him.

CHORUS 2

0:52	A	Evans's solo begins as a loose improvised **counterpoint** between his unaccompanied right hand and LaFaro's bass line.
1:02	A'	As Evans drifts into **double-time**, LaFaro holds on to a syncopated pattern.
1:13	B	Underneath Evans's improvisation, LaFaro repeats a short melodic gesture.
1:25	C	Supported by LaFaro's walking-bass line, Evans's solo reaches a climax.
1:34	A"	LaFaro loosens his walking bass to interact with Evans.

CHORUS 3

1:44	**A**	Evans's melody is occasionally doubled in thirds.
1:53		Having stumbled on a rhythmic idea, he decides to repeat it **polyrhythmically**, supporting it with left-hand chords.
1:55	**A'**	He moves the motive up and down, in accordance with the harmony.
2:05	**B**	Over LaFaro's syncopated bass, Evans plays complex rhythms. The rhythmic descending **riff** from 2:13 to 2:16 is an Evans signature phrase.
2:16	**C**	Propelled by LaFaro's walking bass, the three musicians dig into the groove.
2:26	**A"**	Evans wraps up his solo with more complex rhythms.
2:31		He repeats the polyrhythmic figure (from 1:53), augmented by Motian's accents.

CHORUS 4

2:37	**A**	LaFaro begins his solo, accompanied only by the drummer's brushes. He opens with a challenging triplet motive.
2:47	**A'**	He breaks off a rapid ascent, shifting to shorter, more vocal motives.
2:58	**B**	He plays with a three-note figure.
3:08	**C**	Behind LaFaro's playing, Evans adds a short riff. Within a few measures, it splinters into dissonant chords.
3:19	**A"**	LaFaro returns to his opening triplet motive, which is echoed by Evans.

CHORUS 5 (HEAD)

3:29	**A**	Evans returns to the melody with a startling rhythmic gesture, split between his two hands.
3:39	**A'**	His paraphrase of the melody quickly dissolves into improvisation.
3:50	**B**	He plays the melody's ascending octave, but distorts it with polyrhythm. Motian becomes stronger, lays down a firmer beat, accenting the pianist's accents.
4:00	**C**	LaFaro plays a walking-bass line.
4:11	**A"**	

CODA

4:19		In an arranged coda, the group extends the final **A"** section with new harmonies.
4:24		They reach the final cadence with a firm two-note rhythm.
4:27		In a playful ending, the three musicians quietly improvise to a fade-out.

■ JOHN COLTRANE (1926–1967)

No one motivated a larger circle of major jazz figures than Miles Davis. Unlike most of the great players who populated the Ellington band or Art Blakey's Jazz Messengers, the musicians who passed through Davis's groups would extend his influence beyond his music, creating their own waves and ripples. Even in this fast company, however, John Coltrane holds an exclusive place. His musical and personal impact eventually equaled—some would argue, surpassed—that of Davis. Coltrane became the most intrepid explorer of modal jazz and a cultural-ethical leader of avant-garde jazz in the 1960s. Yet his career was short-lived, barely a dozen years, and his later music alienated most of his early admirers, producing a windstorm of controversy that has not yet completely settled. While both Coltrane and Davis became dissatisfied with the music they were creating, they headed down very different paths. For Davis, this meant examining rock, a fusion that he fully embraced a couple of years after Coltrane's death. For Coltrane, it meant embracing the expressionistic chaos of the avant-garde. Both roads were paved with modality.

Born in Hamlet, North Carolina, John William Coltrane grew up in a racist, hardscrabble community, where his family's precarious situation was devastated by the death of his father when John was twelve. When he wasn't practicing alto saxophone, he took odd jobs, like shining shoes, to help support his family. His musical training began in earnest in Philadelphia, at the Ornstein School of Music and Granoff Studios, where he developed a fascination with scales, tenaciously playing them for hours at a time. After service in the navy, he joined a big band led by a friend, saxophonist Jimmy Heath, the younger brother of Dizzy Gillespie's bassist Percy Heath.

In 1949, Gillespie brought both men to New York. Soon, Coltrane switched to tenor saxophone, and redoubled his obsession with scales. Where Coleman Hawkins had emphasized every chord in a harmonic sequence, Coltrane experimented with a rapid-fire attack in an attempt to play every note in every chord, unleashing what critic Ira Gitler described as "sheets of sound." By the time Miles Davis hired him in 1955, Coltrane's attack was distinctive if not fully formed, but his career was hobbled by narcotics and drink.

© CHUCK STEWART

John Coltrane forged an expressionistic way of improvising that helped to instigate the avant-garde movement and led a classic quartet in the 1960s.

Awakening

Coltrane's dependency on drugs forced Davis to fire him twice. After the second time, in 1957, Coltrane turned his life around. Claiming to have undergone a profound religious experience (the subject of his masterpiece *A Love Supreme*), he renounced all stimulants, devoting himself entirely to music. He spent most of the year working with Thelonious Monk, an education in itself, exhibiting a glowing timbre and emotional perseverance. His freelance work showed his talent as a composer ("Blue Trane," "Moment's Notice") as well as his facility with supersonic tempos and slow romantic ballads.

Early in 1959, Coltrane recorded *Kind of Blue* and albums with Adderley and Milt Jackson. Then, in May, he recorded his own landmark album, *Giant Steps*, backed by leading bebop pianist Tommy Flanagan; Davis's bassist, Paul Chambers; and hard bop drummer Art Taylor. Coltrane composed all the selections, of which three became jazz standards—"Giant Steps," "Naima," and "Mr. P. C." (a tribute to Chambers). The title tune has been called Coltrane's farewell to bebop, because the chord structure is so busy and difficult to play, especially at the roaring tempo he demanded. One of his most influential pieces (it became a test pattern for music students attempting to master fast-moving harmonies), it may be seen as a rejoinder to the scalar concepts of *Kind of Blue*. Most of the remaining selections signify an extension of *Kind of Blue*, with its investigation of scales and chords, and Coltrane's subsequent work demonstrated a deepening interest in the liberating implications of modal jazz.

Giant Steps

🎧 "Giant Steps"

"Giant Steps" is a sixteen-bar composition in which almost every note of the melody is signaled by a new chord—playing the chord changes is practically the same thing as playing the melody. The harmony extends the chord progression between equally distant tonal centers (the giant steps of the title). One goal of this harmonic sequence was to stimulate fresh ideas. Taking a page from Davis, Coltrane decided not to show the piece to the musicians until the day of the recording session, which in this instance turned out to be a disservice to them.

The piece's difficulty is especially evident in the piano solo. The chords alone would not have presented a problem for a pianist as harmonically sophisticated as Tommy Flanagan. The tune consists mostly of half notes, which means a chord change every two beats—no big deal if the tempo is leisurely or medium-fast. But the point of "Giant Steps" lay partly in playing it extremely fast, to trigger a sheets-of-sound jolt. Even for Coltrane, who had been working on these changes for years, the challenge was thorny, and his solo contains many repeated patterns. For Flanagan, the situation was virtually impossible. His solo begins with uncharacteristically jumpy phrases before retreating into a sequence of chords. (Flanagan, a perfectionist, later mastered the piece for his superb 1982 Coltrane tribute album, also called *Giant Steps*.) Coltrane's solo aims for a quite different effect from bebop; unlike most of the improvisations we've heard, including Coltrane's on "So What," the import of his eleven-chorus solo here resides less in details than in the aggregate attack—the overall whooshing energy.

🎧 giant steps

JOHN COLTRANE
John Coltrane, tenor saxophone; Tommy Flanagan, piano; Paul Chambers, bass; Art Taylor, drums

- Label: *Giant Steps,* Atlantic LP311
- Date: 1959
- Style: hard bop
- Form: 16-bar popular song

What to listen for:
- overall energy of Coltrane's 11-chorus solo
- repeated patterns in his solo
- continuous modulation

CHORUS 1 (HEAD)

0:00   Coltrane begins with a rhythmically simple melody disguising the dauntingly difficult chord progression voiced by Flanagan on piano. The tune changes keys 10 times in 13 seconds.

CHORUS 2 (HEAD)

0:13   Beginning of chorus.

0:26   The last two chords serve as the beginning of Coltrane's 11-chorus solo.

CHORUS 3

0:27   Coltrane launches into his solo with a pattern he'll return to again and again. The drummer changes from the open cymbal to a more tightly restrained sound.

CHORUS 4

0:40   Coltrane's intensity increases on a high, held-out note—a melodic peak that he reaches again two seconds later, over a different chord.

CHORUS 5

0:53   Coltrane repeats the opening of chorus 3 before shifting into a new direction.

0:59   A return to the melodic peak of chorus 4, again repeated over two different chords.

CHORUS 6

1:06   Coltrane takes a short break before continuing his solo.

1:11   Another short break may reflect a momentary lapse of attention at such fast speed.

1:18   At the end of the chorus, he reaches a new high note (a **half step** higher than before).

CHORUS 7

1:20   Coltrane's solo remains in the upper register, reaching the highest note at 1:22 and 1:24.

1:29   The end of the chorus settles into a familiar pattern, with one high note being replaced by the next.

CHORUS 8

1:33   Beginning of chorus.

1:40   Coltrane erupts into a rapid ascending E-flat major scale.

1:43   He seems to return to his high-note pattern. But instead of completing it, he dips back down to return to the customary opening for the next chorus.

CHORUS 9

1:46   Beginning of chorus.

CHORUS 10

2:00   His phrasing is choppier and more discontinuous.

CHORUS 11

2:13   The standard opening is interrupted by faster rhythmic gestures.

2:19   As Coltrane looks for ways to intensify his improvisation, the melodic line features **ghosted** notes and half-formed pitches.

CHORUS 12

2:26   Coltrane interrupts his usual chorus opening with a high-note flurry, continually circling his line back toward its melodic goals.

CHORUS 13

2:39   Coltrane's last chorus is built primarily around ever-higher notes, with a throaty timbre.

2:49   He finally tires and brings his line down.

2:52   A series of hard knocks on the side of the drum head signals the end of the solo, which spills over slightly into the next chorus.

CHORUS 14

2:53   Beginning of chorus.

2:55   Announced by a big cymbal crash, Flanagan (piano) starts his solo.

2:57   Early on, it becomes obvious that he can't remember all the chords; when he reaches an unfamiliar spot, his line stops.

CHORUS 15

3:05   Flanagan begins with a **major scale** that quickly becomes out of sync with the changing chords.

CHORUS 16

3:18   He halts his line to reestablish himself with the correct chord.

3:22   The gaps between lines become uncomfortably long.

CHORUS 17

3:31   Flanagan stops trying to create a single-note line, and simply plays chords.

CHORUS 18

3:44   Coltrane returns to solo, taking up his improvisation where he left off.

3:51   Long-held notes add expression to his line.

CHORUS 19

3:57   Coltrane's final chorus begins with a short break before plunging in for another continuous string of notes.

CHORUS 20 (HEAD)

4:10   He returns to the simple melody of the head.

CHORUS 21 (HEAD)

4:23   Beginning of chorus.

CODA

4:35   As the band holds out the final chord, Coltrane plays a skittering run that descends into his lower register. His last note is drowned out by a snare-drum roll.

"My Favorite Things"

Incredibly, Coltrane followed *Giant Steps* in 1960 with the one thing no one could have anticipated: a hit record—perhaps the most improbable jazz hit in the twenty years since Coleman Hawkins's "Body and Soul." His adaptation of "My Favorite Things," a cheerful waltz from Rodgers and Hammerstein's current Broadway blockbuster *The Sound of Music*, was a rarity in every way. With its fifteen-minute running time, it was a particularly unlikely candidate for frequent radio play. Yet it *was* broadcast, making Coltrane a major jazz star while popularizing the use of modes in a more dramatic yet no less accessible manner than "So What." Coltrane's arrangement transformed the piece by accenting the waltz meter with an insistently percussive vamp, and reducing the song's chords to two scales, one major and one minor.

The quintessential John Coltrane Quartet: (left to right) McCoy Tyner, piano; Coltrane; Jimmy Garrison, bass; Elvin Jones, drums. In concert in Indianapolis, 1962.

© DUNCAN SCHIEDT

"My Favorite Things" was also the first recording to document the defining Coltrane quartet, with pianist McCoy Tyner and drummer Elvin Jones. (The quartet reached peak strength a year later with the addition of bassist Jimmy Garrison.) "My Favorite Things" suggested a procedure for interpreting all kinds of songs, which Coltrane applied to the sixteenth-century English folk song "Greensleeves," Sigmund Romberg's "Softly, as in a Morning Sunrise," "Body and Soul," and "Chim-Chim-Cheree" from the movie *Mary Poppins*.

"Chasin' the Trane"

Coltrane had worked with first-rate bop pianists, including Flanagan and Wynton Kelly, but not until McCoy Tyner did he find a true soulmate, with a heavy, harmonically advanced attack, a partiality for vamps, and a rhythmic strength inseparable from his dramatic purpose. Tyner's intensity was matched by that of drummer Elvin Jones, who quickly became known as a drummer's drummer, a master of polyrhythms. Jones used two related approaches to polyrhythms: playing two rhythms simultaneously himself (for example, a three-beat rhythm and a four-beat rhythm) and playing a different rhythm from the rest of the band. He and Coltrane developed a mutual volatility that led them to long improvisational duels; at the height of some of these bombardments, Tyner would stop playing altogether. The cumulative fervor of their performances was liberating and spiritual, especially after Coltrane discovered bassist Jimmy Garrison. Jones called Garrison "the turning point" for the quartet: "His aggressiveness, his attitude toward the instrument gave us all a lift."

In 1961, Coltrane signed a lucrative contract with the fledgling label Impulse!, which began to advertise itself as "The New Wave in Jazz." Recording live at the Village Vanguard, he performed a ferocious sixteen-minute blues, "Chasin' the Trane," so antithetical to "My Favorite Things" that it split his audience in two. Critics who once championed him went on the attack. *Down Beat* magazine accused him of playing "musical nonsense" and "anti-jazz." Others found the performance invigorating and defended him as the new hope of jazz. Occupying one whole side of an LP, the piece is as relentless as it is long and played at tremendous velocity. Coltrane wails some eighty choruses, using **multiphonics** (chords played on an instrument designed to play one note at a time), split tones (cracked notes played that way on purpose), cries, and squeals.

"Chasin' the Trane" requires a new way of listening; without melodic phrases, toe-tapping rhythms, or anything remotely suggesting relaxation, the listener either enters the experience of musical exultation or is left in the cold. The piece doesn't really end, it stops; it doesn't really begin, it starts. The performance is all middle. For the next six years, until his death, Coltrane's audience would be constantly "chasin' the Trane," as he took ever larger steps beyond the rudiments of conventional jazz, challenging the validity of everything he had mastered, and taking another unexpected detour with a series of romantic recordings (including *Ballads*).

McCoy Tyner / Elvin Jones

Jimmy Garrison

Pianist McCoy Tyner and drummer Elvin Jones joined the John Coltrane Quartet in 1960 (with bassist Jimmy Garrison) and transformed jazz utterly with the might and unity of their collaboration. Here, they are pictured, by the great photographer Chuck Stewart, during a coffee break at a 1964 session with Coltrane, whose tenor saxophone shares the bench.

© CHUCK STEWART

In the gatefold cover of his masterpiece *A Love Supreme* (1964), John Coltrane published an open letter describing his triumph over drugs, and a hymn that he interpreted in the work's final movement.

A Love Supreme

In December 1964, Coltrane recorded the autobiographical four-part suite and canticle *A Love Supreme*, a personal outpouring like nothing else in jazz, to enthusiastic reviews. His influence was at this point pervasive. An expanding coterie of musicians looked to him as a leader, and a generation of listeners trusted him to map the no-man's-land of the new music. *A Love Supreme* solemnizes Coltrane's 1957 devotional conversion, and his liberation from addiction, in four movements: "Acknowledgement," "Pursuance," "Resolution," and "Psalm." Though the arc of the piece moves from harmonic stability to chromatic freedom, *A Love Supreme* represented a type of avant-garde jazz that the public found approachable and satisfying; his old and new admirers closed ranks behind it. In retrospect, the album was a spectacular lull before the storm.

"Acknowledgement"

Coltrane's liner notes for *A Love Supreme* describe his religious experience and include a psalm that inspired the fourth movement, which is improvised entirely from the psalm's syllabic content. Unlike the usual canticle, this one is "sung" on the tenor saxophone. The first movement, "Acknowledgement," like the whole work, is a culmination of Coltrane's music thus far, involving scales, pedal points, multiphonics, free improvisation, and shifting rhythms. Toward the end of the movement, a vocal chant signals a harmonic change from one key to another.

Coltrane's sound instantly demands attention, with its heraldic phrases based on the pentatonic scale. It has the feeling of an invocation. Many listeners think the four-note vocal figure is the movement's theme, but in fact it is one of four; the others are motives that spur his improvisation. If the movement opens and closes with incantations, the central section suggests spiritual wrestling as Coltrane works his way through those nagging motives to a final transcendent calm, shadowed by the ever-alert rhythm section. Some critics were repelled by the religious aspect of the piece, arguing that Coltrane abandoned musical coherence for the aesthetics of faith. This view (which drew posthumous support from the 1971 founding of the Church of Saint John Coltrane, in San Francisco) is no more valid or helpful in understanding his music than it is in analyzing J. S. Bach's *B Minor Mass*. "Acknowledgement," including its freest passages, is strictly ordered by musical logic.

LISTENING GUIDE 53

🎧 acknowledgement

JOHN COLTRANE QUARTET
John Coltrane, tenor saxophone, voice; McCoy Tyner, piano; Jimmy Garrison, bass; Elvin Jones, drums

- Label: *A Love Supreme,* Impulse! A(S)77
- Date: 1964
- Style: late Coltrane
- Form: open-ended

> **What to listen for:**
> - open-ended improvisation over an ostinato
> - use of motives (A–D)
> - intense climaxes
> - "A love supreme" motive at 6:06

INTRODUCTION

0:00   The sound of a gong, combined with a piano chord, opens the piece. The music unfolds in free rhythm. Coltrane plays with a few notes from a **pentatonic scale** in the key of E, while the pianist scatters clusters up and down the keyboard.

0:15   The saxophone gently fades out.

0:20   The pianist settles on one chord, playing it with a fast **tremolo**.

0:29   As the bass and drums drop out, the drummer continues tapping on the cymbals.

IMPROVISATION

0:32   Garrison (bass) begins a four-note syncopated **ostinato**, which we'll call motive A.

0:40   Jones plays a Latin-style groove, with bass drum and tom-tom accents coinciding with accents in the ostinato.

0:48   Tyner (piano) enters, playing **quartal** harmonies.

1:00   The drums switch to a more intense, double-time feeling.

1:04   Coltrane enters with a three-note motive, repeated **sequentially** on a higher pitch: motive B.

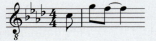

He plays this motive three times, each time with more variation. The bass moves away from the ostinato, improvising within the pentatonic scale.

1:11   Tyner's chords begin to drift, pulling the harmony toward a more dissonant and **chromatic** sound.

1:16   Coltrane plays an ascending pentatonic scale: motive C.

1:21   He returns to motive B.

1:32   Reaching a climax, he ascends to a cadence figure, played with a roughened tone: motive D.

1:35   Coltrane descends with fast passagework, drawn from the pentatonic scale.

2:00   He begins playing with motive C.

2:11	He moves motive C in sequence, shifting the music out of the pentatonic scale. Tyner adjusts his harmonies accordingly. The drums become still more polyrhythmic.
2:31	Coltrane reaches an anguished high note; he descends in pentatonic spirals.
2:44	Again he returns to motive C, quickly sending it into other keys.
3:15	The band finds its way back to the home key.
3:26	For a moment, the intensity and volume begin to fade.
3:37	Coltrane begins again with motive C, once again modulating to new keys.
3:52	He finally reaches motive D, playing it repeatedly with an increasingly torturous sound.
4:13	Coltrane's improvisation renews itself with fragments of motive C. His modulations ascend in a chromatic swirl. On bass, Garrison follows him into the topmost register.
4:22	Coltrane reaches the tonic and falls downward through the pentatonic scale.
4:33	The improvisation gradually subsides.
4:55	He plays motive A, moving it restlessly through all possible keys. The bass and piano follow.
5:50	Finally all instruments come to rest on the tonic. As the mood dies down, Coltrane repeats motive A endlessly.
6:05	The saxophone disappears; in its place, Coltrane's overdubbed voice sings "a love supreme." Its incessant repetition induces a trance-like sense of calm.
6:36	Suddenly the voices sink down a whole step, settling into a new key (which will be the key of the next movement).

CODA

6:44	The voices disappear, leaving Garrison playing his variant of motive A. The piano and drums occasionally add tension, but the bass is at the center.
7:09	The piano drops out.
7:23	The drums drop out. Garrison continues the motive's rhythms, but begins improvising its melody.
7:40	Garrison ends by quietly strumming two notes at once.

Ascension

Within a year of *A Love Supreme*, Coltrane disbanded his quartet for an even more expressionistic group. He replaced Elvin Jones with Rashied Ali, who had been tutored almost exclusively in the avant-garde; on occasion, Coltrane would use two or three drummers. His wife Alice, a former student of Bud Powell, replaced Tyner. Jimmy Garrison continued to play with the group, which became a quintet with the addition of tenor saxophonist Pharoah Sanders. Although the free music Coltrane embraced in his last years was undeniably a product of its time, reflecting the tragedies of the civil rights struggle (his "Alabama" remains an incomparable cry from the heart) and the slaughter in Vietnam, it exerted lasting influence on musicians who adapted free improvisation along with broken notes, squawks, and growls as part of the musician's arsenal.

Coltrane's most extreme work is the 1965 album *Ascension*, a vexatious piece that takes the intensity of "Giant Steps" and "Chasin' the Trane" to the limit of musical reason. The piece, improvised by ten musicians, is based on a minor triad and a couple of ground chords for the ensemble passages; the format consists of free solos that alternate with free ensemble blowouts. Yet even *Ascension* develops an unanticipated logic. Coltrane always claimed not to understand the fuss. "The main thing a musician would like to do," he said, "is to give a picture to the listener of the many wonderful things he knows of and senses in the universe."

After trying various musicians, Miles Davis introduced his second great quintet, with much younger players: (left to right) Herbie Hancock, piano; Tony Williams, drums; Ron Carter, bass; Davis; Wayne Shorter, tenor saxophone. Berlin, 1964.

MILES DAVIS'S SECOND QUINTET

After the back-to-back triumphs of *Kind of Blue* and *Sketches of Spain*, Miles Davis endured a slump of uncertainty. Coltrane, Adderley, and Evans had left to pursue their own careers, and Davis claimed to despise the avant-garde. Then in 1963, once again, he produced magic. He turned to younger musicians who would surely have had important careers on their own but who, under Davis's tutelage, merged into a historic ensemble, greater than its very considerable parts. The rhythm section consisted of three prodigiously skillful musicians: pianist Herbie Hancock, bassist Ron Carter, and seventeen-year-old drummer Tony Williams. Davis auditioned many saxophonists before temporarily settling on George Coleman. In late 1964, Wayne Shorter, who had made his name as a saxophonist and composer with Art Blakey's Jazz Messengers, joined the band, a decision that changed his life and Davis's, and made this second great quintet a worthy follow-up to the 1955 group with Coltrane. This time, however, Davis took as much from his sidemen as he gave, drawing on their compositions (especially Shorter's) and sensibilities. These musicians were keenly interested in the avant-garde, and Davis adjusted his music to assimilate their tastes.

Jazz was beset on one side by avant-garde experimentalism (see Chapter 15) that estranged much of the audience, and on the other by rock, which had matured into the dominant pop music. Davis would eventually inch his way to a fusion of jazz and rock, but first he adapted modal jazz to include elements of the avant-garde in a style far more extreme than anything he had previously done. This approach, known as **postbop**, attracted other accomplished musicians caught between the conventions of modern jazz and the excitement born of the avant-garde. Postbop involved harmonic ambiguity, original compositions with

Postbop

new harmonic frameworks (rather than those built on standard songs), and a radical loosening of the rhythm section. In the most advanced of these pieces, chord progressions were omitted while time, meter, and tonality might evaporate and coalesce several times in the course of a performance.

In the rhythm section, so much was going on between Hancock's unruffled block chords, Carter's slippery bass lines, and Williams's rhythmic brushfires that they all appeared to be soloing all the time. Davis gave them leave, enjoying the excitement they created, but he imposed a discipline that left space for the lyrical drama of his trumpet. Free of chord changes, unapologetic about fluffs, and stimulated by his band's ceaseless energy, Davis became a more expansive trumpet player. He began to forage in the upper register at precipitous tempos, ideas spilling from his horn with spiraling confidence despite occasional technical failings. He cut back on his signature ballads and began to jettison standard tunes and his classics. Between 1965 and 1968, he found his own way to be avant-garde.

🎧 "E.S.P."

The 1965 album *E.S.P.* was a critical event, but not a popular success. It represented the first studio recording by the new quintet, and the seven new compositions, all by members of the group, challenged listeners who expected to hear the tender, meditative Davis who incarnated jazz romanticism. This music is audacious, fast, and free. The title of the album (and first selection) emphasized the idea that extra-sensory perception is required to play this music. Shorter composed "E.S.P." as a thirty-two-bar **A A'** tune, but its harmonic structure is far more complicated than that of "So What."

The melody is based on intervals of fourths (recalling the indefinite quartal harmonies of "So What" and "Acknowledgement"), and is married to a mixture of scales and chords in a way that offers direction to the improvisers without making many demands. The main part of the piece (**A**) hovers around an F major scale, while the **B** sections close with specific harmonic cadences that are handled easily and quickly—especially at this expeditious tempo. The soloists (Shorter for two choruses, Davis for six, Hancock for two) take wing over the rhythm, bending notes in and out of pitch, soaring beyond the usual rhythmic demarcations that denote swing. No less free is the multifaceted work of the rhythm section: the bass playing is startlingly autonomous, and the drummer's use of cymbals has its own narrative logic.

LISTENING GUIDE 54

🎧 e.s.p.

MILES DAVIS QUINTET
Miles Davis, trumpet; Wayne Shorter, tenor saxophone; Herbie Hancock, piano; Ron Carter, bass; Tony Williams, drums

- Label: *E.S.P.* (Sony B00000DCH2)
- Date: 1965
- Style: postbop
- Form: 32-bar popular song (**A A'**)

What to listen for:
- rhythmic freedom and bent notes of soloists: Shorter, Davis, Hancock
- Davis's shrill high notes and short phrases
- imaginative playing of rhythm section

CHORUS 1 (HEAD)

0:00   **A**   The tenor saxophone and trumpet enter with the tune, which initially alternates between three notes. Because the notes harmonize equally well with two different chords, it's hard to determine the piece's key. Underneath, Carter (bass) plays two beats per bar, while Williams rattles busily on the cymbals.

0:07   The melody descends from a high note, while the bass rises chromatically. For several measures, the piano is silent.

0:14   **A'**   The **A** section is repeated with a higher-pitched bass line.

0:21   The bass harmonizes underneath in **tritones** by playing two strings at once (**double stops**).

0:27   The tune ends in a major key that may be the tonic, but the sense of closure lasts less than a second.

CHORUS 2

0:28   **A**   Shorter (tenor saxophone) begins a two-chorus solo with an upward-rising line that ends in a bent note. Carter (bass) begins to walk.

0:35   Shorter plays pitches that are out of time and slightly flat before blending them back into a continuous line.

0:42   **A'**   He improvises an even stream of notes.

CHORUS 3

0:55   **A**   Shorter leaves spaces for Hancock (piano) to enter with chords.

1:02   With a sudden ascent, Shorter returns to the tune's melody. He ends a flurry of notes with a dismissive honk.

1:09   **A'**   Shorter plays with a motive that, in its alternation of two pitches, recalls the theme.

1:15   His melody is **chromatic**, matching the tension of Hancock's dissonant chords.

CHORUS 4

1:22   **A**   Davis begins his six-chorus solo. He concentrates on a few mid-register notes.

1:29   As the harmonies become more tense, Davis rises to a dissonant note.

1:36   **A'**

1:41   Davis suddenly rises into the upper register. He plays a few shrill notes before tumbling, somewhat untidily, back down.

CHORUS 5

1:49   **A**   As Williams (drums) and Hancock play more aggressively, Davis's solo becomes more disjointed, breaking into short fragments.

2:02   **A'**   Davis begins a new phrase with a repeated-note fanfare, followed by a series of short phrases.

CHORUS 6

2:15   **A**   The trumpet hits an accent that coincides spontaneously with a drum accent.

2:29   **A'**   Carter takes his walking-bass line into the upper register.

2:35   As the bass drops back down, Davis rises step by step.

CHORUS 7

2:42   **A**   Davis screeches out a descending four-note line in his upper range. Williams's drumming hits a new level of intensity with powerful drum strokes.

2:55   **A'**   The band retreats to a lower volume. Davis plays a continuous line of notes in his middle register.

CHORUS 8

3:08   **A**   Davis's new motive has a bluesy tinge.

3:21   **A'**

3:31   Davis abruptly drops out; the space is filled by Hancock's **comping**.

CHORUS 9

3:34   **A**   Davis plays a motive that rocks back and forth a half step, interrupting it with several swoops up to his highest register.

3:47   **A'**   He returns to a variant of the bluesy motive from chorus 8.

CHORUS 10

4:00   **A**   Hancock starts his solo, imitating the rhythm of Davis's last motive.

4:13   **A'**   Playing a single-note line, he sounds like a saxophonist or trumpet player.

CHORUS 11

4:27   **A**   Hancock plays a riff, then modifies it subtly to fit the chord progression.

4:40   **A'**   His improvised line interacts with his left-hand chords.

CHORUS 12 (HEAD)

4:53   **A**   As Davis and Shorter reenter with the tune's melody, Carter on bass returns to a slower pattern.

5:00   Carter plays tritone double stops, Williams adding a few cymbal colors.

5:07   **A'**   Williams reestablishes his drum pulse, but fades in and out for the rest of the tune.

CODA

5:20   When the tune ends, Carter is on an unexpected note. He resolves it downward to the opening chord.

The public reception accorded *E.S.P.* and succeeding albums by Davis's quintet (*Miles Smiles, Sorcerer, Nefertiti*) suggested the tremendous changes that had taken place in the cultural landscape in the few years since *Kind of Blue* and *Sketches of Spain*. They were received favorably and sometimes enthusiastically by musicians, critics, and young fans, but achieved nothing of the broader cachet enjoyed by his earlier work: there was nothing easy or soothing about these records. By 1965, rock could no longer be dismissed by jazz artists as music for kids, and Davis was feeling the heat, not least from his disgruntled record company. His response will be discussed in Chapter 17.

MILES DAVIS CHRONOLOGY		
1926	Born May 26 in Alton, Illinois.	
1944	Enrolls at the Juilliard School, New York.	
1945–48	Performs with Charlie Parker.	
1948–50	Befriends Gil Evans, forms the Miles Davis Nonet ("birth of the cool" band).	
c. 1950	Becomes addicted to heroin.	
1954	Kicks drug habit.	"Walkin'" (Prestige)
1955	Forms first quintet, with John Coltrane, Red Garland, Paul Chambers, Philly Joe Jones.	*'Round Midnight* (Columbia)
1957–60	Writes score for French film; records with Evans.	*Miles Ahead* (1957), *Porgy and Bess* (1958), *Sketches of Spain* (1960)

MILES DAVIS CHRONOLOGY		
1958	Adds Cannonball Adderley, expands to sextet.	*Milestones*
1959	Explores modal improvisation.	*Kind of Blue* (with Bill Evans)
1963	Forms second quintet, with Wayne Shorter, Herbie Hancock, Ron Carter, Tony Williams.	
1965–67	Records postbop albums.	*E.S.P.* (1965), *Miles Smiles* (1966), *Nefertiti* (1967)
1968–70	Moves into fusion (Chapter 17).	*Filles de Kilimanjaro* (1968), *In a Silent Way* (1969), *Bitches Brew* (1970, best-seller)
1975–80	Withdraws from music.	
1981	Returns to performing.	
1985	Signs with Warner Bros.	
1989		*Amandla*, *Aura*
1991	Dies September 28 in Santa Monica, California.	

┤ ADDITIONAL LISTENING ├

Charlie Parker	"Donna Lee" (1947)
Miles Davis	"Walkin'" (1954), "'Round Midnight" (1956), "Milestones" (1958), *Kind of Blue* (1959), "Someday My Prince Will Come" (1961), "My Funny Valentine" (1964), "Orbits," "Footprints" (both 1966)
Miles Davis and Gil Evans	*Sketches of Spain* (1959)
Bill Evans	"Peace Piece" (1958), "Blue in Green" (1959), "My Foolish Heart" (1961)
John Coltrane	"Naima" (1959), "My Favorite Things" (1960), "Chasin' the Trane" (1961), "Alabama" (1963), *A Love Supreme: Deluxe Edition* (1964)

ONLINE MULTIMEDIA RESOURCES AND REVIEW MATERIALS

Author Insight Videos

Gary Giddins describes how Miles Davis found his own style—in the middle range with fewer notes, focusing on timbre and feeling—in contrast to Dizzy Gillespie's virtuosity; explains why listening to "So What" is the easiest way to understand modal jazz; and describes how John Coltrane's "Chasin' the Trane" created a kind of Rubicon for his fans.

Interactive Listening Guides

Miles Davis, "So What"
Bill Evans, "Witchcraft"
John Coltrane, "Giant Steps"
John Coltrane, "Acknowledgement"
Miles Davis, "E.S.P."

Jazz Concepts (audio and/or video demonstrations of terms covered here)

backbeat	modal jazz	sequence
block chords	modulation	tonic
call and response	multiphonics	tremolo
chromatic scale	ostinato	triplets
ghosted notes	pentatonic scale	tritone
half, whole steps	polyrhythm	walking bass
Harmon mute	quartal chords	
major scale	(or harmonies)	

- For quick reference, review the **Chapter Overview** and **Chapter Outline**.

- Take the online **Chapter** and **Listening Quizzes**.

- Use the online **Glossary** and **Flashcards** to review important terms.

BEBOP

With the arrival of bebop in the mid-1940s, jazz turned a sharp corner. Emerging from Swing Era jam sessions, bebop was at the same time a rejection of the era's racial prejudice and resulting commercial restrictions. Bebop, with its fast tempos and complex harmonies, failed as popular music, but over sixty years later, young jazz musicians still learn to improvise by studying Charlie Parker and Dizzy Gillespie.

Texture
- homophonic, with occasional monophonic breaks

Rhythm
- unpredictable, extremely fast tempos

Typical instrumentation
- solo: saxophone (alto or tenor), trumpet
- rhythm section: piano, bass, drums
- other possibilities: trombone, vibraphone, electric guitar

Form
- original melodies written over standard forms (12-bar blues, 32-bar popular song)

Special techniques
- heads (unison lines at beginning and end)
- trading fours (between soloists, between soloists and drummer)
- comping (piano, guitar)
- interactive drums ("dropping bombs")

Bebop pioneers
- Kenny Clarke (drums)
- Dizzy Gillespie (trumpet)
- Charlie Parker (alto saxophone)
- Thelonious Monk (piano)
- Art Blakey (drums)
- Wardell Gray (tenor saxophone)
- Dexter Gordon (tenor saxophone)
- Milt Jackson (vibraphone)
- Theodore "Fats" Navarro (trumpet)
- Bud Powell (piano)
- Max Roach (drums)
- J. J. Johnson (trombone)
- Miles Davis (trumpet)
- Red Rodney (trumpet)
- Al Haig (piano)
- Kenny Dorham (trumpet)

COOL JAZZ

Cool (or West Coast) jazz grew out of bebop in the early 1950s. The style is characterized by a light, laid-back, reticent quality.

Texture
- basically homophonic, tending toward polyphonic lines

Rhythm
- unusual meters (five, seven)

Typical instrumentation
- solo: experimental (possible additions: flute, tuba, French horn, oboe)
- rhythm section: piano, bass, drums

Form
- 12-bar blues, 32-bar popular song, classically influenced compositions (fugue, atonal music)

Special techniques
- restrained timbre, vibrato
- limited range
- quiet rhythm section

Cool jazz pioneers
- Lennie Tristano (piano)
- Tadd Dameron (piano)

Important cool bands/musicians

- Miles Davis Nonet ("Birth of the Cool")
- Lee Konitz (alto saxophone)
- Gil Evans (piano/arranger)
- Gerry Mulligan Quartet: Mulligan (baritone saxophone), Chet Baker (trumpet), Chico Hamilton (drums)
- Modern Jazz Quartet: John Lewis (piano), Milt Jackson (vibraphone), Percy Heath (bass)
- Dave Brubeck (piano), with Paul Desmond (alto saxophone)
- "white Lesters": Stan Getz, Zoot Sims, Al Cohn, Allen Eager

HARD BOP

Hard bop, centered on the East Coast, was a counterstatement to cool jazz: it was essentially a revival of bop but with a harder edge.

Texture

- homophonic, with occasional monophonic breaks

Rhythm

- assertive

Typical instrumentation

- solo: trumpet, saxophone, piano, bass, drums
- rhythm section: piano, bass, drums

Form: 12-bar blues, 32-bar popular song

Special techniques

- bop with a rough edge, resisting experimentation
- heavy, dark timbres
- African American aesthetic

Important hard bop bands/musicians

- Jazz Messengers: Art Blakey (drums), Horace Silver (piano)
- Clifford Brown (trumpet), Max Roach (drums)
- Sonny Rollins (tenor saxophone)
- Wes Montgomery (electric guitar)
- Miles Davis Quintet
- "black Lesters": Dexter Gordon, Wardell Gray, Illinois Jacquet, Gene Ammons

JAZZ COMPOSERS

Pianist Thelonious Monk, after Duke Ellington the most widely performed of jazz composers, worked almost exclusively with 12-bar blues and 32-bar **A A B A** tunes. He sometimes altered standard harmonic progressions with whole-tone and chromatic scales, and added quirky dissonances (such as minor seconds and tritones). Monk believed that a meaningful improvisation should flow and develop the composed theme.

Bassist Charles Mingus, among the most accomplished virtuosos of his time, composed in styles as far ranging as the sanctified church, New Orleans polyphony, swing, hard bop, and classical music. He was the first composer of his generation to pay tributes to great musicians of the past, such as Lester Young and Jelly Roll Morton.

Gil Evans "elevated arranging virtually to the art of composition," in the words of Gunther Schuller. His imaginative arrangements were characterized by the use of counterpoint, slow-moving chords, and very low instruments (tuba) combined with very high ones (flute). He's best known for his use of concerto form, featuring a single soloist.

George Russell, who worked exclusively as a composer-bandleader, devoted much of his life to formulating an intricate musical theory known as the Lydian chromatic concept. His ideas were the basis for modalism, which liberated jazz from bebop's harmonic grids and encouraged improvisers to think more melodically.

MILES DAVIS AND JOHN COLTRANE

Miles Davis was the archetypal modern jazz musician, a magnet for artists in and out of music. His unmistakable trumpet style was characterized by emotional and rhythmic restraint, while his continuous rethinking of harmony, melody, rhythm, and instrumentation led to works that changed the ground rules of jazz at least six times.

- 1949–50: "birth of the cool" sessions launched the cool jazz movement.
- 1954: "Walkin'" provided the impetus for hard bop.
- 1957–60: collaborations with Gil Evans enlarged the scope of jazz composition and projected a new meditative mood.
- 1959: *Kind of Blue,* featuring modal improvisation, transformed jazz performance in its favoring of melody and nuance.
- 1963–67: second quintet's postbop style incorporated elements of the avant-garde (*E.S.P., Nefertiti*).
- 1969: *Bitches Brew* initiated an era of jazz-rock fusion.

The pianist on *Kind of Blue* was Bill Evans, one of the most influential musicians of his generation, who in 1959 premiered a new approach to the piano trio (favoring the bass), with Scott LaFaro (bass) and Paul Motian (drums).

Davis's musical and personal impact was equaled (or surpassed) by that of tenor saxophonist John Coltrane, who became the most intrepid explorer of modal jazz. While Davis in later years leaned toward rock, Coltrane embraced the expressionistic chaos of the avant-garde. His "sheets of sound" harmonic improvisation can be heard in *Giant Steps;* modal improvisation in "My Favorite Things," "Chasin' the Trane," and *A Love Supreme*, with his quartet—McCoy Tyner (piano), Jimmy Garrison (bass), and Elvin Jones (drums); and free improvisation in *Ascension*.

PART V

THE AVANT-GARDE, FUSION, HISTORICISM, AND NOW

By the 1960s, jazz had accrued a convoluted history in little more than half a century. There had been so many jazz schools that Duke Ellington spoke for most listeners and musicians when he said, "I don't know how such great extremes as now exist can be contained under the one heading." The most extreme developments were still to come: the avant-garde and fusion. The former seemed to blow all the rules out of the water, advancing improvisation that was free from predetermined harmonies and rhythms. Fusion took a more popular approach, combining improvisation with rock's rhythms and instrumentation. Sometimes, as in the music of Miles Davis and Ornette Coleman, the avant-garde and fusion coalesced.

In a precarious era, defined by an apparently endless occupation in Vietnam and racist atrocities and political assassinations at home, jazz could hardly compete

1939
- *Jazzmen* published: the first book to look back at early jazz.

1940
- The U.S. Good Neighbor Policy begins to have cultural ramifications as Walt Disney and others explore songs from South and Central America.

1940s
- "Jump" music popularized by Louis Jordan.

1942
- Bunk Johnson makes recordings.
- Sarah Vaughan wins talent competition at the Apollo Theater.

1947
- Dizzy Gillespie records "Manteca" (with Chano Pozo).
- University of North Texas, Denton, offers the first degree in jazz studies.

1948
- Machito records "Tanga."

1951
- *I Love Lucy* (with Lucille Ball and Desi Arnaz) debuts on TV, inadvertently spurring interest in Latin music.

1952
- Samuel Beckett's *Waiting for Godot* published.

1954
- Ray Charles's "I Got a Woman" is the No. 1 R&B hit.
- George Wein establishes the Newport Jazz Festival.
- Elvis Presley makes his first records for Sun, in Memphis.
- *The Glenn Miller Story* (with Jimmy Stewart) released.

1955
- Hammond B3 organ introduced.

1956
- Cecil Taylor plays at Five Spot, records *Jazz Advance*.

As John Coltrane forged ever farther into the avant-garde, he recruited his wife Alice Coltrane as pianist, 1966.

Since organizing her own orchestra in 1992, Maria Schneider has been a staple of the New York club scene, conducting her own subtly nuanced compositions and arrangements in weekly engagements while touring the world's festivals. She has won critics' awards (best big band, composer, arranger) year after year and nearly a dozen Grammys, and has innovated fan-funded recordings with her website—offering a successful new template for a faltering industry.

Composer and faculty member Gunther Schuller examines a score with guest "student" Ornette Coleman at the Lenox School of Jazz (Massachusetts), 1959.

in popularity with the accessible, verbal urgency of rock. Still, the avant-garde flourished artistically, expanding its base in Europe and ultimately demonstrating at least as much diversity as its predecessors. Coleman, its most radical yet lyrical proponent, eventually earned establishment plaudits that had been denied earlier jazz artists. His successors used every kind of music, from brass band marches to Javanese gamelan ensembles, to fashion new works and reinterpret old ones. A conservative movement also took hold, presenting big-band classics in repertory and advocating a return to generally accessible styles.

At the same time, jazz began to examine its own history in seminars and clinics, moving into the academy where orchestras were assembled as training grounds for young musicians. Although contrary theories of jazz history were advanced, by the twenty-first century most of the old battles had been settled and a universal modernism predominated, paying homage to the past while keeping its options open. The audience for jazz dwindled as the monopolized airwaves banished it, yet successful jazz festivals proliferated around the world and the overall level of virtuosity and commitment continued unabated.

- Frank Sinatra records *Songs for Swingin' Lovers*, with arranger Nelson Riddle.
- Duke Ellington makes a comeback at Newport.

1957
- Lenox School of Jazz founded in Massachusetts.
- *The Sound of Jazz* broadcast on TV.

1958
- Bossa nova initiated in Rio de Janeiro.
- Ornette Coleman makes his first recordings in Los Angeles.
- Mahalia Jackson brings gospel music, Chuck Berry brings rock, to Newport Jazz Festival.

1959
- Ornette Coleman appears at the Five Spot, records "Lonely Woman."
- Duke Ellington writes score to *Anatomy of a Murder*.

1960
- Coleman records *Free Jazz*.

1961
- Dizzy Gillespie, Charlie Byrd, and other musicians discover bossa nova in Brazil.

1963
- *Getz/Gilberto* is million-selling bossa nova record.

1964
- Albert Ayler records *Spiritual Unity*.
- Louis Armstrong has an unexpected hit with "Hello, Dolly!"
- The Beatles, Rolling Stones tour United States.

1965
- The Association for the Advancement of Creative Musicians (AACM) founded.

1966
- Cecil Taylor records *Unit Structures*.
- Duke Ellington receives President's Medal of Honor.

1967
- Art Ensemble of Chicago (AEC) formed.
- First Montreux Jazz Festival in Switzerland.

PART V

1968
- Martin Luther King Jr. and Robert F. Kennedy assassinated.
- USSR invades Czechoslovakia.

1969
- Anthony Braxton records *For Alto.*
- Miles Davis records *In a Silent Way, Bitches Brew.*
- Woodstock concert in Bethel, New York.
- Neil Armstrong becomes first man to walk on moon.
- Philip Roth's *Portnoy's Complaint* published.

1970
- Supreme Court, in *Roe v. Wade,* affirms abortion rights.
- U.S. invades Cambodia.

1971
- Louis Armstrong dies.

1972
- Mahavishnu Orchestra records *The Inner Mounting Flame.*

- Chick Corea forms Return to Forever.

1973
- George Roy Hill's *The Sting* (with Paul Newman and Robert Redford) revives interest in Scott Joplin and ragtime.
- Vietnam War ends.

1974
- Herbie Hancock records *Head Hunters.*
- Duke Ellington dies.
- President Richard M. Nixon resigns over the Watergate scandal.

1974–86
- The Loft Era takes hold in downtown New York.

1975
- Keith Jarrett records *The Köln Concert.*

1976
- Weather Report records *Heavy Weather.*

He wore a wig and used an electronic pickup, but not even fusion could undermine the unmistakable timbre of Miles Davis, seen at a concert in London, 1989.

At a memorial service for John Coltrane, at St. Peter's Lutheran Church in New York, saxophonist Albert Ayler (in white suit) led his quartet in a dirge of astonishing intensity, July 21, 1967.

After you: Two of the great male vocalists to cross the divide between jazz and pop, Nat "King" Cole and Billy Eckstine, in New York, 1949.

At the time he turned eighty, in 2010, Sonny Rollins was the most honored living jazz artist. That year, he became the first jazz musician to win the annual Edward MacDowell Medal, awarded by the MacDowell Colony; and the National Medal of Arts, which was presented to him the following year at the White House by President Barack Obama. The playful glint in his eye is aimed directly at you.

Berliners celebrate as East Germans (backs to camera) flood through the dismantled Berlin Wall into West Berlin at Potsdamer Platz, November 12, 1989.

Matthew Shipp spent much of his career as pianist with the David S. Ware Quartet, while recording a series of albums that stretched his talents as composer and improviser.

1978
- Pat Metheny Group formed.

1979
- Henry Threadgill's avant-garde group Air records music by Scott Joplin and Jelly Roll Morton.
- Charles Mingus dies.
- Revolution in Iran, Americans held hostage at the U.S. embassy for over a year.

1981
- Sandra Day O'Connor becomes the first female Supreme Court justice.

1982
- Thelonious Monk dies.

1987
- Jazz at Lincoln Center established.
- Soviet prime minister Mikhail Gorbachev institutes policies of *glasnost* and *perestroika.*

1989
- Berlin Wall falls.

1990–94
- Apartheid dismantled in South Africa.

1997
- Wynton Marsalis receives Pulitzer Prize for his oratorio *Blood on the Fields.*

2001
- Terrorists attack World Trade Center and Pentagon.

2002
- Jason Moran records *Modernistic.*

2006
- Thelonious Monk receives a posthumous Pulitzer Prize for his body of work.

2007
- Ornette Coleman receives Pulitzer Prize for his recording *Sound Grammar.*

2008
- Barack Obama is elected the first African American president in U.S. history.

ORNETTE COLEMAN
lonely woman

CECIL TAYLOR
bulbs

ALBERT AYLER
ghosts

ANTHONY BRAXTON/MAX ROACH
spirit possession

WORLD SAXOPHONE QUARTET
hattie wall

15

THE AVANT-GARDE

FORWARD MARCH

The term "avant-garde" originated in the French military to denote troops sent ahead of the regular army to scout unknown territory. In English, the word was adapted to describe innovative composers, writers, painters, and other modernist artists whose work was so pioneering that it pushed the boundaries of contemporary thought. Avant-gardism liberated artists from the restraints of tradition, and often went hand-in-hand with progressive social ideas.

Two especially prominent avant-garde movements gathered steam in the decades following each world war, and jazz was vital to both. The first wave, emerging in the 1920s and including such factions as surrealism, cubism, and imagism, as well as twelve-tone music, consciously sought to rupture artistic conventions. It was a response to the devastation of World War I, the expansion of women's rights, and startling advances in technology—radio, talking pictures, transcontinental flight—that seemed to shrink the world while expanding its potential. Jazz was an integral part of this world, socially daring and emblematic of freethinking young people, and regarded by many as a powerful component of courageous modernism; yet few white Americans took its African American creators seriously.

The second avant-garde movement, of the late 1950s and 1960s, reflected conditions similar to those of the 1920s, only more so. The rebuilding of Europe and Asia

First wave

Second wave

Sonny Rollins combined the harmonic progressions of bop with the freedom of the avant-garde and sustained an international following. He appeared with percussionist Victor See Yuen and trombonist Clifton Anderson at a stadium in Louisiana, 1995.

343

THE FIVE SPOT

Few jazz clubs have had as profound an impact on the development of a particular kind of jazz as the Five Spot, which allowed the avant-garde to develop much as Minton's Playhouse allowed bop to develop. The main difference is that Minton's created a jam-session atmosphere in which individual players proved themselves, while the Five Spot became a showcase for major bands to perfect their music during open-ended engagements. Cecil Taylor, Ornette Coleman, and John Coltrane all had career-changing engagements there, as did Charles Mingus and Eric Dolphy, among others.

The Five Spot began as a family-operated bar on New York's Bowery. The owners, Iggy and Joe Termini, cared little about jazz, but in the middle 1950s a musician who held jam sessions in his loft offered to hold the sessions in their bar if the Terminis would buy a piano. In 1956, the Five Spot played host to two important engagements. Alto saxophonist Phil Woods organized an all-star tribute to Charlie Parker and recorded it—the first of many *Live at the Five Spot* albums. Then Taylor, utterly unknown in the jazz world, began the long residency that attracted a following of painters, writers, actors, and musicians.

The room was unprepossessing, small and dark, with a bar along one wall and the stage at the rear. Filled with smoke and the bohemian chatter of the regulars, it achieved national renown in 1957 when it presented a long engagement by Thelonious Monk's quartet, featuring Coltrane—the first of several extended Monk appearances through 1962, averaging six to eight months a year. In 1959, the Five Spot became the focal point for the jazz world when it presented Coleman in his New York debut, for three months. The club closed for a few years in 1967, for good in 1976.

Outside the Five Spot Café in 1958, tenor saxophonist Lester Young, wearing his porkpie hat, is greeted by pianist Hank Jones. The club was better known for long engagements by modernists like Monk, Coleman, Taylor, and Mingus.

he convinced the Five Spot in New York to hire his quartet—a six-week engagement that turned the neighborhood bar into a home for futuristic jazz and exposed Taylor's music to excited if often bewildered scrutiny.

Jazz Advance

Taylor's success at the club led directly to the recording *Jazz Advance*. His group consisted of Steve Lacy, the first important soprano saxophonist in jazz since Sidney Bechet; a classically trained bassist, Buell Neidlinger; and a self-taught drummer, Dennis Charles, whose inexperience pleased Taylor. Like Coleman, Taylor required malleable musicians who could follow him into new territory. For *Jazz Advance*, the band recorded intense versions of songs by Monk and Cole Porter, but the highlights were original compositions that suggested a free-form atonality and ferocious rhythmic attack. On the basis of that album, Taylor's quartet was invited to play at the 1957 Newport Jazz Festival, where he received respectful if hesitant notices largely concerned with physical descriptions of his rapid attack, creating pealing cascades of notes.

A turning point came in 1961, as he began to work with more accomplished musicians who hastened his break with the last vestiges of bebop principles. These included tenor saxophonist Archie Shepp, who later recorded with Coltrane and made an important series of politically blunt avant-garde recordings (Shepp's 1965 *Fire Music*, perhaps his masterpiece, is an indispensable album of that period), and two musicians who would go on to play critical roles in Taylor's music: alto saxophonist Jimmy Lyons, who remained with him for twenty-five years, and drummer Sonny Murray, who worked with him for only a few years but profoundly influenced his approach to rhythm.

Unit Structures

Rather than writing conventional scores, Taylor preferred an arcane system of sketches, fragments, codes, and arrows. He did not, however, provide his musicians with these scores. Instead, he played episodes on the piano, which the musicians picked up by ear and developed by way of improvisation. As he explained it: "When you ask a man to read something, you ask him to take part of the energy of making music and put it somewhere else. Notation can be used as a point of reference, but the notation does not indicate music, it indicates a direction."

Taylor coined the term "unit structures" (also the title of a celebrated 1966 album) as a means of describing his method. Rather than compose a single theme to spur improvised variations, he constructed his works out of modules, or units; the group worked through each unit in sequence. Because the separate units were flexible (the band could work through any of them quickly or expansively), the performance of a particular piece could run ten minutes or an hour.

Jimmy Lyons, with his quick ear and particular affinity for Taylor's method, became a kind of translator, interpreting Taylor's figures on alto saxophone and showing the other musicians how to phrase and develop them. Sonny Murray, on the other hand, helped to trigger Taylor's most radical departure from the past: a way of playing rhythm based not on a preset meter, but on the energy level of the performance. The center of that force could be the piano or the drummer or another soloist. After he and Murray parted, Taylor developed his second closest association (after Lyons) with the drummer Andrew Cyrille, who worked with him from 1964 to 1975, and then formed his own Taylor-influenced ensemble.

Taylor's rhythmic attack was an example of his fundamental differences with Coleman. Both musicians were emotional, but if Coleman wore his heart on his sleeve, Taylor was virtuosic and intellectual. Coleman avoided the piano, developed his theories outside the framework of the educated tradition, perfected a raw timbre descended from the roots of African American music, and eventually employed relatively conventional notation and a dance-beat fusion. Taylor emphasized the piano's drum-like quality, studied modern classical theory and atonality, and avoided any kind of conventional notation (even in his several big bands). His particular kind of emotional commitment is evident in his method as a performer. His hands work so quickly they become a blur, as he produces great cataracts of sound. He pummels

Cecil Taylor attacked the piano as though it consisted of eighty-eight tuned drums, but could also be lyrical and romantically expansive. Despite his astonishing technique, he confounded the jazz audience for decades. New York, 1970s.

Jimmy Lyons / Sonny Murray

FRANK DRIGGS COLLECTION

VOICES

Drummer Andrew Cyrille, who had played and studied every kind of jazz drumming before joining Cecil Taylor, explained Taylor's process of improvising in a 2001 interview:

> We had a magical dialogue. This kind of improvising is a matter of very close listening and trading of information. It's like a game. We put forth sounds, ideas, rhythms, and melodic fragments that turn into much longer statements, and we surprise each other with replies and continue to evolve within the dialogue. It can be endless. And when we decide to resolve what's happening, it's as though we've finished a conversation. We have grown, matured, to some degree even mellowed.

By 2008, the avant-garde had continued to develop for half a century, influencing every kind of jazz with its treatment of timbre, instrumentation, and repertory. Still, avant-garde jazz today is all but unknown outside of a few American and European cities—an educated taste for a small, ardent audience.

ADDITIONAL LISTENING	
Ornette Coleman	"Turnaround" (1959)
Gunther Schuller	"Variants on a Theme of Thelonious Monk" (1960)
Cecil Taylor	"Rick Kick Shaw" (1956), "Enter, Evening" (1966), "Spring of Two Blue-J's, Part I" (1973), "3 Phasis" (1978)
Eric Dolphy	"Out There" (1960), "Out to Lunch" (1964)
Albert Ayler	"Bells" (1965), "Our Prayer / Spirits Rejoice" (1966)
Sonny Rollins	"The Bridge" (1962)
Andrew Hill	"Point of Departure" (1964)
Sun Ra	"Saturn" (1958), "Space Is the Place" (1972)
Muhal Richard Abrams	"Blues Forever" (1981)
Art Ensemble of Chicago	"Nice Guys" (1978)
Air	"Weeping Willow Rag" (1979)
David Murray	"Flowers for Albert" (1976), "Shakhill's Warrior" (1992), "El Matador" (1996)
World Saxophone Quartet	"I Heard That" (1980)

ONLINE MULTIMEDIA RESOURCES AND REVIEW MATERIALS

Author Insight Videos

Gary Giddins describes how musicians responded to the civil rights movement and the political aspect of "free jazz"; stresses the importance of being open-minded when listening to Ornette Coleman or Cecil Taylor, learning *how* to listen as you learn how to read Shakespeare or *Ulysses*; and recounts his experience as social coordinator at Grinnell, when he booked Taylor for a concert and was almost "impeached" as a result.

Interactive Listening Guides

Ornette Coleman, "Lonely Woman"
Cecil Taylor, "Bulbs"
Albert Ayler, "Ghosts"
Anthony Braxton / Max Roach, "Spirit Possession"
World Saxophone Quartet, "Hattie Wall"

Jazz Concepts (audio and/or video demonstrations of terms covered here)

arpeggio	major scale	polyphonic texture
block chords	minor scale	polyrhythm
call and response	multiphonics	riff
chromatic harmony	octave	rubato
diatonic scale	ostinato	tonic
dissonance	pedal point	whole-tone scale
dominant	pentatonic scale	

- For quick reference, review the **Chapter Overview** and **Chapter Outline**.
- Take the online **Chapter** and **Listening Quizzes**.
- Use the online **Glossary** and **Flashcards** to review important terms.

WES MONTGOMERY/JIMMY SMITH
o.g.d.

SARAH VAUGHAN
all of me

DIZZY GILLESPIE
manteca

STAN GETZ/JOÃO GILBERTO
só danço samba

EDDIE PALMIERI
un día bonito

FUSION I: R&B, SINGERS, AND LATIN JAZZ

NEW IDIOMS

In the late 1960s, as jazz musicians began to employ the instrumentation, rhythms, and repertory of rock in an effort to reposition jazz in the sphere of popular music, the word "fusion" was coined to denote this new synthesis, also known as **jazz-rock**. Yet fusions of one sort or another have always played a role in jazz history. Jazz, after all, emerged as an American phenomenon through the melding of traditions from Africa, Europe, and Latin America, and from an amalgamation of such sources as blues, ragtime, and Tin Pan Alley. In the words of Dexter Gordon, "Jazz is an octopus"—it will take whatever it needs or can use.

In this chapter and the next, we examine jazz's relationship to popular music, beginning in the 1940s. We will use the term **fusion** to describe all music situated on the boundary line between jazz and pop. In the usual narrative of jazz, the music develops in a fairly straight line, from the insular community of New Orleans to the internationally popular swing to the modernist reformation of bop to the art-for-art's sake avant-garde. In looking at jazz from a fusion perspective, however, we find an alternate approach that tacks back and forth between jazz and parallel changes in popular culture. This narrative

Sarah Vaughan was called "the Divine One" in praise of her peerless voice and musicianship, which won over the boppers and the general public. At Birdland, 1949.

focuses on stylistic developments and trends outside the parameters of jazz, including new dance grooves and advances in music technology that have altered jazz itself.

In the early years of the twentieth century, New Orleans musicians played to please audiences and employers, tailoring their music to a specific situation: advertising wagons, street parades, funerals, dancing in saloons or at pavilions. By the middle 1920s, in Chicago, New York, and elsewhere, a split had appeared between musicians who played jazz for the sake of playing jazz and society band leaders who inhibited their rhythms and reduced their improvisations to occasional breaks in otherwise gummy-sweet ballroom arrangements. Attempts to enliven those dance bands with jazzy condiments indicated an early, forced, and frequently awkward fusion of jazz and pop.

With the coming of the Swing Era in the middle 1930s, jazz was thoroughly integrated into the popular entertainment industry. Jazz bands played dance music, performing the latest popular songs, usually with singers. The art vs. commerce chasm continued to divide hot swing bands from sweet ones, yet each borrowed elements from the other—sweet bands ventured cautiously into jazz, and hot bands promoted pop singers, ballads, and novelty songs. There was relative peace in the kingdom until the bands began to fade in popularity, as which point it became evident that bebop would not be their only successor. Specifically, three listener-friendly alternatives emerged to take up the slack, all involving artists grounded in the Swing Era: rhythm and blues, mainstream pop vocals, and Latin jazz. Until the arrival of rock and roll, they would simultaneously dominate American popular music in the postwar era.

THE R&B CONNECTION

During the 1940s, an offshoot of swing called **jump music** was popularized by bandleader Louis Jordan and other former big-band musicians. This kind of "race music," which countered the experimental trends of modern jazz, eventually became known as **rhythm and blues** (R&B). It was only a matter of time before the appeal of R&B reached the white mainstream, with boogie-woogie as one of its primary ingredients.

At first, there wasn't much of a gap between jazz and what would become rhythm and blues. The jump style usually focused on blues played at a fast tempo and featured brash vocals backed with ensemble riffs. Lyrics might be risqué, satirical, serious, or socially relevant, but they were almost always marked by a humorous attitude. Several black bandleaders of the 1930s and 1940s—including Lionel Hampton, Cab Calloway, and Lucky Millinder—made jump blues a part of their repertory, and produced some of R&B's leading lights. But the gap steadily widened until R&B assumed prominence as a black popular music in its own right, and modern jazz went in another direction entirely. The breakthrough for R&B was chiefly engineered by Louis Jordan.

■ LOUIS JORDAN (1908–1975)

Jordan, a saxophonist, singer, and songwriter as well as an influential bandleader, was an unlikely phenomenon in American entertainment history. He recorded nearly sixty charted hits between 1942 and 1951; many of them reached the No. 1 and No. 2 positions on the R&B charts and crossed over to the predominantly white pop charts. Born in Arkansas, Jordan moved to New York in 1936 to play saxophone in Chick Webb's band. Two years

FRANK DRIGGS COLLECTION

Louis Jordan, playing alto saxophone at center stage, was the entertainer and musician who practically invented rhythm and blues. Here, he leads his Tympany Five (Josh Jackson, tenor saxophone; Bill Davis, piano; Jordan; Jesse Simprins, bass; Aaron Izenhall, trumpet; Eddie Byrd, drums) in a 1946 movie.

later, he organized the band that he eventually named Louis Jordan and His Tympany Five (his drummer, Walter Martin, used tympani in his traps set), consisting of two saxophonists, one trumpet player, and a three-man rhythm section. Jordan was a martinet, yet for all his endless rehearsing, the ensemble retained a loose-limbed joy, playing with such zest that it seemed to have the power of a big band.

At the height of the Swing Era, Jordan proved that a small group could achieve great commercial success. Widely imitated in the 1940s, he set the direction that the music industry followed after the war, as small bands took over in jazz and pop. Jordan's music derived much of its appeal and humor from the everyday life and current trends of Southern black culture, which—good, bad, and ridiculous—he often skewed and always celebrated. His songs are about sexual and marital mores, Saturday night parties, the draft, and the church; in emphasizing good times, they explore personal peccadilloes rather than hardship and injustice. Jordan reminded people that African Americans had a life, not just a grievance.

In the 1940s, Jordan's popularity was such that he recorded successful duets with Bing Crosby, Louis Armstrong, and Ella Fitzgerald, and appeared in several movies. His tunes blended elements of jazz, boogie-woogie, and Latin rhythms like the rumba, and he put them over with the kind of showmanship he had learned working on the minstrel and vaudeville circuits—complete with funny hats and comical sketches. No one, however, doubted his craftsmanship. As Sonny Rollins, who called Jordan "my first idol," observed, "He really was a great musician" with "the heart and soul of rhythm and blues." Some of Jordan's songs have endured as all-time standards, including "Is You Is or Is You Ain't My Baby," "Caldonia," "Let the Good Times Roll," and "Don't Let the Sun Catch You Crying." Jordan helped to pioneer the electric guitar in pop music, and the use of the Hammond organ, as he encouraged his pianists Wild Bill Davis and Bill Doggett to master it. Although his career slowed down in 1951 because of illness, his influence carried on in the music of Chuck Berry, T-Bone Walker, Bill Haley, B. B. King, and Ray Charles.

R&B's Influence on Jazz

Rhythm and blues was not only a forerunner of rock; it was also a lateral influence on jazz. Several musicians of Jordan's generation managed to succeed on both sides of the R&B–jazz divide, as the need for a party music increased in direct proportion to the sophisticated challenges proffered by modern jazz. Consider these tangled examples:

The alto saxophonist Earl Bostic studied harmony and theory before he took jobs playing and writing arrangements for big bands, including those of Don Redman, Cab Calloway, Artie Shaw, and Lionel Hampton. He received little popular recognition until 1951, when he recorded an R&B version of a song made famous a decade earlier by Duke Ellington, "Flamingo"; the record established him as the No. 1 instrumentalist of the year. His small band became, in turn, a training ground for such future jazz luminaries as John Coltrane and pianist Jaki Byard.

When Johnny Hodges took his five-year sabbatical from the Ellington orchestra to lead his own small group, he had a hit straightaway (in 1951) with the R&B tune "Castle Rock"; it did so well that even Frank Sinatra recorded a version. Significantly, Hodges didn't solo on his own recording. In a way, he was slumming to attract a mainstream audience. He had come of age in the 1920s; musicians who came up with Jordan in the 1940s recognized that the template for commercial success had changed. The younger audience wanted brazen, brassy music with a strong backbeat. A musician like Hodges, known for the dynamic elegance of his playing, would have to meet that audience on its terms, not his.

The most influential of Jordan's sidemen proved to be the keyboard player and arranger Wild Bill Davis, who had developed a piano style influenced by Fats Waller and Art Tatum. He was hired by Jordan in 1945, and served as his pianist and chief arranger for four years. Upon leaving Jordan in 1949, he began to focus on the organ, an instrument he had played intermittently ever since hearing a recording of Waller on the pipe organ in the 1930s. Davis's work on organ attracted the attention of musicians, but found little commercial success; he's best remembered for adapting his organ arrangements of "April in Paris" for the Count Basie Orchestra—No. 8 on the R&B charts in 1956.

Davis's replacement in Jordan's band (1949–51) was the more experienced jazz pianist and arranger Bill Doggett, who had worked with several big bands; he had arranged Thelonious Monk's " 'Round Midnight" for the Cootie Williams Orchestra. After hearing Davis play the Hammond electric organ, Doggett followed suit, and in 1956 scored the No. 1 record in the country with his rock and roll opus "Honky Tonk (Parts 1 & 1)." The success of that record reflected a period when rock and roll, as yet undefined, sought inspiration from R&B and technical know-how from jazz. In his later years, Doggett returned to the jazz-pop mainstream, writing arrangements for Ella Fitzgerald, Louis Armstrong, and the Ink Spots.

■ RAY CHARLES (1930–2004)

One musician single-handedly represented a fusion between swing, bop, R&B, gospel, and rock: the blind singer and pianist Ray Charles, whose influence was so pervasive that no one contested Frank Sinatra's nickname for him (adopted by his record label), "the Genius." Born to an impoverished family in Georgia, Charles was raised in Greenville, Florida, by his mother, who took him to the Shiloh Baptist Church on Sundays. He went much farther than anyone else in merging pop and gospel; observers said that he was no different from a Baptist church singer, except that he sang "baby" instead of "Jesus." He additionally emphasized the church connection by playing the kind of basic, blues-drenched piano chords associated with gospel music, and creating a backup choir of women singers, called the Raelettes.

On road tours, Charles perfected an original style that combined the blues, progressive bebop harmonies, and the testifying shouts and back-beat rhythms of gospel. His recording of "I Got a Woman" reached the No. 1 slot on the 1954 R&B hit parade, and during the next few years he triumphed in every area of international show business. His 1959 two-part hit "What'd I Say," a rock and roll landmark, firmly secured for him the white audience. And his hugely popular version of Hoagy Carmichael's "Georgia on My Mind" proved that he could sing anything, a point he drove home with albums of country and western songs, many of them adapted to the style of the old swing bands.

Ray Charles and other vocalists reached a larger audience than any jazz musician could. They flourished not as singers with big bands, as in the Swing Era, but instead as solo attractions leading their own groups, usually trios. For jazz musicians who wanted to reach the mainstream audience, the most successful avenue was a hard bop subsidiary called **soul jazz**. An obvious offshoot of music innovated by Art Blakey, Horace Silver, and Cannonball Adderley, this style also relied on a strong backbeat, an aggressive urban sound, and gospel-type chords, but it simplified the result—preferring basic harmonies, short solos, and clearly defined dance rhythms. Song titles paid particular attention to ethnic orientation (Bobby Timmons's "Moanin'") or celebrated the aspects of black life that characterized Louis Jordan's music: soul food, churchgoing, Saturday night parties.

In the 1960s, the exemplary modern jazz label Blue Note enjoyed a series of unlikely hits as successful hard bop records were assimilated into the mainstream: these included Herbie Hancock's "Watermelon Man" (adapted to a Latin style by bandleader Mongo Santamaria), Lee Morgan's "The Sidewinder" (used for a series of razor ads), and Silver's "Song for My Father" (covered by soul singer James Brown). The leaders of soul jazz attempted to cut out the middle man: rather than make records that generated pop versions, they made three-minute singles immediately suitable for pop radio.

PHOTO BY CAROLE REIFF/© CAROLE REIFF ARCHIVE

Blind from early childhood, Ray Charles (1959) combined his love of jazz, R&B, pop, country music, and gospel into a heady brew and often recorded with his vocal group, called the Raelettes.

Soul jazz

■ JIMMY SMITH (1925–2005)

The enormous popularity and influence of organist Jimmy Smith was a direct expression of the fusion between jazz and R&B. His was the kind of music that sustained an audience for jazz in black communities of the 1950s and 1960s. Like "the Genius" Ray Charles, Smith picked up his own nickname, "the Incredible Jimmy Smith"—and his imitators were everywhere. He launched a new kind of trio centered on the Hammond B3 organ, supported

© CHUCK STEWART

Jimmy Smith made the Hammond B3 one of the most popular instruments of his time, sustaining a feeling for soul music amid the complexities of modern jazz. In this 1950s photo, drawbars can be seen at lower left.

by drums and either guitar or tenor saxophone. The music was brash, bluesy, lean, and rocking, and it became ubiquitous in urban bars around the country, whether it was live or on jukeboxes.

Smith was born in Norristown, Pennsylvania, and studied piano with his parents, occasionally getting pointers from a young pianist in nearby Willow Grove, Bud Powell. For several years, Smith played piano with local R&B bands. In 1953, while traveling with one such group, he heard Wild Bill Davis (Louis Jordan's pianist and arranger for four years) play organ and was smitten.

Smith's fascination with the organ coincided with an important technological advance. The inventor Laurens Hammond had introduced the first Hammond organ (model A) in 1935. His goal was to replicate the opulent sound of a pipe organ through purely electronic means, but model A never caught on with the public or musicians: it was expensive, bulky, and complicated, involving two keyboards, foot pedals, and a system of drawbars (similar to stops) to control volume and timbre. In 1955, Hammond presented the model B3, an altogether tidier version that caught Smith's attention—so much so that he went into semi-seclusion for three months to study it. Wild Bill Davis warned him that it might take him a decade just to learn the bass pedals, but Smith wasn't discouraged:

> When finally I got enough money for a down payment on my own organ, I put it in a warehouse and I took a big sheet of paper and drew a floor plan of the pedals. Anytime I wanted to gauge the spaces and where to drop my foot down on which pedal, I'd look at the chart. Sometimes I would stay there four hours or maybe all day long if I'd luck up on something and get some new ideas using different stops.

Smith's mastery of the foot pedals allowed him to play complete bass lines with his feet, setting a powerful precedent for subsequent jazz organists. He also realized that the B3's keyboard, called a "waterfall keyboard" for its light construction, rounded edge, and absence of an overhanging lip, encouraged rapid melody lines and glissandos played with the palm of the hand. His tremendous technique enabled him to develop an attack that combined R&B rhythms and gospel feeling with daunting bebop virtuosity.

Smith introduced his trio in Atlantic City in September 1955. The following January, he scored a much touted New York debut at Harlem's Small's Paradise. Blue Note signed him and promptly released his album *A New Star—A New Sound: Jimmy Smith at the Organ*. He played a torrent of notes with the right hand, supporting chords or drones with the left, and a walking bass with his feet or left hand (on a lower keyboard), often sparking his solos with glissandos that varied in speed (some were sensuously slow-moving) and texture—a consequence of his peerless ability to combine keyboards, drawbars, and pedals. He recorded prolifically, using album titles that echoed the categories Louis Jordan had popularized: leisure time (*House Party*, 1957), church (*The Sermon*, 1958), and food (*Back at the Chicken Shack*, 1960). While the avant-garde was busy splintering the "serious" jazz audience, Smith maintained a fervent popular following.

🎧 "O.G.D."

At a time when jazz stars really were stars, by any measure of commercial or critical success, record producers encouraged pairings; few worked as well as the 1966 sessions by Smith and Wes Montgomery. The matchup was made possible by the fact that both artists were under contract to the same label (Verve), but its success reflected their friendship and genuine enthusiasm for the project. The first meeting of what was billed as "the dynamic duo" used a big band as a framing device, handsomely arranged but unnecessary and even intrusive if you mostly wanted to hear these brilliant musicians interact. On the quartet session that followed, each man became in effect the other's "orchestra"—one of the particular pleasures of "O.G.D" is their cannily inventive accompaniments.

With Montgomery

Montgomery wrote themes considered "tricky" for their harmonic and rhythmic ingenuity, and "O.G.D." exemplifies these traits. It combines minor and major seventh chords, Latin and 4/4 rhythms, and a melody so hummable that two years later he renamed it "Road Song" for an easy-listening rendition (alas, his last album), which became a huge pop hit. The piece, apparently untitled at the time of the session, was labeled "O.G.D." by the producer, an abbreviation for organ, guitar, drums. This version is the alternate take; the original album has a longer, less compelling performance. Many of the details that make this one so absorbing, including Smith's piercing chords in the second **A** section, Montgomery's elegant triplets, and much of the interaction, came to fruition in this take, which was released a few years later on an anthology. Most of their trademark gambits are in evidence: Montgomery's incomparably mellow octaves, rhythmically varied phrases, melodic variations; and Smith's blues-driven riffs and squawks, humorous background figures, incredible speed, and signature tension-raising use of repetition (3:20–3:32), which in concert he sometimes stretched out for a chorus or more, until the audience begged for mercy.

LISTENING GUIDE 60

🎧 o.g.d.

WES MONTGOMERY AND JIMMY SMITH
Jimmy Smith, organ; Wes Montgomery, electric guitar; Grady Tate, drums; Ray Baretto, conga

- Label: Verve (E)VLP9177
- Date: 1966
- Style: hard bop
- Form: 32-bar popular song (**A A B A**)

What to listen for:
- Smith's organ playing (including bass line)
- polyrhythmic playing
- Montgomery's guitar technique (including octaves)

CHORUS 1 (HEAD)

0:00	**A**	Over a relaxed Latin groove, Montgomery plays the melody in **octaves**. Smith plays quiet chords behind him.
0:13	**A**	On its repetition, Smith responds to the melody with biting organ chords.
0:26	**B**	The bridge uses more **chromatic** harmony. Underneath Montgomery's melody, Smith plays a descending **countermelody**.
0:39	**A**	

CHORUS 2

0:52   **A**   Montgomery's solo begins with a broad **triplet** rhythm. Smith comps underneath.

1:04   **A**   Montgomery begins the next phrase with a pair of chords, followed by a blues-tinged high note.

1:11   He begins playing in **double-time**.

1:17   **B**   The double-time rhythmic feeling continues throughout the bridge.

1:27   At the end of the bridge, he returns to normal time.

1:29   **A**

1:32   Montgomery uses a guitarist's version of **false fingering**: playing a repeated note on two different strings with a subtle shift in timbre. The phrase ends with a **blue note** (at 1:35).

CHORUS 3

1:42   **A**   Montgomery starts playing in octaves, occasionally interrupting his simple, direct phrases with fast triplets. (e.g., at 1:45).

1:54   **A**   Searching for a fresh sound, he finds a pair of unusual notes within the scale.

2:07   **B**

2:19   **A**   He returns to the rhythm of the opening of the head, ending his solo on a high pitch.

CHORUS 4

2:32   **A**   Smith echoes the high notes Montgomery had just played; he uses them as a riff, in **call and response** with his lower register.

2:41   He suddenly shifts to a fast, double-time line.

2:44   **A**   Montgomery accompanies Smith's churning line with a **polyrhythmic** bent chord.

2:56   **B**   Over the changing harmonies, Smith plays bluesy lines; yet when the harmony shifts up a half step (3:00), he plays notes that match the chords.

3:08   **A**   On returning to the **tonic**, Smith weaves his line in and around Montgomery's bent chord.

CHORUS 5

3:20   **A**   Smith's second chorus focuses almost exclusively on a short riff.

3:32   **A**   He switches to a two-note chord, again playing it polyrhythmically.

3:45   **B**   Over the chromatic harmonies of the bridge, he plays a blindingly fast line.

3:57   **A**   His last section begins with the same unusual notes Montgomery played at 1:54.

CHORUS 6 (HEAD)

4:09   **A**   Montgomery repeats the head, playing his accompaniment figures more vigorously than before.

4:21   **A**   Smith responds to the melody with a syncopated series of repeated chords.

4:34   **B**

4:46   **A**   Smith's chords echo the rhythm of Montgomery's line.

CODA

4:58   The band repeats the last four bars.

5:04   While Smith holds the last chord, Montgomery plays a descending scale in **tremolo**.

SINGERS IN THE MAINSTREAM

The 1950s are often described as a golden age for singers of the classic American songbook. The claim is justified on several counts, and may be attributed to at least four factors. First, the number of gifted vocalists was remarkable; most of them had apprenticed with big bands and were now aiming for solo careers. After the war, returning servicemen whose musical tastes had been conditioned by prewar band styles and the singers who dominated V-Discs (recordings made expressly for the armed forces) provided a made-to-order audience. Second, in addition to new songs constantly ground out for movies, theater, and record sessions, an astonishingly large repertory of songs written between the 1920s and 1950s had become part of the country's musical diet. Some composers and lyricists (Irving Berlin, Richard Rodgers, Duke Ellington, Hoagy Carmichael, Johnny Mercer, Harold Arlen, and others) were as well known to the public as the performers.

Third, the 45-rpm single furthered the careers of rising stars and encouraged novelty songs and other "one-hit wonders." At the same time, the 33-rpm album attracted an older and more affluent audience, as an ideal forum for mature performers like Ella Fitzgerald and Frank Sinatra. Finally, the rise of television in the 1950s helped sustain the careers of established performers, particularly singers. Variety shows, combining music and comedy, were broadcast nearly every day, in the afternoon as well as during prime time, and most were initially built around singers who had become famous during the war.

Nat "King" Cole (1949) was considered one of the finest pianists in jazz as leader of an influential trio with guitar and bass—then he started to sing and became one of the most successful entertainers of all time.

Rosemary Clooney

Nat "King" Cole

As they supplanted bandleaders as music industry stars, many singers maintained a connection to jazz or swing, because that was the music they had grown up with. To choose one of many examples, Rosemary Clooney was a best-selling recording artist between 1951 and 1954. Her biggest hit, a nonsense song about food, "Come On-a My House," was so popular it put her on the cover of *Time* and led to a film and television career. She had recorded this novelty number under duress; its phenomenal success, however, allowed her to record more personally rewarding LPs, like the 1956 collaboration with Duke Ellington *Blue Rose*. During the last thirty years of her career, she performed almost exclusively with jazz musicians, singing the classic American songbook. Clooney was essentially a popular artist who had learned her trade touring with a big band.

In contrast, Nat "King" Cole was an accomplished jazz pianist who enjoyed an unexpected triumph as one of the most successful pop singers of all time. His singing on the novelty song "Straighten Up and Fly Right" helped him achieve a commercial breakthrough in 1943, yet during the next few years he was still known primarily as an excellent pianist who occasionally sang numbers with an R&B appeal similar to that of Louis Jordan. After the war, however, Cole began recording ballads like "Mona Lisa" and "Too Young," smash hits that outsold most of his white rivals'. His popularity was so great that in 1956 he became the first African American entertainer (and the last for more than a decade) to be offered his own television show, sponsored by Revlon cosmetics. When Southern affiliates protested, though, Revlon withdrew its support, complaining that Negro women did not use cosmetics. Cole's much-quoted response was "Revlon is afraid of the dark."

■ FRANK SINATRA (1915–1998)

No popular singer had a more fabled career than Frank Sinatra, universally admired by jazz artists—from classic prewar figures like Louis Armstrong, Duke Ellington, and Count Basie (all of whom he performed with) to such modernists as Miles Davis and John Coltrane, who acknowledged his influence and recorded several of the songs he introduced. Born in Hoboken, New Jersey,

Sinatra started out as an imitator of his idol, Bing Crosby, but developed a deeply personal style as he listened to the way such singers as Billie Holiday and cabaret performer Mabel Mercer interpreted lyrics, turning them into statements of private anguish. Sinatra believed that every song tells a story and that a singer's phrasing should emphasize the meaning of the lyric. As a young man, he practiced holding his breath under water to increase his lung power so that, like an instrumentalist, he could sing eight-bar phrases without pausing.

Sinatra lacked the rhythmic confidence of Crosby or Holiday, but won immediate recognition as a ballad singer who could delve deeper into the emotional core of a song than anyone else. From 1939 to 1942, he received international acclaim as the "boy singer" with the big bands of Harry James and Tommy Dorsey. His debut as a star in his own right was front-page news, attracting screaming female fans who fainted in his presence; newspapers called them swooners and referred to Sinatra as "Swoonatra." His more enduring nickname was "the Voice." In the early 1940s, Sinatra launched his own radio show and a film career in Hollywood. In those years, he rarely recorded anything at a fast tempo.

With the end of the war, Sinatra's career fell apart. Returning servicemen who resented his failure to serve ignored his recordings and broadcasts. They preferred Crosby, who had made a more vigorous contribution to the war effort, participating in entertainment tours in America and overseas. As Sinatra's career declined, excessive drinking and smoking marred his voice, gossip columnists pursued his rocky personal life (divorces, public brawls), and a newer crop of singers, like Clooney, Cole, Tony Bennett, and Billy Eckstine, won the hearts of younger listeners.

In perhaps the most celebrated comeback in American show business, Sinatra set about reinventing himself. He affected a new persona: the jet-set hipster-gambler-drinker-womanizer, sporting a fedora and holding a trench coat over his shoulder. He rebuilt his film career with powerful dramatic performances, winning an Academy Award as the doomed Maggio in *From Here to Eternity*. His most profound change, however, was musical. Although he remained an unparalleled ballad singer, Sinatra focused increasingly on up-tempo swing numbers, accompanied by studio orchestras arranged by some of the finest writers in popular music—most notably the orchestrator Nelson Riddle, known for his imaginative way of expanding the big-band sound with strings, harp, flutes, and other colorful instruments.

Frank Sinatra (1956) achieved widespread fame as a skinny, bow-tied ballad singer in the early 1940s, but after he remade himself as a jet-set swinger, he became a deeper artist and a stylistic avatar of the era.

© HERMAN LEONARD PHOTOGRAPHY LLC

Sinatra did not improvise as freely as a jazz singer, but he embellished the melodic line to make it more interesting. He continued to phrase in order to accentuate meaning, no matter the tempo. If he failed to swing in the easy legato manner associated with jazz, he did create his own kind of swing: a buoyant, foot-tapping, on-the-beat style that his detractors unfairly characterized as "a businessman's bounce." Ellington got to the root of Sinatra's art when he said, "Every song he sings is understandable and, most of all, believable, which is the ultimate in theater."

Working with Riddle, Sinatra was one of the first artists to make LPs that reflected a particular concept or theme (young love, loneliness, travel, dance). By 1956, Sinatra was king of the LP—he was also the anti–Elvis Presley, who was king of the 45. He remained a major force in the entertainment industry for the rest of his life.

■ SARAH VAUGHAN (1924–1990)

Sarah Vaughan approached jazz-pop fusion from the opposite vantage point. Sinatra was a pop performer steeped in the tradition of Tin Pan Alley and swing. Vaughan was a dedicated jazz singer who applied bop harmonies, rhythms, and improvisational ideas to popular music. The leading figures of bop attempted to make their music accessible (Charlie Parker's strings, Dizzy Gillespie's comical novelties), but they could never reach as far into the mainstream as Vaughan, who had one of the most admired and lustrous voices in twentieth-century music. Jazz musicians crowned her with two enduring nicknames, "Sassy" to denote her artistic temperament, and "the Divine One" to denote her art.

Vaughan was born in Newark, New Jersey, where she sang in the Mt. Zion Baptist Church, and learned piano from her mother, the church organist. Shy and awkward at eighteen, she sang "Body and Soul" at the Apollo Theater's Amateur Night, winning the competition and an important job. In the audience that night was pianist Earl Hines; astonished by her voice, he gave her a spot in his orchestra, playing second piano to Hines and sharing vocals with Billy Eckstine, his popular ballad singer and a lifelong friend to Vaughan. Word of Vaughan's gifts quickly spread, and in 1946 she headlined at New York's Café Society, developing a confident stage presence that eventually became world famous: sensuous, imperious, and yet humorously self-deprecating. One of her characteristic lines, uttered midway through a set as she wiped perspiration from her brow, was "I come up here every night looking like Lena Horne, and go home looking like Sarah Vaughan." Inevitably, she was signed by a major record label, Columbia.

Café Society and Columbia

Vaughan's contralto voice ranged over four octaves with excellent intonation, allowing her to nail far-reaching melodic and harmonic embellishments that were usually the restricted property of instrumentalists. She had a strong feeling for the blues (reflecting her gospel training) and, in marked contrast with Sinatra, an instinctive feel for swing: no businessman's bounce for her. By the time she signed with Columbia, in 1949, Vaughan was admired for her stunning creativity at any tempo.

The record label, however, wasn't looking for that kind of creativity, which it felt would alienate an audience that wanted to hear familiar songs in a familiar style. During her five years with Columbia, Vaughan was allowed to record only one outright jazz session (with sideman Miles Davis, who later compared her brilliance with that of Charlie Parker), but the presence of large string orchestras could not rein in her improvised embellishments. Nor could she fake interest in the kind of novelties that governed the pop charts in the early 1950s—the era of million-sellers like "The Doggie in the Window" and "Hot Diggity, Dog Diggity." When she signed with Mercury Records in 1954, that label acknowledged her dual appeal by having her alternate between jazz and pop record dates. In her first year with Mercury, Vaughan achieved a major hit with the forgettable "Make Yourself Comfortable" and also recorded an ageless jazz classic (called simply *Sarah Vaughan*) featuring trumpet player Clifford Brown. Typically, she refused to sing inferior songs in concert, no matter how well they sold.

Mercury

The 1950s were the years when Ella Fitzgerald expanded her audience with her songbook series, helping to establish the pantheon of American songwriters while sustaining her jazz following with astonishing flights of scat-singing. Some of Vaughan's best work similarly resulted from a fusion of jazz and pop. As long as she could work in both fields, everything was fine. But by the 1960s, a new generation of record executives was less than enchanted by her free-thinking spontaneity and rapier wit. Vaughan complained that producers handed her sheet music for new songs on the day they were to be recorded, depriving her of rehearsal time on the assumption that unfamiliarity with the material would tame her creative impulses.

Reinvention By 1967, she had had enough of their attempts to market her as a middlebrow pop star. When her contract ended, she turned her back on the industry and refused to record for four years. This turned out to be the beginning of the most successful phase in her career. Like Sinatra, Vaughan reinvented herself, but not by changing her music. Instead, she modified her place in the business, working in major concert halls with a trio instead of nightclubs, although she occasionally performed with big bands, guest stars, and even symphonic orchestras. When she resumed recording, she did so on her own terms and continued to successfully combine concerts and recordings for the rest of her life.

🎧 "All of Me"

This version of "All of Me" is from one of Vaughan's greatest albums, *Swingin' Easy*, a title that might incline listeners and particularly fledgling singers to murmur ruefully, "easy for you." The title was undoubtedly chosen by the producer, employing two highly marketable terms targeted at 1950s adults—the first an antidote to "rockin'," the second a hedge against complexity (e.g., bebop), the two together an invitation to chill. Music as sexy sedative: in the same period, Frank Sinatra offered *Songs for Swingin' Lovers* and *Nice 'n' Easy*. The Cold War was roiling; people were nervous.

Of course, there is nothing easy about this performance, least of all the swing, which is about as subtly sophisticated as rhythmic displacement can get. Like any artist of her eminence and skill, Vaughan allows you to take away as much as you bring to the experience. A cursory listener is likely to get caught up in her virtuosity, humor, inventiveness, and rhythmic aplomb. And in 1957, just about every listener had a good idea of what to expect before the needle hit the groove. "All of Me," written in 1931 by Gerald Marks and Seymour Simon, had endured as one of those undying standards, recorded and performed thousands of times. Vaughan lets you hear the song pretty much as written, in the first and third choruses, anyway—although even in them, she alters every phrase and, in some passages, every syllable. The closer you listen, the more rewarding her alchemy. She changes her vocal mask from bluesy to operatic, with several variations in between; revises the chords and melody; and adds intervals of an octave or more that the songwriters never imagined. As for that easy swinging, try this experiment: count four beats to the measure while noting where she places the first note of each phrase ("*all* of me," "*can't* you see," and so on). Does it fall after the beat, before the beat, on the beat? Actually, she switches the placement throughout, always with purpose, occasionally with a wink.

Then there's the second chorus, where she scats with all the freedom and adventure of an instrumentalist. She takes risk after risk, and lest anyone think that some of the grander conceits were worked out in advance, here's another experiment: listen to four or five of her performances of "All of Me," including those recorded in concert. They are markedly different, each with distinct and wildly original inventions. This version is buoyed by the superb trio of Jimmy Jones, Richard Davis, and the brilliant Roy Haynes. The jazz critic Martin Williams liked to tell of an evening when he escorted the opera singer Jan DeGaetani to a Vaughan concert. She was dazzled but concerned, advising him that if she kept stretching across her four octaves, she would quickly wear out her voice. He told her she had been doing it for more than three decades. She continued doing it until her death in 1990.

🎧 all of me

LISTENING GUIDE 61

SARAH VAUGHAN

Sarah Vaughan, vocal; Jimmy Jones, piano; Richard Davis, bass; Roy Haynes, drums

- Label: *Swingin' Easy*, EmArcy MG36109
- Date: 1957
- Style: hard bop
- Form: 32-bar popular song (**A B A C**)

What to listen for:

- **spectacular scat-singing**
- **Vaughan's wide vocal range and variety of timbres**
- **rhythm section as accompaniment**

INTRODUCTION

| 0:00 | | Jones plays a lively vamp over Davis's **pedal point** on bass. |

CHORUS 1

0:07	**A**	Vaughan begins the melody by flattening its contour to a single note. Behind her, Jones alternates **comping** with florid improvised lines.
0:17		On the phrase "*I'm no good without you,*" Vaughan alters her timbre to a more comical nasal sound.
0:22	**B**	She holds out the last note, allowing her timbre to return to normal before beginning the next phrase.
0:37	**A**	Vaughan sings her phrases with vigor, but noticeably behind the beat.
0:51	**C**	For the last, climactic phrase ("*You took the part*"), she returns firmly to the downbeat, abandoning syncopation to exaggerate the groove.
1:02		With a barrage of nonsense syllables, she begins **scat-singing**.

CHORUS 2

1:06	**A**	As Jones drops out, Vaughan's ascending line contrasts sharply with Davis's **walking bass**.
1:13		As she returns to her normal register, Vaughan matches the **dissonance** of her notes with a sharpened timbre.
1:21	**B**	A descent through the **whole-tone scale** takes us to her lowest notes. She follows this by a rapid ascent to two and a half octaves higher.
1:36	**A**	Vaughan repeats a **riff** she had just sung a few seconds before.
1:44		A sequence of **triplets** again explores her lower register, ending with a good example of a **flatted fifth** (1:46–47).
1:50	**C**	As she nears the end of her scat solo, her improvisation becomes more bluesy. She glides up to her high falsetto range, reaching a B-flat (almost two octaves above middle C).

CHORUS 3

| 2:06 | **A** | For the last chorus, Vaughan returns to the song's original melody and text, but continues her athletic improvisation. Jones returns, supporting her with firm comping. |
| 2:21 | **B** | |

2:24		She draws out one word ("I'll") before leaping an octave to continue the phrase.
2:37	A	Davis occasionally adds to the intensity by syncopating his bass notes.
2:52	C	Striking an operatic tone, Vaughan begins her last phrase with a step-by-step ascent.
2:59		With a sudden change of timbre, she returns to a bluesy feeling.
3:05		She holds the last note, giving the rhythm section time to make their last statements.

LATIN JAZZ: CUBA

The dance beats of the Caribbean, which are closely related to actual West African sources, have always exerted a powerful influence on jazz history, beginning with New Orleans. As Jelly Roll Morton counseled: "If you can't manage to put tinges of Spanish into your tunes, you will never be able to get the right seasoning, I call it, for jazz." Yet in the postwar era, the Latin "tinge," especially as developed in Cuba and Brazil, fused with jazz to create riveting new developments.

Cuban music maintained a large following in the United States in the big-band era and after, spurring the rumba in the 1930s, the mambo in the 1940s, and the cha-cha-cha in the 1950s. In those years, Cuba was a popular destination for vacationing Americans, who returned with a taste for those exotic, sexy dances. The most successful of the Cuban bands working in the United States offered little in the way of jazz, but they were much admired for their rhythmic vitality and colorful showmanship, which often entailed extravagant costumes and beautiful dancers and singers.

Xavier Cugat   The most famous of all the Latin bandleaders was Xavier Cugat, a Spanish-born violinist whose family moved to Cuba when he was a boy. His fame peaked in the 1940s, thanks to hit records and frequent appearances on radio and in the movies—he appeared in more Hollywood musicals than any other bandleader. Cugat's band did not play jazz, but it furthered a vogue for Latin music and bandleaders, of which there were soon a great many. (Desi Arnaz popularized that image on television in *I Love Lucy*.) Their success was encouraged by the Good Neighbor Policy, initiated by the United States in the late 1930s to counter its own interventionist policies, combat Nazi propaganda, and promote better relations with countries throughout Latin America.

Hollywood also began promoting a new generation of Latin leading men in musicals and dramas that pretended to take place in Havana or Rio, but were actually filmed on the studio lots. The most prominent Latin import **Carmen Miranda** was the wildly effervescent Brazilian entertainer Carmen Miranda, known for performing her songs in outrageous costumes that involved huge fruit-salad hats. But she insisted on being accompanied onscreen by her own band, performing authentic Brazilian sambas with wit and brio—her expressive arms and facial gestures emphasized the music's stirring rhythms.

■ MARIO BAUZÁ (1911–1993), MACHITO (1908–1984), and the DIZZY FACTOR

A profound realignment of Cuban music and jazz began to take place during the war but was little noticed until the late 1940s. This brew had been fermenting for years, partly in protest against Cugat's showboating, inau- **Cubop** thentic presentations. The new Cuban-jazz fusion was known as **Cubop** or **Afro-Cuban jazz**, and its relatively little-known godfather was the trumpet

Machito (seated far right) pioneered Afro-Cuban jazz and attracted many stars to the Brazil Club in Los Angeles (1946), including radio singer Lina Romay (black jacket) and Bing Crosby (center); also shown are his singer Graciela (to the right of Crosby) and trumpet player and composer Mario Bauzá (seated, second from right).

player and arranger Mario Bauzá. Born in Havana, Bauzá came to New York as a teenager and worked with important big bands, most notably that of Chick Webb. (When you recall that Webb also introduced Louis Jordan and Ella Fitzgerald, his posthumous influence beyond jazz is really quite astonishing.) In 1939, he attempted to form an Afro-Cuban band with Frank Grillo, soon to be known as the bandleader, singer, and maracas player Machito.

Machito was also raised in Havana, where he began performing in the 1920s. He moved to the United States in 1937, and worked with several Latin ensembles before he and Bauzá launched their first band, which was forced to fold for want of steady engagements. Bauzá joined Cab Calloway's orchestra and Machito recorded with Xavier Cugat. A year later, in 1940, everything changed: Machito formed the Afro-Cubans, a ten-piece band (two saxophonists, two trumpeters, pianist, bassist, four percussionists), and never looked back. Bauzá soon left Calloway to become Machito's music director, and hired innovative young arrangers to give the band a jazz sound. The California-based bandleader Stan Kenton later recalled that when he went to see Cugat, a member of the band told him, "Man, if you think this is good, you should go and hear Machito—he's the real thing!"

The foundation of Cuban music, and specifically of Cubop, is the **clave** (Spanish for "keystone"): a time-line pattern on which other rhythms may be stacked. A crucial difference between jazz and Latin rhythms is that jazz has a fairly symmetrical forward momentum (swing), charged by a strong backbeat. Clave is asymmetrical, creating tension within each measure by its fluid, constantly changing nature. It originated in West Africa and was adapted by Cuban musicians as the defining organizing rhythmic principle for their music. There are two widely played clave patterns. The **son clave** is a two-bar phrase that can be notated as

played as shown here or with the measures reversed. The **rumba clave** is similar but with one important change:

That subtle rhythmic shift allows rumba clave to fit compatibly with a more Africanized 6/8 meter. In a Latin band, the rhythm section is larger than the jazz configuration of piano, bass, and drums. In addition to trap drums, the instruments played by a typical Cubop percussion team are timbales, congas, bongos, maracas, claves (short wooden sticks), and guiros.

Gillespie　　　　The breakthrough for the Afro-Cuban jazz movement was triggered by Dizzy Gillespie. Once again, the seeds had been planted by Mario Bauzá. During the two years he spent with the Cab Calloway Orchestra, Bauzá persuaded Calloway to hire the young, untested Gillespie, whom he then privately instructed in the essentials of Cuban music, including clave. In 1946, backed by a contract with RCA-Victor, Gillespie organized a big band and started working toward a fusion of jazz and Cuban music. After Bauzá introduced him to Chano Pozo, the ingeniously flamboyant congas player, Gillespie invited Pozo and bongo player Chiquitico (Diego Iborra) to appear with his band at Carnegie Hall, marking the first public presentation of a serious jazz-Latin fusion.

Gillespie had already displayed a penchant for Afro rhythms in "A Night in Tunisia," but he now delved deeply into the arena of Cuban music, a subject about which he knew virtually nothing—in consulting Bauzá, he initially called the congas "one of those tom-tom things." He was a fast learner, eventually becoming a fair congas player himself. But in Pozo he had a master: a tough, wiry man who had been something of an underground legend in Havana. He had limited command of English, but Gillespie gave him a free reign to instill Latin polyrhythms in his band from 1947 until the end of 1948, when Pozo's life was cut short at age thirty-four by a bullet in a Harlem bar. In December 1947, the Gillespie band recorded their major works together: "Cubana Be" and "Cubana Bop" (arranged by George Russell in an early example of modal jazz), "Algo Bueno," and the instantly influential "Manteca." Recalling the response to "Manteca," Gillespie said, "It was similar to a nuclear weapon when it burst on the scene. They'd never heard a marriage of Cuban music and American music like that before."

🎧 "Manteca"

"Manteca" was originally Pozo's idea. The title, which literally means "grease" or "lard" in Spanish but which was also Cuban slang for marijuana, is loudly invoked by Pozo throughout the recording. We hear his conga drumming from the outset, interlocked with a Latin syncopated bass line strikingly different from the walking-bass line that characterized swing and bebop. The sections of the orchestra add riff upon riff, saturating the musical space with cross-rhythms. Pozo apparently wanted nothing but this tumultuous Latin groove, stretched out over a single tonic chord (another example of modal jazz). "If I had let it go like he wanted it," recalled Gillespie, "it would've been strictly Afro-Cuban, all the way."

Gillespie's job was to link these exotic sounds to jazz. In the introduction, his rapid-fire bebop solo ricochets past the riffs like an express train. Later on, he complements the "Manteca" tune with a sixteen-bar bridge that suddenly shifts to the distant realms of chromatic harmony. The whole piece, it seems, is in constant tension, moving from one world to another, giving the musicians a rhythmic background to challenge them and a harmonic one to comfort them. One of Gillespie's soloists, "Big Nick" Nicholas, was a hard-swinging tenor saxophonist, so the arrangement drops him into an "I Got Rhythm" chord progression with a steady four-four bass—he's so comfortable, he casually interpolates a reference to the song "Blue Moon." There is no better example of cultural fusion in mid-century America.

🎧 manteca

DIZZY GILLESPIE AND HIS ORCHESTRA

Dizzy Gillespie, Dave Burns, Elmon Wright, Benny Bailey, Lamar Wright Jr., trumpets; Bill Shepherd, Ted Kelly, trombones; Howard Johnson, John Brown, alto saxophones; Joe Gayles, George "Big Nick" Nicholas, tenor saxophones; Cecil Payne, baritone saxophone; John Lewis, piano; Al McKibbon, bass; Kenny Clarke, drums; Chano Pozo, congas and vocal

- Label: Victor 20-3023
- Date: 1947
- Style: big-band Latin jazz
- Form: 40-bar popular song (**A A B A**; the bridge lasts 16 bars) with interludes

What to listen for:

- Latin syncopated bass line and conga drumming, alternating with bebop groove and walking bass
- layered riffs supplied by the orchestra
- brilliant Gillespie improvisations, with bebop dissonances
- "I Got Rhythm" chord progression (interlude 2)

INTRODUCTION

0:00		The piece opens with an interlocking duet between the Afro-Cuban drumming of Pozo and the bassist. Pozo's repeated pattern emphasizes a strong **backbeat** on beat 2 (the high-pitched drum), and two drum beats that fall *just before* beat 1. The syncopated bass line falls strongly off the beat.
0:05		The drum set fills in the texture, adding a bass drum accent firmly on the beginning of each measure. Pozo begins chanting, *"Manteca! Manteca!"*
0:08		The baritone saxophone enters with yet another polyrhythmic riff, a two-note riff in **octaves**. It's soon doubled by the tenor saxophones.
0:16		The brass instruments enter: the trombone section on its own riff, the trumpet section doubling the saxophones but adding a chord at the end.
0:19		Gillespie adds his own improvised layer: simple phrases alternating with rapid bebop passages.
0:30		The full band enters with a sudden explosion. The final note is held and decays gradually, with each instrument falling away at its own rate. The texture once again reduces to the bass-conga duet (with the drums playing quietly behind them).

CHORUS 1 (HEAD)

0:38	A	The saxophones play a short riff, answered by the full band. Each line ends in a **shake**—a rapid tremolo that marks the end of the phrase. Behind them, the bass plays various asymmetric riffs.
0:49	A	
1:00	B	Playing a sustained chord, the saxophones **modulate** to a new key. The congas continue their rhythm, but the bassist has shifted to a walking-bass pattern.
1:12		Gillespie takes over the melody on trumpet, the saxophones harmonizing underneath him.
1:22	A	

INTERLUDE 1

1:33		We return to the bass-conga duet, with subtle changes in the bass line.
1:36		As Pozo shouts, *"Manteca!"* the trombones and saxophones reenter on riffs.
1:42		Over a **cross-rhythm**, the full band enters with the high trumpets on top.

INTERLUDE 2 ("I GOT RHYTHM")

1:48	A	With a flourish, Nicholas enters on tenor saxophone, improvising against **block chords** played by the full band. The chord progression is the jam-session favorite "I Got Rhythm," with a walking bass. The background chords, voiced at the peak of the trumpet section's range, feature intense bebop dissonances.
1:54		Nicholas's line lands strongly on the **flatted fifth** (a melodic dissonance).

| 1:59 | **A** | The band is now silent, leaving Nicholas to play with the rhythm section. He quotes the opening of "Blue Moon." The congas are still heard, but they subordinate their Latin rhythms to the prevailing bebop groove. |

CHORUS 2 (abbreviated)

2:10	**B**	The brass play a syncopated version of the melody, backed by a **countermelody** from the saxophones.
2:21		Entering on a stunning high note, Gillespie improvises over the second phrase.
2:32	**A**	The band returns to the opening riff.
2:38		Pozo bellows "*Manteca!*" over the entire band.

CODA

2:43		A conglomeration of riffs gradually declines in volume. Pozo continues to yell, changing his pitch and rhythm. The sound retreats to the bass and congas.
2:55		The bassist, now the focus of attention, plays variations on his line.
3:03		A few short drum strokes end the piece.

■ Bossa Nova: JOBIM, GILBERTO, and GETZ

Samba

A different style of Latin music came from Brazil, where the **samba**, having originated in the nineteenth century as an amalgam of African dances and march rhythms, laid particular emphasis on the second beat of the measure, or more specifically the eighth note leading from beat 1 to beat 2. Although it was grounded on a version of clave, samba does not use clave as an organizing rhythmic principle: the overall feeling is more relaxed than that of Cuban music. The samba found acceptance in the United States in the 1930s and 1940s through hit songs like "Brazil" and "Tico Tico" and the Hollywood stardom of Carmen Miranda, but by the 1950s it had faded into nostalgic memory.

Then in 1958, the revered Brazilian singer and actress Elizete Cardoso released an album (*Canção do Amor Demais*) that introduced Brazil to the most gifted songwriter it had ever produced: Antônio Carlos Brasileiro de Almeida (Tom) Jobim (1927–1994). Cardoso was accompanied on a couple of selections by Jobim's friend guitarist João Gilberto (b. 1931), whose way of playing gave Jobim's tunes a uniquely tranquil style that soon became known as **bossa nova** (new flair).

Antonio Carlos Jobim, Brazil's greatest songwriter (seen here in the 1960s), wrote the melodies and often the lyrics that João Gilberto and other musicians interpreted to launch the bossa nova.

Although detractors claimed that they were merely reinterpreting the traditional samba, Jobim and company insisted that bossa nova represented a break with tradition no less meaningful than bop's break with swing. The public agreed. Bossa nova incarnated a young, innovative attitude with poetic, sometimes self-mocking lyrics and melodies that, though occasionally melancholy, were almost invariably as gentle as a summer's breeze. Rhythmically, bossa nova seemed to sway rather than swing. Harmonically, it delighted in intricate chord changes not unlike those of bop, favoring seventh and ninth chords and melodic dissonances.

As of 1960, bossa nova was a phenomenon largely confined to Brazil. Two factors brought it north. First, as far as the United States was concerned, the 1959 Cuban Revolution put a damper on celebrating anything Cuban, from cigars to music. Brazil was now the logical place to turn to for South American rhythms. Second, touring jazz musicians—often sponsored by the State Department—discovered Jobim's songs and embraced them. Not surprisingly, the first American to seriously study Jobim's music was Dizzy Gillespie, during a visit in 1961. He added such bossa nova benchmarks as "Desafinado" and "Chega de Saudade" to his repertory and recorded them shortly after returning.

Another musician visiting Brazil in 1961 was guitarist Charlie Byrd, who toured South America for three months with his trio. Byrd could not interest an American label in recording bossa nova until he recruited Stan Getz (1927–1991), a musician who ranked with Dexter Gordon, Sonny Rollins, and John Coltrane as one of the most influential tenor saxophonists of the 1950s. When Woody Herman hired Getz in 1947, he placed him in what quickly evolved into the distinctive bebop reed section famously known as the "Four Brothers." Getz's brief solo on Herman's "Early Autumn" made him an overnight jazz star—his supple timbre had a cool, romantic, otherworldly quality that was instantly recognizable. When Getz, who worked with Machito during the Afro-Cuban jazz vogue, listened to recordings Byrd brought back from Brazil, he was sold on bossa nova.

Joining with Byrd's group, Getz recorded *Jazz Samba* early in 1962. A single version of one of the tracks, "Desafinado," became the kind of hit that drives album sales: *Jazz Samba* reached the No. 1 spot on the pop music charts. Within a year, more than two dozen jazz and pop albums claiming to have something to do with bossa nova were released, including creative ventures by Gillespie, Sonny Rollins, Cal Tjader, and Sarah Vaughan. There had been nothing like it in American pop since Elvis Presley triggered rock and roll—and nothing like it in jazz since the Swing Era. In 1963, Getz, aiming for greater authenticity, collaborated with the Brazilians who created bossa nova and had begun performing in New York. The million-selling *Getz/Gilberto* comprised eight songs by Jobim (who played piano), including the track that became a milestone in the globalization of the jazz–bossa nova fusion, "The Girl from Ipanema."

Stan Getz and João Gilberto did not get along very well, though they reunited a few times, including for the 1972 engagement at New York's Rainbow Room (with Chick Corea on piano) pictured here. Surprisingly, their largely one-sided dispute (Gilberto argued that Getz didn't understand his music) added to the magic of their 1963 masterpiece *Getz/ Gilberto*: instead of harmonizing, they played sequential solos, allowing each the freedom to interpret the incomparable songs of Antonio Carlos Jobim, whose piano helped keep both men on track, without either of them compromising.

© BETTMANN/CORBIS

🎧 "Só danço Samba"

The springtime sublimity that made *Getz/Gilberto* one of the most popular albums of its day did not reflect a cozy camaraderie at the recording studio. The notoriously prickly Gilberto felt that Getz, who also had a short fuse, failed to grasp the bossa nova rhythm on one piece. According to Ruy Castro, the Brazilian music historian, Gilberto told Jobim, in Portuguese, "Tom, tell that gringo he's a moron." Jobim translated: "Stan, João said to tell you that he has always dreamed of making a record with you." "Funny," Getz noted, "the tone of his voice" indicated something else. Jobim sent downstairs for a fifth of scotch to loosen everyone up. It did not help. For Gilberto, the essence of bossa nova, the style he virtually invented, was a quiet understatement; Getz, the most lyrical of saxophonists, was known for his use of dynamics, sudden loud reports that could pin your ears back. Somehow they produced eight masterly selections unlike anything else in jazz, and an album that stayed high on the pop charts for ninety-six weeks.

This background helps to explain the unusual structure of "Só danço Samba," which is symptomatic of the

whole album. Although Getz was an inspired accompanist, the performance is essentially bifurcated between Gilberto's presentation of the song and Getz's longer improvisation, with little if any interaction between them. Jobim, the composer (along with Vinicius de Moraes) of the major songs that launched bossa nova as an international sensation, binds the two sections with spare piano chords that highlight the intricate harmonies and laid-back rhythm. One of Jobim's lighter compositions, "Só danço Samba" comments on bossa nova's position within the latest dance crazes. His Portuguese is colloquial and elliptical, and thus sometimes hard to translate. The word "vai" ("go") could be an expression of either enthusiasm ("go, go, go!") or irritated dismissal ("enough, go away"). Either way, the mood is relaxed—the essence of hipster cool.

Jobim was widely regarded as the most original nonrock songwriter of the era, and Gilberto's solo recitals over the next forty-plus years were sold-out, séance-like events. But few musicians understood the songs better than Getz, who realized that their music gave new life to melody at a time when hard bop and avant-gardism favored jazz's rougher edges. Still, although he made several more bossa nova albums, Getz never again repeated the purity and inspiration of this one; nor did Gilberto's later recordings reach as many people. Like it or not, they were made for each other.

🎧 só danço samba

LISTENING GUIDE 63

STAN GETZ AND JOÃO GILBERTO

Stan Getz, tenor saxophone; Antônio Carlos Jobim, piano; João Gilberto, guitar and vocal; Tommy Williams, bass; Milton Banana, drums

- Label: *Getz / Gilberto*, Verve MGV8545
- Date: 1963
- Style: bossa nova
- Form: 32-bar popular song (**A A B A**)

What to listen for:

- Getz's smooth improvisation within the relaxed bossa nova groove
- Gilberto's inimitable reedy vocal and relaxed vibe
- Jobim's skill as a composer (and pianist)
- multiple modulations

INTRODUCTION

| 0:00 | | Gilberto's guitar introduces the samba beat over the bass line, answered by Jobim playing an octave on the piano. |

CHORUS 1

0:06	**A**	Gilberto sings a verse in celebration of the samba dance: "*Só danço samba, só danço samba, vai, vai, vai, vai vai*" ("Only samba dance, just samba dance—go, go, go, go, go").
0:17	**A**	Jobim adds a few notes on piano.
0:29	**B**	The bridge situates the singer's craze for samba amid other popular dances: "*Já dancei o twist até demais / Mas não sei, me cansei / Do calipso ao chá-chá-chá*" ("I danced plenty of twist / But I don't know, I'm tired of it all / From calypso to cha-cha-cha").
0:41	**A**	Gilberto places the text differently against the beat, creating **polyrhythm**.
0:50		Getz responds to the last phrase. The recording suddenly shifts away from the heavy reverberation associated with the vocal.

CHORUS 2

| 0:52 | **A** | Getz immediately **modulates** upward, to the key of F major. |
| 0:57 | | As Getz plays with **double-time** rhythms, Jobim comps on the **offbeat**. |

1:02		The last two notes are humorously placed in the tenor saxophone's lowest register.
1:04	A	A slight change in the bass line adds an additional harmony to the opening phrase.
1:16	B	To mark the bridge, Getz moves to his upper register. He plays a four-note motive, then repeats it, shifting its place in the meter.
1:22		He decorates his line with a short 16th-note figure.
1:27	A	Using a bluesy sound, he plays a short phrase polyrhythmically.

CHORUS 3

1:39	A	Getz modulates up one more time (to A-flat major). On drums, Banana plays more intently.
1:51	A	Focusing on short motives, Getz plays in double-time.
2:02	B	At the bridge, he returns to normal time.
2:08		He once again uses the 16th-note decorative pattern.
2:14	B	To end the solo, he returns to a bluesy figure.

CHORUS 4

2:26	A	Getz plays the head, mimicking Gilberto's rhythmic changes. Banana returns to a more restrained style.
2:38	A	Jobim returns to his consistent offbeat comping.
2:49	B	Getz plays the melody freely in his high register.
3:01	A	The last version of the melody is played **staccato**.

CODA

3:10		The band alternates between the **tonic** and a bluesy sounding IV chord. Getz plays lines that emphasize the **blue third** of the scale.
3:26		In an upward-reaching phrase, Getz plays the **flatted fifth** of the IV chord.
3:31		He descends quietly into his lowest register.
3:37		As he reaches his lowest note, the recording begins to fade.

SALSA

The Latin influence was widespread by 1950. Charlie Parker recorded with Machito, while Bud Powell drew on clave for his trio recording of "Un Poco Loco." But the Latin community itself was undergoing change. When the Cuban Revolution cut off immigration from the island, musical leadership in the barrio of New York shifted to Puerto Rico, and audiences embraced a broader appreciation of Latin American styles, such as the bossa nova, Argentine tango, and Mexican mariachi. Still, dance music in New York was governed by the basic Cuban song structure, the *son*, which consists of two sections: the *canta*, with a melody sung by the vocalist, followed by the *montuno*, named for a short repeating passage. The *montuno* opens up room for solos by both instrumentalists and singers, whose improvisation is framed by a repeating choral refrain (*coro*).

By the mid-1960s, Latin American musicians (who called themselves Nuyoricans) had created a new hybrid style: **salsa**. By the next decade, salsa was a full-blown urban tradition, with several ballrooms accommodating its orchestras and the loyal dancers and fans who followed them. The fact that "salsa" means "sauce," a well-known complement of Latin cuisine, prompted the timbales virtuoso Tito Puente to note, "I'm a musician, not a cook"; still, this spicy condiment matches the music's heat and intensity. Unlike earlier Latin styles, salsa was less a dance rhythm than a marketing concept. Promoted by Fania Records, the term symbolized the tough, uncompromising style of the barrio, home to a new generation of Latin musicians determined to make their mark

Eddie Palmieri's vigorous new salsa style combined intricate Latin rhythms, modern jazz harmonies, and imaginative improvisations. His trademark sound as an arranger, combining trombones and flute, has been widely imitated. He's seen here in the Netherlands, in 1987.

FRANS SCHELLEKENS / REDFERNS / GETTY IMAGES

on the American recording industry. Along the way, the instrumentation changed: the larger, big-band styles of the 1940s and 50s gave way to punchy smaller groups, featuring the brash sound of trombone soloists like Willie Colón.

A different group, La Perfecta, was led by pianist Eddie Palmieri (b. 1936), younger brother of Charlie Palmieri, an early salsa trumpet player. Eddie took his musical direction not only from Latin music but also from a panoply of jazz greats, including Horace Silver, Bud Powell, and McCoy Tyner. His connection to jazz was tenuous: although he was honored in 2013 by the NEA as a Jazz Master, his playing experience was thoroughly encased in salsa. Yet he was fascinated by jazz harmony, and even studied arranging and composition with the Russian music theorist Joseph Schillinger (who earlier taught George Gershwin and Benny Goodman).

La Perfecta also featured a jazz-savvy trombonist named Barry Rogers. Descended from Polish Jews, Rogers grew up surrounded by musical riches in the Bronx—which he absorbed by hanging out on the corner, admiring jazz trombonists, and listening to recordings his schoolteacher mother brought home from field research trips to Mexico and the Caribbean. After hearing Rogers perform one night with John Coltrane at Birdland, and another night at a local Latin dance club, Palmieri hired him for his group. Influenced by R&B singers, Rogers turned the trombone into a powerful, bluesy solo voice, bringing a soulful intensity into Latin music. His tone wasn't subtle—to make his mark in crowded ballrooms, he played at top volume, sounding (according to an awed Willie Colón) "like an elephant." But he learned the rhythmic discipline of Latin music, improvising incisive phrases that linked skillfully to the underlying clave rhythm. With their small, compact band—usually a pair of trombones and flute, plus rhythm—Palmieri and Rogers reproduced in Latin dance halls the improvisational freedom of the jam session.

🎧 "Un día bonito"

When La Perfecta folded in 1968, Palmieri and Rogers went their separate ways. Yet their collaboration continued on recordings, including *The Sun of Latin Music*, a 1974 album that exemplified the experimentalism of Palmieri's musical thought. The highlight of the album was undoubtedly the fourteen-minute masterpiece "Un día bonito" ("My Lovely Day"). When the record company re-released the album, it bowed to popular demand and cut the rambling, eight-minute piano-and-bass preamble. We agree, and have chosen to go with the shorter version, which begins with the tune itself. Like most of salsa, it's in the form of a Cuban *son*: the *canta*, or basic melody, alternates with intense *montunos* that give ample solo space to the singer—Palmieri's sixteen-year-old discovery Lalo Rodriguez—who improvises both words and music in a practice known as *soneo*.

This special album, mixing together elements from jazz and salsa, spurred the Grammy Award committee, which had never recognized Latin music, to create a new category to honor it—Best Latin Performance. "I've never played piano like that," Palmieri later recalled, "and I couldn't do that again if I tried."

🎧 un día bonito

EDDIE PALMIERI

Eddie Palmieri, piano; Lalo Rodriguez, vocal; Peter Gordon, horn; Virgil Jones, Vitin Paz, trumpets; Jose Luis Rodriguez, Barry Rogers, trombone; Tommy Lopez, bongos; Eladio Perez, congas; Nicky Marerro, timbales; Tony Price, tuba; Eddie Rivera, bass; Ronnie Cuber, Mario Rivera, baritone saxophones; Alfredo de la Fe, violin; Jimmy Sabater, Willie Torres, background vocals

- Label: *The Sun of Latin Music*, Coco 061173
- Date: 1974
- Style: salsa
- Form: Cuban *son*

What to listen for:

- **Palmieri's distinctive composition, featuring vocalist Rodriguez**
- **improvisation within a Latin groove**
- **Rogers's superb trombone solo**

INTRODUCTION

0:00   A two-note blast from the brass opens the piece.

0:03   Palmieri enters on piano with a ***montuno***: a short, rhythmically intense phrase, repeated every two bars.

0:09   As the percussion joins in, the rest of the band doubles the *montuno*.

0:14   The full brass section complicates the texture with rich, dissonant voicings.

0:33   A dominant chord prepares for the ***canta*** (melody).

CANTA

0:34   Rodriguez sings the main text for the song. While Palmieri and the bassist (Rivera) anchor the beat, Rodriguez sings his line entirely on the **offbeats**:
"En un día tan bonito como hoy / Yo me encuentro en California"
("On a lovely day like today / I find myself in California").

0:45   In pauses in the vocal line, the brass add interjections.

INTERLUDE

0:52   Over firmly held bass notes, the brass add complex harmonies.

1:01   The band drops out, leaving the percussion: Perez holding a steady pattern on congas, Lopez improvising on bongos, with Marrero keeping time on timbales in the distant background.

1:10   The lower brass and rhythm section play a short pattern of three menacing chords.

1:15   The trombones respond with chords on the offbeat.

1:19   Over both patterns, the trumpets play a dissonant **riff**.

1:26   The brass punch out chords in **call and response** with Palmieri.

1:33   Palmieri returns to the *montuno*.

CANTA

1:39   Rodriguez returns with the second half of his lyrics.

INTERLUDE

1:56   The brass repeat the passage previously heard at 0:52. In response, Sabater and Torres, harmonizing in thirds, sing the *coro* (refrain):
"Qué día bonito" ("What a lovely day").

MONTUNO (improvised section)

2:06   Over Palmieri's new *montuno*, Rogers begins his trombone solo with a bold dissonance. He's answered by the *coro*: "*Qué lindo mi día / Mi día bonito*" ("What a beautiful day / My lovely day").

2:14   Throughout his solo, Rogers plays short but rhythmically incisive phrases, maintaining a call and response with the *coro*.

2:29   In the percussion section, Lopez switches to a handbell.

2:32   Rodriguez begins a **soneo**, in which he improvises text as well as melody: *"Este es un día bonito para mí / Y por eso te lo digo San Francisco"* ("This is a lovely day for me / That's why I tell ya, San Francisco"). As with Rogers, his line continually converses with the *coro*.

INTERLUDE

3:12   The texture is interrupted once again for a return of the interlude passage.

3:19   Instead of the *coro,* Palmieri plays the response on the piano.

MONTUNO

3:22   Perez begins his conga solo by repeating a two-note phrase.

3:32   He alternates a complex pattern with open strokes and closed strokes.

3:46   His short phrases are interrupted by strings of 16th notes, divided between the two drums.

4:03   He uses a quick pair of notes to create polyrhythmic patterns.

4:12   He creates a stronger sense of **cross-rhythm** with another pattern (two high-pitched "closed" strokes, followed by two lower-pitched "open" strokes).

4:40   He builds his line entirely with notes on the offbeat.

4:51   Palmieri disrupts the texture by repeatedly hitting his keyboard with his arm, creating loud crashes.

4:55   While the piano sound slowly fades, the *coro* returns.

5:01   Rogers returns to his solo.

5:09   In the background, de la Fe adds a rhythmically tricky one-note pattern on violin.

5:29   Reaching the climax of his solo, Rogers accentuates his line with **glissandi**.

5:34   As Marrero comments with timbales strokes, the brass intensify the texture with background riffs, or **moña**.

5:47   Once again, Palmieri interrupts by bashing his piano. This time, however, the sound is electronically manipulated. The performance ends in a shimmering wash of noise.

MASS MEDIA JAZZ

Television: Four Clichés

As the gap widened between modern jazz and an increasingly uncomprehending public, jazz began to embody four very different cultural clichés—each far removed from the optimistic "Let's Dance" status that buoyed the music during the Swing Era. The use of jazz on TV in the late 1950s and early 1960s tells the story. In one cliché, jazz was associated with urban mavericks, especially beatniks; these depictions emphasized jive talk, eccentric haircuts and goatees, and aimless scat-singing or crime. The stereotype had nothing to do with music, and underscored the idea that jazz musicians and enthusiasts were cultural outsiders and probably not very bright.

The second cliché, though musical, also fostered a negative image: jazzy sounds—particularly sultry high notes played on alto saxophone—served as cues in dozens of shows to introduce women of doubtful virtue or bad parts of town.

Detective shows almost always featured jazz scores, most famously *Peter Gunn* (1958–61), with a theme by Henry Mancini that became a big hit. *M Squad* (1957–60) had music by Count Basie and Benny Carter, while Nelson Riddle scored *The Untouchables* (1959–63) and *Route 66* (1960–64).

The third cliché was largely positive though no less tiresome. This one postulated that jazz was the exclusive property of the super-hip. If you didn't qualify, you were a square or "out to lunch." Jazz was the antidote to rock and roll, regarded as kids' music. Cutting-edge comedians like Lenny Bruce revered jazz; stylish writers like Jack Kerouac and Norman Mailer pondered its meaning. This sort of jazz lover disappeared in the middle 1960s, as the Beatles, Bob Dylan, and others certified rock's adult bona fides.

The fourth role was the most positive and realistic: the actual presentation of jazz musicians on variety shows, late-night gabfests, and arts programming like *Omnibus* (1953–57), which hired Leonard Bernstein to explain "What Is Jazz?" Isolated one-shot programs were devoted entirely to jazz, including the justly acclaimed *The Sound of Jazz* (1957). The overall portrait, however, was severely circumscribed by mass taste and racial imperatives: singers were favored, blacks were limited to guest appearances, and true modernists were rarely welcome. Even so, more jazz was seen on television in the 1950s and 1960s than in the past forty years of cable TV—it was too much a part of the cultural landscape to ignore.

At the Movies

Jazz has always been part of the mix in Hollywood movies, even in the silent era, when ragtime was played by theatrical pianists and organists. From the beginning, jazz justifiably represented the sound of urban life; with less justification, it also came to signal immorality, in the form of wayward flappers, dissolute roués, and other lost souls.

During the Swing Era, the association between jazz and moral laxity briefly disappeared, as big-band music was celebrated for its all-American vitality, wartime sentimentality, and promise of good times. No sooner did the war end than jazz lost its Hollywood smiley face and came to represent urban decay and despair. Consider the episode in Frank Capra's Christmas perennial *It's a Wonderful Life* (1946), in which Jimmy Stewart is required to experience what his idyllic town would be like if he had never been born. The place has gone to hell, particularly the friendly neighborhood bar, which in his absence has been invaded by bullies, rummies, hookers, and ... Negro jazz!

In the 1950s, jazz stood for the same negative qualities in the movies as it did on television: the humid saxophone glissando became ubiquitous in melodramas whenever the camera turned to a "bad" woman or wandered into the city's tenderloin. Most of the jazzy film scores of the period were created by composers under contract to the Hollywood studios who were masters of their craft, especially as arrangers. Yet when they wrote jazz-influenced scores, they tended to settle for overstatement and hackneyed formulas. A few producers and directors rebelled and hired true jazz composers. A big push in this direction came from

Director Otto Preminger (left) signed Duke Ellington (right) and his aide de camp Billy Strayhorn to score *Anatomy of a Murder*. Ellington plays a pianist named Pie Eye in the 1959 film.

Europe (as we saw in Chapter 14), when French director Louis Malle hired Miles Davis to improvise a score for his 1957 film *Ascenseur pour l'échafaud*.

The Hollywood director Robert Wise, who would go on to direct such blockbusters as *West Side Story* and *The Sound of Music*, initiated a breakthrough for jazz with two films, *I Want to Live* (1958) and *Odds Against Tomorrow* (1959). Both explored the sleaziest elements in society, but the music was exceptional. John Mandel, a swing band arranger in the 1940s, wrote the former, featuring a West Coast "cool" band that included baritone saxophonist Gerry Mulligan, who appeared in the film. *Odds Against Tomorrow* was scored by pianist John Lewis, creator of the Modern Jazz Quartet.

One of the best and most significant scores was composed by Duke Ellington for Otto Preminger's *Anatomy of a Murder,* also in 1959. This assignment was considered unusual because the film is about a Midwestern country lawyer (Jimmy Stewart again), not a city slicker. Ellington was nevertheless encouraged to write in his own style and without restraint. His much-admired score shows that jazz has an emotional resonance that can echo beyond the city's mean streets. Still, the average jazz-style film score can be depended on, even now, to illuminate the travails of drug addicts, prostitutes, and criminals.

To this point, we have seen several different types of jazz fusion, all dealing with the basic elements of pop culture—dance music and popular song—that bebop had left behind. Aside from the brief flurry of enthusiasm for bossa nova, nothing felt like a movement: there was no attempt to reshape the relationship of jazz to society, or to dislodge cool jazz or hard bop from the mainstream. All that would change, however, when the very foundation of popular music was shaken by the rock revolution of the 1960s.

ADDITIONAL LISTENING

Louis Jordan	"Is You Is or Is You Ain't My Baby" (1943), "Caldonia" (1945)
Earl Bostic	"Flamingo" (1951)
Ray Charles	"I Got a Woman" (1958), "Georgia on My Mind" (1960)
Jimmy Smith	"The Sermon" (1958), "The Organ Grinder's Swing (1965)
Rosemary Clooney and Duke Ellington	"Grievin'" (1956)
Nat King Cole	"Sweet Lorraine" (1940), "Straighten Up and Fly Right" (1943)
Frank Sinatra	"The Birth of the Blues" (1952), "I've Got You Under My Skin" (1956)
Sarah Vaughan	"It's Crazy" (1954), "Baby, Won't You Please Come Home?" (1962), "My Funny Valentine" (1973)
Machito	"Tanga" (1949)
Charlie Parker and Machito	"Tico Tico" (1951)
Stan Getz and Charlie Byrd	"Samba Dees Days" (1962)
Stan Getz and João Gilberto	"Desafinado" (1962)
Mongo Santamaria	"Watermelon Man" (1962)
Eddie Palmieri	"Bouncer" (1993)
Rosa Passos	"Por Causa de Você" (2007)

ONLINE MULTIMEDIA RESOURCES AND REVIEW MATERIALS

Author Insight Videos

Gary Giddins traces the connection between jazz and Cuban music, from Dizzy Gillespie's explosive hit "Manteca" (1947) to the 1960s and salsa.

Interactive Listening Guides

Wes Montgomery / Jimmy Smith, "O.G.D."
Sarah Vaughan, "All of Me"
Dizzy Gillespie, "Manteca"
Stan Getz / João Gilberto, "Só danço Samba"
Eddie Palmieri, "Un día bonito"

Jazz Concepts (audio and/or video demonstrations of terms covered here)

backbeat	false fingering	shake
block chords	flatted fifth	staccato
blue note	glissando	tonic
bossa nova	modulation	tremolo
call and response	octave	triplet
chromatic harmony	pedal point	walking bass
clave	polyrhythm	whole-tone scale
countermelody	riff	
dissonance	samba	

- For quick reference, review the **Chapter Overview** and **Chapter Outline**.

- Take the online **Chapter** and **Listening Quizzes**.

- Use the online **Glossary** and **Flashcards** to review important terms.

WEATHER REPORT
teen town

HERBIE HANCOCK
cantaloupe island

JOHN SCOFIELD/MEDESKI, MARTIN AND WOOD
chank

ROBERT GLASPER
why do we try

FUSION II:
JAZZ, ROCK, AND BEYOND

BARBARIANS AT THE GATE

In the middle 1950s, a revolution occurred outside the gates of jazz and popular music. A new sound, **rock and roll**, unsettled the music industry by attracting an ever-growing body of white teenagers to a compelling fusion of the fluid rhythms of black race records and the plaintiveness of white "hillbilly" music. Its leaders included Elvis Presley, a Memphis truck driver who added pelvic gyrations and sensual poses to his mixture of blues, country, and Tin Pan Alley pop; Chuck Berry, a St. Louis bluesman who mimicked white country music, duck-walked through his guitar solos, and showed a real knack for writing songs about adolescents; and Little Richard, a gospel singer from Georgia who had begun recording boogie-woogie-style R&B in 1951 but didn't let loose until five years later, whooping his way onto the pop charts.

In retrospect, it seems that jazz musicians should have been paying attention to this new music, but few did. Early rock and roll was marketed and viewed as music for teenagers, created by amateurs and catering to untutored tastes. As far as most adults were concerned, it was at best errant nonsense, at worst a juvenile plague. Jazz, by contrast, was firmly part of an adult sensibility that surely would triumph over such rubbish. That

Miles Davis, who devoted as much time to his painting as to his music, was a work of art himself. He's seen here in Malibu, California, in 1989, just two years before he died.

illusion crumbled in the 1960s, when rock overwhelmed popular music, and jazz musicians found themselves struggling for survival in a world not of their making. The eventual result was a new jazz-rock fusion, which many assumed was simply the next phase of jazz, a fashion that would, at least for a while, displace all that had come before. For several years, it seemed like no one could escape it. Even bebop legends like Dizzy Gillespie and John Lewis allowed their sideburns to grow and opted for electric bass or electric piano. By the 1980s, the term "fusion" had fallen from favor, replaced by market-driven terms like "smooth jazz" and "contemporary jazz."

Jazz-Rock Background

Rock and roll's success was intertwined with a new generation of songwriters working in the Brill Building on New York City's Broadway. There, Carole King, Neil Sedaka, Neil Diamond, and others churned out hundreds of tunes aimed at the youth market. Few of these songs, with their puerile lyrics (Sedaka's "Stupid Cupid," for example), appealed to jazz musicians still attuned to the sophisticated harmonies and lyrics of Gershwin, Porter, Berlin, and Rodgers. But they created a pop repertory separate from the adult world.

In the same period, a different signal was sent by the collegiate Kingston Trio, which sold 6 million copies of their glossy version of an old folk song, "Tom Dooley," in 1958. Within a few years, a folk revival brought a new aesthetic: austere, simple, and moralistic. Veterans like Pete Seeger and Odetta and fresh-faced singers like Bob Dylan and Joan Baez became the lodestars for politically active youth, who felt it better to make their own music with harmonicas and guitars than to sully themselves with inauthentic "commercial" music. Yet in 1963, Dylan's "Blowin' in the Wind," as sung by Peter, Paul and Mary, sold a million copies, rising toward the top of both *Billboard*'s pop and easy-listening charts.

British invasion In 1964, the rock revolution went into full swing with the British invasion led by the Beatles and the Rolling Stones. They brought back into circulation pop styles from the 1950s that had struck the mainstream as obscure or extreme—those of Chuck Berry and Little Richard, rockabilly pioneers Carl Perkins and Gene Vincent, and Chicago blues artists Bo Diddley and Muddy Waters. If the Beatles made audiences feel safe, with matching suits and haircuts and a cheerful demeanor and repertory, the Stones introduced a note of surly defiance. The Beatles wanted to "hold your hand"; the Stones couldn't "get no satisfaction." These British artists made an anti-establishment attitude synonymous with youth culture.

They also brought their own music. To the surprise of their handlers, John Lennon and Paul McCartney created an astonishing catalog of tunes that were melodic, harmonically fresh, and instantly popular. They triggered a **Singer-songwriters** shift in the music industry that favored **singer-songwriters** over "mere" performers. Recording artists were expected to create their own songs, infusing them through performance with an aura of authenticity. When Bob Dylan went electric in 1965, bringing his heightened, expressive poetry into rock (to the horror of folk purists), it became clear that rock and roll—or **rock**, as it was now known—needed no outside interpreters. This transformation left jazz musicians out in the cold. Throughout the 1960s, they tried giving what they considered the more sophisticated of the new rock tunes their own interpretive spin, but the results (like the 1966 *Basie's Beatles Bag*) were meaningless—not because the performances were inept, but because the jazz-rock enterprise seemed suspect.

To be sure, the music business did not change overnight. Mainstream pop songs in the old tradition continued to be written by the likes of Burt Bacharach ("Raindrops Keep Falling on My Head"). There were new musicals, supplying a steady if narrow stream of hit songs: *My Fair Lady* (1956, filmed in 1964) sold 5 million albums, and *The Sound of Music* (1959, filmed in 1965) and *Camelot* (1960, filmed in 1967) each sold 2 million. Jazz musicians continued to mine them for new material: the 1964 season of musicals generated jazz versions by Cannonball Adderley (of *Fiddler on the Roof*), Duke Ellington (of *Mary Poppins*), and Louis Armstrong (of "Hello, Dolly!"). As the decade went on, even this material dried up. Executives at the major labels nervously watched as soundtrack albums—their bread and butter—declined in sales. The end of an era was in sight.

Record sales overall, however, skyrocketed. Sales broke the $1 billion mark in 1966 and the $2 billion mark by 1972. These staggering increases, obviously due to rock, indicated a greater than ever disparity between pop sales and jazz or classical sales. Record companies that had been indifferent to 1950s rock and roll quickly adjusted, filling their staffs with business-savvy rock enthusiasts. Rock became a sprawling business, swallowing up opera and musicals (*Jesus Christ Superstar, Tommy, Hair*), bluegrass and country music (the folk-rock movement), the avant-garde (Frank Zappa, Captain Beefheart), and race music (Motown, soul). It even collided with world music: after the Indian virtuoso Ravi Shankar took a place of honor at the 1969 Woodstock concert in Bethel, New York, fans began to expect virtuoso rock musicians, like guitarist Eric Clapton, to improvise over long stretches of time.

● Record business

The rock musician who appealed most to jazz musicians was guitarist Jimi Hendrix, who fused the blues with the raw power of amplified sound. Had he not died accidentally in 1970—just days before he was to meet with Gil Evans about a recording session—he may well have played an active role in jazz-rock fusion.

PHOTOFEST

THE CHALLENGE TO JAZZ

In the late 1960s, rock groups began to shift away from the tight pop format of 45-rpm singles in favor of album-oriented improvisation, signaled by the shift from AM to FM radio. Groups like Cream, which teamed Eric Clapton with bassist Jack Bruce and drummer Ginger Baker (all of them jazz or blues fans from England), featured a freewheeling, blues-drenched style that was occasionally characterized as electrified jazz. In San Francisco, Jerry Garcia's Grateful Dead similarly favored jams that embedded improvisation in bluegrass, gospel, country, and blues. In the guitarist, singer, and songwriter Jimi Hendrix, rock had its most formidable virtuoso improviser, stunning audiences with the intensity of his solos.

Jazz musicians who coveted commercial success now faced several obstacles.

YOUTH: Despite its growing appeal to adults, rock remained primarily the music of youth. The word "teenager" had been in existence only since the 1940s, but two decades later it denoted the huge demographic known as the baby boomer generation. These teenagers had affluence, and the musicians they preferred were invariably young.

The phrase "Don't trust anyone over thirty" made it difficult for older jazz musicians, who had spent their lives mastering their idiom, to believe they could ever again be accepted by that audience.

ELECTRONICS AND RECORDINGS: Baby boomers not only looked, dressed, and spoke unlike their parents, but also developed an attachment to musical electronics. Rock was built on the electric guitar and remained indebted to the sheer power of amplification. Thanks to the stacks of amplifiers that now lined every rock stage, an electric guitarist could drown out an entire big band with one chord. Rock musicians brought unbridled enthusiasm to new technologies: their *wah-wah* pedals, phasers, feedback, electric keyboards, and synthesizers produced a dramatically new range of timbres. They depended far more on the studio than on live performance—initially, in some cases, to compensate for weak-voiced singers. But technology allowed the studio much more flexibility. Multitracking opened the way to startling sonic landscapes, and a handful of artists like the Beatles and the Beach Boys made studio production part of their creative process. Jazz musicians had made efforts to master editing, but remained trapped in the belief that recordings should transparently demonstrate what a band sounds like in person.

RHYTHM: Although early rock and roll employed loose rhythms similar to jazz—as Chuck Berry's "Rock and Roll Music" declared, "It's got a backbeat, you can't lose it"—by the 1960s, the rock groove had shifted away from swing toward a steady, pounding, even-eighth-note 4/4. Jazz musicians who had grown up on the more flexible patterns of uneven eighth notes found it hard to adjust. Many refused to do so for aesthetic reasons.

GROUPS: Rock groups were *bands* that submerged individual musicians into a collective sound, something jazz had not seen since swing. It would take a revolution in thought to come up with a new collective aesthetic, one that replaced the improvised solo with a group-oriented creative process.

VIRTUOSITY: Virtually every respectable jazz musician was capable of instrumental feats far beyond the norm. Rock had little patience with that kind of technique. Through the "do-it-yourself" ethos of the folk or blues revival and the naive primitivism of the teenage garage band, rock shifted attention toward other qualities—the band, the song, the singer. Not until rock moved toward instrumental virtuosity, in the work of players like Hendrix and Clapton, would jazz musicians find a place at its table.

The Renewal of Funk

Ultimately, the jazz-rock fusion of the late 1960s was designed to meet each of these obstacles. It was electronic music, created in a studio by younger musicians, often in groups; it fused a strong dance-beat rhythm with a modified cult of jazz virtuosity. The vocabulary that allowed jazz musicians to create this fusion came not from mainstream rock but from the contemporary version of race music, generally known as **soul** or **funk**.

Soul music dated back to the 1950s, when Ray Charles redefined black music by dragging religious grooves into the secular marketplace, and instrumentalists like Horace Silver and Jimmy Smith emphasized backbeat rhythms; but a new and more intense groove, known as funk, was born in the next decade. Specifically, it was the revolutionary music created by James Brown when he entered the national spotlight in 1965 with crossover hits like

James Brown

© CHUCK STEWART

Fusion was inspired by the electrifying James Brown, seen here dancing with his horn section in the 1960s. Jazz musicians adopted his tight, multilayered rhythm section, while his flexible, open-ended tunes were perfect for modal improvisation.

"I Got You (I Feel Good)" and "Papa's Got a Brand New Bag." Brown felt it first in the recording studio: "I had discovered that my strength was not in the horns, it was in the rhythm. I was hearing everything, even the guitars, like they were drums."

Unlike rock, where the 4/4 rhythmic groove dominated the texture, each layer in a funk tune was independent rhythmically, allowing greater possibilities for inventive bassists, guitarists, and drummers to offer fresh support. Jazz drummers interested in this music had to learn to switch from a swing feeling to a new funk groove, but the best of them understood that there was freedom as well as responsibility in this way of playing. Bassists shifted from walking-bass lines to more asymmetric, syncopated lines. Soloists understood that their improvisation was only one part of the overall texture, contributing to but not dominating the groove.

Also unlike rock, which often reduced its chords to their most basic forms, funk was harmonically sophisticated, supporting denser, jazz-oriented harmonies and opening the door for chromatically based semi-atonal sounds, including modal improvisation. In James Brown's hands, a funk tune was flexible and open-ended, typically featuring lengthy stretches on a single harmony. The band would move to a contrasting bridge only on a cue from the vocalist. Funk was a new dance groove, based like rock on the steady eighth note. Young people could relate to it, as could young musicians. One of the most surprising and stimulating things musicians discovered is that a steady beat was enough to hold their audience even when they ventured into extremely dissonant harmonies.

By 1967, jazz was in a state of crisis. Coltrane had died, leaving the free jazz movement without its most charismatic leader. The music was losing its audience, as nightclubs began closing and concerts drying up. Critics had started to take rock artists seriously, and even *Down Beat*, which had become the leading trade magazine for modern jazz, started featuring articles on rock.

Something needed to be done to bridge the gap between jazz and pop. "The prevailing attitude was 'Let's do something different,'" recalled guitarist Larry Coryell. "We were saying, 'We love Wes, but we also love Bob Dylan. We love Coltrane but we also love the Beatles. We love Miles but we also love the Rolling Stones.'"

Charles Lloyd / Tony Williams

The first groups to begin to break down the barriers found opportunities in the California jam-band scene. Charles Lloyd, a Coltrane-influenced tenor saxophonist who had worked with cool jazz drummer Chico Hamilton and soul jazz star Cannonball Adderley, formed his own group in 1965; his killer rhythm section included the then-unknown pianist Keith Jarrett and drummer Jack DeJohnette. Lloyd benefited from the loose cultural boundaries on the San Francisco scene, where jazz drifted into a melting pot with many kinds of music. In 1968, Tony Williams, the dazzling drummer who had recently left the Miles Davis Quintet, formed the groundbreaking trio Emergency, with the electric guitarist John McLaughlin, whom he brought over from the U.K., and organist Larry Young. As an organ trio playing electric music, it was caustic, hard-driving, dissonant, and given to extended improvisations. The group pointed the way toward a style of group improvisation that would form the basis for fusion.

MILES'S MUSICIANS THROUGH THE YEARS

The number of people invited by Miles Davis to play with his band became legend: just to be associated with the "master" was enough to entrance most players, including (for example) Keith Jarrett, a pianist who hated electronic instruments, but who nevertheless played electric piano for Miles. Musicians who played with him during the turbulent period from 1968 through 1971:

Herbie Hancock	Chick Corea
Tony Williams	Keith Jarrett
Wayne Shorter	Benny Maupin
Joe Zawinul	John McLaughlin
Jack DeJohnette	Dave Holland
Billy Cobham	

A different group was added to the ever-changing Davis roster in the 1970s:

John Scofield	Airto Moreira
Sonny Fortune	Michael Henderson
Dave Liebman	Pete Cosey
Steve Grossman	Mike Stern
Kenny Garrett	Bob Berg
Al Foster	George Duke

MILES AHEAD: THE BREAKTHROUGH

The true fusion breakthrough happened only when it captured the attention of the biggest name in jazz—Miles Davis. In 1968, Davis, an old man by baby boomer standards (forty-two), had become dissatisfied with the direction taken by his postbop quintet, and by his steadily decreasing record sales. Searching for something to rescue him from the tired routines of modern jazz, he thought he heard it in the music of Chicago's preeminent bluesman, Muddy Waters, in "the $1.50 drums and the harmonicas and the two-chord blues. . . . I had to get back to that now because what we had been doing was just getting really abstracted." Rock put that kind of simplicity back into the spotlight, and Davis wanted a piece of it. He began changing the instrumentation of his group, pushing his rhythm section to go electric. Ron Carter didn't like the electric bass, so Davis replaced him with a young British player, Dave Holland. Davis similarly put a Fender Rhodes in front of Herbie Hancock for a series of loosely conceived recording sessions. When Hancock failed to return on time from a honeymoon in Brazil, he hired Chick Corea as his replacement at one of those sessions. He also brought in Gil Evans to help arrange the music and forestall imminent chaos.

These experiments produced the 1968 *Filles de Kilimanjaro*, a scintillating yet repetitive blend of modal jazz and abstracted soul rhythm, with the harmonies floating over ostinato bass lines. Tony Williams's drum parts don't sound like rock, but they are clearly influenced by it, and provide a firm foundation for the shifting bass riffs that underscore most of the pieces. Davis realized that by maintaining a steady beat, Williams could hold together complicated textures, retaining the sought-for simplicity no matter how dense and complicated the harmonies became. On the jacket, above the title *Filles de Kilimanjaro* in tiny letters, Davis insisted on the legend "Directions in music by Miles Davis," making it clear that his music could no longer be contained by a single idiom. In case anyone missed the point, he told an interviewer that calling his music jazz was "old fashioned"—"like calling me colored."

More dramatic changes came with his next album, *In a Silent Way*. Among the musicians at this session was John McLaughlin, who added the crucial missing ingredient to the jazz-rock mix: the distorted sound of electric guitar. On the title track, Davis drastically simplified a tune by pianist Joe Zawinul; in place of Zawinul's carefully crafted harmonic progression, Davis asked McLaughlin to play an E major chord, the most basic sound on the guitar. The musicians thought it was a rehearsal, but Davis and his producer, Teo Macero, kept the tapes running, and the musicians' spontaneous interaction over this static harmonic background became part of the finished album.

Increasingly, Davis came to rely on studio post-production. This was hardly new to jazz, but Davis took full advantage of the new technologies firmly in place at Columbia Records. In Macero, he had a producer who did for him what the producer George Martin did for the Beatles. At day's end, Macero cut and spliced the session tapes into unexpected new patterns. Davis's musicians were often surprised and pleased to hear how their work was ultimately combined and recombined. The overall effect sacrificed the intensity of earlier jazz for a deeper sense of groove. *In a Silent Way* consisted of two long tracks, each taking up a full side of the LP. As Davis acknowledged in an interview, "This one will scare the shit out of them." Scarier stuff was to follow.

In a Silent Way

Bitches Brew

Davis's leadership was sparse and intermittent, leaving plenty of room for his musicians. "He'd go out and play, and you'd follow," said Chick Corea. "Whenever he'd stop playing, he never told the group what to do, so we all went and did whatever." Earlier in the 1960s, his rhythm section had learned to take advantage of what they called Davis's "controlled freedom." By the end of the decade, Davis was gathering much larger conglomerations of musicians: two drummers, two bassists, two percussionists, a bass clarinet, an electric guitar, and the three electric keyboards of Hancock, Corea, and Zawinul. The musicians were a full generation younger than Davis and often looked the part, sporting casual hippie clothing and long hair. Yet Davis justly insisted that his music drew less from conventional rock than from the new currents in African American music: "I don't play rock, I play *black*." When a Columbia executive complained of his static sales, Davis retorted, "If you stop calling me a *jazz* man, I'll sell more." He proved his point with his next album, *Bitches Brew*.

Bitches Brew, recorded at three sessions in 1969 and released the following year, looked and sounded nothing like a typical jazz album. "It was loose and tight at the same time," said Davis. "Everybody was alert to different possibilities that were coming up in the music." Some of the tunes came from his then-current band's repertory, but others took shape only after the fact through ingenious editing. No one in their right mind would have considered it a commercial product: it was dissonant, texturally dense, and radio-unfriendly. Nevertheless, *Bitches Brew* found a niche in the new album-oriented rock of the day, selling a half million copies during its first year. Davis pushed forward. So did the music industry, which now loudly trumpeted the new category, marketed in the record store as "Fusion."

Through the teachings of his guru, Sri Chinmoy (whose portrait is prominent in this early 1970s photo), John McLaughlin became devoted to Indian music. He brought Indian tala (meters) into the music of the Mahavishnu Orchestra, and in 1975 formed Shakti, an acoustic group featuring tabla player Zakir Hussain and Ravi Shankar's nephew, the violinist L. Shankar.

■ MAHAVISHNU, RETURN TO FOREVER, and WEATHER REPORT

Bitches Brew may have been the revolutionary album that launched fusion, but it could not serve as a model for other musicians. It was too idiosyncratic and too reliant on the unmistakable sound of Miles Davis's trumpet. Instead, fusion found its template in the intense yet disciplined electric-guitar sound of the Mahavishnu Orchestra, the creation of John McLaughlin (b. 1942), an English guitarist from Yorkshire. Like many young guitarists of the period, he was inspired by the playing of American blues musicians such as Muddy Waters and Lead Belly. But McLaughlin also mastered aspects of flamenco guitar, which showed him how the blues could be linked to blindingly fast passagework and constantly shifting cross-rhythms. He retained an openness to music of all kinds, including 1960s rock; fascinated by Eastern religion, he immersed himself in Indian classical music, which offered the improviser a bewildering variety of unusual meters, or *tala*. The band's first two albums, *The Inner Mounting Flame* (1972) and *Birds of Fire* (1973), sold 700,000 copies—proof that a so-called jazz band could compete in the same commercial league as the rock bands.

Mahavishnu Orchestra was an ideal band for the times. It played loud, fast, intensely distorted music, better suited to concert dates with ZZ Top and Emerson, Lake and Palmer than to the confined quarters of a jazz club. McLaughlin was out in front, playing an electric guitar with two necks—one with six strings, the other with twelve. With lengthy solos, played at sledgehammer volume, McLaughlin raised the level of virtuosity associated with rock guitarists like Hendrix to a new level. A typical Mahavishnu tune featured McLaughlin playing seamlessly alongside the amplified violin of Jerry Goodman, the electric keyboard of Jan Hammer, and drummer Billy Cobham, a powerhouse who, like McLaughlin, had recently worked with Miles.

Although one observer compared Mahavishnu to "a car that could only function at 100 miles per hour," the group's inventiveness was undeniable. Its reliance on *talas* produced rhythmic groupings reminiscent of Dave Brubeck—five, seven, or nine—but could be more complicated: "Birds of Fire" asks the musicians to improvise in a meter of eighteen, while "The Dance of Maya" somehow squeezes a hard-driving boogie-woogie into a meter of twenty. Harmonically, the band played chords that were far removed from the harmonies of popular song, including **slash chords**—triads sitting precariously on top of unrelated bass roots. (The term reflects fake-book notation: an E major triad over a C bass is shown as E/C, pronounced "E slash C.") These chords aren't atonal—the triads offer points of stability—but they propel harmony toward dissonance. Much of Mahavishnu's music was built on such unstable combinations.

Chick Corea

Looking for a band that would prove artistically satisfying and commercially successful, pianist Chick Corea (b. 1941) was among the most influential musicians to adopt the Mahavishnu Orchestra's approach as a prototype to enter fusion. Born in Boston, Corea studied jazz by transcribing the harmonic voicings of Horace Silver and learning to play Bud Powell's solos.

Shortly after leaving Miles Davis in 1970, Corea joined with saxophonist Anthony Braxton and bassist Dave Holland in Circle, an avant-garde group that recorded six albums in one year. Then, just as suddenly, he found free improvisation alienating. "It was like group therapy, just getting together and letting our hair down," he said later. "Everybody yelled and screamed. Then after a while nobody cared." After seeking help in religion, he formed the first of his groups known as Return to Forever in 1972. Hearing Mahavishnu, though, led him "to want to turn the volume up and write music that was more dramatic and made your hair move," he recalled. Jan Hammer's use of the synthesizer as a fluid, singing solo voice inspired him to switch to an entire rack of synthesizers. To capture McLaughlin's lead, he hired guitarist Bill Connors, who was replaced a year later by Al DiMeola, a pyrotechnic soloist who once proclaimed that his goal was "to be the fastest guitarist in the world." Corea continued to call his group Return to Forever, but by the mid-1970s, it was a vehicle for Corea's disciplined compositions, overwhelming audiences with Mahavishnu's crowd-pleasing volume and intensity.

The most artistically and commercially successful fusion group of the 1970s was Weather Report, yet another band with roots in the Miles Davis experience: its founders, Joe Zawinul (1932–2007) (briefly) and Wayne Shorter (b. 1933), were 1960s Davis sidemen, though Shorter had been associated almost exclusively with acoustic jazz—with Art Blakey and Davis, and on his own much-admired series of ten Blue Note albums. While other fusion bands came and went, Zawinul and Shorter's partnership lasted uninterrupted for a decade and a half, evolving from its loose, experimental playing in the early 1970s to a hard-driving funk in the 1980s, topping the charts and selling out stadiums while delighting critics.

Weather Report

The strong hand in the group was Zawinul, who grew up in Austria, where he had survived the war in countryside music camps that sheltered talented youngsters. He came to America in 1959, and a couple of years later became an unlikely member of the Cannonball Adderley quintet, which was largely associated with soul jazz. For the next decade, he was the only white musician in the group—a mutual decision that reflected Adderley's conviction that he played "black," and Zawinul's love of black music and entertainment, cultivated

SHOWTIME MUSIC ARCHIVE, ONTARIO

The mid-1970s version of Return to Forever matched Chick Corea's compositional genius with the volume and intensity of the Mahavishnu Orchestra. Left to right: Lenny White, drums; Corea; Al DiMeola, guitar; Stanley Clarke, bass.

The dominant fusion band of the 1970s and 1980s was Weather Report, which arose from the imaginations of keyboardist Joe Zawinul (seen here in 1972, adjusting the volume on his Fender Rhodes electric piano) and soprano saxophonist Wayne Shorter.

In a career that lasted barely a decade, Jaco Pastorius brought the electric bass (here in its fretted version) to the center of fusion. In a reflective mood, he could play warm melodies with a singing timbre, while on faster tunes he could unleash endless torrents of notes. Philadelphia, 1978.

in Austria as he watched, over and over, movies like the 1942 *Stormy Weather* (featuring Bill "Bojangles" Robinson, Lena Horne, Cab Calloway, Fats Waller, and the amazing dance team the Nicholas Brothers). "To me," he later said, African Americans "are the easiest to understand, the closest to my environment."

Weather Report became a laboratory for new sounds made possible by technology. Inspired by Ray Charles, Zawinul took up electric piano in the mid-1960s, and made it pay off handsomely when he used it to compose and perform Adderley's biggest hit, "Mercy, Mercy, Mercy." He soon mastered the synthesizer; despising its pre-set sounds, he burrowed deep into the equipment to create his own timbres, sometimes detuning the intervals to mimic non-Western instruments. Taking charge of the ARP 2600 even required him to play "backward," using an inverted keyboard with the top notes starting on the left-hand side.

Over time, Weather Report moved from atmospheric jazz improvisations toward straight-ahead Afro-pop rhythmic grooves. But the band did not find its center of gravity until it drafted a new member. Jaco Pastorius, born the same year as the electric bass (1951), was the first jazz bassist who did not play acoustic. He loved electric bass, creating his own version with the frets removed (the holes sealed with wood filler), flying over the soundboard with extraordinary speed. By manipulating the controls on his amplifier, he developed a rich, singing sound: "that ballad voice," Zawinul called it. His virtuoso skills astonished the jazz community. On his first album, *Jaco Pastorius,* he sealed his claim on the jazz tradition by playing an unaccompanied version of the bebop standard "Donna Lee," a notoriously difficult piece even for its composer, Miles Davis, who wrote it for Charlie Parker.

Pastorius became Weather Report's "warhead," grounding its rhythm section while playing fluid melodic lines one might normally expect from a guitarist. (In concert, he even played a feedback solo à la Jimi Hendrix.) "Jaco . . . brought the white kids in," Zawinul remembered. "He was all of a sudden a real white All-American folk hero." Tragically, his fall was as steep as his climb. A few years after joining Weather Report, he surrendered to drugs, almost daring himself to perform his convoluted solos in states of extreme intoxication. He left the group in 1982, and died four years later. Yet with Jaco as its foundation, Weather Report had reached its commercial and some would say artistic zenith, especially with the 1976 album *Heavy Weather*, featuring Zawinul's splendid "Birdland," a tribute to the jazz club named after Parker. Although its overall texture is driving funk, it evokes a genial, big-band feeling in its refrain. Zawinul's skill as a composer is evident throughout: the piece is built on the most basic musical elements, the G major scale and the G blues scale, but in a way that leaves us hanging until the climactic refrain brings us home.

🎧 "Teen Town"

Named after a club in Pompano Beach, Florida, that had been a youthful hangout for the bassist, "Teen Town" is a Pastorius showcase. He plays two roles: the electric bass soloist and the substitute drummer. The tune features a peculiar chord progression, cycling through four major triads. The chords are simple but ambiguous: no one key can contain them all. Over this shifting background, Pastorius plays a melody line that snakes its way through different rhythms with unexpected accents. It sounds improvised but is composed, as becomes clear when it begins to repeat. Still, there are moments when Pastorius the improviser trumps Pastorius the composer, adjusting his line to the heat of performance. While Pastorius is clearly in front, the tune also works as a dialogue—sometimes with Shorter, who plays brief solos that hint at his remarkable melodic invention, but more often with Zawinul. By the end of the performance, the dialogue is wide open. In live performance, Weather Report would extend this last section, allowing room for Shorter and Zawinul to trade melodic and harmonic ideas with Pastorius before the final lick closed the tune off.

LISTENING GUIDE 65

🎧 teen town

WEATHER REPORT

Joe Zawinul, Fender Rhodes piano, melodica, Oberheim polyphonic synthesizer, ARP 2600; Wayne Shorter, soprano saxophone; Jaco Pastorius, electric bass, drums; Manolo Badrena, congas

- Label: *Heavy Weather,* Columbia CK 65108
- Date: 1976
- Style: fusion
- Form: eight-measure cycle

What to listen for:
- up-tempo 1970s dance groove
- peculiar harmonic progression in an eight-bar cycle
- interchange between Pastorius and Shorter and between Pastorius and Zawinul

INTRODUCTION

0:00   Shorter on soprano saxophone and Zawinul on synthesizer play the melody harmonized in thirds (Zawinul on top, Shorter below). Behind them, the drummer begins a rapid, steady pattern with high-hat cymbal accents on the backbeat and the snare falling on the third beat of the measure, while punctuating gaps in the melody with bass-drum accents. Distantly in the background, the percussionist adds Latin rhythms.

CHORUS 1

0:08   An accented pair of high notes announces the first chorus. Pastorius begins a lightning-fast line on electric bass, accompanied by the synthesizer. The chords in the background are **major triads** from different keys: each new chord cancels out the previous one.

CHORUS 2

0:16   The chords begin to repeat, establishing an eight-bar cycle. Pastorius continues his line, changing the rhythm and pitches.

CHORUS 3

0:23   Pastorius's line bridges the boundary between one chorus and the next. Underneath, Shorter emerges from the background with long-held saxophone notes.

CHORUS 4

0:31   On this chorus, Pastorius plays the pair of accented high notes, this time doubled by the drums. His line becomes intensely **syncopated**, prompting a flurry of snare-drum and bass-drum accents.

CHORUS 5

0:39   Pastorius repeats the line from the first chorus note for note, making it clear that the solo is a composed piece, not an improvisation. The first phrase is answered by short decorative passages by Shorter.

CHORUS 6

0:46   Pastorius repeats the second chorus.

CHORUS 7

0:53   His line is temporarily displaced by Zawinul's synthesizer, which is much slower than Pastorius's rapid-fire solo, calling our attention to the increasingly dissonant harmonies.

0:59   Pastorius plays a single phrase before dropping out again.

CHORUS 8

1:01   In the absence of melodic activity, the bass and snare drums add syncopated **fills**.

INTERLUDE (INTRODUCTION)

1:08   Zawinul and Shorter play the introductory melody again, this time with the synthesizer on a softer and more resonant timbre.

1:23   At the end of the second phrase, the harmony suddenly shifts into a new direction: the piece has **modulated** to a new key.

CHORUS 9

1:24   Doubled by synthesizer, the bass plays a mighty ascending line. Each phrase is answered by a loud "boom" from the drums.

CHORUS 10

1:31   Over the bass line, the synthesizer adds a slow line that rises **chromatically**.

CHORUS 11

1:39   The synthesizer line rises until it disappears into the upper range. The background chords, now played by an ethereal electric piano, become more extended and dissonant.

CHORUS 12

1:47   Shorter plays a few tentative notes on saxophone before retreating to silence.

CHORUS 13

1:54   The chord progression is doubled by a slow synthesizer line.

CHORUS 14

2:02   Pastorius begins improvising in the style of the opening chorus. His line is dissonant against the background chords.

CHORUS 15

2:09   Pastorius begins with the phrase that opened the fifth chorus, but sends it off into an unexpected direction.

2:13   Shorter sneaks in with a descending line.

2:16   Pastorius ends the chorus with a closing phrase: a rhythmically catchy lick using just two notes.

CHORUS 16

2:17   The texture thins out. It becomes easier to hear the conga drums improvising alongside the drumming.

2:23   Pastorius repeats the closing phrase from the end of the last chorus.

CHORUS 17

2:24   Shorter plays another short solo.

2:30   Pastorius again repeats the closing phrase.

CODA

2:31   The harmony suddenly comes to a stop on a sustained chord. The drumming continues.

2:38   The drummer adds ferocious bass drum accents, culminating in a cymbal crash. The sound suddenly becomes distant, as if heard from far away.

2:42   The synthesizer enters with the opening of the introduction.

2:46   The harmony shifts in unexpected directions. The final chord is heard over the accented pair of high notes.

■ Chameleons: HERBIE HANCOCK (b. 1940)

One of the ironies of the 1970s is that two of its most popular jazz stars were pianists of extraordinary ability who managed, somehow, to sell their music based on its simplicity. During his years with Miles Davis, Herbie Hancock established himself as a postbop composer of subtlety and bristling complexity, while also showing a talent for writing tunes built on funky vamps, like "Watermelon Man" and "Cantaloupe Island." Yet by the early 1970s, under the name Headhunters, he created a far more elemental mixture of funk and jazz that consisted of little more than syncopated bass lines repeated and extended ad infinitum. He once observed: "We jazz listeners tend, 90% of the time, to like clever, complex treatments of simple ideas. That's what we respect. . . . But what I found out is that . . . there's a much more subtle kind of challenge in going towards the simple."

The title of Hancock's most lucrative recording, "Chameleon," indicates his career-long ability to adapt to new surroundings in an instant. Hancock has balanced several careers simultaneously, sustaining his reputation as a superb modern jazz pianist while also composing film scores and achieving stardom as a pop star in 1970s funk, 1980s hip-hop, and collaborations with performers like Sting, Christina Aguilera, Josh Groban, and Norah Jones. In concert, he will play a Steinway grand and then switch to a "keytar" (a keyboard slung around his neck like a guitar), playing acoustic jazz as well as contemporary R&B. His 2007 album *River: The Joni Letters*, an inventive interpretation of songs by Joni Mitchell (and a couple by Wayne Shorter and Duke Ellington), was the first jazz recording to win the Grammy Award as album of the year since the 1964 *Getz/Gilberto*.

Born in Chicago, Hancock grew up playing classical music well enough to win a competition at age eleven.

The harmonic sophistication of Herbie Hancock, seen here at a 1963 recording session, appealed directly to the jazz aficionado. Yet his best-selling songs fit squarely into pop territory.

PHOTO BY FRANCIS WOLFF© MOSAIC IMAGES LLC

He also played rhythm and blues and drifted toward jazz, listening to Bill Evans and Oscar Peterson and teaching himself how to play the blues. As soon as he arrived in New York, in 1961, Hancock found work with master musicians ranging from Coleman Hawkins to Eric Dolphy. He made his first album as a leader, *Takin' Off*, in 1962, with Dexter Gordon as a sideman and "Watermelon Man" as its lead track. That piece, already popularized by conga player Mongo Santamaria, evoked for Hancock the vendors on Chicago's summer streets, but its title entailed a risk: thanks to minstrel shows, watermelon symbolized decades of racist stereotypes as the favorite and often stolen fruit of plantation "darkies." Hancock remembered, "I looked at myself in the mirror. 'Now wait a minute, man. You are projecting something from the black experience, tell what the thing is. What are you ashamed of?'" His follow-up albums, especially *Maiden Voyage*, with its title track suspended on cool ambiguous harmonies and the innovative use of slash chords on "Dolphin Dance," appealed to jazz fans and became texts for study by countless young musicians.

🎧 "Cantaloupe Island"

Hancock's fourth album as a leader established him as an innovative force beyond his superb work with the Miles Davis Quintet. *Empyrean Isles* explores hard bop, funk, and free jazz, proving that his generation of jazz musicians could assimilate the pop of the 1960s as inventively as previous generations had used standard popular songs. His much-covered "Cantaloupe Island" has a rollicking rhythm created by the contrast between the underlying four-beats-to-a-bar meter and the marvelously distinct piano vamp. Listen to the way Ron Carter's bass underscores the second bass note in the sequence and Tony Williams's drum slap sets the vamp into motion. The rhythm section makes the vamp seem natural, easy, almost spontaneous, yet it's the rigorous interaction between the three instruments that makes it work. It wasn't easy; this performance was the fourteenth take.

"Cantaloupe Island" makes for an interesting contrast with Horace Silver's "Song for My Father," also recorded for Blue Note in 1964 (four months later), though Hancock sounds more modern—in part because he uses advanced harmonies and a keyboard touch that suggests a cooler, clearer attack as compared with Silver's aggressive style. Also, Silver's use of rests calls to mind traditional short jazz breaks, while Hancock's four-bar oases at the end of the choruses hold a more radical element of surprise. In both pieces, exotic rhythms indicate exotic places (the mythological Empyrean Isles, Cape Verde), and the solos are confined to piano and one wind instrument, in this instance the exuberant cornet of Freddie Hubbard. Silver, older by twelve years, influenced Hancock, yet the younger man seems to anticipate elements of Silver's solo when, at 3:07–3:10 and again at 4:03–4:12, he plays chords in like-minded polyrhythms. Both performances devote much space to theme statements, but compare the endings: Silver's full stop vs. Hancock's slow fade, portending the vamp's eternal motion.

Hubbard, with his brilliant sound and stunning technique, dominated jazz trumpet in the 1960s, as he recorded many albums of his own and appeared in support of classic sessions by, among others, Ornette Coleman, John Coltrane, Eric Dolphy, Oliver Nelson, Andrew Hill, Wayne Shorter, Sonny Rollins, and Art Blakey, with whose Jazz Messengers he spent five years. In that period, the mellower cornet, with its conical tubing and larger bell, enjoyed a revival among trumpet players, including Don Cherry, Nat Adderley, and Thad Jones. Hubbard rarely played it—he complained that the sound did not carry well in concert—but on this album he made it resound with warmth, nuance, and crackling vitality.

🎧 cantaloupe island

HERBIE HANCOCK

Herbie Hancock, piano; Freddie Hubbard, cornet;
Ron Carter, bass; Tony Williams, drums

- Label: *Empyrean Isles*, Blue Note BLP4175
- Date: 1964
- Style: hard bop/fusion
- Form: original composition (16 bars)

What to listen for:

- jazz improvisation over a rhythm-and-blues groove
- harmonic progression, loosely based on the blues, that incorporates modern jazz harmonies
- Hubbard and Hancock's bluesy improvisation

0:00   A single drum beat heralds Hancock's distinctive **vamp** figure, setting a slow, funky groove. Williams plays a steady pulse on the ride cymbal, adding offbeat accents on the snare drum.

CHORUS 1 (HEAD)

0:09   The head begins with a pair of notes, played just before the downbeat by Hubbard on cornet (doubled by Hancock). Hubbard continues with a simple bluesy melody.

0:18   The same melody is now harmonized by an unexpected chord.

0:26   The bass shifts upward a half step to a new, unsettled harmony. Hubbard and Hancock play a riff.

0:35   Hancock returns to the vamp and the **tonic** harmony.

CHORUS 2 (HEAD)

0:43   Repeat of chorus 1.

CHORUS 3

1:17   Hubbard's first phrase begins with a long tone.

1:26   As the harmony changes, he plays a sweeping gesture, descending from a high note.

1:34   He contrasts with the new rhythmic accompaniment by using **polyrhythmic** figures.

1:43   He stops playing, leaving the last four bars for the vamp.

CHORUS 4

1:51   Beginning in the upper register of the cornet, Hubbard plays a bluesy figure.

1:59   He creates unusual timbres by **half-valving**.

2:16   The last four bars are once again left empty.

CHORUS 5

2:24   Hubbard opens his third chorus with a few isolated phrases in **double-time**.

2:41   He plays a descending three-note motive, ♪♫, followed by a flurry of 16th notes.

2:53   Hubbard ends his solo with an offhand gesture.

CHORUS 6

2:57   Hancock begins his solo by alternating the vamp with a paraphrase of the melody.

3:05   As the harmony changes, he allows his melody a bit more rhythmic freedom.

3:14	Over the new accompaniment figure, his melody is bare and austere.
3:19	A quick melodic gesture precedes a return to the vamp for the last four bars.

CHORUS 7

3:30	Hancock begins with a brief **tremolo** before turning to a double-time line. For a time, a bass line displaces the vamp.
3:46	Over the new rhythmic accompaniment, he generates a funky 16th-note feeling.

CHORUS 8

4:03	Hancock opens his last chorus with a tricky polyrhythm.
4:25	His solo ends with a brief flurry of fast notes.

CHORUS 9 (HEAD)

4:35	Chorus 1 is repeated.

CODA

5:08	The recording fades out on the vamp.

Headhunters

After leaving Davis in 1970, Hancock formed a highly experimental group, combining his complex postbop jazz impulses with textures created by an array of synthesizers. The group struggled, though, and he came to realize that the music he *really* admired was the heightened funk of James Brown, Sly and the Family Stone, and Tower of Power. "I decided that it was now time to try some funky stuff myself and get me some cats who could play that kind of music."

Hancock recast his band as the Headhunters, finding new musicians with little jazz experience but with a background in funk: the drummer Harvey Mason, who could improvise expertly within a strong funk groove; Paul Jackson, a master of syncopated bass lines; and percussionist Bill Summers, who brought with him an education in traditional West African music. The music on their 1974 album of the same name spoke a new language: simple yet intensely polyrhythmic. The big hit, "Chameleon," was little more than a bass line locked into a steady clave rhythm that cycled back and forth between two chords. On this foundation, Hancock added layer upon layer, recreating the web of sounds that energized a James Brown recording, using electronic keyboards instead of guitars.

"Chameleon"

Some people disliked *Head Hunters*, feeling that in trying to combine jazz and funk, Hancock was doing neither. Hancock was hurt by this criticism, but not by the distinction between the two genres. "Some of the dance music I do," he once said, "is not done for art." When he balanced his inventive complexity with the demands of straightforward funk, the results could be devastating. Albums like *Thrust* (1974) and *Man-Child* (1975) wove a jazz sensibility into modern funk grooves. In the early 1980s, in Los Angeles, Hancock listened to tapes sent to him by Bill Laswell and Michael Beinhorn, then working with the Brooklyn hip-hop group Material, which used the scratching sounds of the turntablist

Grand Mixer DXT. Intrigued, Hancock added his own melody on top. The result, "Rockit" (1983), emerged as an underground success and an MTV video—with robots banging their heads in time to the music. Typically, he toured that same year with an acoustic jazz quartet featuring the young Wynton Marsalis. Hancock has gone back and forth between jazz and pop, and mergers of the two, ever since.

"Rockit"

■ KEITH JARRETT (b. 1945)

Keith Jarrett is a no less idiosyncratic musician, but in a different way. He grunts and yowls when he improvises, and his body seems possessed, gyrating and twisting, rising off the bench or kneeling below it. His fans debate whether this is show business or genuine musical possession. But even his fans can be less tolerant of his boorish behavior in concert, interrupting performances to berate audiences for inattention, coughing, latecoming, and, in stadium settings, photography. Audiences have come to expect such outbursts, and his longtime trio partners—bassist Gary Peacock and drummer Jack DeJohnette—stand or sit mutely by as they run their course. Nevertheless, Jarrett has built and sustained a wide following because he is one of the most resourceful and exciting pianists in jazz.

Jarrett was born in Allentown, Pennsylvania, and, like Hancock, emerged as a musical prodigy with classical training. Along the way he learned to improvise. After a brief stint in Art Blakey's Jazz Messengers, he played in the Charles Lloyd Quartet and then survived a stint with Miles Davis, a remarkable feat for someone who thought fusion was a mistake. "The main reason I joined the band was that I didn't *like* the band," he explained. "I liked what Miles was playing very much and I hated the rest of the band playing together." He tolerated electric pianos out of a desire to help Davis achieve his artistic goals, later writing about the recordings the band made at the Cellar Door, in Washington, D.C.: "You don't usually see this kind of comet go by more than once or twice in a lifetime."

Jarrett's best-known music is restricted to the piano. His improvisations range from the quietly meditative to the blindingly aggressive, but almost always reflect a distinctive melodic sensibility. *The Köln Concert* (1975), a double LP that sold more than 4 million copies, ranks among the top-selling jazz albums of all time. According to Jarrett, everything about the concert was wrong: "It was the wrong piano; we had bad food in a hot restaurant; and I hadn't slept for two days. . . . But I knew something special was happening when I started playing." Recorded live in Cologne, Germany, *The Köln Concert* brought his music to people who were not jazz fans but who were attracted by another kind of fusion, known as New Age. In Jarrett's hands, such freewheeling improvisation brought jazz into a compelling real-time mix with gospel, folk music, and whatever else captured his attention in the spur of the moment.

His subsequent work has been vast and diffuse, ranging from classical music (some of it recorded on pipe organ and clavichord) to avant-garde improvisations to divine

Keith Jarrett, shown playing with bassist Cecil McBee, burst onto the jazz scene in the late 1960s with the Charles Lloyd Quartet. He's probably the most eclectic pianist active today, his irrepressible creativity surfacing in free jazz, acoustic fusion, and traditional jazz standards.

FRANK DRIGGS COLLECTION

© DONNA RANIERI

One of the first members of the rock generation to tackle fusion, Pat Metheny has been recording albums for over thirty years. His distinctive amplified hollow-body guitar has graced many pop-oriented projects, but he has also recorded with avant-garde giant Ornette Coleman. Philadelphia, 1979.

inspirations (he dedicated *Hymns* to the Sufis), though most of his performances during the past quarter-century have involved his Standards Trio.

FROM HARD FUSION TO SMOOTH JAZZ

Fusion entered a new phase when it passed from veterans like Miles Davis and even Herbie Hancock to a generation of musicians who had absorbed rock as the music of their own generation. None achieved a more devoted fan base than guitarist Pat Metheny (b. 1954), originally of Lee's Summit, Missouri, near the very center of the continent. Like most would-be jazz guitarists growing up in the 1960s, Metheny was infatuated with Wes Montgomery (see Chapters 12 and 16), whose *Smokin' at the Half Note* (1965) he called "the absolute greatest jazz guitar album ever made." Listening repeatedly to Montgomery's albums, he learned how to play in octaves and to use his thumb instead of a pick. But he also listened to Bob Dylan, the Beatles, Waylon Jennings, and bossa nova, embracing it all, his guitar drawing jazz into an ongoing dialogue with the whole new landscape of pop music.

Metheny's sound was already fully formed on his first album, *Bright Size Life*, with Jaco Pastorius: a warm tone from a hollow-bodied guitar, spread out through two amplifiers and a delay unit to achieve a rich and ringing voice. His phrases are broad and melodic, and his tunes, often explicitly geographical ("Missouri Uncompromised," "Omaha Celebration"), betray a country-like openness. He found a composing partner in Lyle Mays, an introverted pianist whose intellectual musical ideas fused with Metheny's lyricism. The two formed the Pat Metheny Group in 1977, launching the long-haired guitarist as the fresh face of fusion jazz.

Metheny was the first musician of his generation to reclaim the guitar as a solo jazz voice. His sound is immediately recognizable, despite his use of electronic accoutrements such as the guitar synthesizer. At times, he verges into pop, with backgrounds generated by sequencers spinning out loops created in advance. But he prizes the jazz element most, having familiarized himself with the tradition, from Louis Armstrong to Ornette Coleman. In 1985, on the triumphant *Song X*, he recorded with Coleman himself (and his band Prime Time, with his son Denardo Coleman on drums). Metheny extends the openness and optimism of Coleman's music by adding his own layer to the harmolodic texture.

A different type of fusion pulls in music not only from outside the jazz tradition, but outside the United States, producing a music strongly influenced by the genre known as **world music**. In this realm, not surprisingly, European players have a powerful role, but unlike the musicians of Django Reinhart's generation who aimed chiefly at mastering the American jazz style, these younger musicians use jazz as a platform for understanding other musical cultures. Tenor saxophonist Jan Garbarek, for example, grew up in Norway, where he found his musical idol in John Coltrane, especially for his use of Third World scales and percussion. Garbarek became a jazz ethnomusicologist, learning to sing various folk traditions and infusing his improvisations with

World music ▸

Jan Garbarek ▸

them, recording a long series of albums over thirty years. He refuses to call his distinctive music jazz—he refuses to call *anything* after *Bitches Brew* jazz. It is simply Norwegian music. You could multiply his example by a hundred and not take into account all the music that fuses jazz with overseas traditions.

Another way for jazz to go global was exemplified by Paul Winter, who took on stewardship of the entire earth. He began as a straight-ahead saxophonist who served as cultural ambassador in Latin America and Brazil, where he soaked up local folk traditions. By 1967, his band had morphed into the Paul Winter Consort, a term he borrowed from Elizabethan music to evoke the idea of diversity. Winter drew on the cry of the wolf and the singing of humpbacked whales for recordings like *Common Ground* (1978). Subsequent projects took him from New York's Cathedral of St. John the Divine to the Grand Canyon.

Paul Winter

The Consort's theme, "Icarus," an arching, folk-like melody situated within advanced jazz harmony, was composed by Ralph Towner, who, in 1970, left the Consort with other members to form a group called Oregon. Each musician in Oregon has a primary instrument, but the fluid nature of the band allows them to experiment with other instruments. Ralph Towner was originally a trumpet player and pianist who turned to acoustic guitar. He became a virtuoso on the six-string and twelve-string guitar, though he occasionally played French horn and returned to piano. Bassist Glen Moore also played violin and flute. Paul McCandless specialized in the oboe, an exceedingly rare instrument in jazz. Percussionist Colin Walcott (who never played the trap set) was the group's firmest link to world traditions, as a former student of Alla Rakha on tabla and of Ravi Shankar on sitar. Oregon is closely associated with New Age jazz—quiet, reflective, serene. But its intricate compositions and musicianship warrant attention and respect.

Ralph Towner / Oregon

Smooth Jazz

When Bill Clinton was asked early in his presidency to name his favorite saxophonists, he replied: "Lester Young and Kenny G." The first name points back to the jazz tradition (and to the only saxophonist nicknamed Pres). The second—far better known to voters—points toward **smooth jazz**. This term first appeared in the late 1980s, when the label "fusion" had run out of steam. But the idea behind it—an innocuous, listener-friendly blending of jazz with an upbeat, celebratory brand of R&B and funk—dates back to the 1960s, when producer Creed Taylor helped Wes Montgomery break through with cover versions of the Beatles. Taylor's label, CTI, took off in the early 1970s, offering recordings by George Benson, Freddie Hubbard, Herbie Mann, Antonio Carlos Jobim, and other accomplished musicians in an easy-listening atmosphere. Sometimes the backgrounds were created first; then the soloists were brought in to dub their parts.

In time, the music grew funkier: the rhythms took on a kick and the timbres of the soloists took on grit. It was mood music you could dance to, reflecting a laid-back affluence that appealed especially to black professionals who were turned off by the blaring volume of fusion and the apparent incoherence of the avant-garde. Significantly, this music was radio driven. While record companies prefer broad categories (corresponding to sections of a record store), radio searches for finer and finer divisions of taste. By the late 1980s, a new category had emerged, variously known as "new adult contemporary," "jazz lite," "quiet storm," or "smooth jazz." The target audience was adults aged twenty-five to forty-four (known by professionals as the "money demographic") who had "graduated" from rock to a less abrasive music, but were still shy of embracing jazz. Smooth jazz was supposed to be the perfect soundtrack for their lifestyle. In 1987, *Billboard* amended its charts, placing jazz in the category "traditional jazz," while dubbing its pop-oriented spinoff as "contemporary jazz." As smooth jazz ricocheted back to a predominantly white demographic, the funk receded.

Kenny G   Enter President Clinton's saxophone hero, Kenny G, or Kenneth Gorelick. He is currently ranked No. 25 of all performers by the Recording Industry Association of America—having sold 48 million recordings, including 12 million for *Breathless*, undoubtedly the highest total ever for anyone associated, however fitfully, with jazz. His name evokes howls of derision from jazz musicians, especially when he dubbed his solos—which Pat Metheny memorably described as "his lame-ass, pseudo bluesy, out-of-tune noodling"—over Louis Armstrong's "What a Wonderful World."

There are many things to dislike about smooth jazz—for example, everything. Jazz has always depended on real-time interaction, live or in the studio. Pop recordings long ago dispensed with the concept of live performance. Tunes are constructed in layers, with each musician recorded separately, often wearing headphones, listening and performing with tracks created days or weeks before. The sound may be beautiful, even precise (thanks to digital sampling and synthesized drum tracks), but it comes at the cost of the interaction central to jazz. We can't blame technology per se: many jazz pieces, including "Teen Town," have been recorded in this way. But technology aside, jazz of every school and era is about spontaneous expression, risk-taking, improvisational resourcefulness, rhythmic excitement, and the promise of the unforeseen, all of which is absent from smooth jazz—which exists primarily as musical wallpaper for the Weather Channel, exercise classes, and presumably the Clinton home.

JAM BANDS

If smooth jazz is chiefly consumed through recording and radio, other types of fusion are inescapable from the sweat and noise of contemporary life and music. The **jam band** concept has its roots in 1960s rock bands like the Grateful Dead, which rejected commercial dictates in favor of communal improvisation. Devoted to the freedom of the moment, the band became an international phenomenon. Phish, an improvisational rock group led by guitarist Trey Anastasio, continued the jam band approach. Phish began in the early 1980s as a pick-up band playing gigs in its home state of Vermont; by the time it officially disbanded in 2004 (it has since taken shape again), the group had reached an audience astronomically larger than anything jazz could muster (hundreds of thousands attended its concerts). Like the Dead, Phish could not be construed as a jazz band; but its enthusiasm for open-ended improvisation encouraged jazz-oriented bands to follow in its footsteps.

Medeski, Martin and Wood   One group, Medeski, Martin and Wood, got a direct boost from Phish, which played their tapes between sets. Pianist John Medeski studied at the New England Conservatory, where he began playing with the bassist Chris Wood. On one of their early gigs, they discovered the drummer Billy Martin,

Phish

a New Yorker who brought "that more danceable element" to their music. They came to New York as a conventional piano trio, but in the early 1990s they embarked on a road tour in a van and camper, booking gigs along the way—including bills with alternative rock bands like Los Lobos and the Dave Matthews Band. Medeski, finding electric instruments more suitable to the band's peripatetic existence, became expert on the Hammond B3 organ, the Clavinet, the Wurlitzer electric piano, the Mellotron (another Wurlitzer instrument), the ARP String Ensemble, and the Yamaha synthesizer. Each instrument has its own amplifier. He has said, "I can hit three notes on any of my keyboards, and each will sound different."

John Medeski, flanked by Chris Wood on bass (left) and Billy Martin on drums (right), has brought the Hammond B3 organ sound into a twenty-first-century aesthetic by combining it with the most modern synthesizers and samplers. Cape Cod Music Festival, 1999.

Medeski considers the term "jam band" "demeaning." Yet the music of Medeski, Martin and Wood is very much part of that scene, better suited to coffeehouses and rock clubs than jazz nightclubs. Inevitably, their audiences affect what they create—in part because each night's show is taped, digitized, and loaded onto the Internet for everyone's free use. Much of their music seems retro, but it is also sufficiently modern to incorporate the work of hip-hop artists like DJ Logic and Scott Harding, both of whom help the band conceive of their music as a whole, not just as a collection of individual soloists.

🎧 "Chank"

In 1998, Medeski, Martin and Wood received a phone call from an older musician who had become a fan. John Scofield was an electric guitarist who had played with Miles Davis in the early 1980s. Over the years, Scofield had earned a reputation as a skillful composer as well as performer within the neo-funk groove. His playing combined a searing, distorted blues sound with a deep knowledge of modern postbop scales. His command of chord progressions made him accepted within mainstream jazz, but he yearned for a change of groove. "I'm at a point now where I'm bebopped out," he complained.

John Scofield is a jazz guitarist and composer with a taste for funk and soul. A Miles Davis alumnus from the mid-1980s, he has recorded albums featuring mainstream jazz, drums and bass, and the music of soul genius Ray Charles. At the Blue Note, New York, 1999.

Scofield arranged for Medeski, Martin and Wood to play on his next recording session, which produced the album *A Go Go*. Scofield was the composer for the date, providing tunes that were disarmingly simple, often little more than a few guitar licks set against a funk groove. But the rhythmic flow was designed for improvisation. "I'm not a huge fusion fan per se," Scofield said. "I like swing. But some grooves make you want to play, if you're a jazz musician."

"Chank" was written as a tribute to Jimmy "Chank" Nolen, a guitarist in James Brown's stellar rhythm section. Scofield's part was basically a rhythm line—not necessarily the role most jazz guitarists hanker for. But the line was essential in setting up the overall groove. Scofield remembers the bass line as reminiscent of James Brown's seminal "Cold Sweat" (1967): on the offbeat, except for the first beat of the measure. "[Saxophonist] Maceo Parker and [trombonist] Fred Wesley describe funk as 'about the one,' and on that tune, everything comes back to it. It was a whole way of breaking up the bass and drum rhythm."

The form is simple, derived again from James Brown's practice: an **A** section over a single chord, used for modal improvisation, followed by a

bridge. The bridge is cued by each soloist, who can play as long as he wants: "On 'Chank,' you play four-bar phrases, not choruses." The group, which had played together only three times in rehearsal, mesh beautifully on this tune. The album as a whole jump-started Scofield's career, selling 100,000 copies—nowhere near as much as, say, Hancock's *Head Hunters*, but a quantum leap from his usual sales.

🎧 chank

JOHN SCOFIELD

John Scofield, electric guitar; John Medeski, Hammond B3 organ; Chris Wood, electric bass; Billy Martin, drums

- Label: *A Go Go,* Polygram 539979
- Date: 1998
- Style: jam band fusion
- Form: **A A B A** (**A B** during the solos)

What to listen for:
- Scofield's intricate rhythms and electrified timbres
- each soloist's improvised **A** section, ending with his signal for the bridge
- composed coda, with descending melody

INTRODUCTION

0:00		Scofield (electric guitar) plays a dissonant chord in a syncopated rhythm.
0:02		After a brief pause, he follows with a brief **pentatonic** lick.
0:04		Scofield repeats the guitar chord, this time following with a rhythmically tricky passage.
0:08		Having established the pattern, Scofield plays it repeatedly.
0:15		On an upbeat, the drums enter, followed by the electric bass.
0:16		The drums and bass add their own rhythmic layers, sometimes reinforcing Scofield's syncopations, at other times creating new patterns. The bass begins squarely on the downbeat before shifting to the offbeat.

HEAD

0:32	**A**	Medeski (organ) plays a melody with strong, sustained **blue notes**, in a simple repetitive pattern that contrasts with the syncopated accompaniment.
0:38		The last note of the line dissolves in a bluesy **glissando**.
0:48		Having completed two complete phrases, the organ rests, giving the drums, bass, and guitar room to continue the groove for another eight bars.
0:57	**A**	The melody is repeated in a higher register.
1:05		Medeski begins the melody harmonized in thirds.
1:13	**B**	The bass note moves to IV. After a few beats, the guitar and organ play syncopated chords, followed by a riff.
1:21		The band reaches a **half cadence** (on the dominant chord).
1:22		A brief drum solo closes the bridge after only five bars.
1:24	**A**	Medeski returns to the opening melody, again harmonized in thirds.

SOLO 1

1:40	**A**	Medeski plays a few **staccato** chords.
1:42		Scofield enters for his guitar solo with a forceful electric sound. Some of his phrases are loud, others suddenly quiet.
1:49		As Scofield plays, Medeski **comps** quietly in the background.
1:56		Scofield's lick begins quietly on the downbeat with fast repeated notes.
2:08		Scofield plays a line with expressive, upward-bending blue notes.

2:16	He stitches together several short ideas into a long continuous phrase.
2:28	In the background, the organ holds out sustained notes.
2:44	Scofield returns to the repeated-note idea, interacting aggressively with Medeski's comping.
2:50	As Scofield ends his phrase with a short, distorted passage, the organ plays a brief riff.
2:53	Scofield echoes the riff, adding brief rhythmic decorations.
2:56	His guitar sound becomes more distorted.
3:00	With a change in the timbre of his guitar, Scofield repeats a simple four-note riff, playing it in **call and response** with a lower-pitched blues line.
3:06	At times, his lines become blurred in pitch and rhythm.
3:16	Scofield begins to suggest the tune's opening melody.
3:20	He follows this with a rapid repeated riff.
3:24	By referring once more to the opening melody, he signals the bridge.
3:32 **B**	

SOLO 2

3:43 **A**	Medeski begins his organ solo with a fiercely repeated riff, placed polyrhythmically against the bar.
3:47	In the background, Scofield plays a variant of the line he introduced at the beginning of the tune.
4:00	Medeski's next line is a string of fast notes, moving "outside" the main chord until it descends into the bass register.
4:07	His licks become shorter, interacting more with Scofield's syncopated accompaniment.
4:14	Medeski focuses on a single bluesy note.
4:24	He begins a simple four-note riff, then repeats it at different pitch levels, some dissonant against the prevailing harmony.
4:31	He starts a longer and faster melody that once again moves into dissonant territory.
4:46	To signal the bridge, Medeski plays the opening melody, which quickly disintegrates into polyrhythmic improvisation.
5:01 **B**	

HEAD (abbreviated)

| 5:12 **A** | Medeski leads a version of the head that's reduced to two phrases. |

CODA

5:28	The band moves to a composed passage (lasting nine and a half measures). As the bass slowly ascends, the guitar and organ play a bizarre melody, harmonized in dissonant intervals that fall just short of octaves.
5:32	The melody is repeated, with the bass slightly higher and the intervals slightly more dissonant.
5:40	The melody moves in faster note values.
5:43	The passage comes to rest on a half cadence, followed by a brief drum solo.
5:47	The passage is repeated exactly.
6:06	As the passage is repeated one more time, the guitar begins playing a solo over harmonies played by the organ.
6:24	The bass shifts down **chromatically** to a new harmony; the organ lingers on a fragment of the melody, repeated polyrhythmically against the bass.
6:28	A strange synthesized sound fills up the melody space, gradually growing louder.
6:31	Suddenly the bass rises in pitch as it speeds up, as if the tape were being run faster.
6:40	The bass finally stops, ending the piece.

ACID JAZZ AND HIP-HOP

The term **acid jazz** comes from England's "rave" scene, in dance clubs of the 1980s and early 1990s. Late at night, DJs would draw crowds of dancers with electronic music enhanced by light shows and artificial fog. The music was known as "acid house," and it was hypnotically repetitive, powered by a sturdy bass line. One night, DJ Chris Bangs, tired of the usual selections, offered an alternative woven together from soul jazz tracks in his record collection. He called it acid jazz, and the term spread. Dancers heard the music as retro, an evocation of now-forgotten soul jazz from the 1960s, available only on LPs. For many young people, it was their pathway into the jazz tradition.

The acid jazz craze brought back to life styles that had been shunted to the fringes, like soul jazz. During a time when giants like Coltrane, Mingus, and Coleman roamed the earth, soul jazz received little critical attention, yet it survived the inattention, through the few bands that continued to play it and in private record collections. As DJs hungry for new beats combed through piles of used vinyl looking for material, they discovered boatloads of these albums and recycled them back into dance music. Acid jazz was, in fact, jazz pastiche.

The latest area to be affected by the fusion impulse is black **hip-hop**, which arose from the streets of the Bronx in the 1970s and by the 1980s had spread throughout the country and beyond to make an indelible mark on the entire world. Few jazz musicians had any involvement with it (Herbie Hancock's "Rockit" is a memorable exception, with its turntable scratching), and by the 1990s it had become a symbol of everything jazz was not: young, countercultural, and in touch with the reality of the streets in black communities.

Two things had to happen for jazz/hip-hop fusion to work. First, hip-hop artists had to discover jazz. Musicians from bands like A Tribe Called Quest and Digable Planets began raiding their parents' cabinets, finding old Blue Notes and pulling cuts to use as samples on their own records. The results surprised almost everyone. In 1994, Us3 transformed Herbie Hancock's "Cantaloupe Island" into a new mix called "Cantaloop (Flip Fantasia)," which made it into the top twenty. Blue Note enjoyed unanticipated prosperity as sales of its classics rose dramatically, thanks to their use on hip-hop records.

The second thing was that jazz musicians had to find a way to use hip-hop that went beyond adding spoken rhymes to conventional jazz numbers. The financial incentives were obvious: embracing hip-hop opened up a new, young audience for their music. But success often depends on who is in charge. Recordings controlled by hip-hop artists tend to keep jazz well in the background, reduced to short sampled loops or buried in the mix. That hasn't stopped jazz musicians from trying their damnedest. They are willing to absorb just enough hip-hop to make their own music more stylish. Branford Marsalis's fusion band, for example, Buckshot LeFonque (after one of Cannonball Adderley's pseudonyms), adds a rapper and a turntablist to an otherwise conventional electric jazz ensemble. A more promising approach is suggested by pianist Jason Moran, who in his version of "Planet Rock" and original compositions honestly uses musical elements of hip-hop (rhythms, loops, dubs) to spark his jazz improvisations.

FUSION AND ROCK

The question of repertory has always troubled fusion musicians. As early as the 1930s, jazz musicians showed that anything could be jazzed or swung, just as a few decades earlier ragtime pianists boasted that anything could be ragged. Still, what these musicians chose to play was undisturbed by controversy. Songwriters of the pre-rock era wrote tunes with sophisticated harmonic sequences that appealed to improvisers and arrangers, and they expected their compositions to be performed by everybody, from pop singers to jazz musicians. If there was a divide between jazz and pop, it seemed more a matter of attitude and procedure than of warring tribes.

Rock arrived at the very moment when jazz pushed toward the seeming anarchy of the avant-garde, and perceptions about pop songs changed. Rock fans dismissed the older style of pop song as arty, old-hat, and dull, while jazz musicians, already leaving Tin Pan Alley song behind, derided the new rock tunes as simplistic and childish. Rock developed its own sense of repertory, kept alive by classic albums, oldie stations, and tribute bands; yet very little of it has found its way into jazz. This leaves jazz players who grew up with and maintained affection for rock, hip-hop, and other pop forms struggling to find ways to include contemporary songs in their repertory.

In 1973, the bop saxophonist and flutist Yusef Lateef made an album called *Part of the Search*, exploring his memories of black radio hits, from Billie Holiday and Jimmie Lunceford to Ray Charles and the Five Satins, replacing the silences between tracks with station-tuning static. With his 2012 album *Black Radio*, the pianist Robert Glasper updated the idea with the declared objective of reducing the distance between jazz and black (though not exclusively black) commercial pop. Born (in 1978) and raised in Houston, Glasper developed a love of vernacular music inherited from his mother, a gospel pianist and singer, that fused with his jazz training at Houston's High School of Performing Arts (which also educated Beyoncé as well as fellow jazz musicians Jason Moran, Kendrick Scott, and Eric Harland). His first recordings emphasized the piano trio, yet he loved pop songs: on *In My Element* (2007), he blended the modal harmonies of Herbie Hancock's "Maiden Voyage" with "Everything in Its Own Place" by the indie band Radiohead. Within a few years, he had formed the Robert Glasper Experiment, augmenting his group with electronic resources and recruiting star pop vocalists.

Robert Glasper worked as musical director for Mos Def and toured with prominent hip-hop artists before inaugurating his own series of albums, including *Black Radio*, a classic of jazz-infused rhythm and blues. Here, he's seen leading his more characteristic trio at a New York jazz club, in 2011.

Robert Glasper

🎧 "Why Do We Try"

Before he recorded *Black Radio*, Glasper knew he would have to establish his jazz cred. "Jazz is my first love," he said, "and I just really wanted to solidify myself as a jazz pianist [and] then move on to something else, because the media and everybody, they're quick to peg you as something: 'Oh, the hip-hop guy.' They couldn't wait to do that to me." In a sense, he purposely did what John Coltrane inadvertently did in proving himself a magnificent jazz saxophonist before embarking on the avant-garde. No one could say Coltrane played "out" because he couldn't play "in." No one can say that Glasper is a jazz dilettante or that his method is insincere. By any definition, "Why Do We Try" is an outstanding performance. Is is jazz? It's definitely a kind of jazz: listen to the superb piano solo, the flexibility of the rhythm section, the daring vocal improv by Stokley Williams, the singer and drummer with the

Minnestota-based R&B band Mint Condition. Is it pop? The commercial success of the project (*Black Radio 2* followed in 2013) suggests that it is.

On Mint Condition's 2007 recording, Stokley supports the lead vocal by a guest singer, Ali Shaheed Muhammed. In Glasper's reworking, the tempo is brightened, the rhythm is made more intricate and responsive, and the lyrics are edited down. The theme of love's labors is there, but lines about family breakups are gone in favor of a wordless, melismatic, visceral crooning. Stokley's fans may be surprised to hear him scat. Other jazz musicians have adopted rock and R&B themes, but often press them into a conventional jazz setting, sometimes with new harmonies to facilitate improvisations. Glasper's approach is more radical and more respectful; he tackles these pieces whole, savoring them while recasting them to suit his jazz sensibility. His piano girds and animates the entire performance, and his solo entails an almost casually virtuosic transformation of basic melodic modules (for example, the five-note figure at 2:07). "It's tricking people," he told an interviewer, laughing at the idea. "They aren't even gonna know they have a jazz album." Speaking of tricks, wait for the fake ending.

LISTENING GUIDE 68

🎧 why do we try

ROBERT GLASPER EXPERIMENT
Robert Glasper, piano; Casey Benjamin, synthesizer; Chris Dave, drums and percussion; Stokley Williams, voice and percussion; Derrick Hodge, bass

- Label: *Black Radio*, Blue Note 88333
- Date: 2012
- Form: verse/chorus
- Style: fusion

What to listen for:

- an ingenious jazz arrangement of an R&B pop song
- Stokley's vocal improvisation, including scat-singing
- Glasper's shift from smooth accompaniment to improvised solo

INTRODUCTION

0:00   With hoarse, nasal syllables, Stokley sings a short, repeated **riff**.

0:16   The rhythm section enters: Glasper plays quiet chords on piano; Dave marks the **downbeat** with a pair of bass-drum strokes, followed by snare-drum hits on the **backbeat**; Hodge plays sparely on bass. Stokley's riff is harmonized in **block-chord texture** by a synthesized background line.

0:32   As the rhythm section continues, Stokley sings a wordless melody.

VERSE

0:48   *"Do I continue living by myself? . . ."*

Stokley begins the song's verse, accompanied by Glasper's chords.

CHORUS

1:21   *"So why do we try to let love pass us by . . ."*

The chorus is marked by three strong accents, coinciding with the main words in the title ("Why do we try?").

1:38   A new chord and percussive drum accents herald the end of the chorus.

PIANO SOLO

1:40   At the opening of his solo, Glasper plays quick, disorienting figures with his right hand. The accompaniment is spare—drum patterns, interrupted by occasional bass phrases and a sigh from Stokley every other fourth beat.

1:49   Glasper doubles the melody with his left hand, creating disconnected lines that interact with Hodge's bass line.

2:07   He transforms a five-note pattern into a complex **polyrhythm**, prompting accents from the drummer.

2:19   His rhythmic patterns become more eccentric, adding to the intensity of the passage.

2:29   The rhythmic tension finally resolves on the downbeat.

2:34   Glasper suddenly steps **outside** the tonality to play an unexpected phrase.

2:46   As the tune shifts to a new harmony, his phrases become more **legato** and sustained.

VERSE

3:01   *"Do I continue living by myself?. . ."*

      Stokley returns for the verse with florid, improvised lines. Glasper gently responds with broad chords.

3:18   *"I know I've found someone. . . ."* As Stokley reaches for a high note, Glasper's response is more brittle and **staccato**. Stokley returns with a quick improvised line of his own.

3:27   *"Why do we have to question how it should be?"*

3:31   Dave calls attention to the coming chorus with improvised **fills**.

CHORUS

3:34   *"So why do we try to let love pass us by . . ."*

      Once more the full band enters, including the synthesizer and high-pitched percussion.

3:50   Repeating the words, Stokley aims for higher pitches.

4:08   Loud drum strokes bring the chorus to a close.

VOCAL SOLO

4:10   Stokley's wild, ascending line echoes over a **cross-rhythm** on the snare drum.

4:21   A fast, improvised ornate line ends with an unaccompanied low note.

4:23   The drum line falters, then comes to a complete stop.

4:26   As the rhythm section restarts, Stokley insistently repeats a short line of text ("Why do . . ."), his voice doubled at an upper interval with a voice encoder. In the background, Glasper plays a rhythmic **ostinato**.

4:37   *"It's right there, underneath your nose."* Stokley ends his line with a long **melisma** (several notes sung to one syllable). The synthesizer background returns.

4:48   *"Look to your left."* The doubled voice line is piercing and intense.

4:52   *"Look to your right."* The last syllable is extended with another meandering melisma.

5:00   *"Open your eyes."* Stokley's line reaches its melodic peak.

5:09   He briefly breaks into scat-singing.

5:17   *"Why do we try? Why?"* He latches on to a high note, emphasizing it by bending it with a dissonant **chromatic** note.

5:25   Scat-singing on "Why?," he creates a riff that alternates with the drum's insistent backbeats.

5:31   As the chord changes, Stokley's scat-singing accelerates to match the drummer's improvised accompaniment.

5:35   The tune begins to fade out, leading to an extended period of silence.

CODA

5:52   The song fades in again, with the same chords but at a much slower tempo. Stokley sings a line from the chorus: *". . . question how we feel that love's not real."*

6:05   The background synthesizer plays a slow, lazy polyrhythm.

6:09   Stokley scats on the syllable "now," turning a four-note phrase in and out of tension with the meter.

6:18   Over his wordless syllables, a second fade-out takes us to the end.

If the marketing category "fusion" ran its course decades ago, the broader idea of jazz-pop fusion shows no sign of dissipating. And why should it? Each new generation of jazz musicians comes of age knowing the dance music and pop songs of their day, and it's hard to believe they would not want to share that sensibility with their audience. Granted, jazz musicians have their own way of doing things. Typically, they distance themselves from their pop contemporaries with a barrage of defamiliarizing gestures: complex harmonies, virtuosic solos, rhythmic intensity, all drawn from the jazz tradition. But the energy of change comes from pop rather than jazz.

Not everyone feels this way. Many jazz musicians find their inspiration in the tradition itself.

ADDITIONAL LISTENING	
Tony Williams Lifetime	"Emergency!" (1969)
Charles Lloyd Quartet	"Forest Flower—Sunrise" (1966)
Miles Davis	"Filles de Kilimanjaro" (1968), "Shhh/Peaceful," "Spanish Key" (both 1969)
Mahavishnu Orchestra	"Vital Transformation" (1971)
Return to Forever (Chick Corea)	"Song of the Pharaoh Kings" (1974)
Weather Report	"Birdland," "Black Market" (1976)
Jaco Pastorius	"Donna Lee" (1975)
Pat Metheny	"Have You Heard" (1989)
Herbie Hancock	"Chameleon" (1973), "Palm Grease" (1974)
Keith Jarrett	"Long as You Know You're Living Yours," "The Windup," "Death and the Flower" (all 1974)
George Benson	"This Masquerade" (1976)
Oregon	"Aurora" (1973)
Charlie Hunter	"Mitch Better Have My Bunny" (2001)
Medeski, Martin and Wood	"Beeah" (1993)
Robert Glasper	"Medley: Maiden Voyage / Everything in Its Right Place" (2007)

ONLINE MULTIMEDIA RESOURCES AND REVIEW MATERIALS

Author Insight Videos

Scott DeVeaux describes the origins and nature of fusion; why *Bitches Brew* was a breakthrough album; how smooth jazz fits between rock and jazz and how recording techniques affect the music; and the relation of hip-hop to jazz, a more contested form of fusion.

Interactive Listening Guides

Weather Report, "Teen Town"
Herbie Hancock, "Cantaloupe Island"
John Scofield / Medeski, Martin and Wood, "Chank"
Robert Glasper, "Why Do We Try"

Jazz Concepts (audio and/or video demonstrations of terms covered here)

backbeat	glissando	polyrhythm
block-chord texture	half-valving	staccato
blue notes	legato	syncopation
cadence	major triad	tonic
call and response	modulation	tremolo
chromatic	ostinato	
dissonance	pentatonic scale	

- For quick reference, review the **Chapter Overview** and **Chapter Outline**.
- Take the online **Chapter** and **Listening Quizzes**.
- Use the online **Glossary** and **Flashcards** to review important terms.

18

HISTORICISM: JAZZ ON JAZZ

THE WEIGHT OF HISTORY

In 1925, shortly after joining Fletcher Henderson's big band in New York, Louis Armstrong showed Henderson's arranger, Don Redman, a handbook containing music that he and his mentor, King Oliver, had composed in Chicago. Armstrong encouraged Redman to select a piece to orchestrate. Redman decided on "Sugar Foot Stomp," which Oliver had recorded as "Dippermouth Blues," and wrote an arrangement in which Armstrong would perform Oliver's famous cornet solo.

"Sugar Foot Stomp" helped put Henderson's band on the map: it was a startling example of a modern New York recording based on written and improvised material taken from a traditional New Orleans (by way of Chicago) jazz recording, and the piece quickly became a favorite among dancers and musicians. This was neither the first nor last time Henderson looked to jazz history for inspiration. As we saw in Chapter 5, just the previous year he had recorded "Copenhagen," a piece introduced months before by Chicago's Wolverines (the white band that featured Bix Beiderbecke); Henderson's records served as critiques, showing that New York was paying attention to Chicago even as it moved in a new direction. Then in 1926, Henderson recorded "King Porter

John Lewis, who believed in jazz education, helped launch the Lenox School in the year that he brought the Modern Jazz Quartet to Paris, 1957.

Stomp," based on the third strain of a Jelly Roll Morton piano piece; a decade later, that arrangement would be embraced as a Swing Era anthem.

The two narratives that have dominated our chronicling of jazz thus far are suitable and necessary for a music busy being born. The first presented jazz as an art-for-art's-sake tradition whose masters move the music along with radical leaps of creativity, and the second viewed jazz as a fusion tradition in which jazz evolves in response to contemporary pop culture. The Henderson recordings suggest the foundation for a third way of interpreting jazz history: a historicist narrative, which begins with the precept that jazz creativity is inextricably bound to its past. It's particularly useful in considering today's jazz. Historicism helps to explain how jazz became increasingly self-conscious about its status, and why twenty-first-century jazz is plagued with countless tributes, re-creations, and variations on its past.

Historicism originated in the nineteenth century as an alternative theory to the notion that great men and women and their works arise independently of history. Instead, it connects each new undertaking to its predecessors, emphasizing historical evolution over individual genius, positing an exchange between past and present that philosopher G. W. F. Hegel called a dialectic. In the 1980s, critical theorists put forth a **New Historicism**, which says that a work of art must be viewed within the context of the place and time of its creation. Rejecting the **New Criticism**, which analyzes works of art as sufficient unto themselves, the New Historicists look beyond a work to the historical and social context that conditioned it.

Martin Williams

Perhaps the leading advocate of the New Criticism as applied to jazz was the writer and producer Martin Williams, who always focused on the particularity of a musical work, and paid relatively little attention to historical details that might have furnished a different kind of interpretation. In the 1970s, while working at the Smithsonian Institution, he created *The Smithsonian Collection of Classic Jazz*, an anthology that revolutionized the teaching of jazz. Yet as an example of pitfalls inherent in the New Criticism, consider that Williams included Jelly Roll Morton's "Dead Man Blues" (Chapter 4) while cutting its comic introduction, which he considered irrelevant, dated, and rather embarrassing. A historicist, on the other hand, finds value in that bit of tomfoolery: it tells us something of Morton's times and of his background, intentions, and attitude.

In the twenty-first century, we live in an age of homage and interpretation, with countless writers, filmmakers, composers, choreographers, painters, architects, and others attempting to energize the present by mining the past. In the 1950s and 60s, jazz musicians strove to create new and original works of art; today, musicians are as likely to perform or pay tribute to those same works. The ways in which they apply historicist principles tend to fall into three categories:

- The revival of entire idioms, such as traditional jazz or swing, which usually involves an immersion in jazz repertory and the faithful reproduction of classic or neglected works.

- Original music that celebrates music of the past, which may range from expansive tributes to playful parodies.

- Modernist interpretations of jazz classics as a way of using the past to spur the present.

These principles have found favor throughout jazz history, but largely as a sideshow to the main action. That began to change in the late 1930s, when jazz chroniclers bemoaned the loss of historical perspective and musical styles subsumed by the present-day fashions.

RECLAIMING AND DEFINING THE PAST: FROM BUNK TO THE ACADEMY (1940s and 50s)

The first genuine movement to counter prevailing musical tastes in favor of an older, neglected jazz style did not take place until (and in response to) the height of the Swing Era. The kick-off came with the 1939 publication of *Jazzmen*, edited and partly written by Frederick Ramsey Jr. and Charles Edward Smith. A serious if faultily researched work, *Jazzmen* argued that true jazz was an essentially New Orleans–derived, African American, blues-based music—hardly a controversial position. But in romanticizing jazz's traditional roots while ignoring modern swing stylists (Lester Young, Roy Eldridge, Billie Holiday, and Lionel Hampton are mentioned only in passing or not at all), it created a nostalgic longing for early jazz. In the course of researching a section on New Orleans for *Jazzmen*, the writer William Russell discovered a New Orleans trumpet player named Willie "Bunk" Johnson (1889–1949), and made him one of the book's heroes.

Jazzmen

Bunk Johnson

Johnson, who predated the actual year of his birth by a decade, claimed to have played with Buddy Bolden in 1895 (he would have been six at the time) and to have influenced Louis Armstrong—a boast that Armstrong gently debunked. In 1942, fitted with a new set of teeth, Johnson recorded for the first time in his career; he continued to record over the next five years, while touring the country from San Francisco to New York and spurring a major revival of traditional jazz. Bunk Johnson was exhibited as an uncompromised purveyor of the "real" jazz. Though beset by technical limitations, he had a rosy, glowing tone and an undeniable predilection for the blues and lyricism.

To their credit, Johnson and his admirers forced a reconsideration of early jazz, which was so remote to most swing fans that King Oliver and Jelly Roll Morton died broke and forgotten. Bunk also introduced a clique of veteran New Orleans musicians, born at the turn of the century, who accompanied him on tour and in the studio. They interpreted a narrow traditionalist repertory with sincerity and emotional candor, and they revived elemental musical pleasures—strong backbeats and polyphonic elation—that had fallen by the wayside. The best known among them, clarinetist George Lewis (1900–1968), later played an important role in reestablishing the French Quarter in New Orleans as a destination for tourists. His plaintive sound sustained an international following well into the 1960s, long after the Bunk Johnson phenomenon ended, offering honest refuge for those disinclined to tackle modern jazz, middle-of-the-road pop, or rock.

Bunk Johnson brought his New Orleans Jazz Band to New York and became the focal point for the New Orleans revival: (left to right) Big Jim Robinson, trombone; Johnson, trumpet; Baby Dodds, drums; Lawrence Marrero, banjo; George Lewis, clarinet; Alton Purnell, piano; Alcide "Slow Drag" Pavageau, bass. Decca Records, New York, 1945.

The Lenox School of Jazz

Bunk died in the summer of 1949, around the same time that Miles Davis led the "Birth of the Cool" sessions and Dave Brubeck made his first records. The 1950s

FRANK DRIGGS COLLECTION

Dave Brubeck speaks to a class at the Lenox School in Lenox, Massachusetts, in 1959, while Gunther Schuller and John Lewis look on.

offered a nonstop parade of new styles—cool, hard bop, Third Stream, soul, avant-garde—energized by ingenious improvisers and innovative composers. Not surprisingly, this creative commotion also instigated historical inquiry into older schools seemingly left in the dust.

In 1958, the critic Stanley Dance coined the term **mainstream** to describe that giant swath of jazz situated between reactionary traditionalism and radical modernity—in short, all those musicians, from Louis Armstrong and Duke Ellington to Benny Goodman and Lester Young, who played in prebop styles. Dance, who despised bebop, sought to renew interest in musicians who were still relatively young (not yet fifty, for the most part) but were treated in the jazz press as dinosaurs. He succeeded, but in the 1960s, to his dismay, with the avant-garde at center stage, mainstream came to encompass bop musicians. Then in the 1970s, when fusion or jazz-rock dominated the spotlight, the mainstream was said to include just about everyone who played acoustic jazz. The important thing, however, is that mainstream now represented the ongoing language of jazz creativity while holding it at a distance from the latest trends.

Jazz eventually began making inroads into academia and the arts establishment, but this was an exceedingly slow process. In the unsympathetic atmosphere that would deny Duke Ellington the Pulitzer Prize, jazz activists took matters into their own hands, creating schools and exploring jazz history in books, magazines, and public discussions. At the same time, musicians were crossing stylistic divides. Louis Armstrong and Dizzy Gillespie, who feuded in the early years of bop, played together on television. In the tradition of Ellington's musical portraits, modernists composed tributes to jazz pioneers. John Lewis helped launch the Modern Jazz Quartet with his cortege for Django Reinhardt, while Charles Mingus created a threnody for Lester Young ("Goodbye Pork Pie Hat"), among other salutes.

Much of the historical and educational activity was stimulated in an area rarely singled out in jazz histories: Massachusetts, its eastern (Boston) and western (Lenox) borders. The first dedicated jazz curriculum was launched in 1957 as the Lenox School of Jazz, in the Berkshires near the classical music festival at Tanglewood. Never before had a faculty been convened for the exclusive purpose of teaching jazz; never before had an integrated but largely black faculty been recruited to teach whites anything. The Lenox School, under the direction of John Lewis, offered a star-studded roster of musicians and composers to a small, international selection of students who had submitted audition tapes through the mail. The staff included Dizzy Gillespie, Oscar Peterson, Ray Brown, Jimmy Giuffre, George Russell, Max Roach, Gunther Schuller, J. J. Johnson, and Ornette Coleman (who, although registered as a student, also taught), along with several ensembles. In the first year, there were thirty-four instructors for forty-five students; as the number of students doubled, the staff also increased. For the educators, some of whom continued to teach at other institutions, the experience was a revelation; most of them had learned by doing—now they were at the frontier of discovering how to pass on their knowledge.

Lenox's goal was to combine chronological history with musical technique, and to rid jazz of semi-mystical notions of racial or "natural" talent. The courses ranged from writer Marshall Stearns's "The History of Jazz" to Schuller's "The Analytical History of Jazz." By the time Lenox folded, after the 1960 season, jazz studies had begun to make headway in accredited schools. The most important of these were the Berklee College of Music in Boston and the University of North Texas in Denton. North Texas offered the first degree in jazz studies in 1947, and accumulated one of the largest libraries of American music; its big-band workshop has served as the training ground for a legion of gifted players. Berklee began to offer undergraduate degrees in jazz performance and composition in the middle 1960s, and continues to boast the best-known jazz department in American education. By 2000, countless musicians could claim an undergraduate background in jazz studies. Jazz players now served their apprenticeships not on the road, but in classes and school bands.

Composer Bill Russo (arm raised) rehearses his Choir Ensemble with such notables as cellist-educator David Baker (third from left), Ornette Coleman (center, seated), and pianist Steve Kuhn (right, seated) at the Lenox School, 1959.

The Newport Jazz Festival

Boston probably made its most influential contribution to jazz history with the impresario George Wein, who founded the Newport Jazz Festival, across the state line in Rhode Island. Musicians knew Wein, a pianist and occasional bandleader, primarily as the proprietor of two Boston jazz clubs, Storyville and Mahogany Hall, which specialized in Dixieland and swing. In 1954, Wein answered the call of socialites Elaine and Louis Lorillard, who wanted him to program a jazz festival in one of the least likely, most insular settings imaginable: a tennis and croquet court in Newport, patronized by old money. The shutters of some mansions closed in outrage, but Wein prevailed, and jazz found acceptance as a symbol of postwar social enlightenment and good times.

George Wein

Wein programmed panels and workshops along with the concerts, which presented every major jazz star from Armstrong and Ellington to Miles and Monk. He also invited the participation of musicians not always accepted in the jazz world; his motive may have been commercial, but his choices (including gospel singer Mahalia Jackson, Frank Sinatra, Ray Charles, and Chuck Berry) reflected both the historicist idea of placing jazz in the wider context of contemporary music and the fusion idea of showing how jazz and other music interact. Audience insurrections in the late 1960s caused a suspension of the festival in Newport, but Wein quickly relocated his operation in New York, where it grew far larger, establishing him as the most powerful producer in jazz. He later created festivals in France, New Orleans, and elsewhere, and even rebuilt summer events in Newport. By the time he stepped down in 2006, jazz festivals had become annual events on the cultural calendars of six continents.

George Wein, a Boston-based pianist and club owner, changed the presentation of jazz forever when he produced the Newport Jazz Festival, featuring Count Basie in 1956.

AVANT-GARDE HISTORICISM AND NEOCLASSICISM (1970s and 80s)

Historicism all but vanished during the avant-garde 1960s, when the emphasis in jazz was on pushing boundaries. But it made a major and apparently permanent comeback in the 1970s, as the second-generation avant-garde looked to the past in order to vary its music. The boundless eclecticism favored by New York's loft scene coincided with a significant surge in jazz education, as influenced by Williams's *Smithsonian Collection of Classic Jazz* and similar compilations. Record companies in that period released comprehensive boxed sets encompassing entire careers, movements, and label catalogs.

At the same time, great jazz artists whose careers had faltered during the all-consuming rise of rock in the late 1960s and early 70s returned to jazz, creating tremendous interest in musicians of all eras. Some players had shifted their focus to studio work, the academy, and Broadway or Las Vegas pit bands; others relocated to Europe or simply kept low profiles. Now they were greeted as "living legends" (see p. 441). Suddenly you could see long-absent musicians who had started out in the 1920s, like Benny Carter and Doc Cheatham, or in the bop era, like Dexter Gordon, Red Rodney, and James Moody. In this atmosphere, musicians experimented with the very nature of style, and the audiences seemed ready for almost anything.

Ironically, it was the avant-garde that first located the "jazz tradition" as a new realm for creativity. The Loft Era musicians borrowed from old styles as resources: they combined swing, funk, and free rhythms to create an independent music seasoned with humor, irony, nostalgia, and deep feelings. For them, the aging battle cry of "free jazz" meant the freedom to play whatever they liked—even ragtime, even a march. Startling new recordings by groups such as Air, the spare trio featuring alto saxophonist Henry Threadgill, bassist Fred Hopkins, and drummer Steve McCall, offered visions of early jazz as a new playground. Their album *Air Lore* (1979) was devoted to the music of Scott Joplin (only recently rediscovered in the movie *The Sting*) and Jelly Roll Morton, presented in versions that alternated between precise fidelity and challenging outside playing. Arthur Blythe titled one of his albums *In the Tradition* (1978); its cover showed the stocky saxophonist, in black-and-white photography, dressed to the nines, as if heading to a jam session in 1930s Harlem. The avant-garde composer and saxophonist Anthony Braxton used the same title for his acoustic quartet, devoted to performing jazz and pop standards.

Yet in the long run, the avant-garde invariably triggered (in the manner of Hegel's dialectic) an antithesis in the early 1980s, which may be defined as **neoclassical.** This more conservative approach was predicated on fidelity to a specific canon of masterpieces. Instead of looking at marches or swing or bop as generic styles that could be interpreted and reinterpreted, it paid homage to particular musicians and works, infusing them with a contemporary luster—at best. Yet neoclassicists also argued that jazz must swing in a certain way, that harmonies and melodies had to conform to traditional practices, that jazz had clear-cut borders defined by its key artists.

This kind of traditionalism found acceptance for several reasons, not least the temper of the 1980s. Ronald Reagan had just been elected president, promising to implement (despite his own messy personal life) traditional American values, a harsh approach toward law and order, and a rollback of

1960s Great Society programs, including welfare and civil rights. He precipitated a storm of anti-intellectualism and hostility toward the arts, especially those thought to appeal to an "elitist" (still a prominent code word on the right) audience. Arts funding was reduced, while books and other artworks were censored or removed from public display. In this atmosphere, nostalgia for an orderly, swinging style of jazz was practically a given.

Established players who had been alienated by the avant-garde and fusion began to explore jazz history by paying homage to deceased or neglected musicians. Joe Henderson recorded albums of music by Billy Strayhorn and Miles Davis; Kenny Barron and musicians associated with Thelonious Monk formed a quartet, Sphere, to play his music. Philly Joe Jones organized a big band to play music by Tadd Dameron. Steve Lacy focused on works by the overlooked pianist-composer Herbie Nichols. Keith Jarrett, who almost always played original music as a bandleader, now launched a Standards Trio to reinvestigate classic pop and jazz tunes.

■ WYNTON MARSALIS (b. 1961)

Young neoclassical musicians of the 1980s found an unmistakable leader in Wynton Marsalis, an audacious trumpet virtuoso who loudly denied that avant-garde music and fusion had anything to do with jazz. Marsalis also sought to alter the personal styles of musicians. Ridiculing the dashikis, occasional facial paint, and general informality that characterized the way musicians appeared onstage, he insisted on a suit-and-tie dress code that reinstated the elegance of Swing Era bands. Marsalis launched his recording career with simultaneous jazz and classical releases, winning Grammy Awards in both categories. Highly intelligent, impeccably groomed, and fiercely outspoken, he changed the discussion in jazz from one of progressive modernism—with its liberal borrowings from world, popular, and classical music—to the strict interpretation of mainstream jazz parameters, insisting that jazz had to swing with a particular regularity.

Wynton Marsalis (right), trumpet player, composer, and activist, helped to create the jazz wing at Lincoln Center, emphasizing jazz's swinging tradition and often performing with major figures from earlier eras, including trumpet player Clark Terry and saxophonist Jimmy Heath. New York, 1990.

© ALAN NAHIGIAN

Though lambasted as divisive by many musicians, Marsalis was quickly accepted by the popular culture, frequently appearing in televised concerts, in magazine articles, and as a key voice in Ken Burns's television miniseries *Jazz*. He was the first straight-ahead jazz musician to achieve that degree of renown in more than a decade. As the artistic director of Jazz at Lincoln Center (see p. 438), he conducted dozens of jazz repertory concerts, interpreting composers from Ellington and Armstrong to Mingus and Gil Evans. He recorded fanciful interpretations of Morton and Monk. He created a massive body of original work that probes African American history, tradition, and music in such formats as jazz ensembles, chamber groups, and ballet.

Marsalis was born in New Orleans to a musical family; his father, Ellis Marsalis, a well-known pianist and educator, instilled in him and his gifted brothers a sense of dedication and discipline. In 1980, he alternated classical studies at New York's Juilliard School with hard bop, earning a much-coveted position with Blakey's Jazz Messengers. After making a dynamic showing on Blakey's *Album of the Year*, he toured with a Herbie Hancock quartet and then organized his own quintet with his older brother Branford, an equally skilled saxophonist—a group loosely modeled on the postbop 1963–68 Miles Davis Quintet. Many people found his deliberate turn to the musical past, along with his dark suits and sober demeanor, a delightful return to jazz sanity. If he hadn't used his celebrity to attack less well-placed musicians, setting off a windstorm of petty feuds, his success might have proved even more widespread.

Unfortunately, the mass media that accepted Marsalis as an engaging personality and musical spokesman was no longer responsive to jazz itself. It could absorb Marsalis as a celebrity, but could not roll the clock back to a time when musicians appeared on radio and television and when record releases by its most creative players were well-publicized events. Marsalis's exacting historicism underscored the fact that jazz now competed less with pop or classical music than with its own past. Young fans were challenged with a choice: do you buy a new tribute to Monk, or do you buy Monk? As jazz record sales plummeted, even Marsalis—despite his Grammys and a 1997 Pulitzer Prize for his oratorio *Blood on the Fields*—was dropped by his label, Columbia Records, which turned its corporate back on jazz altogether.

Marsalis, nothing daunted, devoted his energies to tours, education, and fundraising events to ensure the success of Jazz at Lincoln Center. For a while, his trumpet playing turned from Miles Davis to an earlier New Orleans style that employed mutes and vocalized sounds, à la Oliver and Ellington. In time, however, he also developed greater clarity in his improvisations, making the most of long phrases and high-note gambits, and perfecting his highly personal timbre. He also loosened his strictures, though not about the avant-garde, and collaborated on mainstream Americana and vocal projects, including a popular recording with Willie Nelson. Most of his recordings have focused on acoustic jazz, plumbing repertories that range from the contemporary to the antique.

🎧 "The Pearls"

In 1959, Charles Mingus recorded an homage of sorts to Jelly Roll Morton called "Jelly Roll," an original composition that acknowledges superficial elements of 1920s traditional jazz with two-beat bass slapping and a saxophone solo (by John Handy) that begins in a rickety staccato style and then sharply turns modern. Listeners smiled, but were never for a moment lulled into thinking they were hearing anything resembling Morton's music. Forty years later, Wynton Marsalis paid tribute to his fellow New Orleans native with a very different approach, an album devoted to Morton, acknowledging the leap from Morton's generation to his own—not with a few glib reference points, but rather with a conviction that old forms of jazz require their own virtuosity.

Whether or not you are familiar with Morton's celebrated 1926 Red Hot Peppers recording of "The Pearls," with its delightfully lyrical trio theme, you may find Marsalis's take bordering on schizophrenia, at least the first time you hear it. The opening minute, notwithstanding the signature dash and vigor of Marsalis's trumpet playing, promises nothing more than a handsomely played transcription of Morton's performance. This is the approach taken by most jazz repertory ensembles: tidy replication of the original. But then, in the second **A** section, the piece suddenly becomes unstuck in time. Everything changes: the rhythm, articulation, timbre—the saxophone solo unfolds in a series of modernistic sixteenth notes. Then, as we accustom ourselves to the land of modern jazz, the tuba returns to knock off the bass and reclaim Morton's trio as he created it. Perhaps the high point of the performance is the repeat of the trio (**C**), where the band embellishes the music in the style of Morton, as if on further consideration the band decided that this was a more fitting gesture than another abrupt return to modernism. By the coda, the ensemble is firmly committed to Jelly Roll.

What are we to make of this recording: are traditional and modern jazz styles oil and water, or is there mutuality linking them? Does Marsalis's re-creation of Morton's performance risk the pitfall of a cornball mockery? How, after all, does this exercise in historicism compare with the original? What does it add, if anything, and what does it lose, if anything? One thing is clear. When it comes to the jazz canon, Marsalis and company look backward with the same authority they bring to their own music.

🎧 the pearls

WYNTON MARSALIS

Wynton Marsalis, trumpet; Victor Goines, clarinet; Lucien Barbarin, trombone; Wessell Anderson, alto saxophone; Wycliffe Gordon, tuba; Don Vappie, banjo; Reginald Veal, bass; Herlin Riley, drums; Harry Connick Jr., piano

- Label: *Standard Time, Vol. 6: Mr. Jelly Lord*, Columbia CK69872
- Date: 1999
- Style: historicist
- Form: march/ragtime

What to listen for:
- Jelly Roll Morton's composition
- Marsalis's spectacular trumpet technique
- ingenious blending of historicist New Orleans jazz and modern bebop

INTRO

0:01		Marsalis's sound penetrates through a **polyphonic** texture, delivering the melody for the four-bar introduction.
0:07	**A**	Over an extended **stop-time** (with the chord consistently falling on the backbeat), Marsalis plays Jelly Roll Morton's bouncy melody.

0:17		A one-measure **break** features Goines on clarinet.
0:19		Marsalis improvises a new wide-ranging melody that floats rhythmically above the stop-time.
0:26		Toward the end, he returns to the written melody.
0:30		The clarinet briefly overlaps Marsalis's line.
0:32	**B**	The whole band plays the theme in **block-chord** harmony, occasionally devolving into polyphonic **collective improvisation**. In the background, Vapple foregrounds banjo chords prominently on each beat, while Riley hits the snare drum on the backbeat.
0:50		On a monophonic break, Marsalis plays figurations over an unexpected chord (a **diminished seventh**).
0:56	**A**	The groove suddenly shifts to a modern style: the banjo and tuba stop playing, Veal enters with a **walking-bass** line, and the pianist **comps**. Over this texture, Anderson begins his solo on alto saxophone.
1:07		Goines once again takes the break, this time with bebop-style 16th notes.
1:08		As if following suit, Anderson also plays in **double-time**.
1:21	**A**	The pianist plays a riff underneath Anderson's solo.
1:31		Goines's break is harshly **dissonant**.

TRANSITION

| 1:45 | | Framed by dramatic silences, the band signals a change to a new key with block-chord textures and clarinet **trills**. The tuba replaces the bass. |

TRIO (C)

1:51		The trio begins with a steady, marching tuba line.
1:54		Goines and Anderson play the new theme in a loose harmony.
2:04		For a brief time, they move into collective improvisation with the piano.
2:17		Gordon on tuba starts the trio again, but in his accompaniment returns to a two-beat bass line.
2:23		The second half of the trio moves into new harmonic territory.
2:29		In a passage scripted by Morton, the clarinet takes the melody in a brief stop-time passage.
2:33		The entire band, in polyrhythmic block chords, moves to the final cadence.

TRIO (repeated)

2:42		The tuba line is augmented by a soulful note by Barbarin on trombone, and doubled a few seconds later by the bass. Marsalis joins the others, playing the main melody.
3:09		Gordon embellishes his tuba line but drops out, leaving his role to be covered by the bass.
3:20		Marsalis takes the lead, improvising over the stop-time.

CODA

3:32		The tuba line returns (preceded by a **triplet** bass pickup).
3:35		The clarinet responds with a solo trill.
3:40		The entire band sounds a final chord.

Repertory vs. Nostalgia

Harry Conick Jr./Diana Krall

For many popular performers, the turn toward historicism has been nostalgic. Singer-pianists Harry Connick Jr. and Diana Krall demonstrated popular appeal by resurrecting performance styles of the 1940s and 50s. Connick was the first of several male singers to invoke the manner of Frank Sinatra, though he also spiced his performances with piano playing that reflected Monk's percussive wit. Krall initially made her name with a trio that echoed the instrumentation (piano, guitar, bass) and songs of Nat King Cole. She later recorded ballads with lush studio orchestras in the manner of mainstream 1950s singers. Jazz nostalgia even found its way into such movies as Bertrand Tavernier's *'Round Midnight*, in which tenor saxophonist Dexter Gordon created a character based on Bud Powell and Lester Young; Clint Eastwood's *Bird*, a fictionalized biography of Charlie Parker, with Parker's saxophone solos grafted to a modern rhythm section; and Robert Altman's *Kansas City*, in which 1930s musicians were viewed as a positive counterstatement to the city's appalling crime and corruption.

Diana Krall first became famous with a trio and repertory modeled on Nat King Cole, and similarly allowed her vocal talents to obscure her ability as a pianist.

But actual repertory bands—designed to resurrect big-band jazz, either by performing original arrangements or by commissioning new versions of classic works—have also been part of the jazz scene. The **jazz repertory** movement got its start in the middle 1970s, with the debuts of two groups. The New York Jazz Repertory Company, launched by George Wein, produced two seasons of concerts at Carnegie Hall by rotating music directors: Cecil Taylor led a large orchestra that included former students; George Russell conducted a revised version of his album *Living Time*; Paul Jeffrey conducted orchestral versions of music by Thelonious Monk with Monk playing piano; and so forth.

In 1986, the American Jazz Orchestra debuted, conducted by John Lewis, who had managed to create one of the most successful small ensembles of his time, the Modern Jazz Quartet, while pioneering jazz education. In addition to music by Ellington, Goodman, Count Basie, Jimmie Lunceford, Mary

American Jazz Orchestra

The American Jazz Orchestra revitalized jazz repertory in residence at Cooper Union's Great Hall: (first row) Danny Bank, Norris Turney, Loren Schoenberg; (second row) Benny Powell, Eddie Bert, Bob Milliken, John Eckhardt, bassist John Goldsby, pianist Dick Katz. Standing: director of the Great Hall Roberta Swann, artistic director Gary Giddins, music director John Lewis. New York, 1986.

Lou Williams, Woody Herman, Dizzy Gillespie, and Gil Evans, the orchestra performed arrangements that had rarely if ever been heard, including Ellington's *Black, Brown and Beige*. Several composers from various eras of jazz history—Benny Carter, Jimmy Heath, Muhal Richard Abrams, David Murray—were invited to write and conduct new works during the orchestra's seven years. Similar orchestras were created in San Diego, Washington, D.C. (under the aegis of the Smithsonian), and elsewhere.

JLCO But the most durable of the new repertory orchestras debuted in 1987 at New York's leading cultural institution. The Jazz at Lincoln Center Orchestra (JLCO), under the direction of Wynton Marsalis, achieved outstanding successes, musically and in the usually neglected area of education. Encouraged by the Jazz at Lincoln Center program, university and high school music departments introduced classic numbers from jazz repertory in their student orchestras. Firmly ensconced in the Frederick P. Rose Hall, an 100,000-foot concert space overlooking Central Park, the JLCO has become a national institution, spreading its historical re-creations over the country in nationwide tours. Under Marsalis's leadership, it has taken on an aggressively conservative stance, preserving the music of such classic musicians as Duke Ellington.

In recent years, the JLCO has had competition from the West Coast in the form of the SFJAZZ Collective, an eight-person, all-star combo based in San Francisco. Initially under the leadership of tenor saxophonist Joshua Redman (b. 1969), the Collective is a loose, collaborative association of instrumentalists and composers that's seeking its own path to the jazz repertory. Each season has seen the group dedicate its concerts to the works of a jazz composer: Ornette Coleman, John Coltrane, Wayne Shorter, Thelonious Monk—even pop star Stevie Wonder. In 2013, the group acquired its own state-of-the-art performing facility, the SFJAZZ Center in downtown San Francisco. The success of the host organization—which, like Lincoln Center, sponsors educational activities as well as a vigorous series of concerts—suggests that repertory groups may thrive in cities besides New York.

🎧 "Maiden Voyage"

In 2006, the Collective devoted itself to the music of Herbie Hancock, including the title track to his landmark 1965 *Maiden Voyage*. The sales of that album didn't approach those of the Beatles and other rock bands, but the tune "Maiden Voyage" was heard more than was generally realized, if only subliminally: it was conceived for a much televised cologne ad. One musician who heard it first in that context was the great vibes player Bobby Hutcherson (b. 1941), who later described it as "one of the hippest commercials ever!" Less than a year after Hancock completed his breakthrough Blue Note recording, Hutcherson recorded his own version—the first of a good many interpretations—for the same label, with Hancock (a frequent recording partner) on piano. Hutcherson had not yet heard the composer's album, and Hancock did not attempt to take charge in this account of the piece. Forty years later, when the SFJAZZ Collective created its own

Until 2007, the SFJAZZ Collective's artistic director was the brilliantly inventive tenor and soprano saxophonist Joshua Redman, seen here with Eric Harland, the group's drummer from 2005 until 2012. By rethinking music by Ornette Coleman, John Coltrane, Herbie Hancock, Wayne Shorter, and others, SFJAZZ liberates classic jazz from its original context, extending its reach for a new generation of musicians to explore.

HIROYUKI ITO/GETTY IMAGES

arrangement, it had in Hutcherson someone with a direct connection to the composition and the era it helped to define.

It would be difficult to overstate the impact of Hancock's album, as countless jazz musicians who grew up in the 1960s claim *Maiden Voyage* as a personal revelation. Hancock was a member of the Miles Davis Quintet at the time, and the lead-off track represented both the influence of Davis and a distinct step forward. The form is similar to Davis's 1959 "So What": a thirty-two-bar **A A B A** piece with a modal approach to harmony. There are only four chords in the entire piece—all suspended chords (dominant chords without the leading tone), two in the **A** sections and two in the bridge. The challenge is to improvise creatively in a harmonic context that floats beyond the familiar resolutions of chord changes. The harmonically bare setting tends to accentuate dynamics, group interplay, and a kind of programmatic or poetic portraiture. Hancock wrote on the album's jacket that he intended to depict musically "the splendor of a sea-going vessel on its maiden voyage."

The performance by the SFJAZZ Collective, which gets a particular charge from the concert setting, unites Hutcherson with seven formidable musicians born in the 1960s and 70s, as well as the arranger Gil Goldstein—a teenager when "Maiden Voyage" debuted—who provides a loose but decisive map for them to follow. Given the talent on board, including the virtuoso tenor saxophonist Joshua Redman, you might anticipate a succession of brilliant solo turns. But the magic here is genuinely collective. Some of the playing is so understated that the smallest instrumental gesture may generate suspense or surprise. The texture of the first two choruses allows for successive entrances by the wind instruments and an engaging duet by the tenor and alto saxophones, which diverge and unite in starling patterns. But the heart of this performance is reserved for Hutcherson and the rhythm section, a four-and-a-half-minute episode where the vibes lead the way, and each piano chord, bass walk, and shiver of the snares is vital—a confident yet wary series of *crescendos* and *decrescendos* building to an aggressive climax driven by Eric Harland's drums. You can almost hear the audience breathing in sync throughout the performance.

LISTENING GUIDE 70

🎧 **maiden voyage**

SFJAZZ COLLECTIVE
Joshua Redman, tenor saxophone and artistic director; Bobby Hutcherson, vibraphone; Nicholas Payton, trumpet; Miguel Zenón, alto saxophone; Andre Hayward, trombone; Renee Rosnes, piano; Matt Penman, bass; Eric Harland, drums; Gil Goldstein, arranger

- Label: *SFJAZZ Collective, Live 2006: 3rd Annual Concert Tour*, SFJAZZ Records
- Date: 2006
- Style: repertory jazz
- Form: 32-bar popular song (**A A B A**)

What to listen for:

- inventive new arrangement of Herbie Hancock's famous composition
- Redman and Zenón's improvised saxophone duet
- Hutcherson's masterful four-chorus solo

0:00		Rosnes begins to play Hancock's **vamp** on piano. The audience recognizes it, prompting a smattering of applause.
0:08		As the vamp moves to a new chord, Hutcherson plays a chord on the vibes.
0:18		The vamp repeats, supported by the entire rhythm section.

CHORUS 1 (HEAD)

0:35	**A**	Redman plays the song's slow, arching melody, lightly doubled by Hutcherson.
0:52	**A**	Payton takes over the melody on trumpet, leaving Redman room to improvise a **countermelody**.
1:00		The harmony thickens with a trombone line from Hayward.
1:09	**B**	As the volume jumps, the band sustains a full, richly harmonized chord.
1:26	**A**	Hayward takes over the melody.
1:37		Zenón improvises a line on alto saxophone that moves in a **counterrhythm**; he's joined a few seconds later by Redman.

CHORUS 2

1:43	**A**	Zenón and Redman create a constantly changing harmony as they improvise together in whole notes.
2:00	**A**	Zenón devises new melodies, his ideas quickly answered by Redman.
2:17	**B**	Their lines become faster, accelerating into spurts of **double-time**.
2:22		As the two lines decelerate, they synchronize in a new, contrasting meter.
2:33	**A**	Short, disjointed bits are tossed back and forth between the saxophones.
2:43		With Zenón taking the lead, they once again coalesce in a **cross-rhythm**.

CHORUS 3

2:49	**A**	The saxophones fade out to applause.
2:56		Hutcherson's vibes solo starts quietly.
3:00		He focuses on a short two-note motive.
3:06	**A**	Gently, he decorates the motive.
3:23	**B**	He shifts the motive higher, matching the changing harmony, before shifting to more continuous improvising.
3:35		A faster, double-time lick prompts a startled chord from Rosnes.
3:39	**A**	
3:45		Harland plays a gentle offbeat pulse on the drums. Hutcherson picks up on this, improvising off the beat.

CHORUS 4

3:55	**A**	Hutcherson suddenly switches back on the beat, playing a funky motive that locks firmly into Harland's steady pulse on the snare drum.
4:12	**A**	He devises a somewhat dissonant five-note motive, answered by Rosnes's dissonant **comping**.
4:28	**B**	
4:32		Hutcherson returns to his two-note motive, now steadily rising in pitch.
4:38		The motive accelerates to a new counterrhythm.
4:45	**A**	Finally the motive locks in with the steady pulse, prompting a cry of "whoo!" from the audience.

CHORUS 5

| 5:01 | **A** | Hutcherson fastens onto one note, working it into a new rhythmic figure. Rosnes devises a contrasting comping rhythm. |
| 5:17 | **A** | The two continue their improvised dialogue, building tension. |

| 5:32 | **B** | When the harmony shifts, Hutcherson moves to a new, higher pitch. The rhythm section continues its complex interaction. |
| 5:49 | **A** | Harland takes on a leadership role with his increasingly vigorous playing. |

CHORUS 6

6:05	**A**	While Hutcherson continues his solo, the band enters in **block-chord** harmony, paraphrasing the head.
6:21	**A**	The head now returns full force, with Hutcherson still improvising freely.
6:38	**B**	The horns take on a supporting role, sustaining chords beneath Hutcherson's line.
6:54	**A**	
7:06		A sudden ascending series of chords leads to silence, filled by surprised cheering from the crowd.

CHORUS 7 (HEAD)

7:10	**A**	Penman quietly plays the melody on bass (doubled by Rosnes on piano).
7:18		Underneath the horns, Harland plays martial rhythms on the snare drum.
7:26	**A**	
7:43	**B**	With a powerful *crescendo*, the full band trumpets the harmonies of the bridge.
7:59	**A**	Still playing at full volume, they play the head in unison, punctuated by **staccato** strokes on Harland's drums.

CODA

8:16		The band returns to a much quieter groove over the opening vamp. Hutcherson plays fragments that interact with Rosnes's comping.
8:57		Gradually the vamp grows quieter and quieter. Penman becomes almost inaudible, as Hutcherson adds fast counterrhythms.
9:21		A last tap on the cymbal ends the fade-out.
9:24		After a few seconds' pause, the audience greets the ending with laughter and applause.

THE NEW MAINSTREAM: *HOMECOMING*

By the 1970s, when rock had taken over the music business, acoustic jazz was in deep trouble. Clubs closed by the hundreds; entire black neighborhoods were wiped out by urban renewal. All the important independent jazz labels—Prestige, Contemporary, Blue Note, Riverside, Fantasy—went on the auction block and became either reissue labels or fusion outlets, while the major recording labels dropped their jazz departments or signed their few remaining musicians to one-off albums instead of the usual year-by-year contracts. Established older musicians headed for Europe (Phil Woods, Carla Bley, Randy Weston), the academy (Cecil Taylor, Max Roach, Jackie McLean, Jaki Byard), or commercial bands (James Moody in a Las Vegas pit band, Clark Terry and Hank Jones on TV).

All this started to change when tenor saxophonist Dexter Gordon decided to return from Europe in 1976. He had spent the previous fifteen years living in Paris and Copenhagen, preferring life as an expatriate to the racism and drug addiction he had experienced back home. Encouraged by his road manager (and later, wife) Maxine, he scheduled an engagement in Storyville, a short-lived club run by George Wein on Manhattan's East Side. On opening

Gordon's return

night, during a torrential rainstorm that scared no one off, he was stunned to be met with a long and raucous standing ovation: the audience wouldn't let him leave till about 3 a.m. By the time he was scheduled to play the Village Vanguard (in Greenwich Village), Bruce Lundvall of Columbia had signed him to a contract and arranged to record his club appearance live. The two-disc set, called *Homecoming*, became a minor sensation, selling 50,000 copies (when the average jazz album sold 3,000).

Gordon's personal magnetism seemed to open the doors. Soon everyone was coming home from Europe, Las Vegas, academia, for weeklong gigs—including names no one had thought about in decades, like Red Rodney and Ira Sullivan, who formed a quintet, and Jimmy Rowles, Tommy Flanagan, and other pianists who had spent the past twenty years backing singers. New labels sprouted: India Navigation and Arista, Black Saint (in Italy), and eventually Musician and the revived Blue Note, both of which Lundvall headed (after being dispatched from Columbia). New clubs flourished, more than at any other time since the 1950s: Sweet Basil, Fat Tuesdays, Bradley's, Seventh Avenue South, Lush Life. The older clubs that had survived the drought, chiefly the Village Vanguard and Village Gate, became tourist destinations. This turn of events may not have been directly related to Dexter Gordon, but no one can doubt that his *Homecoming* represented not just his own but that of an entire generation of acoustic jazz players.

As historicism continued to play out through the last decades of the twentieth century, these musicians were helping to develop a new mainstream—one that combined innovation, fusion, and aspects of historicism in original and imaginative ways. We will consider three stars of this movement: singer Betty Carter, whose career oscillated between obscurity and stardom; tenor saxophonist Michael Brecker, who late in his career abandoned his earlier orientation to jazz-pop fusion to emerge as a leading model for acoustic jazz; and Jason Moran, the pianist and composer whose artistic approach dissolved all boundaries.

■ BETTY CARTER (1929–1998)

In jazz, as in most vocations, gender is fate and it takes an iron will to take destiny in hand. Betty Carter (born Lillie Mae Jones) grew up in Detroit, where she studied piano at its Conservatory of Music and sat in with Charlie Parker and Dizzy Gillespie. At nineteen, she joined Lionel Hampton's popular orchestra and was given the sobriquet Betty Bebop—a name altogether too cute, and probably as much inspired by her glittery eyes and impossibly wide smile as her penchant for modernism and scat-singing. Her career had a brief, unlikely liftoff in 1961, when she and Ray Charles recorded a superb album of duets, producing a minor hit with "Baby, It's Cold Outside." On the basis of that recording, she was signed to a pop label and handed material like "Theme from Dr. Kildare" and cool lounge arrangements. She quickly rebelled, earned a reputation as "troublesome," and left the business as she raised her two sons.

When this photo was taken at a rehearsal for a 1978 concert in New York, Betty Carter was just beginning to enjoy one of the most productive second acts in jazz history. Her trio became a training ground for generations of young pianists, bassists, and drummers. In 1997, President Bill Clinton presented her with the National Medal of the Arts.

© BETTMANN/CORBIS

Carter orchestrated a surprising return in 1969, when she founded her own record company, Bet-Car. It soon became apparent that, much as Sarah Vaughan was the voice of bop, Carter identified with the slightly younger generation associated with the avant-garde; one of her loyal supporters in this period was Cecil Taylor, her senior by two months. Carter's career zoomed forward, propelled initially by word of mouth. She signed with record labels that let her do it her way, and attracted an international coterie for her concerts, which resembled a cross between séances and religious revivals. Although she wrote songs, most of her material consisted of standards that she deconstructed and reassembled as if they, too, were new compositions. She was always accompanied by a trio, staffed by excellent pianists, bassists, and drummers who were firmly under her artistic control.

VOICES

Detroit offered plenty of opportunities for young musicians who wanted to play jazz, if you knew where to look, as Betty Carter did:

If you wanted to get into jazz, you had to go downtown where the pimps, prostitutes, hustlers, gangsters and gamblers supported the music. If it wasn't for them there wouldn't be no jazz! They supported the club-owners who bought the music. It wasn't the middle-class church people who said, "Let's go hear Charlie Parker tonight."

🎧 "My Favorite Things"

"My Favorite Things," a signature number, has as little to do with John Coltrane's celebrated recording as with its origin in *The Sound of Music*. Carter's 1979 version, from an album appropriately called *The Audience with Betty Carter*, demonstrates her singing in concert in San Francisco's Great American Music Hall. It's fast and furious and ultimately stunning. She revels in the lyrics (even at this tempo, her pronunciations are wittily distinct), the melody, the chords, and the storming rhythm that she and the trio whip to a frenzy. Note the lustrous accompaniment of pianist John Hicks, at once supportive and daringly assertive. The highlight is the long coda, where Carter variously phrases three words ("I just feel") in guiding a free-form *crescendo* to a stormy and entirely satisfying finale.

🎧 my favorite things

LISTENING GUIDE 71

BETTY CARTER

Betty Carter, vocal; John Hicks, piano; Curtis Lundy, bass; Kenneth Washington, drums

- Label: *The Audience with Betty Carter*, Bet-Car MK-1003
- Date: 1979
- Style: postbop
- Form: irregular popular song (**A A A′ B B**, with four-measure vamps)

What to listen for:
- Carter's unusual timbre and sense of timing
- her use of Rodgers and Hammerstein's song as a vehicle for improvisation
- the excellent accompanying group, featuring Hicks on piano

0:00 Applause from the previous tune greets the performers.

INTRODUCTION

0:08 The band enters with a fast triple-meter **vamp** in D minor, reminiscent of the opening of Coltrane's famous 1960 version of this song. While Hicks improvises a string of eighth notes, his left hand (reinforced by Lundy on bass) stresses the **polyrhythm** of two beats per measure over the implied three beats.

CHORUS 1

0:19 **A** The drums drop out as Carter begins to sing. Her timing is deliberately out of whack: she declaims words so slowly that her first phrase ends ("*whiskers on kittens*") where one would expect the second phrase to begin.

0:32 The drums reenter for the vamp. For this normally instrumental section, Carter has reserved the song's refrain: "*These are a few of my favorite things!*"

0:38 **A** The drums once again drop out, highlighting Carter's willful rhythmic reading (note the unexpected emphasis on "Schnitzel").

0:51 Again, the refrain coincides with the vamp.

0:57 **A'** The band suddenly shifts to the **major mode**, a 4/4 meter, and a blisteringly fast tempo. Carter is fully in control, leading the band rhythmically.

1:07 **B** For the song's conclusion, the meter and tempo continue as before.

1:17 **B**

1:27 As the band returns to the triple-meter vamp, Carter takes a deep breath, concluding the stanza with: "*And then I don't feeeeeel . . .*"

CHORUS 2

1:33 **A** The sentence's end ("*so bad!*") coincides with the beginning of the second chorus. After a short break, Carter improvises with loose, low-register **scat syllables**.

1:52 **A** The bass shifts to a steady **walking-bass** line. Carter responds with a strongly focused line.

2:04 She concludes the vamp with two bluesy lines, each reaching emphatically up to the **tonic**.

2:10 **A'** As the fast tempo once again kicks in, she returns to the song's lyrics. Even at this speed, her improvisation is remarkably loose.

2:20 **B**

2:30 **B** To liven up the repetition, she sings the opening line ("*When the dog bites, when the bee stings*") exaggeratedly low.

CODA

2:40 The chord progression stops short of a final cadence. Carter begins her final phrase ("*And then I don't feel . . .*"). Hicks improvises wildly.

2:45 Doubled by the band, Carter sings the short phrase "*I . . . don't . . . feel*" to a sharply accented three-note syncopated motive. This phrase serves as a refrain for the coda.

2:50 While Hicks continues to improvise, Carter intones: "*And then . . .*"

2:55 She sings "*I . . . don't . . . feel*" on new pitches.

3:00 She quickly reprises earlier lyrics: "*I simply remember my favorite things . . . and then . . .*"

3:05 "*I . . . don't . . . feel.*"

3:10 She repeats the lyrics at a higher pitch.

3:15 She gives "*I . . . don't . . . feel*" a longer, more dramatic reading.

3:20 She sings "*And then*" at a lower pitch, and repeats it for emphasis.

3:30 She approaches "*I . . . don't . . . feel*" with a dramatic swoop.

3:45 After sustaining "*And then,*" she moves one last time to "*I . . . don't . . . feel.*"

3:51 She holds out the last note. For the next fourteen seconds, her line interacts with the rhythm section.

4:06 The band finally takes a **break**. With a triumphant bluesy phrase, Carter ends the song: "*I don't feel so bad!*"

4:17 The last cymbal crash leaves the band with thunderous applause.

■ MICHAEL BRECKER (1949–2007)

In the 1970s and 80s, a generation groomed as much in rock as in jazz brought a new virtuosity to jazz/rock fusion. As we have seen, Pat Metheny made his mark at nineteen as a guitarist who had studied Wes Montgomery's octaves but also knew blues and rock guitar and had no intention of being limited to acoustic jazz. Similarly, Michael Brecker made his name on the tenor saxophone at twenty-one, playing with the early jazz-rock band Dreams. Born in Philadelphia, Brecker cut short his studies at Indiana University to pursue a career in music full time. After debuting with Dreams (with trombonist Barry Rogers and drummer Billy Cobham), he was promptly drafted for a recording session by Miles Davis, and achieved commercial success co-leading the Brecker Brothers with his trumpet-player brother Randy, one of the finer fusion groups of the 1970s (1975–82). Brecker's governing influence was John Coltrane, but his increasing, apparently unlimited virtuosity helped lift his playing into a sphere of intense improvisational brilliance, making him an influential figure in his own right. Like Metheny, there was nothing he couldn't play, and he was as much in demand in pop (John Lennon, Steely Dan) as in jazz (Charles Mingus, McCoy Tyner). Probably more people have heard him as a soloist on Paul Simon's 1975 megahit "Still Crazy After All These Years" than on any of his other recordings. He didn't record an album under his own name until he was thirty-eight. "I waited a long time to do this," he said, "because I never felt ready."

By the late 1980s, Brecker began moving forcefully into acoustic jazz—sometimes playing the EWI (short for Electronic Wind Instrument, a synthesizer that uses a mock-up of a soprano saxophone as its trigger), but more often concentrating on his tenor saxophone. Maintaining his high status as a studio musician and earning eleven Grammy Awards along the way, he became more and more influential as an improvisational model for young players. Brecker's career ended suddenly when he was diagnosed with myelodysplastic syndrome (MDS) in 2005, a blood condition resulting in progressive bone marrow failure. After numerous attempts to alleviate his condition, he died at age fifty-seven.

A musician's musician, Michael Brecker created a singular virtuoso path by connecting jazz and rock. In 1970, he and his older, equally gifted brother, trumpeter Randy Brecker, helped to form one of the earliest jazz-rock ensembles, Dreams—a precursor to the more successful Brecker Brothers band. For more than thirty years, he was one of the most in-demand musicians for pop and jazz recording sessions, while also touring with his own groups and constantly expanding and polishing his always formidable technique.

🎧 "Timeline"

For his 1999 album *Time Is of the Essence*, Brecker created a remarkably relaxed ambience, improvising for the most part on original themes based on familiar structures. Teaming with Metheny, he filled out the quartet with organist Larry Goldings (obviating the need for a bassist) and a different drummer at each of three sessions, most notably the incomparable Elvin Jones, Coltrane's ardent partner, in whose band Brecker had toured.

On "Timeline," they rework the twelve-bar blues with substitute chord changes and an unusual sixteen-bar head, half of which is an easygoing, melodic riff and half a repeated rhythmic figure that turns the rhythm inside out. The solos have an almost offhanded vitality and great clarity, calling attention to the harmonic gambits and the way one chorus leads to another—for example, the melodic figures with which Metheny goes from his second chorus to his third, and the high-note flights Brecker sets up between the sixth and seventh and the seventh and eighth choruses. Jones provides a plush rhythmic background, steady and responsive, always ready to intensify the beat when cued by the soloist.

🎧 timeline

MICHAEL BRECKER

Michael Brecker, tenor saxophone; Pat Metheny, electric guitar; Larry Goldings, organ; Elvin Jones, drums

- Label: *Time Is of the Essence*, Verve 5478442
- Date: 1999
- Style: postbop
- Form: 12-bar blues (with a 16-bar head)

What to listen for:
- Brecker's solo style, incorporating and modernizing aspects of John Coltrane's style
- Metheny's polyrhythmic composition
- septuagenarian drummer Jones's rhythmic intensity

HEAD

0:01   Over a crisp, solid beat, Brecker and Metheny play a melody that's built on a simple D minor triad **riff**.

0:10   Goldings begins to **comp**.

0:17   For eight bars, the melody becomes "stuck" in a **polyrhythm**—a repeating rhythmic pattern, reinforced by the bass and drums, that contrasts with the basic meter. Over a simple melody that emphasizes the minor third,

the chords shift **chromatically**.

HEAD

0:33   The melody is repeated, with Metheny adding harmony notes.

CHORUS 1 (BLUES)

1:06   Metheny begins his solo, a single-line accompanied only by bass and drums. After an opening bluesy gesture, he moves to a **double-time** feeling, intensified by Jones's frequent snare-drum hits.

CHORUS 2

1:31

1:37   Goldings, who has been comping quietly, now becomes more audible.

1:44   Metheny ends a phrase in a rhythmic flurry.

1:48   The next phrase reaches a high note.

CHORUS 3

1:56   A snare drum roll leads to a new chorus. Metheny fastens on to a three-note rhythmic figure, taking it into the upper register.

2:12   After deriving his line mostly from the harmonies, he shifts to a bluesy mode.

CHORUS 4

2:20   A repeated figure that Metheny had started in the previous chorus continues, prompting a strong **backbeat** from Jones.

2:36   Metheny finally breaks off the repeated pattern with a bent high note.

CHORUS 5

2:46   Brecker enters on a strident high note.

2:56   He uses several patterns that recall Coltrane: descending flurries, followed by a fast ascending scale (2:59) and complex harmonic improvisation (3:02).

CHORUS 6

3:11   A sharp snare-drum hit on the downbeat prompts a simple motive from Brecker, derived from the head.

3:21   He uses **false fingering** before dissolving his line in a descending flurry.

3:32   An offbeat pattern leads to the next chorus.

CHORUS 7

3:37   Near the top of his register, Brecker plays the motive on the downbeat, then returns to it through a complex ascending scale.

3:43   The same motive, played a half step up, signals the change of harmony to IV.

3:51   Having exhausted his eighth-note lines, Brecker accelerates the pace to even faster note values.

CHORUS 8

4:01   At the climax of his solo, Brecker hits a strained high note, which descends to the motive.

4:12   Gradually he lets the intensity of his solo subside, returning to calmer, more relaxed gestures.

HEAD

4:27   The band returns to the simpler driving groove of the head.

CODA

5:00   The polyrhythm at the end of the head continues, featuring Jones's increasingly frenetic playing.

5:15   Brecker breaks into a solo, matching Jones's percussive outbursts with anguished high notes.

5:37   As Brecker moves into impossibly fast playing, the cut begins to fade out.

■ JASON MORAN (b. 1975)

For a last look at historicism, we consider the exemplary career of pianist Jason Moran. In the years since he made his first album (*Soundtrack to Human Motion*, 1998), Moran has earned nearly unanimous acclaim, demonstrating with wit and imagination the triumphs possible in jazz despite its relatively remote standing in America's cultural life.

Born in Houston, he began playing classical piano at six. When he was thirteen, he heard a Thelonious Monk record, "'Round Midnight," and found himself riveted by Monk's keyboard touch, rhythmic intensity, and melodic playfulness. As he learned more about Monk, he delved deeper into jazz and particularly jazz piano—Bud Powell, Horace Silver, McCoy Tyner, Herbie Hancock. Like any young jazz lover, Moran allowed each musician to lead him to other musicians: soon he was also soaking up older pianists like Art Tatum and Erroll Garner and more obscure or idiosyncratic modernists like Herbie Nichols, Randy Weston, Ahmad Jamal, and Cecil Taylor. This process groomed him with a broader musical platform than that of his predecessors. It could not fail to combine elements of the avant-garde (he searched

Moran was bored with piano lessons as a child until he heard Thelonious Monk, whose flair for haberdashery he also inherited.

out the cutting edge of musical possibilities), fusion (his increasing love of jazz by no means diminished his enthusiasm for modern pop, especially hip-hop), and especially historicism: he roamed as freely through the past as he did the present. Many performances combine two, or even all three, approaches.

Moran's three primary teachers have been Jaki Byard, at the Manhattan School of Music (well known for his longtime association with Charles Mingus and his own records, which revealed a style that combined the techniques of stride, swing, bop, and avant-garde), Andrew Hill, and Muhal Richard Abrams. As he developed his own style, Moran added compositions by these three into his repertory, helping to keep alive a body of work that had been largely neglected.

Keeping it new

As Moran began to release a series of albums in 1998, one a year, it quickly became evident that he saw each one as a distinct project, with its own goals and parameters. Even so, a few characteristics remained stable—the surprising breadth of his repertory, his love of electronic enhancements, and his humor. The albums have included works based on pieces by classical composers, fresh yet faithful renditions of work by Byard and Ellington, movie themes (including *Godfather II* and *Yojimbo*), a collaboration with the veteran saxophonist and pianist Sam Rivers, an album-length exploration of blues forms, and such idiosyncratic original works as "Ringing My Phone," in which he finds notes on the keyboard that match up with the notes of a woman and her mother speaking Turkish in a taped phone conversation. In every instance, the challenge is to mesh contemporary musical ideas with tradition to create music that is recognizable yet new.

James P. Johnson (1921), as we saw in Chapter 5, made the better part of his living as the composer of such Jazz Age anthems as "Charleston," but was also the greatest of stride pianists.

FRANK DRIGGS COLLECTION

🎧 "You've Got to Be Modernistic"

Moran's 2002 solo album *Modernistic* is a benchmark achievement and a profound illustration of his capacity to combine classicism and maverick innovation. Whereas many pianists would be content simply to master James P. Johnson's 1930 "You've Got to Be Modernistic," Moran suggests its essential character while giving it a radical facelift, taking it through so many variations that by the end you suspect that you've been on a completely different trip from the one intended by Johnson. To understand Moran's interpretation, listen again to Johnson's original piece (Chapter 5).

Johnson's "You've Got to Be Modernistic" is basically a ragtime work, made up of three sixteen-bar strains. Moran works with the original material, but adds his own variations (including new **C** and **D** strains) and frequently alters or stops the tempo. Johnson's modernism was apparent in his introduction and the first two strains (**A** and **B**), which are ornamented by augmented chords and the whole-tone scale. Although Moran is basically faithful to Johnson's primary theme, he adds incremental dissonances and extends its final melodic figure. Here and in the subsequent strains, Moran halts the flow in unexpected places, as if to look around and tweak this chord or twist that rhythm before returning to the grid.

Moran's reading suggests an asymmetrical impulsiveness that threatens the integrity of the piece, despite his frequent return to the stride underpinning. The effect is ironic in the sense that he holds the original work at a distance, partaking of it and then rejecting it, as he lingers on passages he wants to emphasize or alters the tempo and harmonies. He defamiliarizes the piece. Passages that seem stable when Johnson plays them now seem unmoored, free to go in any direction the pianist wishes to take them, thanks to his strategically misplaced notes or wildly divergent harmonic progressions. Intermingled with his versions of Johnson's first theme are harmonic cycles that can be considered Moran's own strains, which, like much of his playing, are elusive and unconventional.

LISTENING GUIDE 73

🎧 you've got to be modernistic

JASON MORAN, PIANO
- Label: *Modernistic,* Blue Note 39838
- Date: 2002
- Style: historicist/modernist
- Form: march/ragtime with alterations

What to listen for:
- **theme phrase, from James P. Johnson's A strain (see Chapter 5), recurring throughout**
- **descending chromatic chords in B strain, from Johnson**
- **harmonic cycles within the "C" and "D" strains**
- **disappearing and then returning triple meter in "D" strain**

INTRODUCTION

0:00   After a held-out bass note, Moran plays a series of chords descending the **whole-tone scale.**

A STRAIN

0:06   Moran faithfully plays the first four bars of James P. Johnson's "You've Got to Be Modernistic." This section (we'll call it the *theme phrase*) is his main point of contact with the original.

0:09   On its first appearance in Johnson's composition, the theme phrase ended with the left hand playing a tonic chord with a mild dissonance (we'll call it the *tonic chord passage*). Moran lingers on this passage, repeating it and gradually building in volume.

0:14   Moran defamiliarizes the theme phrase by playing a deliberately inaccurate bass note.

0:18   On its second appearance in Johnson's composition, the theme phrase was followed by chords from the whole-tone scale. Moran extends this passage, pulling it temporarily outside the meter of the piece.

0:21   On its last repetition, Moran plays the theme phrase for six bars, leading through **whole-tone**, or **augmented**, chords (made up of major thirds) to a full cadence.

0:29   He lengthens the tonic chord passage by two bars.

A STRAIN

0:32   Moran plays the theme phrase.

0:37   The left hand suddenly drops to a remote key. Over this harmony, the right hand improvises a wild passage.

0:42	Moran repeats the theme phrase.
0:46	The left-hand chords drop once again. Moran pulls the harmony upward step by step while the right hand plays sharp dissonances.
0:51	Moran repeats the theme phrase; as before, he extends the whole-tone response.
0:57	The last repetition of the theme phrase is undistorted, coming to a full cadence.

B STRAIN

1:06	Moran plays the opening **B** strain: descending chromatic chords divided between the hands, culminating in a bluesy phrase.
1:11	The second time through, the left hand is overwhelmed by dissonant passagework in the right hand. Not until the phrase's end (at 1:15) do the original melody and tempo return.
1:15	For four bars, Moran adheres closely to Johnson's original.
1:20	The third repetition of the opening disintegrates into harsh dissonance and free rhythm.
1:23	Suddenly, Moran returns to the original tempo and meter. Landing on the **tonic**, he plays the note insistently.

INTERLUDE

1:30	Over a **pedal point**, Moran plays a series of descending **tritones**, ending with a simple ragtime cadence and the tonic chord passage (repeated and extended).
1:40	He repeats the descending tritones.
1:47	Suddenly he inserts a passage that sounds as though it might **modulate** to a new key; but it resolves quietly back to the tonic.
1:54	He repeats the tonic chord passage to support bizarre right-hand improvising.
2:10	The harmony works its way back to the descending tritones, followed by a **turnaround**— a short concluding chord progression. We can now recognize an **eight-bar cycle:** six bars of pedal point with descending tritones, followed by two bars of turnaround.

"C" STRAIN

2:19	(cycle 1) As the left hand settles into a familiar routine, Moran begins improvising with his right hand.
2:29	(cycle 2)
2:38	(cycle 3) His left hand remains constant, but his right hand becomes increasingly wild, spreading dissonant flurries across the chord progression.
2:47	(cycle 4)
2:57	(cycle 5) He batters several notes at the top of the keyboard.
3:06	(cycle 6) The texture on the piano thickens as Moran adds complex passagework.
3:12	At the climax, we suddenly return to the simple ragtime cadence, now densely voiced at top volume. It is followed by a thunderous repetition of the tonic chord passage.

A STRAIN

3:17	Moran returns to the theme phrase.
3:21	The left-hand chords become loosened from their moorings, moving up or down a half step in a spastic rhythm.
3:34	He repeats the theme phrase, followed by the whole-tone chords.
3:41	He again repeats the theme phrase, this time reaching a full cadence.

"D" STRAIN

3:49	(cycle 1) The tonic chord drops down, then moves back up step-by-step in a triple meter. This establishes yet another cycle, six bars long.
3:54	(cycle 2) Moran adapts **stride** technique to this unusual meter: the bass line is played not on the downbeat, but in the middle of the measure (chord–bass–chord). He begins improvising within the cycle with his right hand.
4:00	(cycle 3)
4:05	(cycle 4) His lines grow faster, occasionally disrupting the left-hand foundation.
4:10	(cycle 5) The right hand becomes thickened with chords, which interrupt and displace the left-hand chords.

4:15	(cycle 6) Gradually, the stride accompaniment and triple meter disappear into a complex, disjointed rhythmic flux. We still hear Moran moving slowly through the chords, however, and can recognize the end of each cycle by the return to the tonic.
4:25	(cycle 7)
4:34	(cycle 8)
4:42	(cycle 9) Finally, Moran settles back into a smooth stride accompaniment, once again in triple meter. The right hand improvises rich, mellifluous chords.
4:50	(cycle 10)
4:58	(cycle 11) The right hand begins to play behind the beat, distorting our sense of meter.
5:05	(cycle 12) The stride foundation dissolves into left-hand chords.

CODA

5:12	Before the cycle is complete, the theme phrase from strain **A** slips back in. The tempo slows down dramatically, and the piano texture is simplified.
5:16	The music becomes hushed, as if Moran were preparing for a big cadence.
5:22	He plays the upward-rising whole-tone chords quietly and slowly.
5:26	A sudden loud octave jolts us awake. Moran plays the final cadence with a certain bluesy bluntness.
5:30	He continues to fool us, however, dropping from the tonic to remote harmonies.
5:40	The piece ends on an unresolved V7 chord.

The Historicist Present

When musicians get together and grouse about the current state of jazz, they almost invariably reserve a generous amount of derision for waves of historicist tributes and interpretations. In 2008, the Grammy Awards, which has always treated jazz as a poor relation, awarded its most coveted prize, Album of the Year (for 2007), to Herbie Hancock's *River: The Joni Letters*. It was the first time in forty-three years that the accolade had gone to a jazz recording—since the 1964 bossa nova classic *Getz/Gilberto*.

No one contested the merit of Hancock's album, which consists of highly inventive interpretations of Joni Mitchell songs, performed by a quartet featuring no fewer than three Miles Davis alums (Hancock, saxophonist Wayne Shorter, and bassist Dave Holland). But neither could anyone imagine a jazz album even being nominated that did not offer either a fusion with pop or a historicist tribute—unlike *Getz/Gilberto*, which celebrated a new idiom in jazz and pop. With *River*, Hancock brought off a jazz-pop fusion *and* a memorial to another era. How long jazz can continue gazing into a rear-view mirror while gliding forward is anyone's guess.

⊣ ADDITIONAL LISTENING ⊢	
Fletcher Henderson	"Sugar Foot Stomp" (1925)
Charles Mingus	"My Jelly Roll Soul" (1959)
Don Byron	"The Dreidel Song" (1992)
Bill Frisell	"Shenandoah" (1999)
Cassandra Wilson	"Dust My Broom" (2007)
Marc Ribot	"St. James Infirmary" (2001)
Nicholas Payton	"Wild Man Blues" (1995)
Uri Caine	"Symphony No. 2 (Resurrection) / Primal Light" (1996)
Francisco Cafiso	"Just Friends" (2008)
Gerry Mulligan (with Wallace Roney)	"Godchild" (1992)
Anthony Braxton	"Piece Three" (1976), "Donna Lee" (2002)
Wynton Marsalis	"Processional" (1993), "Donna Lee" (2002)
Ronald Shannon Jackson	"Now's the Time" (1994), "American Madman" (2000)
James Carter	"'Round Midnight" (1994), "Nuages" (2000)
Betty Carter	"Sounds (Movin' On)" (1979)
Michael Brecker	"Escher Sketch (A Tale of Two Rhythms)" (1990)
SFJAZZ Collective	"Brilliant Corners" (2007)
Jason Moran	"Planet Rock" (2001), "Gangsterism on a Lunchtable," "Ringing My Phone" (both 2002)

ONLINE MULTIMEDIA RESOURCES AND REVIEW MATERIALS

Author Insight Videos

Gary Giddins discusses how knowledge of the social context of a piece can open up a different way of listening; how, in the 1950s, jazz became comfortable with its own history and musicians felt free to play in any earlier style; and what the term "mainstream" has come to mean.

Interactive Listening Guides

Wynton Marsalis, "The Pearls"
SFJAZZ Collective, "Maiden Voyage"
Betty Carter, "My Favorite Things"
Michael Brecker, "Timeline"
Jason Moran, "You've Got to Be Modernistic"

Jazz Concepts (audio and/or video demonstrations of terms covered here)

backbeat	false fingering	staccato
block chords	major scale	stop-time
break	modulation	tonic
cadence	pedal point	triplets
countermelody	polyphonic texture	tritone (flatted fifth)
chromatic harmony	polyrhythm	walking bass
dissonance	riff	whole-tone scale

- For quick reference, review the **Chapter Overview** and **Chapter Outline**.
- Take the online **Chapter** and **Listening Quizzes**.
- Use the online **Glossary** and **Flashcards** to review important terms.

JAZZ TODAY

PARADIGMS LOST AND FOUND

In the 1990s, a new term became fashionable: "post-historical." Intended to convey the essentially insupportable idea that history is somehow over, that the great political and cultural movements are behind us, it was applied to every aspect of modern life, including jazz. The concept's appeal lies in two liberating illusions: first, that our generation is perched atop the historical mountain, looking down at the past, like gods; and second, that history's afterlife is a clean slate, upon which we are free to scrawl our own blueprints for the future. A cursory glance at post-post-historical history confirms that (as throughout human history) such arrogance leads to military debacles and moral chaos. No surprise there.

Even so, the post-historical perspective may provide a helpful way of sorting through the three narratives we have followed in order to define jazz in the twenty-first century. So let's pretend we are looking down from the mountain crest. Now we do have a surprise. It turns out that even in the context of the post-historical, movements and fashions continue to arise, roiling the waters, then abating, then recharging, so that any general statement we make one year is almost certain to require qualifications the next. Take the art-for-art's-sake account, in which jazz is seen to have evolved in a whirlwind

Esperanza Spalding found her true instrument in her teens, when she switched from cello to bass, but that was only one step in a transformation that found her blossoming into a composer, vocalist, bandleader, lyricist, and all-around booster for genre-straddling music and international amity.

455

of inspired innovations, from Buddy Bolden's slow blues to Charlie Parker's ferocious bop to Ornette Coleman's free jazz. By the end of the twentieth century, that lineage seemed to be at an impasse if not at an end: after the avant-garde era, musicians freely mined the idioms of jazz's past, but the next movement, neoclassicism, represented a retrenchment—away from the avant-garde, not a continuation toward another frontier.

What a difference a decade makes. A new generation arrives, born and raised after the old debates about jazz vs. rock and progressive vs. traditional have been quelled if not resolved. The best of its jazz visionaries are neither avant-garde nor neoclassical. They may not, as a group, qualify as a movement with a handy tag (like swing or bop), but neither are they weighed down by parameters of the past. The baton has been passed, as witness the annual polls of the best jazz recordings. The best-of lists during the first decade of the present century were invariably topped by Sonny Rollins, Cecil Taylor, Ornette Coleman, Carla Bley, Wayne Shorter, Roy Haynes, Herbie Hancock, Chick Corea, Shirley Horn, and other masters who had been breaking ground since the 1950s and 60s. By 2012 and 2013, however, the lists were dominated by relative newcomers (we will meet a few in this chapter), some with debut recordings. You might argue that this turnover was biologically inevitable, but no one could see ten years ago where the new action would come from or what form it would take.

The second narrative, fusion, took us beyond the avant-garde into diverse attempts to combine the practices of jazz with those of rock, soul, hip-hop, and other kinds of pop music, domestic and international. A few years back, that also seemed a dead end, as the farther pop music departed from melody and harmony, the less it appeared to offer useful source material for jazz. Some observers thought that the pinnacle of jazz-rock fusion was created by Miles Davis more than forty years ago. The jazz performance of a song by, say, Radiohead signified an isolated stunt rather than a true meeting of minds. When Herbie Hancock adapted pop songs as jazz's "new standards," he added new harmonies to make them feasible for improvised variations. Yet as we've seen, a younger provocateur like Robert Glasper demonstrated in 2012 that unlikely pop material might offer jazz artists genuine inspiration.

Perhaps fusion, in the general and literal sense of the word, is the key to understanding the current wave in jazz. As a marker in jazz history, fusion was coined in the late 1960s to describe the rapprochement between jazz and rock. Yet as we've also seen, fusion of one kind or another has been crucial to the development of jazz aesthetics since the beginning. (Remember Dexter Gordon's axiom: "Jazz is an octopus.") It's more evident now than ever that jazz acknowledges no barriers of style, time, or place in making and remaking itself.

An ongoing source of inspiration for young musicians is the work of the old masters, which triggers our third narrative. The historicist model is very much alive, yet not nearly as prevalent as it was a decade ago. The inclination to pay homage to the past is curtailed in periods of renewed creativity, so while an occasional reclamation project may attract much attention (for example, Ryan Truesdell's *Centennial: Newly Discovered Works of Gil Evans*, in 2012), there is nothing like the slew of jazz repertory tributes to Morton, Ellington, Goodman, Monk, and other giants that appeared in the 1990s and early 2000s. Now soundings of the past are more focused on goals of inspired renewal.

CLASSICAL JAZZ

While each of these paradigms gives us a way of understanding jazz history, none provides us with a label that satisfactorily describes the broad canvas of contemporary jazz. In the absence of warring factions, a live-and-let-live accord has taken over. If jazz is in a post-historical phase, it's generally a reign of peace—jazz offers something for everyone, and hardly anyone feels obliged to declare allegiance to or rail against one canon rather than another. So a different, encompassing narrative may offer a better sense of the present situation. Some commentators have described jazz as America's classical music, but what exactly does that mean? Throughout this book, we refer to classical music as the European tradition of composed music that produced the great symphonic, chamber, and operatic repertories. Here we let "classical" represent no particular style or movement or time period, but rather the status to which all serious and lasting music (including rock) aspires. Bach, known to his contemporaries as a player and repairer of organs, was not considered classical in his day; time and semantics defined the tradition in which we place him.

Four Phases

In this classical formulation, jazz has undergone four phases of development. These phases are not aesthetic schools, like bebop or fusion; instead, they signify broader stages that mark jazz's overall place in the cultural world.

1. The first phase (1890s–1920s) was the period of genesis. Every musical idiom begins in and reflects the life of a specific community where music is made for pleasure and to strengthen social bonds. Jazz's primary breeding ground was the black South, especially New Orleans, where a mixture of musical and cultural influences combined to create a freewheeling, largely improvised, blues-based music that suited every social gathering, entertaining the living and commemorating the dead. The strength and originality of this music allowed it to spread beyond geographical, racial, and cultural boundaries.

2. In the second phase (1920s–50s), jazz was transformed from a community-based phenomenon to an authentic art of unlimited potential. Speedily spreading around the world, it revolutionized musical performance and conception, extending its influence into the classical and popular fields, spurred by remarkable individuals who expressed singular artistic visions within its generally stable yet constantly shifting parameters. Within twenty years, jazz achieved popular acceptance as a generation's dance music, and immediately thereafter generated intellectual interest during the modernist reformation of bebop and its offshoots.

3. The third phase (1950s–70s) tackled the limits of modernism, which increased artistic possibilities while alienating the general public. Jazz had become primarily a listener's music. It continued to sustain a large following (the years 1954 to 1964 in particular were extraordinarily flush), but passed from center stage. Newer and more popular styles (R&B, rock and roll) fulfilled the unchanging social needs—they suited dancing and singing and required little in the way of virtuoso technique or imaginative concentration on the part of listeners. In this period, jazz also moved into the classroom.

4. In its fourth stage (1970s–), jazz has moved so far from center stage that its survival is largely dependent on an infrastructure of academic study and institutional support, including public and private grants. In some—indeed, most—areas of the United States, people live their lives without encountering jazz; it has disappeared from most of the nation's radio, television, and jukeboxes. It is a specialty interest, like European classical music. Jazz and its musicians have to assimilate the glories of the past without getting weighted down by them. Virtually every young jazz artist is defined in part by the presumed influences of his or her predecessors. These musicians are obliged to compete with the past in a way that did not exist in jazz before the 1990s.

On the other hand, the classical status is liberating for upcoming jazz artists, who range freely between past and present, creating their own narratives as they attempt to forge new techniques, or to fuse jazz techniques with those of popular and classical music, or to elaborate on acknowledged jazz masterworks. Viewed in this context, the final (specialty) stage offers a more reasonable way of anchoring jazz in history than the post-historical analysis: it assumes evolving growth within its new status, leaving open the promise of waves of performers, some of whom will be admirably accomplished in established idioms while others will continue to forge daring explorations.

Lingua Franca

In the absence of one governing jazz school, the present era enjoys something akin to a universal *lingua franca*—a useful term coined in seventeenth-century Europe to describe the hybrid language that developed between different nationalities interacting in Mediterranean seaports. Whatever their stylistic preferences, today's jazz musicians can all speak the same language, a consequence of jazz education: a musical patois grounded in bebop, with respect for previous jazz schools and knowledge of later ones. In the past, musicians learned by doing. They traveled in bands or memorized solos from recordings, and almost always leaned toward the style that was dominant at the time

Pianist Brad Mehldau brought a powerfully meditative approach to pop standards, jazz classics, and original pieces in a series of five albums called *The Art of the Trio*.

they came of age. Now musicians are less likely to pick up the latest chord changes by ear than to learn them as homework.

At a time when pop squeezes every other kind of music into the slimmest margin of commercial significance, jazz students are motivated to master the shared pool of styles and techniques to survive as professional musicians. Yet neither near-universal education nor the marketplace has succeeded in making them assembly-line performers—a fact that, perhaps more than any other, testifies to jazz's inviolable fortitude. Something at the heart of jazz, and every kind of art worth its name, rejects slavish imitation. It thrives on a mixture of individualism and compatibility. Twenty-first-century jazz has unquestionably produced one of the best-equipped musical generations ever. Its members all know the lingua franca, but are highly particular in the way they develop it.

Keep in mind that this hasn't always been the case. Consider the pianists Bill Evans and Cecil Taylor, born within a few months of each other in 1929, though we don't think of them as sharing much common ground. Yet even the most stylistically disparate of today's jazz pianists—from the studied lyricism of

Brad Mehldau and neoclassical proficiency of Danilo Pérez to the percussive idiosyncrasy of Matthew Shipp and geometric intricacy of Vijay Iyer—suggest a common grounding in jazz classicism that might allow them to cross over into each other's realms in a way that would be unthinkable for Evans and Taylor or, for that matter, Thelonious Monk and Oscar Peterson, or Earl Hines and Meade Lux Lewis (who were both born in 1905). This extraordinary unity of purpose helps to sustain jazz as a singular, stirring, and still surprising art.

Dizzy Gillespie hired the astonishing pianist Danilo Perez in 1989 and mentored him until his death in 1992, at which time Pérez organized his own groups and freelanced with countless musicians. His virtuoso bop-based style is flexible enough to suit almost any jazz setting.

■ VIJAY IYER (b. 1971)

Vijay Iyer, a prolific and multifaceted pianist, exemplifies the way contemporary jazz artists may inch forward by tracking backward and laterally, while expanding on personal roots. Throughout the past century, the brunt of American jazz innovation was borne by a few ethnicities, chiefly African American but also Jewish American, Italian American, Irish American, Latin American, Native American, and others. The 1990s introduced another hyphenate: Indian American.

The emergence of Iyer, who was born and raised in New York, and alto saxophonist Rudresh Mahanthappa, who was born the same year and raised in Colorado, spurred an intense consideration of the relationship between jazz and the classical music of Southern India, called Carnatic music. In the 1960s, the Carnatic idiom was popularized in the United States by the sitar virtuoso Ravi Shankar, and jazz musicians occasionally reflected their fascination with his music by adding cosmetic touches to what they were doing—for example, long improvisations that superficially borrow from the scalar intricacies of the raga, or the addition of a tabla player to the rhythm section. When Iyer first met Mahanthappa while performing in Chicago, he could hardly believe there was another Indian American jazz musician. But as they began to work together, other kindred souls emerged, including the guitarist Rez Abassi and the drummer Dan Weiss, who has become a dedicated proponent of the tabla.

Though Iyer and Mahanthappa do indeed explore their familial heritage, which reflects the changing demographics in America, they are first and foremost dyed-in-the-wool jazz musicians who have studied its history deeply. Iyer is more involved with the patterns of piano trio music, including the mastery of dynamics as perfected by such virtuoso jazz pianists as Ahmad Jamal (b. 1930), and the poetic-rhythmic possibilities of hip-hop than with pursuing the orthodoxies of centuries-old ragas. In the liner notes to his first album, titled with characteristic ingenuity *Memorophilia* (1995), he lists nearly eighty of his jazz heroes.

With his assured attitude and finely controlled sense of dynamics, Iyer belongs to the percussive school of jazz piano, a lineage that ranges from Duke Ellington, Earl Hines, and Thelonious Monk to Jamal, Cecil Taylor, and Abdullah Ibrahim. Trained in mathematics and physics, he applied his studies to music. Shortly after completing his dissertation on musical cognition, he began to perform with such respected musicians as alto saxophonist Steve Coleman

One of the brainiest musicians of his generation, Vijay Iyer has created a startling variety of ensembles and projects, each with a different mission, ranging from trio to orchestra, song cycles to ballet. He has won a shelf full of international prizes and shows no signs of slowing down.

and trombonist George Lewis, as well as Mahanthappa and others of his own generation. He has won several grants and commissions (including, in 2013, a MacArthur "genius grant"), taught at universities (Harvard as of 2014), and divided his concerts and recordings among various small ensembles— including the Carnatic-influenced Tirtha; the avant-garde Fieldwork; the politically engaged collaborations with hip-hop librettist Mike Ladd; and the trio with Stephan Crump and drummer Marcus Gilmore, which brought him much critical success and a Grammy nomination.

🎧 "Lude"

"Lude" is a highlight of the Vijay Iyer Trio's second album, *Accelerando*, and has become a particular favorite at concerts, where its repetitive chords, insistent rhythms, and three-way interplay can create a trancelike sense of engagement. This performance shows Iyer's confident touch, his penchant for vamps and ostinatos (note the unusual three-note figure with which he launches the piece), and the intimate, unswerving unity of the three musicians, who rise and fall as one through diverse stops and starts and rhythmic changeups. The influence of Ahmad Jamal's trio is evident, and a comparison with the elder statesman's work (his celebrated 1958 live performances of "Poinciana," an unlikely hit, and "But Not for Me" are good starting points) is illuminating, though Iyer's keyboard attack is more introverted.

Iyer's music often suggests a mathematic precision, as though numbers danced in his head before he found the notes to illuminate them, but ultimately his reliance on tightly structured patterns and complementary ostinatos is put in service of a knowing groove, which becomes increasingly apparent on repeated hearings. "Lude" combines rigorous discipline with spontaneous give-and-take. The piece is structured as a diptych, built on two eight-bar patterns, the second of them introduced at 3:16 and the first reprised in the coda. Each number in the Listening Guide, 1 to 19 and 1 to 8, indicates an eight-bar cycle. The cycles control the flow of the piece while encouraging the musicians to respond freely within its parameters. Not the least pleasurable aspect of their playfulness is the now-you-see-it-now-you-don't treatment of the backbeat.

LISTENING GUIDE 74

🎧 lude

VIJAY IYER TRIO

Vijay Iyer, piano; Marcus Gilmore, drums; Stephan Crump, bass

- Label: *Accelerando*, ACT Music + Vision ACT95242
- Date: 2012
- Style: contemporary
- Form: short composed cycles

What to listen for:
- updating of the piano trio for the 21st century
- complex structures, inspired by Indian classical music
- intense rhythmic interaction between the three instruments

CYCLES

0:03 **1** Iyer plays a series of chords, loosely related to one another harmonically. Although they seem to appear in a random rhythmic sequence, they fit within an eight-bar pattern.

0:13	2	The chords repeat. Against them, Crump plays a tricky **ostinato** pattern on bass (doubled by Iyer's left hand), using only three pitches. This pattern is played three times (the last pattern is cut short to fit an eight-bar cycle) before ending on the downbeat of the next cycle. The chords' pattern and the bass line fit together to form a complex composite.
0:23	3	Gilmore enters on drums, clarifying the overall eight-bar structure by playing accents on the backbeat.
0:34	4	As Crump takes over the bass line, Iyer begins playing a simple melody against the chords (still played strictly in sequence).
0:44	5	Iyer continues playing the melody, with slight variations.
0:54	6	
1:04	7	He begins to improvise over the changes.
1:15	8	His improvisation turns to fast 16th-note runs.
1:25	9	
1:32		Iyer plays and repeats a four-note **sequence**; the last time, the new cycle begins on the third note.
1:35	10	
1:45	11	The volume and intensity continue to rise.
1:53		Crump's bass line begins to rise, finally reaching the upper octave by the next cycle's downbeat.
1:55	12	
2:05	13	
2:12		Crump departs from the ostinato, playing a pickup to the next cycle's downbeat.
2:15	14	The line stays up an octave, repeating many notes.
2:25	15	Iyer plays his chords twice, until reaching the next chord at 2:29.
2:35	16	As he returns to the head, he intensifies the groove by playing chords on each beat.
2:45	17	
2:53		Iyer repeats the head's high note several times
2:55	18	
3:06	19	
3:16	1	The texture is suddenly interrupted by a new pattern, played (again) by the bass and the pianist's left hand—rising and falling an octave, then moving up a major third. As before, the pattern repeats three times (the last time shortened) to fit an eight-bar cycle.
3:26	2	Gilmore enters, sharply accenting the backbeat. Against this, Iyer plays a high note twice, followed by a note a fourth below. This pattern reinforces the bass line, making the backbeat sound as if it were irregular, rather than the bass line and high piano line.
3:36	3	Crump maintains the bass line, while Iyer improvises a complex line in octaves between his two hands.
3:47	4	Iyer's line is loose, and shifts unexpectedly between **ghosted** and accented notes.
3:58	5	Crump omits part of his ostinato, momentarily exposing the backbeat.
4:08	6	
4:18		He repeats the last phrase, leading to the next cycle.
4:19	7	
4:30	8	

CODA

| 4:40 | | With a sudden hush, the musicians return to the first cycle. |
| 4:49 | | Iyer plays the last note in three octaves. |

■ ESPERANZA SPALDING (b. 1984)

The apprenticeship of Esperanza Spalding could hardly be more different from that of Vijay Iyer. Raised in a comfortable immigrant family in Rochester, New York, Iyer studied classical violin from the age of three and enjoyed a brilliant educational career at Yale and the University of California at Berkeley. Spalding, whose ethnic background is a mix of African American, Native American, Welsh, and Hispanic, was raised along with her brother by their single mother in an area of Portland, Oregon, that she later described as a "pretty scary" ghetto. Because of illness, she was home-schooled in her early years, and despite her obvious gifts did not take to school until she auditioned at the Berklee College of Music and received a full scholarship. Even then she considered switching to political science until guitarist Pat Metheny, a Berklee alum, and vibist Gary Burton (then Berklee's vice-president) encouraged her to stay the course.

Like Iyer, Spalding exhibited precocious musical talent but did not find her true instrument until her mid-teens. Initially drawn to the cello at the age of four, after seeing Yo-Yo Ma perform on television, she taught herself violin, picked up music theory by observing her mother's guitar lessons, and within a year—she was now five years old—joined the Chamber Music Society of Oregon, which appointed her concertmaster by the time she was fifteen. By then she had come across a string bass in a high school practice room, an encounter she characterized as finding true love. Knowing only one blues progression in F, she sat in at a local blues club and, instead of getting gonged off the bandstand like Charlie Parker, was invited to join the band's rehearsals. She also took voice lessons and began writing lyrics.

If Esperanza Spalding was by no means the first jazz artist to appear on the Academy Awards, she remains the only one to perform at Oslo's Nobel Peace Prize ceremony, where this ecstatic 2009 photo was taken.

ALBERT NIEBOER/DPA/PICTURE ALLIANCE/NEWSCOM

Spalding blossomed at Berklee, studying and touring with saxophonist Joe Lovano and singer Patti Austin, and was hired as an instructor after she graduated at age twenty. Two years later, she released her first CD, *Junjo*, a trio session, followed by *Esperanza*, in which the trio is amplified by various guest performers. Embracing fusion in all its motley and functioning as her band's bassist, singer, and chief composer, she combined jazz, funk, bossa nova, neo-soul, hip-hop, and other primarily rhythmic styles while underscoring her penchant for lush melodies with arrangements that use violin and cello. She has echoed Robert Glasper in her stated intention to revive jazz as an essential part of today's black musical life, and has expressed the breadth of her diversity by citing, among others, Wayne Shorter, Milton Nascimento (Brazilian music is a vital part of her repertory), Madonna, and Ornette Coleman as career archetypes.

In 2011, Spalding stunned the music business by unexpectedly winning the Grammy Award as Best New Artist (incredibly, she was the first jazz musician to do so). She also made several internationally publicized appearances, including the 2009 Nobel Peace Prize ceremony in Oslo and the 2012 Academy Award broadcast in Hollywood. The scope of her musical ambitions became evident as she released two widely acclaimed albums, titled in accordance with the featured ensemble: *Chamber Music Society* and *Radio Music Society*, accompanied by a series of music videos, a medium usually ignored by jazz artists. In 2013, Spalding created a song and video called "We Are America," to protest the incarcerations at Guantanamo Bay. The striking refrain goes: "We are America / In our America / We don't stand for this."

🎧 "Short and Sweet"

"Short and Sweet," the closing selection on *Chamber Music Society*, displays Spalding's talents as bassist, singer, bandleader, and composer-arranger. In the opening measures, we notice three components that help make this performance distinctive: first, the poised lyricism of the lovely introductory melody and vamp, to which the subsequent improvisations allude; second, the canny use of three bowed instruments—violin, viola, and cello—to create a rich texture that suggests a larger ensemble than the one at hand (in this, she was aided by Gil Goldstein, whose skills we previously encountered in "Maiden Voyage"); and third, the tropical, waving 6/8 waltz rhythm that reflects her love of Brazilian music. In contrast to the sweetly bowed strings, she introduces the first chorus with a bold, plucked-bass arpeggio.

The combination of strings and Spalding's wordless crooning may set off warning bells that we are on the terrain of easy-listening pop. Yet as she la-la-las, the ensemble tills an ever-deeper groove, defined by her first-beat-of the-measure bass notes and Terri Lyne Carrington's expert drumming. A jazz bassist-leader is uniquely confronted by the challenge of creating effective settings for an instrument that is usually consigned to the background and brought to the fore in occasional solos that too often sound like obligatory episodes. Duke Ellington once likened recurring bass solos to television commercials.

In "Short and Sweet," Spalding answers the challenge by contrasting high/bowed and low/plucked strings, and by creating a twelve-bar composition with limited harmonic movement—a context in which the value and meaning of her every note is emphasized. This is especially evident in the marvelously interactive choruses by Spalding and the Argentinian pianist Leo Genovese. They respond so surely and promptly that they seem to anticipate each other's moves. Some of Genovese's passages (the polyrhythms at the three-minute point, the turnback into chorus 5) evoke the influence of Bill Evans, and the entire passage from chorus 3 to chorus 6 may be seen as an extension of the piano and bass dialogue of "Witchcraft"—only this time the bassist provides the cues.

LISTENING GUIDE 75

🎧 short and sweet

ESPERANZA SPALDING

Esperanza Spalding, acoustic bass, voice; Leo Genovese, piano; Terri Lyne Carrington, drums; Entcho Todorov, violin; Lois Martin, viola; David Eggar, cello; strings arranged by Gil Goldstein and Spalding

- Label: *Chamber Music Society*, Heads Up HUI-31810-02
- Date: 2010
- Style: fusion
- Form: 12-bar form

What to listen for:

- Spalding's expressive composition
- her unusual use of the voice as a melody instrument
- the piano trio ensemble (piano, bass, drums), which steadily builds the music to a climax

INTRODUCTION

0:00   In a slow tempo, Genovese plays a wistful chord progression in G minor.

0:07   The melody is doubled by the viola and cello.

0:14   As Carrington enters on drums, the violin adds a **countermelody**.

0:26   A descending **arpeggio** in the bass signals Spalding's entrance.

CHORUS 1

0:27   With Genovese doubling her on piano, Spalding sings the wordless melody.

0:41   As the harmony temporarily returns to the **tonic**, the strings bring back their melodies from the Introduction.

INTERLUDE

1:10   The Introduction serves as an interlude, with Spalding playing the bass line (six bars).

CHORUS 2

1:31   The strings drop out, leaving the trio to improvise. Spalding begins her solo with descending melodies.

1:59   As the harmonic pace accelerates, her line becomes livelier, reaching into the bass's upper register.

CHORUS 3

2:13

2:17   In her second chorus, Spalding responds imaginatively to Genovese's chords.

2:32   She plays a **triplet** figure on two strings, which she adjusts as the chords change.

2:42   Her line speeds up into **double-time**.

CHORUS 4

2:56   Genovese begins with a four-note motive: he repeats it **polyrhythmically**, then speeds it up over unpredictable chords.

3:11   At the end of the phrase, Genovese and Spalding let their notes fade into silence. Carrington fills in with quiet strokes on the cymbal.

3:24   While Spalding plays the roots of the chords, Genovese adds dissonant harmonic substitutions.

CHORUS 5

3:38   Genovese begins with a **staccato** idea, prompting Spalding and Carrington to match his intensity. The passage fades once again to a brief silence.

3:48   Genovese plays chords that temporarily disrupt the texture, leading to a wild display of virtuosity.

3:59   Spalding plays a new bass note, repeating it with a harsher timbre. Genovese responds to her idea, leading to a new explosion of activity.

CHORUS 6

4:20

4:40   Halfway through the chorus, Spalding reenters on voice with the melody, accompanied by the strings.

CODA

5:02   The Introduction is repeated again, this time to close out the piece.

5:30   Spalding's bass drops to its lower octave.

5:37   The strings drop out, leaving the texture bare.

5:44   Spalding and Genovese sustain the last chord of the **vamp**, its dissonance unresolved.

■ CÉCILE McLORIN SALVANT (b. 1989)

The sudden appearance of a terrifically gifted singer tends to create a seismic wave of delight in jazz because it happens so rarely and because the pantheon of jazz singers is so forbiddingly secure, especially the women. What young aspirant expects to mount an Olympus that, after more than half a century, is still ruled by Bessie Smith, Billie Holiday, Mildred Bailey, Ella Fitzgerald, Sarah Vaughan, Anita O'Day, Carmen McRae, Dinah Washington, Betty Carter, Abbey Lincoln, and few others—all born long before World War II? Singers have had a rough time keeping up with instrumental jazz; the great standards have been done to death, postwar songwriters are frequently their own best interpreters, and decades of avant-gardism have marginalized the human voice.

Cécile McLorin Salvant's first album, *WomanChild*, caused much excitement, not least for her intrepid tackling of a diverse repertory, her aversion to cliché, and the kind of rhythmic confidence that won't be denied. Here she is with pianist Aaron Diehl at Harlem's Richard Rodgers Amphitheater, participating in the annual Charlie Parker Jazz Festival.

Since 1970, a handful of jazz singers have made a serious impression and maintained durable careers, validating their inventive approaches to style and repertory. The most prominent of these include Dee Dee Bridgewater, Dianne Reeves, Cassandra Wilson, and Diana Krall, all born between 1950 and 1964. Most key singers in that era belonged to pop, even if jazz profoundly shaped their music, as it did for Norah Jones and Amy Winehouse.

The release in 2013 of the album *WomanChild* by a virtually unknown twenty-three-year-old singer of French and Haitian parentage generated much excitement, and perhaps a touch of hyperbole. No one wanted to jinx her with inflated claims—there have been too many one-hit wonders, too much promise unfulfilled—but neither could anyone listen to the American-label debut recording by Cécile McLorin Salvant and fail to acknowledge an outsize talent that radiates authority and authenticity. If the pantheon singers are unmistakably alive in her work, so is the determination to make her own way. Indeed, some of her reworking of classic material may be faulted as too strenuously dramatized. Yet Salvant has an immediately recognizable sound and style; it's there in her timbre and the way she modulates it; in her rhythmic confidence; in her bold explorations of repertory; and, perhaps most of all, in her determination to heed Ezra Pound's exhortation to "make it new!" What she has gleaned from the past she uses to address the present. For Esperanza Spalding, vocalizing is an element in the fabric of her music. Salvant's total dedication to singing is evident in every syllable.

Born and raised in Miami, she studied piano from the age of five and three years later successfully auditioned for the Miami Choral Society. At eighteen, she moved to France to study law, and as a sideline enrolled in courses in classical singing at the Darius Milhaud Conservatory. One of her teachers, the saxophonist Jean-François Bonnel, introduced her to jazz and improvisation, playing stacks of records by great jazz singers. In an interview, she recited an unusually expansive list of her favorites: Louis Armstrong, Betty Carter, Bessie Smith, Billie Holiday, Sarah Vaughan, Blanche Calloway, Lil Hardin Armstrong, Blossom Dearie, Bing Crosby, and Abbey Lincoln, who inspired her to write her own songs. She also stresses the influence of her multicultural upbringing: "My friends growing up were Colombian, Mexican, Argentine, Cuban, Haitian, Jamaican, so I don't know what it is like to be raised in a situation where everybody is like you and has your same background. . . . I don't know how that shapes my music, but it definitely shapes my personality."

In France, Salvant earned her degree but dropped the law and began examining traditions of popular songs dating back more than a century. In 2009, she recorded an album (*Cécile*) with Bonnel's quintet, and a year later entered and won the annual Thelonious Monk International Jazz Competition in Washington, D.C. (the jurors included Bridgewater, Reeves, Patti Austin, Kurt Elling, and Al Jarreau)—an event that has launched the careers of several noted artists since its 1987 inception. Salvant soon began headlining at jazz festivals around the world.

🎧 "John Henry"

The first thing one is likely to notice about *WomanChild* is the nervy repertory. In addition to original songs (including one in French), Salvant deconstructs and reassembles pieces associated with Bessie Smith, Fats Waller, Billie Holiday, and Bert Williams, the blackface comedian who was the first African American to star on Broadway. An undoubted highlight is her treatment of a nineteenth-century folk song narrating the life and death of John Henry, the legendary black steel driver who insists that "a man ain't nothin' but a man" and lays down his life engaging in a competition with a steam drill. While a great deal of scholarship has been devoted to tracking down the real John Henry, now thought to be an unfairly arrested convict from New Jersey who died drilling holes in Virginia's Appalachian Mountains in 1871, the fabled John Henry looms as the most renowned mythic figure in American history—a subject of books, plays, paintings, sculpture, and several songs, most famously the one recorded by Salvant and hundreds of other performers, from Lead Belly to Paul Robeson to Bruce Springsteen, though rarely by jazz singers.

The arrangement begins with an attention-grabbing funk rhythm, played with flawless, impeccable aplomb by the frequently teamed drummer Herlin Riley and bassist Rodney Whitaker. Salvant performs the traditional folk-blues arrangement in which the last line of each four-line verse (two measures per line) is sung four times, extending the chorus to fourteen measures. Aaron Diehl's piano solo, however, is structured as a twelve-bar blues, and given a startling resonance by his dampening the piano strings to produce a percussive, choked sound, somewhat redolent of a banjo. His witty use of a phrase from "Arkansas Traveler" adds to the sense of another time and place, at once icily modern yet weirdly nostalgic. Salvant's interpretation is rigorous and commanding. She frequently alters her timbre (favoring, like Sarah Vaughan, her low register) and her rhythmic accents, especially in her assertive breaks and the repeated tag line in each chorus.

🎧 john henry

CÉCILE McLORIN SALVANT
Cécile McLorin Salvant, vocal; Aaron Diehl, piano; Rodney Whitaker, bass; Herlin Riley, drums

- Label: *WomanChild*, Mack Avenue Records MAC 1072
- Date: 2013
- Style: contemporary
- Form: traditional ballad

What to listen for:

- a traditional ballad in a jazz context
- subtle and expressive changes in vocal timbre
- piano solo featuring unusual technique (dampening of strings)

INTRODUCTION

0:00   A four-stroke drum blast initiates the funk groove. Riley plays two syncopated strokes on the bass drum, the backbeat on the side of the snare, and a tightly muted rhythm on the high-hat cymbal.

0:04   At the end of the two-measure cycle, he adds more syncopated bass-drum rhythms, and lets the cymbal escape for a brief "whoosh."

0:09   Whitaker enters on an **ostinato** figure, the first two notes of which coincide with the bass-drum accents.

0:12   He plays an obvious blue note.

0:17   Whitaker and Riley continue their figures as a **vamp**.

CHORUS 1

0:25   Salvant enters on an **offbeat**, in her upper register:
"John Henry was a little baby / Sittin' on his papa's knees."
The word "baby" coincides neatly with the bass-drum figure.

0:34   The band stops for a **break**, allowing her to continue unaccompanied.
"Well, he picked up a hammer and a little piece of steel,
Said 'This hammer's gonna be the death of me.'" The line descends into her lower register, which turns deliberately to a harsher timbre on "death."

0:42   She repeats the last line four times, often ending it with lazy blue notes.

CHORUS 2

0:55   *"John Henry said to his captain,*
'Now a man ain't nothing but a man.'" Salvant continues the arrangement.

1:03   *" 'Before I let your steel drill bring me down,*
I will die with a hammer in my . . .'" On her second break, she teases the listener by omitting the last word in the line.

1:14   Upon repetition, she finally ends with "*hand.*"

CHORUS 3

1:25   *"John Henry said to his shaker,*
'Now shaker, why don't you sing?
Shakin' twelve pounds from my hip bone down,
Now don't you hear that cold steel ring?'"

Behind Salvant, Diehl plays a repeated string of notes with his right hand, while his left hand dampens some strings inside his piano.

1:33   On her third break, Salvant's line is **polyrhythmic**:

The break's end is signaled by a cymbal crash.

1:37   As she repeats the last line, Diehl plays a vigorous **countermelody**, the equal temperament of the piano clashing subtly with her bent notes.

CHORUS 4 (12-BAR BLUES)

1:54   Diehl begins his first blues chorus by agitatedly repeating the **blue third** of the scale.

2:07   He quotes "Arkansas Traveler."

2:15   He marks a return to the tonic by lingering on a short motive. Riley adds a few variants to his ostinato.

CHORUS 5 (12-BAR BLUES)

2:19   Diehl's short motive continues.

2:24   The repeated note that opened chorus 4 returns.

2:27   The move to IV is marked by a brief five-note descending scale. Diehl plays with this motive.

CHORUS 6

2:44   *"John Henry hammered in the mountain,*
        And the mountain it was so high,
        And the last words I heard that poor man cry, he said,
        'Gimme a cool drink of water 'fore I die!'"

2:53   Salvant's break begins with a high, drawn-out phrase.

CHORUS 7

3:14   *"John Henry went down that railroad track*
        With a twelve-pound hammer by his side,
        Yes, he went down that track but he never came back
        Because he laid down his hammer and he
        He laid down his hammer and he
        He laid down his hammer and he died,
        He laid down his hammer and he died."

3:25   On "never came back," Salvant's vocal timbre gets nasty.

3:29   Again, she builds tension by stopping before the last (emotional) word in the line: "died."

3:38   The word finally emerges on the third attempt.

CHORUS 8 (INTERLUDE)

3:44   Riley raises the intensity by playing his drum strokes on the now-open ride cymbal.
        Diehl plays with a simple motive. Unlike in the blues choruses, the harmony refuses
        to budge from the **tonic**.

3:55   Diehl switches to his repeated-note idea.

CHORUS 9

4:09   *"John Henry had a little woman,*
        And the dress that she wore was red,
        And the last words that I heard that poor girl said, she says,
        'I'm going where John Henry fell dead.'"

4:20   The last break is surprisingly interrupted by a few soulful piano chords.

4:25   Salvant ends each repetition of the last line in a flat and neutral tone, with few
        pitch variations.

CODA

4:39   Riley returns to his more open cymbal sound. Both Diehl and Riley play with the
        same melodic motive.

4:57   Diehl drops out.

5:01   Riley drops out, leaving the drums.

5:09   The pattern suddenly stops on its last beat.

ENJOYING THE SHADOWS

Each of the previous three selections can be considered in terms of one, two, and possibly all three of the narratives we've cited for the evolution of jazz: art, fusion, historicism. Yet another narrative, deserving a volume of its own, would chronicle jazz's global reach. We've alluded to this subject (chiefly Django Reinhardt, João Gilberto, Eddie Palmieri, Jan Garbarek), but have by no means done it justice. Jazz had hardly burst out of New Orleans when it began to travel the world, first by way of recordings and then by constant international touring, beginning in 1919 when the Southern Syncopated Orchestra (featuring Sidney Bechet) and the Original Dixieland Jazz Band were quartered in London. Everywhere they visited, jazz musicians planted seeds. At first, native musicians of Europe, Asia, and South America copied the Americans to master the idiom, but soon they began to use jazz as a way of interpreting their own musical heritage.

Today, American jazz musicians depend on foreign travel—specifically, the summer jazz festivals that attract tens of thousands of visitors—to secure their livelihood. But now the cultural exchange goes both ways, and an American musician is as likely to pick up ideas as leave them. Jazz in most nations on six continents maintains connections to the American tradition, especially in sustaining as core principles the African American polyrhythms and distinctive sound and qualities of the blues, as well as mastery of the art of improvisation. Yet each place also draws on its own traditions in pop, folk, classical, and, not least, jazz. Each has its own past and its own future.

Duke Ellington, as usual, was ahead of the game in absorbing or translating various musical cultures with his particular musical palette. He may have been speaking facetiously when he remarked of his first visit to Africa, that he had been "writing African music for thirty-five years." But as we noted in Chapter 9, he gave a more thoughtful formulation in introducing his 1970 suite *The Afro-Eurasian Eclipse*, when he remarked on the fluidness of cultural identity and concluded, "It's most improbable that anyone will ever know exactly who is enjoying the shadow of whom." To sketch out this idea, we will focus on one remarkable musician, the pianist and composer Abdullah Ibrahim, who has come to represent the South African subgenre of Cape Jazz. Ellington figures in his story, too.

■ ABDULLAH IBRAHIM (b. 1934)

Ibrahim was born Adolph Johannes Brand in Cape Town and took the nickname Dollar Brand when he began playing professionally in the mid-1950s, initially with a swing band and later as the leader of a trio with bassist Johnny Gertze and drummer Makaya Ntshoko. In 1959, he co-founded The Jazz Epistles, a cornerstone ensemble in South African music, with other musicians and composers who would achieve international renown, including saxophonist Kippie Moeketsi, trombonist Jonas Gwangwa, and trumpeter Hugh Masakela. Brand's musical influences typify the diverse traditions competing for attention. Through recordings, he dedicated himself to jazz and grew particularly enamored of Ellington and Thelonious Monk. No less profound was the impact of Cape Town's African Methodist Episcopal Church, where his grandmother played piano, the instrument he took up at age seven. He was steeped in traditional South African songs, which had a long-standing penchant for chordal harmonies and repetitive rhythms that he would refine into irresistible ostinatos and vamps.

Brand left South Africa after the Sharpeville Massacre of 1960 to lead his trio (with Gertze and Ntshoko) at clubs in European capitals, including the African Club in Zurich. Early in 1963, Ellington and his orchestra played a concert in Zurich. Backstage, a young woman—the singer Sathima Bea Benjamin, who married Brand two years later—insistently made Ellington promise to visit the African Club. He obliged, reluctantly, and was so

When this picture of Abdullah Ibrahim was taken in the 1960s at London's Roundhouse, a venue more accustomed to rock bands like the Doors and Pink Floyd, he was still known as Dollar Brand, the musician who so impressed Duke Ellington. After converting to Islam, Ibrahim returned to Cape Town, where his recording of "Mannenberg" was adopted as an anthem of the resistance to apartheid.

© ARENAPAL/TOPHAM/THE IMAGE WORKS

impressed that he convinced Frank Sinatra's Reprise Records to record Brand's trio for a session that was released as *Duke Ellington Presents the Dollar Brand Trio*. That was the beginning of his international recognition, though by the time he came to the United States, Brand encountered the same uphill battle that beset all jazz musicians. In the 1970s, feeling lost, he and his wife attempted to resume their lives in South Africa, where he converted to Islam and adopted the name Abdullah Ibrahim. Following the bloody Soweto Uprising in 1976, they returned to the United States, where his career finally took off with a series of successful albums and several assignments to score movies. He formed his own record label and, in 1983, introduced his signature septet, Ekaya, which means "home." With the end of apartheid, Ibrahim resettled in Cape Town for good, while maintaining an international schedule of touring and recording.

🎧 "Calypso Minor"

During most of its history, Ekaya included well-known American musicians, even a few bona fide jazz stars. The edition of the septet heard on the acclaimed 2010 album *Sotho Blue* features highly accomplished, younger American musicians whose résumés chronicle their work in jazz, rhythm and blues, pop singing, academia, and everywhere else a gifted musician can find work. Under Ibrahim's tutelage, the ensemble work on "Calypso Minor" is stunningly precise and the improvisations richly satisfying. This is a slow, finger-snapping groove tune that must be played with impeccable finesse or it will fall apart. Although Ibrahim's piano is well featured in the album, this track—the album's lead-off number—has him only in a supporting role. But he makes his every note count, so much so that although the solos are performed by saxophones, flute, and trombone, he remains the music's driving personality, his every chord and fillip incarnating an almost epigrammatic prudence.

As is the case with "John Henry," the performance is set in motion with a powerful rhythmic figure, and this time the backbeats fall like an axe. "Calypso Minor" originated in one of Ibrahim's cinema scores, the 1990 French film *No Fear, No Die*, but it might well have been conceived as a gospel piece, with the harmonization of the wind instruments filling the expanse between baritone saxophone on the bottom and trombone and flute on top, all breathing as one. It's an ideal example of the notion that jazz is an international music, united by backbeat rhythms, plush harmonies, racy dissonances, blues locutions, freely expressed improvisations, and a unifying commitment that never sacrifices a sense of humor and a determination to surprise, as witness the very last chord.

LISTENING GUIDE 77

🎧 calypso minor

ABDULLAH IBRAHIM AND EKAYA
Abdullah Ibrahim, piano; Belden Bullock, bass; George Gray, drums; Cleave Guyton, alto saxophone and flute; Keith Loftis, tenor saxophone; Jason Marshall, baritone saxophone; Andrae Murchison, trombone

- Label: *Sotho Blue*, Sunnyside 1276
- Date: 2010
- Style: South African jazz
- Form: 64-bar popular song (**A A B A**)

What to listen for:
- Ibrahim's ingenious composition and arrangement
- the ensemble solos by Ekaya
- the South African rhythmic groove

INTRODUCTION

0:00		Bullock enters on bass. His ascending line is heard against the backbeat, played by Gray on the drums.
0:13		The second phrase ends with a descending **chromatic** line.
0:15		As the bass repeats the phrase, Gray marks the moment with a stroke on the crash cymbal.
0:29		The first two notes of the bass line are answered by a **dissonant** chord in the horns; they add a four-note phrase a measure later.
0:43		The horns and bass repeat the phrase.

CHORUS 1 (HEAD)

0:57	**A**	The horns, doubled by the drums, mark the chorus with an accent just before the downbeat. Ibrahim responds with a single note on the piano.
1:01		Ibrahim's short phrase is answered by a four-note unison horn line.
1:11		With a change in harmony, the horns play a chord that swells until it reaches its resolution, a **V** chord.
1:18		Ibrahim plays another quizzical phrase.
1:25	**A**	A new section is marked by a prolonged cymbal crash. Ibrahim's responses are short and laconic.
1:46		He plays a bluesy phrase.
1:53	**B**	Ibrahim plays a descending chromatic line that leads to the bridge. He comps underneath Loftis, who begins his tenor saxophone solo by mimicking Ibrahim's phrase.
2:07		The harmony temporarily lands on a **major** chord, only to return to the **tonic minor**.
2:21	**A**	Ibrahim plays a clanging chord, which resolves into an unexpected note.
2:45		The bass concludes the opening chorus with a **syncopated** line.

CHORUS 2

2:49	**A**	Guyton begins his solo with a single, sharp note—as if imitating Ibrahim's acerbic phrases.
3:16	**A**	As Ibrahim repeats a semi-dissonant chord, Murchison improvises on trombone.
3:43	**B**	Marshall, on baritone saxophone, solos over Ibrahim's constantly changing accompaniment.
4:10	**A**	Guyton, on flute, enters over silence.
4:19		Here (and again at 4:32), he **flutter-tongues** to create an unusual timbre.

CHORUS 3

4:37	**A**	Over an empty downbeat, Bullock begins his solo on bass.
4:58		He accents the return to the tonic by playing in **double stops**.
5:03	**A**	
5:24		At the end of his solo, he returns to the rhythm of the opening bass line.
5:30	**B**	Loftis returns for another tenor solo. Underneath him, Ibrahim's accompanying voice can be heard and felt.
5:50		The background horns return for their swelled chord, doubled by Ibrahim's **tremolo**.
5:57	**A**	Once again, the bass line is heard in dialogue with the horns.
6:17		The tune ends suddenly on an unexpected note.

No one has ever successfully predicted the future of jazz. It's unlikely that Buddy Bolden could have foreseen the worldwide acceptance of music he played to entertain dancers in the tenderloin district of *fin de siècle* New Orleans. Louis Armstrong helped to spur the Swing Era, but he could not have seen it arising from his Hot Five recordings of the 1920s—no more than swing musicians could have predicted bop or bop musicians the avant-garde or free jazz proponents the turn to fusion. We began by evoking Sidney Bechet's observation about being in the sun to feel the sun. Many people today believe that jazz is dead or no longer relevant, citing its absence from commercial radio and television outlets as proof. Evidence to the contrary is in the hands of an incredible number of young, ambitious, innovative musicians, the majority of them pouring forth from colleges and music schools, determined to make a contribution to jazz's unfolding history. It may require more of an effort to step into the sunshine of contemporary jazz, but it is there, bright and welcoming.

ADDITIONAL LISTENING

Brad Mehldau	"The Very Thought of You" (2006)
Danilo Pérez	*Panamonk* (1996)
Vijay Iyer	"Imagine" (2004), "Big Brother" (2009)
Esperanza Spalding	"Radio Song" (2012)
Cécile McLorin Salvant	"Le front cache sur tes genoux" (2013)
Lead Belly	"John Henry" (1994)
Johnny Cash	"The Legend of John Henry's Hammer" (1963)
Abdullah Ibrahim	"Mannenberg" (1974), "The Wedding," "African Marketplace" (both 1980)

ONLINE MULTIMEDIA RESOURCES AND REVIEW MATERIALS

Author Insight Videos

Gary Giddins explains how jazz has achieved its "classical" status and how musicians today, rather than creating exclusively new works, interpret the past as well; and reflects on Jason Moran as a symbolic figure in contemporary jazz.

Interactive Listening Guides

Vijay Iyer, "Lude"
Esperanza Spalding, "Short and Sweet"
Cécile McLorin Salvant, "John Henry"
Abdullah Ibrahim, "Calypso Minor"

Jazz Concepts (audio and/or video demonstrations of terms covered here)

arpeggio	dissonance	sequence
backbeat	ghosted notes	staccato
blue third	major mode	syncopation
break	minor mode	tonic
chromatic scale	ostinato	tremolo
countermelody	polyrhythm	triplet

- For quick reference, review the **Chapter Overview** and **Chapter Outline**.
- Take the online **Chapter** and **Listening Quizzes**.
- Use the online **Glossary** and **Flashcards** to review important terms.

AVANT-GARDE JAZZ

Avant-garde jazz (1950s–60s) was no longer light entertainment but serious and challenging music, requiring the listener's full concentration; in a performance, anything could be tried. It also became increasingly entrenched in the racial and antiwar struggles of the time.

Texture
- varies widely, but tends toward polyphony (independent lines)

Rhythm
- free

Instrumentation
- varies widely, including instruments from all over the world

Form
- original compositions

Special techniques
- free improvisation, dispensing with harmonic background
- use of timbre as an improvisational device
- ambiguous rhythmic pulse rather than steady dance beat

Pioneers of avant-garde jazz
- Ornette Coleman (alto saxophone)
  Quartet: Billy Higgins (drums), Charlie Haden (bass), Don Cherry (pocket trumpet)
- Cecil Taylor (piano)
  Jimmy Lyons (alto saxophone), Sonny Murray (drums), Steve Lacy (soprano saxophone), Archie Shepp (tenor saxophone), Andrew Cyrille (drums)
- Eric Dolphy (alto saxophone, clarinet, flute)
- Albert Ayler (tenor saxophone)

- Herbie Nichols (piano)
- Andrew Hill (piano)
- Sun Ra (piano)

Older musicians attracted to avant-garde jazz
- John Coltrane, Charles Mingus, Sonny Rollins

Avant-garde collectives

Underground Musicians' Association, Los Angeles

Association for the Advancement of Creative Musicians (AACM), Chicago
- Muhal Richard Abrams (piano)
- Anthony Braxton (saxophone)
- Leroy Jenkins (violin)
- Henry Threadgill (saxophone)
- Art Ensemble of Chicago: Joseph Jarman (saxophone), Roscoe Mitchell (saxophone), Lester Bowie (trumpet), Malachi Favors Maghostut (bass), Famoudou Don Moye (percussion)

Black Artists Group (BAG), St. Louis
- World Saxophone Quartet: David Murray, Julius Hemphill, Oliver Lake, Hamiet Bluiett, Arthur Blythe

Loft jazz (1970s)
- David Murray (tenor saxophone)
- Arthur Blythe (alto saxophone)
- Ed Blackwell (drums)
- James Newton (flute)
- Butch Morris (trumpet)
- John Zorn (saxophone)
- James Blood Ulmer (guitar)
- Beaver Harris (drums)

FUSION

Fusions of some kind have always played a role in jazz history. Symphonic jazz in the 1920s and the Third Stream in the late 1950s attempted to merge the techniques of jazz and classical music. And from the beginning, jazz has had an ongoing relationship to popular music. As jazz has responded to contemporary pop culture over the years, new schools of music have emerged, along with musicians at home in both worlds.

1940s–1960

Rhythm and blues, or "jump music" (blues played at a fast tempo, boogie-woogie rhythm)
- Louis Jordan (alto saxophone)
- Earl Bostic (alto saxophone)
- Wild Bill Davis (organ)
- Bill Doggett (piano)

Soul jazz (gospel-type chords, basic harmonies, clearly defined dance rhythms)
- Ray Charles (piano, vocal)
- Jimmy Smith (organ)

Singers
- Rosemary Clooney
- Nat King Cole
- Frank Sinatra
- Sarah Vaughan

Latin jazz

Cubop/Afro-Cuban jazz/salsa (asymmetrical clave rhythm, large percussion section)
- Mario Bauzá (trumpet)
- Machito (bandleader)
- Dizzy Gillespie (trumpet)
- Chano Pozo (percussion)
- Cal Tjader (vibraphone)
- Eddie Palmieri (piano)

Brazilian bossa nova (more relaxed and melodious)
- Luiz Bonfá (guitar)
- Vinícius de Moraes (composer)
- Antônio Carlos Jobim (composer)
- João Gilberto (guitar)
- Stan Getz (tenor saxophone)
- Charlie Byrd (guitar)

FROM 1960

Jazz-rock fusion

Texture
- homophonic

Rhythm
- rock-based (even eighth notes)

Instruments
- electronically amplified bass, guitar, keyboards, synthesizers, "bottom-heavy" rhythm section

Form
- contemporary popular song (verse-chorus), original compositions

Special techniques
- high volume
- modern recording techniques (editing, sampling)

Early jazz-rock fusion bands
- Charles Lloyd Quartet
- Emergency (Tony Williams, drums)
- Miles Davis: *Filles de Kilimanjaro* (1968), *In a Silent Way* (1969), *Bitches Brew* (1970)

1970s–80s jazz-rock fusion
- Mahavishnu Orchestra: John McLaughlin (guitar), Jan Hammer (keyboard), Billy Cobham (drums)
- Chick Corea (keyboard) and Return to Forever
- Weather Report: Wayne Shorter (saxophone), Joe Zawinul (keyboard), Jaco Pastorius (electric bass)
- Herbie Hancock (keyboard) and Headhunters
- Keith Jarrett (piano)
- Pat Metheny Group: Metheny (guitar), Lyle Mays (keyboards)
- Brecker Brothers: Michael Brecker (tenor saxophone), Randy Brecker (trumpet)

World music
- Jan Garbarek (saxophone), Paul Winter Consort, Oregon

Smooth jazz
- Grover Washington Jr. (saxophone), George Benson (guitar), Donald Byrd (trumpet), Kenny G (saxophone)

Jam-band jazz
- Charlie Hunter (guitar), Medeski, Martin and Wood

Acid jazz
- Groove Collective

Jazz/hip-hop
- Us3, Buckshot LeFonque (Branford Marsalis), Herbie Hancock, Miles Davis

HISTORICIST JAZZ

Throughout much of jazz history, musicians have faithfully reinterpreted classic or neglected works (from the jazz repertory), written original music that celebrates music of the past, and created modernist interpretations of jazz classics. By looking at ways musicians have followed these principles, we find a new way of interpreting jazz history: the historicist narrative.

Avant-garde historicist (1970s)
- Anthony Braxton (saxophone, clarinet, flute, piano)
- Arthur Blythe (alto saxophone)
- Henry Threadgill (saxophone) and Air

Neoclassicist (1980s)
- Wynton Marsalis (trumpet)

Repertory groups
- American Jazz Orchestra
- Carnegie Hall Jazz Band
- Jazz at Lincoln Center Orchestra
- SFJAZZ Collective
- Mingus Big Band

Nostalgia
Harry Connick Jr., Diana Krall (singer-pianists)

Experimental historicist
- Don Byron (clarinet)
- Uri Caine (piano)
- Cassandra Wilson (singer)
- Dave Douglas (trumpet)
- Bill Frissell (guitar)
- Mark Ribot (guitar)
- Nicholas Payton (trumpet)
- Francisco Cafiso (alto saxophone)
- Ronald Shannon Jackson (drums)
- James Carter (saxophone)

Selected Musicians on Primary Jazz Instruments

Trumpet/Cornet

Nat Adderley (1931–2000)
Henry "Red" Allen (1908–1967)
Franco Ambrosetti (b. 1941)
Louis Armstrong (1901–1971)
Chet Baker (1929–1988)
Mario Bauzá (1911–1993)
Bix Beiderbecke (1903–1931)
Bunny Berigan (1908–1942)
Sonny Berman (1925–1942)
Terence Blanchard (b. 1962)
Buddy Bolden (1877–1931)
Lester Bowie (1941–1999)
Bobby Bradford (b. 1934)
Ruby Braff (1927–2003)
Randy Brecker (b. 1945)
Clifford Brown (1930–1956)
Clora Bryant (b. 1927)
Teddy Buckner (1909–1994)
Billy Butterfield (1917–1988)
Donald Byrd (1932–2013)
Roy Campbell (1952–2014)
Conte Candoli (1927–2001)
Pete Candoli (1923–2008)
Benny Carter (1907–2003)
Doc Cheatham (1905–1997)
Don Cherry (1936–1995)
Buck Clayton (1911–1991)
Bill Coleman (1904–1981)
Johnny Coles (1926–1996)
Ted Curson (1935–2012)
Olu Dara (b. 1941)
Miles Davis (1926–1991)
Wild Bill Davison (1906–1989)
Sidney De Paris (1905–1967)
Bill Dixon (1925–2010)
Kenny Dorham (1924–1972)
Dave Douglas (b. 1963)
Harry "Sweets" Edison (1915–1999)
Roy Eldridge (1911–1989)
Don Ellis (1934–1978)
Pee Wee Erwin (1913–1981)
Jon Faddis (b. 1953)
Art Farmer (1928–1999)
Maynard Ferguson (1928–2006)
Dizzy Gillespie (1917–1993)
George Girard (1930–1957)
Bobby Hackett (1915–1976)
Tim Hagans (b. 1954)
Roy Hargrove (b. 1969)
Tom Harrell (b. 1946)

Eddie Henderson (b. 1940)
Kid Howard (1908–1966)
Freddie Hubbard (1938–2008)
Harry James (1916–1983)
Bunk Johnson (1889–1949)
Sean Jones (b. 1978)
Thad Jones (1923–1986)
Taft Jordan (1915–1981)
Freddie Keppard (1890–1933)
Ryan Kisor (b. 1973)
Nick LaRocca (1889–1961)
Yank Lawson (1911–1995)
Booker Little (1938–1961)
Brian Lynch (b. 1956)
Wingy Manone (1904–1982)
Wynton Marsalis (b. 1961)
Howard McGhee (1918–1987)
John McNeil (b. 1948)
Jimmy McPartland (1907–1991)
Bubber Miley (1903–1932)
Blue Mitchell (1930–1979)
Lee Morgan (1938–1972)
Ray Nance (1913–1976)
Fats Navarro (1923–1950)
Joe Newman (1922–1992)
King Oliver (1885–1938)
Jimmy Owens (b. 1943)
Oran "Hot Lips" Page (1908–1954)
Nicholas Payton (b. 1973)
Manuel Perez (1871–1946)
Hannibal (Lokumbe) Peterson (b. 1948)
Marcus Printup (b. 1967)
Red Rodney (1927–1994)
Shorty Rogers (1924–1994)
Wallace Roney (b. 1960)
Randy Sandke (b. 1949)
Arturo Sandoval (b. 1949)
Charlie Shavers (1920–1971)
Woody Shaw (1944–1989)
Jabbo Smith (1908–1991)
Valaida Snow (1900–1956)
Lew Soloff (b. 1944)
Muggsy Spanier (1906–1967)
Terell Stafford (b. 1966)
Bobby Stark (1906–1945)
Rex Stewart (1907–1967)
Idrees Sulieman (1923–2002)
Ira Sullivan (b. 1931)
Clark Terry (b. 1920)
Kid Thomas (1896–1987)
Malachi Thompson (1949–2006)

Charles Tolliver (b. 1942)
Warren Vache (b. 1951)
Freddie Webster (1916–1947)
Joe Wilder (1922–2014)
Cootie Williams (1910–1985)
Snooky Young (1919–2011)

Trombone

Clifton Anderson (b. 1957)
Ray Anderson (b. 1952)
Dan Barrett (b. 1955)
Eddie Bert (1922–2012)
Bob Brookmeyer (1929–2011)
Lawrence Brown (1907–1988)
George Brunis (1902–1974)
Sam Burtis (b. 1948)
Jimmy Cleveland (1926–2008)
Willie Dennis (1926–1965)
Wilbur De Paris (1900–1973)
Vic Dickenson (1906–1984)
Tommy Dorsey (1905–1956)
Eddie Durham (1906–1987)
Honoré Dutrey (1894–1935)
Robin Eubanks (b. 1955)
John Fedchock (b. 1957)
Carl Fontana (1928–2003)
Curtis Fuller (b. 1934)
Tyree Glenn (1912–1974)
Wycliffe Gordon (b. 1967)
Bennie Green (1923–1977)
Urbie Green (b. 1926)
Al Grey (1925–2000)
Slide Hampton (b. 1932)
Bill Harris (1916–1973)
Craig Harris (b. 1953)
Jimmy Harrison (1900–1931)
Conrad Herwig (b. 1959)
J. C. Higginbotham (1906–1973)
Quentin "Butter" Jackson (1909–1976)
Jack Jenney (1910–1945)
J. J. Johnson (1924–2001)
Jimmy Knepper (1927–2003)
George E. Lewis (b. 1952)
Melba Liston (1926–1999)
Albert Mangelsdorff (1928–2005)
Delfeayo Marsalis (b. 1965)
Glenn Miller (1904–1944)
Miff Mole (1898–1961)
Grachan Moncur III (b. 1937)
Benny Morton (1907–1985)

Joe "Tricky Sam" Nanton (1904–1946)
Ed Neumeister (b. 1952)
Kid Ory (1886–1973)
Benny Powell (1930–2010)
Big Jim Robinson (1892–1976)
Frank Rosolino (1926–1978)
Roswell Rudd (b. 1935)
Jack Teagarden (1905–1964)
Juan Tizol (1900–1984)
Steve Turre (b. 1948)
Bill Watrous (b. 1939)
Dicky Wells (1907–1985)
Sandy Williams (1906–1991)
Kai Winding (1922–1983)
Britt Woodman (1920–2000)
Trummy Young (1912–1984)

Saxophone

George Adams (1940–1992)
Pepper Adams (1930–1986)
Cannonball Adderley (1928–1975)
Gene Ammons (1925–1974)
Fred Anderson (1929–2010)
Albert Ayler (1936–1970)
Charlie Barnet (1913–1991)
Bill Barron (1927–1989)
Gary Bartz (b. 1940)
Sidney Bechet (1897–1959)
Tim Berne (b. 1954)
Leon "Chu" Berry (1908–1941)
Walter Blanding Jr. (b. 1971)
Jane Ira Bloom (b. 1955)
Hamiet Bluiett (b. 1940)
Arthur Blythe (b. 1940)
Earl Bostic (1913–1965)
Anthony Braxton (b. 1945)
Michael Brecker (1949–2007)
Willem Breuker (1944–2010)
Nick Brignola (1936–2002)
Tina Brooks (1932–1974)
Peter Brotzmann (b. 1941)
Pete Brown (1906–1963)
Jane Bunnett (b. 1956)
Abraham Burton (b. 1971)
Don Byas (1912–1972)
Scoops Carey (1915–1970)
Harry Carney (1910–1974)
Benny Carter (1907–2003)
James Carter (b. 1969)
Serge Chaloff (1923–1957)
Arnett Cobb (1918–1989)
Tony Coe (b. 1934)
Al Cohn (1925–1988)
George Coleman (b. 1935)
Ornette Coleman (b. 1930)

Steve Coleman (b. 1956)
John Coltrane (1926–1967)
Ravi Coltrane (b. 1965)
Junior Cook (1934–1992)
Hank Crawford (1934–2009)
Sonny Criss (1927–1977)
Eddie "Lockjaw" Davis (1921–1986)
Jesse Davis (b. 1965)
Paul Desmond (1924–1977)
Eric Dolphy (1928–1964)
Arne Domnérus (1924–2008)
Lou Donaldson (b. 1926)
Jimmy Dorsey (1904–1957)
Paquito D'Rivera (b. 1948)
Allen Eager (1927–2003)
Bill Easley (b. 1946)
Teddy Edwards (1924–2003)
Marty Ehrlich (b. 1955)
Booker Ervin (1930–1970)
Herschel Evans (1909–1939)
Joe Farrell (1937–1986)
Ricky Ford (b. 1954)
Jimmy Forrest (1920–80)
Sonny Fortune (b. 1939)
Frank Foster (1928–2011)
Bud Freeman (1906–1991)
Chico Freeman (b. 1949)
Von Freeman (1923–2012)
Jan Garbarek (b. 1947)
Kenny Garrett (b. 1960)
George Garzone (b. 1950)
Charles Gayle (b. 1939)
Stan Getz (1927–1991)
John Gilmore (1931–1995)
Jimmy Giuffre (1921–2008)
Benny Golson (b. 1929)
Paul Gonsalves (1920–1974)
Dexter Gordon (1923–1990)
Wardell Gray (1921–1955)
Johnny Griffin (1928–2008)
Gigi Gryce (1925–1983)
Lars Gullin (1928–1976)
Shafi Hadi (b. 1929)
Scott Hamilton (b. 1954)
Craig Handy (b. 1962)
John Handy (b. 1933)
Billy Harper (b. 1943)
Eddie Harris (1934–1996)
Donald Harrison (b. 1960)
Michael Hashim (b. 1956)
Antonio Hart (b. 1968)
Coleman Hawkins (1904–1969)
Tubby Hayes (1935–1973)
Jimmy Heath (b. 1926)
Julius Hemphill (1938–1995)
Joe Henderson (1937–2001)

Ernie Henry (1926–1957)
Vincent Herring (b. 1964)
Fred Ho (1957–2014)
Johnny Hodges (1906–1970)
Javon Jackson (b. 1965)
Willis "Gator" Jackson (1928–1987)
Illinois Jacquet (1922–2004)
Joseph Jarman (b. 1937)
Hilton Jefferson (1903–1968)
Budd Johnson (1910–1984)
Howard Johnson (b. 1941)
Phillip Johnston (b. 1955)
Clifford Jordan (1931–1993)
Louis Jordan (1908–1975)
Talib (T. K. Blue) Kibwe (b. 1953)
Rahsaan Roland Kirk (1936–1977)
Lee Konitz (b. 1927)
Steve Lacy (1934–2004)
Oliver Lake (b. 1944)
Ralph Lalama (b. 1951)
Harold Land (1928–2001)
Yusef Lateef (1920–2010)
Dave Liebman (b. 1946)
Charles Lloyd (b. 1938)
Joe Lovano (b. 1952)
Frank Lowe (1943–2003)
Jimmy Lyons (1931–1986)
Rudresh Mahanthappa (b. 1978)
Joe Maini (1930–1964)
Branford Marsalis (b. 1960)
Warne Marsh (1927–1987)
Hal McKusick (1924–2012)
Jackie McLean (1931–2006)
Charles McPherson (b. 1939)
Roscoe Mitchell (b. 1940)
Hank Mobley (1930–1986)
James Moody (1925–2010)
Frank Morgan (1933–2007)
Bob Mover (b. 1952)
Gerry Mulligan (1927–1996)
David Murray (b. 1955)
Ted Nash (1959–2011)
Oliver Nelson (1932–1975)
David "Fathead" Newman (1933–2009)
Big Nick Nicholas (1922–1997)
Sal Nistico (1940–1991)
Greg Osby (b. 1960)
Harold Ousley (b. 1939)
Charlie Parker (1920–1955)
Evan Parker (b. 1944)
Leo Parker (1925–1962)
Cecil Payne (1922–2007)
Art Pepper (1925–1982)
Flip Phillips (1915–2001)
Odean Pope (b. 1938)
Chris Potter (b. 1971)

Russell Procope (1908–1981)
Ike Quebec (1918–1963)
Gene Quill (1927–1988)
Dewey Redman (1931–2006)
Joshua Redman (b. 1969)
Mario Rivera (1939–2007)
Sam Rivers (1923–2011)
Adrian Rollini (1904–1956)
Sonny Rollins (b. 1930)
Charlie Rouse (1924–1988)
David Sanborn (b. 1945)
David Sanchez (b. 1968)
Pharoah Sanders (b. 1940)
Loren Schoenberg (b. 1958)
Gene Sedric (1907–1963)
Bud Shank (1926–2009)
Archie Shepp (b. 1937)
Sahib Shihab (1925–1989)
Mark Shim (b. 1973)
Wayne Shorter (b. 1933)
Zoot Sims (1925–1985)
Buster Smith (1904–1991)
Gary Smulyan (b. 1956)
James Spaulding (b. 1937)
Sonny Stitt (1924–1982)
John Surman (b. 1944)
Lew Tabackin (b. 1940)
Buddy Tate (1913–2001)
Joe Temperley (b. 1929)
Joe Thomas (1909–1986)
Lucky Thompson (1924–2005)
Henry Threadgill (b. 1944)
Frank Trumbauer (1901–1956)
Mark Turner (b. 1965)
Stanley Turrentine (1934–2000)
Charlie Ventura (1916–1992)
Eddie "Cleanhead" Vinson (1917–1988)
David S. Ware (1949–2012)
Earle Warren (1914–1994)
Ben Webster (1909–1973)
Frank Wess (1922–2013)
Bobby Watson (b. 1953)
Rudy Williams (1919–1954)
Dick Wilson (1911–1941)
Steve Wilson (b. 1961)
Chris Woods (1925–1985)
Phil Woods (b. 1931)
Lester Young (1909–1959)
John Zorn (b. 1953)

Clarinet

Buster Bailey (1902–1967)
George Baquet (1883–1949)
Alvin Batiste (1932–2007)
Barney Bigard (1906–1980)

Peter Brötzmann (b. 1941)
Don Byron (b. 1958)
John Carter (1928–1991)
Eddie Daniels (b. 1941)
Kenny Davern (1935–2006)
Buddy DeFranco (b. 1923)
Johnny Dodds (1892–1940)
Paquito D'Rivera (b. 1948)
Irving Fazola (1912–1949)
Pete Fountain (b. 1930)
Jimmy Giuffre (1921–2008)
Benny Goodman (1909–1986)
Edmond Hall (1901–1967)
Jimmy Hamilton (1917–1994)
Stan Hasselgard (1922–1948)
Woody Herman (1913–1987)
George Lewis (1900–1968)
Joe Marsala (1907–1978)
Matty Matlock (1909–1978)
Mezz Mezzrow (1899–1972)
Don Murray (1904–1929)
Albert Nicholas (1900–1973)
Jimmy Noone (1895–1944)
Ken Peplowski (b. 1959)
Alphonse Picou (1878–1961)
Perry Robinson (b. 1938)
Leon Roppolo (1902–1943)
Pee Wee Russell (1906–1969)
Louis Sclavis (b. 1953)
Tony Scott (1921–2007)
Artie Shaw (1910–2004)
Larry Shields (1893–1953)
Omer Simeon (1902–1959)
Wilbur Sweatman (1882–1961)
Frank Teschemacher (1906–1932)
Dr. Michael White (b. 1954)
Putte Wickman (1924–2006)
Bob Wilber (b. 1928)
Lester Young (1909–1959)

Flute

George Adams (1940–1992)
Jane Bunnett (b. 1956)
Wayman Carver (1905–1967)
Buddy Collette (1921–2010)
Eric Dolphy (1928–1964)
Joe Farrell (1937–1986)
Sonny Fortune (b. 1939)
Holly Hofmann (b. 1956)
Paul Horn (1930–2014)
Rahsaan Roland Kirk (1936–1977)
Moe Koffman (1928–2001)
Yusef Lateef (1920–2013)
Hubert Laws (b. 1939)
Herbie Mann (1930–2003)

James Moody (1925–2010)
Sam Most (1930–2013)
David "Fathead" Newman (1933–2009)
James Newton (b. 1953)
Jerome Richardson (1920–2000)
Sam Rivers (1923–2011)
Ali Ryerson (b. 1952)
Albert Socarras (1908–1987)
Jeremy Steig (b. 1942)
Lew Tabackin (b. 1940)
Dave Valentin (b. 1952)
Frank Wess (1922–2013)
Elise Wood (b. 1952)
Leo Wright (1933–1991)

Piano/Keyboard

Muhal Richard Abrams (b. 1930)
Toshiko Akiyoshi (b. 1929)
Joe Albany (1924–1988)
Monty Alexander (b. 1944)
Geri Allen (b. 1957)
Mose Allison (b. 1927)
Chris Anderson (1926–2008)
Albert Ammons (1907–1949)
Lil Hardin Armstrong (1898–1971)
Lynne Arriale (b. 1957)
Kenny Barron (b. 1943)
Count Basie (1904–1984)
Jonathan Batiste (b. 1986)
Richie Beirach (b. 1947)
Walter Bishop Jr. (1927–1998)
Eubie Blake (1887–1983)
Ran Blake (b. 1935)
Paul Bley (b. 1932)
Stefano Bollani (b. 1972)
Joanne Brackeen (b. 1938)
Dave Brubeck (1920–2012)
Dave Burrell (b. 1940)
Joe Bushkin (1916–2004)
Henry Butler (b. 1949)
Ray Bryant (1931–2011)
Jaki Byard (1922–1999)
George Cables (b. 1944)
Michael Cain (b. 1966)
Uri Caine (b. 1956)
John Campbell (b. 1955)
Barbara Carroll (b. 1925)
Marc Cary (b. 1967)
Bill Charlap (b. 1966)
Ray Charles (1930–2004)
Cyrus Chestnut (b. 1963)
Sonny Clark (1931–1963)
Gerald Clayton (b. 1984)
Nat "King" Cole (1919–1965)
Alice Coltrane (1937–2007)

Harry Connick Jr. (b. 1967)
Marc Copland (b. 1948)
Chick Corea (b. 1941)
Eddie Costa (1930–1962)
Stanley Cowell (b. 1941)
Marilyn Crispell (b. 1947)
Albert Dailey (1939–1984)
Tadd Dameron (1917–1965)
Walter Davis Jr. (1932–1990)
Armen Donelian (b. 1950)
Kenny Drew (1928–1993)
Kenny Drew Jr. (b. 1958)
Eliane Elias (b. 1960)
Duke Ellington (1899–1974)
Bill Evans (1929–1980)
Victor Feldman (1934–1987)
Tommy Flanagan (1930–2001)
Joel Forrester (b. 1946)
Don Friedman (b. 1935)
Dave Frishberg (b. 1933)
Hal Galper (b. 1938)
Red Garland (1923–1984)
Erroll Garner (1921–1977)
Giorgio Gaslini (b. 1929)
Robert Glasper (b. 1978)
Vince Guaraldi (1928–1976)
Al Haig (1924–1982)
Bengt Hallberg (1932–2013)
Herbie Hancock (b. 1940)
Sir Roland Hanna (1932–2002)
Barry Harris (b. 1929)
Hampton Hawes (1928–1977)
Kevin Hays (b. 1968)
Fred Hersch (b. 1955)
Eddie Heyward (1915–1989)
John Hicks (1941–2006)
Andrew Hill (1931–2007)
Earl Hines (1903–1983)
Jutta Hipp (1925–2003)
Art Hodes (1904–1993)
Elmo Hope (1923–1967)
Dick Hyman (b. 1927)
Abdullah Ibrahim (b. 1934)
Ethan Iverson (b. 1973)
Vijay Iyer (b. 1971)
D. D. Jackson (b. 1967)
Ahmad Jamal (b. 1930)
Keith Jarrett (b. 1945)
James P. Johnson (1894–1955)
Pete Johnson (1904–1967)
Hank Jones (1918–2010)
Duke Jordan (1922–2006)
Dick Katz (1924–2009)
Wynton Kelly (1931–1971)
Rodney Kendrick (b. 1960)
Dave Kikoski (b. 1961)

Kenny Kirkland (1955–1998)
Diana Krall (b. 1964)
Steve Kuhn (b. 1938)
Billy Kyle (1914–1966)
Ellis Larkins (1923–2002)
John Lewis (1920–2001)
Meade "Lux" Lewis (1905–1964)
Ramsey Lewis (b. 1935)
Harold Mabern (b. 1936)
Pete Malinverni (b. 1957)
Dodo Marmarosa (1925–2002)
Ronnie Mathews (1935–2008)
Dave McKenna (1930–2008)
Jim McNeely (b. 1949)
Marian McPartland (1918–2013)
Jay McShann (1916–2006)
John Medeski (b. 1965)
Brad Mehldau (b. 1970)
Misha Mengelberg (b. 1935)
Mulgrew Miller (1955–2013)
Thelonious Monk (1917–1982)
Tete Montoliu (1933–1997)
Jason Moran (b. 1975)
Jelly Roll Morton (1890–1941)
Marty Napoleon (b. 1921)
Phineas Newborn Jr. (1931–1989)
Herbie Nichols (1919–1963)
Walter Norris (1931–2011)
Eddie Palmieri (b. 1936)
Horace Parlan (b. 1931)
Danilo Perez (b. 1966)
Oscar Peterson (1925–2007)
Michel Petrucciani (1962–1999)
Enrico Pieranunzi (b. 1949)
Bud Powell (1924–1966)
Mel Powell (1923–1998)
Clarence Profit (1912–1944)
Don Pullen (1941–1995)
Freddie Redd (b. 1928)
Eric Reed (b. 1970)
Luckey Roberts (1887–1968)
Marcus Roberts (b. 1963)
Joe Robichaux (1900–1965)
Ted Rosenthal (b. 1959)
Renee Rosnes (b. 1962)
Jimmy Rowles (1918–1996)
Gonzalo Rubalcaba (b. 1963)
Hilton Ruiz (1952–2006)
Alex Von Schlippenbach (b. 1938)
George Shearing (1919–2011)
Matthew Shipp (b. 1960)
Horace Silver (1928–2014)
Pine Top Smith (1904–1929)
Willie "the Lion" Smith (1893–1973)
Martial Solal (b. 1927)
Mark Soskin (b. 1953)

Jess Stacy (1904–1994)
Billy Strayhorn (1915–1967)
Joe Sullivan (1906–1971)
Sun Ra (1914–1993)
Ralph Sutton (1922–2001)
Horace Tapscott (1934–1999)
Art Tatum (1909–1956)
Billy Taylor (1921–2010)
Cecil Taylor (b. 1929)
Jacky Terrasson (b. 1966)
Sir Charles Thompson (b. 1918)
Bobby Timmons (1935–1974)
Lennie Tristano (1919–1978)
McCoy Tyner (b. 1938)
Mal Waldron (1925–2002)
Fats Waller (1904–1943)
Cedar Walton (1934–2013)
Michael Weiss (b. 1958)
Kenny Werner (b. 1951)
Randy Weston (b. 1926)
Gerald Wiggins (1922–2008)
James Williams (1951–2004)
Jessica Williams (b. 1948)
Mary Lou Williams (1910–1981)
Teddy Wilson (1912–1986)
Richard Waynds (b. 1928)
Jimmy Yancey (1898–1951)
Joe Zawinul (1932–2007)
Denny Zeitlin (b. 1938)

Organ

Count Basie (1904–1984)
Milt Buckner (1915–1977)
Wild Bill Davis (1918–1995)
Joey DeFrancesco (b. 1971)
Barbara Dennerlein (b. 1964)
Bill Doggett (1916–1996)
Charles Earland (1941–1999)
Larry Goldings (b. 1968)
Richard Groove Holmes (1931–1991)
Jack McDuff (1926–2001)
Jimmy McGriff (1936–2008)
Don Patterson (1936–1988)
Shirley Scott (1934–2002)
Jimmy Smith (1925–2005)
Johnny Hammond Smith (1933–1997)
Dr. Lonnie Smith (b. 1942)
Fats Waller (1904–1943)
Larry Young (1940–1978)
Joe Zawinul (1932–2007)

Bass

Mickey Bass (b. 1943)
Aaron Bell (1922–2003)

Jimmy Blanton (1918–1942)
Wellman Braud (1891–1966)
Cameron Brown (b. 1941)
Ray Brown (1926–2002)
Steve Brown (1890–1965)
Red Callender (1916–1992)
Ron Carter (b. 1937)
Paul Chambers (1935–1969)
Avishai Cohen (b. 1970)
Greg Cohen (b. 1953)
Joe Comfort (1917–1988)
Curtis Counce (1926–1963)
Bob Cranshaw (b. 1932)
Israel Crosby (1919–1962)
Bill Crow (b. 1927)
Art Davis (1934–2007)
Richard Davis (b. 1930)
Mark Dresser (b. 1952)
Ray Drummond (b. 1946)
George Duvivier (1920–1985)
Malachi (Maghostut) Favors
    (1927–2004)
George "Pops" Foster (1892–1969)
David Friesen (b. 1942)
Larry Gales (1936–1995)
Jimmy Garrison (1933–1976)
Eddie Gomez (b. 1944)
Larry Grenadier (b. 1966)
Henry Grimes (b. 1935)
Charlie Haden (1937–2014)
Bob Haggart (1914–1998)
Percy Heath (1923–2005)
Milt Hinton (1910–2000)
Dave Holland (b. 1946)
Major Holley (1924–1990)
Dennis Irwin (1951–2008)
Chuck Israels (b. 1936)
David Izenzon (1932–1979)
Bill Johnson (1872–1972)
Marc Johnson (b. 1953)
Sam Jones (1924–1981)
John Kirby (1908–1952)
Steve Kirby (b. 1956)
Peter Kowald (1944–2002)
Scott LaFaro (1936–1961)
Jay Leonhart (b. 1940)
Ahmed Abdul-Malik (1927–1993)
Wendell Marshall (1920–2002)
Tarus Mateen (b. 1967)
Cecil McBee (b. 1935)
Christian McBride (b. 1972)
Pierre Michelot (1928–2005)
Charles Mingus (1922–1979)
Red Mitchell (1927–1992)
Charnett Moffett (b. 1967)
George Mraz (b. 1944)

John Ore (b. 1933)
Walter Page (1900–1957)
William Parker (b. 1952)
Jaco Pastorius (1951–1987)
John Patitucci (b. 1959)
Alcide "Slow Drag" Pavageau
    (1888–1969)
Gary Peacock (b. 1935)
Niels-Henning Ørsted Pedersen
    (1946–2005)
Oscar Pettiford (1922–1960)
Tommy Potter (1918–1988)
Gene Ramey (1913–1984)
Rufus Reid (b. 1944)
Larry Ridley (b. 1937)
Curly Russell (1917–1986)
Eddie Safranski (1918–1974)
Arvell Shaw (1923–2002)
Esperanza Spalding (b. 1984)
Slam Stewart (1914–1987)
Steve Swallow (b. 1940)
Jamaaladeen Tacuma (b. 1956)
Reginald Veal (b. 1963)
Leroy Vinnegar (1928–1999)
Miroslav Vitous (b. 1947)
Wilbur Ware (1923–1979)
Peter Washington (b. 1964)
Buster Williams (b. 1942)
Reggie Workman (b. 1937)

Drums/Percussion

Rashied Ali (1935–2009)
Carl Allen (b. 1961)
Barry Altschul (b. 1943)
Paul Barbarin (1899–1969)
Joey Baron (b. 1955)
Ray Barretto (1929–2006)
Louie Bellson (1924–2009)
Han Bennink (b. 1942)
Dick Berk (1939–2014)
Denzil Best (1917–1965)
Ed Blackwell (1929–1992)
Brian Blade (b. 1970)
Art Blakey (1919–1990)
Willie Bobo (1934–1983)
Roy Brooks (1938–2005)
Alvin Burroughs (1911–1950)
Candido Camero (b. 1921)
Terri Lyne Carrington (b. 1965)
Michael Carvin (b. 1944)
Sid Catlett (1910–1951)
Joe Chambers (b. 1942)
Kenny Clarke (1914–1985)
Terry Clarke (b. 1944)
Jimmy Cobb (b. 1929)

Billy Cobham (b. 1944)
Cozy Cole (1909–1981)
Denardo Coleman (b. 1956)
Jerome Cooper (b. 1946)
Jimmy Crawford (1910–1980)
Andrew Cyrille (b. 1939)
Alan Dawson (1929–1996)
Jack DeJohnette (b. 1942)
Warren "Baby" Dodds (1898–1959)
Hamid Drake (b. 1955)
Billy Drummond (b. 1959)
Frankie Dunlop (b. 1928)
Al Foster (b. 1944)
Vernel Fournier (1928–2000)
Panama Francis (1918–2001)
Gerry Gibbs (b. 1964)
Milford Graves (b. 1941)
Sonny Greer (1895–1982)
Chico Hamilton (1921–2013)
Jake Hanna (1931–2010)
Eric Harland (b. 1979)
Winard Harper (1962)
Beaver Harris (1936–1991)
Billy Hart (b. 1940)
Louis Hayes (b. 1937)
Roy Haynes (b. 1925)
Al "Tootie" Heath (b. 1935)
Billy Higgins (1936–2001)
Gregory Hutchinson (b. 1970)
Susie Ibarra (b. 1970)
Ronald Shannon Jackson (1940–2013)
Gus Johnson (1913–2000)
Elvin Jones (1927–2004)
Jo Jones (1911–1985)
Philly Joe Jones (1923–1985)
Tiny Kahn (1924–1953)
Connie Kay (1927–1994)
Gene Krupa (1909–1973)
Cliff Leeman (1913–1986)
Mel Lewis (1929–1990)
Victor Lewis (b. 1950)
Shelly Manne (1920–1984)
Ray Mantilla (b. 1934)
Marilyn Mazur (b. 1955)
Steve McCall (1933–1989)
Charles Moffett (1929–1997)
Airto Moreira (b. 1941)
Joe Morello (1928–2011)
Paul Motian (1931–2011)
Famoudou Don Moye (b. 1946)
Sonny Murray (b. 1936)
Lewis Nash (b. 1958)
Adam Nussbaum (b. 1955)
Tony Oxley (b. 1938)
Sonny Payne (1926–1979)
Walter Perkins (1932–2004)

Charli Persip (1929)
Ralph Peterson (b. 1962)
Chano Pozo (1915–1948)
Tito Puente (1923–2000)
Buddy Rich (1917–1987)
Dannie Richmond (1935–1988)
Ben Riley (b. 1933)
Herlin Riley (b. 1957)
Max Roach (1924–2007)
Mongo Santamaria (1922–2003)
Zutty Singleton (1898–1975)
Grady Tate (b. 1932)
Art Taylor (1929–1995)
Dave Tough (1907–1948)
Kenny Washington (b. 1958)
Freddie Waits (1943–1989)
Nasheet Waits (b. 1972)
Jeff "Tain" Watts (b. 1960)
Chick Webb (1909–1939)
Jackie Williams (b. 1933)
Tony Williams (1945–1997)
Shadow Wilson (1919–1959)
Sam Woodyard (1925–1988)

Guitar/Banjo

John Abercrombie (b. 1944)
Howard Alden (b. 1958)
Oscar Aleman (1909–1980)
Derek Bailey (1930–2005)
Danny Barker (1909–1994)
George Barnes (1921–1977)
Billy Bauer (1915–2005)
George Benson (b. 1943)
Gene Bertoncini (b. 1937)
Bobby Broom (b. 1961)
Kenny Burrell (b. 1931)
Charlie Byrd (1925–1999)
Charlie Christian (1916–1942)
Joe Cohn (b. 1956)
John Collins (1913–2001)
Eddie Condon (1905–1973)
Larry Coryell (b. 1943)
Pierre Dorge (b. 1946)
Ted Dunbar (1937–1998)
Eddie Duran (b. 1925)
Eddie Durham (1906–1987)
Herb Ellis (1921–2010)
Kevin Eubanks (b. 1957)
Tal Farlow (1921–1998)
Bill Frisell (b. 1951)
Barry Galbraith (1919–1983)
Arv Garrison (1922–1960)
João Gilberto (b. 1931)
Egberto Gismonti (b. 1947)
Freddie Green (1911–1987)

Grant Green (1935–1979)
Tiny Grimes (1916–1989)
Lonnie Johnson (1899–1970)
Robert Johnson (1911–1938)
Jim Hall (1930–2013)
Charlie Hunter (b. 1967)
Barney Kessel (1923–2004)
Carl Kress (1907–1965)
Biréli Lagrène (b. 1966)
Eddie Lang (1902–1933)
Russell Malone (b. 1963)
Pat Martino (b. 1944)
John McLaughlin (b. 1942)
Pat Metheny (b. 1954)
Wes Montgomery (1923–1968)
Joe Morris (b. 1955)
Mary Osborne (1921–1992)
Joe Pass (1929–1994)
Les Paul (1915–2009)
Bucky Pizzarelli (b. 1926)
John Pizzarelli (b. 1960)
Jimmy Raney (1927–1995)
Django Reinhardt (1910–1953)
Emily Remler (1957–1990)
Marc Ribot (b. 1954)
Emanuel "Manny" Sayles (1907–1986)
John Scofield (b. 1951)
Bolo Sete (1928–1987)
Sonny Sharrock (1940–1994)
Floyd Smith (1917–1982)
Johnny Smith (1922–2013)
Johnny St. Cyr (1890–1966)
Leni Stern (b. 1952)
Toots Thielemans (b. 1922)
Ralph Towner (b. 1940)
James "Blood" Ulmer (b. 1942)
George Van Eps (1913–1998)
T-Bone Walker (1910–1975)
Muddy Waters (1913–1983)
Chuck Wayne (1923–1997)
Mark Whitfield (b. 1966)
Jack Wilkins (b. 1944)

Vibraphone

Karl Berger (b. 1935)
Gary Burton (b. 1943)
Teddy Charles (1928–2012)
Eddie Costa (1930–1962)
Don Elliott (1926–1984)
Victor Feldman (1934–1987)
Terry Gibbs (b. 1924)
Gunter Hampel (b. 1937)
Lionel Hampton (1908–2002)
Stefon Harris (b. 1973)
Jay Hoggard (b. 1954)

Bobby Hutcherson (b. 1941)
Milt Jackson (1923–1999)
Khan Jamal b. 1946)
Joe Locke (b. 1959)
Steve Nelson (b. 1955)
Red Norvo (1908–1999)
Warren Smith (b. 1934)
Cal Tjader (1925–1982)
Lem Winchester (1928–1961)

Violin

Svend Asmussen (b. 1916)
Billy Bang (1947–2011)
Regina Carter (b. 1966)
Johnny Frigo (1916–2007)
Stephane Grappelli (1908–1997)
Leroy Jenkins (1932–2007)
Joe Kennedy Jr. (1923–2004)
Ray Nance (1913–1976)
Jean-Luc Ponty (b. 1942)
Jenny Scheinman (b. 1973)
Stuff Smith (1909–1967)
Eddie South (1904–1962)
Joe Venuti (1903–1978)

Singers

Mose Allison (b. 1927)
Karrin Allyson (b. 1963)
Ernestine Anderson (b. 1928)
Ivie Anderson (1905–1949)
Louis Armstrong (1901–1971)
Mildred Bailey (1907–1951)
Chet Baker (1929–1988)
Tony Bennett (b. 1926)
Andy Bey (b. 1939)
Connee Boswell (1907–1976)
Boswell Sisters
    Martha (1905–1958)
    Connee
    Helvetia "Vet" (1911–1988)
Dee Dee Bridgewater (b. 1950)
Jeanie Bryson (b. 1958)
Cab Calloway (1907–1994)
Betty Carter (1929–1998)
Ray Charles (1930–2004)
June Christy (1925–1990)
Jay Clayton (b. 1941)
Rosemary Clooney (1928–2002)
Freddy Cole (b. 1931)
Nat King Cole (1919–1965)
Chris Connor (1927–2009)
Bing Crosby (1903–1977)
Meredith D'Ambrosio (b. 1941)
Bob Dorough (b. 1923)

Billy Eckstine (1914–1993)
Roy Eldridge (1911–1989)
Ella Fitzgerald (1917–1996)
Dave Frishberg (b. 1933)
Slim Gaillard (1916–1991)
Teddy Grace (1905–1992)
Nancy Harrow (b. 1930)
Johnny Hartman (1923–1983)
Jon Hendricks (b. 1921)
Woody Herman (1913–1987)
Al Hibbler (1915–2001)
Billie Holiday (1915–1959)
Stevie Holland (b. 1967)
Shirley Horn (1934–2005)
Helen Humes (1913–1981)
Alberta Hunter (1895–1984)
Jackie and Roy
    Jackie Cain (b. 1928)
    Roy Kral (1921–2002)
Denise Jannah (b. 1956)
Eddie Jefferson (1918–1979)
Herb Jeffries (1913–2014)
Etta Jones (1928–2001)
Louis Jordan (1908–1975)
Sheila Jordan (b. 1928)
Diana Krall (b. 1964)
Lambert, Hendricks & Ross
    Dave Lambert (1917–1966)
    Jon Hendricks
    Annie Ross
Barbara Lea (1929–2011)
Jeanne Lee (1939–2000)
Julia Lee (1902–1958)
Peggy Lee (1920–2002)
Abbey Lincoln (b. 1930)
Bobby McFerrin (b. 1950)
Carmen McRae (1920–1994)
Helen Merrill (b. 1930)
Mills Brothers
    John (1882–1967)
    John Jr. (1910–1936)
    Herbert (1912–1989)
    Harry (1913–1982)
    Donald (1915–1999)
Anita O'Day (1919–2006)
Jackie Paris (1926–2004)
Rosa Passos (b. 1952)
John Pizzarelli (b. 1960)
King Pleasure (1922–1981)
Ma Rainey (1886–1939)
Dianne Reeves (b. 1956)
Annie Ross (b. 1930)
Jimmy Rushing (1903–1972)
Cécile McLorin Salvant (b. 1989)
Kendra Shank (b. 1958)
Daryl Sherman (b. 1949)

Nina Simone (1933–2003)
Frank Sinatra (1915–1998)
Carol Sloane (b. 1937)
Bessie Smith (1894–1937)
Clara Smith (1894–1935)
Mamie Smith (1883–1946)
Jeri Southern (1926–1991)
Jo Stafford (1917–2008)
Kay Starr (b. 1922)
Maxine Sullivan (1919–1987)
Sister Rosetta Tharpe (1921–1973)
Big Joe Turner (1911–1985)
Sarah Vaughan (1924–1990)
Eddie "Cleanhead" Vinson (1917–1988)
Fats Waller (1904–1943)
Dinah Washington (1924–1963)
Ethel Waters (1896–1977)
Leo Watson (1898–1950)
Lee Wiley (1908–1975)
Joe Williams (1918–1999)
Cassandra Wilson (b. 1955)
Nancy Wilson (b. 1937)

Composers/Arrangers/ Leaders

Muhal Richard Abrams (b. 1930)
Manny Albam (1922–2001)
Van Alexander (b. 1915)
David Baker (b. 1931)
Bob Belden (b. 1956)
Carla Bley (b. 1938)
Francy Boland (1929–2005)
Anthony Braxton (b. 1945)
Bob Brookmeyer (1929–2011)
Dave Brubeck (1920–2012)
Ralph Burns (1922–2001)
Benny Carter (1907–2003)
Bill Challis (1904–1994)
Al Cohn (1925–1988)
Ornette Coleman (b. 1930)
Al Cooper (1911–1981)
Chick Corea (b. 1941)
Tadd Dameron (1917–1965)
Miles Davis (1926–1991)
Eddie Durham (1906–1987)
Duke Ellington (1899–1974)
Mercer Ellington (1919–1996)
James Reese Europe (1881–1919)
Gil Evans (1912–1988)
Bill Finegan (1917–2008)
Frank Foster (1928–2011)
Gil Fuller (1920–1994)
Dizzy Gillespie (1917–1993)
Gil Goldstein (b. 1950)

Benny Golson (b. 1929)
Gigi Gryce (1925–1983)
George Handy (1920–1997)
Herbie Hancock (b. 1940)
Neal Hefti (1922–2008)
Fletcher Henderson (1897–1952)
Horace Henderson (1904–1988)
Bill Holman (b. 1927)
Budd Johnson (1910–1984)
Sy Johnson (b. 1930)
Quincy Jones (b. 1933)
Thad Jones (1923–1986)
Louis Jordan (1908–1975)
Stan Kenton (1911–1979)
Andy Kirk (1898–1992)
Bill Kirchner (b, 1953)
Papa Jack Laine (1873–1966)
Michel Legrand (b. 1932)
John Lewis (1920–2001)
Abbey Lincoln (1930–2010)
Jimmie Lunceford (1902–1947)
Teo Macero (1925–2008)
Machito (1912–1984)
Johnny Mandel (b. 1925)
Wynton Marsalis (b. 1961)
Gary McFarland (1933–1971)
Tom McIntosh (b. 1927)
Jim McNeely (b. 1949)
Glenn Miller (1904–1944)
Lucky Millinder (1900–1966)
Charles Mingus (1922–1979)
Thelonious Monk (1917–1982)
Butch Morris (1947–2013)
Jelly Roll Morton (1890–1941)
Bennie Moten (1894–1935)
Gerry Mulligan (1927–1996)
Jimmy Mundy (1907–1983)
David Murray (b. 1955)
Oliver Nelson (1932–1975)
Red Nichols (1905–1965)
Chico O'Farrill (1921–2001)
Sy Oliver (1910–1988)
Hall Overton (1920–1972)
Marty Paich (1925–1995)
Charlie Parker (1920–1955)
Duke Pearson (1932–1980)
Hannibal (Lokumbe) Peterson (b. 1948)
Bud Powell (1924–1966)
Boyd Raeburn (1913–1966)
Don Redman (1900–1964)
Johnny Richards (1911–1968)
Nelson Riddle (1921–1985)
Sonny Rollins (b. 1930)
Pete Rugolo (1915–2011)
George Russell (1923–2009)
Luis Russell (1902–1963)

Edgar Sampson (1907–1973)
Heikki Sarmanto (b. 1939)
Eddie Sauter (1914–1981)
Lalo Schifrin (b. 1932)
Maria Schneider (b. 1960)
Gunther Schuller (b. 1925)
Wayne Shorter (b. 1933)
Don Sickler (b. 1944)

Horace Silver (1928–2014)
Billy Strayhorn (1915–1967)
Cecil Taylor (b. 1929)
Claude Thornhill (1909–1965)
Henry Threadgill (b. 1944)
Charles Tolliver (b. 1942)
Fats Waller (1904–1943)
Randy Weston (b. 1926)

Paul Whiteman (1890–1967)
Ernie Wilkins (1922–1999)
Clarence Williams (1898–1965)
Mary Lou Williams (1910–1981)
Gerald Wilson (1918–2014)
John Zorn (b. 1953)

Glossary

I chord chord built on the first degree of the scale; known as the *tonic.*

IV chord chord built on the fourth degree of the scale; known as the *subdominant.*

V chord chord built on the fifth degree of the scale; known as the *dominant.*

A A B A form the most common 32-bar *popular song* form, referring to melody and harmonic progression (but not text). Each portion is eight bars long, with B, the *bridge,* serving as the point of contrast. A = statement, A = repetition, B = contrast, A = return.

A B A C form the second most common 32-bar *popular song* form, referring to melody and harmonic progression (but not text). Each portion is eight bars long, with the A section returning in the song's middle. Can also be considered A A′ form.

accelerando a gradual speeding up of *tempo.*

acid jazz a form of contemporary music created by DJs in the 1990s, relying heavily on samples taken from jazz recordings from the 1950s and 1960s.

alto saxophone one of the most common saxophones used in jazz performance, smaller and higher-pitched than the tenor.

arpeggio the notes of a chord played in quick succession rather than simultaneously.

arrangements composed scores for big bands, with individual parts for each musician.

arco a stringed instrument (such as the string bass) played with a bow.

art music a form of music with high aesthetic standards and social prestige, created by professional artists for a well-educated public and insulated from the commercial world.

atonal music with no key center.

augmented chord an unstable chord made up of two major thirds; found in the whole-tone scale.

avant-garde jazz a modernist style of jazz exploring new methods that radically oppose existing traditions; among the elements of jazz undermined by the avant-garde are rhythm, harmony, melody, structure, instrumentation, manner of presentation, and politics.

backbeat a simple *polyrhythm* emphasizing beats 2 and 4 of a 4/4 measure (rather than 1 and 3).

ballad (1) a slow, romantic *popular song;* (2) a long, early type of folk song that narrated a bit of local history.

bar see *measure.*

baritone saxophone the largest and deepest saxophone used in jazz performance.

bass in the *rhythm section* of a jazz band, an instrument—*string bass, electric bass,* or *tuba*—that supports the harmony and plays a basic rhythmic foundation.

bass clarinet a *wind instrument* pitched lower than a standard *clarinet.*

bass drum the large drum front and center in a jazz *drum kit,* struck with a mallet propelled by a *foot pedal;* it produces a deep, heavy sound.

bebop A style of modern jazz pioneered in the mid-1940s; it has become the basis for most contemporary jazz.

bell the flared opening at the end of a brass instrument.

bent notes see *blue notes.*

big bands large jazz orchestras featuring sections of saxophones, trumpets, and trombones, prominent during the Swing Era (1930s).

block chords a *homophonic texture* in which the chordal accompaniment moves in the same rhythm as the main melody.

blue notes notes in which the pitch is bent expressively, using *variable intonation;* also known as blue notes.

blues a musical/poetic form in African American culture, created c. 1900 and widely influential around the world.

blues form a twelve-bar *cycle* used as a framework for improvisation by jazz musicians.

blues scale the melodic resources for the *blues;* includes simple *pentatonic* and *diatonic* scales combined with *blue notes.*

blue third the lowered third degree of the scale, featured in the *blues.*

bongos in *Latin percussion,* an instrument with two drumheads, one larger than the other, compact enough to sit between the player's knees.

boogie-woogie a blues piano style in which the left hand plays a rhythmic *ostinato* of eight beats to the bar.

bossa nova "new flair"; Brazilian form of *samba* music.

bottleneck guitar *guitar* played with a glass slide over the finger to create a *glissando* effect.

bow a string instrument, such as a *string bass,* played by drawing a bow with horsehair across the strings; also known as *arco.*

brass instruments *wind instruments,* some of which are indeed made of brass, that use a cuplike *mouthpiece* to create the sound.

break a short two- or four-bar episode in which the band abruptly stops playing to let a single musician solo with a *monophonic* passage.

bridge (release) the middle part (or B section) of 32-bar *A A B A form,* which connects, or "bridges," between the A sections; it typically ends with a *half cadence.*

broken octaves a form of left-hand piano accompaniment that alternates the lower note of an octave with the higher one.

cadence stopping places that divide a *harmonic progression* into comprehensible *phrases.* See *half cadence, full cadence.*

cadenza a classical-music word for a monophonic solo passage that showcases the performer's virtuosity.

cakewalk ragtime dancing featuring *syncopated* rhythms.

call and response a pervasive principle of interaction or conversation in jazz: a statement by one musician or group of musicians is immediately answered by another musician or group.

changes jazz slang for a harmonic progression. See *rhythm changes*.

Charleston rhythm a dance rhythm from the 1920s, consisting of two emphatic beats followed by a rest.

chart a shorthand musical score that serves as the point of reference for a jazz performance, often specifying only the melody and the harmonic progression; also known as a lead sheet.

Chicago style style of jazz in the 1920s that imitated the New Orleans style, combining expansive solos with *polyphonic* theme statements.

chord a combination of notes performed simultaneously.

chord clusters *dissonant* chords with closely spaced notes.

chorus (1) a single statement of the harmonic and rhythmic jazz *cycle* defined by the musical form (e.g, 12-bar blues, 32-bar popular song); (2) the repeated portion of a *popular song*, often introduced by its *verse*.

chromatic harmony complex harmony based on the *chromatic scale*.

chromatic scale the scale containing twelve *half steps* within the *octave*, corresponding to all the keys (black and white) within an octave on the piano (e.g., from C to C).

clarinet a *wind instrument* consisting of a slim, cylindrical, ebony-colored wooden tube that produces a thin, piercing sound.

classic blues see *vaudeville blues*.

classical music *art music* from the European tradition.

clave a Latin *time-line pattern*.

clusters see *chord clusters*.

coda Italian for "tail": a concluding section to a musical performance.

collective improvisation method of improvisation found in New Orleans jazz in which several instruments in the *front line* improvise simultaneously in a dense, *polyphonic* texture.

comping a rhythmically unpredictable way of playing chords to accompany a soloist; typically one of the *variable layers* in the *rhythm section*.

congas in *Latin percussion*, two tall drums of equal height but different diameters, with the smaller one assigned the lead role.

consonant the quality of a harmony that's stable and doesn't need to *resolve* to another chord.

contrapuntal adjectival form of *counterpoint*.

cool jazz a style of modern jazz in the 1950s that used a "cool," relaxed approach to timbre and experimented with such basic elements as form, texture, instrumentation, and meter.

coon song an early form of *ragtime* popular song that yoked polyrhythmic accompaniments to grotesque racial stereo-types.

cornet a partially conical *brass instrument* used often in early jazz and eventually supplanted by the *trumpet*.

countermelody in *homophonic texture,* an accompanying melodic part with distinct, though subordinate, melodic interest; also known (especially in classical music) as obbligato.

counterpoint *polyphonic texture,* especially when composed.

counterrhythm see *cross-rhythm*.

country blues an early style of blues, first recorded in the 1920s, featuring itinerant male singers accompanying themselves on guitar.

crash cymbal a cymbal that produces a splashy, indeterminate pitch, not unlike a small gong, used for dramatic punctuations.

crescendo an increase in volume.

cross-rhythm a rhythmic layer that conflicts with the underlying meter.

cup mute an orchestral *mute* with an extension that more or less covers the *bell* of a *brass instrument*.

cycle a fixed unit of time, repeated indefinitely, that's used as the framework for improvisation in jazz.

cymbals broad-rimmed, slightly-convex circular plates that form part of the jazz *drum kit*. See also *crash cymbal, high-hat,* and *ride cymbal*.

decrescendo a decrease in volume.

degree individual notes in a scale (e.g., the first note of a scale is the first degree).

diatonic scale the seven-note scale most commonly used in Western music. See *major scale, minor scale, Dorian mode*.

diminished (or diminished-seventh) chord an unstable chord made up entirely of minor thirds.

discography the science of record classification.

dissonant the quality of an unstable harmony that *resolves* to another chord.

dominant a chord built on the fifth degree of the scale that demands resolution to the tonic chord.

Dorian mode a diatonic scale with an arrangement of half and whole steps (found on the piano white keys from D to D) that falls between major and minor.

double (1) to play more than one instrument; (2) to reinforce a melody with one or more different instruments.

double bass see *string bass*.

double stop on a bowed string instrument (violin, bass), two strings played at the same time.

double time a technique in which a jazz ensemble, especially the *rhythm section*, plays twice as fast without changing the length of the overall cycle.

downbeat the first beat of a *measure*, or bar.

dropping bombs a technique devised in *bebop* in which the bass drum plays strong accents.

drum kit (or drum set, trap set, traps) a one-man percussion section within the rhythm section of a jazz band, usually consisting of a *bass drum, snare drum, tom-toms,* and *cymbals*.

duple meter the most common form of *meter*, grouping beats into patterns of twos or fours; every *measure*, or bar, in duple meter has either two or four beats.

dynamics volume, or loudness.

electric bass a four-stringed guitar used in popular music, amplified through an electric speaker.

electric piano an electrically amplified keyboard, such as the Fender Rhodes, capable of producing piano sounds.

Ellingtonians musicians who played with Duke Ellington for years or even decades.

embouchure the shaping and positioning of the lips and other facial muscles when playing wind instruments.

extended chords *triads* to which additional pitches, or *extensions,* have been added.

extensions notes added to extend a chord beyond the triad (such as the sixth, seventh, ninth, or thirteenth).

fake book a collection of *charts* or lead sheets used by jazz musicians (so-called because jazz musicians improvise, or "fake," their way through a performance).

false fingerings on a reed instrument (especially the saxophone), playing the same note with different fingers, often producing unusual timbres or slight pitch differences.

field holler an unaccompanied, rhythmically loose vocal line sung by a field worker.

fill a short drum solo performed to fill in the spaces in an improvised performance.

fixed intonation a tuning system that fixes pitches at precise frequencies. See *variable intonation.*

flat a musical symbol (♭) that lowers a note by a half step.

flatted third the lowered third degree of the scale, typically found in the blues.

flatted fifth see *tritone.*

flatted scale degree note played a half step lower.

flugelhorn brass instrument with a fully conical bore, somewhat larger than a trumpet and producing a more mellow, rounded timbre.

folk music a form of music created by ordinary people for their own use, insulated from the commercial world and the world of social elites.

foot pedal the mechanism that propels the mallet to hit a *bass drum.*

form the preconceived structures that govern improvisation in jazz. These may include *cycles* of various kinds, popular song (like *A A B A*), or compositional forms such as *march/ragtime.*

forte a loud dynamic.

foundation layers continuous, unchanging patterns whose very repetition provides a framework for a musical piece.

free improvisation improvisation in an atonal context, where the focus shifts from harmony to other dimensions of music: timbre, melodic intervals, rhythm, and the interaction between musicians.

free rhythm music that flows through time without regularly occurring pulses.

frequency the vibrations per second of a musical note.

front the nominal star of a jazz band, but not really its leader or music director.

front line in *New Orleans jazz,* the melody instruments: trumpet (or cornet), trombone, and clarinet.

fugue a Baroque polyphonic form in which a short melody or phrase (the subject) is introduced in one part, or voice, and successively taken up by others.

full cadence a musical stopping point on the *tonic* that marks the end of a phrase.

funk a type of groove with a highly sycopated bass line and multiple contrasting rhythmic layers, favored by jazz musicians after about 1970.

fusion the joining of two types of music, especially the mixing of jazz and rock in the 1970s.

ghosting playing notes so lightly that they are almost inaudible.

glissando sliding seamlessly from one note to another, as exemplified on the trombone; also known as smear.

grace note a short, decorative note sounded either immediately before or simultaneously with a longer melodic note.

groove a general term for the overall rhythmic framework of a performance. Grooves include *swing, funk, ballad,* and *Latin.*

guiro in *Latin percussion,* a scraped gourd with ridges.

guitar a plucked string instrument with waisted sides and a fretted fingerboard; the acoustic guitar was part of early jazz *rhythm sections,* while the electric guitar began to be used in the late 1930s and came to dominate jazz and popular music in the 1960s.

half cadence a musical stopping point on the *dominant.* Half cadences sound incomplete; they serve like a comma or a semicolon in punctuation, providing a stop but not signaling full closure.

half-valving depressing one or more of the valves of a brass instrument only halfway, producing an uncertain pitch with a nasal sound.

half step the smallest interval possible in Western music.

hard bop a *bebop* style of the 1950s that refused the experiments of *cool jazz* and linked its aesthetic with African American culture; included the more populist *soul jazz* and was played by great bebop artists of the day.

Harlem Renaissance an artistic movement of the 1920s that attempted to display African American abilities in painting, drama, literature, poetry, criticism, and music; jazz was usually not included by critics of the time, although in retrospect the music of Duke Ellington seems central.

harmonic improvisation a new melodic line created with notes drawn from the underlying *harmonic progression;* also known as running the changes.

harmonic progression a series of chords placed in a strict rhythmic sequence; also known as changes.

harmonic substitution the substitution of one chord, or a series of chords, for harmonies in a progression.

Harmon mute a hollow mute, originally with a short extension but usually played without it, leaving a hole in the center and creating a highly concentrated sound.

head a composed section of music that frames a small-combo performance, appearing at the beginning and again at the end.

head arrangement a flexible, unwritten arrangement created by a band.

high-hat two shoulder-level *cymbals* on an upright pole with a foot pedal at its base; the pedal brings the top cymbal crashing into the lower one with a distinct *thunk.*

hip-hop a form of contemporary music that arose in the 1970s, featuring rapping, turntable styling, and the dance and fashion of inner-city youth.

Historicism the theory that artistic works do not rise independently of history but must be understood in relation to the past.

homophony a *texture* featuring one melody supported by harmonic accompaniment.

horns jazz slang for *wind instruments*.

inside see *playing inside*.

interval the distance between two different pitches of a scale.

irregular meter a meter featuring beats of unequal size (some are divided into twos, others into threes). A meter of five, for example, features two beats—one divided into three notes, the other divided into two notes (as in Dave Brubeck's "Take Five"). Similar combinations of seven, nine, and eleven are possible.

jam session an informal gathering at which musicians create music for their own enjoyment.

Jazz Age the 1920s; the era in which jazz became a popular, prominent form of music.

jazz repertory a movement that arose in the mid-1970s to critically examine and perform jazz from earlier eras.

keeping time playing the *foundation layers* for a musical piece.

klezmer a Jewish dance music.

Latin music dance grooves from the Caribbean, Central America, or South America (such as rumba, samba, mambo, bossa nova, or merengue) that feature syncopated bass lines and lively polyrhythm.

Latin percussion a wide variety of instruments including congas, bongos, timbales, maracas, and guiro.

legato a smooth, unbroken connection between notes.

licks short melodic ideas that form a shared basic vocabulary for jazz improvisers.

mainstream term first coined for music during the 1950s that was neither modernist (bebop, cool jazz, hard bop) or historicist (New Orleans jazz); today, it refers to styles that are neither aggressively innovative nor backward-looking, but falling in the center of the tradition.

major scale or mode the most common scale in Western music, sung to the syllables *do, re, mi, fa, sol, la, ti do*. The pattern of whole and half steps is W W H W W W H.

major second a whole step, or an interval made up of two half steps.

major triad a triad featuring a major third between the two lower notes.

maracas in *Latin percussion,* a gourd filled with beans and shaken.

march form a musical form exemplified by composers like John Philip Sousa, consisting of a series of sixteen-bar *strains,* usually repeated once and not brought back; for example, **A A B B C C D D**; the third strain, or *trio, modulates* to a new key (usually *IV*) and is often twice as long.

march/ragtime form *march form* as adopted by ragtime composers like Scott Joplin.

measure (or bar) a rhythmic unit lasting from one downbeat to the next.

melismatic several notes sung to a single syllable.

melodic paraphrase a preexisting melody used as the basis for improvisation.

meter the organization of recurring pulses into patterns. See also *duple meter, irregular meter,* and *triple meter.*

microtones melodic intervals smaller than a half step.

minor scale or mode a diatonic scale similar to the *major scale,* but with a different pattern of half steps and whole steps (W H W W H W W); normally used in Western music to convey melancholy or sadness.

minor triad a triad featuring a minor third between the two lower notes.

modal improvisation the process of using a scale as the basis for improvisation.

modal jazz a style of jazz devised in the 1950s that relied heavily on *modal improvisation.*

modulate to move from one key (B-flat, G, D minor, etc.) to another.

monophony a *texture* featuring one melody with no accompaniment. See also *break, stop-time.*

montuno a syncopated *vamp* that serves as a rhythmic foundation in Latin music.

motive a short melodic or rhythmic idea.

mouthpiece on a brass instrument, a cuplike rest for the musician's lips, into which air is blown; on a reed instrument, the piece of hard plastic to which a reed is attached.

multiphonics complicated sounds created on a wind instrument (through intense blowing) that contain more than one pitch at the same time; used often in avant-garde jazz.

mutes physical devices inserted into the bell of brass instruments to distort the timbre of the sounds coming out. See *cup mute, Harmon mute, pixie mute, plunger mute,* and *straight mute.*

neighbor note a note one half or whole step away; neighbor notes leave and return to a note by step.

New Criticism criticism that emphasizes close examination of a work of art with little concern for the cultural or biographical circumstances under which it was created.

New Orleans jazz the earliest jazz style, developed early in the twentieth century and popularized after 1917 in New York and Chicago; native to New Orleans, it features *collective improvisation.*

ninth an interval a step larger than an octave, used to create *extended chords.*

obbligato see *countermelody.*

octave two notes with the same letter name; one pitch has a frequency precisely twice the other (in a ratio of 2:1).

offbeat a note that falls in between the basic beats of a measure.

organ in jazz, an electrically amplified keyboard with *pedals* that imitates the sound of a pipe organ; used in *soul jazz* in the 1950s and 1960s.

ostinato (Italian for "obstinate") a repeated melodic or rhythmic pattern.

ostinato riff a riff that's repeated indefinitely.

outside see *playing outside.*

pedals the bass notes on an *organ,* played on a keyboard with the feet.

pedal point a passage in which the bass note refuses to move, remaining stationary on a single note.

pedal tone the bass note that creates a *pedal point.*

pentatonic scale a scale of five notes; for example, C D E G A.

percussion in the *rhythm section* of a jazz band, the drums, cymbals, congas, and other instruments that are struck to provide the music's rhythmic foundation.

phrase a musical utterance that's analogous to a sentence in speech.

phrasing the manner of shaping phrases: some musicians play phrases that are short and terse, while others are garrulous and intense.

piano a stringed keyboard instrument on which a pressed key triggers a hammer to strike strings; a standard part of the *rhythm section.*

piano a soft dynamic.

pickup a small microphone attached to the bridge of a *string bass* or to an acoustic *guitar* to amplify its sound.

pitch the vibrations per second, or *frequency,* of a sound.

pixie mute a small mute inserted into the bell of a brass instrument; players like Cootie Williams and "Tricky Sam" Nanton modified its sound further with a *plunger mute.*

pizzicato the technique of playing a string instrument by plucking the strings with the fingers; usually the preferred method in jazz for playing the *string bass.*

playing inside improvising within the structure of a *tonal* harmonic progression

playing outside improvising outside the structure of a *tonal* harmonic progression.

plunger mute the bottom end of a sink plunger (minus the handle), used as a mute for a brass instrument.

polyphony *texture* in which two or more melodies of equal interest are played at the same time.

polyrhythm the simultaneous use of contrasting rhythms; also known as rhythmic contrast.

popular song a type of song created by professional songwriters, especially in the period from the 1920s to the 1960s; usually falls into one of the basic song forms, such as *A A B A* or *A B A C.*

press-roll an intense rumbling on the *snare drum.*

programmatic music that attempts to link itself to specific places, people, or events.

quartal chords (or harmonies) chords built using the interval of a fourth (rather than a third).

quarter tone a *microtone* that divides the half step into equal parts.

ragtime a style of popular music in the early twentieth century that conveyed African American polyrhythm in notated form; includes popular song and dance, although it's primarily known today through compositions written for the piano.

reed instruments *wind instruments* whose *mouthpieces* are inserted between the lips, with the player blowing a stream of air into a passageway between a thin, limber reed and the hard part of the mouthpiece.

refrain in *popular song* or *folk music,* a musical section that returns regularly.

register the range of an instrument or voice: upper register means its highest notes, lower register its lower notes.

resolve what an unstable (or *dissonant*) note or chord does when it moves to a stable (or *consonant*) note or chord.

rest a moment of silence, indicated by a sign in musical notation; for example, indicates a quarter rest (a quarter note's duration of silence).

retro-swing a form of dance music popular toward the end of the twentieth century that appropriated dances from the Swing Era with musical accompaniment from 1940s rhythm and blues.

rhythm changes a harmonic progression based on the George Gershwin tune "I Got Rhythm."

rhythmic contrast see *polyrhythm.*

rhythmic layers in the repetitive cyclic structures of jazz, highly individualized parts that contrast with one another, even as they create a unified whole. See also *polyrhythm.*

rhythm section instruments that provide accompaniment for jazz soloing: harmony instruments (piano, guitar), bass instruments (string bass, tuba), and percussion (drum set).

ride cymbal a cymbal with a clear, focused timbre that's played more or less continuously.

ride pattern a steady pulsation played on the ride cymbal that forms one of the foundations for modern jazz.

riff a short, catchy, and repeated melodic phrase.

ring shout an African American religious dance, performed in a circle moving counterclockwise; often cited as the earliest and most pervasive form of African survival in the New World.

rip a strong *glissando* rising to the top of a note, especially on a trumpet.

ritard a gradual slowing down of *tempo.*

rock and roll a form of contemporary music, combining rhythm and blues with elements from popular song and country music and marketed at white teenagers; since the 1960s, when it became known simply as rock, it has been the dominant form in the music industry.

root the bottom note of a *triad.*

rubato (Italian for "stolen") an elastic approach to rhythm in which musicians speed up and slow down for expressive purposes; rubato makes musical time unpredictable and more flexible.

rumba clave a slight variation of the *clave* pattern, used in the rumba.

salsa a form of Latin popular music, founded in the 1970s.

samba a traditional Latino music with African roots.

saxophone invented by Adophe Sax in the 1840s, a family of single-reed *wind instruments* with the carrying power of a brass instrument. See *alto saxophone, tenor saxophone, soprano saxophone,* and *baritone saxophone.*

scale a collection of *pitches* within the *octave,* forming a certain pattern of whole and half steps, from which melodies are created.

scat-singing improvising by a vocalist, using nonsense syllables instead of words; popularized by Louis Armstrong.

secondary ragtime a pattern of *polyrhythm* in which a short motive of three pitches, implying a meter of three, is superimposed on a duple meter.

send-off riffs ensemble *riffs* played in the first few bars of a *chorus* by the entire band. They interrupt or immediately precede a solo, "sending" the soloist off on his way; the soloist then completes the rest of the chorus.

sequence a short melodic pattern repeated on different pitches. See also *transpose.*

seventh an *interval* one step smaller than an *octave,* often used as an *extension* for chords.

shake for *brass instruments,* a quick *trill* between notes that mimics a wide *vibrato,* often performed at the end of a musical passage.

sharp a music symbol (♯) that raises a note a half step.

shuffle rhythms slow, powerfully syncopated rhythms derived from *boogie-woogie.*

sideman any musician employed by a bandleader; often used to describe members of a swing band.

singer-songwriter in contemporary popular music, a perfomer who creates his or her own music; this contrasts with the practice in the music industry before the 1960s that set songwriters apart from performers.

single reed a *reed instrument,* such as the *clarinet* or *saxophone,* that uses only one reed; in jazz, double-reed instruments such as the oboe or bassoon are rarely used.

slash chords complex *extended chords* in which the root is a note not normally part of the *triad* (e.g., an A major chord with an F root, written as A / F and spoken as "A slash F").

slide an elongated trombone tube that adjusts the length of a column of air when the player slides it.

small combo the standard small group for jazz, combining a few *soloists* with a *rhythm section.*

smear see *glissando.*

smooth jazz a highly popular form of contemporary jazz, featuring inoffensive soloing and digitally processed rhythm tracks, favored on some radio stations.

snare drum smaller drum in a jazz *drum kit,* either standing on its own or attached to the *bass drum,* and emitting a penetrating, rattling sound.

soli a passage for a section of a jazz band (saxophones, trumpets, trombones) in block-chord texture.

soloist any instrument in the jazz ensemble whose improvisation is featured in a performance.

son clave the standard version of the *clave* pattern.

soprano saxophone the smallest and highest-pitched saxophone used in jazz performance.

soul jazz a popularized form of *hard bop* that employs a strong backbeat, an aggressive urban sound, and gospel-typechords.

spiritual African American religious song.

staccato a short, detached way of playing notes or chords.

standard a popular song that has become part of the permanent repertory for jazz musicians.

stepwise in melody, moving from one note in the scale to the next.

stock arrangements standard arrangements of popular songs made available by publishing companies for swing bands.

stop-time a technique in which a band plays a series of short chords a fixed distance apart (e.g., a measure), creating spaces for an instrument to fill with monophonic improvisation; often used in early jazz.

straight mute a standard orchestral mute that dampens the sound of a brass instrument without much distortion.

strain in *march form,* a 16- or 32-bar section.

stride piano a style of jazz piano relying on a left-hand accompaniment that alternates low bass notes with higher chords.

string bass the most common bass used in jazz, the same acoustic instrument found in symphony orchestras; also known as double bass.

subdominant the fourth degree of the scale, or the chord built on that scale degree.

swing (1) jazz from the period 1935–1945, usually known as the Swing Era; (2) a jazz-specific feeling created by rhythmic contrast within a particular rhythmic framework (usually involving a walking bass and a steady rhythm on the drummer's ride cymbal).

swing eighth notes a jazz soloist's flexible division of the beat into unequal parts.

symphonic jazz a form of jazz popular in the 1920s that attempted to elevate the music through symphonic arrangements.

syncopation an occasional rhythmic disruption, contradicting the basic meter.

synthesizer an electronically amplified keyboard that creates its own sounds through computer programming.

tailgate trombone (or smears) exaggerated *glissandos.*

tempo the speed of a piece of music.

tenor saxophone a common type of saxophone, larger and deeper than the alto.

territory bands in the 1920s and early 1930s, dance bands that serviced a "territory," defined by a day's drive from an urban center.

texture the relationship between melody and harmony: a melody supported by harmonic accompaniment (*homophony*), a melody by itself (*monophony*), or two or more melodies played at the same time, creating their own harmonies (*polyphony*).

third the basic interval for tonal harmony; in a major scale, it's formed by skipping over a scale degree (e.g., moving from *do* to *mi*).

thirty-two-bar popular song a standard song form, usually divided into shorter sections, such as **A A B A** (each section eight bars long) or **A A′** (each section sixteen bars long).

timbales in *Latin percussion,* two drums mounted on a stand along with a cowbell, played with sticks by a standing musician.

timbre the quality of sound, as distinct from its pitch; also known as tone color.

timbre variation the use of a wide range of *timbres* for expressive purposes.

time-line pattern a repeated, asymmetric pattern that serves as a basic foundation layer in African (and, to a lesser extent, African American) music.

tom-toms cylindrical drums with no snare used in a *drum kit*, typically tuned to different pitches.

tonal music music characterized by an overall tonal center (the *tonic*) that serves as the center of gravity: all other harmonies are more or less dissonant in relation to this tonal center.

tonic the first degree of the scale, or the chord built on the first scale degree.

tonic triad the chord built on the first scale degree.

trading fours in a jam session, "trading" short (usually four-bar) solos back and forth between the drums and the soloists, or between soloists.

transpose to shift an entire musical phrase to a higher or lower pitch. See also *sequence*.

traps see *drum kit*.

trap set see *drum kit*.

tremolo the speedy alternation of two notes some distance apart; on a piano, this action imitates a brass vibrato.

triad the standard three-note chord (e.g., C-E-G) that serves as the basis for tonal music.

trill the rapid alternation of two adjacent notes.

trio (1) the third, or C section of *march* or *march/ragtime form*, usually twice as long (32 bars), *modulating* to a new key, and offering contrast; (2) a group with three members.

triple meter a *meter* that groups beats into patterns of threes; every *measure*, or bar, of triple meter has three beats.

triplet a note divided into three equal parts.

tritone a dissonant *interval* made up of three *whole steps* (e.g., C to F-sharp). also known as flatted fifth.

trombone a low-pitched *brass instrument* that uses a *slide* to adjust the column of air. See also *valve trombone*.

trumpet the most common *brass instrument*; its vibrating tube is completely cylindrical until it reaches the end, where it flares into the instrument's *bell*.

tuba a large, low-pitched *brass instrument* with an intricate nest of tubing ending in an enormous bell; often used in early jazz groups as a bass instrument because of its powerful volume.

turnaround (or turnback) a faster, more complex series of chords used in the last two bars of a blues or the last A section of an A A B A form, leading back to the beginning of the chorus.

twelve-bar blues see *blues form*.

unison the "interval" formed by two different instruments performing the same pitch.

upbeat note or notes that precede the *downbeat*.

valve trombone a *trombone* that uses valves rather than a *slide* to change the length of the tube.

valves controls in *brass instruments* that shunt air into a passageway of tubing, altering a pitch.

vamp a short, repeated chord progression, usually used as the introduction to a performance.

variable intonation a tuning system that allows for certain pitches to fluctuate by microtones, thus creating *blue notes*.

variable layers contrasting parts played above the *foundation layers* in a piece.

vaudeville blues an early theatrical form of the blues featuring female singers, accompanied by a small band; also known as classic blues.

verse the introductory portion of a *popular song*, preceding the *chorus;* usually omitted by jazz musicians.

vibraphone (vibraharp) an amplified metallophone (metal xylophone) with tubes below each slab; a disc turning within each tube helps sustain and modify the sound.

vibrato a slight wobble in pitch produced naturally by the singing voice, often imitated by wind and string instruments.

voicing distributing the notes of a chord on a piano, or to different instruments in an arrangement.

walking bass a bass line featuring four equal beats per bar, usually used as a rhythmic foundation in jazz.

whole note the longest possible rhythmic note; in a four-beat *duple meter*, it would fill up an entire *measure*.

whole step an interval made up of two half steps; the distance between *do* and *re*.

whole-tone chord an *augmented chord* made up of *intervals* (major thirds) from the *whole-tone scale*.

whole-tone scale a six-note *scale* made up entirely of *whole steps*; because it avoids the *intervals* of a perfect fourth or fifth (the intervals normally used to tune instruments), it has a peculiar, disorienting sound.

wind instruments in jazz, instruments that are played by blowing air into a tube; also known in jazz as horns.

wire brushes drumsticks—actually hollow handles with thin wire strands—used to strike or brush the drumheads.

work song a type of folk song used during work to regulate physical activity or to engage the worker's attention.

Primer on Music Notation

Jazz is a largely improvised music, but much of it is also composed, from the **heads**, or themes that kick off the solos, to big-band orchestrations. Today, nearly all jazz musicians are fluent in the traditional forms of music notation. While we don't expect readers of this textbook to know how to read music, a few pointers about how it works may prove helpful.

There are two ways music notation is used in jazz. The first operates according to the same principles as classical music: a composer writes music on a page for instrumentalists to translate into sound. Jazz notation, though, sometimes lacks the kind of details that indicate dynamics, articulation, or even melodic notes (a jazz chart may consist exclusively of chord symbols). Rather than providing painstaking instructions, jazz composers rely on musicians to know how to interpret their symbols, as in the example below.

Charlie Parker, "Billie's Bounce"

The second approach puts into notation a musical work that already exists, perhaps as a spontaneously created arrangement like Count Basie's "One O'Clock Jump," or as an ad lib solo like Coleman Hawkins's improvisation on "Body and Soul." These works have then been **transcribed**. They can be simple or elaborate, depending on what the transcriber wants to show, and will *always* be incomplete—nothing in writing can capture the totality of sound or the rhythmic nuance of swing as heard in a performance.

Both ways rely on the traditional forms of music notation. The basic guidelines that follow will allow you to make sense of written music, or perhaps even write or transcribe some of your own.

Pitch

Pitches, or notes, are written on five lines grouped together as a **staff** or in the spaces in between.

Each line or space represents a different note—A, B, C, D, E, F, or G. Pitches that lie outside the range of the staff can be added by drawing extra lines (called **ledger lines**) above or below the staff.

The precise range of pitches is defined by the **clef** written at the far left of the staff: the **treble clef** for the higher pitches, the **bass clef** for the lower. The treble clef, also called the G clef, curls around the second line from the bottom of the staff, marking the G above middle C. The bass clef, also called the F clef, has two dots that enclose the second line from the top of the staff, the F below middle C.

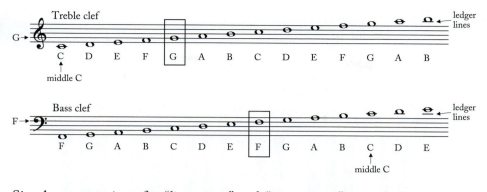

Simple mnemonics—for "line notes" and "space notes"—can help you remember where the notes fall on the staff.

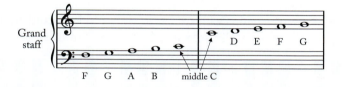

The two clefs combined make the **grand staff**, with middle C (notated with a ledger line) lying precisely in the middle; it can be written in either the treble or bass staff.

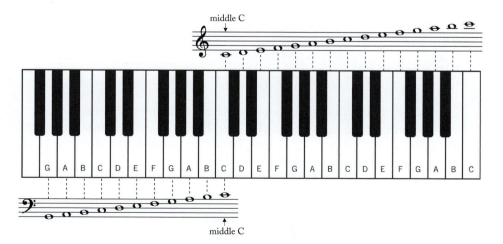

The keyboard below shows over three octaves of notes and how they are notated on the musical staff.

Major and Minor Scales

Seven-note major and minor scales, called **diatonic scales**, are the basis of melodies in Western music. As noted in Chapter 1, the piano white keys from C to C make up a **major scale** (or **mode**), with C as the **tonic**, or home, pitch.

Any major scale is constructed by a pattern of half (H) steps and whole (W) steps: W W H W W W H. (A half step is the shortest distance between any two notes, white or black, in either direction; a whole step is equal to two half steps.) The pattern is easy to see on a keyboard if you start from C and play the white keys up to the next C.

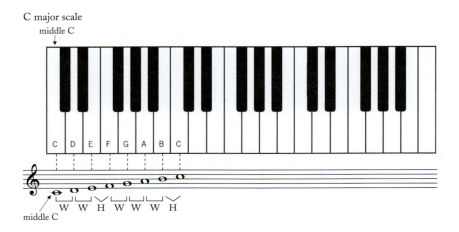

To preserve this pattern, all other scales will necessarily need some of the black keys—either **sharps** (♯), which raise a pitch by a half step, or **flats** (♭), which lower a pitch by a half step. A major scale starting on E, for example, requires four sharps (F♯, C♯, G♯, D♯).

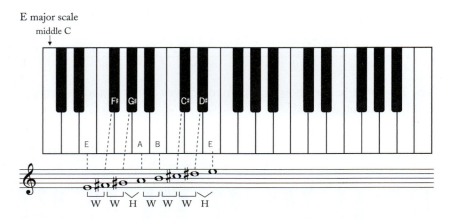

To convey music in E major, or any other key besides C, musicians use a **key signature**, to the right of the clef. The E major key signature automatically ensures that every F, C, G, and D will be raised a half step—unless a natural sign (♮) restores the note to its white key.

E major key signature

Key signatures range from blank (for C major) to up to seven sharps (for C♯ major) or six flats (for G♭ major). To tell what key corresponds with a certain key signature, use a simple bit of mnemonics: the tonic (starting pitch) of the major scale is either the next-to-last flat, or one half step higher than the last sharp.

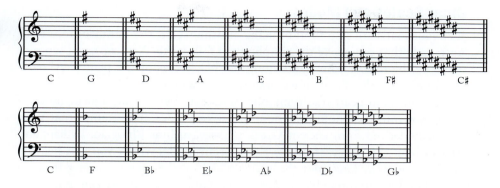

When building a major scale, how do you know when to use sharps and when to use flats? The main thing to remember, in addition to the whole- and half-step pattern, is that each scale contains all seven letter names. So starting on F, for example, the major scale is F, G, A, B♭, C, D, E, F. The fourth note has to be B♭, not A♯, because there's already an A.

F major scale

Each major scale has a **relative minor** scale: a minor scale that uses the same key signature. To find a major scale's relative minor, take the tonic (beginning) pitch of the major scale and count down one and a half steps. (Do this process in reverse to find a minor scale's relative major.) The relative minor of F major is thus D minor. The key signature for both scales is one flat, B♭.

The minor scale has its own pattern: W H W W H W W. The difference in sound between major and minor results mostly from the interval between the first and third notes of the scale. This interval in a major scale is a **major third** (two whole steps) and in a minor scale is a **minor third** (a whole and half step).

You can't tell what key a piece is in *just* by looking at the key signature; one flat, for example, could indicate either F major or D minor. You need to also look at the beginning and especially the end of the piece, which will usually feature the tonic note and harmony.

Western musical notation assumes **fixed intonation**: there are no notes smaller than a half step. Yet we know that in playing **blue notes**, jazz musicians often make use of **microtones**. To show tiny variations in pitch requires the use of idiosyncratic notation: arrows, downward slurs, lines from one note to the next.

Other Scales and Modes

Jazz musicians are also fond of using another scale, the **pentatonic**, a five-note scale that can evoke the simplicity of folk music. You can get a sense of its sound by rolling your hand along the black keys of the piano keyboard. But musicians also favor other diatonic (seven-note) scales, some of which come from European traditions but were abandoned long ago in favor of the major/minor dichotomy. These scales, or modes, have names that were originally derived from ancient Greek practice, such as Phrygian, Lydian, and Mixolydian. "So What" features the **Dorian mode**, which you can hear by playing the *white* keys (not the major scale) on the piano running from D to D. The Dorian mode has a pattern that falls curiously between major and minor. Jazz thus blurs the major/minor dichotomy of classical music, creating many shades of emotional nuance.

A scale made up entirely of whole steps may seem to have a certain logic, but the sound it produces is deeply unsettling. Only well-trained musicians can sing the **whole-tone scale** with any accuracy. But in the hands of composers like Thelonious Monk and the classical composer Claude Debussy, it creates a musical effect that's easy to recognize. We don't need to follow musicians into these arcane nuances, but it helps to know that scales are an infinite resource.

Rhythm

Staves are divided by vertical **bar lines** into **measures**, or **bars**, which allow musicians to keep regular beats and accents throughout the piece.

bar line   measure, or bar

The longest-held note is normally the **whole note**, an oval that usually fills up a measure. From there, notes are divided in half: a whole note equals two **half notes**, a half note two **quarter notes**, a quarter note two **eighth notes**, an eighth note two **sixteenth notes**, and so on. Each division marks a smaller amount of time. At a moderate tempo, the beat will usually be assigned to the quarter note, with sixteenth notes moving by at blinding speed.

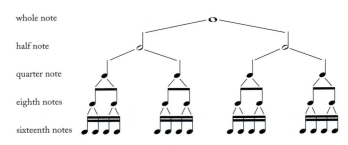

The parts of a note are shown below. Eighth and sixteenth notes are written with a flag attached to the stem or, when two or more are joined together, with beams. Each note value has a corresponding **rest**, indicating a silence that lasts as long as the equivalent note.

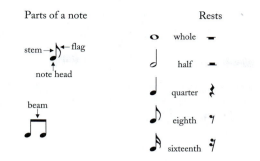

Beats usually divide into two, but when a note is (exceptionally) divided into threes, it's called a **triplet**, and special notation is required: the three notes grouped together are marked by a bracket with the number 3 attached.

Meter

Most jazz is in duple meter, which is indicated by the **meter signature** 4/4 (sometimes abbreviated as *C*) to the right of the key signature. The top number shows the number of beats to the measure (four), while the lower number designates which note gets one beat (the quarter note). Another form of duple meter (with two beats to the measure) is 2/4; triple meter, with three beats to the measure, is 3/4.

Vernon Duke, "I Can't Get Started"

Ludwig van Beethoven, Symphony No. 9, 4th movement

Richard Rodgers, "My Favorite Things"

When the beat is divided into three instead of two throughout a whole piece, however, a different meter signature is required. In a duple meter of four beats, with each beat divided into threes, a **dot** is added to the quarter note, which makes it equal to three eighth notes rather than two. (A dot attached to any note adds half that note's value; so a dotted half note would be equal to three quarter notes.) Such a measure is notated as 12/8; each measure contains the equivalent of twelve eighth notes, or four dotted quarter notes.

The first example below shows a measure of 4/4 and a measure of 12/8, with the beats written below; in 4/4 the quarter note divides in twos, and in 12/8 it divides in threes.

George David Weiss, "What a Wonderful World"

A **tie** mark, seen in the example above, is an arc that connects two identical notes and adds the duration of the second note to the first; the second is not played.

Jazz musicians don't rigidly divide the beat up into twos or threes, but use an infinite variety of divisions, known as **swing eighth notes**. In Miles Davis's solo on "So What" at 1:45, he plays notes that would be notated as

But in practice, the passage sounds more like this:

Such rhythmic nuances are usually not written out—partly to simplify the notation, but also because they are infinitely variable. Musicians decide by feeling the rhythmic groove just how uneven they want their eighth notes to sound.

Western notation can't show the continuous cycles of African American music, but it does include a symbol for repetition, **repeat marks**: double bar lines with two dots at the beginning and end of a passage, instructing the performer to play that passage twice. We can also use this notation to show cycles that repeat indefinitely.

Count Basie, "Splanky"

An arc that connects *different* notes, seen in the example above, is known as a **slur**. A slur instructs the performer to play smoothly, or **legato**. **Accent marks** emphasize a given note. And notes underscored with small dots are meant to be played crisply, with little sustain; this is known as **staccato** playing.

Dizzy Gillespie, "Salt Peanuts"

Harmony

Harmony is created by combining several notes at once to make **chords**. The most common type of chord is the **triad**, three alternate notes: for example, C-E-G, D-F-A, E-G-B, and so on. Numbers in the examples below indicate **scale degrees** (in a scale, *do* = 1, *re* = 2, and so on).

Triads in C major

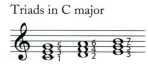

A chord can be built on any note, but be sure to check the key signature of the key you are in; if you're playing in F major, remember that every B is flatted.

Triads in F major

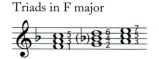

The chords built from notes in the C major scale, using only white keys, are shown below. They are all either major chords (with a major third as the bottom interval) or minor chords (a minor third is the bottom interval)—except for the chord built on B, the "leading tone," which is a **diminished** chord. As the diagram shows, chords are identified with a Roman numeral that signifies the scale degree, the first, second, third (and so on) note of the scale: I for the chord built on scale degree 1, V for the chord built on scale degree 5, and so on. Uppercase numerals indicate major chords, lowercase minor or diminished.

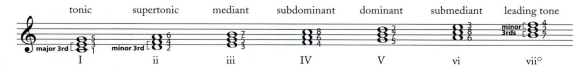

If you have access to a piano, play these chords to get a sense of major, minor, and diminished. Then try adding another third to a chord—for example, 1-3-5-7 or 5-7-2-4. These are **seventh chords**, reflecting the interval from the bottom note to the top. Continue to experiment, using your ear to add notes, and you will quickly find your way to the rich colors that are part of every jazz musician's harmonic palette.

Jazz musicians don't stick with the chords written in a book. They have the right to make **harmonic substitutions**: replacing chords with ones they happen to like, inserting more to enliven a slow spot, making chords more complex, or even removing them to simplify the progression. These are things that can be done spontaneously, or they can be worked out in advance as part of an arrangement. One common way to increase the complexity of chords, besides extending them, is to base them on the chromatic scale (rather than a diatonic scale). Thus, when we speak of **chromatic harmony**, we are referring to harmony that sounds more complex. Finally, as noted in Chapter 1, jazz musicians may sometimes play **outside** a tonal harmonic progression altogether, usually finding a way back in before long.

This primer is just a starting point. Many of the elements discussed here can be heard online in the demonstrations in "Jazz Concepts." You might want to further expand your understanding by investigating a music theory site on the Internet, or taking a course in music fundamentals. The more you know about music and how it works, the greater appreciation you will have for the spontaneous, creative art of jazz.

Collecting Jazz Recordings

Notes for Beginners and Prompts for Connoisseurs

The process of collecting music or anything else tends to combine dedication (as in "I'm going to acquire every record Dinah Washington ever made") and serendipity (as in "While searching for Dinah Washington, I discovered a really obscure and wonderful singer named Teddy Grace"). This book—with its Listening Guides and passing references to other works—should serve as a fairly comprehensive beginning, whether you find yourself drawn to particular pieces, and the styles and eras they represent, or have a more capacious interest in confronting jazz whole. Jazz is a blend of art and entertainment, and its first objective is to give pleasure. In pursuing it, trust your instincts and go with what you like. If Artie Shaw's "Star Dust" makes you want to look more deeply into bands of the Swing Era, you're not required to give equal time to the avant-garde. And if Cecil Taylor's "Bulbs" blows your mind, you don't have to feign a love of soul jazz. Even those of us who are seemingly enamored of every facet of jazz are likely to roll our eyes at a facet or two. On the other hand, everyone has to venerate Louis Armstrong; it's a law, punishable by loss of affect.

Tastes change, and if you are lucky, yours will expand rather than diminish in its curiosity and receptiveness. We subscribe to the advice of Sidney Bechet, this book's sole epigraph: "You got to be in the sun to feel the sun. It's that way with music, too." That means listen to everything with empathy. On the other hand, don't be intimidated into letting go of your bullshit detector—this applies to arts and to arts criticism, including this book, which only pretends to be objective. Jazz criticism and reference works are a good way to expand knowledge and find recommendations for recordings. Monthly magazines like *Jazz Times, Down Beat, Jazziz,* various online sites, and a very few urban newspapers have reviewers who are dedicated and opinionated listeners. After reading the same bylines again and again, you find yourself trusting some more than others, either because their tastes prove similar to yours or you find their perspectives and styles of articulation companionable and persuasive. You know soon enough whose passions and discontents ring true.

Unhappily, criticism has a larger role in introducing jazz records and reissues than it should, owing to jazz's low (almost nonexistent in many places) profile on radio and television. Record stores have listening apparatuses, and just about every online music service allows you to sample tracks, but part of the fun of collecting jazz is occasionally taking a flyer because you like the cover design or have heard someone mention the artist's name or you recognize a few of the tunes or just want to hear something new. It is now a sad reality that retail stores have disappeared from the musical landscape in many areas. Most of us buy records online, as CDs or MP3s, sacrificing the pleasure of shuffling through bins and racks and coming across a gem we didn't know existed. Yet the advantages of online shopping are obvious, not the least of which is that we can buy a single track before investing in an album. In doing that, we are replicating the experience of our ancestors, who bought 78s: those primitive discs consisting of a hit side and a flip side.

Almost all records made before 1948 were sold as single discs, so it is logical—especially when looking for music from that era—to sample a selection or two by an artist before springing for a collection of two dozen or so tracks. From the early 1950s until the middle 1980s, the industry was dominated by the LP; many of those albums ought to be considered as integrated works. If a track may be compared to a short story or bagatelle, an album may be thought of as a novel or symphony. Works such as Miles Davis's *Sketches of Spain*, Duke Ellington's *Far East Suite*, and John Coltrane's *A Love Supreme*, among hundreds more, should be experienced in their entirety—no less than a Beethoven symphony or a Verdi opera or *Sgt. Pepper's Lonely Hearts Club Band.*

The album concept remained in force in the CD era, but its hold began to slacken, especially in jazz. Why? For one thing, the playing time got so long that it surpassed the average listener's attention span, and musical dullness spread. In introducing CDs, the recording industry elected to *double* the price of vinyl LPs, even though the digital audio quality was initially much inferior to analog engineering and despite the fact that CDs were far less costly to manufacture. The record companies hoped to compensate for this shameless flimflam with semantic pomp and extended playing time. They even devised a laughably devious euphemism for those crappy plastic CD cases: "jewel boxes." In an exercise akin to price-fixing, they settled on an arbitrary CD playing time of about seventy-five minutes.

Extended play is a good thing for an opera, symphony, jazz suite, or anthology of short selections, but it isn't a virtue when it's turned into a rule. As the producers of jazz albums felt increasingly obliged to offer maximum-time discs (critics actually grumbled about discs that played under an hour), they achieved their goal by encouraging long individual tracks. The art of economy, the philosophy of less-is-more, the goal of improvising a perfect solo in one or two choruses, the showbiz adage of "Always leave them wanting more," gave way to long improvisations that were motivated not by the fever of inspiration but by the need to fill up the disc. Not surprisingly, a later generation of listeners preferred to download tracks rather than albums.

Meanwhile, the record labels began offering elaborate boxes, dumping material onto discs, including rejected takes, false starts, unedited session tapes, and random recording session chatter. One notorious knucklehead even restored to classic concert recordings longer applause interludes and the sounds of roadie labor, as a chair was pushed around or another mike brought to the stage. Some of these makeshift documentary recordings are extremely interesting, others are simply annoying. Gerry Mulligan, confronted with a boxed set of his "complete" sessions (the tracks arranged in the order they were recorded rather than as they were sequenced for the original album), was appalled: "Do you know how much time we spent arranging the tunes so they would be fun to listen to? They've turned it into homework."

Special editions are for specialist interests. For one artist, you may be satisfied with a greatest-hits-type collection; for another, you may want everything the artist ever released; for yet another, you may want the released stuff plus those newly excavated alternate takes and false starts. Bigger is not necessarily better. Some classics have been rendered virtually unlistenable by the addition of scraps from the cutting-room floor. To pick one of many examples, in 1959 Verve released the beloved album *Gerry Mulligan Meets Ben Webster*. In 1997, that same label issued *The Complete Gerry Mulligan Meets Ben Webster*, a two-disc CD in which the original tracks are cluttered with twenty rejected takes. Only a truly obsessed fan is likely to enjoy four consecutive versions of the same tune. One of Ellington's great late-period triumphs, the 1967 "*. . . and his mother called him Bill*," a tribute to Billy Strayhorn, ended with an unplanned Ellington piano rendition of Strayhorn's "Lotus Blossom," played quietly at the end of a session as the other musicians packed up; it serves as an emotionally devastating *l'envoi*. A CD producer, noting that "Lotus Blossom" was played at the end of a middle session, mindlessly programmed it midway on the CD.

You need to examine an album's contents, even in the case of a genuine classic, before buying it. Are you getting the original work, or the original work with new tracks, and are the new tracks added at the end (a bonus that no one is likely to complain about) or scattered throughout? On the list below, we intended to include Bill Evans's 1961 album *Waltz for Debby*, recorded live at the Village Vanguard, and were saddened to find that the only versions presently in print are an admirable but expensive "complete" three-disc set of the Vanguard engagement, or a single-disc version with consecutive performances of the same tunes, destroying the concentrated beauty of the original LP. In this book, we discuss the original version of Charles Mingus's "Boogie Stop Shuffle," which Mingus approved for release. That track is difficult to find now, because after Mingus's death a producer spliced back the passages that Mingus had edited out (in his approved release, the saxophone solo begins with a shout rather than a warm-up chorus). You may prefer the longer version, but we believe the record label also ought to offer the album as initially conceived. We've included the false start to Charlie Parker's "Ko Ko" because it provides fascinating insight into how that masterpiece was created. We've used the rejected take of Jelly Roll Morton's "Dead Man Blues" because, despite the flawed trumpet solo, we think it a more effective performance than the one chosen for release in 1926. (The Morton album in the list below offers both takes.) The point is that there is a sensible way to program reissues, and as sensibleness is in short supply, the consumer is obliged to do some digging to learn exactly what is being offered.

One way to check recording information is by consulting a discography—a book or site that lists all of an artist's record sessions (and surviving concert performances) chronologically, with the recording dates, band personnel, and catalog numbers. A discography for all of jazz, collating tens of thousands of sessions, is expensive, but dozens of individual jazz artists are represented by free online discographies (see the indispensable website www.jazzdisco.org). Ellington recorded several performances of "Mood Indigo," and if you are looking for a particular one, you need to know the label (he recorded five versions in 1930 alone, for Victor, OKeh, and Brunswick), the present owner of the labels (Victor and OKeh now belong to Sony, Brunswick to Sony and Verve), the full date, and the matrix or catalog number to be certain of getting the desired take.

For the most part, however, buying jazz records is a straightforward business. Reliable mail-order companies often have people who can answer questions, as retail stores once did. The best and easiest way to get advice is to solicit it from the large and passionate circle of fellow jazz enthusiasts. A few decades ago, this would have presented a challenge—many jazz lovers, especially in small towns, were as isolated as atheists or gays or gourmands or readers of Homeric Greek. Yet cyberspace is rich in jazz sites (including allaboutjazz.com, jerryjazzmusician.com, and jazzcorner.com) and chat groups. The population of dedicated jazz fans may be small, and at times cranky, but it is also ardent and helpful—most jazz lovers love to be in touch with other jazz lovers. It's them against the world.

Go for Broke

Meanwhile, here is a list of 106 albums by 106 artists. Two things make this discography unusual and potentially useful beyond the recommendation of good records. First, it is not a 106-best list. No artist is represented by more than a single work as a leader—a serious library of recorded jazz would include many recordings by central figures like Ellington and Miles Davis, whose influence and achievement represent artistic growth over decades. In fact, by sticking to our rule, which favors variety over prominent individuals and acknowledged masterworks, we were obliged to exclude some of our favorite records, some of which figure as Listening Guides in the text.

With this list, we offer a way to look at the jazz map from several perspectives; all these albums are excellent, and each one may lead you—through sidemen, arrangers, songs—to others, in an ever-expanding web that touches on most of the major avenues and side streets that make up the jazz world of the past century. (Admittedly, some areas are underrepresented, most conspicuously foreign jazz.) Each entry represents a way to explore a part of jazz and, with it, your own emotional and intellectual responses to it. In keeping with that idea, the second unusual aspect of this list is that it's alphabetical rather than chronological. The idea here is to distract you from the customary tendency to pigeonhole musical works according to the eras that produced them. It is one thing, for example, to study 1950s jazz and listen to Art Blakey as an example of hard bop, and another to encounter him on his own, possibly in tandem with Bix Beiderbecke and Arthur Blythe, who are connected to him on this list through the juxtapositions of alphabetical serendipity.

Not that you ought to start at number one and work down the list. Start anywhere you like. The point is to create a fourth narrative for jazz, unique to your experience. Unlike the first three—jazz as artistic progression, fusion, and historicism—this narrative is as random as life, and may well provide the most rewards. Included with each entry on the list is the year in which it was recorded, so that if you find yourself favoring a particular period, you can pursue it by reading the list from the right rather than the left. Note that this list includes no catch-all collections, like Martin Williams's *Smithsonian Collection of Classic Jazz* or *Ken Burns's Jazz: The Story of American Music*. In fact, there are no boxed sets and no items with more than two discs. Our selections, especially in cases where the same music is available in various formats from multiple labels, were influenced by audio quality, price, and availability. They are intended to encourage you to investigate the market on your own. If you search for the single-disc Dizzy Gillespie compilation of his 1940s RCA recordings, you will discover that a superior two-disc edition exists for those who would rather get the complete works.

Some of these albums survey entire careers, while others are classic LPs. Some capture the early work that established an artist's reputation, while others exemplify autumnal maturity (see, for example, Ornette Coleman, Stan Getz, Sonny Rollins). All these items were available in one form or another in the late months of 2014. (A few, like Lee Konitz's *Motion* and Roy Eldridge's *Uptown*, no longer exist as domestic CDs, but can be purchased as MP3s from iTunes.) By the time you read this, it is certain that some of these recordings will *not* be readily available, while others, left off the list, will be back in catalog. The record business has never been more volatile than it is now, when technology and changes in ownership have brought it to a point of crisis. At this moment, the entire Black Saint catalog of loft jazz from the

1970s and 80s is out of print but has recently been purchased by a company that will soon rerelease it; also missing is the Commodore catalog of 1930s and 40s swing and Dixieland classics, and no one knows when or how it will reemerge. We were astonished that we could not find—as CDs or MP3s—suitable anthologies or classic albums by Jack Teagarden, Randy Weston, Henry Threadgill, Anthony Braxton, and, incredibly, the prewar Lester Young (though his major solos are collected on the Count Basie, Billie Holiday, and Jimmy Rushing discs). Yet record company executives complain when jazz fans trade and download favorite recordings! They have made us that way. Every jazz lover is a sleuth. Your sleuthing may as well begin here.

1. Muhal Richard Abrams: *Blu Blu Blu* (Black Saint), 1990
2. Cannonball Adderley: *Mercy, Mercy, Mercy!* (Capitol), 1966
3. Gene Ammons and Sonny Stitt: *Boss Tenors* (Verve), 1961
4. Louis Armstrong: *The Complete Hot Five & Hot Seven Recordings,* vol. 3 (Columbia), 1928
5. Albert Ayler: *Spiritual Unity* (ESP-Disk), 1964
6. Count Basie: *One O'Clock Jump: The Very Best of Count Basie* (Sony), 1936–42
7. Mildred Bailey: *The Rockin' Chair Lady* (Verve), 1931–50
8. Sidney Bechet: *The Legendary Sidney Bechet* (RCA), 1932–41
9. Bix Beiderbecke: *At the Jazz Band Ball* (ASV Living Era), 1924–28
10. Art Blakey: *Mosaic* (Blue Note), 1961
11. Arthur Blythe: *Focus* (Savant), 2002
12. Lester Bowie: *The Great Pretender* (ECM), 1981
13. Clifford Brown and Max Roach: *Clifford Brown and Max Roach* (EmArcy), 1954
14. Dave Brubeck: *Time Out* (Columbia), 1959
15. Jaki Byard and Roland Kirk: *The Jaki Byard Experience* (Prestige), 1968
16. Don Byron: *Bug People* (Nonesuch), 1996
17. Benny Carter: *Further Definitions* (Impulse!), 1961
18. James Carter: *Chasin' the Gypsy* (Atlantic), 2000
19. Bill Charlap: *Live at the Village Vanguard* (Blue Note), 2007
20. Charlie Christian: *The Benny Goodman Sextet Featuring Charlie Christian* (Sony), 1939–41
21. Nat King Cole: *After Midnight: The Complete Session* (Blue Note), 1956
22. Ornette Coleman: *Sound Grammar* (Sound Grammar), 2006
23. John Coltrane: *A Love Supreme* (Impulse!), 1964
24. Chick Corea: *Now He Sings, Now He Sobs* (Blue Note), 1968
25. Sonny Criss and Horace Tapscott: *Sonny's Dream* (Prestige OJC), 1968
26. Bing Crosby: *Jazz Singer* (Retrieval), 1931–41
27. Miles Davis: *Kind of Blue* (Columbia), 1959
28. Eric Dolphy: *Out There* (Prestige), 1960
29. Roy Eldridge: *Roy Eldridge with the Gene Krupa Orchestra Featuring Anita O'Day Uptown* (Sony), 1941–49
30. Duke Ellington: *The Essential Duke Ellington* (Sony), 1927–60
31. Bill Evans: *The Paris Concert, Edition One* (Blue Note), 1979
32. Gil Evans: *Out of the Cool* (Impulse!), 1960
33. Ella Fitzgerald: *Something to Live For* (Verve), 1937–66
34. Erroll Garner: *Concert by the Sea* (Sony), 1955
35. Stan Getz and Kenny Barron: *People Time* (Verve), 1992

36. Dizzy Gillespie: *A Night in Tunisia: The Very Best of Dizzy Gillespie* (RCA), 1946–49
37. Robert Glasper: *Black Radio* (Blue Note), 2012
38. Benny Goodman: *Carnegie Hall Jazz Concert* (Sony), 1938
39. Dexter Gordon: *Go!* (Blue Note), 1962
40. Herbie Hancock: *Maiden Voyage* (Blue Note), 1965
41. Roy Hargrove: *Habana* (Verve), 1997
42. Johnny Hartman: *John Coltrane and Johnny Hartman* (Impulse!), 1963
43. Coleman Hawkins: *The Centennial Collection* (BMG), 1929–56
44. Roy Haynes: *Roy Haynes Trio Featuring Danilo Perez and John Pattitucci* (Verve), 2000
45. Fletcher Henderson: *Ken Burns Jazz Collection* (Sony), 1924–40
46. Woody Herman: *Blowin' Up a Storm: The Columbia Years* (Sony), 1945–47
47. Andrew Hill: *Point of Departure* (Blue Note), 1964
48. Billie Holiday: *Lady Day: The Best of Billie Holiday* (Sony), 1935–42
49. Dave Holland: *Conference of the Birds* (ECM), 1972
50. Abdullah Ibrahim: *Sotho Blue* (Sunnyside), 2010
51. Vijay Iyer, *Accelerando* (ACT Music + Vision), 2012
52. Keith Jarrett: *Whisper Not* (ECM), 1999
53. Stan Kenton: *Contemporary Concepts* (Blue Note), 1955
54. Lee Konitz: *Motion* (Verve), 1961
55. George Lewis: *Jazz in the Classic New Orleans Tradition* (Riverside OJC), 1950
56. Abbey Lincoln: *You Gotta Pay the Band* (Verve/Gitanes), 1991
57. Joe Lovano: *Joyous Encounter* (Blue Note), 2005
58. Jimmie Lunceford: *Rhythm Is Our Business* (ASV Living Era), 1933–40
59. Rudresh Mahanthappa: *Kinsmen* (PI), 2008
60. Wynton Marsalis: *Standards & Ballads* (Sony), 1983–97
61. John McLaughlin: *Live at the Royal Festival Hall* (JMT), 1989
62. Brad Mehldau: *Live* (Nonesuch), 2008
63. Charles Mingus: *The Black Saint & the Sinner Lady* (Impulse!), 1963
64. Roscoe Mitchell: *Sound* (Delmark), 1966
65. Modern Jazz Quartet: *Django* (Prestige), 1953–54
66. Thelonious Monk: *The Best of the Blue Note Years* (Blue Note), 1947–52
67. Wes Montgomery: *Smokin' at the Half Note* (Verve), 1965
68. Jason Moran: *Modernistic* (Blue Note), 2002
69. Lee Morgan: *The Sidewinder* (Blue Note), 1963
70. Jelly Roll Morton: *Birth of the Hot* (RCA Bluebird), 1926–27
71. Gerry Mulligan: *The Concert Jazz Band at the Village Vanguard* (Verve), 1960
72. David Murray: *Shakill's Warrior* (Sony), 1991
73. Fats Navarro and Tadd Dameron: *The Complete Blue Note and Capitol Recordings* (Blue Note), 1947–49
74. Oliver Nelson: *The Blues and the Abstract Truth* (Impulse!), 1961
75. King Oliver: *Off the Record: The Complete Jazz Band Recordings* (Archeophone), 1923
76. Charlie Parker: *Best of the Complete Savoy and Dial Studio Recordings* (Savoy), 1944–48
77. Bud Powell: *Jazz Giant* (Verve), 1949–50

78. Joshua Redman: *Back East* (Nonesuch), 2007
79. Django Reinhardt: *The Best of Django Reinhardt* (Blue Note), 1936–48
80. Sam Rivers: *Fuchsia Swing Song* (Blue Note), 1964
81. Sonny Rollins: *Road Shows*, vol. 1 (EmArcy/Doxie), 1980–2007
82. Jimmy Rushing: *Mr. Five by Five* (Pearl), 1929–42
83. George Russell: *Ezz-Thetics* (Riverside), 1961
84. Cécile McLorin Salvant: *WomanChild* (Mack Avenue), 2013
85. John Scofield and Pat Metheny: *I Can See Your House from Here* (Blue Note), 1994
86. Artie Shaw: *Begin the Beguine* (RCA), 1938–41
87. Archie Shepp: *Fire Music* (Impulse!), 1965
88. Wayne Shorter: *Footprints Live!* (Verve), 2002
89. Horace Silver: *Song for My Father* (Blue Note), 1964
90. Bessie Smith: *The Essential Bessie Smith* (Sony), 1923–33
91. Jimmy Smith: *The Sermon* (Blue Note), 1958
92. Esperanza Spalding: *Chamber Music Society* (Heads Up), 2010
93. Art Tatum: *Piano Starts Here* (Columbia), 1933–49
94. Cecil Taylor: *Unit Structures* (Blue Note), 1966
95. Lennie Tristano: *The New Tristano* (Atlantic), 1955–62
96. Joe Turner: *The Boss of the Blues* (Atlantic/Collectables), 1956
97. Sarah Vaughan: *Sarah Vaughan with Clifford Brown* (EmArcy), 1954
98. Fats Waller: *The Very Best of Fats Waller* (RCA), 1929–42
99. David S. Ware: *Go See the World* (Columbia), 1998
100. Dinah Washington: *The Essential Dinah Washington* (Verve), 1952–59
101. Weather Report: *Heavy Weather* (Sony), 1977
102. Chick Webb: *Stompin' at the Savoy* (ASV Living Era), 1934–39
103. Ben Webster and Oscar Peterson: *Ben Webster Meets Oscar Peterson* (Verve), 1959
104. Cassandra Wilson: *Belly of the Sun* (Blue Note), 2002
105. World Saxophone Quartet: *Revue* (Black Saint), 1980
106. Lester Young and Teddy Wilson: *Pres and Teddy* (Verve), 1956

Jazz on Film

In 1981, a British researcher, David Meeker, published his second edition of *Jazz in the Movies*, listing 3,724 feature films, short subjects, television shows, and documentaries with jazz content, however little it might be. That was nearly thirty-five years ago, and even then his work had dozens of unavoidable lapses. Hardly a year goes by when significant jazz footage, unknown to the most zealous collectors, isn't discovered—often from long forgotten television programs languishing in European broadcasting archives. Here is an introductory guide to jazz-related movies, divided into four categories: feature films with jazz as the subject; feature films with jazz scores; documentaries and performance films; and television series. Most of these films have been available on one or more home video formats over the years, usually on DVD. Those that are not presently in catalog may be found in libraries or are likely to be reissued.

Feature Films with Jazz Stories

Jazz has had a rather twisted relationship with Hollywood dating back to the silent era, when jazz, blues, and ragtime themes were often used to indicate the wanton or dissolute (see p. 393). During the Swing Era, Hollywood imported jazz orchestras to suggest optimism and good times. As bandleaders achieved national recognition, it was good business to banner them on movie marquees. After the war, jazz usually signified the denizens of urban blight. Some of the movies listed here are unintentionally hilarious, but they all have savory musical moments.

The Benny Goodman Story (1955, Valentine Davis): Cliché-ridden idiocy at every turn and a stupefying lead performance, but worthy music makes it endurable.

Bird (1988, Clint Eastwood): A powerful, partly factual and partly imagined telling of the Charlie Parker story with much music and an eye-popping studio recreation of New York's 52nd Street.

Birth of the Blues (1941, Victor Schertzinger): One of several films reflecting the historicist New Orleans revival, with Bing Crosby, Jack Teagarden, and a game Mary Martin inventing jazz as only Hollywood Caucasians could.

Black Orpheus (1959, Marcel Camus): A visually and musically thrilling version of the Orpheus legend told against the Brazilian Carnival and introducing several of the sambas that helped to launch bossa nova.

Blues in the Night (1941, Anatol Litvack): A Warner Bros. gangster film from the perspective of white jazz musicians, inspired by authentic Negro "misery"; this is a revealing curio, briskly directed, with a cameo appearance by Jimmie Lunceford's band.

Cabin in the Sky (1942, Vincente Minelli): A brilliant all-black musical with production numbers featuring Ethel Waters, Duke Ellington, Lena Horne, Eddie "Rochester" Anderson, the wickedly cool tap dancer John Bubbles, and a funny cameo by Louis Armstrong.

The Connection (1961, Shirley Clarke): The garrulous junkies waiting for their connection, in this film version of Jack Gelber's play, include the Freddie Redd Quartet, playing a celebrated score and featuring saxophonist Jackie McLean.

The Gig (1985, Frank Gilroy): A smart, realistic comedy about a group of white professionals who play jazz for fun, until they get a gig at a Catskills resort working with a pro.

The Glenn Miller Story (1953, Anthony Mann): A nostalgic fabrication in which Miller explains his radical musical ideas: "To me, music is more than just one instrument. It's a whole orchestra playing together!" Louis Armstrong and Gene Krupa drop by.

Hollywood Hotel (1937, Busby Berkeley): This is the way Hollywood packaged swing for the masses, salvaged by Benny Goodman's integrated quartet at its absolute peak.

Jazzman (1983, Karen Shakhnazarov): Hard to find, but keep an eye out for this superb Russian film about musicians risking their freedom to play hot jazz in the Soviet Union of the 1920s.

Low Down (2014, Jeff Preiss): A credible if superficial look at the life of bebop pianist Joe Albany (John Hawkes), from the perspective of his daughter A. J. Albany (Elle Fanning), on whose brief memoir the film is based. It's more about the pathology of addiction than the art of jazz, and the moral seems to be: jazz is a blood sport and think twice about having children.

A Man Called Adam (1966, Leo Penn): Sammy Davis Jr. plays an overwrought trumpet player in an overwrought film made memorable by Louis Armstrong, in a straight acting role, and a musical score by Benny Carter.

Murder at the Vanities (1934, Mitchell Leisen): A backstage murder mystery immortalized by Duke Ellington playing his take on Liszt (classical musicians mow his band down with machine guns) and the production number "Sweet Marijuana"—those were the days.

New Orleans (1947, Arthur Lubin): More New Orleans revivalism, purportedly from the black perspective, as Louis Armstrong leads his people in an exodus from Storyville and Billie Holiday shows up as a maid who sings as she dusts.

Orchestra Wives (1942, Archie Mayo): An underrated, surprisingly well-written story in which Glenn Miller's band hits the road (look sharp for Bobby Hackett), and the great Nicholas Brothers steal his thunder with acrobatic jazz dancing.

Passing Through (1977, Larry Clark): Difficult to see, this stunning student film, with a musical score by Horace Tapscott along with records by Charlie Parker and Eric Dolphy, captures the dilemma of the Los Angeles jazz avant-garde struggling to survive.

Pennies from Heaven (1936, Norman Z. McLeod): A Depression fable that may strike a relevant note today, with Bing Crosby in excellent voice and Louis Armstrong, making his first feature film, performing "A Skeleton in the Closet."

Paris Blues (1961, Martin Ritt): Not much plot animates this soap opera, but when Paul Newman and Sidney Poitier shut up, Duke Ellington's all-star orchestra takes over, including sequences featuring Louis Armstrong.

Pete Kelly's Blues (1955, Jack Webb): A splendidly photographed and scored saga of Kansas City in the 1920s, in which a white jazz band battles racketeers while Ella Fitzgerald operates a speakeasy, Peggy Lee goes insane, and Lee Marvin plays clarinet and is punched out by a little Jack Webb.

A Song Is Born (1948, Howard Hawks): A remake of the comedy *Ball of Fire* (which has a Gene Krupa solo played on a matchbox) in which cloistered professors, led by Danny Kaye, investigate jazz with the help of Benny Goodman, Louis Armstrong, Lionel Hampton, Tommy Dorsey, and others.

Ray (2004, Taylor Hackford): Jamie Foxx's uncanny imitation of Ray Charles traces his career from swing to gospel-infused R&B to his unique amalgamation of jazz, R&B pop, and rock—interrupted by narcotics, sex, and other domestic interludes.

'Round Midnight (1986, Bertrand Tavernier): Dexter Gordon's performance, in a role based on the lives of Bud Powell and Lester Young, is astonishing; Bobby Hutcherson, Herbie Hancock, Wayne Shorter, and others also appear.

Stormy Weather (1943, Andrew L. Stone): This all-black musical loosely touches on the early years of jazz, including James Reese Europe, but is best savored for performances by Bill Robinson, Lena Horne, Fats Waller, Cab Calloway, and the Nicholas Brothers.

Sweet Love, Bitter (1966, Herbert Danska): Melodrama of a black genius, thinly based on Charlie Parker (he's called Eagle), as experienced by his concerned white friend; score by Mal Waldron, alto saxophone solos by Charles McPherson.

Sweet Smell of Success: (1957, Alexander Mackendrick): A dark, caustic classic that involves an incestuous columnist framing a jazz musician for marijuana use; Elmer Bernstein's score is complemented by the on-screen Chico Hamilton Quintet.

Tap (1989, Nick Castle): The modest story is an excuse to gather several of the greatest jazz or tap dancers assembled in a Hollywood film, including star Gregory Hines, Sandman Sims, Bunny Briggs, Sammy Davis Jr., and the young Savion Glover.

The Tic Code (2000, Gary Winick): A young boy suffering from Tourette's syndrome learns to express himself through jazz, with Gregory Hines as a jazz star who learned to cover-up his own TS and a score by pianist Michael Wolff.

Whiplash (2014, Damien Chazelle): An absorbing yet often ludicrous melodrama about a music student (Miles Teller) who is determined to be the next Buddy Rich if it kills him, which it almost does—and his psychotic teacher, superbly played by J. K. Simmons, even if he does seem closer to, say, Joseph Goebbels than to, say, David Baker. The moral seems to be: jazz is a blood sport and stay the hell away from band practice.

Feature Films with Jazz Scores

Hollywood soundtracks often employed jazz or jazzy touches, but not until the 1950s did composers start using jazz as the governing style for film scores. Not surprisingly, the plots of most of these films concern junkies, sexual deviants, and murderers. In the late 1950s and 1960s, genuine jazz composers were also hired. Here are a few benchmarks in chronological order.

A Streetcar Named Desire (1951): Often cited as the first film to use a jazz-style score for a nonjazz-themed story, fittingly set in New Orleans, and composed by Alex North.

The Man with the Golden Arm (1955): Elmer Bernstein's score is mostly pseudo-jazz, but it conveys a kick as the basic blues theme comes up during the opening credits. Frank Sinatra is the junkie who wants to play drums with the on-screen Shorty Rogers band.

Elevator to the Gallows (*Ascenseur pour l'echafaud*, 1957): For Louis Malle's first thriller, one of the most piquant and influential film scores of all time was entirely improvised by Miles Davis during an all-night session.

I Want to Live! (1958): Director Robert Wise hired former big-band composer Johnny Mandel to write the first true jazz score in a Hollywood feature, a brilliant achievement, underscored by on-screen performances by an all-star Gerry Mulligan band—the film opens with four minutes of music before a line of dialog is spoken.

Touch of Evil (1958): The prolific Henry Mancini is best known for his movie ballads, like "Moon River" (from *Breakfast at Tiffany's*), but he used ingenious jazz scoring in several 1950s works, including this Orson Welles classic and the TV series *Peter Gunn*.

Anatomy of a Murder (1959): Director Otto Preminger made a counterintuitive decision in hiring Duke Ellington to score a film about a Midwestern trial lawyer; Ellington wrote a superb score, and appears onscreen as the local pianist, Pie Eye.

Odds Against Tomorrow (1959): Robert Wise's race-conscious heist film is luminously scored by the Modern Jazz Quartet's John Lewis, including his tender ballad "Skating in Central Park"—Bill Evans and Jim Hall play in the soundtrack orchestra.

Shadows (1961): Charles Mingus never completed his score for John Cassavetes's film about racial conflict in New York, so the director created a soundtrack out of Mingus's bass solos and Shafi Hadi alto saxophone solos.

Mickey One (1961): Arthur Penn's surreal showbiz fantasy boasts an Eddie Sauter score with improvised solos by Stan Getz—a musical sequel to their renowned album *Focus*.

The Cincinnati Kid (1965): Lalo Schifrin, the former pianist for Dizzy Gillespie, wrote more than 200 film scores; this one uses Ray Charles on the title song and various New Orleans traditionalists—Cab Calloway has an acting role.

In the Heat of the Night (1967): One of the best of Quincy Jones's many scores employs Ray Charles on the title song, and bassist Ray Brown and flutist Roland Kirk throughout.

The Young Girls of Rochefort (1968): Michel Legrand, a French jazz pianist and songwriter, scored several New Wave classics by Jean Luc Godard, Agnes Varda, and Jacques Demy—his swinging take on the MGM musical in this Demy film is irresistible.

The Gauntlet (1977): Clint Eastwood used jazz in most of his films, never more memorably than in this Jerry Fielding score, with expansive solos by trumpeter Jon Faddis and alto saxophonist Art Pepper.

Naked Lunch (1991): For David Cronenberg's adaptation of William Burroughs's novel, Howard Shore wrote a suitably mind-bending score constructed around improvisations by the Ornette Coleman Trio.

Documentaries and Performance Films

Although the market for jazz documentaries is small, the field has attracted dozens of filmmakers. Many of their films were made initially for television, a few had theatrical releases, some were conceived for educational purposes, and others went directly to home video. Note that the following list, the tip of a rapidly expanding iceberg, excludes all but a few short subjects: many early jazz bands were filmed for one-reelers by Vitaphone and other movie companies. Anthologies of these films occasionally appear (see *The Best of Jazz & Blues* below), and individual shorts are often included as extras on DVDs of classic movies—especially by Warner Bros. Also worth noting are cartoons of the 1930s and 40s. Warner Bros. (Looney Tunes and Merrie Melodies), Disney, and other studios frequently used jazz—none as cannily as Fleischer Studio, which produced the great Betty Boop series: "Snow-White," "I Heard," "I'll Be Glad When You're Dead You Rascal You," and "The Old Man of the Mountain" (1932–33) are among the best of the risqué Bettys, using on-screen and traced (rotoscoped) images of Cab Calloway, Don Redman, and Louis Armstrong.

"After Hours" and *"Jazz Dance"* (1961/1954): The former was created as a television pilot but never broadcast, probably because of inane narration and a terrible singer. But Roy Eldridge and especially Coleman Hawkins *kill*.

Art Blakey: The Jazz Messenger (1987): A documentary of the drummer whose band became a graduate school for young musicians, by Dick Fontaine and Pat Hartley.

The Art Ensemble of Chicago (1981): A live performance at Chicago's Jazz Showcase.

Artie Shaw: Time Is All You've Got (1985): Brigitte Berman's Oscar-winning life of a great clarinetist and bandleader who gave up music because he hated being a celebrity.

Barry Harris: The Spirit of Bebop (2000): Interviews, performances, classic footage.

Benny Carter: Symphony in Riffs (1989): Harrison Engle's life of a musician for all seasons.

The Best of Jazz & Blues (2001): An indispensable Kino Video compilation of short films from 1929–41, including Bessie Smith's *St. Louis Blues* and others featuring Duke Ellington, Louis Armstrong, Fats Waller, Cab Calloway, and more.

Billie Holiday: The Long Night of Lady Day (1984): Though hard to find, this BBC film by John Jeremy remains the best biographical portrait of the singer.

Bix: Ain't None of Them Play Like Him Yet (1981): Brigitte Berman's detailed biographical portrait of Bix Beiderbecke.

Buena Vista Social Club (1999): Wim Wenders's multiple prize-winning and hugely popular study of Cuban music as seen through some of its aging masters.

Celebrating Bird: The Triumph of Charlie Parker (1987): Gary Giddins's biographical portrait includes Parker's 1952 television performance (with Dizzy Gillespie) of "Hot House."

Ella Fitzgerald: Something to Live For (1999): Charlotte Zwering's PBS documentary, narrated by Tony Bennett, traces the First Lady of Song's career from her discovery at the Apollo Theater.

Erroll Garner in Performance (1964): Two sets initially broadcast by the BBC.

Fred Anderson, Timeless (2005): The avant-garde saxophonist leading his trio in concert in Chicago.

A Great Day in Harlem (1995): Jean Bach's Oscar-nominated documentary, centered on a celebrated 1958 photograph, is a treasure brimming with anecdotes; it's improved on a two-disc DVD with hours of added footage.

Imagine the Sound (1981): Ron Mann's beautifully photographed film includes uninterrupted performances by Cecil Taylor, Bill Dixon, Paul Bley, and Archie Shepp.

Jammin' the Blues (1941): The best ten minutes of jazz ever filmed—a Vitaphone short with Lester Young and other swing greats (including drummers Jo Jones and Sid Catlett)—can be found as an extra on the DVD of *Blues in the Night* (see above).

Jazz '34 (1996): Robert Altman's superior companion piece to his film *Kansas City* focuses on music, as such modernists as Joshua Redman, James Carter, and Geri Allen revisit 1930s swing.

The Jazz Master Class Series (2007): Seven double-disc sets explore the lives and artistry of Barry Harris, Jimmy and Percy Heath, Hank Jones, Cecil Taylor, Clark Terry, Toots Thielemans, and Phil Woods though extensive interviews and master class sessions with student musicians.

Jazz on a Summer's Day (1958): The first great music video, exquisitely photographed by Bert Stern at the 1958 Newport Jazz Festival, capturing classic performances by Louis Armstrong, Anita O'Day, Mahalia Jackson, Gerry Mulligan, and others.

Jazz (2001): Ken Burns's PBS epic, written by Geoffrey C. Ward, is the most ambitious film ever made about jazz (nineteen hours long, more than 2,000 film clips); criticized for cutting the story off in the 1960s, it remains a remarkable, matchless achievement.

John Hammond: From Bessie Smith to Bruce Springsteen (1990): Hart Perry's Peabody-winning film, written by Gary Giddins, traces the life of jazz's most influential talent scout and record producer.

Last Date: Eric Dolphy (1991): Hans Hylkema's life of the great and tragic saxophonist and flutist.

Last of the Blue Devils (1979): Bruce Ricker's expansive look at the history and ongoing influence of Kansas City jazz, focusing on Jay McShann, Count Basie, and Big Joe Turner.

Norman Granz Presents Improvisation (2007): Long-suppressed material from the 1940s and 50s, including Jazz at the Philharmonic sequences and previously unknown footage of Charlie Parker and Coleman Hawkins.

Ornette: Made in America (1985): Shirley Clarke's study of Ornette Coleman, with recreations of his early years and extensive interviews with Coleman.

The Miles Davis Story (2001): A lively documentary by Mike Dibb with interviews of more than a dozen of Davis's associates.

Mingus (1968): A controversial, riveting film by Thomas Reichman, capturing Mingus at home, on the bandstand, and in the process of being evicted from his studio.

Satchmo (1989): Gary Giddins's award-winning PBS documentary on Louis Armstrong, based on his book, with much rare footage.

Sonny Rollins: Saxophone Colossus (1986): Robert Mugge's film features archival footage and interviews but is best remembered for the concert footage in which Rollins suddenly leaps from a precipice, finishing his solo lying on the ground with a sprained ankle.

The Sound of Jazz (1957): The best hour of jazz ever broadcast on American television (on a Sunday afternoon), with an all-star cast, including a legendary Billie Holiday blues with Lester Young, Coleman Hawkins, Ben Webster, Gerry Mulligan, and Roy Eldridge.

Thelonious Monk: Straight, No Chaser (1988): Peerless concert footage shot by Charlotte Zwerin is edited, with many interviews, into a gripping portrait of an enigmatic genius on tour.

Television Series

Jazz Casual: In the 1960s, critic Ralph J. Gleason produced twenty-eight half-hour shows, all issued on DVD. They include performances by and interviews with John Coltrane, Sonny Rollins, Louis Armstrong, Dizzy Gillespie, Carmen McRae, Jimmy Rushing, the Modern Jazz Quartet, and Dave Brubeck.

Jazz Icons: A magnificent, ongoing series of concert performances, shot live or in the studio for European television between the late 1950s and the early 1970s; these broadcasts were largely unknown here, and include first-class work by such figures as Dizzy Gillespie, Louis Armstrong, Sonny Rollins, Art Blakey, Bill Evans, Thelonious Monk, Buddy Rich, Dexter Gordon, Sarah Vaughan, Dave Brubeck, Wes Montgomery, Charles Mingus, Roland Kirk, and Nina Simone.

Jazz Scene USA: A short-lived 1962 series, shot in California, with two half-hour segments on each DVD, including shows with Cannonball Adderley, Jimmy Smith, Teddy Edwards, and Stan Kenton.

Selected Readings

In these pages, we have done our best to provide a basic outline of jazz history. Anyone interested in doing further research in jazz will encounter a vast and uneven literature—some of it decades old, some of it recently published. This selected bibliography is an attempt to provide you with a guide to the most relevant and interesting books on the subject. A few older volumes may be difficult to find in a bookstore, but are likely to be held by public libraries.

We begin with discographies, reference books, and works covering the entire range of jazz history. Thereafter, the list is organized by chapter. Note that the earlier chapters are more complete: anyone wishing to explore more contemporary forms of the music will have to rely on databases providing links to the broader periodical literature.

Discography

Bruyninckx, Walter. *90 Years of Recorded Jazz and Blues* (CD-ROM). Mechelen, 2007.

Jazz Discography Project: www.jazzdiscog.org.

Rust, Brian. *Jazz Records, 1917–1942*. New Rochelle, N.Y.: Arlington House, 1978.

Reference

Chilton, John. *Who's Who of Jazz: Storyville to Swing Street*. Philadelphia: Chilton, 1972.

Feather, Leonard. *The Encyclopedia of Jazz*. New York: Bonanza, 1960.

Kernfeld, Barry, ed. *The New Grove Dictionary of Jazz*. New York: Macmillan, 1988.

General

Balliett, Whitney. *American Musicians: Fifty-six Portraits in Jazz*. New York: Oxford University Press, 1986.

———. *American Singers: Twenty-Seven Portraits in Song*. New York: Oxford University Press, 1988.

Feather, Leonard G. *The Encyclopedia of Jazz*. New York: Da Capo Press, 1984 (originally Horizon, 1960).

———, and Ira Gitler. *The Biographical Encyclopedia of Jazz*. New York: Oxford University Press, 1999.

Gabbard, Krin, ed. *Jazz Among the Discourses*. Durham, N.C.: Duke University Press, 1995.

Gennari, John. *Blowin' Hot and Cool: Jazz and Its Critics*. Chicago: University of Chicago Press, 2006.

Giddins, Gary. *Riding on a Blue Note: Jazz & American Pop*. New York: Oxford University Press, 1981.

———. *Visions of Jazz: The First Century*. New York: Oxford University Press, 1998.

———. *Weather Bird: Jazz at the Dawn of Its Second Century*. New York: Oxford University Press, 2004.

Gioia, Ted. *The History of Jazz*. New York: Oxford University Press, 1997.

Gottlieb, Robert, ed. *Reading Jazz: A Gathering of Autobiography, Reportage, and Criticism from 1919 to Now*. New York: Pantheon, 1996.

Hinton, Milt, and David G. Berger. *Bass Line: The Stories and Photographs of Milt Hinton*. Philadelphia: Temple University Press, 1988.

Hobsbawm, Eric. *The Jazz Scene*. Rev. ed. New York: Pantheon, 1993.

Hodeir, André. *Jazz: Its Evolution and Essence*. Trans. David Noakes. New York: Grove Press, 1956.

Kart, Larry. *Jazz in Search of Itself*. New Haven: Yale University Press, 2004.

Kirchner, Bill, ed. *The Oxford Companion to Jazz*. New York: Oxford University Press, 2000.

Morgenstern, Dan. *Living with Jazz*. New York: Pantheon, 2004.

Murray, Albert. *Stomping the Blues*. New York: McGraw-Hill, 1976.

O'Meally, Robert, ed. *The Jazz Cadence of American Culture*. New York: Columbia University Press, 1998.

Shapiro, Nat, and Nat Hentoff. *Hear Me Talkin' to Ya: The Story of Jazz as Told by the Men Who Made It*. New York: Rinehart, 1955.

Stokes, W. Royal. *The Jazz Scene: An Informal History from New Orleans to 1990*. New York: Oxford University Press, 1991.

Walser, Robert, ed. *Keeping Time: Readings in Jazz History*. New York: Oxford University Press, 1999.

Ward, Geoffrey C., and Ken Burns. *Jazz: A History of America's Music*. New York: Knopf, 2000.

Williams, Martin. *Jazz Heritage*. New York: Oxford University Press, 1985.

———. *The Jazz Tradition*. 2nd rev. ed. New York: Oxford University Press, 1993.

———. *Where's the Melody? A Listener's Introduction to Jazz*. New York: Pantheon, 1969.

———, ed. *Jazz Panorama: From the Pages of the "Jazz Review."* New York: Da Capo Press, 1979 (reprint of Crowell-Collier, 1962).

Chapter 3 The Roots of Jazz

Albertson, Chris. *Bessie*. New York: Stein and Day, 1972.

Badger, Reid. *A Life in Ragtime: A Biography of James Reese Europe*. New York: Oxford University Press, 1995.

Bebey, Francis. *African Music: A People's Art*. Westport, Conn.: Hill, 1999.

Berlin, Edward A. *King of Ragtime: Scott Joplin and His Era*. New York: Oxford University Press, 1994.

Blesh, Rudi, and Harriet Janis. *They All Played Ragtime*. New York: Oak, 1971.

Bushell, Garvin. *Jazz from the Beginning*. As told to Mark Tucker. Ann Arbor: University of Michigan Press, 1988.

Chernoff, John Miller. *African Rhythm and African Sensibility*. Chicago: University of Chicago Press, 1979.

DeVeaux, Scott. *Jazz in America: Who's Listening?* Carson, Calif.: Seven Locks Press, 1995.

———, and William Howland Kenney, eds. *The Music of James Scott*. Washington, D.C.: Smithsonian Institution Press, 1992.

Emerson, Ken. *Doo-Dah! Stephen Foster and the Rise of American Popular Culture*. New York: Da Capo Press, 1998.

Erenberg, Lewis A. *Steppin' Out: New York Nightlife and the Transformation of American Culture, 1890–1930*. Chicago: University of Chicago Press, 1981.

Gioia, Ted. *Delta Blues: The Life and Times of the Mississippi Masters Who Revolutionized American Music*. New York: Norton, 2008.

Handy. W. C. *Father of the Blues: An Autobiography*. New York: Macmillan, 1941.

Jones, LeRoi (Amiri Baraka). *Blues People: Negro Music in White America*. New York: Morrow, 1963.

Lott, Eric. *Love and Theft: Blackface, Minstrelsy, and the American Working Class*. New York: Oxford University Press, 1993.

Nelson, Scott Reynolds. *Steel Driving Man: John Henry, the Untold Story of an American Legend*. New York: Oxford University Press, 2006.

Wald, Elijah. *Escaping the Delta: Robert Johnson and the Invention of the Blues*. New York: Amistad, 2004.

Waldo, Terry. *This Is Ragtime*. New York: Da Capo Press, 1991.

Chapter 4 New Orleans

Bechet, Sidney. *Treat It Gentle*. New York: Hill and Wang, 1960.

Charters, Samuel. *A Trumpet Around the Corner: The Story of New Orleans Jazz*. Oxford: University of Mississippi Press, 2008.

Chilton John. *Sidney Bechet: The Wizard of Jazz*. Basingstoke, Eng.: Macmillan, 1997.

Foster, Pops. *Pops Foster: The Autobiography of a New Orleans Jazzman*. Berkeley and Los Angeles: University of California Press, 1971.

Gushee, Lawrence. *Pioneers of Jazz: The Story of the Creole Band*. New York: Oxford University Press, 2005.

Lomax, Alan. *Mr. Jelly Roll: The Fortunes of Jelly Roll Morton, New Orleans Creole and "Inventor of Jazz."* New York: Duell, Sloan and Pearce, 1950.

Marquis, Donald. *In Search of Buddy Bolden, First Man of Jazz*. Baton Rouge: Louisiana State University Press, 1978.

Schuller, Gunther. *Early Jazz: Its Roots and Musical Development*. New York: Oxford University Press, 1968.

Turner, Frederick. *Remembering Song: Encounters with the New Orleans Tradition*. New York: Viking Press, 1982.

Williams, Martin. *Jazz Masters of New Orleans*. New York: Da Capo Press, 1978 (reprint of Macmillan, 1967).

Chapter 5 New York in the 1920s

Appel, Alfred. *Jazz Modernism: From Ellington and Armstrong to Matisse and Joyce*. New York: Knopf, 2002.

Brooks, Tim. *Lost Sounds: Black and the Birth of the Recording Industry, 1890–1919*. Urbana: University of Illinois Press, 2004.

Brown, Scott E. *James P. Johnson: A Case of Mistaken Identity*. Metuchen, N.J.: Scarecrow Press, 1986.

Charters, Samuel B., and Leonard Kunstadt. *Jazz: A History of the New York Scene*. Garden City, N.Y.: Doubleday, 1962.

DeLong, Thomas A. *Pops: Paul Whiteman, King of Jazz*. Piscataway, N.J.: New Century, 1983.

Giddins, Gary. *Bing Crosby: A Pocketful of Dreams*. Boston: Little, Brown, 2001.

Hadlock, Richard. *Jazz Masters of the Twenties*. New York: Macmillan, 1965.

Haskins, James. *The Cotton Club: A Pictorial and Social History of the Most Famous Symbol of the Jazz Era*. New York: Random House, 1977.

Jasen, David A., and Gene Jones. *Spreadin' Rhythm Around: Black Popular Songwriters, 1880–1930*. New York: Schirmer, 1998.

Kenney, William H. *Chicago Jazz: A Cultural History, 1904–1930*. New York: Oxford University Press, 1993.

Tucker, Mark. *Ellington: The Early Years*. Urbana: University of Illinois Press, 1991.

Chapter 6 Louis Armstrong and the First Great Soloists

Armstrong, Louis. *Satchmo: My Life in New Orleans*. New York: Da Capo Press, 1986 (reprint of Prentice-Hall, 1954).

Berrett, Joshua, ed. *The Louis Armstrong Companion*. New York: Schirmer, 1999.

Brothers, Thomas. *Louis Armstrong in His Own Words: Selected Writings*. New York: Oxford University Press, 1999.

———. *Louis Armstrong: Master of Modernism*. New York: Norton, 2014.

———. *Louis Armstrong's New Orleans*. New York: Norton, 2006.

Cogswell, Michael. *Louis Armstrong: The Offstage Story of Satchmo*. Portland, Ore.: Collector's Press, 2003.

Dance, Stanley. *The World of Earl Hines*. New York: Scribner, 1977.

Dickerson, James. *Just for a Thrill: Lil Hardin Armstrong, First Lady of Jazz*. New York: Cooper Square Press, 2002.

Giddins, Gary. *Satchmo*. New York: Doubleday, 1988.

Jones, Max, and John Chilton. *Louis: The Story of Louis Armstrong, 1900–1971.* Boston: Little, Brown, 1971.

Kennedy, Rick. *Jelly Roll, Bix, and Hoagie: Gennett Studios and the Birth of Recorded Jazz.* Bloomington: Indiana University Press, 1994.

Lion, Jean Pierre. *Bix: The Definitive Biography of a Jazz Legend.* New York: Continuum, 2005.

Mezzrow, Mezz, and Bernard Wolfe. *Really the Blues.* Garden City, N.Y.: Anchor, 1972.

Riccardi, Ricky. *What a Wonderful World: The Magic of Louis Armstrong's Later Years.* New York: Pantheon, 2011.

Von Eschen, Penny. *Satchmo Blows Up the World: Jazz Ambassadors Play the Cold War.* Cambridge: Harvard University Press, 2004.

Chapter 7 Swing Bands

Barnet, Charlie. *Those Swinging Years: The Autobiography of Charlie Barnet.* With Stanley Dance. Baton Rouge: Louisiana State University Press, 1984.

Calloway, Cab, and Bryant Rollins. *Of Minnie the Moocher and Me.* New York: Crowell, 1976.

Collier, James Lincoln. *Benny Goodman and the Swing Era.* New York: Oxford University Press, 1989.

Dance, Stanley. *The World of Swing.* New York: Da Capo Press, 2001.

Erenberg, Lewis. *Swingin' the Dream: Big Band Jazz and the Rebirth of American Culture.* Chicago: University of Chicago Press, 1998.

Hampton, Lionel, and James Haskins. *Hamp: An Autobiography.* New York: Warner, 1989.

Levinson, Peter. *Tommy Dorsey: Living in a Great Big Way.* New York: Da Capo Press, 2006.

Magee, Jeffrey. *The Uncrowned King of Swing: Fletcher Henderson and Big Band Jazz.* New York: Oxford University Press, 2008.

McCarthy, Albert. *Big Band Jazz.* New York: Berkley, 1977.

Schuller, Gunther. *The Swing Era: The Development of Jazz, 1930–1945.* New York: Oxford University Press, 1989.

Shaw, Artie. *The Trouble with Cinderella: An Outline of Identity.* New York: Da Capo Press, 1979.

Simon, George T. *The Big Bands.* New York: Schirmer, 1981.

Stowe, David. *Swing Changes: Big-Band Jazz in New Deal America.* Cambridge: Harvard University Press, 1994.

Chapter 8 Count Basie and Duke Ellington

Basie, Count. *Good Morning Blues: The Autobiography of Count Basie.* With Albert Murray. New York: Random House, 1985.

Dahl, Linda. *Morning Glory: A Biography of Mary Lou Williams.* New York: Pantheon, 1999.

———. *Stormy Weather: The Music and Lives of a Century of Jazzwomen.* New York: Pantheon, 1984.

Dance, Stanley. *The World of Count Basie.* New York: Scribner, 1980.

———. *The World of Duke Ellington.* New York: Scribner, 1970.

Driggs, Frank, and Chuck Haddix. *Kansas City Jazz: From Ragtime to Bebop—A History.* New York: Oxford University Press, 2005.

Ellington, Duke. *Music Is My Mistress.* Garden City, N.Y.: Doubleday, 1973.

———, and Stanley Dance. *Duke Ellington in Person: An Intimate Memoir.* Boston: Houghton Mifflin, 1978.

Hajdu, David. *Lush Life: A Biography of Billy Strayhorn.* New York: Farrar, Straus and Giroux, 1996.

Hammond, John. *John Hammond on Record: An Autobiography.* With Irving Townsend. New York: Penguin, 1977.

Kirk, Andy. *Twenty Years on Wheels.* As told to Amy Lee. Ann Arbor: University of Michigan Press, 1989.

Pearson, Nathan W. *Goin' to Kansas City.* Urbana: University of Illinois Press, 1994.

Russell, Ross. *Jazz Style in Kansas City and the Southwest.* Berkeley and Los Angeles: University of California Press, 1971.

Schiff, David. *The Ellington Century.* Berkeley and Los Angeles: University of California Press, 2012.

Tucker, Mark, ed. *The Duke Ellington Reader.* New York: Oxford University Press, 1993.

Tucker, Sherrie. *Swing Shift: "All-Girl" Bands of the 1940s.* Durham, N.C.: Duke University Press, 2000.

Van de Leur, Walter. *Something to Live For: The Music of Billy Strayhorn.* New York: Oxford University Press, 2002.

Chapter 9 A World of Soloists

Berger, Morroe, Edward Berger, and James Patrick. *Benny Carter: A Life in American Music,* vols. 1 and 2. Metuchen, N.J.: Scarecrow Press, 1982.

Büchmann-Möller, Frank. *Someone to Watch Over Me: The Life and Music of Ben Webster.* Ann Arbor: University of Michigan Press, 2006.

Chilton, John. *Roy Eldridge: Little Jazz Giant.* New York: Continuum, 2003.

———. *The Song of the Hawk: The Life and Recordings of Coleman Hawkins.* London: Quartet, 1990.

Clarke, Donald. *Wishing on the Moon: The Life and Times of Billie Holiday.* New York: Viking Press, 1994.

Cohodas, Nadine. *Queen: The Life and Music of Dinah Washington.* New York: Pantheon, 2004.

Daniels, Douglas Henry. *Lester Leaps In: The Life and Times of Lester "Pres" Young.* Boston: Beacon Press, 2002.

Friedwald, Will. *Jazz Singing: America's Great Voices from Bessie Smith to Bebop and Beyond.* New York: Da Capo Press, 1996.

Gourse, Leslie, ed. *The Billie Holiday Companion: Seven Decades of Commentary.* New York: Schirmer, 1997.

Holiday, Billie. *Lady Sings the Blues.* With William Dufty. London: Abacus, 1975.

Nicholson, Stuart. *Ella Fitzgerald: A Biography of the First Lady of Jazz.* New York: Scribner, 2004.

O'Meally, Robert. *Lady Day: The Many Faces of Billie Holiday.* New York: Da Capo Press, 1991.

Porter, Lewis, ed. *A Lester Young Reader.* Washington, D.C.: Smithsonian Institution Press, 1991.

Stewart, Rex. *Boy Meets Horn.* Ann Arbor: University of Michigan Press, 1991.

———. *Jazz Masters of the Thirties.* New York: Macmillan, 1972.

Chapter 10 Rhythm in Transition

Burke, Patrick. *Come In and Hear the Truth: Jazz and Race on 52nd Street.* Chicago: University of Chicago Press, 2008.

Crowther, Bruce. *Gene Krupa: His Life and Times.* New York: Universe, 1987.

Dregni, Michael. *Django: The Life and Music of a Gypsy Legend.* New York: Oxford University Press, 2004.

Korall, Burt. *Drummin' Men: The Heartbeat of Jazz—The Swing Years.* New York: Schirmer, 1990.

Lester, James. *Too Marvelous for Words: The Life & Genius of Art Tatum.* New York: Oxford University Press, 1994.

Sallis, James, ed. *The Guitar in Jazz: An Anthology.* Lincoln: University of Nebraska Press, 1996.

Shaw, Arnold. *52nd Street: The Street of Jazz.* New York: Da Capo Press, 1991.

Shipton, Alyn. *Fats Waller: His Life and Times.* New York: Universe, 1988.

Waller, Maurice, and Anthony Calabrese. *Fats Waller.* New York: Schirmer, 1977.

Chapter 11 Bebop

DeVeaux, Scott. *The Birth of Bebop: A Social and Musical History.* Berkeley and Los Angeles: University of California Press, 1997.

Feather, Leonard. *Inside Jazz.* New York: Da Capo Press, 1977. Reprint of *Inside Be-Bop* (New York: Robbins, 1949).

Giddins, Gary. *Celebrating Bird: The Triumph of Charlie Parker.* Minneapolis: University of Minnesota Press, 1987; rev. ed. 2013.

Gillespie, Dizzy. *To Be or Not . . . to Bop: Memoirs.* With Al Fraser. Garden City, N.Y.: Doubleday, 1979.

Gitler, Ira. *The Masters of Bebop: A Listener's Guide.* New York: Da Capo Press, 2001.

———. *Swing to Bop: An Oral History of the Transition in Jazz in the 1940s.* New York: Collier, 1985.

Hirshorn, Tad. *Norman Granz: The Man Who Used Jazz for Justice.* Berkeley and Los Angeles: University of California Press, 2011.

Korall, Burt. *Drummin' Men: The Heartbeat of Jazz—The Bebop Years.* New York: Oxford University Press, 2002.

Owens, Thomas. *Bebop: The Music and the Players.* New York: Oxford University Press, 1995.

Paudras, Francis. *Dance of the Infidels: A Portrait of Bud Powell.* New York: Da Capo Press, 1998.

Pullman, Peter. *Wail: The Life of Bud Powell.* New York: Bop Changes, 2012.

Ramsey, Guthrie P. Jr. *The Amazing Bud Powell: Black Genius, Jazz History, and the Challenge of Bebop.* Berkeley and Los Angeles: University of California Press, 2013.

Reisner, Robert George. *Bird: The Legend of Charlie Parker.* New York: Da Capo Pres, 1977.

Shipton, Alyn. *Groovin' High: The Life of Dizzy Gillespie.* New York: Oxford University Press, 1999.

Woideck, Carl, ed. *The Charlie Parker Companion: Six Decades of Commentary.* New York: Schirmer, 1998.

———. *Charlie Parker: His Music and Life.* Ann Arbor: University of Michigan Press, 1996.

Chapter 12 The 1950s: Cool Jazz and Hard Bop

Bryant, Clora, ed. *Central Avenue Sounds: Jazz in Los Angeles.* Berkeley and Los Angeles: University of California Press, 1998.

Combs, Paul. *Dameronia: The Life and Music of Tadd Dameron.* Ann Arbor: University of Michigan Press, 2012.

Cook, Richard. *Blue Note Records: The Biography.* Boston: Justin, Charles, 2003.

Gioia, Ted. *West Coast Jazz: Modern Jazz in California, 1945–1960.* New York: Oxford University Press, 1992.

Goldberg, Joe. *Jazz Masters of the Fifties.* New York: Macmillan, 1965.

Goldsher, Alan. *Hard Bop Academy: The Sidemen of Art Blakey and the Jazz Messengers.* Milwaukee: Hal Leonard, 2002.

Hamilton, Andy. *Lee Konitz: Conversations on the Improviser's Art.* Ann Arbor: University of Michigan Press, 2007.

Klinkowitz, Jerome. *Listen: Gerry Mulligan—An Aural Narrative in Jazz.* New York: Schirmer, 1991.

Maggin, Donald L. *Stan Getz: A Life in Jazz.* New York: Morrow, 2003.

Nisenson, Eric. *Open Sky: Sonny Rollins and His World of Improvisation.* New York: Da Capo Press, 2000.

Pepper, Art, and Laurie Pepper. *Straight Life: The Story of Art Pepper.* New York: Schirmer, 1979.

Rosenthal, David H. *Hard Bop: Jazz and Black Music, 1955–1965.* New York: Oxford University Press, 1992.

Silver, Horace. *Let's Get to the Nitty Gritty: The Autobiography of Horace Silver.* Phil Pastras, ed. Berkeley and Los Angeles: University of California Press, 2006.

Chapter 13 Jazz Composition in the 1950s

Crease, Stephanie Stein. *Gil Evans: Out of the Cool—His Life and Music.* Chicago: A Cappella, 2002.

De Wilde, Laurent. *Monk.* Trans. Jonathan Dickinson. New York: Marlowe, 1997.

Easton, Carol. *Straight Ahead: The Story of Stan Kenton.* New York: Da Capo Press, 1981.

Fitterling, Thomas. *Thelonious Monk: His Life and Music.* Berkeley, Calif.: Berkeley Hills, 1997.

Kelley, Robin. *Thelonious Monk: The Life and Times of an American Original.* New York: Free Press, 2009.

Mingus, Charles. *Beneath the Underdog: His World as Composed by Mingus.* New York: Vintage, 1971.

Priestly, Brian. *Mingus: A Critical Biography.* New York: Da Capo Press, 1982.

Russell, George: *Lydian Chromatic Concept of Tonal Organization.* New York: Choice, 1959.

Solis, Gabriel. *Monk's Music: Thelonious Monk and Jazz History in the Making.* Berkeley and Los Angeles: University of California Press, 2008.

Van der Bliek, Rob, ed. *The Thelonious Monk Reader.* New York: Oxford University Press, 2001.

Chapter 14 Modality: Miles Davis and John Coltrane

Carner, Gary, ed. *The Miles Davis Companion: Four Decades of Commentary.* New York: Schirmer, 1997.

Carr, Ian. *Miles Davis: A Critical Biography.* London: Paladin, 1982.

Chambers, Jack. *Milestones: The Music and Times of Miles Davis.* Toronto: University of Toronto Press, 1985.

Davis, Miles. *Miles: the Autobiography.* With Quincy Troupe. New York: Simon and Schuster, 1989.

Early, Gerald, ed. *Miles Davis and American Culture.* St. Louis: Missouri Historical Society Press, 2001.

Heath, Jimmy, and Joseph McLaren. *I Walked with Giants: The Autobiography of Jimmy Heath.* Philadelphia: Temple University Press, 2010.

Kahn, Ashley. *Kind of Blue: The Making of the Miles Davis Masterpiece.* Boston: Da Capo Press, 2000.

———. *A Love Supreme: The Story of John Coltrane's Signature Album.* New York: Penguin, 2002.

Kirchner, Bill, ed. *A Miles Davis Reader.* Washington, D.C.: Smithsonian Institution Press, 1991.

Pettinger, Peter. *Bill Evans: How My Heart Sings.* New Haven: Yale University Press, 1998.

Porter, Lewis. *John Coltrane: His Life and Music.* Ann Arbor: University of Michigan Press, 1998.

Szwed, John. *So What: The Life of Miles Davis.* New York: Simon and Schuster, 2002.

Chapter 15 The Avant-Garde

Anderson, Iain. *This Is Our Music: Free Jazz, the Sixties, and American Culture.* Philadelphia: University of Pennsylvania Press, 2007.

Giddins, Gary. *Rhythm-a-ning: Jazz Tradition and Innovation in the '80s.* New York: Oxford University Press, 1985.

Jones, LeRoi (Amiri Baraka). *Black Music.* New York: Morrow, 1967.

Jost, Ekkehard. *Free Jazz.* Graz: Universal Edition, 1974.

Lewis, George. *A Power Stronger Than Itself: The AACM and American Experimental Music.* Chicago: University of Chicago Press, 2008.

Litweiler, John. *The Freedom Principle: Jazz After 1958.* New York: Morrow, 1984.

———. *Ornette Coleman: A Harmolodic Life.* New York: Morrow, 1992.

Mandel, Howard. *Miles, Ornette, Cecil: Jazz Beyond Jazz.* New York: Routledge, 2008.

Radano, Ronald M. *New Cultural Figurations: Anthony Braxton's Cultural Critique.* Chicago: University of Chicago Press, 1993.

Spellman, A. B. *Four Lives in the Bebop Business.* New York: Pantheon, 1966.

Such, David. *Avant-Garde Musicians: Performing "Out There."* Iowa City: University of Iowa Press, 1993.

Szwed, John. *Space Is the Place: The Lives and Times of Sun Ra.* New York: Pantheon, 1997.

Williams, Martin. *Jazz Masters in Transition, 1957–69.* New York: Macmillan, 1970.

Wilmer, Valerie. *As Serious as Your Life: The Story of the New Jazz.* Westport, Conn.: Hill, 1980.

Chapter 16 Fusion I: R&B, Singers, and Latin Jazz

Castro, Ruy. *Bossa Nova: The Story of the Brazilian Music That Seduced the World.* Chicago: A Capella, 2000.

Charles, Ray, and David Ritz. *Brother Ray: Ray Charles's Own Story.* New York: Dial Press, 1978.

Chilton, John. *Let the Good Times Roll: The Story of Louis Jordan and His Music.* Ann Arbor: University of Michigan Press, 1994.

Epstein, Daniel Mark. *Nat King Cole.* Boston: Northeastern University Press, 1999.

Fernandez, Raoul A. *From Afro-Cuban Rhythms to Latin Jazz.* Berkeley and Los Angeles: University of California Press, 2006.

Friedwald, Will. *Sinatra! The Song Is You—A Singer's Art.* New York: Da Capo Press, 1997.

Gourse, Leslie. *Sassy: The Life of Sarah Vaughan.* New York: Scribner, 1993.

Petkov, Steven, and Leonard Mustazza, eds. *The Frank Sinatra Reader.* New York: Oxford University Press, 1997.

Roberts, John Storm. *Latin Jazz: The First of the Fusions, 1880s to Today.* New York: Schirmer, 1999.

Sublette, Ned. *Cuba and Its Music: From the First Drums to the Mambo.* Chicago: Chicago Review Press, 2004.

Washburne, Christopher. *Sounding Salsa: Performing Latin Music in New York City.* Philadelphia: Temple University Press, 2008.

Wexler, Jerry, and David Ritz: *Rhythm and the Blues: A Life in American Music.* New York: Knopf, 1993.

Chapter 17 Fusion II: Jazz, Rock, and Beyond

Coryell, Julie, and Laura Friedman. *Jazz-Rock Fusion: The People, the Music*. Milwaukee: Hal Leonard, 2000.

Freeman, Phil. *Running the Voodoo Down: The Electric Music of Miles Davis*. San Francisco: Backbeat, 2005.

Mercer, Michelle. *Footprints: The Life and Works of Wayne Shorter*. New York: Tarcher, 2004.

Milkowski, Bill. *Jaco: The Extraordinary and Tragic Life of Jaco Pastorius*. New York: Backbeat, 1995.

Nicholson, Stuart. *Jazz-Rock: A History*. New York: Schirmer, 1998.

Pond, Steven. *Head Hunters: The Making of Jazz's First Platinum Album*. Ann Arbor: University of Michigan Press, 2005.

Tingen, Paul. *Miles Beyond: The Electric Explorations of Miles Davis, 1967–1991*. New York: Billboard, 2001.

Chapter 18 Historism: Jazz on Jazz

Berry, Jason, Jonathan Foose, and Tad Jones. *Up from the Cradle of Jazz: New Orleans Music Since World War II*. Athens: University of Georgia Press, 1986.

Bethell, Tom. *George Lewis: A Jazzman from New Orleans*. Berkeley and Los Angeles: University of California Press, 1977.

Burton, Gary. *Learning to Listen: An Autobiography*. Boston: Berklee Press, 2013.

Gabbard, Krin. *Jammin' at the Margins: Jazz and the American Cinema*. Chicago: University of Chicago Press, 1996.

Gennari, John. *Blowin' Hot and Cold: Jazz and Its Critics*. Chicago: University of Chicago Press, 2006.

Hazeldine, Mike, and Bill Russell. *Bill Russell's American Music*. New Orleans: Jazzology, 1993.

Lock, Graham. *Forces of Motion: The Music and Thoughts of Anthony Braxton*. New York: Da Capo Press, 1988.

Marsalis, Wynton, and Frank Stewart. *Sweet Swing Blues on the Road*. New York: Norton, 1994.

Ramsey, Frederic Jr., and Charles Edward Smith, eds. *Jazzmen*. New York: Harcourt, Brace, 1939.

Wein, George, and Nate Chinen: *Myself Among Others: A Life in Music*. New York: Da Capo Press, 2004.

Chapter 19 Jazz Today

Carver, Reginald, and Lenny Bernstein. *Jazz Profiles: The Spirit of the Nineties*. New York: Billboard, 1998.

Mandel, Howard. *Future Jazz*. New York: Oxford University Press, 1999.

Nicholson, Stuart. *Is Jazz Dead? (or Has It Moved to a New Address)*. New York: Routledge, 2005.

Stokes, W. Royal. *Living the Jazz Life: Conversations with Forty Musicians About Their Careers in Jazz*. New York: Oxford University Press, 2000.

Weston, Randy, and Willard Jenkins. *African Rhythms: The Autobiography of Randy Weston*. Durham, N.C.: Duke University Press, 2010.

End Notes

Chapter 1 Musical Elements and Instruments

8. "You got to be in the sun": Sidney Bechet, *Treat It Gentle* (Hill and Wang, 1960), p. 2.

Chapter 3 The Roots of Jazz

43. "They were led by a long-legged chocolate boy": W. C. Handy, *Father of the Blues: An Autobiography* (Collier, 1941), pp. 80–81.
44. Jazz is an "art form": Robert Walser, ed., *Keeping Time* (Oxford University Press, 1999), p. 333.
45. The blasting of a railroad tunnel: Scott Reynolds Nelson, *Steel Drivin' Man: John Henry—The Untold Tale of an American Legend* (Oxford University Press, 2006).
46. "The Buzzard Lope" is a spiritual dance: Mark Knowles, *Tap Roots: The Early History of Tap Dancing* (McFarland, 2002), p. 320.
47. African American society had shifted: Lawrence Levine, *Black Culture and Black Consciousness* (Oxford University Press, 1978), pp. 222–23.
53. "When a good orchestra": Lewis A. Erenberg, *Steppin' Out: New York Nightlife and the Transformation of American Culture* (Greenwood Press, 1981), p. 153.
54. "a town without its brass band": Raoul Camus, "Band," in *The New Grove Dictionary of American Music*, ed. H. Wiley Hitchcock and Stanley Sadie (Macmillan, 1986), 1:133.

Chapter 4 New Orleans

64. The jazz guitarist Danny Barker: Alan Lomax, *Mister Jelly Roll* (Duell, Sloan and Pearce, 1950), p. 61.
66. "Everybody got up quick": *Down Beat,* December 15, 1940.
66. "You never had to figure": Nat Shapiro and Nat Hentoff, *Hear Me Talkin' to Ya: The Story of Jazz as Told by the Men Who Made It* (Rinehart, 1955), pp. 66–67.
74. "I was sitting at the piano": Shapiro and Hentoff, *Hear Me Talkin' to Ya*, pp. 45–46.
77. "He was standing there": Richard Merryman, *Louis Armstrong—A Self-Portrait* (Eakins Press, 1971), pp. 48–49.
79. "I wish to set down": Ralph de Toledano, ed., *Frontiers of Jazz* (Durrell, 1947; trans. and revised), p. 122.

Chapter 5 New York in the 1920s

87. "Negroes playing it": *San Francisco Examiner,* April 11, 1928, p. 6.

Chapter 6 Louis Armstrong and the First Great Soloists

107. "had the potential capacity": Gunther Schuller, *Early Jazz* (Oxford University Press, 1968), p. 89.

Chapter 7 Swing Bands

137. In 1939, two-thirds of the public: Russell B. Nye, *The Unembarrassed Muse: The Popular Arts in America* (Dial, 1970), p. 384.
137. "fancy wall decorations all over": Clyde Bernhardt, *I Remember: Eighty Years of Black Entertainment, Big Bands, and the Blues* (University of Pennsylvania Press, 1986), pp. 149–50.
138. "to observe the Lindy Hop": ibid., p. 210.
138. "If you were on the first floor": Count Basie (with Albert Murray), *Good Morning Blues: The Autobiography of Count Basie* (Random House, 1985), p. 120.
138. "a lot of kids playing": Dickie Wells, quoted in Jeffrey Magee, *The Uncrowned King of Swing: Fletcher Henderson and Big Band Jazz* (Oxford University Press, 2005), p. 171.
142. "get a Harlem book": James Maher, transcript from *Ken Burns's Jazz* (www.pbs.org/jazz/about/pdfs/Maher.pdf).
143. "He arrived with 'Blue Skies'": ibid.
145. "There was no white pianist": John Hammond, *John Hammond on Record: An Autobiography* (Penguin, 1977), pp. 68, 32–33.
147. "I was actually living": Artie Shaw, *The Trouble with Cinderella: An Outline of Identity* (Farrar, Straus, and Young, 1952), p. 228.
148. "We arrived in one town": Nat Shapiro and Nat Hentoff, *Hear Me Talkin' to Ya: The Story of Jazz as Told by the Men Who Made It* (Rinehart, 1955), pp. 328–30.
150. "Until I met Jimmie": Sy Oliver, quoted in Alyn Shipton, *A New History of Jazz* (Continuum, 2001), p. 299.
150. "They would come out and play a dance routine": Eddie Durham, National Endowment for the Arts/Smithsonian Institution Jazz Oral History Project.

Chapter 8 Count Basie and Duke Ellington

161. Sometimes they were paid: Linda Dahl, *Morning Glory: A Biography of Mary Lou Williams* (Pantheon, 1999), p. 85.
161. "She'd be sitting": Andy Kirk (as told to Amy Lee), *Twenty Years on Wheels* (University of Michigan Press, 1989), p. 73.
162. "I listened to how a pianist": Dahl, *Morning Glory,* pp. 87, 77.

164. "I had never heard": Count Basie (with Albert Murray), *Good Morning Blues: The Autobiography of Count Basie* (Random House, 1985), pp. 4–5.

164. "Whenever we wanted to do something": Frank Driggs, *Kansas City Jazz: From Ragtime to Bebop—A History* (Oxford University Press, 2005), p. 121.

165. "might as well have been": Roy Wilkins, quoted in Douglas Henry Daniels, *Lester Leaps In: The Life and Times of Lester "Pres" Young* (Beacon Press, 2002), p. 182.

165. This tiny, L-shaped salon was so small: Basie, *Good Morning Blues*, p. 164.

165. "I don't think we had": ibid.

165. "It wasn't unusual": Nat Shapiro and Nat Hentoff, *Hear Me Talkin' to Ya: The Story of Jazz as Told by the Men Who Made It* (Rinehart, 1955), p. 291.

165. "revival meetings": Gene Ramey, National Endowment for the Arts/Smithsonian Institution Jazz Oral History Project.

166. "I don't think I even knew": Basie, *Good Morning Blues*, p. 137.

166. "By the time you read this": ibid., p. 180.

166. "It was like the Blue Devils": ibid., p. 199.

168. "just like you were mixing": Stanley Dance, *The World of Count Basie* (Scribner, 1980), p. 103.

170. "You know, don't you": Albert McCarthy, *Big Band Jazz: The Definitive History of the Origins, Progress, Influence and Decline of Big Jazz Bands* (Berkley, 1974), p. 207.

170. "Negro folk music": Richard Boyer, "The Hot Bach," in *The Ellington Reader*, ed. Mark Tucker (Oxford University Press, 1993), p. 218.

170. "beyond category": Edward Kennedy Ellington, *Music Is My Mistress* (Doubleday, 1973), p. 237.

171. "I'm supposed to remember": Dizzy Gillespie (with Al Fraser), *To Be, or Not . . . to Bop* (Doubleday, 1979), p. 184.

172. "at the height of his creative powers": Irving Townsend, "When Duke Records," in *The Ellington Reader*, p. 320.

172. "You've got to write": Boyer, "The Hot Bach," p. 229.

174. "Duke merely lifts a finger": *Down Beat*, November 5, 1952, p. 18.

175. "It was a happy day": Duke Ellington, "We, Too, Sing 'America,'" in *The Ellington Reader*, p. 146.

175. "Where in the white community": Ralph Ellison, "Homage to Duke Ellington on his Birthday," in *The Ellington Reader*, pp. 96–97.

176. "I guess *serious* is a confusing word": "Why Duke Ellington Avoided Music Schools," in *The Ellington Reader*, p. 253.

176. "I don't feel the pop tunes": Boyer, "The Hot Bach," p. 231.

176. Playing by ear: Mercer Ellington, in Stanley Dance, *The World of Duke Ellington* (Scribner, 1970), p. 39.

180. "That was the last thing": David Hajdu, *Lush Life: A Biography of Billy Strayhorn* (Farrar, Straus and Giroux, 1996), p. 253.

180. "His greatest virtue, I think": ibid., p. 257.

Chapter 9 A World of Soloists

186. "People always say I invented the jazz tenor": Hawkins on the album *Coleman Hawkins: A Documentary* (Riverside Records, 1956).

190. "Man, this cat ain't playing harsh": Gary Giddins, *Visions of Jazz* (Oxford University Press, 1998), p. 191.

192. "I'm looking for something soft": Francois Postif, "Lester Paris 59," in *Jazz Hot* (Paris), April 1959.

192. "Zoot and I worked in a club in Hollywood": Giddins, *Visions of Jazz*, p. 331.

194. "it's most improbable that anyone will ever know": Duke Ellington on the album *The Afro Eurasian Eclipse* (Fantasy Records, 1976).

198. "Have you ever heard": "Why Women Musicians Are Inferior" (unsigned article), *Down Beat*, February 1938, p. 4.

198. While touring with the Count Basie band: Billie Holiday (with William Dufty), *Lady Sings the Blues* (Abacus, 1975), p. 56.

198. "What does a jacket": Anita O'Day (with George Eells), *High Times, Hard Times* (Putnam, 1981), pp. 101–102.

199. "I missed a lot of opportunities": Linda Dahl, *Stormy Weather: The Music and Lives of a Century of Jazzwomen* (Pantheon, 1984), p. 216.

203. "For my money": Holiday, *Lady Sings the Blues*, p. 58.

Chapter 11 Bebop

231. "entirely separate and apart": Charlie Parker, "No Bop Roots in Jazz: Parker," *Down Beat*, September 9, 1942, p. 12.

232. "Man, is that cat crazy?": Nat Shapiro and Nat Hentoff, *Hear Me Talkin' to Ya: The Story of Jazz as Told by the Men Who Made It* (Rinehart, 1955), p. 356.

233. "Stop that crazy boppin'": ibid., p. 351.

234. "That's what I've been hearing": Ira Gitler, *Jazz Masters of the Forties* (Collier, 1974), p. 20.

234. "With bop, you had to *know*": Scott DeVeaux, "Conversation with Howard McGhee," *Black Perspective in Music* 25 (September 1987), p. 73; italics added.

236. "real advanced New York style": Leonard Feather, *Inside Be-Bop* (Robbins, 1949), p. 15.

237. "I worked hard": Dizzy Gillespie (with Al Fraser), *To Be, or Not . . . to Bop* (Doubleday, 1979), p. 218.

237. "head and hands": Miles Davis (with Quincy Troupe): *Miles: The Autobiography* (Simon and Schuster, 1989), p. 64.

237. "Charlie Parker brought the rhythm": Gillespie, *To Be, or Not*, p. 232.

238. "As we walked in": Marshall Stearns, *The Story of Jazz* (Oxford University Press, 1956), pp. 224–25.

239. "I had never heard": DeVeaux, interview with Howard McGhee, December 20, 1980.

239. "Naming-day at Savoy": Douglass Parker, in *The Bebop Revolution in Words and Music*, ed. David Oliphant (University of Texas Press, 1994), p. 165.

244. "The one was jazz": Teddy Reig (with Edward Berger), *Reminiscing in Tempo: The Life and Times of a Jazz Hustler* (Scarecrow Press, 1990).

248. "I listened to bebop after school": Imanu Amiri Baraka, *The Autobiography of LeRoi Jones / Amiri Baraka* (Freundlich, 1984), pp. 57–58, 60.

249. "one with the music itself": Gitler, *Jazz Masters of the Forties*, p. 110.

252. "When Pres appeared": ibid., p. 205.

255. "There was no such thing": Gillespie, *To Be, or Not*, p. 343.

Chapter 12 The 1950s: Cool Jazz and Hard Bop

260. "One countered racial provocation": Ralph Ellison, *The Collected Essays of Ralph Ellison* (Modern Library, 1995), p. 631.

262. "Diz and Bird play a lot of real fast notes": Miles Davis (with Quincy Troupe), *Miles: The Autobiography* (Simon and Schuster, 1989), pp. 219–20.

267. "We had a hard time": author interview, Gary Giddins, *Visions of Jazz* (Oxford University Press, 1998), p. 384.

Chapter 13 Jazz Composition in the 1950s

290. "I say play your way": Grover Sales, "I Wanted to Make It Better: Monk at the Blackhawk," in *Jazz: A Quarterly of American Music* 5 (Winter 1960).

290. "I used to have a phobia": Nat Hentoff, *The Jazz Life* (London: P. Davies, 1962), p. 203.

291. "I always had to be alert": Nat Hentoff, liner notes to *Giant Steps* (Atlantic Records, 1959).

296. "Now, Charles" he says: Charles Mingus, *Beneath the Underdog: His World as Composed by Mingus* (Vintage, 1991), pp. 323–35.

299. "When I first met him": Miles Davis (with Quincy Troupe), *Miles: The Autobiography* (Simon and Schuster, 1989), p. 122.

303. "It's not like when you base stuff on chords": ibid., p. 225.

303. "The challenge here": ibid.

Chapter 14 Modality: Miles Davis and John Coltrane

310. "My ultimate culture hero": William C. Banfield, *Black Notes* (Scarecrow Press, 2004), p. 148.

318. "hears an idea": Peter Pettinger, *Bill Evans: How My Heart Sings* (Yale University Press, 1998), p. 91.

318. "ideas were rolling out": ibid., p. 94.

325. "the turning point": Ian Carr, Digby Fairweather, and Brian Priestley, *Jazz: The Essential Companion* (London: Grafton, 1897), p. 182.

325. "musical nonsense": John Tynan, "Take Five," *Down Beat*, November 23, 1961.

328. "The main thing a musician would like to do": John Coltrane, liner notes to *Crescent* (Impulse Records, 1964).

Chapter 15 The Avant-Garde

345. "Musicians tell me, if what I'm doing": Ornette Coleman at World Jazz Scene, "Great Quotes of and About Musicians" (www.worldjazzscene.com/quotes).

345. "Bebop is like playing scrabble": Duke Ellington, *Look* Magazine, August 10, 1954.

345. "It's like not having anything to do with what's": Charles Mingus, quoted in Gary Giddins, *Visions of Jazz* (Oxford University Press, 1998), p. 445.

346. "You can always reach into the human sound": Ornette Coleman, quoted in Nat Hentoff, liner notes to Coleman's *Something Else!!!!* (Contemporary Records, 1958).

351. "We had a magical dialogue": Andrew Cyrille, quoted in an interview by Ted Panken, *Jazziz*, March 16, 2001.

355. "screaming the word 'FUCK'": Ted Joans, review of Albert Ayler in *Coda* Magazine (Canada), 1971.

355. "coonish churchified chuckle tunes": Leroi Jones (Amiri Imamu Baraka), *Black Music* (Morrow, 1968), p. 126.

355. "Salvation Army band on LSD": Dan Morgenstern, "Concert Review: Newport '67," *Down Beat*, August 10, 1967.

359. "The musicians don't know how": Sun Ra, quoted in John F. Szwed, *Space Is the Place* (Da Capo Press, 1998), pp. 235–36.

359. "Until I had the first meeting": Joseph Jarman, quoted in J. B. Figi, liner notes to Jarman's *Song For* (Delmark Records, 1967).

Chapter 16 Fusion I: R&B, Singers, and Latin Jazz

369. "Jazz is an octopus": Dexter Gordon, quoted in Gary Giddins, *Visions of Jazz* (Oxford University Press, 1998), p. 330.

374. "When finally I got enough money": Jimmy Smith, quoted in Leonard Feather, liner notes to *The Sounds of Jimmy Smith* (Blue Note Records, 1957).

378. "Every song he sings is understandable": Duke Ellington, *Music Is My Mistress* (Doubleday, 1973), p. 239.

382. "If you can't manage to put tinges": Jelly Roll Morton, in *The Complete Library of Congress Recordings*, 1938 (released in 2005 by Rounder Records).

384. "It was similar to a nuclear weapon": Dizzy Gillespie, in *Routes of Rhythm*, PBS series (telecast 1997).

384. "If I had let it go": Dizzy Gillespie (with Al Fraser), *To Be, or Not . . . to Bop* (Doubleday, 1979), p. 321.

390. "like an elephant": Willie Colon, quoted in David M. Carp, "Salsa Symbiosis: Barry Rogers, Eddie Palmieri's Chief Collaborator in the Making of La Perfecta," *Centro Journal*, vol. XVI, no. 2 (Fall 2004), p. 55.

Chapter 17 Fusion II: Jazz, Rock, and Beyond

401. "I had discovered that my strength": James Brown (with Bruce Tucker), *James Brown: The Godfather of Soul* (Thunder's Mouth, 1997), p. 158.
402. "the $1.50 drums and the harmonicas": Miles Davis (with Quincy Troupe): *Miles: The Autobiography* (Simon and Schuster, 1989), p. 288.
403. "He'd go out and play": *Down Beat,* March 28, 1974, p. 15.
403. "If you stop calling me a jazz man": Clive Davis, *Clive: Inside the Record Business* (Morrow, 1975), p. 260.
403. "It was loose and light at the same time": Davis, *Miles: The Autobiography,* p. 299.
405. "It was like group therapy": *Down Beat,* October 21, 1976, p. 14.
405. "to be the fastest guitarist": Stuart Nicholson, *Jazz Rock: A History* (Schirmer, 1998), p. 203.
406. "To me," he later said: *Down Beat,* June 15, 1978, p. 21.
406. "Jaco . . . brought the white kids in": *Down Beat,* April 1988, p. 17.
409. "We jazz listeners tend": Herbie Hancock, in *Down Beat,* September 8, 1977, p. 56.
410. "I looked at myself in the mirror": *Down Beat,* October 24, 1974, p. 44.
412. "I decided that it was now time": *Time,* July 8, 1974.
413. "The main reason I joined the band": *Down Beat,* October 24, 1974, p. 17.
413. "You don't usually see": *Down Beat,* August 2005, p. 43.
413. "It was the wrong piano": *Jazz Times,* June 2001, p. 73.
417. "that more danceable element": *Down Beat,* November 2000, p. 28.
417. "I can hit three notes on any of my keyboards": *Electronic Musician,* September 2005, pp. 85–86ff.
417. "I'm at a point now": *Guitar Player,* June 1998, p. 40.
421. "Jazz is my first love": Bill Beuttler, "Renegade of Funk," *Jazz Times,* May 2012.
422. "It's tricking people": Jazz Line interview (www.youtube.com/watch?v=NEIETra3hOY).

Chapter 18 Historicism: Jazz on Jazz

438. "one of the hippest": liner notes to Bobby Hutcherson, *Happenings* (Blue Note, 1966).
439. "The splendor of a sea-going vessel": liner notes to Herbie Hancock, *Maiden Voyage* (Blue Note, 1965).
443. "If you wanted to get into jazz": Linda Dahl, *Stormy Weather: The Music and Lives of a Century of Jazz Women* (Pantheon, 1984), p. 237.
445. "I waited a long time": Shloto Byrnes, "Michael Brecker," *The Independent,* January 15, 2007.

Credits

Part Opener Photos

I: p. 2: Gertrude "Ma" Rainey: Frank Driggs Collection. **3 (left):** Oran Page jam session: © Charles Peterson, courtesy of Don Peterson. **3 (right):** Henderson/ Webb poster: Frank Driggs Collection. **4 (top):** Cab Calloway: Frank Driggs Collection. **4 (bottom):** Horace Silver with quintet: © Carole Reiff, courtesy of the Carole Reiff Archive. **5 (top):** Cecil Taylor: Frank Driggs Collection. **5 (bottom left):** Thelonius Monk and Charlie Rouse: © Paul Hoeffler, courtesy of the Frank Driggs Collection. **5 (bottom right):** Wynton Marsalis: © Herman Leonard Photography LLC.

II: p. 38: Primrose and West's Big Minstrels: Frank Driggs Collection. **39 (left):** Mamie Smith: Frank Driggs Collection. **39 (right):** Paul Whiteman: Frank Driggs Collection. **40 (top):** Cotton Club: Frank Driggs Collection. **40 (bottom):** Freddy Keppard and Sidney Bechet: Frank Driggs Collection. **41 (top):** Prohibition image: © Imagno/Ullstein, courtesy of The Granger Collection. **41 (bottom left):** Vernon & Irene Castle: Frank Driggs Collection. **41 (bottom right):** Vincent Youman's *Great Day*: Frank Driggs Collection.

III: p. 130 (left): Roy Eldridge: © Timme Rosenkrantz, courtesy of the Duncan Schiedt Collection. **130 (right):** Rosie the Riveter: © The Granger Collection, New York. **131 (left):** Benny Goodman Band: © Duncan Schiedt Collection. **131 (right):** Mary Lou Williams: © Frank Driggs Collection. **132 (top):** Ella Fitzgerald: © Herman Leonard Photography LLC. **132 (bottom):** The Blue Devils: © Duncan Schiedt Collection. **133 (top):** Fats Waller: © Frank Driggs Collection. **133 (bottom left):** The Savoy Ballroom: © Frank Driggs Collection. **133 (bottom right):** *Swing Time*: © John Kobal Foundation, courtesy of Getty Images.

IV: p. 226: Coleman Hawkins: © Frank Driggs Collection. **227 (left):** 1963 civil rights activists: © Bettmann, courtesy of CORBIS. **227 (right):** Cannonball Adderley: © Herman Leonard Photography LLC. **228 (top):** John Lewis: © Frank Driggs Collection. **228 (bottom):** Royal Roost: © Herman Leonard Photography LLC. **229 (top left):** Woody Herman: © Herman Leonard Photography. **229 (top right):** Gil Evans: © Frank Driggs Collection. **229 (bottom left):** Dizzy Gillespie and Charlie Parker: © Frank Driggs Collection. **229 (bottom right):** Gerry Mulligan: © Chuck Stewart.

V: p. 338: John Coltrane and wife: © Chuck Stewart. **339 (left):** Maria Schneider: © Dina Regine. **339 (right):** Gunther Schuller: © Carole Reiff, courtesy of the Carole Reiff Archive. **340 (top left):** President Obama awarding medal to Sonny Rollins: © Dennis Brack, courtesy of Newscom. **340 (top right):** Berlin Wall falls in 1989: © Lionel Cironneau, courtesy of the Associated Press. **340 (bottom):** Miles Davis in London, 1989: © Herman Leonard Photography LLC. **341 (top):** Matthew Shipp: © Jimmy Katz. **341 (bottom left):** John Coltrane memorial: © Neal Boenzi, courtesy of The New York Times and Redux. **341 (bottom right):** Nat King Cole and Billy Eckstine: © Herman Leonard Photography LLC.

Color Insert Photos

Pp. 1–8: Courtesy of the Gary Giddins Collection. **9 (top):** John Coltrane: © Savoy Records. **9 (middle):** Bobby Hackett: © Gary Giddins Collection / Permission of SONY-BMG. **9 (bottom):** Lady Day: © Gary Giddins Collection / Permission of SONY-BMG. **10 (top):** Chico Hamilton Quintet: © Gary Giddins Collection / Permission of SONY-BMG. **10 (bottom):** Don Redman: © Gary Giddins Collection / Permission of SONY-BMG. **11 (top):** Sonny Rollins: © Blue Note Records. **11 (middle):** John Coltrane: © Blue Note Records. **11 (bottom):** *Undercurrent*: © Blue Note Records. **12 (top):** Getz/Gilberto: © The Verve Music Group. **12 (bottom):** Dave Brubeck Quartet: © Columbia Records / SONY-BMG. **13 (top):** *Sketches of Spain*: © Columbia Records / SONY-BMG. **13 (middle):** *Love for Sale*: © Blue Note Records. **13 (bottom):** *Out There*: Courtesy of Concord Music Group, Inc. **14 (top):** *Mingus*: © Courtesy of The Verve Music Group. **14 (middle):** Albert Ayler: © Courtesy of The Verve Music Group. **14 (bottom):** *Attica Blues*: © Courtesy of The Verve Music Group. **15 (top):** Mary Lou Williams: © Courtesy Chiaroscuro Records. **15 (bottom):** *Bitches Brew*: © Columbia Records / SONY-BMG. **16 (top):** Diana Krall: © Courtesy of The Verve Music Group. **16 (middle):** Danilo Perez: © Courtesy of The Verve Music Group. **16 (bottom):** Jason Moran: © Blue Note Records.

Music

Leon Berry and Andy Razaf: "Christopher Columbus," Lyric by Andy Razaf, Music by Leon Berry. (c) 1936 (Renewed) Edwin H. Morris & Company, A Division of MPL Music Publishing, Inc. All Rights Reserved. Reprinted by permission of Hal Leonard Corporation.

Walter Donaldson: "Changes," by Walter Donaldson. © 1927, Renewed 1983 Donaldson Publishing Co. LLC (ASCAP). Reprinted by permission.

Fred Longshaw and Jack Gee: "Reckless Blues," by Fred Longshaw and Jack Gee, as performed by Bessie Smith. Reprinted by permission of C.R. Publishing Company.

Big Joe Turner and Pete Johnson: "It's All Right, Baby." Words and Music by Pete Johnson and Joe Turner. Copyright © 1938 Universal Music Corp. Copyright Renewed © *1956 MCA Music* Limited. All Rights Reserved. International Copyright Secured. Reprinted by permission of Hal Leonard Corporation and Music Sales Limited.

Index

Page numbers in *italics* indicate illustrations.